The Buddhist Dead

STUDIES IN EAST ASIAN BUDDHISM 20

The Buddhist Dead

Practices, Discourses, Representations

EDITED BY

Bryan J. Cuevas and Jacqueline I. Stone

A KURODA INSTITUTE BOOK
University of Hawai'i Press
Honolulu

Printed in the United States of America

Paperback edition 2011
16 15 14 13 12 11   6 5 4 3 2 1

Library of Congress Cataloging-in-Publication Data

The Buddhist dead : practices, discourses, representations / edited by
Bryan J. Cuevas and Jacqueline I. Stone.
p. cm. — (Studies in East Asian Buddhism ; 20)
"A Kuroda Institute book."
Includes bibliographical references and index.
ISBN-13: 978-0-8248-3031-1 (hardcover : alk. paper)
ISBN-10: 0-8248-3031-8 (hardcover : paperback alk. paper)
ISBN 978-0-8248-3599-6
1. Death—Religious aspects—Buddhism. 2. Buddhism—Customs and
practices. I. Cuevas, Bryan J., 1967– II. Stone, Jacqueline Ilyse.
III. Kuroda Institute.
BQ4487.B82 2007
294.3'423—dc22
2006027683

The Kuroda Institute for the Study of Buddhism and Human Values
is a nonprofit educational corporation founded in 1976. One of its
primary objectives is to promote scholarship on the historical,
philosophical, and cultural ramifications of Buddhism. In association
with the University of Hawai'i Press, the Institute also publishes
Classics in East Asian Buddhism, a series devoted to the translation
of significant texts in the East Asian Buddhist tradition.

University of Hawai'i Press books are printed on acid-free
paper and meet the guidelines for permanence and
durability of the Council on Library Resources.

Based on design by Kenneth Miyamoto
Printed by The Maple-Vail Book Manufacturing Group

Contents

List of Illustrations vii

Acknowledgments ix

Introduction 1
Bryan J. Cuevas and Jacqueline I. Stone

1 The Buddha's Funeral 32
John S. Strong

2 Cross-Dressing with the Dead: Asceticism, Ambivalence, and Institutional Values in an Indian Monastic Code 60
Gregory Schopen

3 The Moment of Death in Daoxuan's Vinaya Commentary 105
Koichi Shinohara

4 The Secret Art of Dying: Esoteric Deathbed Practices in Heian Japan 134
Jacqueline I. Stone

5 The Deathbed Image of Master Hongyi 175
Raoul Birnbaum

6 Dying Like Milarépa: Death Accounts in a Tibetan Hagiographic Tradition 208
Kurtis R. Schaeffer

7 Fire and the Sword: Some Connections between Self-Immolation and Religious Persecution in the History of Chinese Buddhism 234
James A. Benn

8 Passage to Fudaraku: Suicide and Salvation in Premodern Japanese Buddhism 266
D. Max Moerman

9 The Death and Return of Lady Wangzin: Visions of the Afterlife in Tibetan Buddhist Popular Literature 297
Bryan J. Cuevas

10 Gone but Not Departed: The Dead among the Living in Contemporary Buddhist Sri Lanka 326
John Clifford Holt

11 Mulian in the Land of Snows and King Gesar in Hell: A Chinese Tale of Parental Death in Its Tibetan Transformations 345
Matthew T. Kapstein

12 Chinese Buddhist Death Ritual and the Transformation of Japanese Kinship 378
Hank Glassman

13 Grave Changes: Scattering Ashes in Contemporary Japan 405
Mark Rowe

14 Care for Buddhism: Text, Ceremony, and Religious Emotion in a Monk's Final Journey 438
Jason A. Carbine

Chinese and Korean Character Glossary 457

Japanese Character Glossary 461

Contributors 467

Index 471

Illustrations

5.1. Master Hongyi on his deathbed 176
5.2. Hongyi in 1937 177
5.3. Vinaya master Guanghua at the moment of death 188
5.4. Hongyi in 1941 191
8.1. Image of *Fudaraku tokai* based on Jesuit accounts 278
8.2. *Nachi Pilgrimage Maṇḍala* (*Nachi sankei mandara*) 280
8.3. Detail from *Nachi Pilgrimage Maṇḍala* 281
8.4. Diagram of funerary ground from *Shugendō mujō yōshū* 282
8.5. *Manifestation of Kannon at Nachi* 288
8.6. Detail of *Fudaraku bune* sails from *Nachi Pilgrimage Maṇḍala* 289
12.1. Marriages among Reishi's close relatives 383

Acknowledgments

We wish to express our deepest appreciation to the fine scholars whose excellent contributions appear in this volume and for their patience in awaiting its publication. The essays that appear in this collection were prepared initially for a conference on "Death and Dying in Buddhist Cultures" held at Princeton University in May 2002. The conference was organized by the two editors and sponsored by Princeton's Center for the Study of Religion (CSR), along with the Council on Regional Studies, the Department of Religion, the East Asian Studies Program, the Humanities Council, and the Stewart Fund for Religion. We are grateful for the generous support of these institutional centers. In particular, we would like to thank Robert Wuthnow, director of the Center for the Study of Religion, and Stephen ("Buzzy") Teiser of the CSR executive committee for their support and encouragement of the initial proposal for the conference. Moreover, the conference could not have succeeded without the gracious and tireless administrative and organizational efforts of Anita Kline, Lorraine Fuhrmann, Micah Auerback, and Paul Copp.

We especially wish to thank the following individuals for their lively discussion during the three-day event and for their insightful comments, all of which helped to improve the essays included here: James Boon (Princeton), David Germano (University of Virginia), Phyllis Granoff (Yale), Yang Lu (Harvard), Reiko Ohnuma (Dartmouth), and Liz Wilson (Miami of Ohio). Kevin Carr, now assistant professor at the University of Michigan, deserves our special praise for his fine artistic sensibilities, for designing the conference Web site and posters, and for his assistance in selecting and securing the image of the Yatadera bodhisattva Jizō saving evildoers from the hells, which graces the cover of this book. We would like to thank the Nara National Museum and Yatadera for permission to use this image. A few of the essays included here, or portions thereof, represent revisions of earlier published works. We gratefully acknowledge permission from the University of Chicago Press, University of Hawai'i Press, Princeton University Press, Harvard University Asia Center, and the *Japanese Journal of Religious Studies*.

We are greatly indebted to Peter Gregory, editor in chief of the Kuroda Institute for the Study of Buddhism and Human Values, and to Patricia Crosby, executive editor at the University of Hawai'i Press, for their unflagging support of this project and for seeing it through to publication. We wish also to thank the Kuroda Institute's editorial board and our two anonymous manuscript reviewers, whose suggestions substantially improved the quality of the essays. We also extend our appreciation to the staff of the University of Hawai'i Press; to Bojana Ristich, our copy editor; to Mary Mortensen, who prepared the index; and to Frank Macreery for his much valued technical assistance in encoding the diacritics on the final version of the manuscript. Last but not least, we would like to thank Princeton University's Committee on Research in the Humanities and Social Sciences for a subvention grant that contributed to the publication of this volume.

Introduction

Bryan J. Cuevas
Jacqueline I. Stone

From its beginnings in India to its varied cultural and regional forms throughout Asia, Buddhism has been and continues to be a religion concerned with death and with the dead. Buddhist doctrines, practices, and institutions all bear some relation to this theme. Doctrinal teachings speak of death as occurring at each moment, as one causally dependent set of conditions passes away and another arises. In this sense, death is simply change, the way things are. Unawakened persons, failing to apprehend this, read into the flux of momentary events illusory objects such as "self" or "others" and cling to them, although such objects cannot last and are not under our control. As one may read in any introductory textbook on Buddhism, attachments to possessions, relationships, and especially notions of a perduring self are deemed unwholesome, inevitably producing frustration and misery and binding one to saṃsāra, the cycle of deluded rebirth. From this perspective, as indicated by its presence among the four sufferings—birth, old age, sickness, and death—death becomes emblematic of the whole samsaric process. "Death" is suffering, both as an end, separating one from all that one cherishes, and as a revolving door, spinning one back into yet another round of unsatisfactory rebirth, up or down in accordance with one's deeds, until ignorance and craving are finally eradicated. In this sense, death is not merely the way things are, but it also exemplifies the very problem that the Buddhist soteriological project is to overcome. The Buddha has "attained to the deathless"; his conquest of Māra just before his awakening was not merely the conquest of desire, but of death itself. In the words of Frank E. Reynolds, Buddhism has held forth the promise of "insight into a larger reality within which the power of death could be domesticated and defeated"[1]—no small part of its attraction as a religious system.

Death also figures as a recurring theme in specific Buddhist practices. Because death represents both the transient, unstable nature of things and the suffering born of ignorance and craving, which is to be overcome, the sight or thought of death can, to the reflective mind, act as a spur to religious endeavor. We see this in the story of Prince Siddhārtha, the Buddha to be, who is prompted by the sight of a corpse being borne along in a funeral procession to leave his father's palace and become a wandering ascetic. Death reminds the practitioner both that work remains to be done and that the time to accomplish it is fleeting. Thus Buddhaghosa, in the fifth century, recommended death, together with universal good will (Pāli *metta*), as one of two meditation topics suitable to persons of all temperaments.[2] Buddhist death contemplations have assumed many forms, from simple reflections on death's inevitability to yogic techniques for rehearsing the stages of dissolution at death to the graphic charnel ground meditations (sometimes performed using paintings or, more recently, photographs in lieu of corpses), designed to cultivate aversion to the body (*asubhabhāvanā*).[3] Specific "deathbed" practices aim at using the liminal potential of life's last moments to effect a soteriologically advantageous rebirth or even to achieve liberation. And since actions in this life are said to affect one's condition in the next, in a broad sense, all forms of Buddhist practice might be said to include an element of death preparation.

Death also plays a vital role in Buddhism's social and institutional dimensions. Rites for the deceased have been deemed most efficacious when performed by those purified by ascetic discipline —the Buddhist clergy or other local adepts and thaumaturges.[4] The performance of funerary and memorial ritual represents a chief social role of Buddhist clerics and strengthens ties between saṅgha and laity. Funerary rites reaffirm both the message of impermanence and the need for religious endeavor, as well as the promise that if one follows the Buddhist path, death can in some sense be overcome. They reinforce the authority of Buddhist clerics by highlighting their ritual power to benefit the deceased and also constitute a major source of revenue for Buddhist temples. Death, in short, generates the underlying urgency that sustains the Buddhist tradition and also provides the paradigmatic occasion for reasserting its normative ideals, often with particularly dramatic force.

The essays in this volume shed light on a rich array of traditional Buddhist practices for the dead and dying; the sophisticated but often paradoxical discourses about death and the dead in Buddhist texts; and the varied representations found in Buddhist funerary art and popular literature about the dead and the places they are believed to inhabit. Before introducing the individual chapters, however, we shall touch briefly on the place of "death" in the study of Buddhism and the perspectives that inform this volume.

Death as a Topic in Buddhist Studies

Despite its centrality to Buddhist traditions, until recently death has received surprisingly little attention in the field of Buddhist Studies as a theme in its own right.[5] While a full investigation of the reasons for this neglect would require a separate essay, we suspect that it may stem, at least in part, from a legacy of modernist assumptions about what Buddhism is "supposed" to be. Since the late nineteenth century, proponents of Buddhist modernism, in Asia and the West, have sought to reconfigure Buddhism as rational, empirical, and fully compatible with science—in short, a religion preeminently suited to the modern age.[6] "The message of the Buddha I have to bring to you," wrote the Sinhalese reformer Anagārika Dharmapāla (1864–1933), "is free from theology, priestcraft, rituals, ceremonies, dogmas, heavens, hells and other theoretical shibboleths."[7] Traditional Buddhist depictions of the afterlife, with its radiant pure lands, heavens, and terrifying realms of rebirth among demons, hell dwellers, or hungry ghosts, simply did not fit this picture and so had to be "explained away," either as accommodations to the uneducated masses or as popular accretions unrelated to Buddhism's putative original form. Buddhist clerical involvement in funerals and the economic reliance of Buddhist temples on rites for the dead also drew charges that Buddhism was archaic, superstitious, and socially non-productive. Such criticisms posed a serious obstacle to Asian Buddhist leaders intent on demonstrating the relevance of their tradition to modernizing projects. Central to Buddhist modernism is a rhetoric lamenting clerical preoccupation with funerals and promoting Buddhism as a religion first and foremost for the present world. Tanaka Chigaku (1861–1939), an advocate of lay Buddhism in modern imperial Japan, lamented that in the eyes of the laity, the Buddhist clergy had become little more than undertakers, forced to absent themselves from auspicious occasions such as weddings and New Year's celebrations because their presence was associated with funerals. "They [the clergy] abandon the most important period of human existence, life, and purposefully labor at explaining the silence after death. Truly this is an extremely major force in misleading the secular nation."[8] Holmes Welch records the explanation of Buddhist rites for the dead given by one of his monk informants, a disciple of the Chinese Buddhist reformer Taixu (1890–1947): "The Chinese sangha has never opposed them, but we who expound the sutras and spread the dharma often criticize them. They were not a feature of Buddhism in ancient times, yet because people think they were, they look down on Buddhism as superstition. When you write about this, you must make it clear that these things are old Chinese customs, but do not belong to Buddhist thought."[9]

Discomfort with traditional Buddhist notions of the afterlife also influenced modern presentations of Buddhism to a non-Asian general readership. We see this, for example, in the repeated assertion, contrary to historical and ethnographic evidence, that the *Tibetan Book of the Dead* was really intended for the living. First put forth in Lama Anagarika Govinda's (Ernst Lothar Hoffman, 1895–1985) "Introductory Foreword" to the 1957 edition of the Evans-Wentz translation, this odd claim recurs in the introduction to the 1987 Freemantle and Trungpa version: "Although this book is ostensibly written for the dead, it is in fact about life. The Buddha himself would not discuss what happens after death, because such questions are not useful in the search for reality here and now. But the doctrine of reincarnation, the six kinds of existence, and the intermediate bardo state between them, very much refer to this life, whether or not they also apply after death."[10] Since around the 1990s, in the context of the "death awareness" movement, the topic of death in Buddhism has suddenly come to the fore in a plethora of therapeutic "self-help" books introducing Buddhist (typically Tibetan) perspectives on death and dying to the spiritual seeker. Yet even in these works one often detects an awkwardness regarding traditional notions of the afterlife; cosmological descriptions of postmortem realms are attenuated and psychologized, and the ontological status of rebirth occasions debate, apologetics, and extensive reinterpretation.

Scholars of Buddhism have not failed to note that the marginalizing of Buddhist death rites and afterlife concerns in the rhetoric of Buddhist modernism is profoundly at odds with the actual practice of most traditional Buddhists, historically and in the present. Yet we too have not proved altogether immune to modernist emphases on Buddhism for the "here and now." While not necessarily in the business of promulgating normative definitions of what Buddhism "should" be, we *are* committed—especially where the broader field of religious studies remains dominated by the study of Christianity and other Western traditions—to the often uphill struggle of promoting Buddhism as a worthy area of inquiry. This concern may have helped to shape a broad scholarly preference for areas in which Buddhism could be shown to be "relevant"—its ethical discourses, its cogent philosophical insights, and its social and political formations—while its approaches to so commonplace a matter as death have failed for a long time to garner sustained interest.[11]

Another factor contributing to a long neglect of death in Buddhist Studies may lie in a perceived incompatibility of many Buddhist death-related practices with the doctrine of "not-self" (Skt. *anātman*; Pāli *anattā*), the denial of any permanent essence, such as a soul. While the philosophical and soteriological importance of this unique doctrine is beyond dispute, in the modern period, it has often been lifted out of any specific context and virtually enshrined as the sole standard for judging what is authentically Buddhist. "With this doctrine of egolessness, or *anattā*, stands or falls the entire Buddhist structure," as Nyanatiloka has it.[12] This move was neither simply an artifact of the now much maligned "textual Buddhism," whose study long dominated the field, nor solely a "Protestant presupposition" privileging doctrine over practice.[13] Rather it represents a singling out, from more diverse canonical material, of a particular strand against which all aspects of the tradition were to be measured. Just as the *anattā* doctrine in a classical context once represented "an intransigent symbolic opposition to the belief system of the Brahmin priesthood,"[14] so in the late nineteenth and early twentieth centuries, we suspect, it expressed an intransigent symbolic opposition to Christian hegemony, deployed by both Asian and Western spokespersons for the Buddhist cause. As a rhetorical strategy, this was little short of genius: the God of Western religion, along with the embarrassing ghosts and spirits of Buddhism's own "superstitious" past, could be dismissed at a single stroke. However, modernist deployment of the *anattā* doctrine did not stop with its traditional use as an identity marker for the Buddhist tradition or as a support for specific forms of meditation and scholastic analysis, but elevated it to an all-encompassing, normative measure of everything claiming to be "Buddhist"—an inflated and distorting burden that, historically, it had seldom been made to carry.[15] The reduction of all that is properly Buddhist to discourses of not-self and non-attachment tends to erase death in particular as an issue of any significance. In the words of Walpola Rahula, "The difference between death and birth is only a thought-moment: the last thought-moment in this life conditions the first thought-moment in the so-called next life, which, in fact, is the continuity of the same series. . . . So from the Buddhist point of view, the question of life after death is not a great mystery, and a Buddhist is never worried about this problem."[16]

Not only that, but ubiquitous Buddhist death-related practices, including the placation of unhappy ghosts, funeral prayers, and rites of merit transference for the deceased, along with cults of the holy dead centered on the worship of relics and icons, seem to be more concerned with achieving permanence and stability than with underscoring egolessness or themes of evanescence and decay. From a "not-self"-centered perspective, the pervasive presence of these seemingly heterogenous elements could be explained only as a concession to the ignorant or by appeal to decline rhetoric, in which early Buddhism's pure and lofty quest for nirvāṇa was said to have gradually become obscured by rites and folk elements imported from the broader religious cultures of Vedic India and other regions where Buddhism had spread.[17]

From around the 1960s, scholars conducting anthropological research, chiefly in Theravāda countries, began to address seriously the on-the-ground beliefs and practices of actual Buddhist communities, including their death rites, and devised models to illuminate how these beliefs and practices coexisted with doctrinal teachings of impermanence and not-self. Yet though heuristically useful, their models still tended to take not-self doctrine as a normative standard and to relegate death-related rites and discourses to an opposing category. Thus in Melford Spiro's famous tripartite typology of nibbanic, kammaic, and apotropaic Buddhism, Buddhist death rites transferring merit to the deceased and placating their potentially hostile spirits are assigned to the latter two systems, in contrast to the "nibbanic" position: "In normative Buddhism there is no soul; hence, nothing survives the death of the body. Rebirth is caused by the deceased's craving for existence; the nature of his rebirth is determined by his personally created karma. This being so, the bereaved has no power to do good or ill for the deceased. Keeping these normative assumptions in mind, it will be noted that they are all inverted by the assumptions underlying the Burmese death and burial ceremonies."[18] In Richard Gombrich's schema, a clash between "cognitive" and "affective" religious systems has its roots in Sinhalese Buddhist attitudes toward death; these emphasize survival of the personality rather than *anattā*-based views of the individual as constituted solely by a series of karmically linked momentary psychophysical formations: "I think that this affective belief in personal survival, clashing with the cognitive belief in merely karmic survival, is the basis for a whole system of affective religion which diverges from official doctrine."[19] Such models are heuristically useful, and at the time they were proposed, they represented a significant advance in that they took the practices of living Buddhists seriously. Nonetheless, by their very structure, they inevitably implied an unequally weighted polarity in which Buddhism's "orthodox" soteriological project stood on one side, while death rites and on-the-ground beliefs about the dead represented "other stuff."[20] From that perspective, to study death was still, by implication, to study a second-tier phenomenon.

Over roughly the last two decades, in Religious Studies generally, the "other stuff" has achieved respectability. What we may call "popular religion" (though the term itself is contested) is no longer understood as a leftover or marginal category posited in contradistinction to "official religion."[21] Other, older schema of "folk" versus "elite" or "great" and "little" traditions have been critiqued and largely abandoned. Buddhist Studies scholars, actively contributing to this shift, have begun to claim as legitimate topics for study a range of hitherto marginalized areas, including Buddhist funerary and mortuary culture. Indeed, few topics pose so devastating a challenge to two-tiered official/popular or elite/folk distinctions. We now know, for example, that Buddhist death rites in India, far from being concessions to an uneducated laity, were instituted by monastics. Monks initiated Buddhist funerals within the monastery, placated unhappy ghosts, and practiced burial *ad sanctos* in the vicinity of their holy dead; the cult of stūpas and donations for merit transference to the deceased similarly appear to have been first practiced not by the laity but by monks and nuns, some of them learned doctrinal specialists.[22]

We are in sympathy with those who see religious culture not as a static or unified field but as inevitably entailing differences, disputes, and oppositions. The antinomy between teachings of impermanence (of which the *anattā* doctrine represents an especially rigorous formulation) and discourses and practices stressing the continuity of the deceased represents a real and near ubiquitous feature of Buddhist funerary contexts. Once we break free of the assumption that one pole of this antinomy should be understood as "normative" (thus casting the other in a problematic light), we can begin to recognize the very tension between them as itself constitutive of Buddhist approaches to death.[23] Death, as anthropologists have long recognized, brings together a number of contradictory logics, and Buddhism is no exception in this regard, juxtaposing a number of strikingly disparate elements in death-related settings. One might note, for example, the tension between strict readings of karmic causality, according to which the individual's own acts are solely determinative of his or her postmortem fate, and belief in the power of ritual action, performed by others on the deceased's behalf, to eradicate that person's misdeeds and guide him or her to a superior rebirth. (This particular tension has a counterpart in Hindu tradition, where the teaching that the soul transmigrates in accordance with inexorable karmic law coexists with notions that the postmortem well-being of the deceased depends on rites performed by their descendants.)[24] Another recurring tension can be found between Buddhist ideals of world renunciation and the lingering pull of family obligations. Still others could be named. Indeed, death represents an ideal lens through which to examine how diverse, even contradictory elements have been drawn together in the dynamic, ongoing processes by which specific Buddhist cultures are formed, challenged, and redefined—a major premise that informs our collection.

"Death in Buddhism": A Cross-Cultural Category?

Since the late 1980s and 1990s, the subject of death in Buddhism has at last begun to draw scholarly attention, especially in the areas of funerary and mortuary practice.[25] However, the majority of these studies have tended to focus on a particular geographic or cultural area, mirroring broader, field-wide trends. Once dominated chiefly by textual, philological, and doctrinal concerns, Buddhist Studies has expanded in recent decades to include the methods of history, anthropology, and sociology, as well as literary criticism, cultural studies, gender studies, and other disciplines. Buddhologists are no longer required to have reading knowledge of several Buddhist languages or to be versed in multiple canons; instead, they are increasingly expected to be familiar with the historical and social specifics of particular Buddhist cultures. Recognition of local diversity has led to an emphasis on "buddhisms" rather than a unitary "Buddhism," and some of the most intense areas of inquiry and debate in recent years have centered around efforts to understand more precisely how Buddhism as a pan-Asian tradition has transformed, and been transformed by, local religious cultures. (One thinks, for example, of recurring tropes of "foreign impact" versus "sinification" in the study of Buddhism in medieval China or of the discovery of "combinatory paradigms" by which local *kami* were identified with buddhas and bodhisattvas in premodern Japan.) Scholars in Religious Studies have occasionally even suggested that "Buddhism" is too diverse to be of use as an analytic category and should be abandoned in favor of "Indian religion," "Japanese religion," and the like.[26] While few would endorse so extreme a position, the vast range of regional and historical variation embraced by the rubric "Buddhism" has for some time represented scholarly common sense. And nowhere does such local diversity appear more strikingly than in connection with beliefs and practices surrounding death. As Mark Blum reminds us, "In every society in Asia that may be considered traditionally Buddhist, indigenous belief structures regarding the dead that were operative before the assimilation of Buddhism persist and form an integral part of that assimilation."[27] Do the varied Buddhist discourses, practices, and representations associated with death in fact show sufficient consistency across cultures to warrant grouping them as "death and Buddhism"? Or do they differ so radically according to cultural context as to render such a rubric misleading?

This became a pressing problem for us, the volume editors, in the course of our personal research. We have both been engaged for some time in the study of death-related practices in specific Buddhist cultures, one of us focusing on medieval Tibet (Cuevas) and the other on premodern Japan (Stone), and we felt a growing need to learn whether, and if so, to what extent, our research findings were specific to these particular cultural settings or reflected broader, transregional patterns. We consequently organized a conference called "Death and Dying in Buddhist Cultures," held at Princeton University in May 2002. Our aim was to provide a venue for methodological reflection on how we, as scholars of Buddhism working in diverse cultural settings, could most effectively address the study of Buddhist approaches to death and the afterlife. In light of the thematic continuity that emerged, the conference participants concluded that while still sustaining a rigorous historical or social focus on the specifics of particular areas, it was now appropriate to move discussions of Buddhism and death into a wider conversational arena and to launch a more comparative investigation into the issue of death across the major Buddhist cultures. This conclusion provided the impetus that carried the project beyond the initial conference and led to the compilation of this volume.

The Buddhist Dead

We have already noted the pervasive tension between Buddhist doctrinal teachings of transience and non-attachment and the emotional adherence to stability and permanence found in multiple aspects of Buddhist funerary practices and attitudes toward the deceased. Buddhist societies have shared widespread assumptions about the prolonged "liveliness" of the Buddhist dead and their persistent ties to the living. This raises some fascinating problems, especially for those interested in the social and historical dimensions of Buddhist attitudes toward death and the dead or in how doctrine is appropriated in social practice. Are the dead ever truly dead in Buddhism? Just who are the Buddhist dead? Where are they, and what forms do they take? And in what ways do those who are still alive relate to them?

The "Buddhist dead" who appear in the essays collected here may be divided broadly into two groups: the "special dead" and the "ordinary dead."[28] While the distinction is by no means confined to Buddhism, these two categories assume particular meanings in Buddhist contexts. All beings, both deluded and enlightened, eventually vanish from this world, but their departure is understood in radically different terms. For the special dead—those who have achieved awakening or accumulated significant merit—death is a liberation. Special vocabulary is often employed to distinguish the exit of enlightened beings from ordinary samsaric death. Indeed, such persons are not said to have "died" at all but rather to have entered final nirvāṇa, as in the case of the Buddha, or to have gone to a pure land; alternatively, buddhas and bodhisattvas are sometimes said to manifest death as a form of religious instruction, a skillful means to awaken others to the truth of impermanence. Pāli sources use the technical term "dying by extirpation of saṃsāra" (*samuccheda-maraṇa*) to indicate the particular death of buddhas and arhats that will not lead to another rebirth, while Mahāyāna exegetes distinguished between ordinary, deluded rebirth, driven by the forces of karma (in Japanese, *bundan shōji*) and the voluntary rebirth of bodhisattvas, chosen out of compassion in order to benefit beings (*hennyaku shōji*). However their liberation may be understood, the special dead are said to have escaped the samsaric cycle once and for all, putting an end to suffering. As though to demonstrate their spiritual status, such individuals are often represented as having died exemplary deaths, in a state of calm meditative focus and accompanied by wondrous signs. The extraordinary nature of their attainments is also mapped onto their physical remains. Buddhist hagiography abounds with fantastic tales of the bodies of dead sages and adepts behaving quite differently from those of ordinary people. The paradigmatic example is of course the Buddha, whose body is said to have produced jewel-like relics (Skt. *śarīra*) in the crematory fire. So too have the bodies of many subsequent Buddhist saints. Such relics were believed to retain the charisma of the original living person and to be able to multiply, respond to prayers, and even move under their own volition. The remains of the Buddhist special dead, in short, behave in a manner quite opposite to the inertness and decay that one expects from an ordinary corpse. The extraordinary status of the special, or enlightened, dead is further represented in Buddhist societies by the production of paintings and photographic images of ideal deaths; by the stories recorded and repeated about exemplary lives and spectacular exits; and even by the special clothing worn in life and left behind in death. Several essays in this volume deal with the social, political, and symbolic power of the Buddhist "remarkable" dead.

But these are the elite among the dead. In contrast, the far more numerous, unenlightened dead are said to be still bound to the rebirth process by craving and attachment; they will be born in yet another realm of samsaric existence in accordance with their prior deeds. Many are represented as living painful and desperate lives as hungry ghosts, animals, and denizens of hell. Those with a slightly greater stock of merit may be living as gods or demi-gods or, better yet, may be reborn as humans—the most advantageous state, from a Buddhist perspective, for cultivating religious practice. These ordinary, not yet enlightened dead, and especially those suffering in inferior realms, serve routinely as cautionary examples in Buddhist didactic literature and artistic representations. They are also the objects of the extensive and varied funerary and mortuary rites of merit transference that have flourished in all Buddhist cultures and provided a major economic base for Buddhist institutions.

Having noted the distinction between the "remarkable" and the "ordinary" Buddhist dead, however, we must also stress that the line between them is often blurred or even deliberately collapsed. Funerary and mortuary rites performed by the living have sometimes been thought to elevate the status of the ordinary dead, eradicating their sins and enabling their relocation to a buddha land or other superior realm. Death itself has also been understood in Buddhist cultures as a unique and potent juncture when even those who have done evil can potentially escape samsaric rebirth by right contemplation in their last moments. And finally, whether we speak of the special dead or the ordinary dead, they are by no means lost to the living. The enlightened dead can in some cases respond to prayers, and their spiritual power remains in their relics and images and narratives about them, while the ordinary dead are able to communicate their condition to surviving relatives, receive their memorial offerings, and sometimes watch over and protect them.

The essays contained in this collection, each with its own thematic focus, historical period, and geographical setting, deal with both the remarkable and the ordinary dead. To underscore our cross-cultural concerns, we have deliberately avoided grouping them by geographical region or by strict chronological order of their subject matter. While readers will undoubtedly discover multiple connections among the individual chapters for themselves, we may note here some of the larger thematic considerations that inform the volume's content and organization.

The Buddha as Paradigm and New Readings of Mortuary Sites

The two opening chapters of this volume deal with the figure of the historical Buddha, who in death, as in other matters, has been paradigmatic for the entire tradition. They also offer insights into the social practices of Buddhist communities by suggesting new readings of the mortuary sites that figure prominently in Buddhist literature: the cremation pyre and the charnel ground. John Strong's opening essay on the Buddha's death and funeral underscores the importance of the Buddha as the model for all extraordinary Buddhist deaths. Strong argues that the Buddha's death should be understood not merely as his entry into final nirvāṇa, the end of the visible life of a blessed figure, but rather as a rite of passage in which the Buddha and his body undergo a significant change of status, highlighting the tension between the impermanence illustrated by the Buddha's departure from this world and his continued material presence in the form of relics and the stūpas enshrining them. Once dismissed as a concession to popular piety, relics have now begun to draw scholarly attention commensurate with their importance in Buddhist practice and institutions.[29] Buddha relics were seen as functionally equivalent to the living Buddha, imbued with his virtues; deposited in stūpas at monasteries, they possessed legal personhood and were able to hold property.[30] Readily portable, they facilitated the spread of Buddhism throughout Asia, aided in the formation of pilgrimage routes, and lent stature to the temples and monasteries that housed them.[31] Relics also extend the narrative of the Buddha's biography in the world, continuing to spread the dharma in lands he never visited; at the kalpa's end, it is said, they will reassemble beneath the bodhi tree and undergo a *parinirvāṇa* of their own, demonstrating just as the living Buddha did that all conditioned things must eventually perish.[32] Anthropological perspectives suggest that the enshrining of relics can be seen as a form of "secondary burial," marking the successful transit of the deceased through a polluted, liminal state to a purified and stable condition and thus linked to themes of regeneration.[33] While the crematory fire that consumed the Buddha may have vividly demonstrated the truth that all things are impermanent, Strong argues that it also generated for the Buddha a "new body" in the form of relics. Indeed, he suggests that the primary purpose of the Buddha's funeral, especially the burning of his body, was to ensure the production of these relics. Other essays in this collection similarly suggest that "cremation-productive-of-relics" has been an essential function of funerals for the Buddhist "special dead." Strong also analyzes specific elements in the symbolism of accounts of the funerary treatment of the Buddha's corpse, treatment modeled on the funeral rites reserved for great Indian monarchs. The multiple layers of shrouds, prescribed for royal funerals, in which the Buddha's body was cremated were reduced by the flames to just two robes, as in monastic garb; thus the cremation, Strong argues, in effect signals a transformation of the Buddha from the status of monarch to that of monk. Throughout the Buddhist world, death and funerals have often been thematically assimilated to monastic ordination—another, soteriologically meaningful way of "leaving the world."[34] Strong's essay suggests that this symbolic association may have its beginnings in the Buddha's funeral.

The second chapter, by Gregory Schopen, also begins with a story of the Buddha, a controversial narrative from the *Lalitavistara*. Here too we see the symbolism of a transformation in the Buddha's status marked by dress—in this case, his changing of clothes just prior to his awakening. However, as might be expected, the clothes into which he changes are no ordinary garments. On the contrary, much to the surprise of his witnesses, the Buddha dons the discarded and thoroughly polluted shroud of a recently deceased village girl. Wearing only robes made of the shrouds of corpses is celebrated in some texts as one of the *dhūtaguṇa*s or extra ascetic practices that a monk might undertake. Schopen shows us that the symbolic import of the Buddha's act, while in one sense exemplifying an ascetic ideal, also reveals on close reading of Indian Buddhist Vinaya texts just how anxious Buddhist monks were to preserve an impeccable public profile. Acceptable public impressions, Schopen argues, were important for gaining and keeping lay sponsors, whose support was crucial to the maintenance of monastic institutions. At the same time, Schopen draws attention to the anxiety and horror that surrounded death and the dead in Indian society. The pervasive sense of the impurity and contagion of death is what gave the tale of the Buddha's change of dress so much power and left many of the more conservative Buddhist monks (i.e., those image brokers and rule makers in monastic administrative positions) uncomfortably ambivalent about how best to explain and justify the Buddha's daring to pollute himself in such a dangerous manner. What Schopen exposes here is an undercurrent of opposition between those seeking to live the Buddhist monk-ascetic ideal and those responsible for maintaining the monasteries. For the latter, those Buddhist ascetics who lived with the dead in cemeteries or wore the contaminated shrouds of corpses threatened to tarnish the image of Buddhism in a society of potential patrons who could in no way tolerate exposure to death or contact with the dead.

Exemplary Deaths and Their Legitimizing Power

Chapters 3 through 8 deal with the possibility of acquiring meditative and ritual control over one's own death process; the remarkable deaths of Buddhist adepts said to have achieved such control; and the value that narrative accounts and visual representations of such extraordinary deaths have held for disciples and devotees, both as sources of inspiration and for the religious authority that they conferred on the community to which the deceased had belonged. Across Buddhist cultures, committed practitioners have sought to die with a calm and focused mind, not only to follow the Buddha's example or to demonstrate their own attainments, but also because it was believed that the quality of a dying person's last thoughts exerted a determinative influence on that individual's next rebirth. Dying well means approaching the final moments with a pure and virtuous mind. To ensure right mindfulness at the time of death, sūtras, Vinaya texts, and ritual manuals have recommended attending the sick and dying, whether they are monastics or lay people, and exhorting them to cultivate wholesome thoughts in their critical last moments. The ideal of a mindful death was by no means confined to Buddhism but was part of the broader Indian religious culture and persists to the present day.[35] Here we find another set of contradictory logics recurring in Buddhist approaches to death: in the juxtaposition of the ideas that an individual's postmortem fate would be determined by the sum of his or her acts throughout life and that proper ritual action at the last moment, on the part of the dying person or of those in attendance, could at once dissolve that person's accumulated sins and enable his or her birth in a superior realm.

Koichi Shinohara's chapter analyzes instructions for deathbed practices to be conducted in the monastic setting as set forth by the Chinese Vinaya authority Daoxuan (596–667) in his commentary on the *Dharmaguptaka vinaya*. Drawing extensively on both Indic and Chinese sources, Daoxuan's recommendations include removing a dying monk to a separate hall, placing him in a prescribed posture, and having him hold a five-colored cord or pennant attached to the hand of a buddha image, so as to help him to form the thought of following the Buddha to his buddha land. Attendants should also offer the dying monk sermons and encouragement to assist his mental focus at the end. Daoxuan's instructions for deathbed practice would exert a far-reaching influence on rites for the time of death throughout East Asian Buddhism, especially in Pure Land circles. In analyzing Daoxuan's sources and other related Chinese Buddhist texts, Shinohara notes the recurrence of two contrasting themes: one emphasizeing the impermanence of all things and the need to relinquish attachments at the time of death and the other stressing the importance of one's final thoughts as a way of securing rebirth in a pure land or other superior realm. He suggests that while both views can be found in Indian Buddhist sources, the growing momentum of Pure Land beliefs and practices in Chinese Buddhist circles in Daoxuan's time heightened the tension between them. For Daoxuan, as for later commentators, the tradition of deathbed reflections on impermanence was subordinated to the goal of birth in a pure land. Shinohara's chapter underscores the fact that even within the Buddhist tradition of a specific time and place, aspirations concerning one's postmortem state and understandings of the significance of deathbed practice were not necessarily uniform but might be contested and redefined.

Tensions between differing soteriological goals are also addressed in Jacqueline Stone's essay, which focuses on the use, in medieval Japan, of deathbed practices associated with esoteric Buddhism (*mikkyō*). From a purely doctrinal standpoint, esoteric Buddhism was understood as the vehicle for realizing buddhahood in this very body, while hopes for the next life were commonly framed in terms of birth in Amida Buddha's Pure Land. While a modern Buddhist sectarian reading might see these two goals as mutually incompatible, Stone finds that the picture was far more complicated. For the most part, medieval Japanese Buddhists freely combined esoteric practices with Pure Land aspirations in the deathbed context with no evident sense of contradiction. However, some thinkers of the esoteric Shingon tradition sought to reinterpret both the concept of "birth in the Pure Land" and deathbed ritual practice in light of esoteric models of the direct realization of buddhahood. Stone's chapter explores three such attempts that approach the problem in strikingly different ways: by reinterpreting deathbed practice as a form of esoteric ritual union with the Buddha; by rejecting aspiration to specific pure lands as inconsistent with the esoteric teaching that all reality is the realm of the cosmic Buddha Mahāvairocana; and by a creative "double logic" that simultaneously acknowledges both birth in the Pure Land and the realization of buddhahood with this very body, holding these two goals in a dynamic tension without resolving the opposition between them.

Chapters 5 and 6 focus on representations of ideal deaths and the roles they have played in the lives of Buddhist communities. Raoul Birnbaum's chapter details the death of the modern Chinese Buddhist master Hongyi (1880–1942). Hongyi's death was distinctive in a number of ways, one of which was that his appearance in death was captured in a remarkable photograph. This picture of Master Hongyi portrays the "beautiful death" of an extraordinary Buddhist figure, inspired by representations of the Buddha's own death, and incidentally demonstrates that Buddhist ideals about dying in an exemplary manner have by no means been confined to premodern times. Birnbaum reminds us, however, that an image is meaningful only to the extent that it is seen by an audience. The symbolic power of Hongyi's image takes form in the eyes of its viewers and provides for them both a model *of* and a model *for* the ideal Buddhist death. In this way, Birnbaum argues, the photograph of the dead master Hongyi also serves as a form of relic. As in John Strong's essay, we see here the power of the materially present relic to help maintain the connection between a deceased Buddhist master and his devoted followers.

Kurtis Schaeffer's chapter extends the category of sacred relic to include the published life story of an extraordinary Buddhist teacher. Schaeffer takes this notion as his central theme in his examination of the Tibetan hagiographical literature narrating the death of the twelfth-century yogi Milarépa (ca. 1052–1135), one of Tibet's most beloved Buddhist saints. In an insightful analytical twist, Schaeffer also examines the biography of the biographer, comparing details of Milarépa's remarkable death with those of the death of his most renowned hagiographer, Tsangnyön Heruka (1452–1507). Tibetan accounts of the deaths of both Milarépa and his biographer mirror in several essential ways the traditional accounts of the Buddha's death, again stressing, as do other essays in this volume, the paradigmatic importance of the Buddha's example. But, as Schaeffer points out, the death of the biographer Tsangnyön Heruka is modeled more on Milarépa than on the Buddha, though at the level of ultimate reality the latter two are understood to be essentially one and the same.

Schaeffer's primary focus, however, is the hagiographical texts themselves and the relationship between physical texts and revered relics. Echoing Strong's argument that the main goal of the Buddha's cremation was to ensure the production of relics, Schaeffer suggests that one of the prime purposes of hagiographical writing was to produce a relic of sorts for veneration, again underscoring the importance of relics as reinstantiating the continued presence of the absent Buddhist master. Strong, in another context, has interpreted relics as an extension of the Buddha's biography;[36] Schaeffer here considers biography as a form of relic. He also shows how, in the aftermath of the master's death, the relic, as well as the hagiographical text *as relic*, could be used to serve political and economic agendas. He concludes that relics, either in corporeal or textual form, were particularly effective in gaining patrons and sponsors and even in promoting the superiority of one Buddhist group over another.

"Giving Up the Body"

Chapters 7 and 8 deal with the controversial subject of religious suicide or—more appropriately in a Buddhist context, "giving up the body"—a particular category of exemplary death in which the ascetic exercises control over his or her death by deliberate self-sacrifice for soteriological aims. Liz Wilson has recently argued that buddhas, strictly speaking, "die by choice, voluntarily giving up a portion of their allotted span of life," and thus display their mastery over life and death.[37] From this perspective, religious suicide reenacts the Buddha's passing and homologizes the ascetic's death to the Buddha's *parinirvāṇa*. Historically, sacrifice of the body has been undertaken in Buddhist contexts as an offering to the Buddha or to his relics, to demonstrate his teachings, or to seek the Pure Land; it has been seen as the ultimate ascetic act, which, if carried out for pure motives and in a proper state of mind, could bring about birth in a superior realm or even liberation itself. Yet as Reiko Ohnuma has demonstrated about the Buddhist "gift" more generally, the sacrifice of the body, even when performed in the purest renunciatory spirit, still retains something of the "logic of exchange": one gives up the present body, subject to decay, to receive the adamantine body of an enlightened one.[38] James Benn's chapter turns to the political dimensions of this act and considers in what ways the deliberate self-sacrifice of Chinese monks could be understood as a type of Buddhist martyrdom. Focusing on accounts in Daoxuan's *Xu gaoseng zhuan* (Continued biographies of eminent monks), Benn examines six cases, dating from the sixth and seventh centuries, of monks who sacrificed their lives in a dramatic statement of resistance to anti-Buddhist policies of the Chinese state. The disciples of these monks and the devoted consumers of their remarkable stories all viewed these deaths as exemplary. Here too we see how representations of the ideal deaths of Buddhist teachers could serve as models on which future deaths might be patterned. As in the case of Tsangnyön Heruka's biography of Milarépa, discussed by Kurtis Schaeffer, the hagiographical narratives of these ideal Buddhist deaths were used to construct and promote the identity and status of specific Buddhist communities.

D. Max Moerman's chapter discusses an alternate form of Buddhist self-immolation—"death by water"—in premodern Japan, where birth in a pure land became the dominant reason given for Buddhist ascetic suicide. Along with the method of auto-cremation discussed in Benn's chapter, that of self-drowning (*jusui*) is well attested in Japan and was often carried out at sites having cultic associations with specific pure lands. Moerman's chapter focuses on a variant of this practice known as "sailing to Potalaka" (*Fudaraku tokai*), in which ascetics set out from various points along the southern coast of western Japan in small, rudderless boats, hoping to reach Potalaka (J. Fudaraku), the island paradise of the bodhisattva Kannon (Skt. Avalokiteśvara). None of them returned. In tracing resonances with non-Buddhist notions of realms of the dead located on islands or across the sea, or the ritual use of boats to send disease and defilement away from the community, Moerman reminds us that Buddhist cosmologies and death-related rites were often informed by those of other traditions. His study of "sailing to Potalaka" draws on examples of this practice spanning the medieval period, using both visual representations and textual accounts, including the reports of Jesuit missionaries. This practice was at once both "personal devotion and public spectacle," as the departure of the boats bound for Potalaka would typically be witnessed by crowds of devotees, prompted by the desire to form karmic connections with the ascetic and share in the merit of his act. Like Raoul

Birnbaum's account of the death photograph of Master Hongyi, Moerman's chapter underscores the point that exemplary deaths, to be exemplary, require witnesses and that the seemingly personal act of dying in ideal Buddhist fashion had a profoundly social dimension. This observation also raises some questions about the term "voluntary death," by which ascetic suicide is often described. As Moerman notes, the presence of insistent crowds determined to gain merit from witnessing the act may have rendered some instances of religious suicide not quite so voluntary.

The Dead and the Living

One recurring theme of the essays collected here is that the Buddhist dead are seldom really "dead" in the sense of being utterly gone and inaccessible. Chapters 9 through 11 address the ongoing relations between the dead and those still living. They treat examples of those special individuals who are able to mediate between the two realms, by either journeying to the realm of the dead or otherwise making contact with the deceased and relaying their messages to those left behind. Such individuals may operate within the context of established Buddhist institutions or on their periphery. Historically, they have played, and continue to play, key roles in Buddhist cultures by providing "proof" of recompense for good and evil deeds and thus reinforcing Buddhist ethical norms.

The chapter by Bryan Cuevas examines narratives of Tibetan *délok* (Tib. *'das log*), people who pass into the world of the dead and then return to recount their experiences. Cuevas focuses on one such story in particular, that of an ordinary Buddhist laywoman named Karma Wangzin, who lived in the seventeenth century, and examines the main features of this woman's narrative, including her intimate account of her own death, her journey to hell, and her eventual return to the world of the living. He analyzes the remarkable tale of Karma Wangzin within a social-historical framework and sifts through the details of her story for evidence of popular Tibetan attitudes toward death. Cuevas notes that perceptions of death and of the postmortem realms that emerge in *délok* narratives, while rooted in formal Buddhist doctrine, also diverge from it in significant ways, being at once both more vague and ambiguous and yet fleshed out with local specifics in a way not seen in formal treatises. These informal notions, which are shared across gender groups and social-religious classes in Tibetan Buddhist society, constitute what he defines as "popular" religious belief. At the same time, Cuevas shows that even formal teachings about the fate of the deceased in the *bardo* were compounded not only from Indian Buddhist Abhidharma concepts of the interim state but also from indigenous ideas of the soul (*bla*) and its vulnerability to demonic attack, underscoring the extent to which Buddhist traditions are inextricably embedded in the matrices of local traditions.

Similar interactions with local practices and similar confluences and divergences between formal doctrine and informal ideas are highlighted in John Holt's chapter, which examines relationships between the living and the dead as expressed in the activities of the lay village priestess Viṣṇu Kalyāni in contemporary Buddhist Sri Lanka. This priestess is revered for her seemingly astounding ability to communicate with the recently deceased, and, like the *délok* Karma Wangzin in Cuevas' essay, she functions as a sort of "communications broker" between the two worlds. Holt demonstrates how common fears of the "restless dead" in a Sri Lankan village and appeals to Buddhist principles of merit and karmic retribution work together to empower this priestess in the eyes of her community and authenticate her otherwordly communications as manifestly true. At the same time, he notes, her activities also indicate that after death, links to relatives are not altogether severed; the deceased actually remains an important and interactive member of the family left behind. Holt argues that such concerns about how the living relate to the dead are not merely a feature of the contemporary "spirit religion" emerging as a byproduct of social change in urban areas, but they have also formed a central focus of Sinhala lay Buddhist piety since ancient times.

Matthew Kapstein's chapter concerns one of the most celebrated journeys in the shared Buddhist tradition to the world beyond: the descent into hell of the Buddha's disciple Maudgalyāyana (Ch. Mulian) to save his mother. In East Asia, the legend is most fully elaborated in two Chinese Buddhist texts, the *Yulanpen jing* and the *Damuqianlian mingjian jiumu bianwen* (Transformation text on Mulian saving his mother from hell). Kapstein considers the place of this popular Chinese literature in Tibet and demonstrates how the narrative of Mulian's heroic descent, transformed and reformulated by Tibetans, was assimilated into a distinctively Tibetan Buddhist framework. In so doing, he contributes a significant Tibetan example to recent scholarship analyzing how Buddhist practices and discourses emphasizing filial piety coexisted with the tradition's renunciate ideal.[39] In China, the Mulian story gave rise to the popular "ghost festival," which centered on Chinese concerns for the salvation of deceased relatives and ancestors. In Tibet, Kapstein notes, no such festival ever took root, but the Chinese legend did spawn Tibetan analogues to Mulian, such as the thirteenth-century visionary Guru Chöwang (1212–1270) and the epic hero Gesar of Ling. Moreover, the legend of Mulian helped to inspire the development of the Tibetan *délok* literature.

"Placing" the Dead

As anthropologists have long recognized, the dead, despite the fact of being dead, continue to be present among the living. Thus, the dead are always in need of care and a suitable "place" in society. Chapters 12–14 address the social and physical locations of the Buddhist dead through examination of funerary and mortuary rites. Hank Glassman's chapter investigates the role of Japanese Buddhist funerary and mortuary practices in shaping norms of family and kinship in the eleventh and twelfth centuries. New practices that emerged at this time—including the separate burial of husbands and wives of different family origins; the preservation and enshrining of bones, often identified with Buddhist relics; and calendrically determined visits to family grave sites—both reflected and stimulated a growing consciousness of ancestors, lineage, and the importance of the paternal line. Glassman's essay focuses in particular on the female dead. He suggests that as emphasis on the patriarchal household grew and women's legal, social, and familial status correspondingly declined, married women came with growing frequency to be buried with their husbands' families, leading eventually to the early modern system of family graves and memorial rites that persists to the present. Where and in what manner the dead are placed, Glassman argues, tells us much about how society is structured and how particular representations of family identity are reinforced. Glassman shows that the place of the female dead in Japanese society, and of married women in particular, shifted over time, and these shifts have both marked and helped to bring about specific changes in the Japanese family and the status of women within it.

Mark Rowe's chapter explores recent controversy over the problem of "placing" the dead in contemporary Japan. Decreasing grave space, the graying of society, and changes in women's status and in concepts of the individual have been accompanied by a growing disaffection with the family grave system and the Buddhist memorial rites that support it. Rowe examines the new and highly politicized practice of scattering the ashes of the dead, as conducted by the Grave Free Promotion Society, founded in 1991, as an alternative to what many perceive as a Buddhist monopoly on death ritual. The varied responses of Buddhist priests that Rowe analyzes show how foundational doctrines can be deployed to legitimate widely divergent practices: while some priests endorse the scattering of ashes as consistent with normative Buddhist doctrines of impermanence and non-attachment, others invoke dependent origination (Skt. *pratītya-samutpāda*) to argue the importance of ancestral ties and thus the importance of preserving family-based graves and traditional Buddhist memorial rites. Rowe also discusses innovative voluntary burial societies, introduced by some Buddhist temples as an alternative to family graves, where the system of memorial rites is supported not by preestablished bonds of kinship and locality, but by ties of voluntary association. Like Glassman's essay, Rowe's chapter suggests that funerary and memorial rites not only reflect social change but also constitute a vital arena in which social norms may be challenged and reshaped.

In the final chapter, Jason Carbine examines a concern with "caring for Buddhism" in contemporary Myanmar (Burma), as seen in a monastic "cremation volume" recording the grand public funeral of the Sudhammā monk Bhaddanta Indācāra (1897–1993). Through its account of Bhaddanta Indācāra's life, photographic record of the funeral rites, and ceremonial eulogies, this volume, Carbine argues, constitutes a work of pedagogy for the care of the monastic dead, illustrating by example the roles that various sectors of Burmese Buddhists—monks and nuns, military officials, and the laity in general—should play in paying reverence to the special dead. Carbine suggests that caring for the monastic dead is understood as caring for and sustaining the very ideals of Buddhism, though this ethos may be subject to varying interpretation by different social constituencies. With Carbine's essay, the volume comes full circle: the last rites of the high-ranking Buddhist figure Bhaddanta Indācāra reenact the paradigm of the Buddha's own funeral, with which Strong's opening chapter begins. Like the Buddha, Bhaddanta Indācāra's body produced relics in testimony to his attainment, and, like those who tended to the body of the Buddha, Bhaddanta Indācāra's followers, in properly memorializing him and caring for his remains, demonstrate their commitment to preserving the Buddhist ideals that he exemplified in life and in death.

WHAT THIS collection of essays demonstrates most strikingly is the recurrence of common themes in death-related discourses, practices, and representations across Buddhist cultures. These include pervasive tensions between the message of impermanence and the desire for continuity and stability; the ideal of the exemplary death, modeled upon that of the Buddha, as an index to an individual's spiritual state and as a source of legitimation for the followers of particular Buddhist teachers; the importance of relics, whether cremated remains, hagiographical texts, or even photographs, in demonstrating a teacher's attainments and in some sense reestablishing his presence in the world; the liminal power of the moment of death itself, when proper meditative and ritual practice can direct one toward a favorable rebirth or even liberation; and the ongoing relationship between the dead and the living, whether mediated by religious specialists or by funerals and memorial rites, in which concern for the well-being of the deceased becomes a powerful motive for moral conduct and merit-making. Other persistent themes may be adduced as well. These essays demonstrate that approaches to death in Buddhist societies have typically brought together multiple and at times paradoxical logics drawn from diverse doctrines and theoretical systems, as well as from local religious traditions and, most recently, from discourses of modernity. They also shed light on the role of Buddhist memorial rites in the construction of social identities, gender categories, and kinship ties. In the end, all the contributions to this book reveal just how integral matters of the dead have been and continue to be to Buddhists everywhere.

While the essays in this volume represent a range of methods and subjects, we have made no attempt to be comprehensive. Some comment on the more obvious gaps may be in order. For example, our collection does not include an essay focusing on the more technical aspects of doctrine, such as Abhidharmic analyses of death, discussion of death consciousness and rebirth-linking consciousness, or the interim state.[40] This lack does not reflect an antidoctrinal bias on our part but is rather an artifact of our initial question about the feasibility of studying "death in Buddhism" in a way that is both transregional and culturally and historically grounded—a focus that, in retrospect, may have discouraged contributions with a more exclusively doctrinal orientation. We deliberately chose not to engage in comparison with death practices in non-Buddhist cultures. Some of the individual chapters have noted points of potential comparison with late antiquity or medieval Europe; James Benn, for example, suggests a possible comparison between some Buddhist self-immolators and the martyrs of Christian and Islamic traditions. In the wake of the shift away from the largely text- and doctrine-based approaches characterizing an earlier generation of Buddhist Studies and the move to include ritual, devotional, and material culture as areas of study, Robert Sharf has noted, "Buddhism may no longer resemble European humanism, mysticism (the "perennial philosophy"), or enlightened rationalism, but it has come to bear an uncanny resemblance to medieval Christianity: both were preoccupied, at some level, with saints, relics, and miraculous images."[41] Last rites and *ars moriendi* for the dying, along with notions of purgatorial realms, form other suggestive points of comparison. Scholars of premodern forms of Buddhism who have also looked into the work of Peter Brown, Carolyn Walker Bynum, Patrick Geary, Jacques Le Goff, Frederick Paxton, Jean-Claude Schmitt, and others cannot help but notice parallels. But whether such "uncanny resemblances" will prove to be methodologically fruitful in light of disciplined comparative study or merely instances of the "nagging issue of universal, or at least general, features of behavior" is a question that must await a different volume.[42]

Notes

1. "Death as Threat, Death as Achievement: Buddhist Perspectives with Particular Reference to the Theravada Tradition," in *Death and the Afterlife: Perspectives of World Religions*, ed. Hiroshi Obayashi (New York: Greenwood Press, 1992), 158.

2. *Visuddhimagga* III: 57–59.

3. On Buddhist death meditation, see, for example, Edward Conze, "The Meditation on Death," in *Thirty Years of Buddhist Studies: Selected Studies*, ed. Edward Conze (Columbia: University of South Carolina Press, 1968), 86–104, and George D. Bond, "Theravada Buddhism's Meditations

on Death and the Symbolism of Initiatory Death," *History of Religions* 19, no. 3 (1980): 237–58. A contemporary version of the charnel ground meditations in Sri Lanka, conducted in the morgue rather than the cemetery, is discussed in Mathieu Boisvert, "Death as Meditation Subject in the Theravāda Tradition," *Buddhist Studies Review* 13, no. 1 (1996): 37–54.

4. On Buddhist monks as the mediators of merit transference to the dead, see John Holt, "Assisting the Dead by Venerating the Living: Merit Transfer in the Early Buddhist Tradition," *Numen* 28, no. 1 (1981): 1–28.

5. Recent overviews of the subject include John Bowker, "Buddhism," chap. 6 in his *Meanings of Death* (New York: Cambridge University Press, 1991), 168–205; Carl B. Becker, *Breaking the Circle: Death and the Afterlife in Buddhism* (Carbondale: University of Southern Illinois Press, 1993); Charles Hallisey, "Buddhism," in *Death and the Afterlife*, ed. Jacob Neusner (Cleveland: Pilgrim Press, 2000), 1–29; Mark Blum, "Death," in *Encyclopedia of Buddhism*, ed. Robert E. Buswell, Jr. (New York: Macmillan Reference, 2004), 203–210; and Jacqueline I. Stone, "Death," in *Critical Terms for Buddhist Studies*, ed. Donald S. Lopez, Jr. (Chicago: University of Chicago Press, 2005), 56–76.

6. The term "Buddhist modernism" was coined by Heinz Bechert in his *Buddhismus, Staat und Gesellschaft in den Ländern des Theravāda-Buddhismus* (Hamburg: Schriften des Instituts für Asienkunde, 1966). The very similar term "Protestant Buddhism" was first employed by Gananath Obeyesekere in his "Religious Symbolism and Political Change in Ceylon," *Modern Ceylon Studies* 1, no. 1 (1970): 43–63.

7. From *Return to Righteousness*, ed. A. Guruge (Colombo, 1965); quoted in Steven Collins, *Selfless Persons: Imagery and Thought in Theravāda Buddhism* (New York: Cambridge University Press, 1982), 14.

8. *Bukkyō fūfu ron* (1887); trans. from Richard M. Jaffe, *Neither Monk nor Layman: Clerical Marriage in Modern Japanese Buddhism* (Princeton: Princeton University Press, 2001), 176–77; see also 169–70.

9. *The Buddhist Revival in China* (Cambridge, MA: Harvard University Press, 1968), 209.

10. Francesca Fremantle, "Introduction," in *The Tibetan Book of the Dead: The Great Liberation through Hearing in the Bardo*, trans. with commentary by Francesca Fremantle and Chögyam Trungpa (Boston: Shambala, 1987), xix–xx. Lama Angarika Govinda's remarks appear in his "Introductory Foreword" in *The Tibetan Book of the Dead: The After-Death Experiences on the* Bardo *Plane, according to Lama Kazi Dawa-Samdup's English Rendering*, comp. and ed. W. Y. Evans-Wentz (1927; repr. New York: Oxford University Press, 2000), lix–lx. On this and other problems in the Western reception of the *Tibetan Book of the Dead*, see Donald S. Lopez, Jr., "The Book," chap. 2 in his *Prisoners of Shangri La: Tibetan Buddhism and the West* (Chicago: University of Chicago Press, 1998), 46–85, and

Bryan J. Cuevas, "Introduction: The Saga of *The Tibetan Book of the Dead*," in his *Hidden History of the Tibetan Book of the Dead* (New York: Oxford University Press, 2003), 3–24.

11. We are indebted to Robert Gimello for suggesting to us a connection between the marginalizing of death rites and the afterlife in discourses of Buddhist modernism and the long neglect of death in Buddhist Studies.

12. Buddhist Publication Society (1973), 2–3; cited in Collins, *Selfless Persons*, 5.

13. Gregory Schopen traces the textual emphasis of early Buddhist Studies to a "Protestant presupposition," dating back to the Reformation, that seeks the essence of religion, not in the activities of its followers, but in its sacred texts ("Archaeology and Protestant Presuppositions in the Study of Indian Buddhism" [1991]; reprinted in his *Bones, Stones, and Buddhist Monks: Collected Papers on the Archaeology, Epigraphy, and Texts of Monastic Buddhism in India* [Honolulu: University of Hawai'i Press, 1997], 1–22). Others have seen "textual Buddhism" as a construct informed by colonial ideology, in that a Buddhism of texts could be located in, and thus defined, curated, and mediated by, the West. See Philip C. Almond, *The British Discovery of Buddhism* (Cambridge: Cambridge University Press, 1988), 13, and Donald S. Lopez, Jr., "Introduction" to his edited volume, *Curators of the Buddha: The Study of Buddhism under Colonialism* (Chicago: University of Chicago Press, 1995), 1–29.

14. Collins, *Selfless Persons*, 12.

15. Collins has shown that even in the Pāli canon (by no means as univocal a corpus as is often imagined), the *anattā* doctrine and related discourses do not by any means "exhaust the range of psychological and behavioural concern of the individual Buddhist, however much of a meditative or scholastic specialist he might be" (*Selfless Persons*, 70).

16. *What the Buddha Taught* (1959; 2nd ed. Grove Press, 1974), 34.

17. Stanley Tambiah, a pioneer in the critique of two-tiered elite/folk models of religion, has lambasted this position as "Pāli Text Society mentality" (while acknowledging "those extraordinary individuals belonging to this society who did not merit this opprobrium") (*The Buddhist Saints of the Forest and the Cult of Amulets* [New York: Cambridge University Press, 1984], 7). At the same time, however, such assumptions of decline uncannily mirror contemporaneous Protestant accounts of a pristine, original Christianity corrupted by rituals deriving from late antiquity and perpetuated by the Roman Catholic Church (see Jonathan Z. Smith, *Drudgery Divine: On the Comparison of Early Christianities and the Religions of Late Antiquity* [Chicago: University of Chicago Press, 1990]). We thank Donald S. Lopez, Jr. for pointing out this parallel to us.

18. *Buddhism and Society: A Great Tradition and Its Burmese Vicissitudes* (1970; rev. ed. Berkeley: University of California Press, 1982), 248.

19. *Precept and Practice: Traditional Buddhism in the Rural Highlands of Ceylon* (Oxford: Clarendon Press, 1971), 73.

20. One might wonder if such models were informed to any extent by the dual-path structure set forth in Pāli sources, with good rebirth as a proximate goal and nibbāna as the ultimate goal. However, scholarly discourses positing a dichotomy between normative doctrine and traditional Buddhist death rites are by no means limited to Theravāda contexts. A striking case may be seen in the Buddhist sectarian research centers of contemporary Japan, where many Buddhist scholars (often Buddhist priests themselves) have come to be troubled by what they see as a profound disjuncture between "orthodox" doctrines of emptiness and not-self and the rites of merit transfererence to the spirits of the deceased, which parishioners expect of them. See, for example, Mark Rowe, "Where the Action Is: Sites of Contemporary Sōtō Buddhism," *Japanese Journal of Religious Studies* 31, no. 2 (2004): 362–69.

21. For a cogent discussion of the development of "popular religion" as a category of analysis, see Catherine Bell, "Religion and Chinese Culture: Toward an Assessment of 'Popular Religion,'" *History of Religions* 29, no. 1 (1989): 35–57; cf. also Natalie Z. Davis: "Some Tasks and Themes in the Study of Popular Religion," in *The Pursuit of Happiness in Late Medieval and Renaissance Religion*, ed. Charles Trinkaus and Heiko A. Oberman (Leiden: E. J. Brill, 1974), 307–36, and "From 'Popular Religion' to Religious Cultures," in *Reformation Europe: A Guide to Research*, ed. Steven Ozment (St. Louis: Center for Reformation Research, 1982), 321–41.

22. The work of Gregory Schopen on Indian Buddhism has been groundbreaking in this regard. See, for example, the following, all reprinted in his *Bones, Stones, and Buddhist Monks*: "Burial *Ad Sanctos* and the Physical Presence of the Buddha in Early Indian Buddhism: A Study in the Archaeology of Religions" (1987), 114–47; "On Avoiding Ghosts and Social Censure: Monastic Funerals in the *Mūlasarvāstivāda-vinaya*" (1992), 204–37; "An Old Inscription from Amarāvatī and the Cult of the Local Monastic Dead" (1991), 165–203; and "Two Problems in the History of Indian Buddhism: The Layman/Monk Distinction and the Doctrines of the Transference of Merit," 23–55.

23. This is in no way to deny doctrine's own claim to normative status, which is very different from assumptions on the researcher's part that doctrine necessarily will, or even should, play a normative role for actual Buddhists.

24. See David M. Knipe, "*Sapiṇḍīkaraṇa*: The Hindu Rite of Entry into Heaven," in *Religious Encounters with Death: Insights from the History and Anthropology of Religions*, ed. Frank E. Reynolds and Earle E. Waugh (University Park: Pennsylvania State University Press, 1977), 111–24. We thank Phyllis Granoff and Gregory Schopen, who both independently called this reference to our attention.

25. Representative book-length studies dealing wholly or substantially with Buddhist death-related practices or discourses include Bernard Faure, *La mort dans les religions d'Asie* (Paris: Flammarion, 1994); Stephen F. Teiser, *The Scripture on the Ten Kings and the Making of Purgatory in Medieval Chinese Buddhism* (Honolulu: University of Hawai'i Press, 1994); Liz Wilson, *Charming Cadavers: Horrific Figurations of the Feminine in Indian Buddhist Hagiographic Literature* (Chicago: University of Chicago Press, 1996); Glenn H. Mullin, *Living in the Face of Death: The Tibetan Tradition* (Ithaca, NY: Snow Lion Publications, 1998); and Alan Klima, *The Funeral Casino: Meditation, Massacre, and Exchange with the Dead in Thailand* (Princeton, NJ: Princeton University Press, 2002). Individual articles and chapters on Buddhist death-related topics are too numerous to list exhaustively. Some significant examples not otherwise cited in this volume include Charles F. Keyes, "Tug-of-War for Merit: Cremation of a Senior Monk," *Journal of the Siam Society* 63 (1975): 44–62; Elisabeth Benard, "The Tibetan Tantric View of Death and the Afterlife," in Obayashi, ed., *Death and the Afterlife*, 169–80; Stephen F. Teiser: "Hymns for the Dead in the Age of the Manuscript," *Gest Library Journal* 5, no. 1 (1992): 26–56, and "The Growth of Purgatory," in *Religion and Society in T'ang and Sung China*, ed. Patricia Buckley Ebrey and Peter N. Gregory (Honolulu: University of Hawai'i Press, 1993), 115–45; William M. Bodiford, "Zen Funerals," chapter 14 in his *Sōtō Zen in Medieval Japan* (Honolulu: University of Hawai'i Press, 1993), 185–208; Alan Cole, "Upside Down/Rightside Up: A Revisionist History of Buddhist Funerals in China," *History of Religions* 35, no. 4 (1996): 307–28; Frederic J. Kotas, "The Craft of Dying in Late Heian Japan," in *Bukkyō bungaku no kōsō*, ed. Imanari Genshō (Tokyo: Shintensha, 1996), 598–71 (reverse pagination); David Germano, "Dying, Death, and Other Opportunities," in *Religions of Tibet in Practice*, ed. Donald S. Lopez, Jr. (Princeton, NJ: Princeton University Press, 1997), 458–93; Liu Shufen, "Death and the Degeneration of Life: Exposure of the Corpse in Medieval Chinese Buddhism," *Chinese Religions* 28 (2000): 1–30.

26. See, for example, Robert D. Baird, *Category Formation and the History of Religions* (The Hague: Mouton, 1971), 138–41.

27. "Death," 206.

28. We were inspired here by Peter Brown's category of the "very special dead." See his *Cult of the Saints: Its Rise and Function in Latin Christianity* (Chicago: University of Chicago Press, 1981), 69–85.

29. See, for example, Bernard Faure, "Relics and Flesh Bodies: The Creation of Ch'an Pilgrimage Sites," in *Pilgrimage and Sacred Sites in China*, ed. Susan Naquin and Chun-fang Yü (Berkeley: University of California Press, 1992); Kevin Trainor, *Relics, Ritual, and Representation in Buddhism: Rematerializing the Sri Lankan Theravāda Tradition* (Cambridge: Cambridge University Press, 1997); Brian K. Ruppert, *Jewel in the Ashes: Buddha Relics and Power in Early Medieval Japan* (Cambridge, MA: Harvard University

Press, 1997); Gregory Schopen: *Bones, Stones, and Buddhist Monks* (see especially the essays "Burial *Ad Sanctos*," 114–47; "On the Buddha and His Bones: The Conception of a Relic in the Inscriptions of Nāgārjunikoṇḍa," 148–64; and "The Buddha as an Owner of Property and Permanent Resident in Medieval Indian Buddhist Monasteries," 258–89), and "Relic" in *Critical Terms for Religious Studies*, ed. Mark C. Taylor (Chicago: University of Chicago Press, 1998), 256–68; Robert H. Sharf, "On the Allure of Buddhist Relics," *Representations* 66 (1999): 75–99; John S. Strong, *Relics of the Buddha* (Princeton, NJ: Princeton University Press, 2004); and Peter Skilling, "Cutting across Categories: The Ideology of Relics in Buddhism," *Annual Report of the International Research Institute for Advanced Buddhology at Soka University* 8 (2005): 269–322.

30. Schopen: "Burial *Ad Sanctos*," esp. 125–33, and "The Buddha as an Owner of Property."

31. See, for example, Faure, "Relics and Flesh Bodies."

32. Strong, *Relics of the Buddha*, approaches relics as "expressions and extensions of the Buddha's biographical process" (5). On the *parinirvāṇa* of the relics, see 221–26. See also Skilling, "Cutting across Categories," 282–83.

33. See the classic studies, on secondary burial, by Robert Hertz, "A Contribution to the Study of Collective Representations of Death," in *Death and the Right Hand*, trans. Rodney and Claudia Needham (Glencoe: Free Press, 1960 [1907]), 27–86, and, on rites of passage, by Arnold van Gennep, *The Rites of Passage*, trans. Monika B. Vizedom and Gabrielle L. Caffee (Chicago: University of Chicago Press, 1960 [1909]), 146–65. On death ritual and symbols of stability and regeneration, see also *Death and the Regeneration of Life*, ed. Maurice Bloch and Jonathan Parry (Cambridge: Cambridge University Press, 1982).

34. Stone, "Death," 63–64.

35. For references to this idea in early Indian sources, see Franklin Edgerton, "The Hour of Death: Its Importance for Man's Future Fate in Hindu and Western Religions," *Annals of the Bhandarkar Institute* 8, part 3 (1927): 220–49. On contemporary Hindu practice, see Jonathan P. Parry, *Death in Banaras* (Cambridge: Cambridge University Press, 1994), 158–66.

36. Strong, *Relics of the Buddha*.

37. "Introduction" to *The Living and the Dead: Social Dimensions of Death in South Asian Religions*, ed. Liz Wilson (Albany: State University of New York Press, 2003), 4. See also Wilson's own essay in the same volume, "Human Torches of Enlightenment: Autocremation and Spontaneous Combustion as Marks of Sanctity in South Asian Buddhism," 29–50.

38. See Reiko Ohnuma, "Gift," in *Critical Terms for Buddhist Studies*, ed. Donald S. Lopez, Jr. (Chicago: University of Chicago Press, 2005), 103–23.

39. See, for example, Gregory Schopen, "Filial Piety and the Monk in the Practice of Indian Buddhism: A Question of 'Sinicization' Viewed from the Other Side" (1984); reprinted in his *Bones, Stones, and Buddhist Monks*, 56–71; Stephen F. Teiser, *The Ghost Festival in Medieval China* (Princeton, NJ: Princeton University Press, 1988); Alan Cole, *Mothers and Sons in Chinese Buddhism* (Stanford, CA: Stanford University Press, 1998); Hank Glassman, "The Religious Construction of Motherhood in Medieval Japan," Ph.D. diss., Stanford University, 2001; and Reiko Ohnuma, "Debt to the Mother: A Neglected Aspect of the Founding of the Buddhist Nuns' Order, *Journal of the American Academy of Religion* 74: 4 (2006), forthcoming.

40. Useful introductions to these topics include L. De la Vallée Poussin: "Death and Disposal of the Dead," in *Encyclopaedia of Religion and Ethics*, ed. James Hastings (New York: Charles Scribner's Sons, 1912), 4:446–49, and "Death," in *Encyclopaedia of Buddhism*, ed. Jotiya Dhirasekera (Government of Sri Lanka, 1979), 4:331–35. For doctrinal discussions of the *antarābhava*, see Alex Wayman, "The Intermediate-State Dispute in Buddhism," in *Buddhist Studies in Honour of I. B. Horner* (Dordrecht: D. Reidel Publishing, 1974), 227–39, and Robert Kritzer, "Rūpa and the Antarābhava," *Journal of Indian Philosophy* 28 (2000): 235–72.

41. "On the Allure of Buddhist Relics," 79. For an example of a comparative study, see John S. Strong, "Buddhist Relics in Comparative Perspective: Beyond the Parallels," in *Embodying the Dharma: Buddhist Relic Veneration in Asia*, ed. David Germano and Kevin Trainor (Albany: State University of New York Press, 2004), 27–49.

42. Peter Metcalf and Richard Huntington, *Celebrations of Death: The Anthroplogy of Mortuary Ritual*, 2nd ed. (Cambridge: Cambridge University Press, 1991), 63.

1

The Buddha's Funeral

John S. Strong

Ever since the work of Arnold van Gennep, historians of religion have known that funerals do not just mark the end of a life. They are, rather, rites of passage, transitions into another state or status.[1] This, of course, is perfectly obvious in the case of deceased persons who are moving on to heaven (or to hell) or who will be reincarnated again on earth or in some other realm. In the case of the Buddha or other enlightened beings who have transcended saṃsāra, however, the nature of the afterlife is slightly different; it is characterized not by rebirth in some other state but by continued existence as relics. In this chapter I would like to examine the Buddha's funeral as a rite of passage that looks forward to the production and preservation of buddha relics and so ensures the transition of the Blessed One to a new state. By viewing the Buddha's funeral in this way, I believe we can begin to make sense out of some of the admittedly bizarre details of his obsequies that are recounted in various versions of *Mahāparinirvāṇa sūtra*, a text that recounts not only the Buddha's final days but also his death and funeral.[2]

First, we are told that, overall, the body of a tathāgata should be treated in the same manner as that of a cakravartin king.[3] This general injunction recalls a parallelism that spans the whole of the Buddha's biography. As is well known, shortly after the Buddha's birth, the soothsayers who examined his body saw on it the marks of a great man (Skt. *mahāpuruṣa*) and proclaimed that he had a double potential: he would become either a buddha or a cakravartin. Here, at the end of his life, the same duality is recalled.[4] Usually, this association with kingship is said to be intended to enhance the Buddha's prestige. In the context at hand, however, it may have a more particular implication connected to the cult of relics.

Jean Przyluski, who has argued that the cakravartin ideal stems, at least in part, from Hellenistic and ultimately ancient Near Eastern notions of kingship,[5] claims that it also went hand in hand with the practice of venerating the remains—i.e., the relics—of royal persons. In support of his case, he cites the example of

Alexander the Great, who was divinized and whose body, it was thought, would bring happiness and prosperity to the land where it was kept. There consequently erupted a dispute among the Macedonians over the disposal of Alexander's bodily remains—not unlike the so-called "war" over the relics of the Buddha, which I will touch on below. In a slightly different vein, Przyluski further cites Plutarch's statement that after the death of King Menander, the cities of Northwest India divided among themselves his ashes and built *mnêmeia* (memorials—i.e., caityas) over each portion.[6] These examples are important because they may imply that Buddhist relic veneration (basically an anomaly in Indian culture, where dead bodies or their remains were viewed as impure and dangerous)[7] was part of a package deal defined by practices associated with kingship. The prescription that the Buddha's funeral should be conducted as though it were the funeral of a cakravartin, therefore, may generally be related to the later injunction that his relics be preserved and that his body not be handled like those of mere mortals (or of non-Buddhist *saṃnyāsin*s), whose remains were not generally preserved.

But it is the specific elements of the prescribed cakravartin's funeral that most interest me here. In the *Mahāparinirvāṇa sūtra*, these are said to constitute a ritual sequence of acts that is called a "*śarīra-pūjā*," a word that literally means "the worship of the body" but that more generally might be translated as "the funeral arrangements."[8] First, the body of a cakravartin (and consequently the body of the Buddha) should be wrapped in five hundred double-layers of shrouds made of two kinds of cotton cloth. Second, it should be placed in an iron coffin filled with oil and covered with an iron lid. Third, though not explicitly prescribed, it is understood that various ritual forms of veneration of the Buddha's body (pūjā) will be carried out during this time. Fourth, the tathāgata/cakravartin is to be cremated on a fire made with various kinds of sweet-smelling woods. Fifth, his relics/remains are to be gathered. Finally, a stūpa (funerary mound) is to be erected for him at a crossroads.[9] In what follows, I want to examine in turn each of the elements of this sequence so as to form a better impression of the Buddha's funeral as a whole.

The Shrouds

The first specification in this list of items is that the Buddha's body should be wrapped in five hundred pairs of shrouds or pieces of cloth before being placed in an iron sarcophagus filled with oil. This peculiarity has been the subject of much scholarly discussion. Those inclined to read the text historically find it difficult to imagine the Buddha's body as "an enormous mummy, enshrouded in a thousand cotton sheets,"[10] and ask how it could possibly have fit into a normal-sized coffin. Like André Bareau, they may prefer the one Chinese textual variant that puts the number of pairs of shrouds at ten rather than at five hundred.[11] Ernst Waldschmidt, taking a functionalist view, suggests that the multiple shrouds were meant to preserve the body from decay during the seven days in which it was venerated prior to its cremation.[12] Others are more exegetically adventuresome. Jean Przyluski, for instance, while dismissing the number five hundred as hyperbole, argues that what is significant is the notion of a *pair* of cloths, which, as we shall see, he understands to be garments rather than shrouds.[13] Charlotte Vaudeville, on the other hand, interprets the five hundred pairs of "shrouds" as five hundred layers of flowers rained down upon the body of the Buddha by the arboreal divinities resident in the twin *śāla* trees between which the Blessed One passed away.[14]

All of the versions of the *Mahāparinirvāṇa sūtra* state that the fabric (or at least one of the fabrics when two types of cloth are specified) out of which the shrouds were made was cotton.[15] In the Pāli text, a differentiation is made between alternating layers of cotton (*kappāsa*) that is "unbeaten" or "untorn" (*ahata*)—that is, never washed, i.e., new—and cotton that is "beaten" or "torn" (*vihata*)—that is, some sort of cotton wool.[16]

It is customary to think of these layers as so many winding sheets, but they may also have served another function. At least since the time of Buddhaghosa (fifth century CE), it has been suggested that these types of cloth—especially the teased cotton wool (*vihata kappāsa*)—were chosen because they could better soak up the oil in the iron coffin.[17] Apparently, it was thought that this would make the body burn better. More specifically, the description of the wrapping of the Buddha's corpse suggests that his body was being made into a sort of human torch or oil lamp. The metaphor is not without its reverberations. On the one hand, it recalls the well-known comparison of the *parinirvāṇa* (final extinction) to a fire or lamp going out when all its fuel has been spent, when there is no remainder. This image is, in fact, invoked in the Pāli account of the Buddha's own cremation, where we are told that after being completely burned, his body left no ash or soot, "just as an oil or butter [lamp] leaves none when it is burned."[18] On the other hand, the wrapping of the Buddha's body in cotton and the soaking of it in oil reminds one of other legendary Buddhist examples in which kings or great devotees transform themselves into lamps or torches and set themselves on fire as self-sacrificial expressions of devotion. Thus, the past Buddha Mangala, in one of his previous existences, is said to have "wrapped his whole body in the manner of making a torch" and to have set it ablaze, along with a golden thousand-wick butter lamp, as an offering to the stūpa of another buddha.[19] Similarly, the *Lotus Sūtra* recalls the example of the bodhisattva Sarvasattvapriyadarśana, who ate resins and drank oil for twelve years and then wrapped his body in garments and bathed in oil before setting himself ablaze in honor of a buddha; he burned, we are told, for twelve thousand years. In the verse repeat of the story, he is said to burn off an arm in honor of eighty-four thousand stūpas, which he had erected to enshrine the relics of the same buddha.[20] Sarvasattvapriyadarśana's name is reminiscent of that of King Aśoka (Priyadarśa), as is his act of building eighty-four thousand stūpas, so it is perhaps not surprising to find that Aśoka, at least in one tradition, is also said to have honored the relics of the Buddha by setting himself on fire after "having his own body wrapped in cotton . . . and having himself soaked with five hundred pots of scented oil."[21]

In China, such great acts became models for all sorts of related devotional practices, such as suicides by fire or the burning off of fingers or arms. Virtually all of these auto-cremations—whole or partial—were done in honor of buddha relics, and it was expected that relics would be found in the postmortem remains of those who undertook them.[22] Moreover, as John Kieschnick has shown, these practices were closely connected to the memory of the Buddha's funeral and should be seen not only as sacrifices but also as acts of imitation and appropriation—attempts to repeat the Buddha's own cremation and creation of relics.[23] Retrospectively, then, it can be said that the enveloping of the Buddha's body in layers of cotton and the soaking of it in oil are not unconnected to practices that later were seen to be not simply like cremations but also like cremations-productive-of-relics.

There is another complication to the question of the Buddha's multiple shrouds, however. In most of our sources, once the Buddha's cremation fire goes out, it is cryptically declared that all the enveloping layers of cloth were burnt up except for two of them—the innermost and the outermost ones.[24] Again, scholars considering this detail have taken a number of interpretative tacks. Bareau suggests that the non-burning of these shrouds may be related to a prudish monastic desire to hide the Buddha's "nudity," even though his body has been reduced to nothing but ashes and bones.[25] The point may well be valid; as we shall see, the Buddha was thought to still be present in his relics, and the issue of the "exposure" of his body/relics after death was not without controversy. Vaudeville's approach to this matter is somewhat more esoteric. Focusing on the Pāli variant of the story (which indicates that of the thousand layers of cloth, *only* the inner and the outer were burned), she takes the view that the Buddha's cremation was the result of a double fire: the exterior flames of the funeral pyre and the interior heat (*tejas*) of the Buddha's own body.[26] Przyluski goes off on a rather different tangent. As mentioned, he considers the two layers of cloth left on the Buddha's body to be garments rather than shrouds and argues that, as garments, they replicated the traditional double-garb of royalty.[27] For him, then, the Buddha was cremated dressed as a cakravartin king rather than as a monk, and the two unburnt robes are symbolic of this fact.

Unfortunately, as Przyluski himself admits, things are not as clearcut as this, for in a number of Mūlasarvāstivādin versions of the story, the inner and outer layers of cotton cloth that are left unconsumed by the cremation fire are suddenly given a rather specific name; they are called "*cīvara*,"—i.e., monastic robes.[28] More specifically, the fact that there are two pieces of cloth involved here makes these unburnt shrouds homologizable with the "double robe" that the Buddha wore for much of his career.[29] Przyluski seeks to explain these sources away as reflecting an earlier anomalous tradition that was generally rejected but preserved in a few Mūlasarvastivādin sources.[30] Rather than look for layers of tradition here, however, it may be better to read these accounts of the Buddha's cremation as symbolic of a transformation. The five hundred double layers of shrouds (or of princely garments) are prescribed as one of the features of a royal funeral—the obsequies of a cakravartin. The double monastic robe (*cīvara*) that is left is, however, characteristic of monastic life, and is, in fact, reminiscent of the "dustheap robes" (*pāṃśukūla*) of monks that were sometimes gleaned from cremation grounds. The change in the Buddha's dress brought about by his cremation thus reflects a change in status from monarch to monk. Simply put, it can be viewed as an ordination, as a replication of his own great departure, during which he exchanged his princely garb for the robes of an ascetic. Indeed, the recall of this event seems perfectly appropriate at this final moment of his life; kings, unlike buddhas, "stay at home," not only during their lifetime but after their death—i.e., they are reborn in saṃsāra. Buddhas, of course, do not and are not. The garb of a cakravartin is thus wrong for them, especially at this moment when they have "left home" for good and will be reborn no more. The two unburnt shrouds-become-monastic-robes, then, represent a first point in which the Buddha's funeral departs from the model of that of a cakravartin; they make it clear, when the fire is extinguished, that this was the cremation of a buddha and not of a great king.

The two robes, however, are not just the dress of the Buddha; they are also the dress of his relics. And here we come to a different aspect of this whole "miracle" of the unburnt shrouds. In at least one Chinese version of the *Mahāparinirvāṇa sūtra*, the Buddha's relics are found, after the extinction of the cremation fire, neatly enveloped in the two pieces of cloth—the outermost and innermost ones. In this account, then, there is no need to hunt through the ashes for the Buddha's relics; prepackaged, they are placed directly in a golden casket.[31] It may be, then, that the non-burning of the two shrouds is also intended to keep the relics distinct from the ashes of the fire, something which, as we shall see, was of importance to relic gatherers. In this light, we can see that this tradition of the Buddha's shrouds can be understood, not simply as having to do with the wrapping of his body, but also anticipatorily with the wrapping of his relics.

The Sarcophagus

Much the same thing can be said in the case of the double iron oil vessel (Skt. *taila-droṇī*; Pāli *tela-doṇī*) that serves as the Buddha's coffin.[32] Like the five hundred double layers of shrouds, this second feature of the funeral arrangements (Skt. *śarīra-pūjā*) of a cakravartin/tathāgata has been the subject of much discussion. André Bareau is disturbed by the oil-filled coffin, which, he claims, is contrary to the Indian practice of placing corpses directly on the cremation fire, at most on a bier; it makes him think of the Buddha's body being deep-fat fried "like a fish."[33] Bareau is also unconvinced that the original tradition was that the coffin was made of iron; for him, the word "*droṇa*" (Pāli *doṇa*) implies something made out of wood—a vessel or a box—and so he speculates that the coffin was originally wooden and came to be seen as made of iron only because that was the new prestige metal at the time and in the place of the composition of the text. Later, when iron was dethroned from its position of preeminent value, the coffin was said to be made of silver or gold.[34]

Ernst Waldschmidt, on the other hand, claims that the oil-filled sarcophagus, like the thousand shrouds, was needed in order to preserve the Buddha's body from decay, since the cremation of the Blessed One did not take place for a whole week after his death owing to the absence of his chief disciple, Mahākāśyapa. In this Waldschmidt sees a parallel to the case of King Daśaratha in the *Rāmāyaṇa*, whose body was kept from decomposing in a vat of oil (Skt. *taila-droṇī*) while awaiting the arrival of his son, whose participation in the funeral was ritually essential. Mahākāśyapa, as chief disciple, would be the monastic equivalent of the Buddha's eldest son.[35]

A somewhat different interpretative line is take by Jean Przyluski. He also believes the oil-filled vessel was used to preserve the body from decay, not so much to await the arrival of Mahākāśyapa as to transport the Buddha's corpse some distance to the Ganges. The Buddha's disciples, Przyluski suggests, may have wanted to follow the time-honored custom—for ascetics—of disposal of the body by immersion, or by burial "in the banks of a river that flowed to the sea."[36] And he speculates they would have chosen to carry the Buddha's corpse from Kapilavastu all the way to the Ganges, traditionally an important place for the disposal of the dead in India, especially the remains of renunciants. As supportive evidence, Przyluski further points out that one of the meanings of the word "*droṇī*" is a trough-shaped canoe,[37] and he muses that the Buddha's disciples may even have wished to dispose of their master's remains in the manner of a funeral custom described by Xuanzang: "those who are . . . very old . . . or suffering from incurable disease," the Chinese pilgrim tells us, whether already dead or about to be so, are put in a boat (= canoe = *droṇī*) and rowed to the middle of the Ganges, where they are abandoned.[38] But even if the Buddha's *droṇī* was not actually used as a boat, Przyluski concludes, it must still have had a certain metaphorical thrust, for "this coffin in the form of a canoe did not go without recalling the voyage to the land of the dead."[39]

Przyluski's suggestions are imaginative, but his views, as well as those of Waldschmidt, run into certain contextual difficulties. First of all, the tradition that the *droṇī* was made of iron lessens the likelihood that it was viewed as a boat. Second, although it is true that there is non-Buddhist evidence for the use of an iron oil vessel as a means of preserving a corpse in India (e.g., the case of Daśaratha in the *Rāmāyaṇa*), Buddhism ideologically would seem to be opposed to such a practice. Indeed, one of the themes of the *Mahāparinirvāṇa sūtra* itself is its repeated call for the acceptance of death and the recognition of impermanence, especially the impermanence of the body. It would seem strange, therefore, for this text suddenly to advocate a procedure intended to combat impermanence. More pertinently, much the same point is made in the only other Buddhist story I have found that features a *taila-droṇī*. This is the Pāli tale of the wife of King Muṇḍa, a descendant of Ajātaśatru. When Muṇḍa's wife, Bhaddā, dies, her husband is so distraught that he seeks to preserve her corpse so that he can continue to gaze upon her. He therefore orders his minister to put her body "in an oil vessel (*tela-doṇī*) made of iron and covered with another iron vessel."[40] His minister, however, is reluctant to do this, thinking it an unhealthy attachment and preoccupation on the part of the king. He arranges, therefore, for a Buddhist elder to come and preach on the impermanence of the body and the necessity of accepting the fact of death. Moved by this sermon, King Muṇḍa agrees to have Bhaddā's body cremated and a stūpa erected for her.[41] In this story, then, in language that specifically recalls the text of the *Mahāparinirvāṇa sūtra,* we have expressed a more typical Buddhist sentiment against the very notion of the preservation of a body in an iron oil vessel.

Finally and most tellingly, there is also a narrative problem with Przyluski's and Waldschmidt's assumption that the purpose of the oil vessel was to preserve the Buddha's body (either until the arrival of Mahākāśyapa or in order to transport it elsewhere). In all versions of the story, as Waldschmidt himself admits, the Buddha's body is not actually put into the *taila-droṇī* until seven days after his death, *after* it has been transported from the *śāla* grove to the site of his cremation.[42] If the intent of this placement was preservation, such timing simply makes no sense. The iron oil vessel, then, must have been intended to serve another purpose.

As we have seen, one of the problems with cremations in which the body is placed on a pyre, either uncovered or in a simple wooden casket, is the possible mixing that may occur between the remains of the person and the ashes of the fire.[43] That this was an important distinction is made clear in the *Mahāparinirvāṇa sūtra* itself, where, as we shall see, a differentiation is made, at the time of the distribution of the Buddha's relics, between his bodily remains (*śarīra*) and the "ashes of the fire" (*jvalanasya aṅgāra*).[44] There must, therefore, have been some way for keeping the Buddha's relics apart from the remains of the fire, especially when the latter got doused by a rain shower or a spontaneously appearing flood of water (or milk).[45] We have already seen that one of the purposes of the unburnt top and bottom shrouds wrapping the Buddha's body may have been to serve as a sort of envelope for the relics. It is possible that the Buddha's iron *taila-droṇī*, which would presumably not burn either, may have been intended to serve the same function.[46]

This view is reinforced if we consider that the *taila-droṇī* not only serves as a coffin but also anticipates the need for a reliquary container for the relics. And here we need to return to the importance of the word "*droṇī*," which is used to designate the Buddha's sarcophagus. It is surely not insignificant that this term, meaning "vessel," is closely connected to the name of the brahmin Droṇa (Pāli Doṇa), who, as we shall see, is responsible for dividing the Buddha's relics.[47] The word "*droṇa*" also means a wooden box or bucket used for measuring grain, and it is often thought that Droṇa used such a measure in portioning out the relics, since each of the eight kings coming to the Buddha's funeral is said subsequently to have built a stūpa over one "*droṇa*" of relics.[48] Alternatively, the vessel used by Droṇa to divide the relics is said to be a "*kumbha*," a clay pot or jar.[49] It would seem, then, that in this context, "*droṇa*" and "*kumbha*" are homologizable.[50] This is significant because "*kumbha*" more specifically designates not just a measuring jar but also a receptacle for relics. In the Sanskrit text of the *Mahāparinirvāṇa sūtra*, it is in a golden *kumbha* that the Mallas first place the relics of the Buddha, and the same term comes to be used to designate the part of the stūpa that contains the relics.[51] Through these associations, the connotations of the Buddha's *droṇī* shift from referring to his sarcophagus to indicating precursorially a receptacle for his relics.

These connections between coffin and reliquary are reinforced in other ways. Not only do both vessels have lids, but in one of the Chinese versions of the *Mahāparinirvāṇa sūtra,* the Buddha's body is also said to have been put first in a gold casket, which was then placed in an iron *droṇī,* which in turn was put in a sandalwood coffin.[52] In another, the innermost gold coffin was placed in a silver one, which was put in a copper one, which was put in an iron one.[53] Such multiple coffins are strongly reminiscent of the multiple nesting reliquaries, often made of different metals or woods, that are commonly used to enshrine relics.[54]

The Veneration of the Buddha's Body

We have seen above that the Buddha is not put into his iron sarcophagus for seven days after his demise. During this time, his body "lies in state" and is the object of much veneration and lamentation by devotees. Though these acts are not actually specified in the description of a cakravartin's *śarīra-pūjā*, in the case of the Buddha's funeral, they are implicit throughout.

The first to mourn the Blessed One are his disciples and the divinities who are present at his deathbed. They are said to utter verses mostly expressive of sorrow and impermanence. These have been studied by Przyluski and others and need not detain us here.[55] I do, however, want to examine the pūjā paid to the Buddha's body by the Mallas of Kuśinagarī during the week in between his death and his cremation. Learning of the Blessed One's passing, they flock to his body, lying between the two *śāla* trees, and do it honor with a series of rituals that may be seen as precursors to the later veneration of relics. These include offerings of flower garlands, cloth, perfumes, music, dance, and lights. The seven-day delay in cremating the Buddha is, in fact, linked to these celebrations. In the Pāli tradition, for example, the Mallas are said to get so caught up each day in their devotional activities that by the time it occurs to them that they ought to move on to the cremation of the body, it is too late to do so, and they have to put it off until the next day. On the morrow, however, exactly the same thing happens, until a whole week has passed. On the seventh day, when they do manage to resolve early enough to transport the Buddha's body to the cremation ground, they find they cannot lift it. This is said to be because the gods have in mind a different route for the funeral procession than that envisaged by the Mallas, and until the latter acquiesce to their divine intent, they "freeze" the body and prevent its movement.[56]

This, of course, is not the usual way of conducting a funeral in India, where the cremation of the body is rarely delayed.[57] Some of the Buddha's disciples might have expressed strong grief at the passing of their teacher, but the Mallas appear to use the occasion for merit making and celebration. As Alfred Foucher has pointed out, we seem to be dealing here with something akin to a village fair, and "we must understand that, over the course of time, the Buddha's obsequies were no longer conceived of as being funereal; they had rather been transformed . . . into a festival of the sort that was to be celebrated in honor of the relics of the Blessed One."[58]

In the midst of these festivities, however, there does occur one event that is marked by mournful emotionality. Realizing that the Malla women might not be forceful enough to push their way to the front of the crowd in order to venerate the Buddha's body and so might miss out on this rare opportunity to gain merit by making offerings to the Blessed One at the time of his *parinirvāṇa*, Ānanda clears a passage for the women and invites them to approach. Once they have come forward, they circumambulate the Buddha, break into lamentations, and make all sorts of offerings, except for one elderly and very poor widow, who is horribly distraught because she has nothing to give at all. Carried away by emotion, she bursts out crying, and her tears run down and wet the Buddha's feet.[59]

Ānanda's action in letting the elderly widow's tears fall on the Buddha's feet eventually gets him into trouble with the Buddha's disciple Mahākāśyapa. As we shall see, when Mahākāśyapa himself later venerates the feet of the Buddha, he notices that they are spotted and that the mark of the wheel on them has been discolored. "The Buddha body shone like gold," he declares; "why are his feet now different?"[60] Ānanda then explains that the stains and discoloration are due to the old woman's crying on them, and he gets reprimanded for dereliction of duty.[61] Later, at the First Council in Rājagṛha, Mahākāśyapa brings up the same episode again as one of a series of faults committed by Ānanda,[62] only this time the severity of the charge has been increased, and Ānanda is accused of having shown the Malla women the Buddha's sheath-encased penis. The Buddha's peculiar male organ was one of the thirty-two marks of the Great Man (*mahāpuruṣa*), and Ānanda seeks to justify his action by claiming that by showing the women the Buddha's penis, he was merely trying to get them to be ashamed of their female bodies so that they would plant roots of merit that would enable them to be reborn as men.[63]

The opposition between Ānanda and Mahākāśyapa is given another expression in the episode in which Mahākāśyapa worships the feet of the Buddha. As mentioned, Mahākāśyapa comes late to the site of the Buddha's funeral, since he is on the road and does not find out about the *parinirvāṇa* until a week after it occurs.[64] In the meantime, in his absence, the Mallas of Kuśinagarī prepare the Buddha's body for cremation. They enshroud it in the thousand layers of cloth and encoffin it in the *taila-droṇī*, only to find then that they cannot light the pyre. This is said to be owing to the power of the gods who do not want the fire lit until after the arrival of Mahākāśyapa. This is intended to give him the opportunity to see and venerate the feet (or the whole body) of the deceased master one last time before consigning it to the flames. In fact, he is described in our sources as doing this in a variety of ways. In the Pāli tradition, he merely uncovers the Buddha's feet and venerates them before proceeding with the cremation.[65] In the Sanskrit, he actually opens the coffin and unwraps the whole of the Buddha's body in order to venerate it. He then rewraps and re-encoffins it before lighting the pyre.[66] In several Chinese accounts, he asks Ānanda for permission to view the body, but Ānanda refuses, apparently because it would be too difficult to take the coffin down from the pyre, open it, and unwrap the thousand shrouds.[67] This scene, as Waldschmidt has pointed out, once again underlines the rivalry between Ānanda and Mahākāśyapa,[68] but it also serves to set up the episode of the appearance of the Buddha's feet, which in these, and in the remainder of our sources, miraculously poke through the shrouds and emerge from the coffin so that Mahākāśyapa is able to venerate them.[69]

The miracle of the apparition of the Buddha's feet to Mahākāśyapa is significant not only as a first example of the Buddha's posthumous powers but also because it foreshadows magical movements that, later, are commonly attributed to Buddhist relics. In fact, it may be said that the Buddha's feet here, though attached to his body, are a sort of relic and that, as Alexander Cunningham pointed out long ago, their veneration by Mahākāśyapa acts as a paradigm for the later cult of the Buddha's footprints, which becomes an important and early form of relic worship in Buddhism.[70]

Cremation

Generally speaking, Mahākāśyapa's veneration of the Buddha's feet is the last act prior to the igniting of the funeral pyre.[71] In most versions of the story, the fire ignites spontaneously, although sometimes it is lit by the Mallas or by Mahākāśyapa acting as the master's eldest "son."[72] Cremation, which is specified as the fourth element in the *śarīra-pūjā* of a cakravartin/tathāgata, became the norm for Buddhists—at least for Buddhist monks—in ancient India, even though various other means of disposing of dead bodies (such as immersion in a river, or burial, or exposure in a deserted place) were recognized.[73]

Cremation, of course, was also (and remains) the norm for Hindus in India. Yet the parallelism between the two traditions should not mislead us. First of all, cremation, for ordinary Hindus, is a sacrificial rite intended to ensure rebirth and generally results in the eradication of all bodily remains.[74] Cremation for Buddhist monks is a ritual hopefully productive of relics. Second, one important thing about the cremation of the Buddha (and, after him, of his monks) is that it symbolically distinguishes him (and them) from *saṃnyāsin*s, orthodox brahmanical ascetics, and renunciants. *Saṃnyāsin*s, because they have already performed their own mortuary rite at the time of their wandering forth, and because they have abandoned their families and hence no longer recognize any relatives who can perform their cremation, and because they have given up their sacrificial fires needed to kindle the cremation pyre, are typically not cremated but buried in sand or abandoned in a river.[75] We come here to the flip side of the injunction on how to conduct the funeral of a tathāgata; not only is he to be cremated *like* a cakravartin king, but he is also to be cremated *unlike* a *saṃnyāsin*.

Almost one hundred years ago, Robert Hertz highlighted the importance of exhumation and secondary burial in helping the body (as well as the soul and the relatives) of the deceased make a transition through liminality to a final stable state.[76] In some cultures, the completion of this passage—marked by the decay of all flesh and the exhumation of pure white bones—could take some time, several years in fact.[77] In this light, cremation may be seen as a rite that accelerates this transition to a stable state and makes secondary burial—of the relics—possible almost immediately.[78] In this regard, it is important to note that the relics that result from the Buddha's cremation are not just ashes and calcined body parts but somatic substances of a radically different nature. According to the Pāli tradition, the Buddha's body (*sarīra*) was entirely consumed by the fire: "skin, under-skin, flesh, sinew, joint-fluid," etc., were completely burnt up, leaving not even a residue of ashes or soot. Only the relics (*sarīrāni*) remained.[79] Walshe, Davids, and Bareau all translate "*sarīrāni*" here as "bones."[80] However, Buddhaghosa's description of them as being like jasmine buds, washed pearls, and nuggets of gold, and as coming in three sizes (as big as mustard seeds, broken grains of rice, and split green peas),[81] suggests that something less osseous than bones or teeth may be meant here. To be sure, teeth and other identifiable bones of the Buddha did go on to become significant relics, but for the most part, texts describing this phase of the Buddha's funeral are careful to distinguish them from the "*sarīrāni*" that are collected immediately after the Buddha's cremation.[82] It is apparent that if these relics are bones, they are bones that have been transmuted and are much more akin to the shiny bead- or gem-like relic-grains that are commonly featured in East Asian Buddhism.[83] Such transmutations are indicative of the transformation undergone by the Buddha in his passage to a final state beyond death and rebirth.

The Collection and Distribution of the Relics

The Buddha's relics, though symbolic of his "transcendence," are still subject to adventures in this world. The fifth element in the funeral of a cakravartin/tathāgata is said to be the gathering of his remains/relics, preliminary to their distribution and enshrinement in various places. In all versions of the story, the collection is done by the Mallas of Kuśinagarī, who, generally, are said to put all of the relics in a casket that they transport to the center of their city and enshrine in a structure that is variously described as a great building, a high tower, or their own assembly hall.[84] There, according to the Pāli text, the relics are surrounded by "a lattice-work of spears" and a "wall of bows."[85] Later texts go on to elaborate on this theme and portray the relics as being closely guarded by a whole fourfold army consisting of elephants, horses, chariots, and foot soldiers.[86]

These defensive preparations make sense in view of the fact that the relics are said, almost immediately, to become the subject of a dispute—the so-called "war of the relics"—among eight principalities. Indeed, news of the Buddha's death and cremation and of the Mallas' actions spreads quickly throughout Northern India and is greeted with strong emotions. The first to react is said to be King Ajātaśatru of Magadha. After recovering from the shock of learning of the Buddha's demise,[87] he resolves to have the Buddha's relics brought to his kingdom, arguing that they (or at least a portion of them) should be his since the Buddha was a kṣatriya and so is he. Accordingly, he sends a message to the Mallas, asking for the relics, but, suspecting that they are unlikely to comply with his request, he also sets out for Kuśinagarī himself, together with his own fourfold army.[88]

Much the same sequence of emotions and actions is then attributed to no fewer than six other kings, who all head for Kuśinagarī to lay claim to the relics. The lists of these contenders vary somewhat, but in general it can be said that those involved are, in addition to the Mallas of Kuśinagarī and Ajātaśatru of Magadha, the Licchavis of Vaiśalī, the Śākyas of Kapilavastu, the Mallas of Pāvā, the Bulakas of Calakalpa, the Krauḍyas of Rāmagrāma, and the brahmins of Viṣṇudvīpa.[89] All of these groups proclaim their right to at least a share of the Buddha's relics, which they stand ready to take by force if necessary.[90] The Mallas, on the other hand, respond by reaffirming their claim, refusing outright even to consider surrendering the relics, and, according to some accounts, beginning to train their women and children in the art of warfare so as to make up for their inferiority in numbers.[91]

Hostilities, however, never quite break out, and the "war of the relics" never actually takes place, for the decision is made to resolve the matter by arbitration. All parties agree to let the brahmin Dhūmrasagotra (as noted above, also known as Droṇa [Pāli Doṇa]), decide the matter, which he does in an apparently equitable and satisfactory fashion by dividing the relics into eight equal shares, each of which will then be taken away to be enshrined in a stūpa in the recipient's home country.[92] After completing this division, Droṇa then asks the assembly for, and is granted, the urn (*kumbha*) with which he measured out the relics, over which he resolves to build his own stūpa. Finally, at the end of the episode, a young brahmin from Pippalāyana arrives and, upon his request, is granted the ashes of the cremation fire, which he likewise takes away to enshrine in a stūpa. Thus, there is an initial division of the Buddha's relics into ten portions.[93]

Phyllis Granoff has suggested that in this, we may have a parallel with Brahmanical/Hindu *navaśrāddha* rites, in which ten rice balls (*piṇḍa*) are formed and laid out over a period of ten days after a death in order to build a new body for the deceased and help prevent him from becoming a preta (malignant departed spirit). Indeed, some Gandhāran depictions of Droṇa's dividing of the relics show him shaping the *śarīra* into what look like balls of rice.[94] This would reinforce the notion, in a funeral context, of the relics being a "new body" for the Buddha.

The theme of latecomers (or at least of others besides the initial eight North Indian rulers) getting relics was, however, to give rise to several other traditions. Xuanzang, for example, tells the story of King Uttarasena of Udyāna, who comes late to Kuśinagarī but who declares that while the Tathāgata was alive, he had promised the king a portion of his bones. This claim is apparently backed by some monks because Uttarasena *is* then given a share of relics, although Xuanzang adds that he was greatly resented by the other kings because of this.[95] A more radical variant is found in another tale in which the latecomers are divinities. In this story, once all eight kings agree to the division effectuated by Droṇa, the god Indra arrives and says that the deities in heaven also have rights to a share of the relics. He is followed by three nāga kings, who similarly say that they merit some relics and who indicate in no uncertain terms that they are stronger than the combined kings. Droṇa then has to rearbitrate the matter, resolving things by getting everyone to agree to a new division of the relics into three portions—one for the gods, one for the nāgas, and one for humans.[96] Phyllis Granoff has further likened this tripartite division of the relics to the Hindu *sapiṇḍīkaraṇa* ceremony, in which the body of the deceased, represented by a ball of rice (the *pretapiṇḍa*), is divided and then conjoined with others to make three *piṇḍa*s, representing three generations of male ancestors.[97]

In all these stories, Droṇa is presented as an honest arbitrator, but in other traditions, he himself is not immune from suspicion. In one tale, for example, he is portrayed as smearing honey inside the urn that he uses to measure out the relics so that some grains of relics will stick to the container. This, it is implied, is the real reason he then asks for the urn as payment for his arbitration.[98] In another story, Droṇa secretly hides the Buddha's right eyetooth in his turban, intending to keep it for himself. His action is observed, however, by Indra, who then comes down from his heaven and steals the tooth in turn, unbeknownst to Droṇa, who is busy dividing up the rest of the relics.[99] Another Pāli tradition expands on this scenario and portrays Droṇa as stealing three tooth relics, hiding one in his turban, one between his toes, and one in his clothes. Indra then takes the first one, the nāga Jasyasena takes the second, and a man from Gandhāra takes the third.[100] Here we would seem to have another reflection of the tripartite division hinted at by Xuanzang above.

The Stūpas

We come finally to the last element in the funeral of a cakravartin/tathāgata—the injunction that the relics, once collected, are to be enshrined in a single stūpa at a crossroads. The defensive tower in the middle of Kuśinagarī, in which the Mallas initially house the relics, whether conceived to be at a "crossroads" or not, is not really a stūpa. Given this, and given the subsequent division of the relics and the building of no fewer than eight stūpas for their enshrinement in different countries, it is legitimate to wonder whether or not we have here another departure from the prescribed set of events that is supposed to make up the Buddha's funeral.[101]

There are some indications of possible concern about this. André Bareau, for example, has detected, in one of the Chinese versions of the *Mahāparinirvāṇa sūtra,* traces of a tradition of a single sepulcher, which may have been built at a village near Kuśinagarī ninety days after the cremation.[102] On rather different grounds, Jean Przyluski has argued that the most ancient tradition was that of a single stūpa, which he is inclined to locate at Rāmagrāma on the Ganges.[103] Moreover, a later Theravāda tradition affirmed that even after the construction of the various stūpas, Mahākāśyapa decided to enshrine the bulk of the relics in one place, leaving only token amounts to the eight countries.[104]

Generally speaking, however, the tradition of a single sepulcher did not take hold, and instead we find the common affirmation of the construction of the eight or ten stūpas—one in each of the eight lands that received a portion of the relics, one over the urn kept by Droṇa, and one over the ashes of the pyre.[105] The different versions of the *Mahāparinirvāṇa sūtra* are somewhat terse about the transportation of the relics to their places of enshrinement in the eight countries. Later traditions, however, were to expand on this at some length. Thus in the *Commentary on the Dīgha Nikāya*, we find a tale told about the share of relics taken by Ajātaśatru for enshrinement back in Magadha. Ajātaśatru has the two hundred miles of road between Kuśinagarī and his capital of Rājagṛha leveled and spruced up. He orders bazaars to be set up for the people all along the route. The relics themselves are carried in a golden casket (*doṇī*) and put down wherever there are lots of flowers. At such places, people come and make offerings to them until all the flowers are exhausted. Then the procession resumes. This turns out to be a very slow process, for according to the text, after seven years, seven months, and seven days, the relics have still not reached Rājagṛha. Worse, non-believers along the way start complaining about being forced to join in the sacred festivities, and, as a result, many of them are reborn in hell. Worried that the whole situation is about to go awry, the monks talk to Ajātaśatru and, after some effort, manage to get him to agree to take the relics directly to the city, where he promptly has them enshrined in a stūpa. Exactly the same thing, the text implies, happens in the case of the seven other shares of relics, as well as Droṇa's measuring urn and the ashes of the fire.[106]

Conclusion

There are many ways to read the *Mahāparinirvāṇa sūtra*. In addition to the perspectives of Bareau, Foucher, Przyluski, Snellgrove, Vaudeville, and Waldschmidt touched on above, mention might be made of those who have approached the text as an important early segment of the Buddha's sacred biography;[107] or those who have looked at it for its symbolic and social context[108] or for what it can tell us about the causes of the Buddha's death;[109] or those who have connected it to art and iconography[110] or to oral history;[111] or who have examined it for its doctrinal thrusts.[112] In this chapter, I have sought to look at several versions of the sūtra, as well as at related texts about the obsequies of the Buddha, from the perspective of relic traditions and to interpret several of its features in that light.

Thus, we have seen that virtually all of the steps in the prescribed funeral rituals for a buddha or a cakravartin—his *śarīra-pūjā*—have in mind the production and preservation of his relics. The shrouds may be viewed as transforming the Buddha's body into a torch—a form of auto-cremation that in East Asia was seen as devoted to and productive of relics. The sarcophagus may have served the purpose of keeping the relics separate from the ashes of the fire and may have symbolically anticipated the reliquaries that later contained those remains. The acts of veneration (pūjā) paid to the Buddha's body after death by the Mallas of Kuśinagarī are reminiscent less of a typical Indian funeral and more of festivities in honor of relics. The Buddha's cremation itself may have been chosen as a method of disposing of his body because it was transformative and quickly productive of relics. Finally, the collection of the Buddha's relics, their distribution, and the building of stūpas may be seen not only as the culmination and end point of the Buddha's funerary sequence (*śarīra-pūjā*) but as indicative of its whole aim and concern.

Gregory Schopen has criticized scholars who have translated "*śarīra-pūjā*" as the "cult of the relics," in an effort to contradict those who would claim that the Buddha thought that monks (such as Ānanda) should have nothing to do with relic worship.[113] He was surely right in doing so. But some have taken his point too far to suggest that the Buddha's "funeral arrangements" (*śarīra-pūjā*) had nothing at all to do with relics. As I have sought to argue here, this is far from the truth. The *śarīra-pūjā* may not be a "cult of relics," but it is certainly possible to think of it as a "cult productive and predictive of relics."

Indeed, the centrality of this preoccupation with relics in the Buddha's funeral seems to me to be reinforced in the verses that are attached to the very end of the *Mahāparinirvāṇa sūtra*. Buddhaghosa, in his commentary, does not deal with this final stanza because, he says, it was "added by elders in Sri Lanka,"[114] but the same verses are also found in the Sanskrit and Tibetan texts.[115] They state once more the fact that eight measures of relics have been enshrined in stūpas. They make no mention of the stūpa over Droṇa's measuring box (the *kumbha-thūpa*) or that over the ashes (the *aṅgāra-thūpa*), but they do include, this time, a list of the four tooth relics of the Buddha. And then, the Pāli text, at least, adds a parting recommendation:

> Because of this his glory, this great earth is embellished by excellent offerings.
> Thus the collection of relics (*sarīra*) of the all-seeing Buddha is well honored by those who are most honored;
> It is worshipped by the lord of gods, the lord of nāgas, and the lord of men; it is thus worshipped by the best of humans.
> Bow down, therefore, with folded hands, for it is difficult indeed to meet a buddha through hundreds of aeons.[116]

With this injunction to venerate the remains of the Buddha's body—an act made possible, I have argued, by the very nature of the Buddha's obsequies—the *Mahāparinirvāṇa sūtra* finally ends.

Notes

Parts of this article represent a revision of materials already considered in the fourth chapter of my book, *Relics of the Buddha* (Princeton, NJ: Princeton University Press, 2004).

1. Arnold van Gennep, *The Rites of Passage*, trans. Monika B. Vizedom and Gabrielle L. Caffee (Chicago: University of Chicago Press, 1960 [1909]), 146–65.

2. The text exists in multiple renditions. For the Sanskrit version, see Ernst Waldschmidt, *Das Mahāparinirvāṇasūtra*, Abhandlungen der deutschen Akademie der Wissenschaften zu Berlin, philosophisch-historische Klasse, 1949, no. 1, and 1950, nos. 2–3 (Berlin: Akademie Verlag, 1950–51), 102–453. For the Pāli see J. Estlin Carpenter, *Dīgha Nikāya* (London: Pāli Text Society, 1911), 2:71–168, trans. in T. W. Rhys Davids, *Dialogues of the Buddha* (London: Pāli Text Society, 1899–1924), 2:78–191, and in Maurice Walshe, *Thus Have I Heard: The Long Discourses of the Buddha* (London: Wisdom Publications, 1987), 231–77. For Chinese versions, see *T* no. 1, 1:11–30, trans. Friedrich Weller, "Buddhas letzte Wanderung," *Monumenta Serica* 4 (1939): 40–84, 406–40 and 5 (1940): 141–207; *T* no. 5, 1:160–75; *T* no. 6, 1:176–90; *T* no. 7, 1:193–207; and *T* no. 1451, 24:382–402, trans. Waldschmidt, *Mahāparinirvāṇasūtra*, 103–496. The Tibetan text of the *Mūlasarvāstivāda vinaya* version is edited in Waldschmidt, *Mahāparinirvāṇasūtra*, summary trans. W. Woodville Rockhill, *The Life of the Buddha and the Early History of His Order* (London: Kegan Paul, Trench, Trübner, 1907), 122–47. For studies of these sources, see Jean Przyluski, *Le parinirvāṇa et les funérailles du Buddha* (Paris: Imprimerie Nationale, 1920); Ernst Waldschmidt, *Die Überlieferung vom Lebensende des Buddha: Eine vergleichende Analyse des Mahāparinirvāṇasūtra und seiner Textentsprech-*

ungen, Abhandlungen der Akademie der Wissenschaften in Göttingen, philologisch-historische Klasse, nos. 29–30 (Göttingen: Vandenhoeck and Ruprecht, 1944–48); Charlotte Vaudeville, "La légende de Sundara et les funérailles du Buddha," *Bulletin de l'École Française d'Extrême-Orient* 52 (1964): 73–91; André Bareau: *Recherches sur la biographie du Buddha dans les sūtrapiṭaka et les vinayapiṭaka anciens: II. Les derniers mois, le parinirvāṇa et les funérailles*, 2 vols. (Paris: École Française d'Extrême-Orient, 1970–71); "Les récits canoniques des funérailles du Buddha et leurs anomalies: Nouvel essai d'interprétation," *Bulletin de l'École Française d'Extrême-Orient* 62 (1975): 151–89; David L. Snellgrove, "Śākyamuni's Final Nirvāṇa," *Bulletin of the School of Oriental and African Studies* 36 (1973): 399–411; Alfred Foucher, *La vie du Bouddha d'après les textes et les monuments de l'Inde* (Paris: Adrien Maisonneuve, 1987), 314–23, and Gregory Schopen, "Monks and the Relic Cult in the Mahāparinibbāna-sutta," in *From Benares to Beijing: Essays on Buddhism and Chinese Religion*, ed. Koichi Shinohara and Gregory Schopen (Oakville: Mosaic Press, 1991), 187–201.

3. Waldschmidt, *Mahāparinirvāṇasūtra*, 360, 410; Carpenter, *Dīgha*, 2:141–42, 161, trans. Davids, *Dialogues*, 2:155–56, 182–83.

4. Moroever, in the *Mahāparinirvāṇa sūtra*, the association with kingship is reinforced by the claim that the site of the Buddha's death and funeral—Kuśinagarī—was itself once the capital of a great cakravartin king, Mahāsudarśana, who is then revealed to have been the Buddha himself in a past life. In the *Dīgha nikāya*, the "Mahāsuddassana sutta" highlighting this myth forms a separate sūtra immediately following the "Mahāparinibbāna sutta," (see Carpenter, *Dīgha*, 2:169–200, trans. Walshe, *Thus Have I Heard*, 279–90). In other sources, however, it is incorporated as a whole into the account of the Buddha's *parinirvāṇa* (see Waldschmidt, *Mahāparinirvāṇasūtra*, 304–55).

5. Jean Przyluski, "La ville du cakravartin: Influences babyloniennes sur la civilisation de l'Inde," *Rocznik Orjentalistyczny* 5 (1927): 165–85. See also K. A. Nilakanta Sastri, "Cakravartin," *New Indian Antiquary* 3 (1940): 307–21.

6. Jean Przyluski, "Le partage des reliques du Buddha," *Mélanges chinois et bouddhiques* 4 (1935–36): 354–55. See also Alfred Foucher, "A propos de la conversion au bouddhisme du roi Indo-Grec Ménandre," *Mémoires de l'Académie des Inscriptions et Belles Lettres* 48, part 2 (1943): 2.

7. See, on this, Strong, *Relics of the Buddha*, Introduction.

8. That is the term selected by Walshe (*Thus Have I Heard*, 264) and suggested by Gregory Schopen in *Bones, Stones, and Buddhist Monks: Collected Papers on the Archaeology, Epigraphy, and Texts of Monastic Buddhism in India* (Honolulu: University of Hawai'i Press, 1997), 103.

9. Waldschmidt, *Mahāparinirvāṇasūtra*, 360, 410, trans. Snellgrove,

"Final Nirvāṇa," 405–6, and Carpenter, *Dīgha* 2:141–42, 161, trans. Davids, *Dialogues*, 2:155–56, 182–83. See also *T* no. 1, 1:20a–b, trans. Weller, "Letzte Wanderung," 434–35; *T* no. 5, 1:169a–b; *T* no. 6, 1:186c; *T* no. 7, 1:199c–200a; and *T* no. 1451, 24:394c–95a, trans. Waldschmidt, *Mahāparinirvāṇasūtra*, 359–61. See also Waldschmidt, *Überlieferung*, 213–16, and Bareau, *Recherches*, 2:35–50. At one point, Schopen seeks to divorce the erection of a stūpa from the *śarīra-pūjā* but later corrects that view. See Gregory Schopen, "Ritual Rights and Bones of Contention: More on Monastic Funerals and Relics in the *Mūlasarvāstivāda-vinaya*," *Journal of Indian Philosophy* 22 (1994): 39.

10. Foucher, *La vie*, 318.

11. Bareau, *Recherches*, 2:39.

12. Waldschmidt, *Überlieferung*, 264.

13. Przyluski, *Parinirvāṇa*, 143.

14. Vaudeville, "Sundara," 84–85. Vaudeville bases her argument on a study of the account of the Buddha's *parinirvāṇa* as found in the *Avadānaśataka*, for which see P.L. Vaidya, *Avadānaśataka* (Darbhanga: Mithila Institute, 1958), 260–63, trans. Léon Feer, *Avadāna-çataka: Cent légendes (bouddhiques)* (Paris: Ernest Leroux, 1891), 430–36.

15. See Bareau, *Recherches*, 2:39–41.

16. See Waldschmidt, *Überlieferung*, 211, and Walshe, *Thus Have I Heard*, 264. See also Thanissaro Bhikkhu, *Handful of Leaves* (Santa Cruz: Sati Center for Buddhist Studies, 2002), 1:105, who translates the terms as "new linen cloth" and "teased cotton-wool." For the Pāli text, see Carpenter, *Dīgha*, 2:141–42.

17. William Stede, *Sumangalavilāsinī: Buddhaghosa's Commentary on the Dīgha Nikāya*, 2nd ed. (London: Pāli Text Society, 1971), 2:583. One of the Chinese versions of the story (*T* no. 5, 1:169, trans. Bareau, *Recherches*, 2:43) likewise specifies that the cotton is to be sprinkled with oil and fat.

18. Carpenter, *Dīgha*, 2:164, trans. Walshe, *Thus Have I Heard*, 275.

19. V. Fausboll, *The Jātaka Together with Its Commentary* (London: Pāli Text Society, 1877–96), 1:31, trans. N.A. Jayawickrama, *The Story of Gotama Buddha* (*Jātaka-nidāna*) (London: Pāli Text Society, 1990), 40. See also I.B. Horner, *Madhuratthavilāsinī nāma Buddhavaṇsaṇṭhakatha of Bhadantācariya Buddhadatta Mahāthera* (London: Pāli Text Society, 1978), 143–44, trans. I.B. Horner, *The Clarifier of the Sweet Meaning* (*Madhuratthavilāsinī*) (London: Pāli Text Society, 1978), 206–7.

20. Hendrik Kern and Bunyo Nanjo, *Saddharmapuṇḍarīka Sūtra* (Saint Petersburg: Bibliotheca Buddhica, 1912), 405–9, trans. Hendrik Kern, *Saddharma-Puṇḍarīka or the Lotus of the True Law* (Oxford: Clarendon Press, 1884), 377–83.

21. Eugène Denis, *La Lokapaññatti et les idées cosmologiques du bouddhisme ancien*, 3 vols. (Lille: Université de Lille, 1977), 1:174, 2:152.

22. Jacques Gernet, "Les suicides par le feu chez les bouddhistes chinois du Ve au Xe siècle," *Mélanges publiés par l'Institut des Hautes Études Chinoises* (Paris: Presses Universitaires de France, 1960), 2:542–43; Jan Yün-hua, "Buddhist Self-Immolation in Medieval China," *History of Religions* 4, no. 2 (1965): 243–68.

23. John Kieschnick, *The Eminent Monk: Buddhist Ideals in Medieval Chinese Hagiography* (Honolulu: University of Hawai'i Press, 1997), 44. See also James A. Benn, "Where Text Meets Flesh: Burning the Body as an Apocryphal Practice in Chinese Buddhism," *History of Religions* 37, no. 4 (1998), 296, and Benn's chapter in this volume. In this context, we should remember that in most accounts of the Buddha's funeral, his cremation is actually an auto-cremation since his pyre is finally said to light itself, spontaneously erupting into flames through his supernatural power (see Bareau, *Recherches*, 2:255).

24. See Bareau, *Recherches*, 2:260–61. The Pāli text, however, anomalously states just the opposite: that only the innermost and outermost shrouds were consumed. Przyluski (*Parinirvāṇa*, 38n1) suspects a negative participle has disappeared from the text by mistake, but see also Waldschmidt, *Überlieferung*, 306n114.

25. Bareau, *Recherches*, 2:261.

26. Vaudeville, "Sundara," 84–85. This duality would then be symbolized by the fact that only the inner and the outer shrouds were burned.

27. Przyluski, *Parinirvāṇa*, 102–67, esp. 145–46. Foucher (*La vie*, 318) makes much the same point.

28. See Waldschmidt, *Mahāparinirvāṇasūtra*, 430–31, and Vaidya, *Avadānaśataka*, 261, trans. Feer, *Cent légendes*, 432. See also Waldschmidt, *Üerlieferung*, 306, 310, and Bareau, *Recherches*, 2:259. Waldschmidt, it should be pointed out, wants to argue that *cīvara* here has the more generic meaning of a "piece of cloth." See, however, Snellgrove, "Final Nirvāṇa," 407.

29. On the double robe of the Buddha, see Hermann Oldenberg, *Vinaya piṭakam* (London: Pāli Text Society, 1969–84), 1:288–89, trans. I. B. Horner, *The Book of the Discipline* (London: Pāli Text Society, 1938–52), 4:411, and Stede, *Sumangalavilāsinī*, 5:1128.

30. Przyluski, *Parinirvāṇa*, 39.

31. *T* no. 7, 1:207a, trans. Przyluski, *Parinirvāṇa*, 38. In *T* no. 1435, 23:436a (see Waldschmidt, *Überlieferung*, 312), they are wrapped in the cloths before being put in the urn. Archaeologists have occasionally found relics still wrapped in cloth inside their reliquaries.

32. For a depiction of the Buddha's coffin in the Gandhāran style, see Foucher, *La vie*, 305.

33. Bareau, *Recherches*, 2:43.

34. Ibid., 2:43–44.

35. Waldschmidt, *Überlieferung*, 263–64. See also *Rāmāyaṭa* II, 66, 14–

15, trans. Sheldon I. Pollock, *The Rāmāyaṇa of Vālmīki: An Epic of Ancient India*, vol. 2: *Ayodhyākāṇḍa* (Princeton, NJ: Princeton University Press, 1986), 213.

36. Przyluski, "Le partage," 365.

37. He does this on the basis of apparently cognate words in a host of non-Indo European South Asian languages (see Przyluski, "Le partage," 341–42).

38. Przyluski, "Le partage," 345. See also Li Ronxi, *The Great Tang Dynasty Record of the Western Regions* (Berkeley: Numata Center for Buddhist Translation and Research, 1996), 62; text in *T* no. 2087, 51:878a.

39. Przyluski, "Le partage," 366.

40. F. L. Woodward and E. M. Hare, *The Book of the Gradual Sayings*, 5 vols. (London: Pāli Text Society, 1932–36), 3:48; text in R. Morris and E. Hardy, *Anguttara Nikāya* (London: Pāli Text Society, 1885–1900), 3:58.

41. Morris and Hardy, *Anguttara Nikāya* 3:57–62, trans. Woodward and Hare, *Gradual Sayings*, 3:48–51.

42. Waldschmidt, *Überlieferung*, 273. See also Bareau, *Recherches*, 2:193.

43. For this reason, in the Brahmanical tradition, a winnowing basket was sometimes used to separate the calcined bones from the wood ash. See Pandurang Vaman Kane, *History of Dharmaśāstra*, 2nd ed. (Poona: Bhandarkar Oriental Research Institute, 1973), 4:241.

44. Waldschmidt, *Mahāparinirvāṇasūtra*, 448. See also Waldschmidt, *Überlieferung*, 327–28, and Bareau, *Recherches*, 2:303–8.

45. On the different ways in which the cremation fire is extinguished, see Waldschmidt, *Überlieferung*, 307–8, and Bareau, *Recherches*, 2:261–62.

46. This suggestion was already made by Foucher (*La vie*, 318).

47. In the Sanskrit tradition (see Waldschmidt, *Mahāparinirvāṇasūtra*, 442), he is also called Dhūmrasagotra, although he is said to come from Droṇa village.

48. Waldschmidt, *Mahāparinirvāṇasūtra*, 450; Carpenter, *Dīgha*, 2:167, trans. Davids, *Dialogues*, 2:191.

49. Waldschmidt, *Mahāparinirvāṇasūtra*, 442; Carpenter, *Dīgha*, 2:166, trans. Davids, *Dialogues*, 2:189. See also Bareau, *Recherches*, 2:289.

50. On this, see also Michael Willis, *Buddhist Reliquaries from Ancient India* (London: British Museum Press, 2000), 19.

51. See Heino Kottkamp, *Der Stupa als Repräsentation des buddhistischen Heilsweges* (Wiesbaden: Otto Harrassowitz, 1992), 74, and Peter Harvey, "The Symbolism of the Stūpa," *Journal of the International Association of Buddhist Studies* 7 (1984): 72–73.

52. *T* no. 1, 1:20a, trans. Weller, "Letzte Wanderung," 435.

53. *T* no. 7, 1:199c, trans. Bareau, *Recherches*, 2:41.

54. For a good picture of such a set, see Zhang Tinghao, *Fa-men ssu/*

Famen Temple/Homon-ji (Xian: Shanxi Tourist Publishing House, 1990), 73–74.

55. See Przyluski, *Parinirvāṇa*, 5–46; Waldschmidt, *Überlieferung*, 254–60; and Bareau, *Recherches*, 2:161–71. See also Waldschmidt, *Mahāparinirvāṇasūtra*, 398–402, and Snellgrove, "Final Nirvāṇa," 403–6.

56. Carpenter, *Dīgha*, 2:160, trans. Walshe, *Thus Have I Heard*, 273. On the various routes to be taken by the funeral cortège, see Waldschmidt, *Überlieferung*, 273–85; Bareau, *Recherches*, 2:195–96, 205; and Gregory Schopen, "Relic," in *Critical Terms for Religious Studies*, ed. Mark C. Taylor (Chicago: University of Chicago Press), 261.

57. See Kane, *Dharmaśāstra*, 212. In this light, it may be said that the Buddha's funeral resembles more the often delayed cremations of great Buddhist monks in parts of Southeast Asia, on which see Charles F. Keyes, "Death of Two Buddhist Saints in Thailand," *Journal of the American Academy of Religion, Thematic Studies* 48 (1981): 149–80.

58. Foucher, *La vie*, 317.

59. See Waldschmidt, *Überlieferung*, 267–70, and Bareau, *Recherches*, 2:185–86.

60. *T* no. 1, 1:28–29, trans. Weller, "Letzte Wanderung," 197.

61. For other versions of the story, see Bareau, *Recherches*, 2:249–51, and Emile Senart, *Le Mahāvastu* (Paris: Imprimerie Nationale, 1882–97), 1:68, trans. J. J. Jones, *The Mahāvastu*, 3 vols. (London: Pāli Text Society, 1949–56), 1:55.

62. For an account and a bibliography, see Étienne Lamotte, *Le Traité de la grande vertu de sagesse*, 5 vols. (Louvain: Institut Orientaliste, 1949–80), 1:94–96.

63. See the sources cited in ibid., 1:96–97n2. One wonders whether this baring of the body of the Buddha may have been related to a rite of washing the corpse, normally undertaken in the Indian context by women relatives.

64. On the various traditions explaining where Mahākāśyapa is and how he finds out about the Buddha's death, see Waldschmidt, *Überlieferung*, 185–89, and Bareau, *Recherches*, 2:215–22.

65. Carpenter, *Dīgha*, 2:163, trans. Walshe, *Thus Have I Heard*, 275.

66. Waldschmidt, *Mahāparinirvāṇasūtra*, 428–29.

67. See Bareau, *Recherches*, 2:243. See also *T* no. 1, 1:28c, trans. Weller, "Letzte Wanderung," 197, and *T* no. 2087, 51:904b, trans. Li Ronxi, *Great Tang Record*, 191.

68. Waldschmidt, *Überlieferung*, 300.

69. See Bareau, *Recherches*, 2:241–42. It is at this point that Mahākāśyapa notices the stains and/or discoloration of the Buddha's feet discussed above.

70. Alexander Cunningham, *The Bhilsa Topes, or Buddhist Monuments*

of Central India (London: Smith, Elder, 1854), 112–13. On Buddha footprint relics in general, see Anna Maria Quagliotti, *Buddhapadas* (Kamakura: Institute of the Silk Road Studies, 1998).

71. In some Chinese sources, the miracle of the feet is followed by one or two other similar postmortem events: the Buddha sticks out his hand to signal Ānanda, and, more commonly, he sits up in his coffin in order to preach to his mother, Mahāmāyā, who has come down from heaven for his funeral. See *T* no. 2087, 51:904b–c, trans. Li Ronxi, *Great Tang Record*, 191. Xuanzang's account appears to be based on the *Mahāmāyā sūtra* (*T* no. 383), on which see Hubert Durt, "L'apparition du Buddha à sa mère après son nirvāṇa dans le *Sūtra de Mahāmāyā* et le *Sūtra de la mère du Buddha*," in *De Dunhuang au Japon: Études chinoises et bouddhiques offertes à Michel Soymié*, ed. Jean-Pierre Drège (Geneva: Droz, 1996), 1–24.

72. See Bareau, *Recherches*, 2:254–65; and Waldschmidt, *Überlieferung*, 305–13.

73. See Schopen, *Bones, Stones, and Buddhist Monks*, 217–19; Anna Seidel, "Dabi," in *Hōbōgirin* (Paris: Adrien Maisonneuve, 1983), 6:578, and *T* no. 2087, 51:877c, trans. Li Ronxi, *Great Tang Record*, 62.

74. Jonathan P. Parry, *Death in Banaras* (Cambridge: Cambridge University Press, 1994), 187–88.

75. See Kane, *Dharmaśāstra*, 229–31, and Parry, *Death in Banaras*, 184.

76. Robert Hertz, "A Contribution to the Study of Collective Representations of Death," in *Death and the Right Hand*, trans. Rodney and Claudia Needham (Glencoe: Free Press, 1960 [1907]), 27–86.

77. See Loring M. Danforth, *The Death Rituals of Rural Greece* (Princeton, NJ: Princeton University Press, 1982), 35–69.

78. On this, see also Bernard Faure, *The Rhetoric of Immediacy: A Cultural Critique of Chan/Zen Buddhism* (Princeton, NJ: Princeton University Press, 1991), 134–35.

79. Walshe, *Thus Have I Heard*, 275; text in Carpenter, *Dīgha*, 2:164.

80. Walshe, *Thus Have I Heard*, 275; Davids, *Dialogues*, 2:186; Bareau ("Os"), *Recherches*, 2:260.

81. Stede, *Sumangalavilāsinī*, 2:603–4.

82. See, for example, N. A. Jayawickrama, *The Chronicle of the Thūpa and the Thūpavaṃsa* (London: Pāli Text Society, 1971), 172.34. See also A. P. Buddhadatta, *Jinakālamālipakaraṇam* (London: Pāli Text Society, 1962), 37–38, trans. N. A. Jayawickrama, *The Sheaf of Garlands of the Epochs of the Conqueror* (London: Pāli Text Society, 1968), 53–54.

83. This is not to deny that bona fide bones and teeth are also sometimes featured in China and Japan.

84. See Waldschmidt, *Überlieferung*, 309. See also Rockhill, *Life*, 145, and Bareau, *Recherches*, 2:262–63.

85. Walshe, *Thus Have I Heard*, 275; text in Carpenter, *Dīgha*, 2:164.

86. Jayawickrama, *Thūpavaṃsa*, 174, 36.

87. For an elaboration on Ajātaśatru's intense emotions, see Jayawickrama, *Thūpavaṃsa*, 174–75.36–38, and Stede, *Sumangalavilāsinī*, 2:605–6.

88. Carpenter, *Dīgha*, 2:164, trans. Davids, *Dialogues*, 2:187. See also Jayawickrama, *Thūpavaṃsa*, 175.38.

89. On this and other versions of the list (including the Pāli), see Waldschmidt, *Überlieferung*, 314.

90. See Bareau, *Recherches*, 2:284–85. In a variant text, however, the Buddha himself predicts the distribution of his relics. See Ernst Waldschmidt, "Der Buddha preist die Verehrungswürdigkeit seiner Reliquien," *Vom Ceylon bis Turfan* (Göttingen: Vandenhoeck and Reprecht, 1967), 417–27.

91. See Waldschmidt, *Mahāparinirvāṇasūtra*, 440–41, and Bareau, *Recherches*, 2:284.

92. See Waldschmidt, *Überlieferung*, 321–24, and Bareau, *Recherches*, 2:288–303.

93. See Waldschmidt, *Überlieferung*, 324–28, and Bareau, *Recherches*, 2:303–8.

94. Phyllis Granoff, oral communication, Princeton, NJ, 18 May 2002. See also Kane, *Dharmaśāstra*, 262.

95. *T* no. 2087, 51:883b, trans. Li Ronxi, *Great Tang Record*, 87.

96. *T* no. 2087, 51:904c, trans. Li Ronxi, *Great Tang Record*, 192. The same division is found in *T* no. 2122, 53:599b, trans. in Brian D. Ruppert, *Jewel in the Ashes: Buddha Relics and Power in Early Medieval Japan* (Cambridge, MA: Harvard University Press, 2000), 290. Bernard Faure cites yet another tradition, according to which the humans get eight shares of relics, the gods three, and the nāgas twelve. See his "Relics, Regalia, and the Dynamics of Secrecy in Japanese Buddhism," in *Rending the Veil*, ed. Elliot R. Wolfson (New York: Seven Bridges Press, 1999), 174.

97. Phyllis Granoff, oral communication, Princeton, NJ, 18 May 2002. See also Kane, *Dharmaśāstra*, 520–23.

98. *T* no. 2087, 51:908a, trans. Li Ronxi, *Great Tang Record*, 209. See also *T* no. 2122, 53:599b, trans. in Ruppert, *Jewel in the Ashes*, 290–91.

99. Jayawickrama, *Thūpavaṃsa*, 177.41.

100. See Kevin Trainor, *Relics, Ritual, and Representation in Buddhism: Rematerializing the Sri Lankan Theravāda Tradition* (Cambridge: Cambridge University Press, 1997), 132.

101. Later, of course, the number of stūpas over the Buddha's relics would be expanded to eighty-four thousand by King Aśoka (see John S. Strong, *The Legend of King Aśoka* [Princeton, NJ: Princeton University Press, 1983], 109–19).

102. See Bareau, *Recherches*, 2:314–20. The text is *T* no. 5, 1:174b (see Waldschmidt, *Überlieferung*, 311).

103. Przyluski, "Le partage," 353. Rāmagrāma, to which one of the eight shares of relics is said to be taken, is featured in later tradition as a most important depository of relics. See Strong, *Relics of the Buddha*, chap. 5.

104. Jayawickrama, *Thūpavaṃsa*, 181.44.

105. See Bareau, *Recherches*, 2:311, and Waldschmidt, *Überlieferung*, 329–30.

106. See Stede, *Sumangalavilāsinī*, 2:610. The same story is found in Jayawickrama, *Thūpavaṃsa*, 178–79.42–43.

107. See, for example, Frank E. Reynolds, "The Many Lives of Buddha: A Study of Sacred Biography and Theravada Tradition," in *The Biographical Process*, ed. Frank E. Reynolds and Donald Capps (The Hague: Mouton, 1976), 37–61.

108. Most recently, see Gananath Obeyesekere, "The Death of the Buddha: A Restorative Interpretation," in *Approaching the Dhamma*, ed. Anne M. Blackburn and Jeffrey Samuels (Seattle: BPS Pariyatti Editions, 2003), 17–45.

109. For example, see Mettanando Bhikkhu and Oskar Von Hinüber, "The Cause of the Buddha's Death," *Journal of the Pāli Text Society* 26 (2000): 105–17; R. Gordon Wasson, "The Last Meal of the Buddha," *Journal of the American Oriental Society* 102 (1982): 591–603; Arthur Waley, "Did Buddha Die of Eating Pork?" *Mélanges chinois et bouddhiques* 1 (1931–32): 343–54; and D. G. Koparkar, "Sūkara-maddava," *Poona Orientalist* 9 (1944): 34–42.

110. Jorinde Ebert, *Parinirvāṇa: Untersuchungen zur ikonographischen Entwicklung von den indischen Anfängen bis nach China* (Stuttgart: Franz Steiner Verlag, 1985).

111. See Raymond B. Williams, "Historical Criticism of a Buddhist Scripture: The *Mahāparinibbāna Sutta*," *Journal of the American Academy of Religion* 38 (1970): 156–67.

112. See Paul Williams, *Buddhist Thought* (London: Routledge, 2000), 30.

113. Schopen, *Bones, Stones, and Buddhist Monks*, 103.

114. Stede, *Sumangalavilāsinī*, 2:615.

115. Waldschmidt, *Mahāparinirvāṇasūtra*, 450, trans. Bareau, *Recherches*, 2:331. See also Rockhill, *Life*, 147.

116. Carpenter, *Dīgha*, 2:167–68, trans. Davids, *Dialogues*, 2:191. These very final lines are not found in the Sanskrit text, but, as Bareau (*Recherches*, 2:337n1) points out, they are contained in the Chinese and Tibetan.

2

Cross-Dressing with the Dead

Asceticism, Ambivalence, and Institutional Values in an Indian Monastic Code

GREGORY SCHOPEN

—To the memory of W. W. Rockhill, probably the only rancher from New Mexico who worked on the *Mūlasarvāstivāda vinaya**

THERE CAN BE very little doubt that the most visible development in the archaeology and epigraphy of Indian Buddhism in the period between the Mauryan and Gupta empires is the fact that Buddhist communities came to be fully monasticized, permanently housed, landed, propertied, and—to judge by almost any standard—very wealthy. There also can be very little doubt that these developments occurred unevenly in both time and geography and did not everywhere follow the same pattern nor reach the same degree of elaboration. What we see now are widely scattered and not easily explainable pockets: the astonishing proliferation of monastic sites—after Aśoka—in Andhra around the Krishna and Godavari Rivers, for example, with records of land grants and permanent endowments (*akṣayanīvī*);[1] the equally astonishing number of monastic complexes of various sizes in and around Taxila;[2] and a much thinner but still impressive distribution in the "heartland." Needless to say, we do not understand well—if at all—why what we see had happened, or how, nor do we have as yet any precise idea of its consequences, though such consequences must have been far-reaching and must have impacted very heavily on Buddhist values and on a Buddhist monk's self-understanding and, indeed, must have created unforeseen problems of group identity. Being a Buddhist monk in these new settings must of necessity have meant something very different from being a Buddhist monk in "the old days," and "corporate" concerns must have begun to override individual lifestyles. It is not hard to imagine that Buddhist monks in these new settings would have had—in every sense of the term—an "identity" problem.

There is no evidence for Buddhist monasteries either before or during the Mauryan period. To judge by his inscriptions and the language used in them, Aśoka himself did not know anything about Buddhist monasteries. When, for example, he grants a tax reduction in conjunction with his personal visit to what he declared to be the place of the Buddha's birth, he does not grant it to a monastery or even to a monastic group, but to the village of Lumbini itself[3]—we know, incidentally, from their own texts that, unlike *saṃnyāsin*s or renouncers, Buddhist monks remained subject to a variety of taxes.[4] Even in the later inscriptions from Bharhut and Sanchi there are no references to vihāras, and they begin to appear—though still rarely—only in Kharoṣṭhī records of a little before and a little after the Common Era, about the same time that the first indications of permanent monastic residential quarters begin to appear in the archaeological record for the Northwest, and this is not likely to be mere coincidence.[5] Some of the Western caves have, of course, been assigned to an earlier date, but such dating is very far from secure.

Needless to say, then, when precisely Buddhist groups begin to live in permanent quarters we do not know, although it seems virtually certain that this did not occur on any scale until well after Aśoka and probably nearer to the beginning of the Common Era. Some systemic consequences of this development, however, might be more easy to surmise. Once Buddhist groups—we might now even call them "monks"—settled in permanent quarters, they would almost certainly have been confronted with a series of interlocking problems. Permanent quarters, to remain so, required upkeep and maintenance; such maintenance required donations beyond mere subsistence; such donations required the further maintenance of long-term relationships with donors. But permanent quarters and the maintenance of relationships with the same donors over prolonged periods also exposed monastic doctrine, attitudes, and practices to prolonged and close observation by those donors and necessarily required that monastic doctrine and practice conform to, or at least not collide with, lay values. Considerations of this sort alone, it seems, can account for one of the most striking characteristics of all Buddhist Vinayas as we have them. Already long ago I. B. Horner, in speaking only of the Pāli Vinaya, had said:

> For the believing laity, though naturally not to the forefront in the Vinaya, are in a remarkable way never absent, never far distant. They perpetually enter into the life of the Order as supporters, critics, donors, intensely interested;...What was important [for the compilers of the Pāli Vinaya, we might add] was that the monks should neither abuse their dependence on the former [i.e., lay supporters], nor alienate the latter [i.e., the lay population as a whole], but should so regulate their lives as to give no cause for complaint.

And also:

> It must be remembered that it was considered highly important [again by the compilers of the Pāli Vinaya] to propitiate these [lay followers], to court their admiration, to keep their allegiance, to do nothing to annoy them....Historically, the success of the Early Buddhist experiment in monasticism must be in great part attributed to the wisdom of constantly considering the susceptibilities and criticisms of the laity.[6]

These same remarks apply, it seems, with equal, if not even greater, force to all the Vinayas that have come down to us, particularly perhaps to the Mūlasarvāstivādin Vinaya, which reveals, for example, several efforts to adjust Buddhist monastic practices to larger Indian values and attitudes in regard especially to the thorny "social" issue of the dead.[7] This in and of itself may be important. If the compilers of the various Vinayas considered it "highly important" to construct or adjust monastic practice so as to give no cause for complaint to the laity and if considerations of this sort could only have assumed high importance after Buddhist groups had permanently settled down, then, since the latter almost certainly did not occur until well after Aśoka, it would be obvious that all the Vinayas that we have are late, precisely as both Wassilieff and Lévi suggested a hundred years ago. Indeed, it could be argued—and should be, but not here—that far from being early, the composition and compilation of the enormous Vinaya literature that has come down to us is in fact one of the major achievements of monastic Buddhism during the Middle Period, the period between the end of the Mauryans and the time of the Guptas.

These are, of course, big issues, but regardless of how they might eventually be sorted out, at least one other thing in regard to Horner's remarks needs to be addressed. She talks about the historical "success" of the monastic Buddhist preoccupation with lay values and sensibilities; she talks—if you will—about its survival value but not about its costs, not about its impact on what it meant to be a Buddhist monk or about the way in which it must have put limits on the choices of individual monks and foreclosed some old or previously available options. These too need to be brought into some kind of focus, and a start in this direction might be made by trying to see the ways in which these monastic codes deal with asceticism, and in particular with ascetic practices that involve some sort of contact with the dead or with dead bodies. Asceticism was—and probably still is even in modern India—dangerously individualistic, prone to excess, culturally powerful, and not easy to predict: precisely the sort of thing that could create problems for an institution. Buddhist attitudes toward it are still not well understood, in part, perhaps, because even the finished biographies of the Buddha are still struggling with it, and in part because these attitudes have not yet been very closely studied and were probably always ambivalent. Still, watching how even one of our monastic codes—one that was certainly compiled in the Middle Period—dealt with a particularly troubling element of asceticism in India involving contact with the dead will perhaps tell us a great deal about how the Buddhist monastic institution tried to contain the individual monk. It might also tell us more fully what that institution valued and where it stood in regard to the Indian attitude toward what is dead.

The *Lalitavistara* is not a Vinaya text, but it probably comes from the same period as the Vinayas that we have,[8] and it contains a curious episode that concerns a particularly offensive and culturally dangerous element of ascetic practice, one that tangles together issues of group identity and public image, lay values, pollution, death, and how a monk should dress. It is strikingly ambivalent and nicely sets the stage for what we will see in our monastic code.

The Buddha tells his monks that when, just prior to his awakening, he had determined to end his six years of extreme ascetic practices, the yellow garments (*kāṣāyāṇi vastrāṇi*) he had worn for those six years were completely worn out (*parijīrṇa*); *kāṣāya* can of course mean "impure," and here the ambiguity starts. As a consequence, he says, it occurred to him: "It would be good if I could obtain a loin-cloth (*kaupīnapracchādana*)." And the text continues with the Buddha speaking:

> At that time a slave girl of the village girl Sujātā had died who was named Rādhā. She, having been wrapped in hemp cloths and carried to the burning ground (*śmaśāna*), had been abandoned (*parityakta*) there. I myself saw that refuse rag (*pāṃśukūla*). Then I, stepping on that refuse rag with my left foot, and reaching out with my right hand, had bent down to pick it up. Then the earthly gods proclaimed to the gods in the sky—"Amazing, sirs! This, sirs, is astonishing, when indeed the off-spring of a great royal family, one who has abandoned the rule of a wheel turning king, has turned his attention toward a refuse rag!"[9]

The news is then shouted from one group of gods to another. They are clearly stunned, and so too might we be, if perhaps for other reasons: the message here seems to be strikingly odd. The Bodhisattva here is starting to change clothes and, as for example in the Buddha's initial "going forth," in Buddhist narrative literature a change of clothes invariably marks a change in character and course. But here, when the Bodhisattva should be ending his period of radical asceticism, the change would seem to be going socially from bad to worse. He is changing from tattered rags, which are offensive enough, to dressing in a shroud, which—given Indian fastidiousness about death pollution—would seem to have been entirely off-putting. More particularly, he would appear to be putting his body in close and direct contact with cloth that had not only been in direct contact with a dead body, but also with a woman's dead body and all its effluents. His asceticism would seem, in short, not to be decreasing but increasing in its social offensiveness. This is very odd, and there are signs that the author of the *Lalitavistara* knew it. Notice, for example, that he avoids words for "corpse" or "shroud" and seems to refer almost immediately not only to the cloth, but also to the body, as a "refuse rag," although technically—as we will see—according to Vinaya law even the cloth cannot be so designated. Our author may also be showing his uneasiness in the way he continues the story.

Immediately following the divine shouting, the author puts into the mouth of the Buddha an elaborate account of how he immediately washed the cloth in a pond especially created by the gods for that purpose, and this is a good, but—again as we will see—not a sufficient alteration of a shroud according to Vinaya rule. The most telling indication of the author's unease, however, may be the fact that he appears to have the Buddha, with some more divine intervention, in effect, conceal what he will be wearing. After washing the shroud, the Buddha, according to the text, made it into a *saṃghāṭī*. Edgerton gives "waist-cloth" for *saṃghāṭī*, but it is likely here to have been similar to a *kaupīnapracchādana*, or simply *kaupīna* (loin-cloth), and our text itself would seem to go some ways toward showing that—it was after all a *kaupīna* that the Bodhisattva was after when he initially picked up the shroud.[10] In any case, it appears here to have been an inner or under garment, and this apparently is all the Bodhisattva has—an inner garment made out of a shroud—as he is about to reenter the social world. That is until the author—not the Buddha—has recourse to a *deus ex machina* with the very probable name Vimalaprabha:

> Then a son of a god who lived in the pure abodes named Vimalaprabha placed before the Bodhisattva divine robes, dyed with ocher dye, proper, appropriate to a *śramaṇa* (*divyāni cīvarāṇi kāṣāyaraṅgaraktāni kalpikāni śramaṇasārūpyāṇi bodhisattvāyopanāmayati sma*). And the Bodhisattva, having taken them, having dressed in the morning, having covered the loin-cloth, turned toward the village within his range (*bodhisattvaś ca tāni gṛhītvā pūrvāhne nivāsya saṃghāṭī prāvṛtya gocaragrāmābhimukho 'bhūt*).

Although the difference in the end may not be significant, it should be first noted that the final sentence here allows for two readings. A strong reading, which is represented in the translation, takes *prāvṛtya* as the gerund of *prā*$\sqrt{}$*vṛ*, "to cover" or, even stronger, "to conceal." But *prā*$\sqrt{}$*vṛt*, which might mean "wrap around," would produce exactly the same form, and the two verbs are, it seems, already confused in the *Veda*. However—and this is the crucial point—even if the author intended "wrapped around," the fact remains that he also apparently felt that robes that were "proper" and "appropriate to a *śramaṇa*" were still required, that, in effect, the *saṃghāṭī* or shroud by itself, and wherever it was worn, was not proper.[11] Moreover, that monastic robes could conceal as much as they reveal, and that Buddhist authors were as aware as we are that clothes are intimately linked with questions of identity, are both clear from other texts. The most straightforward of such texts is perhaps one that occurs in the *Kṣudrakavastu* section of the *Mūlasarvāstivāda vinaya*:

> The Buddha, the Blessed One, was staying in Śrāvastī, in the Jetavana, in the Park of Anāthapiṇḍada.
>
> Since the cold season had descended the monks, being afflicted by the cold, stayed in bed. But when the householder Anāthapiṇḍada came to the monastery and saw them, he said: "Noble Ones, why do you lie around when the teaching is all about effort, and not work toward the good?"
>
> "Although those who are comfortable might call to mind the dharma," they said, "we are freezing!"
>
> Anāthapiṇḍada returned to his house and sent them five hundred woolen garments. The monks put on the householders' clothes, but when they went outside, and brahmins and householders saw them, they scoffed at them and said: "So, Noble Ones, you have fallen?!"
>
> The monks said: "You, sirs, must not speak that way—we have only done this because we were cold," and they abused them in return.
>
> The monks reported this matter to the Blessed One, and the Blessed One said, "Monks must not wear householders' clothes! Should similar circumstances arise, they must be worn when monastic robes have been put on over them."[12]

The implications of this little sketch probably do not require an elaborate exegesis, nor, perhaps, does the rule it delivers. What the text establishes at a minimum is that at least one literate monk who was in a position to redact the rules in the Middle Period thought, or wanted others to think, that in the "outside" world you were what you wore. That, in effect, clothes made the monk, and that anything that might threaten a Buddhist monk's identity as a monk must—quite literally—be covered up or concealed. This, in fact, is made a rule.

In light of Vinaya texts like this one, it is difficult not to see a similar message in the passage from the *Lalitavistara*. Here too the individual (in this case the Buddha himself) is about to enter the "outside" social world. Here too he has—prior to the divine intervention—clothes that would mark him as a specific type. Here too these clothes must be—narratively—either covered up or at the very least supplanted by clothes that are, apparently, "appropriate" to another type. In the case of the Vinaya text, it is clear enough what types are being forcibly distinguished by the concealment: the monk from the layman. In the case of the *Lalitavistara*, things appear to be considerably more complex. Here, at the very least, one type of "renouncer" is being distinguished from another; "appropriate" attire for a renouncer is being distinguished from what, by implication, is not appropriate; at least a neutral, if not positive, image is being distinguished from a threatening, highly polluting one; the dress of the living is being distinguished from the clothes of the dead. And the *Lalitavistara* is, of course, not simply distinguishing. The narrative appears to be describing in effect the concealment of what is inappropriate by that which is "proper"; the addition to that which is threatening and polluting of that which is not; the emergence of a body wrapped (*prāvṛtya* in the second sense) in a shroud for the dead wearing as well a costume of the living presented by a god. If you are what you wear, this is a decidedly mixed message—perhaps even an intentionally scrambled one.

The monks in the Vinaya text have a good reason for wearing laymen's clothes under their religious robes—they are freezing. Curiously, there is no equally good or at least obvious reason why in the *Lalitavistara* the Bodhisattva—once supplied with "appropriate" robes—should retain the *saṃghāṭī* that he had made from the shroud, but its author seems to go out of his way to say explicitly that he did. Indeed, there is no obvious reason why the incident involving the shroud should have been included here at all—leave it out, and with the account of Vimalaprabha alone, you still have a stirring scenario. But the fact that the incident is nowhere else certainly found in Buddhist "canonical" narrative would seem to suggest that it had been intentionally added by the Mahāyāna author or redactor who reshaped another or earlier tradition into the Mahāyāna *Lalitavistara* that we have, and this apparently intentional addition may require that the narrative be read in still another way: the shroud may not be covered up or be concealed; it may undergird or hold everything together. The message here may be, not that radical ascetic, socially dangerous practices must be covered up, but rather that even with the appearance of the conventionally "proper" monk there is a body wrapped in a shroud and that in fact the latter is the foundation or integument of the former, that, in spite of appearances, radical ascetic and socially dangerous practices connected with the dead still underlie or surround Buddhist monasticism.

But whichever reading be preferred, the mere existence of this curious incident must indicate that the place of radical asceticism and the practice of dressing like the dead remained an issue—and a difficult one—for the redactor of our *Lalitavistara*.[13] Moreover, the fact that his rehandling has Mahayanized his text, and the increasing scholarly awareness of an early Mahāyāna tilt toward, or back toward, radical asceticism, might combine to support the second reading and provide some support for seeing in the shroud incident a soft and carefully phrased, if not intentionally ambiguous, assertion of the underlying importance of ascetic practice. All of this, however, remains only possible. What is certain is that Buddhist monks dressing like the dead was also an issue for the redactors of at least one important Sanskrit Vinaya.

THE *Mūlasarvāstivāda vinaya* contains numerous indications that its redactors were keenly aware of the connections between what a monk wore and how he was perceived, the connections between clothes and identity. They also understood, it seems, that clothing, or what you wore, and appearances had consequences. One such indication has already been cited: in the *Kṣudrakavastu*, when monks *wear* laymen's clothes "outside," they are immediately *perceived* there as no longer being monks. But this same awareness also lies at the root of the "origin tale" in this Vinaya, which delivers the authorization and rule requiring Buddhist monks to wear robes of a distinctive pattern so that they are clearly distinguishable from other religious men of the same type. The tale occurs, appropriately enough, in the *Cīvaravastu* and starts this way:

> It was the usual practice (*ācarita*) of King Bimbisāra when he saw a monk or nun to dismount from his elephant and to venerate their feet. On one occasion he had mounted his elephant and set out to venerate the feet of the Blessed One. Along the way he saw an Ājīvaka in the middle of the road. Bimbisāra, being thoroughly confused (*jātasaṃbhrama*) in regard to him, dismounted from his elephant and fell at his feet. The non-believers (*aśrāddha*) there thought to themselves: "So, the king is not devoted (*abhiprasanna*) only to Buddhist monks. He is also devoted to Ājīvakas!"

> But the believers there thought: "Surely the king, thinking, 'This is a monk,' was thoroughly confused when he dismounted from his elephant and fell at his feet." They, in their consternation (*sandigdhamanas*), said to the king: "To whom did the lord show veneration?"
>
> And he said: "To a disciple (*śrāvaka*) of the Blessed One."
>
> "But, lord, that was an Ājīvaka, not a disciple of the Blessed One!"
>
> Then it occurred to King Bimbisāra: "I must certainly do something about this! (*etad eva me karaṇīyaṃ bhavatv iti*)."[14]

He then goes to the Buddha, explains what happened, and requests that the Buddha insist on some distinctive mark on the robes of the monks (*aho vata bhagavann āryakāṇāṃ cīvarakeṣu kiṃcic cihna prajñāpayed ...*). The Buddha, being so prompted, does so, and Buddhist monks end up with robes of a distinctive pattern.

The recognition on the part of the *vinayadhara*s who redacted this text of the causal link between what a monk wore and his public image and social identity could, of course, hardly be more explicit. And the problem here is not in doubt: in the "outside," in the eyes and minds of the state (i.e., the king), of non-Buddhist and Buddhist alike, there is altogether too much confusion and consternation, and this confusion has serious consequences. It makes the king look foolish in supporting the Buddhists; it misleads nonbelievers in regard to the position of the state; and it upsets believers. What is more practically at stake is perhaps clearer in yet another case of mistaken identity, this one found in the *Bhaiṣajyavastu*.[15]

This second case of mistaken identity is purely narrative. The donor Anāthapiṇḍada invites the Buddha and the community of monks to his house for lunch. They come and Anāthapiṇḍada gives instructions to his doorman, saying: "Adherents of other religious groups (*anyatīrthyaka*) are not to be admitted so long as the Community of monks headed by the Buddha has not eaten. Only after that will I give to them." While the group is still eating, the great ascetic monk Mahākāśyapa, who has just returned from living in the forest (*āraṇyaka*), comes to Anāthapiṇḍada's door. He is described as "having long hair and beard and disreputable robes" (*dīrghakeśaśmaśrulūhacīvara*) and is, of course, turned away for reasons he himself expresses: "brahmins and householders do not recognize me as a Buddhist monk (*māṃ brāhmaṇagṛhapatayaḥ śramaṇaśākyaputrīya iti na jānate*)." Here, it seems, the messages are many. A monk who lives in the forest will not be recognized or acknowledged to be a Buddhist monk—this is of a piece with a deeply ambivalent if not outright negative attitude toward monks spending time in the forest, which is expressed in a variety of ways in this Vinaya.[16] To be accepted as a Buddhist monk one must not present in public an unkempt appearance nor be seen in disreputable robes. If one appears unkempt and wears disreputable—"coarse" or "bad" or "pernicious" or even "evil"—robes, one will be taken for a *tīrthyaka* or "heretic."[17] But however the messages be taken, the final one must certainly be this: the doors of wealthy, respectable donors will be shut to such a monk, and this is a message that is hard to miss.

Given the obvious sensitivity to the issue of a monk's appearance in the "outside" world on the part of Vinaya writers, it is easy to see why the author or redactor of the *Lalitavistara* might have structured his text as he did and why wearing a shroud would have to be handled with circumspection. Moreover, if even generically disreputable (*lūha*) robes were a problem, it is not hard to see how robes made from the garments of the dead would have been even more so. One does not have to look very far in at least this Vinaya, for example, to find evidence for the fact that the Buddhist monks who compiled it shared the broad brahmanical aversion and dread of any contact with a corpse. Only a single instance need be cited.

The redactors of the *Mūlasarvāstivāda vinaya* framed a set of rules that could only have been designed to bring Buddhist monastic practice in regard to handling a dead body into line with brahmanical notions of purity and pollution, and these rules had a long shelf life, being picked up and perpetuated in Mūlasarvāstivādin monastic handbooks. In the canonical version, the text says that after the monks had performed the full complement of rituals for the sake and benefit of their deceased fellow monk, they simply dispersed without further ceremony. But this met, according to the text itself, with "outside," social disapproval: "But then brahmins and householders derided them, saying: 'Buddhist monks (Tib. *śā-kya'i bu'i dge sbyong*; Skt. *śramaṇaśākyaputrīya*), after carrying away a corpse, do not bathe and yet disperse like that—they are polluted (*gtsang sbra med pa, aśauca*).'" Such a characterization or claim would be, of course, both dangerous and deleterious for any sedentary and dependent monastic community, and the response put into the Buddha's mouth is unequivocal. When informed of the situation, he is made to say:

> "Monks must not disperse in that manner, but must bathe!" They all started to bathe, but the Blessed One said: "Everyone need not bathe. Those who came in contact [with the corpse] must wash themselves together with their robes! Others need only wash their hands and feet!"[18]

This becomes, in Guṇaprabha's *Vinaya-sūtra*, for example:

> *spṛṣṭavadbhiḥ sacelasnānasya / anyair hastapādaprakṣālanam /*

> For those who had contact [with the corpse, there is the requirement] of bathing with their clothes. For others, washing the hands and feet.[19]

There can, it seems, be very little doubt that the values behind this rule—and a rather large number of other rules in this same Vinaya—are brahmanical, not Buddhist, and this widespread sensitivity to and awareness of brahmanical values on the part of the redactors of this Vinaya make it difficult to maintain that they were unaware of what wearing the clothes of the dead would have signaled or meant to an even moderately brahminized "outside."

One again does not have to look very far in brahmanical normative literature to discover the starkly negative value associated with the clothes of the dead and the living who wore them. In the *Mānavadharma-śāstra*, for example, in its catalogue of the excluded and low-born, it is *āyogava* (unfit) women, "who are non-*ārya*s" and who "eat despicable food," who "wear the clothes of the dead (*mṛta-vastrabhṛt*)."[20] A little later in the same chapter it says:

> *Cāṇḍāla*s *and śvapaca*s [dog-cookers], however, must live outside the village;... Their property consists of dogs and donkeys; their garments are the clothes of the dead (*mṛtacela*); they eat in broken vessels; their ornaments are of iron; and they constantly roam about. A man who follows the law should never seek any dealings with them (*na taiḥ samayam anvicchet puruṣo dharmam ācaran*).... They should carry away the corpses of those without relatives—that is the settled rule.[21]

There is obviously more than one way to understand the expressions *mṛtavastra* and *mṛtacela*. Both could be taken to refer to clothes that belonged to the deceased, without necessarily implying that his corpse was dressed or wrapped in them. But Kullūka glosses the second of these with *śavavastra*, which would seem more certainly to mean "shroud"—*śavavastra* is in fact the first Sanskrit equivalent that Monier-Williams gives for English "shroud."[22] Moreover, Buddhist sources—as we will see—and brahmanical sources too seem to collapse the two possibilities or to refer to both the deceased's clothing and what he or she is wrapped in as being left in the "burning grounds."

But if some ambiguity must remain in regard to "the clothes of the dead" or "a shroud for a corpse," there is no doubt about the associations of wearing either or both: such apparel is associated with "non-*ārya*s," eaters of "despicable food," *cāṇḍāla*s, and dog-cookers—clearly not the sort that a respectable person would want to have anything to do with. It is also virtually certain that Buddhist authors in the Middle Period would have known this, whether they were redacting the *Lalitavistara* or compiling the *Mūlasarvāstivāda vinaya*. And while this might account for some of the ambiguity in the former in regard to the shroud taken from the dead girl's body, it does not account for why it was worn at all or why this Vinaya—as we will see—did not categorically forbid the wearing of such stuff. In other, seemingly more positive cases the compilers of the *Mūlasarvāstivāda vinaya* show no such hesitation to do so. They categorically rule, for example, that a monk must not wear the *yajñopavīta*, or "sacred thread," which they—like the *Yājñavalkyasmṛti* —call the *brahmasūtra*:[23]

> The Buddha, the Blessed One, was staying in Śrāvastī, in the Jetavana, in the Park of Anāthapiṇḍada.
>
> The Group-of-Six monks went into Śrāvastī in the morning for alms. They saw a brahmin wearing the sacred thread (Tib. *tshang pa'i skud pa*; Skt. *brahmasūtra*) who had gone for alms and had received a great deal of both food and drink. The Group-of-Six said, "O Joy, O Rapture! This is a fine method. We too should do it thus!"
>
> The next day unbelievers saw them coming for alms wearing sacred threads. They were contemptuous, saying, "Salutations, salutations!"
>
> The Group-of-Six retorted: "You wretches, do you not even

know to whom salutation is to be made, and to whom reverence is to be paid?"

They said, "In this case, how could we know? Since elder brahmins are those to whom salutation is made, and monks those who are to be reverenced, why did we make salutation to you monks, not reverence?—Noble Ones, we took you to be brahmins, not monks (*'phags pa dag bdag cag gis khyed bram ze lags par 'tshal gyi dge slong du ni ma lags so*). Since it was so, and since we did not know, you really must forgive us!"[24]

The Group-of-Six remained silent.

The other monks, having heard about this, reported the matter to the Blessed One. The Blessed One thought to himself: "How could what is a fault appear small, since this is what follows from wearing the sacred thread? Henceforth, a monk must not wear the sacred thread! If he does so, he comes to be guilty of an offense."[25]

The rule here is also digested in the *Vinaya-sūtra*, where it appears as *na brahmasūtraprāvṛtiṃ bhajeta* (They must not resort to wearing the sacred thread!),[26] but the canonical account that delivers it, like several we have already seen, would again appear to indicate a clear awareness on the part of the compilers of this code that what their "monks" wore determined how they were socially perceived and behaved toward. There is further acknowledgment here, moreover, that what you wore could determine what you received. But the focus here is on the issue of confusion or the clouding of identity and, as in previous cases, the response is unequivocal: a rule is made that Buddhist monks must not wear what blurs their social identity.

The redactors of our code, then, show themselves to be perfectly capable of directly legislating against elements of appearance and apparel that could affect the public image of a monk that they thought appropriate. The obvious willingness to do so both here and in other cases, however, only renders their approach to the question of the "clothes of the dead" that much more curious.

THE MOST easily locatable Buddhist monk who wore "the clothes of the dead" is undoubtedly the *śmāśānika* monk, the monk "who frequents cemeteries." This type of practice is, of course, one of the *dhūtaguṇa*s, a more or less standard list of ascetic—even radically ascetic—practices that are referred to throughout much of Buddhist literature. But while this list of ascetic practices is well known, their role and place in the history of Indian Buddhist monasticism is not, and in fact we know very little for certain about them.[27] At least two things, however, seem to be relatively sure: the authors of a strong, seemingly early strand of Mahāyāna sūtra literature advocated their undertaking or appear to have been "attempting to re-invent, revitalize or resurrect these extreme ascetic practices";[28] and the compilers of the *Mūlasarvāstivāda vinaya*—as we shall see—seem to have been intent on doing everything they could do to demonize and discourage their practice; to poke fun at them; and to erect legal, economic, and social barriers to their undertaking.

While the advocacy of these practices in a significant part of "early" Mahāyāna sūtra literature is visible enough in general outline, like almost everything connected to this literature, it needs to be much more carefully and comprehensively studied, and that is not possible here: it will be a large project. Even a comprehensive treatment of the handling of these practices in the *Mūlasarvāstivāda vinaya* is not feasible here—it too is not a small project. Fortunately, however, the redactors of this Vinaya focused with particular vigor on the one *dhūtaguṇa* that is of specific interest here—dressing like the dead. This practice, the practice of monks wearing shrouds or the clothes of the dead, seems to have attracted the attention of the compilers of this Vinaya to a much greater degree than any other single ascetic practice and seems to have become for them emblematic of all *dhūtaguṇa*s. They return to it again and again.

A presentation of their views on this practice—in fact, a presentation of their presentations—must be shaped, however, by the nature of our surviving sources. None of the major presentations of this issue has come down to us in its Sanskrit original, so the first step is simply to make these presentations available, and at this stage, the most effective way of doing that is, perhaps, to translate into English the Tibetan translations of them that we have. This, of course, means that we see them through a particular filter, but the Tibetan translations of Buddhist Sanskrit texts are, on the whole, notoriously excellent and close, and we have enough of this Vinaya in Sanskrit to allow us to see that its Tibetan translation is also of this sort. Indeed, in most instances the original Sanskrit vocabulary can be reconstructed with some assurance. Moreover, the texts alone—even in translation—can carry much of the exposition or argument; they are in their main thrust remarkably straightforward and, again, do not require a labored exegesis. But perhaps the greatest advantage in presenting the texts *in extenso* is that this will allow the reader to catch something of their *tone*, and this, in the end, may be one of the most important things about them. It might as well reveal, at least indirectly, something of the literary qualities of this Vinaya. Sylvain Lévi in describing this monastic code said, already long ago:

> Un écrivain dont la fougue verbale et l'imagination surabondante évoquent le souvenir de Rabelais, et du meilleur de Rabelais, a pris prétexte des récits ternes et desséchés qui se répétaient dans le couvent à l'appui des prescriptions de la discipline ecclésiastique, pour en tirer une succession de contes qui veulent être édifiants, mais qui sont surtout amusants, pittoresques ou émouvants à souhait. Le Vinaya des Mūlasarvāstivādin's est une espèce de Bṛhatkathā à l'usage des moines.[29]

Lévi in fact called this compilation "un des chefs-d'oeuvre de la littérature sanscrite," and whatever one thinks of this claim, it is not improbable that this Vinaya does indeed represent one of the single most important *literary* achievements of the Buddhists in the Middle Period. This too it is important to see.

THE *Mūlasarvāstivāda vinaya* has a particularly rich cycle of stories, mostly preserved in Sanskrit, about the Buddha's "evil" and none too bright cousin, named—very likely with tongue in cheek—Devadatta, or "John Doe." His attempts to emulate the Buddha are often ridiculous and have disastrous consequences. When he has engineered Ajātaśatru's rise to kingship, for example, he says to him, "I have established you in kingship. You must also establish me in buddhahood (*tvam mayā rājye pratiṣṭhāpitaḥ tvam api mām buddhatve pratiṣṭhāpaya iti*)." The silliness of such a statement could not have been lost on anyone. But Ajātaśatru also at this stage appears as a dope—he thinks buddhahood is a state of the body and says in response, for example, that the (or a) Blessed One has as a characteristic mark (*lakṣaṇa*), the shape of a wheel on the sole of his feet. Devadatta, undeterred, summons a blacksmith and insists that he brand the soles of his feet with the mark of a wheel. The result, of course, is only intense and excruciating pain.[30]

With this and similar stories it is obvious that the redactors of this Vinaya went to particular trouble to set Devadatta up as a bozo—not so much evil as stupid—and it is almost certainly not accidental that it is he, and he alone in this Vinaya, who forcefully advocates and insists on the necessity of the *dhūtaguṇas*, or extreme ascetic practices for Buddhist monks, or that it is this insistence that is also said to have been the cause of the first serious split in the monastic community.[31] The implied association of stupidity and disruption with these practices also must have been obvious.

If there are discernible elements of slapstick in the stories concerning Devadatta, there are also similar elements in the account of a monk, forebodingly named Mahākāla, that occurs in the *Vibhaṅga* section of our Vinaya. Mahākāla is a quintessential *śmāśānika* cemetery monk—in fact, he defines the type in this Vinaya. But not only does his story end with a rule that would have been—and was probably designed to be—a formidable obstacle to the practice of this "ideal," but it is also a story about misunderstandings and perceptions gone awry, about rumors of cannibalism, and about Buddhist monks scaring the bejeezus out of children.

> The Buddha, the Blessed One, was staying in Śrāvastī, in the Jetavana, the Park of Anāthapiṇḍada. The Venerable Mahākāla then was one who obtained everything from the cemetery. His alms bowl was from the cemetery (Tib. *dur khrod pa*; Skt. *śmāśānika*); his robe too was from the cemetery; his alms, his bedding and seat were all from the cemetery as well.
>
> And what is an alms bowl from a cemetery? It is like this—the relatives cast the pot of one who has died and passed away into the cemetery. Then the Venerable Mahākāla, squaring the pieces and having heated them, takes possession of it (*byin gyis brlabs pa, adhitiṣṭhati*) as an alms bowl and keeps it.[32] Just so is an alms bowl from a cemetery.
>
> What is a robe from a cemetery? It is like this—the relatives cast the garments (*gos dag, vastra*) of one who has died and passed away into the cemetery. The Venerable Mahākāla washes and stitches them, and, having altered them, he takes possession of them as a robe and keeps them. Just so is a robe from a cemetery.[33]
>
> What are alms from a cemetery? It is like this—the relatives

cast five balls of food (*zas*, *piṇḍaka*) for one who has died and passed away into the cemetery. The Venerable Mahākāla takes them and makes them his food. Just so are alms from a cemetery.

What are bedding and seat from a cemetery? It is like this—the Venerable Mahākāla lives in the cemetery. Just so are bedding and seat from a cemetery.

When there were epidemics (*mi ngas*, *māri*) among the majority of people, then the Venerable Mahākāla grew in fatness, skin, muscle, and blood, and occasionally he did not even enter the village for alms. But when there were no epidemics among the majority of people, then the Venerable Mahākāla became emaciated, weak, lean, dehydrated, and feeble, and again and again he entered the village for alms.

The village door-keeper, having noticed this pattern, thought: "This Noble One Mahākāla, when there are epidemics among the majority of people, grows in fatness, skin, muscle, and blood. He occasionally does not even enter the village for alms. But when there are no epidemics, then this Noble One Mahākāla becomes emaciated, weak, lean, dehydrated, and feeble. Then again and again he enters the village for alms. Since this is so, I wonder if this Noble One Mahākāla is not eating human flesh?"

Soon everywhere it was heard, "The Noble One Mahākāla eats human flesh."

Now in Śrāvastī there lived a brahmin. He took a wife from a family of equal standing. He played, enjoyed himself, and made love with her. From that dallying, playing, and making love a daughter was born. She was looked after, nurtured, and grew up.

At a later time that brahmin died. His relatives adorned a bier with blue and yellow and red and white cloths and carried him to the cemetery. When they had cremated him, they dispersed. But the dead brahmin's wife and daughter went to one side and sat down.

The Venerable Mahākāla was sitting there staring into her face. The daughter saw the Venerable Mahākāla sitting there staring into her face. Having seen him, she said to her mother: "Mother, this Venerable Mahākāla sits there ruminating like a half-blind old female crow."

The Blessed One then said to the monks: "Monks, a certain brahmin's daughter speaks and reviles. Because she has made this abusive remark in regard to a great disciple who is like Mt. Meru, this brahmin's daughter will be reborn in five hundred births as a half-blind old female crow."

Everywhere it was heard: "The Blessed One has predicted that this brahmin's daughter will be reborn in five hundred births as a half-blind old female crow."

That brahmin's wife too heard that the Blessed One had predicted that her daughter would be reborn in five hundred births as a half-blind old female crow. Then that brahmin woman, taking her daughter, went to the Blessed One. Having arrived there, she honored with her head the feet of the Blessed One, and she said to him: "Blessed One, I beg you to forgive my daughter. She did not make this abusive remark with much ill-will."

"Brahmin woman, did I pronounce a curse in regard to someone?[34] If in fact your daughter had made this abusive remark with much ill-will, the situation would have been such that she would have been reborn in hells."

Brahmin boys in Śrāvastī also heard it said that the Noble One Mahākāla ate human flesh. They said, "Guys, we should put the Noble Mahākāla to a test and see whether or not it's true. One of us should pretend to be a dead person; the rest of us will then perform the honors in the cemetery!"

One of them was to pretend to be dead—"You," they said, "must pretend to be dead!"

He said: "But will I be eaten?"

They said: "We will protect you."

He pretended to be dead, and the others, anointing him with bdellium and oil, having put him on a bier, began to leave Śrāvastī. The Venerable Mahākāla was at the same time entering Śrāvastī for alms. When he saw them he thought: "Why should I, for a purpose hard to fulfill, enter the village for alms when—should I turn back—the five *piṇḍaka*s are to be had?" So thinking, he turned back.

The brahmin boy said to the others: "You guys, the Noble One Mahākāla is coming back—will I not be eaten?"

They said: "If you are, so will we be eaten."

They threw him into the cemetery and, going to one side, they sat hiding their heads in the brush and in their cloaks. A jackal started to wander around there, and the Venerable Mahākāla thought: "That jackal will eat the five *piṇḍaka*s—should I not preserve my food?" Thinking that, he began to run back very fast,

> and the brahmin boy, being terrified, began to cry, "I am being eaten! I am being eaten!"
>
> The other brahmin boys, grabbing sticks, rushed forward saying: "How can the Noble One bear the banner of a *ṛṣi* and still do such awful evil things?"
>
> He said: "What have I done?—Has human flesh been eaten? Did you boys see me holding a sword, or cutting off any flesh, or eating it?"
>
> They said: "But why did you hurry back so fast?"
>
> "You should have known, boys, that a jackal was eating the five *piṇḍaka*s, and thinking, 'Should I not preserve my food?' I ran back very fast."
>
> But because it still was not clear whether the Noble One Mahākāla ate the five *piṇḍaka*s or ate human flesh, the monks reported to the Blessed One that it was said thus everywhere: "The Noble Mahākāla eats human flesh."
>
> Then the Blessed One considered: "How could what is a danger appear small—this is what occurs when monks eat what has not been rendered 'received as a gift' (*apratigrāhita-bhukti*)."[35] Having considered: "Only that food which monks render 'received as a gift' is properly possessed." He said: "Henceforth, only that is to be eaten which monks render 'received as a gift.'"[36]

This is by almost any standards a curious text. It starts with a detailed definition of a cemetery-dwelling monk but ends with a formal rule that would in effect deny such a monk what is said to be his primary means of sustenance. The rule says—using the technical language of donation—that a monk can eat only what he has formally received—i.e., what has been given to him—and that by definition excludes the *piṇḍaka*s—those, as the text says, are "for the one who has died." This, at least at first sight, is odd. Equally odd, however, is the fact that between the initial account of Mahākāla's weight changes, the rumors to which they give rise, and the rule designed to avoid such rumors are two seemingly gratuitous tales about a cemetery monk inadvertently, but none the less surely, terrifying a little girl and stimulating in her a thought that sends her on a long series of unpleasant rebirths, and both scaring a bunch of boys and being the object of their pranks. The Buddha's defense of Mahākāla in the first tale is decidedly weak—he says he "is like Mt. Meru," but since, as we will see, cemetery-dwelling monks are routinely described as tough customers, this does not necessarily make him admirable, and the Buddha does not indicate that he is, or should be, an object of reverence. This first tale, moreover, seems oddly unconnected with the rest of the text, but even more gratuitous, perhaps, is the second tale. When all is said and done, the "test" devised by the boys to see if Mahākāla eats corpses is itself—as the text explicitly indicates—utterly inconclusive: it has no narrative function. Indeed, if both tales were entirely omitted, the rule would follow naturally from the gatekeeper's reasoned suspicions, and nothing would have been lost. Nothing, that is, except for some veiled but visibly unkind characterizations of ascetic monks and the clear implication that they are the source of damaging rumors. Indeed, since the rule itself is about food in general and since the *śmāśānika* monk is only one of a list of monks who might eat food that was not formally given, the redactors' inclusion of the account of Mahākāla here must have been intended to make it perfectly clear that the rule applied with particular force to the practice of *śmāśānika* monks. To see more clearly what is going on here, it might, however, be advantageous to look as well at some other texts in this Vinaya that deal with the same kind of monk.

The above text from the *Vibhaṅga* does not, of course, deal directly with taking cloth from a cemetery—its focus is on food. This does not mean, however, that the issue of cloth is ignored. In fact the *Mūlasarvāstivāda vinaya* addresses the issue over and over again but always, it seems, with the same intent: to make the practice of taking cemeterial cloth difficult, if not impossible, and to marginalize, if not ostracize, Buddhist monks who engage in it. The redactors of this Vinaya appear to have taken several different approaches to "the problem," one of which was connected with property law and the definition of property. The rudiments of this approach are already visible in a little text from the *Uttaragrantha*:

> Some in Śrāvastī conjured corpses, and when a householder conjured for a certain end, and that end was accomplished, he covered the corpse with a white cloth and left it there.
>
> When a monk named Kālananda came there he took that cloth. But the other monks said: "For you an offense leading to expulsion (*pārājika*) has occurred."
>
> "On what grounds?"
>
> "You took the cloth of a corpse that had not been given."

> When the monk felt remorse, the Blessed One said: "There is no offence leading to expulsion, but there is a gross offense (*sthūlātyaya*)."[37]

Here, at least initially, the monk who takes cloth from a cemetery is charged with a *pārājika*, the most serious category of offenses in Buddhist Vinayas. He is charged in effect with theft, and theft is defined in the Vinaya in purely secular terms: theft for Buddhist Vinaya is what the state classifies as theft.[38] If this classification of the act were allowed to stand, it would, of course, have rendered the practice of taking cloth from a cemetery legally impossible for any monk who wanted to remain in good standing (*prakṛtisthaka*), at least in communities where the rules were actually implemented. The Buddha's judgment, however, weakens or lessens the charge, but only slightly. He declares—and the role of the monk's "remorse" (*kaukṛtya*) may here be causal—that it is not a *pārājika*, but it is a "gross offence." Without going into the minutiae of Vinaya classification schemes, suffice it to say that it still remains a serious infraction of monastic rule.

This little text, then, provides a first indication of the complicated attitude that the redactors of this Vinaya had in regard to monks taking cloth from cemeteries. They either do not want to, or cannot, forbid the practice outright. But they also, apparently, do not want to encourage it. Here it totters on the edge of infractions leading to expulsion and is freighted with consequences. It is, it seems, to be avoided by "good" monks. This, however, is not the end of the legal maneuvering.

ANOTHER, somewhat longer text from the *Uttaragrantha* is much more explicitly legalistic and definitional in its apparent attempts to restrict the practice of Buddhist monks taking cloth from cemeteries. It also introduces an additional complication: it at least narratively asserts that other groups or individuals have, by virtue of secular law ("the order of the king"), prior rights to property left in cemeteries, and it severely narrows the range of funereal cloth to which Buddhist monks have access.

> The setting was in Rājagṛha.
>
> The Group-of-Six monks went to the Śītavana cemetery and when they saw that many possessions of the dead had been left—umbrellas, wood, and cloth—one among them said: "O Joy, O Rap-

ture! Since we have found cloth from a rubbish heap (*pāṃśukūla*), we should carry it off!" Saying, "O Joy, that is good, that is good, let us carry it off," they took it and left.

When the outcaste (*cāṇḍāla*) keepers of the cemetery came they thought: "There is nothing at all in the cemetery—someone has surely robbed it!" So thinking, they also thought: "Since whoever robbed it will be inclined to do it again, and will surely return, we should hide and wait." Thinking that, they got into the thick brush and continued to wait every day.

When seven or eight days had passed, the Group-of-Six said: "O Joy, O Rapture, since we have not gone to the cemetery for a long time now, there is a good chance of getting a little something —we should go again!" Saying that, they went.

When the monks began to take the cloth, umbrellas, and wood that had been left, the outcastes in the thick brush saw them, rushed out, and confronted them, saying, "Noble Ones, since we—our brothers, kinsmen, and companions—have been designated according to the order of the king for this cloth from the burning ground (*śmāśānika*), how can you carry away the possessions of the dead from a cemetery that has a proprietor (*svāmika*)?"

The Group-of-Six said, "Sirs, we take cloth from a rubbish heap (*pāṃśukūlika*)!"

But the outcastes said: "This, however, is cloth from a cemetery, so that is certainly wrong."

The Group-of-Six, having no response, stood there saying nothing.

The monks reported to the Blessed One what had occurred, and the Blessed One said: "Criticism by outcastes is a serious accusation, monks. Therefore, monks must not take from a cemetery that has a proprietor cloth from a rubbish heap! If monks take from a cemetery that has a proprietor cloth from a rubbish heap, they come to be guilty of a transgression."

Then, further, the truly devout said in regard to such cloth, "Noble Ones, carry it away as it pleases you!" But the monks had some doubts and did not accept it.

The Blessed one said: "If it is said 'accept it as it pleases you,' it should be accepted, and there must be no doubt in that case!"[39]

In the end, after presenting certain Buddhist monks as thieves and *cāṇḍāla*s as lawyers, this is a story about classificatory confusions and the conflict of monastic and secular law that results. The Group-of-Six—as is their wont—justify their actions (though not their rapacity) by invoking a perfectly legitimate, if largely rhetorical, Buddhist monastic ideal: they claim to be those who "take cloth from a rubbish heap (*pāṃśukūla*)." This source of cloth is, moreover, the one that every Buddhist monk is told about as a part of his ordination when he is asked, "Are you . . . able to subsist, for as long as you live, with cloth from a rubbish heap (*utsahase tvam . . . yāvajjīvaṃ pāṃśukūlena cīvareṇa yāpayituṃ*)?"[40] It does not matter for our purposes that as soon as the newly ordained says that he is *able*, the necessity to do so is immediately removed—apparently in all Vinayas as we have them—by allowing a long list of permissible options (*atireka-lābha*): silk, muslin, fine Benares cloth, etc.[41] What matters in our story is that the Group-of-Six classifies cloth from a cemetery as cloth from a rubbish heap, and it is this classification that the *cāṇḍāla*s—invoking secular law—reject. If they are correct, and it appears that they are, then the practices of a *śmāśānika* monk described in the *Vibhaṅga* are again, actually or potentially, from the point of view of secular law, illegal. Since there is ample evidence elsewhere indicating that the compilers of this Vinaya were well aware of secular law, there is a very good chance that they knew this and either felt a need to resolve the issue of illegality, or saw in it an opportunity to undercut practices of which they also did not approve. They were, however, careful or could only go so far. They did not, perhaps could not, completely forbid the practice, but they did put in place a rule that would have narrowly contained it and at the same time skirted the legality issue. The redactors of our Vinaya had the Buddha allow monks to take cloth only from a cemetery that had no proprietor or when they had formal permission—i.e., when it was in effect given to them—and although we obviously have no statistics here, these conditions would almost certainly have been in effect in only a tiny minority of cases.

What is established by narrative and rule in the story of the Venerable Mahākāla or the tale of the Group-of-Six is, moreover, elsewhere established by straightforward definition, and the "debate" about whether cemeterial cloth can be classified as *pāṃśukūla*, or "cloth from a rubbish heap," is solved by lexicographical fiat. In both the *Bhikṣu-vibhaṅga* and the *Bhikṣuṇī-vibhaṅga*, for example, *śmāśānika*, or cemeterial cloth, is defined as *only* "that which is taken from a cemetery that has no keeper (*parigraha*)." Both sources, moreover, give detailed definitions of *pāṃśukūla*—it is cloth from a highway or thrown out in the forest or on a river bank, etc., cloth that is torn or rotten, eaten by rats, etc.—but any reference to cemeterial cloth is notable by its absence: *pāṃśukūla* does not, by Vinaya definition, therefore include *śmāśānika* cloth; *śmāśānika* cloth is therefore not *pāṃśukūla*.[42] But both sources also include what appears to be, at first sight, a curious concession. Both list as a separate category of cloth what is called in Tibetan *gos bor blangs* or *blangs pa*, and while there is not yet an attested certain Sanskrit equivalent for this expression, there is little doubt about what it means and none about what the redactors of this Vinaya thought it was. *Gos bor blangs pa* must mean "discarded cloth that is brought or carried off" or "discarded cloth that is taken or accepted," and it is described with some precision:

> What is discarded cloth that is brought? Namely, when kinsmen know that one of their kin has been struck, died, and passed away, they wrap him in cloth and, after they have carried him out to the cemetery, they carry that cloth back again. Then coming [to the monastery], they give that cloth to the monastic Community—that is called "discarded cloth that is brought."[43]

This kind of cloth is, again, in a separate and distinct category: it is neither, by definition, *pāṃśukūla* nor *śmāśānika*. It is also not, quite clearly, the clothing of the dead, but probably something more like a pall, and we may already see here the beginnings of a practice described for modern Theravādin Thailand by Wells, who notes that although called *paṅsukula*, the cloth "presented" to monks in connection with Thai funerals is today "fresh new robes laid across the coffin—not the dusty rags once left at the cremation grounds."[44] This categorization also radically transforms the role of the monks in a direction already present in the final rule of the story of the Group-of-Six: it moves the monks from the role of scavengers to the role of recipients of gifts, and—by interjecting the kinsmen into the process—it separates the monks from the cemetery and, presumably, the impurity. It is now the kinsmen who must initially handle the cloth, and this, again presumably, makes it "presentable." But the procedure required by the definition of this category not only interjects the kinsmen, it also completely removes the individual monk: this cloth is not taken or given to an individual but to the community as a whole, and that too is a very different matter. Finally, the procedure required by the definition of this kind of cloth—like, but even more so than, the required permission in the *Uttaragrantha*—renders the entire transaction publicly visible and open to observation. Here there are no possibilities for rumors as in the case of the monk Mahākāla, no grounds for the charge of theft as in the cases of Kālananda and the Group-of-Six. Here the corporate image of the community is protected, and that almost certainly was the point.

One might have thought that all this maneuvering and its consequent rulings and requirements would have covered all the bases, but not, apparently, for our redactors. They were nothing if not thorough, and several gaps remained. What, for example, happens when monks find the clothes of the dead outside a cemetery, on a road, for example? They could then be, by Vinaya definition, *pāṃśukūla,* and that is a problem. Hence, yet another text in the *Uttaragrantha*:

> The setting was Śrāvastī.
>
> A rich man seized a debtor and then said to him: "You must repay in this amount of time!" Having fixed the time, he let him go.
>
> The debtor thought to himself: "Even though the time has been fixed in such a way, I still will not be able to repay it at that time—surely, then, when the time comes, I should go and run away." Having thought that, however, he considered further: "But there will still be much suffering just through being separated from my country and going away—I must surely kill him."
>
> When he had so determined, then he killed him on the road leading to the Jetavana Monastery.
>
> In time, when the Group-of-Six saw him [i.e., the dead man] they thought: "We have got here some cloth from a rubbish heap (*pāṃśukūla*)!" So thinking, they began to strip him. But when his kinsmen came there, when they saw him and were made to weep, they said to the Group-of-Six: "You have murdered him!"
>
> The Group-of-Six said: "Although we did not murder him, he was surely murdered by a foe!"

> The monks reported to the Blessed One what had occurred and the Blessed One said, "Monks, that his relatives are apprehensive is itself an accusation."
>
> Therefore, monks must not take cloth from a rubbish heap (*pāṃśukūla*) of this kind. It must be taken only when many people know about it! If it is not done in this way, one comes to be guilty of an offense!"[45]

This text too delivers a little tale about classification, potential confusion, and damaging public perceptions of the actions of monks. The Group-of-Six here is—as it usually is—technically correct. Their classification of the cloth as *pāṃśukūla* corresponds with the definition of *pāṃśukūla* in the *Vibhaṅga*: it is what has been left on a road. The fact that it is still on a body is—technically—immaterial. The Buddha himself is not made to contest the classification. In fact, his initial ruling tacitly accepts it. What he is made to do—and this would seem to be the main goal of the redactors—is introduce a distinction between permissible and impermissible kinds of *pāṃśukūla* that once again would make it difficult for Buddhist monks to obtain and use the clothing of the dead: "cloth from a rubbish heap of this kind"—i.e., still on a body—must not be taken, even if it is found at a site that would otherwise render it *pāṃśukūla*.

The "problem" addressed in the present tale is also once again familiar. Buddhist monks stripping corpses in this not yet regulated context would still leave members of the monastic community open to serious charges of criminal activity, charges that would necessarily reflect back on the community as a whole. The list of possible charges or public rumors to which the use of cloth or clothing of the dead could give rise is now in fact an impressive one: cannibalism, theft, and murder. And all of this does not include the fact that the practice would also necessarily equate Buddhist monks with *cāṇḍāla*s, the very lowest and most despised of the "mixed tribes." Ironically, the second ruling delivered by our text would seem to solve the first problem of accusation or rumor as well as the first ruling did and still allow the practice to continue. But the continuance of the practice under the conditions imposed by the second ruling would also render it publicly visible and therefore reinforce the identity of any monks who engaged in it with *cāṇḍāla*s: many people would necessarily know where their robes came from. That, however, may have been exactly what the redactors of this Vinaya may have wanted. Certainly our final text would seem to make it very clear that they were trying to arrange things so that any monk who wore clothing of or from the dead would be clearly visible and would pay a heavy price *both* within the community *and* outside it.

THE TALES and texts seen so far are almost exclusively focused on the social consequences, outside the monastery, of Buddhist monks wearing the clothes of the dead. Those consequences—rumor, accusations, confusion—are, of course, damaging and dangerous to the community as a whole, but these texts say very little about the specific consequences for the individual monks who might undertake the practice within the monastery or inside the community, and these consequences are, if anything, far more severe. These are the focus of our last text, a text from the *Kṣudrakavastu*:

> The Buddha, the Blessed One, was staying in Śrāvastī, in the Jetavana, in the Park of Anāthapiṇḍada.
>
> At that time there was a young son of a perfumer in Śrāvastī who had gotten a woolen blanket (Tib. *la ba*; Skt. *kambala*). He was extremely attached to it. After some time he fell ill—and he grieved far more for that woolen blanket than for riches.
>
> Although he was treated with medicines made from roots, stalks, leaves, flowers, and fruits, it was no use. When he himself discerned his physical condition, he assembled his relatives and said: "When I die you must not cremate me, but wrap me in this blanket and take me out!"
>
> They, trying to assure him, said: "Do all those who get sick die? You will get better, you must not worry."
>
> But his lifespan was exhausted, and in spite of being attended to and nursed, it was again no use. When he died, because of his excessive attachment to that woolen blanket, he was reborn among the hungry ghosts (Skt. preta) who have goiters (*galagaṇḍin*). His relatives decorated a bier with blue and yellow and red and white cloths and, wrapping him in that blanket, took him out to the cemetery. When the monks had seen that, they said to Kālananda, a cemetery-dwelling monk (*śmāśānika*): "Venerable, the young son of a perfumer has died. His relatives have wrapped him in a woolen blanket and taken him out to the cemetery. You should go and get that discarded cloth (*pāṃśukūla*)."

Kālananda hurried to the cemetery and grabbed it, but that non-human who had formerly been the boy said: "Noble Kālananda, you must not take my woolen blanket!"

But a cemetery-dwelling monk generally has a lot of nerve (*sattvavat*), so Kālananda said to him: "Hungry one, you were reborn among the hungry ghosts who have goiters because of your excessive attachment to this woolen blanket. Do you now want to be reborn in hell, too? Let go!"

But the hungry ghost did not let go. Because of his own excessive attachment to that blanket, the monk kicked him with his foot and stripped the blanket off. Then, taking it with him, he went to the Jetavana Monastery.

The hungry ghost followed behind him howling, saying, "Noble Kālananda, return the woolen blanket!" Furious, he too went to the Jetavana.

Because gods and nāgas and yakṣas who were devoted to the Buddha were staying in the Jetavana, the hungry ghost, being considered of little power, was not able to enter and sat howling at the door.

Since buddhas, the Blessed Ones, although they know the answers still make inquiries, the Venerable Ānanda was asked: "Ānanda, why is that non-human wailing at the door?"

Ānanda said: "Reverend, Kālananda has taken his woolen blanket."

The Blessed One thought to himself: "It is the case that this non-human wails through such attachment that, if he does not get his blanket, he will vomit warm blood and die." When he had considered that, he said to the Venerable Ānanda: "Go, Ānanda! Say this to the monk Kālananda: 'You must give the blanket back to this non-human! If it is not given back, he will certainly vomit warm blood and die. When you are going to give it back, then you must also say: "First you must go!" When he has gone back to the cemetery, then you must also say, "Lie down!" When he has lain down, then you should spread the blanket on top of him!'"

Saying, "Yes, Blessed One," the Venerable Ānanda assented to the Blessed One and went to the Venerable Kālananda. When he arrived, he said this to him: "You should understand that this is from the mouth of the Blessed One: 'The blanket must be returned to this non-human! If it is not given back, he will certainly vomit warm blood and die. When you are going to give it back, then you must also say: "First you must go!" When he has gone back to the cemetery, then you must also say, "Lie down!" When he has lain down, then you should spread the blanket on top of him!'" The Venerable Ānanda repeated thus the words of the Blessed One as he had spoken them and departed.

Kālananda then said this to that non-human: "If you want the woolen blanket, first you must go and then I will return it." When he went back, then Kālananda also said: "If you want the blanket, you must lie down!" When he had lain down, Kālananda covered him. The non-human, however, gave him a kick with his foot. But because Kālananda was tough, it did not bother him.

The monks heard what had occurred and they told the Blessed One.

The Blessed One said, "Monks, a shroud (Tib. *ro'i gos*; Skt. *śavavastra*) should neither be too quickly taken or returned. Should it be taken, one must remove it starting from the feet and working up to the head. But should one replace a shroud, he should start from the head and work down to the feet. Monks, there are five bad things about shrouds. What are they? Their color is bad; they smell bad; they are old; they are full of lice; they are full of malicious yakṣas. Moreover, so long as it has no holes, a shroud must not be taken by a rag-wearing monk (*pāṃśukūlika*)."

The Blessed One had said that a shroud without holes must not be taken, so the Group-of-Six took dogs to the cemetery with them. When those who were not believers saw this, they verbally abused them, saying, "So you Venerable Ones setting off with dogs for the wilderness must be going hunting!" The Group-of-Six answered them. The monks reported this matter to the Blessed One.

The Blessed One said: "You should not go out taking dogs with you!"

They cut holes in the shrouds with sharp instruments, then took them.

The Blessed One said: "Shrouds should not be taken after cutting them with sharp instruments! But only when small insects and ants have eaten them, then are they to be taken!"

They took them and wore them as they were.

The Blessed One said: "They should not be put on like that. Rather, they must be set out in an out of the way spot for seven or eight days. When they have been bleached out by the wind and sun, then, after being washed and dyed, they are to be worn!"

When they had put on such garments they entered the vihāra and worshipped the stūpas. The monks reported this matter to the Blessed One.

The Blessed One said, "I will designate the rules of customary behavior for a cemetery-dwelling monk: a cemetery-dwelling monk wearing a shroud must not go to a monastery (*vihāra*). He must not venerate a stūpa or, if he does, he must stay a fathom (*vyāma*) away from it. He must not use a cell (*layana*). He must not sit on seats and bedding. He must not sit among the community. When brahmins and householders have come and assembled, he must not teach the dharma to them. He must not go to the houses of brahmins and householders. If he does he must stay at the door. If they say, 'Come in, Noble One!,' he must say, 'I am a cemetery-dwelling monk.' However, if they say, 'Noble One, if those like you who have taken up and entered into the ascetic practices (*dhūta-guṇa*) come into our house, have we not obtained what is well obtained?,' then he should go in, but he must not sit on a seat. If they say, 'Noble One, sit on this seat!' he should say, 'I am a cemetery-dwelling monk.' However, if they then say, 'Noble One, if those like you who have taken up and entered into the ascetic practices use our seats and house, have we not obtained what is well obtained?,' then he should sit down there. In this there is no cause for remorse. But if a cemetery-dwelling monk who has taken up these rules of customary behavior as they were designated were not to enter into them, he would come to be guilty of an offense."[46]

Like that of many of the Mūlasarvāstivādin monastic texts dealing with *śmāśānika* monks, the structure of this text appears, at least at first sight, a bit disjointed and more than a little odd. The story of the monk Kālananda—like the "test" of the monk Mahākāla by the village boys—is narratively inconclusive: he takes the blanket but cannot keep and wear it and has to return it. The cloth ends up, in effect, where it belongs, and the story produces a ruling that seems to take as a given that all such cloth that is taken will potentially have to be returned. The whole procedure—the point seems to be—is an exercise in futility. But along the way, the redactor took every possible opportunity to dump on monks who engage in this practice: the monk Kālananda does not just go to the cemetery to get the blanket, but he also "hurries" or "scurries" there—Tib. *myur ba myur bar*; Skt. *tvarita, śīghraṃ śīghraṃ*. This is exactly the same expression used to describe the action of Mahākāla in trying to beat the jackal to the food, and in both cases the intent was almost certainly to make such monks look ridiculous—"good" monks do not run at any time. Our redactors also subtly but surely equate the monk Kālananda with the boy who became the hungry ghost (preta)—both are described in almost exactly the same terms as excessively attached to the same blanket, and the parallel does not stop there. Both monk and hungry ghost behave in the same way. The redactors make a point of having Kālananda kick the ghost when he is down, and the ghost, then, kick him back in the end. But perhaps the most obvious point to the tale—and it takes almost two-thirds of the text—would seem to be that monks who take cemetery cloth bring foul and pernicious things (pretas), quite literally, to the monastery's door. This quite clearly was not wanted.[47]

Apart from the very brief and curious rules about stripping a corpse *and* dressing it again (!), the whole of the tale of Kālananda seems to function only as a preamble to a very unflattering description of the defects of shrouds, followed by a rule stating that they can only be taken when they are in really bad shape. The Group-of-Six then—in their characteristic way—insists on the rule while trying at the same time to get around it, forcing the rules in which the redactors seem to be most interested.

The final rules delivered by our text survive in Sanskrit in a very condensed form in, again, Guṇaprabha's *Vinaya-sūtra*. The first set of rules requires that any shroud that was actually to be worn—and note that in none of our texts have monks yet done this—must undergo a long process of transformation. It must be temporally and spatially dislocated from its source of origin—i.e., the cemetery—and allowed to remain for a relatively long time in a neutral and probably neutralizing space; Guṇaprabha words this as *parivāsyābhyavakāśe vṛkṣādyupari*, "after leaving it out in the open on a tree, etc."[48] This, of course, in some ways shifts it from the category of *śmāśānika* to, or toward, the category of *pāṃśukūla*. But even when that has been done, it must still be submitted to further transformative processes: it must be washed and dyed—i.e., rendered visually indistinguishable from any other kind of robe material. It must, in short, be well sanitized.

Oddly enough, and in contrast to the case of the dyed and

"proper" robes presented to the Bodhisattva by the god Vimalaprabha in the *Lalitavistara*, which appear to publicly obscure the shroud, the redactors of the Vinaya text go on to indicate that here dyeing is not meant to effect this or that if it did, the monk himself was under obligation to counteract any such effect. Even when the shroud is washed and dyed, the monk is under obligation to publicly declare what he is, and thereby, what he is wearing; he must say, "I am a cemetery dweller," *pravedite smāśāniko 'ham ity*, in Guṇaprabha. The monks must do, in other words, what the *Mānavadharma-śāstra* says *cāṇḍāla*s must do—they must make their presence known to any they encounter. Although what exactly *cihnita* meant for Manu is not certain—"wearing distinguishing marks," "recognizable by distinctive marks"—and although Faxian reports in his day (399–413 CE) that when *cāṇḍāla*s entered into towns they had to "strike a piece of wood to announce their presence,"[49] the rules required by our redactors of Buddhist monks who wore shrouds would seem to go beyond even that: they had to verbally announce, individually and face to face, that they were, in effect, *cāṇḍāla*s. This could not have been comfortable for either party. The rules for such a monk in the larger social world—"outside"—in fact require that the announcement be repeatedly made. In a typically dharmaśāstric fashion—"You must not do x. But if you do, . . ."—these rules require first that the monk "must not go to the houses of brahmins and householders," period. But if he does, he must stay outside—any further, more intimate contact must be by invitation (*upanimantrita*), and each phase must be preceded by another repetition of his character. What is most striking here, in addition to the obvious and compulsory self-"candalization" of the monk in any interaction with the laity is, perhaps, the tacit acknowledgment by the redactors that such monks might still be admitted into the homes of the laity and allowed to "use" their belongings. This is in stark contrast to the rules pertaining to monasteries. The *śmāśānika* monk is absolutely forbidden to go to a vihāra or to use anything that belongs to the monastic community;[50] here nothing is said about any invitation, and there are no contingency clauses whatsoever. Such monks, it appears, are more welcome in lay houses than in monasteries. This impression can only be reinforced by the fact that other provisions systematically disenfranchise the monk who wears the cloth of the dead and even deny him access to objects of veneration: he cannot venerate the stūpa or can only do so at a specified distance; he cannot have a room in the monastery, sit with other monks, or teach. The exclusion of this kind of Buddhist monk from meaningful participation in his own monastic community is virtually complete.

What can be seen in these texts from the *Mūlasarvāstivāda vinaya* is, I would suggest, emblematic or symptomatic or representative of what much of mainstream Buddhist monasticism had become in the Middle Period. We see one group of Buddhist monks, the monks who redacted this Vinaya and were in a position to make the rules, who are concerned with or preoccupied with issues of social identity and the public image of the members of their community, trying to contain or marginalize another group or type of Buddhist monks, monks who were *śmāśānika*s, monks who wore the clothing of the dead. There are no good or apparent doctrinal reasons for objecting to *śmāśānika* monks, of course, and our redactors do not make even the slightest effort to provide any. What they are concerned with and appear to want to avoid, as virtually all of the texts cited here would seem to make clear, are unfriendly and damaging accusations of cannibalism, theft, murder, association with foul pretas, and, importantly, impurity connected with the anonymous dead. But while the specifics here are connected with monks who wear shrouds, the pattern of containment, distancing, and marginalization of certain types of monks, and the overarching concern with public image that overrides the value of individual religious practice, are not. They appear as well, and as clearly, in this Vinaya in regard to other socially "dangerous" practices—dwelling alone in the forest, engaging in individual unsupervised meditation, etc. Indeed, monks who practice meditation alone in the forest are almost always presented as sexual deviants and troublemakers who give the order a bad name. But these monks cannot be considered here.[51] This same pattern, moreover, has also already been detected in regard to the monastic disposal of their dead and monastic inheritance law and could easily be demonstrated in regard to a very broad range of other, seemingly more mundane, matters like washing bowls and providing drinking water.[52]

But if—as seems certain—the *Mūlasarvāstivāda vinaya* is a major literary product of the Middle Period, of the period that used to be thought of as the period of the Mahāyāna, so too must obviously be considered major the rules that it promulgated, the monasticism it was trying to construct, the tone it set toward ascetic practices, the obsession with public image it betrays on almost every one of its very numerous pages, and the fastidiousness, if not dread, of contact with the dead. What emerges from this enormous compilation overall is the picture of a profoundly conservative, socially timid group intent on rocking no boats. This, moreover, is the Buddhism that succeeded in India, that, for example, built and ran Sāñci, the monasteries of Taxila and Pitalkhora. It did so, it seems, because it had learned how to write a loan contract and how to behave "properly." Those monks who could not do the latter—while never formally disallowed—were by their own monastic rules effectively excluded from the very places that we study.

A FEW points remain. Given that the rules that have been cited here governing the behavior of monks who lived in cemeteries and cross-dressed with the dead present us with a representative snapshot of what monastic Buddhism had become, it might be of interest to at least ask about their chronological reach and influence. Their chronological reach or shelf life, it seems, was long. These rules were picked up and carried on by a wide range of medieval monastic handbooks like Guṇaprabha's *Vinaya-sūtra*, Viśākhadeva's *Vinaya-kārikā*, and Viśeṣamitra's *Vinaya-saṃgraha*.[53] At least the first two of these then continued to be copied—we have a surviving manuscript of the first that was copied at Vikramaśīla and has been dated to the eleventh or twelfth century and several folios of the second of about the same period.[54] The question of the influence of such rules is, of course, more complicated. But that they may have cast a long shadow might well be indicated by an unlikely source.

It has already been noted that one thick strand of Mahāyāna sūtra literature openly and strongly advocates or extols the practice of the *dhūtaguṇa*s. One such Mahāyāna sūtra—little studied now but cited by Śāntideva almost thirty times in his early medieval *Śikṣāsamuccaya*[55]—is called the *Ratnamegha sūtra*. Like all Mahāyāna sūtras, its dating is difficult. The text could be late—it was first translated into Chinese only in the sixth century; it could also be relatively early—it is quoted three times in the *Sūtrasamuccaya*, which might be by Nāgārjuna (second century?).[56] But early or late, the *Ratnamegha* is of particular interest here because it outlines in some detail how a bodhisattva should undertake the ascetic practices, one of which is, of course, the practice of a *śmāśānika*.

In treating the bodhisattva as a *śmāśānika*, the *Ratnamegha* first indicates that wherever he is, he must always and uninterruptedly fix in mind in regard to all men the idea of them dying, being devoured (by animals), being bloody corpses, discolored, putrefying corpses, etc. Then it says:

> Son of good family, the bodhisattva who is a cemetery dweller (*śmāśānika*) must develop thoughts of benevolence; he must be endowed with thoughts of benefit and compassion toward living things, morality and purity (*śuci*), and be unpolluted by meat. And what is the reason for that, son of good family? If a bodhisattva were to be seen eating meat in the vicinity of the cemetery, there could be non-human beings (*amanuṣya*) who would give rise to a lack of faith and think to harm him.[57]

Although the spin here is clearly different, it is difficult not to recall the story of Mahākāla and the rumors of cannibalism, in this case explicitly leading to a loss of faith (*aśraddha*) on the part of those who could be potentially beneficial. Here, too, the rule restricting what the *śmāśānika* can eat is even more closely tied to possible misunderstandings about cannibalism. But the text goes on:

> Son of good family, the bodhisattva who is a cemetery dweller, when entering a vihāra, venerating a stūpa of the Tathāgata, venerating the senior monks, or even being agreeable to the junior monks, must stand and remain so! He must not sit on seats and bedding belonging to the Community! And why is that, son of good family? A bodhisattva must adapt to the mind of the world. Although the bodhisattva who is a cemetery dweller does not adapt to the unnoble (*anārya*) world, he does adapt to the noble (*ārya*). If a bodhisattva who is a cemetery dweller is invited to bedding and seats that belong to an individual, he must by all means feel no compunction, but when he has clearly determined that the other would not object, and he knows the intention of that monk, then he must sit before him on that seat with a lowly mind like a child of a *cāṇḍāla*.[58]

Here the echoes of rules like those found in our Vinaya are even stronger and their force clear. Even in a Mahāyāna text that advocates the cemetery ideal and even when the *śmāśānika* is allowed into the vihāra and permitted access to the stūpa, still he is left standing, denied use of the monastic community's goods, and therefore marked as an outsider. Our rules were clearly a force to be reckoned with and not easily got around. But a final irony, perhaps, is the fact that whereas our Vinaya rules only imply that the *śmāśānika* is to be identified with a *cāṇḍāla*, the *Ratnamegha* requires that he actually think like one, and this, indeed, might give us cause for thought. Such a practice would have had a powerful effect on an individual of any standing in classical India.[59]

Finally—as seems only fit—we are left with the dead. The dead that Buddhist monks encounter and interact with in the texts examined here are not persons but objects, and not even objects of concern or compassion. Although we are sometimes told a bit about them, they are largely just corpses, corpses to be stripped. They are discarded objects—once ritually "disposed of," they are no longer of any particular interest. Although perhaps unsettling for some modern Western sensibilities, this is undoubtedly an important aspect of Buddhist—indeed Indian—attitudes toward the dead.

The objectification of the dead and their physical discarding, however, does not render them powerless in the Indian world. At least one of our texts, for example, refers to the instrumental use of corpses in "conjuring," and this dark side of corpses had a long cultural life—one need only refer here to the many versions of the *Vetālapañcaviṃśatikā* and its spread across Central Asia.[60] In fact it is the dark side that renders dead bodies powerful and dangerous cultural objects even apart from such usage: perhaps because they are in the end almost casually discarded, they are an ever-present source of impurity, pollution, and anxiety. Although deeply Indian, there is of course nothing particularly Buddhist about such attitudes and values. And yet it is almost certainly this generically Indian dread of contact with the dead, with dead bodies, that gives, ironically, *both* urgency to the Vinaya masters' concerted and repeated attempts to contain and restrain the wearing of shrouds by Buddhist monks *and* ascetic meaning to the fact that some did. Without Indian notions of purity and pollution, there is no need to curb the practice. Without Indian notions of purity and pollution, much of the meaning of engaging in it is lost.[61] Once again, it seems, Buddhist practices—whether they are of avoidance or embrace—are Indian in . . . the end.

Notes

*Rockhill in fact had already brought together in a footnote two of the passages that are treated in this chapter in his *Life of the Buddha and the Early History of His Order* (London: Kegan Paul, Trench, Trübner, 1907), 29n2.

1. See, for example, the map (fig. 1) at the end of B. S. L. Hanumantha Rao et al., *Buddhist Inscriptions of Andhradesa* (Secunderabad: Ananda Buddha Vihara Trust, 1998), which is captioned "Buddhist Sites in Andhra Pradesh" and where fifty-two such sites are marked. For the land grants and permanent endowments, see, most recently and well, Harry Falk, "The Pātagaṇḍigūḍem Copper-plate Grant of the Ikṣvāku King Ehavala Cāntamūla," *Silk Road Art and Archaeology* 6 (1999/2000): 275–83.

2. See, for convenience, John Marshall, *A Guide to Taxila*, 4th ed. (Cambridge: Cambridge University Press, 1960); Ahmad Hasan Dani, *The Historic City of Taxila* (Paris and Tokyo: UNESCO and Centre for East Asian Cultural Studies, 1986); Shoshin Kuwayama, "Buddhist Establishments in Taxila and Gandhara: A Chronological Review," in his *Across the Hindukush of the First Millennium: A Collection of Papers* (Kyoto: Institute for Research in Humanities, Kyoto University, 2002), 1–11.

3. See, most recently, Harry Falk, *The Discovery of Lumbinī*, Lumbini International Research Institute Occasional Papers 1 (Lumbini: Lumbini International Research Institute, 1998), 18–20.

4. Gregory Schopen, "Dead Monks and Bad Debts: Some Provisions of a Buddhist Monastic Inheritance Law," *Indo-Iranian Journal* 44 (2001): 139n8; reprinted in his *Buddhist Monks and Business Matters: Still More Papers on Monastic Buddhism in India* (hereafter *BMBM*) (Honolulu: University of Hawai'i Press, 2004), 160n8.

5. Gregory Schopen, "Doing Business for the Lord: Lending on Interest and Written Loan Contracts in the *Mūlasarvāstivāda-vinaya*," *Journal of the American Oriental Society* 114 (1994): 527–54; esp. 547–52 (*BMBM*, 73–79); Kuwayama, *Across the Hindukush*, 3–8; Pier Francesco Callieri, *Saidu Sharif I (Swat, Pakistan)*, vol. 1: *The Buddhist Sacred Area, the Monastery*, Centro Scavi e Ricerche Archeologiche, Reports and Memoirs, vol. 23, 1 (Rome: Istituto Italiano per il Medio ed Estremo Oriente, 1989), 113–16. A good history of the Buddhist monastery in India has yet to be written.

6. I. B. Horner, *The Book of the Discipline* (London: Luzac, 1938), pt. 1, xvi–xvii, xxix.

7. See, for example, Gregory Schopen, "On Avoiding Ghosts and Social Censure: Monastic Funerals in the *Mūlasarvāstivāda-vinaya*," in his *Bones, Stones, and Buddhist Monks: Collected Papers on the Archaeology, Epigraphy, and Texts of Monastic Buddhism in India* (Honolulu: University of Hawai'i

Press, 1997), 204–37; and Schopen, "Dead Monks and Bad Debts," 130–38 (*BMBM*, 151–59).

8. The discussion of the date and "composition" of the Sanskrit text of the *Lalitavistara* that we have has not progressed much beyond where it was fifty years ago. It is now generally accepted that the *Lalitavistara* that we have is—as Winternitz said long ago—"a recast of an older Hīnayāna text, the Buddha biography of the Sarvāstivāda school, enlarged and embellished in the spirit of the Mahāyāna." See Maurice Winternitz, *A History of Indian Literature*, trans. S. Ketkar and H. Kohn (Calcutta: University of Calcutta, 1927), 2:252; also Edward Joseph Thomas, "The Lalitavistara and Sarvāstivāda," *Indian Historical Quarterly* 16 (1940): 239–45; Étienne Lamotte, *Histoire du bouddhisme indien: Des origines à l'ère Śaka* (Louvain: Publications Universitaires, 1958), 636, 691. But—again as Winternitz said, and still—"When the Lalitavistara was finally edited, we do not know."

9. Salomon Lefmann, *Lalita Vistara* (Halle: Buchhandlung des Walsenhauses, 1902), part 1, 265, l. 19.

10. Franklin Edgerton, *Buddhist Hybrid Sanskrit Dictionary* (New Haven, CT: Yale University Press, 1953), 549. Edgerton's "waist-cloth" is, of course, reflective of the normal technical sense of *saṅghāṭī* (translated now more commonly as "outer robe"), but its usage here may have to be seen in light of the fact that the events being described are, in Buddhist "narrative time," prior to the promulgation of the formal rules concerning robes and, therefore, any technical sense for the term *saṃghāṭī*.

11. The Tibetan translation of the *Lalitavistara* is of little help in all of this. It may have been based on a different reading or may have simply avoided the ambiguities. It reads: *byang chub sems dpas kyang de dag blangs te / snga dro sham thabs dang chos gos bgos nas spyod yul kyi grang du phyogs pa* (Derge *mdo*, Kha 131b.5; cf. Nicholas Poppe, *The Twelve Deeds of Buddha: A Mongolian Version of the Lalitavistara* [Wiesbaden: Otto Harrassowitz, 1967], 142–43). Philippe Édouard de Foucaux (*Le Lalitavistara: Développement des Jeux* [Paris: Ernst Leroux, 1884–92, reprinted 1988], 230), in his old translation from the Sanskrit, also seems to gloss over the ambiguities: "Le Bodhisattva, les ayant pris et s'étant, le matin, revêtu de ses habits de religieux, se dirigea. . . ." Lefmann, however, gives no significant variants for the passage. Note that all references to Tibetan texts are to the Derge printing reprinted in *The Tibetan Tripitaka, Taipei Edition*, ed. A.W. Barber (Taipei: SMC Publishing, 1991). Canonical Vinaya are cited according to the letter of the volume in the *'dul ba* section, original folio number, and line. For texts in other sections, the same format is followed, but the section name is given first. Texts from the *bstan 'gyur* are marked as such.

12. *Kṣudrakavastu*, Derge Tha 67b.4–68a.1.

13. As just one example, see Gregory Schopen, "The Mahāyāna and the

Middle Period in Indian Buddhism: Through a Chinese Looking Glass," *The Eastern Buddhist*, n.s. 32, no. 2 (2000): 1–25, esp. 21–23, and the textual sources cited in the notes there. See also the passage from the Mahāyāna *Ratnamegha sūtra* cited below.

14. *Cīvaravastu*, Nalinaksha Dutt, *Gilgit Manuscripts* (Srinagar: Calcutta Oriental Press, 1942), vol. 3, pt. 2:49.1–51.7.

15. *Bhaiṣajyavastu*, Nalinaksha Dutt, *Gilgit Manuscripts* (Srinagar: Calcutta Oriental Press, 1947), vol. 3, pt. 1:79.1–80.14.

16. For just two striking examples, see *Kṣudrakavastu*, Derge Tha 102a.5–104b.2, and Da 35b.2–36a.2, in both of which staying in the forest is associated with monks getting into sexual difficulties.

17. For the range of meanings for Sanskrit *lūha*, see Edgerton, *Buddhist Hybrid Sanskrit Dictionary*, under both *lūha* and *lūkha*, as well as the related forms cited there.

18. This set of rules is treated at some length in Schopen, *Bones, Stones, and Buddhist Monks*, 215–21, and is again available in translation in Gregory Schopen, "Deaths, Funerals, and the Division of Property in a Monastic Code," in *Buddhism in Practice*, ed. Donald S. Lopez, Jr. (Princeton, NJ: Princeton University Press, 1995), 488–89 (*BMBM*, 107–8). For the handbooks, see next note.

19. *Vinaya-sūtra* (Sankrityayana), 119.28, Tib. *'dul ba'i mdo*, Derge, *bstan 'gyur, 'dul ba* Wu 99a.3 (see also Viśākhadeva, *Vinaya-kārikā*, Derge, *bstan 'gyur, 'dul ba* Shu 54b.6). Note that the abbreviated form used here will be used throughout for all references to Rahul Sankrityayana, *Vinaya-sūtra of Bhadanta Gunaprabha* (Singhi Jain Śāstra Śiksāpītha, Singhi Jain Series 74, Bombay: Bharatiya Vidya Bhavan, 1981).

20. Patrick Olivelle, *Manu's Code of Law: A Critical Edition and Translation of the Mānava Dharmaśāstra* (Oxford: Oxford University Press, 2005), X.35.

21. Ibid., X.51–55. For the status—or lack thereof—of *cāṇḍāla*s and the stridently negative cultural attitudes against them, see Ram Sharan Sharma, *Śūdras in Ancient India: A Social History of the Lower Order down to circa A.D. 600*, 2nd rev. ed. (Delhi: Motilal Banarsidass, 1980), 139–50; for how these horrific attitudes might be translated into modern terms, see Tom O'Neill, "Untouchables," *National Geographic* (June 2003): 2–31. See also n. 59 below for the literary use of elements of the image of the *cāṇḍāla*, particularly in some Mahāyāna sūtra literature.

22. Monier Monier-Williams, *English-Sanskrit Dictionary* (Oxford: Oxford University Press, 1851), 740.

23. Pandurang Vaman Kane, *History of Dharmaśāstra* (Poona: Bhandarkar Oriental Research Institute, 1941), vol. 2, pt. 1, 293.

24. All of this said with, presumably, no little irony.

25. *Kṣudrakavastu*, Derge Tha 6a.3–6b.2. For the "Group-of-Six" monks

met both here and below, a group of amusing, disruptive, but learned monks who manipulate the rules in such a way that they must be continually clarified and emended, see Gregory Schopen, "On Buddhist Monks and Dreadful Deities: Some Monastic Devices for Updating the Dharma," in *Gedenkschrift J. W. de Jong*, ed. H. W. Bodewitz and Minoru Hara, Studia Philologica Buddhica Monograph Series 17 (Tokyo: International Institute for Buddhist Studies, 2004), 161–84, esp. 176–78.

26. *Vinaya-sūtra* (Sankrityayana), 55.5; Tib. *'dul ba'i mdo*, Derge, *bstan 'gyur, 'dul ba* Wu 43b.5.

27. See Jean Dantinne, *Les qualités de l'ascète (dhutaguṇa): Étude sémantique et doctrinale* (Bruxelles: Editions Thanh-long, 1991), which—while rich in detail—still does not take us very far. More interesting—if justifiably tentative—is Reginald A. Ray, *Buddhist Saints in India: A Study in Buddhist Values and Orientations* (New York: Oxford University Press, 1994), 293–323.

28. Schopen, "The Mahāyāna and the Middle Period in Indian Buddhism," 22, and the textual sources cited in note 41 there.

29. Sylvain Lévi, "Note sur des manuscrits sanscrits provenant de Bamiyan (Afghanistan) et de Gilgit (Cachemire)," *Journal Asiatique* (1932): 23.

30. Raniero Gnoli, *The Gilgit Manuscript of the Saṅghabhedavastu*, Serie Orientale Roma vol. 49, 2 (Rome: Instituto Italiano per il Medio ed Estremo Oriente, 1978), pt. 2, 164–65.

31. Ibid., 204, 271. See also—without necessarily accepting their relative chronology for the various accounts—Biswadeb Mukherjee, *Die Überlieferung von Devadatta, dem Widersacher des Buddha in den kanonischen Schriften* (Münchener Studien zur Sprachwissenschaft, Beiheft J. Munich: J. Kitziner, 1966), esp. 74–86; André Bareau, "Les agissements de Devadatta selon les chapitres relatifs au schisme dans les divers *vinayapiṭaka*," *Bulletin de l'École Française d'Extrême-Orient* 78 (1991): 87–132.

32. For the process of repairing a bowl by the application of heat, see P. V. Bapat and V. V. Gokhale, *Vinaya-sūtra*, Tibetan Sanskrit Works Series no. 22 (Patna: Kashi Prasad Jayaswal Research Institute, 1982), xxxiv, 37.20–39.3.

33. For a text in this same Vinaya in which laymen appear to deny that they routinely discard "vessels and garments" with the deceased, see Schopen, "Dead Monks and Bad Debts," 132–33 (*BMBM*, 152–54).

34. What lies behind this seemingly curious rhetorical question is almost certainly a Buddhist "refutation" of a pervasive Indian cultural expectation. Goldman, for example, has said: "The motif of a curse pronounced in return for some insult or injury to a venerable personage is, to be sure, enormously common in the Sanskrit epics," and "Indian tradition has made a literary convention of representing the father/guru/sage as a distant, irascible, and terrifying figure ready to explode with the most nightmarish

curses for the most trivial provocation." See Robert P. Goldman, "Karma, Guilt, and Buried Memories: Public Fantasy and Private Reality in Traditional India," *Journal of the American Oriental Society* 105 (1985): 413–25, esp. 422, 425. Our text, in effect, has the Buddha deny that he is such a figure.

35. This is a technical way of saying "what has been specifically given to him."

36. *Vinaya-vibhaṅga*, Derge Ja 154b.2–156b.7. It should be noted that, here and throughout, I have generally rendered the Sanskrit *śmaśāna* (or its Tibetan equivalent, *dur khrod pa*) as "cemetery." It is also frequently translated as "cremation ground" or "burning ground," but it is clear from a variety of literary sources that bodies were often not cremated at such places but simply deposited or left there; see Gregory Schopen, "Hierarchy and Housing in a Buddhist Monastic Code: A Translation of the Sanskrit Text of the *Śayanāsanavastu* of the *Mūlasarvāstivāda-vinaya*, Part One," *Buddhist Literature* 2 (2000): 163–64 (vi.7).

37. *Uttaragrantha*, Derge Pa 4a.5–4b.1.

38. See the wording of the second *pārājika* in Lokesh Chandra, "Unpublished Gilgit Fragment of the Prātimokṣa-sūtra," *Wiener Zeitschrift für die Kunde Süd- und Ostasiens* 4 (1960), 2; L. Finot, "Le prātimokṣasūtra des sarvāstivādins," *Journal asiatique* (1913): 477.

39. *Uttaragrantha*, Derge Pa 164a.7–165a.2.

40. B. Jinananda, *Upasampadājñaptiḥ*, Tibetan Sanskrit Works 6 (Patna: Kashi Prasad Jayaswal Research Institute, 1961), 20.1.

41. Ibid., 20.3; Léon Wieger, *Bouddhisme chinois*, I: *Vinaya: Monachisme et discipline*; Hīnayāna, Véhicule inférieur (Paris: E. Guilmoto, 1910), 201; and I. B. Horner, *The Book of the Discipline* (London: Luzac, 1951), 4:75.

42. See *Vinaya-vibhaṅga*, Derge Cha 61b.5–7, and *Bhikṣuṇī-vinaya-vibhaṅga*, Derge Ta 159b.7–160a.1, for the definitions of both *śmāśānika* and *pāṃśukūla*.

43. *Vinaya-vibhaṅga*, Derge Cha 61b.4; *Bhikṣuṇī-vinaya-vibhaṅga*, Derge Ta 159b.6.

44. Cited in Phra Khrū Anusaranaśāsanakiarti and Charles F. Keyes, "Funerary Rites and the Buddhist Meaning of Death: An Interpretative Text from Northern Thailand," *Journal of the Siam Society* 68 (1980): 12n61. For the vagaries of the term *pāṃśukūla* in East Asia, see Bernard Faure, "Quand l'habit fait le moine: The Symbolism of the Kāṣāya in Sōtō Zen," *Cahiers d'Extrême-Asie* 8 (1995): 335–69; John Kieschnick: "The Symbolism of the Monk's Robe in China," *Asia Major*, 3rd ser. 12 (1999): 9–32; and—with little modification—*The Impact of Buddhism on Chinese Material Culture* (Princeton, NJ: Princeton University Press, 2003), 86–107. Both Faure and Kieschnick refer to the controversy in East Asia about the use

of silk for a monk's robes, but silk (*paṭṭaka, kauśeya, koseyya,* etc.) is already allowed for such a purpose in several of the lists of "permissible options" referred to above; Xinru Liu (*Silk and Religion: An Exploration of Material Life and the Thought of People, A.D. 600–1200* [Delhi: Oxford University Press, 1998], 54) must be corrected in this regard.

45. *Uttaragrantha,* Derge Pa 111b.6–112a.4.

46. *Kṣudrakavastu,* Derge Tha 222b.2–24b.1. There is what appears to be a badly bowdlerized version of this text in the Pāli Vinaya. As it stands, and without reference to the commentary, the Pāli text is narratively incoherent; see Horner, *The Book of the Discipline* (1938), pt. 1, 97, and notes 1–5 there.

47. The specificity of the commands to be uttered, as well as the details of the procedure involved in the return of the cloth, leave the impression, at least, that we may have here something like an exorcistic rite for expelling unwanted "spirits" from the monastery.

48. *Vinaya-sūtra* (Sankrityayana), 88.16–.20; Tib. *'dul ba'i mdo,* Derge, *bstan 'gyur, 'dul ba* Wu 71b.2–.4.

49. Olivelle, *Manu's Code of Law,* X.55. For Faxian, see Li Yung-hsi, *A Record of the Buddhist Countries* (Beijing: Chinese Buddhist Association, 1957), 35.

50. This is made explicit at *Vinaya-sūtra* (Sankrityayana), 88.19: *na sāṃghikaṃ śayanāsanaṃ paribhuñjīta.*

51. For some textual references, see note 16 above and also Gregory Schopen, "The Good Monk and His Money in Buddhist Monasticism of the 'Mahāyāna Period,'" *The Eastern Buddhist,* n.s. 32, no. 1 (2000): 104n34 (*BMBM,* 18n34).

52. For the first two, see note 7 above; for the last two, *Kṣudrakavastu,* Derge Tha 226a.2–27a.3 and Tha 108a.6–110a.4.

53. For the *Vinaya-sūtra,* see note 48 above; *Vinaya-kārikā,* Derge, *bstan 'gyur, 'dul ba* Shu 19a.2. and *Vinaya-saṃgraha,* Derge, *bstan 'gyur, 'dul ba* Nu 111a.5; 145a.6.

54. For the first, see the colophon in *Vinaya-sūtra* (Sankrityayana), 124; for the second, Rahul Sāṅkṛityāyana, "Second Search of Sanskrit Palm-leaf Mss. in Tibet," *Journal of the Bihar and Orissa Research Society* 23 (1937): 23 and note 1 (no. 195); these folios remain unpublished.

55. Cecil Bendall, *Çikshāsamuccaya: A Compendium of Buddhistic Teaching,* Bibliotheca Buddhica I (St. Petersburg: Commissionaires de l'Académie Impériale de Sciences, 1897–1902), 370 s.v. *Ratnamegha.*

56. Paul Demiéville, Hubert Durt, and Anna Seidel, *Répertoire du canon bouddhique sino-japonais, Édition de Taishō* (Paris and Tokyo: Adrien-Maisonneuve and Maison Franco-Japonaise, 1978), nos. 489, 658–60. On the still vexing question of the "author" of the *Sūtrasamuccaya,* see, at least, Bhikkhu Pāsādika: "The Concept of Avipraṇāsa in Nāgārjuna," in *Recent*

Researches in Buddhist Studies: Essays in Honour of Professor Y. Karunadasa, ed. Bhikkhu Kuala Lumpur Dhammajoti et al. (Hong Kong: Y. Karunadasa Felicitation Committee, 1997), 516–23, esp. the references in note 5; and "Tib J 380, A Dunhuang Manuscript Fragment of the Sūtrasamuccaya," in *Bauddhavidyāsudhākaraḥ: Studies in Honour of Heinz Bechert on the Occasion of His 65th Birthday* (Indica et Tibetica 30), ed. Petra Kieffer-Pülz and Jens-Uwe Hartmann (Swisttal-Odendorf: Indica et Tibetica Verlag, 1997), 483–94. If it can be convincingly determined that the *Sūtrasamuccaya* is the work of Nāgārjuna, then much of the early "history" of Mahāyāna sūtra literature will have to be rethought.

57. *'Phags pa dkon mchog sprin zhes bya ba theg pa chen po'i mdo*, Derge *mdo* Wa 89b.1. Śāntideva quotes a small part of this: *yady apy āryaratnameghe 'bhihitaṃ śmāśānikena nirāmiṣeṇa bhavitavyam iti*; Bendall, *Çikshāsamuccaya*, 135.1. The *Ratnamegha* devotes nearly five and a half folios to describing the bodhisattva's practice of the *dhūtaguṇa*s.

58. *'Phags pa dkon mchog sprin*, Derge *mdo* Wa 89b.3.

59. The exhortation to assume the mentality of a *cāṇḍāla* is in fact found widely in Mahāyāna sūtra literature: at least twice more in the *Ratnamegha* (quoted in Bendall, *Çikshāsamuccaya*, 150.12, 150.18); in the *Ratnarāśi* (also quoted in Bendall at 129.16); in the *Maitreyasiṃhanāda* (Derge, *dkon brtsegs* Ca 89a.1); and in the *Suvikrāntavikrāmi* (Ryusho Hikata, *Suvikrāntavikrāmiparipṛcchā Prajñāpāramitā-sūtra* [Fukuoka: Committee of Commemoration Program for Dr. Hikata's Retirement from Professorship, 1958], 5:20). But see also Edmund Hardy, The *Aṅguttara-nikāya* (London: Pāli Text Society, 1899), 4:376.11. This "idolization" of the *cāṇḍāla*, however, must be set alongside a harsher textual reality found elsewhere. Guṇaprabha, for example, still does not allow *cāṇḍāla*s to be admitted into the religious life: *na rathakāra-caṇḍāla-pukkasa-tadvidhān pravrājayet*, *Vinaya-sūtra* (Sankrityayana), 4.27.

60. See, most conveniently, Murray B. Emeneau, *Jambhaladatta's Version of the Vetālapañcaviṅśati* (New Haven, CT: American Oriental Society, 1934); J. A. B. van Buitenen, *Tales of Ancient India* (Chicago: University of Chicago Press, 1959), 11–64. For the spread of the same or similar "tales" outside India, see David S. Ruegg, *Ordre spirituel et ordre temporel dans la pensée bouddhique de l'Inde et du Tibet* (Paris: Collège de France, 1995), 115–16, and the sources cited in the notes; Raffaella Riva, "The Tales of the Bewitched Corpse: A Literary Journey from India to China," in *India, Tibet, China: Genesis and Aspects of Traditional Narrative*, Orientalia Venetiana 7, ed. Alfredo Cadonna (Florence: Leo S. Olschki Editore, 1999), 229–56. For yet another use of corpses but the same cultural unease, see Kenneth G. Zysk, "Some Observations on the Dissection of Cadavers in Ancient India," *Ancient Science of Life* 2, no. 3 (1983): 187–89.

61. The same cultural values, of course, play a significant, although ne-

glected, role in the far better known use of corpses as objects of meditation. See the classical description of this practice in Henry Clarke Warren and Dharmananda Kosambi, *Visuddhimagga of Buddhaghosācariya*, Harvard Oriental Series 41 (Cambridge, MA: Harvard University Press, 1950), 144–61, and now Liz Wilson, *Charming Cadavers: Horrific Figurations of the Feminine in Indian Buddhist Hagiographic Literature* (Chicago: University of Chicago Press, 1996), 41–56.

3

The Moment of Death in Daoxuan's Vinaya Commentary

Koichi Shinohara

The "moment of death" (Ch. *linzhong*; J. *rinjū*) is a familiar topic in Pure Land Buddhist literature. According to this tradition, correct practice in one's final moments can enable one to escape the cycle of samsaric rebirth and be born in the pure realm of a buddha or bodhisattva. Deathbed practices associated with Pure Land aspirations have become familiar to scholarship chiefly through the famous treatise *Ōjō yōshū* (Collection on the essentials of birth in the Pure Land) by the Japanese monk Genshin (942–1017). Genshin, however, was extensively indebted to Chinese sources, which have not yet been thoroughly investigated. In consequence, very little attention has been paid to how understandings of the moment of death as determinative in achieving birth in a pure land gained widespread currency. A seminal work for understanding this development in medieval Chinese Buddhism is a brief chapter titled "Attending to the Sick and Sending off the Dead" (Ch. *zhanbing songzhong*) in the Vinaya commentary *Sifenlü shanfan bujue xingshi chao* (Commentary on monastic practices based on the *Dharmaguptaka vinaya*, unnecessary details deleted and missing information added) by the Chinese Vinaya authority Daoxuan (596–667).[1] Known for his Vinaya studies and his role in the formation of Chinese Buddhist monasticism, Daoxuan was also instrumental in the development of deathbed practices and of thought concerning the "moment of death." His commentary was to exert considerable influence on later East Asian Buddhist figures who addressed this topic, Genshin among them. At the same time, it drew, explicitly or otherwise, on a great range of earlier Vinaya and sūtra literature, not necessarily connected with Pure Land thought, that addressed the issue of deathbed contemplations, sometimes with different or even competing emphases. These competing understandings also appear to have been current in Daoxuan's day.

This chapter will provide a close reading of that portion of Daoxuan's chapter devoted to "Attending to the Sick," focusing on his treatment of the moment of death and what immediately precedes it. It will also investigate Daoxuan's sources and his reception of their different understandings of proper mental focus at the time of death as a window onto broader shifts that were occurring in beliefs and practices surrounding the moment of death in medieval Chinese Buddhism. Specifically, I will argue that in Daoxuan's presentation, we can see how an earlier emphasis on the soteriological value of contemplating impermanence at the time of death was becoming marginalized by an overriding concern with death as a uniquely potent juncture for achieving birth in a superior realm. At the end of the chapter, I will touch briefly on a further work about deathbed practice by another authority on Vinaya literature, the *Linzhong fangjue*, or "Instructions for the Moment of Death," by Yijing (635–713), to show how Daoxuan's emphasis on the determinative nature of the last moment in achieving a pure land birth was developed by a slightly later Chinese Buddhist figure.

"Attending to the Sick" in Daoxuan's Vinaya Commentary

As indicated by its title, "Attending to the Sick and Sending off the Dead," Daoxuan's chapter consists of two distinct parts: the first deals with the treatment of sick monks, and the second, with the funeral and disposition of the corpse. It is the first part that will form the focus of my discussion here. As the phrase "attending to the sick" suggests, the discussion of the moment of death here is closely tied to the issue of caring for sick monks, an important theme in Vinaya literature generally.[2]

This first part of Daoxuan's chapter consists of four sections. The chapter's opening paragraph enumerates them as follows: introductory comments on the concept of attending to the sick; the choice of an attendant and the ways of looking after the sick; the place where the sick monk is to be placed; and the teaching preached to the sick monk to help him control his thoughts at the moment of death. The first two sections focus on sick monks in general; these sections first describe how the Buddha came to deliver instructions on the treatment of the sick and then explain how an attendant monk is to be selected and how he is to carry out his task. Here Daoxuan cites passages from the Vinayas of different schools that had been translated in China. The focus then shifts in the succeeding two sections from sick monks in general to those gravely ill monks who are about to die. The third section stipulates that the dying must be taken to a special location. Here Daoxuan cites from a work "transmitted in China" (*zhongguo benzhuan*) a passage describing a deathbed ritual, said to have been performed at the Hall of Impermanence at the Jetavana Monastery in Śrāvastī in India to secure birth in a buddha land. The fourth section discusses the sermon to be given to the dying monk, highlighting the importance of his reflections at the moment of death. In addition to citations from Vinayas and related sources, passages from well-known Mahāyāna sūtras appear here. The "Attending to the Sick" section in Daoxuan's commentary is thus constructed by combining passages on the treatment of the sick quoted largely from the Vinayas, with instructions for the moment of death quoted from a wider range of sources. Now let us consider in some detail Daoxuan's treatment of key themes in this section.

The Origin of the Practice of Attending to Sick Monks

In the introductory section of his chapter, Daoxuan first briefly refers to a passage from the *Dharmaguptaka vinaya* describing how the Buddha came to instruct the monks on "attending to the sick." The passage in question reads:

> One time, when the Buddha was at Śrāvastī, he did not go out to beg for food. As is the practice of the buddhas when they do not go out to beg for food, he visited the cells where the monks lodged. In one place he came upon a sick monk. Without an attendant, the sick monk was lying in the midst of his feces and urine. When the Buddha asked why, the monk replied, "While I myself was not sick, I failed to attend to other monks who were sick. Therefore, now that I am sick, no one is attending to me to look after my needs." The Buddha said, "You did not attend to the sick to look after their needs. Therefore, you do not benefit [from this practice] and you gain nothing [from it]. If you monks do not look after each other, who will look after the sick ones?"
>
> Then, the Buddha helped the sick monk to rise and wiped the uncleanliness from his body. After wiping him, the Buddha washed him. After washing him, the Buddha washed the sick monk's robe and spread it to dry. Throwing away the soiled grass

> bedding, the Buddha swept the dwelling space clean and plastered it with mud, making it very beautiful. He then put down fresh grass and spread a robe over it. Having laid the sick monk upon it, he covered him with another robe.
>
> After the meal, the Buddha gathered the monks to instruct them on account of this matter, and having explained what he had done while they were begging for food, he instructed them, saying, "From now on you should look after sick monks and attend to their illness. If anyone wants to look after me, he should look after the sick."[3]

The story in the *Dharmaguptaka vinaya* goes on to describe how the attendant monk is to be chosen and how he is to look after the sick. In Daoxuan's commentary, this topic comprises the second section of "Attending to the Sick."[4] There Daoxuan begins with a brief quotation from the *Dharmaguptaka vinaya* and then moves on to cite passages from a variety of other sources.

The Jetavana Hall of Impermanence

The third section of Daoxuan's discussion of "attending to the sick" shifts focus to monks who are dying and thus begins the portion of Daoxuan's commentary especially relevant to our investigation of his understanding of the moment of death. At the beginning of this section, he quotes extensively from a Chinese source that he refers to as "a Chinese tradition" (*Zhongguo benzhuan*); the source purports to describe how deathbed practice was conducted at Jetavana, the famous monastery in Śrāvastī presented to the Buddha by the wealthy donor Anāthapiṇḍada. This passage has become extremely well known, owing in part to the fact that Genshin quotes it in the *Ōjō yōshū* at the beginning of his discussion of deathbed practices.[5] It reads as follows:

> In the northwest corner of the Jetavana [Monastery], at the place where the sun sets, is the Hall of Impermanence. The sick are placed there. Sentient beings are affected by greed, and when [dying monks] see their robes, bowl, and other implements in their own cell, they often give rise to the feeling of attachment. [Then] the feeling of repugnance [directed toward life in the world] disappears. For this reason, the rule was established to place the sick in a separate hall. The hall is designated "Impermanence." Many

go there, but few return. Facing the matter that confronts them [death and rebirth], the dying monks single-mindedly meditate on the dharma.

Inside the hall is placed a standing [buddha] image, covered with gold leaf. It faces the direction of the west. The right hand of the image is raised, and to the left hand is fastened a five-colored pennant, whose end trails on the ground. The sick monk is to be placed behind the image. Holding the tail of the pennant with his left hand, he is to think of following the Buddha to the buddha land. The attendant monk (*zhanbingzhe*) burns incense and scatters flowers to adorn [the place]. If the sick monk soils himself, urinates, throws up, or spits, it is to be cleaned up, and he is not held responsible for any transgression.[6]

Two points immediately call for comment here. The first is the treatment of bodily impurity, noted in the final sentence of the quoted passage. As we have seen above, in the earlier portions of Daoxuan's chapter, which are based primarily on the *Dharmaguptaka* and other Vinayas, "attending to the sick" is described primarily as a matter of cleaning a sick monk's body, robe, bedding, and monastic cell, although other forms of assistance are also specified. Keeping the sick clean of feces, urine, and other impurities is given repeated emphasis in the Vinaya literature.[7] The passage from the "Chinese tradition" cited by Daoxuan describing practice at the Jetavana Monastery also clearly reflects this concern. Following this strikingly explicit reference to the sick monk's physical defilements, Daoxuan again quotes from the "tradition," probably the same "Chinese tradition," as follows:

The Buddha patiently guides sentient beings in this world with the intention of removing their suffering (*fannao*). [Even] removing excrement is not repugnant to him. To gods, human beings are smelly and filthy in the way that latrines are to human beings. The smell is indescribable, and yet [the gods] do not think of [human beings] as repugnant but constantly protect them. How much less, in the case of the Buddha's virtue, could he [arbitrarily] love some and hate others? He saves all who follow him. When they become sick, he teaches them according to their capacity. [Thus] when their lives come to an end, they are placed for the duration in the Buddha's presence and are not removed elsewhere.[8]

Here, the specific impurities produced by the incontinent sick are reframed as the unavoidable impurities and repugnant smell of all human beings as their universal condition, and the Buddha's willingness to clean the sick, as described in the *Dharmaguptaka vinaya* passage on the origin of his teachings concerning treatment of sick monks, is doctrinally reinterpreted as expressing the all-inclusiveness of his compassionate teaching of salvation. Nevertheless, the incorporation in Daoxuan's commentary of the specific reference to cleaning up the feces, urine, and other bodily discharges of dying monks in the Hall of Impermanence suggests that the larger Vinaya discussion of "attending to the sick" (*zhanbing*) was here being subsumed within the specific context of ritual practice for the moment of death, both in the "tradition" upon which Daoxuan based himself and in his own thinking.

Another key issue in the discussion of the Hall of Impermanence—one not immediately obvious from the "Chinese tradition" that Daoxuan cites—is its broader associations with reflections on impermanence in the deathbed context. To begin with, the reference to impermanence in the name of the hall may be related to the famous verse concerning impermanence that appears consistently in varying accounts of the Buddha's entry into final nirvāṇa. According to the Chinese version of the *Sūtra of the Great Nirvāṇa* (Skt. *Mahāparinirvāṇa sūtra*; Ch. *Dabanniepan jing*), this verse is uttered by the Buddha immediately before his death. It states:

> All conditioned things are impermanent.
> It is their nature to arise and perish.
> When arising and perishing have ceased,
> There is peace, there is happiness.

The Buddha then comments on the verse he has spoken, saying that even his diamond body is subject to decay.[9] But the *Mahāparinirvāṇa sūtra* passage is only one instance within a much larger scriptural tradition emphasizing impermanence in the deathbed context. Notably, the practice of reminding sick monks of the impermanence of the body and of worldly matters appears repeatedly in the Chinese *āgama*s, particularly the *Za ahan jing* (Saṃyuktāgama) and in their parallels in the Pāli *nikāyas*.[10] In these sūtras, monks are often said to have died shortly after receiving this instruction, though in some cases they are also said to have recovered.[11] Although Daoxuan does not specifically refer to these sūtra passages, his comments on deathbed practice would surely have evoked associations with them for readers familiar with the Buddhist canon. Let me now turn to this broader scriptural tradition.

Sickness Scriptures in Chinese *Āgamas*

As we have seen, Daoxuan begins his discussion of "attending to the sick" with a quotation from the *Dharmaguptaka vinaya*, perhaps because his commentary names this Vinaya as its primary basis. However, his actual approach is to draw relevant passages from a range of scriptural sources, including not only the Vinayas of other schools but also sūtras, Abhidharmas, and Mahāyāna treatises.[12] The initial quotation from the *Dharmaguptaka vinaya* in this chapter, recounting the story of how the Buddha one day chose not to go out on his begging round but instead visited a sick monk, is thus followed by a number of passages from other scriptural sources. But here in the third section, dealing with the treatment of terminally sick monks in the Hall of Impermanence, Daoxuan curiously cites almost exclusively from the Vinayas of different schools and not from sūtras.[13] It is particularly noteworthy that he fails to mention the sūtras on illness scattered in many parts of the Chinese *āgama*s, because a common formulaic treatment of the theme of visiting a sick monk appears in these sūtras, with many parallels in the Pāli *nikāya*s. The frame story in these sūtras often begins by describing how the Buddha took the trouble to visit a sick monk, though in some sūtras he is said to have sent someone else as his representative. Thus, although Daoxuan cites only from the Vinayas and does not refer to these sūtras, his discussion of the topic of "attending to the sick" nonetheless appears to have been informed by a long-standing and familiar sūtra tradition. Let me illustrate this with a few examples.

Za ahan jing, entry 1028

This story begins with the standard formula, "Thus have I heard."

> At one time, the Buddha is said to have been staying at Jetavana in Śrāvastī. Many monks gathered at the Hall of Sickness (Gilāna-sālā), and there were many sick monks. Late in the afternoon, the Buddha rose from meditation and went over to the Hall of Sick-

ness. Seated before the assembly, the Buddha told the following to the monks. They should wait for their time [of death] with "right meditation" (*zhengnian*) and "right wisdom" (*zhengzhi*).[14]

An explanation of these two terms, enumerating a wide range of objects of meditation and noting that correct insight, or mindfulness, must be maintained at all times in all activities, is then followed by a formulaic description of how this practice works:

> When a pleasant sensation arises to one who practices right meditation and right wisdom, [he knows that] it arises by causes and conditions. It is conditioned by the body. Then he entertains the following thought: "This body of mine is impermanent and compounded. It has arisen because of mental conditions. The pleasant sensation, therefore, is also impermanent and compounded. It [too] is mentally conditioned." The contemplation of the body and the pleasant sensation [is followed by] the contemplation (*guancha*) of impermanence, the contemplation of arising and destruction, the contemplation of transcending desires, the contemplation of cessation [of desires], and the contemplation of indifference [to pleasure or pain]. After the monk has contemplated all these, the greed that craves for a pleasant sensation in the body loses its controlling power.[15]

The same account is repeated for the cases of a painful sensation and a sensation that is neither pleasant nor painful. The Buddha then notes that such contemplation leads to revulsion against form (Skt. *rūpa*) and then to revulsion against the remaining four skandhas: perception (*vedanā*), representation (*saṃjñā*), impulse (*saṃskāra*), and consciousness (*vijñāna*). This then leads to the eradication of desires and to liberation. Liberated, the practitioner will know, "My life is finished. The pure practice is established. All that has to be done is done."[16] He will know that there will be no further rebirth. The Buddha is then said to have uttered a verse summarizing the teaching he had presented.

In this entry, the setting of the Buddha's preaching to sick monks in the Hall of Sickness is connected with the content of his sermon, which emphasizes the truth of impermanence. All things that arise in dependence upon conditions, particularly one's body, are impermanent, and knowing this truth frees one from attachment driven by desire. For one who contemplates in this way, the end of life will constitute liberation and will not lead to further rebirths. The name "Hall of Impermanence" at Jetavana, which appears in the "Chinese tradition" cited by Daoxuan, would seem to have been rooted in this tradition of preaching the doctrine of impermanence to dying monks and not just in the passage on impermanence in the *Mahāparinirvāṇa sūtra* relating to the death of the Buddha.

***Za ahan jing*, entry 1025**

In another striking example from the Chinese *āgamas*, a parallel may be seen with Daoxuan's discussion in his Vinaya commentary in a common emphasis on the importance of the last moment in achieving a good rebirth:

> At one time the Buddha was staying at the Jetavana garden in the country of Śrāvastī. At that time there was a monk, young in age and new to the teaching; not many years had passed since he had left the householder's life, and he had few acquaintances. He was travelling alone with no one attending to his needs. While he was staying in a monastic cell in a remote village, he became ill, and his condition grew critical. A group of monks came to the Buddha and, noting that the monk was near death, asked him to go visit the sick monk. In the afternoon of the same day, the Buddha rose from meditation and went to the monk. Seeing the World Honored One from a distance, the sick monk tried to sit up. The Buddha told the monk, "Rest and do not get up. How is it, monk? Is the suffering of illness bearable or not?"[17]

At this point, a conversation between a visiting monk and the sick monk, Khema, described in another entry, is mentioned,[18] with a note that a similar exchange takes place between them, the sick monk answering three times that his suffering is only intensifying.

> Then the Buddha asked the monk, telling him to answer as he saw fit, "Are you free of regrets (Ch. *bianhui*)?" The sick monk replied, "Indeed, I have regrets, World Honored One." The Buddha said to the monk, "You have not violated the precepts, or have you?" The monk said, "World Honored One, indeed, I have not violated the precepts." The Buddha said, "If you have not violated the precepts,

why do you have regrets?" The sick monk told the Buddha, "World Honored One, I am young, and it has not been long since I renounced the householder's life. I have not achieved an understanding of the dharma that is superior to others. When I entertain the following thought, I experience regrets: 'After my life ends, in which realm will I be reborn?'"

The Buddha told the monk, "I will now ask questions. You should answer me as you see fit. What do you think, monk? It is because there is [the sense organ of] the eye that there is eye consciousness, is it not?" The monk said, "It is so, World Honored One." The Buddha asked again, "Monk, what does this mean? [According to the teaching of the twelve-linked chain of causes and conditions,] it is because there is eye consciousness (Skt. *cakṣurvijñāna*) that there is eye contact (*sparśa*). Eye contact gives rise to internal perception (*vedanā*) such as pain or pleasure, or no pain or no pleasure. Is it not so?" The monk said, "It is so, World Honored One." [The Buddha] spoke in the same way about the ear, the nose, the tongue, the body, and the mind. [The Buddha continued,] "What do you think, monk? If there is no eye, there will be no eye consciousness, is it not so?" The monk said to the Buddha, "It is so, World Honored One." [The Buddha] asked again, "Monk, if there is no eye consciousness, there is no eye contact, is it not so? If there is no eye contact, then there will be no inner perceptions caused by eye contact such as pain or pleasure, or no pain or no pleasure, is it not so?" The monk said to the Buddha, "It is so, World Honored One." [The Buddha] spoke in the same way about the ear, the nose, the tongue, the body, and the mind. "For this reason, monk, you should think well about the following teaching. If you achieve a good end to this life, the life that follows will also be good." At that time, the World Honored One preached various dharmas to the sick monk. Having instructed him, causing illumination and joy to arise, the Buddha rose and left.

Shortly after the Buddha left, the sick monk died. At the moment of death, his sense organs were filled with joy, his appearance was pure, and the color of his skin was freshly white. Then, a group of monks came to the Buddha. Having greeted him, showing utmost respect, they reported to the Buddha that the young monk had now died and described the condition of his sense organs, his appearance, and the color of his skin at the moment of death, and asked about the place of his rebirth. The Buddha told

> the monks, "The monk whose life just ended was a truly authentic being (Ch. *zhenshiwu*). Having heard my sermon, he understood it clearly, and, remaining in the dharma, he had no fear and achieved nirvāṇa. You should worship his remains (relics)."[19]

In the first part of the Buddha's sermon, the topic appears, as in entry 1028 discussed above, to be the rise of pleasant or painful, or neither pleasant nor painful, sensations, though their conditioned character is described somewhat differently here, in terms of the functioning of the sense organs. In the Pāli sutta that parallels *Za ahan jing* entry no. 1025, the Buddha's teaching centers around the theme of impermanence, presented in connection with the sense organs of the eye, the ear, the nose, the tongue, the body, and the mind. Noting that it is not proper to regard what is impermanent as one's self or belonging to the self, the sutta concludes: "Whatsoever is of a nature to arise, all that is of a nature to cease."[20]

However, the main purpose of the sermon in *Za ahan jing* entry 1025, attributed to the Sarvāstivāda school, is to teach not the doctrine of impermanence of the body but rather a distinctly different doctrine—namely, that a good death leads to a good rebirth. The dying monk is anxious about his future rebirth and, after receiving the Buddha's instruction, is said to have achieved a good death: "His sense organs were filled with joy, his appearance was pure, and the color of his skin was freshly white." The entry concludes with the Buddha praising the dead monk, saying that he understood the Buddha's teaching well and achieved nirvāṇa and instructing other monks to worship his relics. The Buddha is also said to have prophesied ultimate attainment of buddhahood (*diyiji*) for the dead monk. In this entry, then, the discussion that began with comments on the conditions that give rise to pleasant, painful, or neither pleasant nor painful sensations is in the end assimilated to the quest for a good rebirth. The observations about causally conditioned relationships do not lead here to the realization of the impermanence of one's body or the absence of a substantial self. Rather, the conclusion drawn is that this same causal relationship will extend beyond death to determine the rebirth that immediately follows. The dying monk, anxious about his future destination, receives the Buddha's assurance that by facing the moment of death in the right way, he can be guaranteed a happy rebirth. And yet there is still some ambiguity in this story in that it concludes by noting that the dead monk achieved not a better rebirth but nirvāṇa, and that the Buddha further prophesied his attainment of buddhahood.

The Buddha's sermon in *Za ahan jing* entry 1025 thus suggests that two separate themes competed in discussions of the moment of death in Buddhist scriptural sources. In some cases the impermanence of the body, often connected with the teaching of "no self," is stressed; in others the emphasis is on securing a superior rebirth. The two themes may not necessarily have been understood as mutually contradictory. In the passage on the Jetavana Hall of Impermanence in Daoxuan's Vinaya commentary, references to impermanence—for example, in the name of the hall to which the sick and dying are taken—are combined with a description of a ritual that appears to be exclusively oriented toward the goal of achieving birth in a pure land. The discussion in the following section, on sermons to be given to dying monks, also reflects the competition of these two themes.

The Moment of Death in Daoxuan's Chapter

The fourth and final long section in the first part of Daoxuan's chapter, his treatment of "attending to the sick," is designated in the chapter's table of contents as "preaching the dharma and controlling thought" (*shuofa liannian*) and later, at the beginning of the section itself, as "preaching the dharma and commending good works" (*shuofa quanshan*).[21] The subject of this section is the practice of teaching the dharma to someone approaching death. "Commending good works" in this context appears to mean reminding that person of the good works he has performed during his lifetime. "Controlling thought" at the moment of death becomes an especially important concern in light of Daoxuan's emphasis on the power of one's mind at the last moment to bring about one's birth in a pure realm.

The first large segment in this section is formulated as an extended commentary on a passage from the *Sarvāstivāda vinaya*. In the *Sarvāstivāda vinaya*, this passage occurs in the context of another version of the story from the *Dharmaguptaka vinaya* that Daoxuan presented earlier in explaining the origin of the practice of "attending to the sick." In the *Sarvāstivāda vinaya* version, detailed instructions about how to look after sick monks are followed by the statement: "The monk attending to a sick monk should go frequently to his bedside and preach the profound dharma to him, distinguishing correct teachings from wrong ones and letting him give rise to wisdom." Then follows a paragraph of instructions for encouraging the sick monk.[22] Daoxuan summarizes these as follows: "The [dying] monk may have studied the solitary practice of a forest dwelling monk, or recited scriptures, or upheld the Vinaya, or be specialized in the Abhidharma of dharma masters, or in assisting in the affairs of the monastery. The attendant monk should praise the practice according to the specialization [of the dying monk]."[23]

This summary is followed by Daoxuan's own commentary, which takes up each of the categories of the possible accomplishments of the dying monk and elaborates on them in sequence. For example, in the case of a monk who has cultivated "forest dwelling" (Skt. *araṇyaka*), the attending monk should say to him, "Your illness has now become as serious as this. You should entertain good thoughts and not fear [rebirth in] the evil paths. Why is this so? Before you became ill, you carried out the great *dhūta* practice. Among the Buddha's disciples, it was only Kāśyapa whom the Buddha continually praised before the assembly [for his devotion to this ascetic practice]. The Buddha offered his seat and passed his own robe on to this disciple.[24] This is the model that all holy ones follow in carrying out the superior practices. In your practice you have inherited this holy precedent. You will certainly be reborn in a superior realm. You should not fear death's approach. The only fear is that you might lose control of your thoughts [at the last moment] and become deluded by worldly conditions, which are phantom-like existences. Do not think about them."[25] Daoxuan then explains how to speak to dying monks who engaged in other forms of practice. The instruction for encouraging those who recited scriptures explicitly includes assurance of rebirth in superior realms, while the instruction for encouraging those who upheld the Vinaya speaks of the danger of being misled at the time of death by illusory conditions.[26]

Here, in describing how this practice of "praising" should be conducted for each category of monks, Daoxuan interprets the corresponding Vinaya passage as explicitly addressing anxiety about future rebirth at the moment of death. In the Vinaya passage itself, the attendant monk is told to praise "in front of [the sick monk]"

(Ch. *xianqian*) the various practices in which he specialized; the attendant monk is then told to ask, in the case of great monks known to many, whether they have achieved the first, second, third, or fourth *bhūmi*, or obtained one of the "four fruits" from the status of a stream enterer to arhatship. The issue of the realm of rebirth is hardly mentioned. In contrast, in Daoxuan's own commentary, the attending monk is to praise the meritorious activities in which the dying monk specialized, assuring him that because of these works he will be reborn in a superior realm. From this perspective, the warning against the loss of mental control suggests that one's thought at the moment of death will determine one's place of rebirth, while the instruction to remind dying monks of the meritorious deeds they performed over their lifetime would imply that thinking of these deeds would make the merit they generated effective at the crucial moment of death, thus assuring a superior rebirth. In this way, the Vinaya instruction about preaching to dying monks appears to have been more sharply focused by Daoxuan in terms of a theory that connects one's thought at the moment of death with achieving a particular postmortem destination.

Daoxuan's extended comments on the *Sarvāstivāda vinaya* passage are followed by other scriptural quotations that speak of the importance of recalling at the time of death the meritorious deeds that one performed in life. Without providing a source, Daoxuan cites a short phrase, "recall the meritorious deeds already cultivated and think of pure life," from the *Vimalakīrti-nirdeśa sūtra*. The phrase occurs in a passage where Mañjuśrī, acting under the Buddha's instruction, visits Vimalakīrti, who has let it be known that he is sick, and asks him how to console a sick bodhisattva. Vimalakīrti then tells Mañjuśrī that, among other things, one should remind the sick bodhisattva of the meritorious deeds he has performed earlier in life.[27]

Daoxuan also returns in this section to the "[Chinese] tradition," from which he earlier cited the passage concerning deathbed practice at the Jetavana Hall of Impermanence. In China, the "tradition" says, when someone is about to die (*linzhong*), whether a monastic or a layperson, his or her close associates should stand by the bedside, watching over and guarding that individual. While the dying person's organs and consciousness are still sound, they should recite the good deeds he or she has cultivated throughout life. The intention is to let the dying person be delighted at heart and not fear what lies ahead. Then that individual's thoughts will be correct and undisturbed at the moment of death, and, for that reason, he or she will be reborn in a good realm.

Daoxuan then cites from the *Dazhidulun* (Treatise on perfection of great wisdom) a passage addressing a fundamental difficulty raised by this emphasis on one's thought at the moment of death.[28] The larger context of this passage is a discussion of the Buddha's "ten powers," specifically the "second power," which enables him to know karmic retribution. The *Dazhidulun* here bases itself on the *Fenbie[da]ye jing*, or *Karmavibhaṅga sūtra* (Sūtra on the [greater] analysis of deeds).[29] In explaining the seemingly paradoxical cases of those who have committed evil deeds but receive good rebirths and of those who have done good deeds but receive evil rebirths, this sūtra mentions as one of the possible causes one's thoughts at the moment of death: those who entertain good thoughts at the end are reborn in good realms, while those who entertain evil thoughts are reborn in evil realms. Using a question-and-answer format, the *Dazhidulun* here raises an issue not addressed in the sūtra passage—namely, how can a brief thought at the moment of death possibly supersede the influence of actions carried out over the course of one's lifetime? In answer, it asserts that the power of one's mental state at the moment of death outweighs the effect of even a hundred years' practice. This mental state is compared to fire or poison, which, even in small amounts, can produce major effects; therefore it is called the "Great Mind." It is like the mind of a brave soldier going into battle or that of an arhat who has abandoned all attachments to the body.[30] In his Vinaya commentary, Daoxuan summarizes this reply rather indirectly: Because it is the moment that penetrates both life and death, and because it is the point when it is critically important that one give up attachment to sense objects, one's thought at that moment can induce a particular outcome, which may be filled with either pleasure or suffering.[31] Daoxuan then adds, clearly alluding to his earlier comments, that this need to protect one's mental focus at the end is why the sick must be taken to a separate place and kept there securely.

As we have seen, Daoxuan's first quotation from the "Chinese tradition," concerning the Hall of Impermanence, refers to the danger of a monk's attachment to his robe and bowl were he to remain in his own cell. Daoxuan may be echoing this reference when he next quotes a passage from the *Mulian wen jielü zhong wubai jing-*

zhong shi (Mulian's five hundred questions on precepts), which tells the story of a monk attached to his copper begging bowl. He was reborn as a hungry ghost, and when the ghost licked the dead monk's bowl clean, the bowl developed an exceedingly foul smell. Another monk, attached to his robe, wondered at his last moment who would venture to wear his robe once he had died. After his death, he came back as a snake.[32] Referring again, this time explicitly, to the passage concerning the Jetavana Hall of Impermanence, Daoxuan concludes that it is essential for dying monks to be removed to a separate hall where they will not see their own possessions and arouse thoughts of attachment.

At this point Daoxuan introduces an instruction of his own. The sick person's illness may be grave or light, his mind sharp or dull, his karmic makeup crude or subtle, and his emotions commendable or reprehensible. Whatever the situation of dying persons, the attendant (*zhanbing*) should take into account their abilities and conditions and talk to them according to their aspirations, speaking to some about Amitābha Buddha of the west, to others of Maitreya Buddha in the Tuṣita Heaven, and to others of the original teacher Śākyamuni Buddha of Vulture Peak. To still others, the attendant will explain that while there is ultimately no essential "self" or person in our body, we form the delusion of a self; or that although from outside there appears to be a self, in fact there is no self, and so on; or that there is only consciousness and no external objects, but the deluded mind sees external objects. Each person is to be guided in light of his capacity. Here again we see an implicit tension between emphasis on the contemplation of impermanence at the moment of death and aspiration for birth in a superior realm. In this passage, particularly in the contrast that Daoxuan draws between those who seek help from different buddhas and those who seek the teaching of emptiness of the self and of external objects, Daoxuan may be addressing different groups of practitioners. Contemporary "eminent monks," whose biographies Daoxuan collected, often sought birth in the realms of different buddhas. Others, however, were openly critical of such aspirations, as we shall see below.

As another important example of guidance taking into account the abilities and conditions of dying monks, Daoxuan then discusses the issue of attachment to material possessions. Here he quotes a passage from the *Dharmaguptaka vinaya* criticizing the practice of a sick monk wearing an inferior robe or sending his robe and bowl to another place for fear that the attendant monk might appropriate them after his death.[33] Daoxuan discusses this passage with a reference to the monk Mogharāja, known for his willingness to wear inferior robes. Resuming the format of his earlier comments on the *Sarvāstivāda vinaya* passage about encouraging the sick, Daoxuan again spells out what the attendant should tell (*gaoyun*) the dying monk—in this case, one who happens to be particularly greedy and lacks the will to seek higher goals. He should be told that all such material possessions are illusory; a person is born without owning any goods and does not take anything with him beyond death.[34] One should not trouble oneself with money or possessions, which are illusory and unreal, but rather concentrate on superior, spiritual practices; one should not privately entrust (*fuzhu*) one's property to others but rather have it distributed according to the prescriptions of the Vinaya; by the merit acquired in this way, one can be reborn in a superior realm. Here again, emphasis on impermanence and non-attachment—in this case, to possessions—is subsumed within the aspiration for superior rebirth.

At the moment of death, Daoxuan's instruction continues, deluded thoughts and deeds appear one after another; many people thus fail to maintain their will to seek spiritual goals. This is a singularly important moment that will determine the circumstances of one's rebirth, whether for good or evil. One should take the scripture in one's hand, pointing to the Buddha's name, and gaze at the buddha image. Only good words—i.e., words concerning spiritual matters—should be spoken; worldly affairs should not be discussed. Three scriptural passages are then cited that support different aspects of this instruction. For example, in the first passage, from the *Huayan jing*, or *Flower Garland Sūtra*, a ray of light is said to appear to one who realizes the approaching end of life and guide him so that he will be born in the presence of a buddha. The light will also make the image of a buddha appear and cause the dying person to see it.[35] This section concludes with the statement that when a monk dies, the "bell of impermanence" (*wuchang qing*) is to be struck.[36] The moment of death, when this bell is sounded, marks the conclusion of Daoxuan's discussion of "attending to the sick" and the segue to the next section, on the funeral and disposal of the body.

Daoxuan's discussion of the sermon to be preached to dying monks appears to have been written as an extended commentary, based on a variety of scriptural sources, on the importance of the moment of death. In his reading, it is the thought entertained at that final moment that determines one's rebirth. This is no doubt the reason why he considered helping sick monks to die in a proper frame of mind as a vital component of "attending to the sick." In the section of his commentary that speaks of instructing the dying in light of their abilities and conditions, the positing of a self in the body is said to be illusory, and detachment from worldly possessions and wealth is encouraged, as in some sickness scriptures in the Chinese *āgama*s and Pāli *nikāya*s. The name "Hall of Impermanence" and the mention of the "bell of impermanence," to be sounded at the time of a sick monk's death, evoke similar associations. But these are merely passing references. In Daoxuan's chapter as a whole, the emphasis on the impermanent character of the body that appears as the central lesson of the "sickness scriptures" appears to have been superseded by a very different understanding of the moment of death, in which the thought held at that final moment conditions one's ensuing rebirth. Reflections on impermanence at the end of life are thus subordinated to the aim of achieving birth in a superior realm. To a lesser extent, this may also be true of some Indic sources, such as the *Za ahan jing* story mentioned above about the dying young monk anxious about his rebirth destination. In Daoxuan's case, however, the emphasis is far more pronounced. This move on his part would in turn appear to reflect larger trends in medieval Chinese Buddhism accompanying the rise of aspirations for birth in a pure land.

Yijing's *Linzhong fangjue* (Instruction for the moment of death)

As a way of further illuminating the larger context of Daoxuan's treatment of the moment of death in his Vinaya commentary, I will here briefly compare it with a similar discussion that appears in an essay by another Vinaya authority, Yijing, who lived about half a century after Daoxuan and is famed as the translator of the *Mūlasarvāstivāda vinaya* into Chinese. Yijing's essay, the *Linzhong fangjue*, or "Instruction for the Moment of Death," is appended to his translation of the short sūtra *Foshuo wuchang jing*, or *Scripture on Impermanence*.[37] In his "Instruction," Yijing first describes the deathbed ritual. Like Daoxuan, Yijing here shapes his discussion of deathbed practice around the aim of achieving birth after death in a buddha land. But then, as the setting shifts to the point after death has taken place, Yijing turns his focus to the *Scripture on Impermanence*, explaining how this scripture is to be recited by a monk and how members of the audience are to meditate on impermanence as they listen to it. In other words, in Yijing's essay, the preaching on impermanence shifts venue, from the sickbed of the dying person to the funeral after that person's death.

Yijing begins his "Instruction" by noting that on seeing a person about to die and suffering from physical and mental pains, a monk, nun, *upāsaka*, or *upāsikā* should give rise to compassion and come to the dying person's rescue (*baji raoyi*).[38] Yijing's "Instruction" thus appears to be addressed generally to all people, both those who have renounced the householder's life and those who have not. The sick person is to be bathed in fragrant water and clothed in fresh robes. He or she should sit in the correct posture and meditate. If the dying person is unable to sit up unaided, someone else should provide assistance. If still unable to sit, the dying person may lie on his or her right ride, holding the palms together and concentrating the mind.

An altar is to be set up in front of the sick person, and a painted image is hung inside it. The sick person should mentally visualize and contemplate the primary and secondary marks of the painted buddha image. This will cause the sick person to give rise to the intention of seeking enlightenment (Skt. *bodhicitta*; Ch. *putixin*).

Then the attendant looking after the dying individual is to say to that person: "It is difficult to live in the three realms [of samsaric existence]. The three inferior realms of rebirth [among hell dwellers, animals, or hungry ghosts] are nothing but pain and suffering. These are not [desirable places] in which to be reborn. We can only rely on the enlightened wisdom (bodhi) of the Buddha. If one takes refuge in it, one will surely be born in the buddha lands of the ten directions. There one will dwell beside bodhisattvas and enjoy marvellous pleasures."[39] Exchanges with the dying person then follow. The person attending to the dying should ask, "In what buddha land do you now wish to be born?" The sick person answers, "I intend to be born in the world of such-and-such buddha."[40] Then, according to the sick person's wishes, the attendant should explain how the buddha land in question was established and give instructions on how to achieve birth there—for example, by explaining the sixteen contemplations in the case of the western land of Amitāyus (Sukhāvatī, Wuliangshouguo) or their counterparts in other cases. Detailed instruction on these topics will cause the sick person to experience mentally the happiness of birth in that buddha land.

The dying person is then instructed to visualize the primary and secondary marks of the buddha who presides over the buddha land to which he or she aspires. He or she is to make a request to that buddha and his attendant bodhisattvas, saying, "I worship (*jishou*) the Tathāgata, Arhat and Correctly Enlightened One, and the bodhisattvas, great beings. Take pity on me and rescue me (*baji raoyi*). I now request to have my sins removed and, as a disciple, [be allowed to] follow the Buddha and bodhisattvas and be born in the buddha land."[41] The person is instructed to repeat these words a second and third time. The sick person is then to recite the appropriate buddha's name. After reciting this name for "ten thought moments," the dying person receives the three refuges and confesses his or her sins extensively. After repentance, the sick person receives the bodhisattva precepts. If the sick person is unable to speak, someone else is to receive the precepts in his or her place.

After receiving the precepts, the sick person is helped to lie down, head to the north and face turned toward the western direction. With eyes either open or closed, the person should then visualize the Buddha's thirty-two primary marks and eighty secondary marks. This is done for any of the various buddhas of the ten directions. The dying person should be instructed in the four noble truths, causes and effects, the twelve links of dependent origination from ignorance to old age and death, and contemplations of suffering and emptiness.

When the time of death comes, the person attending to the sick, as well as others, should recite the name of the Buddha for the sick person without interruption, while the sick person mentally recites the name. One should not recite the name of any buddha other than the one in whose realm land the dying person wishes to be born; otherwise the sick person may give rise to doubt.

In this way, when the sick person's life is about to end, he or she will see a buddha, manifesting himself by transformation, along with his attendant bodhisattvas. Holding incense and flowers, they will arrive to welcome the dying practitioner. On beholding them, the dying person will be delighted and will be freed from both physical pain and mental distraction, as insight into the truth (*zhengjian*) emerges in that person's mind. Shortly thereafter that person's life will come to an end, just as though he or she had entered into a meditative state of samādhi. Never again will that person fall back and be reborn to suffer in the realms of the hells, animals, or hungry ghosts. By virtue of the teaching he or she received earlier, in an instant, in the time a warrior takes to flex or extend his arm, the deceased will be reborn in the presence of a buddha.

References to the sixteen contemplations, the western kingdom of Amitāyus, and "the ten thought moments" in this passage are all familiar elements associated with aspiration for the Pure Land of Amitāyus or Amitābha, although here, as in Daoxuan's comments on encouraging the dying in light of their different abilities and conditions, this realm is listed only as one of the many buddha lands to which one might aspire.[42]

This reference to the moment of death is immediately followed by instructions for the disposition of the robe and other objects worn by the deceased. In cases where the dead person is a lay *upāsaka* or *upāsikā*, the fresh new robe in which the person was dressed shortly before death should be divided into three parts and donated for his or her benefit to the Buddha, the Dharma, and the Saṅgha. Because of this gift, the deceased's hindrances will be removed, and meritorious benefits will be secured. Yijing states explicitly that the corpse should not be sent away wearing a good robe. In the case of monastics, the possessions of the deceased should be disposed of according to the rules given in the Vinaya.

These instructions are followed by an account of the ceremony of sending off the dead (*song wangren*) as follows. At the place of burial, the body should be placed downwind, lying down with the right side touching the ground and the face turned toward the sun. Upwind, a high seat is set up and decorated elaborately. Those whom the deceased has left behind are instructed to invite one monk who can recite scriptures to go sit on the dharma seat and recite the *Scripture of Impermanence* for the dead person's sake. This appears to be the sūtra translated by Yijing, to which this "Instruction for the Moment of Death" is appended.[43] The scripture in question is a meditation on death, in which the theme that all living beings must inevitably die is repeated; only the Buddha's wisdom is the true source of support.[44]

> The filial son puts an end to his sorrow and does not wail anymore. As for others, they concentrate their minds. For the sake of the dead person, they burn incense and scatter flowers, making offerings to the high seat and the marvellous scripture. They scatter flowers and incense on the [deceased] monk. Then they return to their seats. They hold their palms together and pay their respects. Single-mindedly they listen to the scripture. The monk slowly and thoroughly recites the scripture. Those who hear it each contemplate that their own body is impermanent and will be destroyed shortly. With their thought transcending the world, they enter samādhi. When the reading of the scripture comes to an end, more flowers are scattered and incense burned as offerings.[45]

Then the monk recites mantras and sprinkles water and scatters yellow soil over the body of the deceased. The body is placed inside a stūpa, cremated, left in the woods (Skt. *śītavana*), or buried in the ground.

The power of the merit produced in this way is said to be such that all the negative karmic burden of the deeds committed by the deceased over a vast number of kalpas will instantly disappear, including such major sins as the ten evil deeds, the four *pārājika* offenses, the five grave crimes that result in rebirth in the Avīci hell, and reviling the Mahāyāna scriptures. Born in a buddha's presence, the deceased is said to acquire merits, give rise to wisdom, cut off delusions, and obtain the six supernatural powers and the three supernatural knowledges; entering the first *bhūmi*, the deceased will travel everywhere, making offerings to the buddhas and listening to the correct teaching; gradually progressing in cultivation and gathering infinite merits and wisdom, in the end the deceased will realize the supreme enlightenment, turn the wheel of the dharma, save innumerable sentient beings, and proceed to the great nirvāṇa and the highest enlightenment of the buddhas.[46]

In this "Instruction for the Moment of Death," Yijing discusses the last moment in terms of a deathbed ritual aimed at securing birth in a buddha land, just as does Daoxuan's chapter in his Vinaya commentary. At the same time, as an appendix to the *Scripture on Impermanence*, Yijing's "Instruction" also specifies when this scripture is to be recited—not at the deathbed, but at the funeral. Yijing thus highlights equally two different points in the ritual sequence that begins with illness and ends with the disposition of the body, specifying both the instruction to be given to the dying, which occurs before that person's death, and that to be heard after the death by those who are left behind, when the *Scripture on Impermanence* is recited. In examining Daoxuan's discussion of illness and death, we saw that impermanence, both of the body and of material possessions in general, and the importance of one's thought at the moment of death for securing birth in a pure land coexist as two important concerns in the instruction to be given to the dying, although the latter theme receives the greater emphasis. In Yijing's "Instruction for the Moment of Death," however, the two concerns are separated into distinct segments of the ritual sequence and addressed to different audiences. Yijing's prescriptions for deathbed practice are clearly aimed at securing birth in a buddha realm, and the benefits of the funeral, including the effects of the spells pronounced by the presiding monk as water and soil are sprinkled over the corpse, are also said to remove the deceased person's sins and ensure his or her ultimate enlightenment. The recitation of the *Scripture on Impermanence*, however, would appear to be directed primarily to the living persons attending the funeral and not to the deceased. Although the merit generated by reciting it may be for the sake of the dead person, its message is clearly intended for the living auditors, who are instructed to listen to it while contemplating the impermanence of their own existence. Thus the instructions for the dying are devoted solely to securing birth in a pure land, while the setting of the preaching on impermanence appears to have shifted from the sickbed to the funeral after the death.

Conclusion

In thinking about the moment of death, medieval Chinese Buddhist monks appear to have been somewhat torn between two potentially conflicting ideas, one emphasizing the realization of impermanence and the other closely connecting the last thought at the moment of death with determination of the realm of rebirth. While these two emphases may not necessarily have been seen as contradictory or mutually exclusive, a degree of tension may still have existed between them. Medieval Chinese monks appear to have inherited this tension from their Indian sources. In the sūtras in the Chinese *āgama*s and their equivalents in the Pāli *nikāya*s, attendant monks are typically said to preach on impermanence, or on closely related topics, as a sick monk approaches his death. However, as we saw above in the story told in the *Za ahan jing*, entry 1025, where the Buddha guides the dying reflections of a young monk, the emphasis on impermanence seems in some cases to have been accompanied by concerns about the realm of rebirth. In Daoxuan's discussion of instructions to be given to the dying, this latter concern becomes paramount. Daoxuan was no doubt aware that there may have been objections to this emphasis, as suggested, for example, by his citing of the *Dazhidulun* passage explaining how it is that one's thought at the last moment can surpass the influence of even a hundred years of practice. The apparent tension between these two emphases may well have been a matter of genuine concern for many medieval Chinese monks, particularly in connection with Pure Land teachings. Daoxuan in fact highlights this concern, perhaps deliberately, in some of the biographies he compiled of the eminent monks of his time.

While stories of monks who achieved birth in the western Pure Land or in other superior realms appear frequently in Daoxuan's biographical collection, *Xu gaoseng zhuan*, in a few of the biographies, the subject is openly critical of this goal. Two such stories take as their polemical foil the well-known Pure Land teacher Daochuo (562–645). Zhiman's biography records a remarkable exchange between himself and Daochuo, in which Zhiman is angered by Daochuo's suggestion to pay attention to the appropriate moment [of death] (*qi*). Taking issue with Daochuo's insistence that sentient beings should be guided in accordance with their conditions and capacities, Zhiman argues that such "conditions" are unreal, and in fact there is nothing that is to be "guided" (*yin*) into the Pure Land. Thus, to place emphasis on the single moment of death (*yiqi yaofa*) is in fact to be buried in bondage over many world cycles. Saying this, Zhiman asks Daochuo to leave.[47] In another biography, after a prolonged illness, in front of the visitors filling his residence and lying down in the posture of the deceased, Tanxuan says, "My life is about to end. Where shall I be reborn?" Daochuo, who is also present, suggests that he make a vow to be born in the western Pure Land, or "the land of happiness," but Tanxuan contemptuously rejects the idea of seeking happiness for himself. To Daochuo's question whether he would then have no rebirth, Tanxuan responds by asking whether there is a self that is reborn.[48] These stories concerning Zhiman and Tanxuan attest not only to the popularity of the Pure Land teaching of Daochuo—for whom Daoxuan wrote a biography while the subject was still alive, perhaps as an exceptional tribute[49]—but also to the fact that there was significant opposition to it.

The evidence reviewed above suggests that discussion about the moment of death became controversial as Daochuo's Pure Land movement gained momentum, and Daoxuan, sharply aware of the issues at stake and personally sympathetic to the discourse about the importance of the moment of death, nevertheless himself remained somewhat ambivalent. Yijing was free from such ambivalence.

Notes

1. *T* no. 1804, 40:143a–145b. On the date of composition of this commentary, see Fujiyoshi Masumi, *Dōsenden no kenkyū* (Kyoto: Kyoto Daigaku Gakujutsu Shuppankai, 2002), 112–16. Daoxuan's commentary and its influence are discussed in Satō Tatsugen, *Chūgoku bukkyō ni okeru kairitsu no kenkyū* (Tokyo: Mokujisha, 1986).

2. The treatment of illness in the Vinaya is addressed in some detail in Paul Demiéville's extensive discussion of illness, or *Byō*, in *Hōbōgirin: Dictionnaire Encyclopédique du Bouddhisme d'après les sources chinoises et japonaises* (Paris: Hōbōgirin, 1974), 3:236–40. This essay has been translated by Mark Tatz as *Buddhism and Healing: Demiéville's Article "Byō" from Hōbōgirin* (Lanham, MD: University Press of America, 1985).

3. *Sifenlü* 41, *T* no. 1428, 22:861b21–c10, partly abbreviated. Daoxuan's reference to this passage in the introductory section of his chapter appears at *T* 40:143a28–b11. A passage from the *Mūlasarvāstivāda vinaya* closely paralleling this *Dharmaguptaka* passage has been translated by Gregory Schopen in "The Good Monk and His Money in Buddhist Monasticism of the 'Mahāyāna Period'" (2000), reprinted in his *Buddhist Monks and Business Matters: Still More Papers on Monastic Buddhism in India* (Honolulu: University of Hawai'i Press, 2004), 8.

4. *T* 40:143b11–144a9.

5. *Ōjō yōshū* 2, *Nihon shisō taikei* 6, ed. Ishida Mizumaro (Tokyo: Iwanami Shoten, 1970), 206.

6. *T* 40:144a13–20. Daoxuan's reference to the "Chinese tradition" occurs at *T* 40:144a12–13. A similar description of death ritual at the Jetavana Hall of Impermanence appears in the *Fayuan zhulin* (Jade forest in the dharma garden), an encyclopedic scriptural anthology attributed to Daoshi, Daoxuan's collaborator at the Ximingsi monastery, where the anthology

was later produced (*T* no. 2122, 53:987a9–20). Daoshi refers to his source as the "Diagram of the Jetavana monastery in the western region" (987a9).

The two passages are clearly related, and the substance of Daoshi's *Fayuan zhulin* quotation closely parallels the quotation in Daoxuan's Vinaya commentary, although sentences are often rephrased slightly. The *Fayuan zhulin* version is introduced immediately following a quotation from the *Mahāsaṃghika vinaya* (*Mohesengqilü*, *T* no. 1425); this quotation also appears in Daoxuan's commentary as one of two short scriptural quotations placed immediately before the passage about Jetavana. However, there are also some notable differences between the two versions. In the *Fayuan zhulin* passage, the buddha image enshrined in the Hall of Impermanence is said to stand "facing the eastern direction" (*T* 53:987a13), while in Daoxuan's Vinaya commentary, it faces toward the western direction (*T* 40:144a17–18). If the image is that of Amitābha, then "facing the eastern direction" would suggest that the Buddha is coming from the west to welcome the sick monk, while "facing the western direction" would indicate that the Buddha is drawing the sick monk along with him back to the Pure Land. The *Fayuan zhulin* passage also contains an additional statement that if the sick monk is too weak to sit facing the image, he is to lie down, facing west and contemplating the marks of the Buddha. Finally, the *Fayuan zhulin* passage ends by noting that the image may take the form of Amitābha, Maitreya, Akṣobhya, or Avalokiteśvara, while in Daoxuan's commentary, its identity is unspecified. Daoxuan's version thus appears here to have been modified to include the possibility of birth in the lands of other buddhas or bodhisattvas.

The Hall of Impermanence is also described in considerable detail in another text attributed to Daoxuan, titled *Zhong tianzhu Sheweiguo Qihuansi tujing* (Diagram and scripture of the Jetavana Monastery in Śrāvastī in Central India, *T* no. 1899). While Daoxuan is said to have based this essay on a miraculous instruction given to him, it also mentions other sources such as the *Shengji ji* and *Sigao* attributed to Lingyu (519–605) (*T* 45:883c21–22). The hall is described differently here, though birth in a pure land is also mentioned (893c10–894a8; cf. 811a). On this text, see Zhihui Tan's recent Ph.D. dissertation, "Daoxuan's Vision of Jetavana: Imagining a Utopian Monastery in Early Tang" (University of Arizona, 2002).

The original "Chinese tradition" concerning Jetavana appears to have been a work underscoring the importance of the moment of death as a uniquely powerful juncture. Daoxuan cites two other passages from it in this section of his Vinaya commentary, referencing them simply as *zhuan*, or "tradition" (*T* 40:144a22 and c6). As we shall see below, the passage given in 144c speaks explicitly of securing right mental concentration at the moment of death in order to achieve rebirth in a superior realm.

7. Schopen, again citing the *Mūlasarvāstivāda vinaya*, has called atten-

tion to the broader social significance of this practice. Brahmanical groups, concerned over pollution, appear not to have been willing to provide care for the sick, who were often soiled by vomiting and diarrhea ("The Good Monk and His Money," 7–8).

8. *T* 40:144a22–27.

9. *T* no. 7, 1:191b–207c; cf. 193c. The verse is at 204c23–24, and the reference to the impermanence even of the Buddha's diamond body, at 204c26–27. Cf. Ernst Waldschmidt, *Das Mahāparinirvāṇasūtra,* (Berlin: Akademie-Verlag, 1951), 3:399.

10. For example, in the story of Kṣemaka (entry 103, *T* 2:29c–30c; cf. *Saṃyutta nikāya* 22.89), the deathbed reminder of impermanence is framed in terms of the relationship between the self and the five skandhas. In entry 1028, to be discussed in more detail below, it is explicitly formulated as a matter of the impermanence of the body. The *Za ahan jing* sūtra collection (*T* no. 99) was translated by Guṇabhadra in the fifth century and has been identified as a Sarvāstivāda work. On this latter point, see *Bussho kaisetsu daijten,* ed. Ono Genmyō (Tokyo: Daitō Shuppansha, 1933–36; rev. 1964–67), 7:61c–d, which lists parallels between scriptural citations attributed to the Sarvāstivāda school in other works and corresponding passages in this collection.

11. E.g., *Za ahan jing,* entry 103, *T* 2:30c6.

12. Satō, *Chūgoku bukkyō ni okeru kairitsu no kenkyū,* 86–100.

13. In contrast, other types of scriptural sources are extensively cited in the corresponding section on "Attending to the Sick" in Daoshi's *Fayuan zhulin* (*T* 53:985–87).

14. *T* no. 99, 2:268b–269a; cf. *Saṃyutta nikāya* 36.7 Gelañña. In F. L. Woodward's translation of the corresponding *Saṃyutta nikāya sutta,* the term *sata* (remembering), corresponding to *zhengnian,* is translated as "collected," and *sampajāna* (mindful), corresponding to *zhengzhi,* is translated as "composed." See *The Book of Kindred Sayings,* part 4 (London: Pāli Text Society, 1927; reprinted 1972), 142.

15. *T* 2:268c11–17.

16. *T* 2:268c28.

17. *T* no. 99, 2:267c7–17, partly abbreviated. Cf. *Saṃyutta nikāya* 35.74, Gilāna.

18. *T* 2:29c; cf. *Saṃyutta nikāya* 22.89.

19. *T* 2:267c19–268a17, partly abbreviated.

20. *Saṃyutta nikāya* 22.89; Woodward, *Kindred Sayings,* 4:25.

21. *T* 40:143a20 and 144a27.

22. *Shisonglü,* *T* no. 1435, 23:205c20–206a1.

23. *T* 40:144a29–b1.

24. Kāśyapa's *dhūta* practice is mentioned in *Za ahan jing* (*T* 2:115b1–3) and *Zengyi ahan jing* (*T* no. 125, 2:795b10–11). The story of the Buddha

offering half his seat to Kāśyapa appears in the *Zhong benqi jing* (*T* no. 196, 4:161a21). Different versions of the story of the Buddha offering his robe to Kāśyapa are listed in Jonathan Silk, "Dressed for Success: The Monk Kāśyapa and Strategies of Legitimation in Earlier Indian Mahāyāna Buddhism," *Journal Asiatique* 29, nos. 1–2 (2003): n. 23. Silk lists *Za ahan jing*, *T* no. 99 (1144), 2:303a22–b29; *T* no. 100 (119), 2:418a23–c14; and *Dazhidulun*, *T* no. 1509, 25:225a4–5 as sources for this story.

25. *T* 40:144b2–7.

26. In this section of his commentary, Daoxuan includes instructions for encouraging dying monks who were meditation masters (144b19–24), a category found neither in the original *Sarvāstivāda vinaya* passage nor in Daoxuan's summary of it. For a discussion of Daoxuan's interest in meditation practices, see Chen Jinhua, "An Alternative View of the Meditation Tradition in China: Meditation in the Life and Works of Daoxuan (596–667)," *T'oung Pao* 88, nos. 4–5 (2002): 332–95.

27. *Weimojie soshuo jing*, *T* no. 475, 14:544c22–23; cited by Daoxuan at *T* 40:144c5–6.

28. *T* no. 1509, 25:238b15–c1.

29. *Zhong ahan jing*, *T* no. 26, 1:706b12–708c28; *Majjhima nikāya* III, 207–15. For a translation of the *Dazhidulun* passage itself, see Étienne Lamotte, *Le Traité de la grande vertu de sagesse* (Louvain: Institut Orientaliste, Bibliothèque de l'Université, 1970), 3:1534–49.

30. *T* 25:238b23–29.

31. *T* 40:144c12–13.

32. *T* no. 1483, 24:982c11–29.

33. *T* 22:862b–c.

34. A story from the *Dazhuangyan jing* (Ornament of sūtras) is cited in this connection (*T* no. 201, 4:272c).

35. *T* no. 278, 9:437b1–4. The other two passages are from the *Shanjian lüpiposha* (*Samantāpāsādikā*), which also speaks of praising the dying and instructing them to free themselves from attachment to dwelling places, robes, other objects, and friends; to concentrate their thought on the three jewels; and to entertain the thought that the body is impure (*T* no. 1462, 24:752b), and the *Pinimu [jing]*, which appears to refer back to an instruction given earlier in Daoxuan's commentary (*T* 40:146a11) to speak gently to the dying and not openly disagree with them (unidentified; possibly *T* no. 1463?).

36. *T* 40:145a22–23.

37. *T* no. 801, 17:745b–746b. Yijing's instructions are at 746b–747a.

38. *T* 17:746b9–11.

39. *T* 17:746b18–21.

40. *T* 17:746b21–22.

41. *T* 17:746b27–c1.

42. Daoshi too, in his account of deathbed practice at the Jetavana Hall of Impermanence, lists the realm of Amitāyus or Amitābha as only one of the buddha realms where one might seek to be born (*T* 53:987a19). See note 6 above.

43. The *Wuchang jing* is also mentioned in Yijing's account of the cremation of a monk in the *Nanhai jigui neifa zhuan* (*T* no. 2125, 54:216c6–12), trans. Junjirō Takakusu, *A Record of the Buddhist Religion as Practised in India and the Malay Archipelago (A.D. 671–695)* (Oxford, 1896), 82. I would like to thank Yang Lu for kindly calling this passage to my attention. Recitation of the *Wuchang jing* is mentioned repeatedly in Yijing's translation of the *Mūlasarvāstivāda vinaya*, *Genben shuoyjiyoubu pinaye* (*T* no. 1442, 23:652b18, 864c7; cf. *T* no. 1451, 24:287a2, and no. 1459, 24:587b26).

44. *T* 17:745b21, 746a19, and 746a27.

45. *T* 17:746c27–747a4.

46. *T* 17:746c24–747a14.

47. *T* no. 2060, 50:583b29–c5. Zhiman summarizes Daochuo's position with the expression "*yiqi yaofa*," the essential teaching of the one period of time, or opportunity (583c4). A similar expression, *yiqi dayao*, appears in Daoxuan's Vinaya commentary (*T* 40:145a11), which there appears simply to mean "the great importance of the one moment [of death]."

48. *T* 50:641c5–10. On the issue of "no birth," see Daochuo, *Anleji*, *T* no. 1958, 47:11c–12a7. Tanxuan's reply is somewhat obscure, and I offer this reading tentatively.

49. *T* 50:594a29.

4

The Secret Art of Dying

Esoteric Deathbed Practices in Heian Japan

JACQUELINE I. STONE

DURING THE LATTER part of the Heian period (794–1185), death came to be conceived in Japan's Buddhist circles as a critical juncture when devout practitioners might escape saṃsāra altogether by achieving birth in the pure land (J. *ōjō*) of a buddha or bodhisattva. Once born in a pure land, one's own eventual attainment of buddhahood was said to be assured. "Pure Land" teachings did not yet have the exclusivistic connotations that they would later assume in the sectarian movements of Hōnen (1133–1212) and Shinran (1173–1262); aspirations for *ōjō* were embraced by Buddhists of all schools, and a range of practices was directed toward that end. Nor did all devotees seek the same pure land. Some aspired to birth in the Tosotsu (Skt. Tuṣita) Heaven, where the future Buddha Miroku (Maitreya) dwells; or the Fudaraku (Potalaka) paradise of the bodhisattva Kannon (Avalokiteśvara) discussed in D. Max Moerman's chapter in this volume; or other superior realms. But by far the most popular postmortem destination—and the one usually designated by the term "Pure Land"—was the Land of Utmost Bliss (Sukhāvatī, Gokuraku) presided over by the Buddha Amida (Skt. Amitābha, Amitāyus), said to lie in the western quarter of the cosmos. Popular songs, hymns, poetry, art, and liturgical performances, as well as doctrinal writings, celebrated Amida's "welcoming descent" (J. *raigō*), together with his holy retinue, to meet practitioners at the time of death and escort them to his realm. The first instructions for deathbed practice (*rinjū gyōgi*) ever compiled in Japan—which appear in the famous *Ōjō yōshū* (Essentials of birth in the Pure Land, 985), a manual of Pure Land practice by the Tendai scholar-monk Genshin (942–1017)—were framed in an Amidist mode. Genshin explained how dying monks should hold a five-colored cord fastened to a buddha image, visualize Amida's coming, and chant the *nenbutsu*, the invocation of Amida's name ("Namu Amida butsu"), so as to generate the all-important "last thought" that would ensure birth in his Pure Land. Several Heian-period hagiographical collections called *ōjōden* (accounts of those born in the Pure Land) were compiled, recording the exemplary deaths of monks, nuns, and laypersons believed to have achieved this goal. It is no exaggeration to say that Pure Land imagery and rhetoric dominated the ways in which people thought about and prepared for dying.

And yet, other strands of Buddhism also played a role in preparations for the next life and in deathbed practice. Perhaps the most prominent of these was *mikkyō*, or esoteric Buddhism. This might at first seem surprising, in that *mikkyō*, in terms of its formal doctrine, has so often been represented as a teaching for this world. Kūkai (774–835), the founder of the esoteric Shingon school who played a key role in the formation of esoteric Buddhist discourse, had stressed that *mikkyō* is the "lightning-fast vehicle" (Skt. *vajrayāna*) of enlightenment, superior in this regard to the gradual path of the lesser, exoteric teachings (J. *kengyō*).[1] Through performance of the "three secrets" (*sanmitsu*)—the forming of mudrās or scripted ritual gestures (*in*), the chanting of mantras (*shingon*), and the contemplation of esoteric deities or their symbolic representations—the body, mouth, and mind of the practitioner were said to be identified with those of the cosmic Buddha Dainichi (Skt. Mahāvairocana), thus "realizing buddhahood with this very body" (J. *sokushin jōbutsu*).[2] Notions of birth after death in a pure land find only the briefest mention in Kūkai's works.[3] A decidedly this-worldly character is also suggested by the various *mikkyō* rites (*shuhō*), sponsored by the court or privately by aristocrats, which were thought to influence the natural and political spheres. Both of the major streams of esoteric Buddhism that took shape during the Heian period—Tōmitsu, or Kūkai's esoteric Shingon school, and Taimitsu, the esoteric branch of the Tendai school—developed complex ritual techniques intended to alleviate drought, quell epidemics, cure illness, secure the birth of male heirs, subdue enemies, and achieve other pragmatic aims. Thus one might expect that esoteric Buddhism would play little or no role in the sort of deathbed practices that Genshin had introduced, since these were framed in terms of liberation after death in a separate buddha realm and an ethos of "loathing this defiled world and aspiring to the Pure Land" (*onri edo gongu jōdo*). On closer examination, however, the reification of esoteric and Pure Land teachings into the opposing polarities of "world affirmation" and "world denial" proves to have been largely a product of modern Shingon sectarian scholarship.[4] A number of esoteric sūtras, ritual manuals, and other works imported during the Nara (710–794) and Heian periods contain spells and rites said to bring about birth after death in Amida's realm.[5] For example, the *Rishushaku* (Ch. *Liqushi*), a commentary on the esoteric scripture *Rishukyō* (*Liqu jing*, Sūtra of the guiding principle), expounds on the seed syllable HRĪḤ that represents Amida, also known as Muryōju Nyorai (Tathāgata of Immeasurable Life); by upholding this one-syllable mantra, it says, one can avoid illness and disaster in this life and, in the next, achieve the highest level of birth in that buddha's land.[6] The *Muryōju giki* (Ch. *Wuliangshou yigui*), an influential ritual text, sets forth a meditation ritual, along with accompanying mudrās and mantras, for achieving birth after death in the Land of Utmost Bliss, as well as for transforming one's present reality into the Pure Land.[7] Whether based upon texts such as these or through their own innovation, a significant number of practitioners drew on esoteric Buddhism in their preparations for the next life. *Mikkyō* influences on Heian-period deathbed ritual ranged from the simple incorporation, without explicit theoretizing, of esoteric incantations or other elements into end-of-life practices for achieving birth in the Pure Land, to very detailed reformulations in esoteric doctrinal terms of both the concept of *ōjō* and the deathbed practices for achieving it. This chapter will consider some of these esoteric forms of deathbed practice, with particular attention to the question of whether or not a tension or contradiction was perceived between the goals of birth in the Pure Land and the realization of buddhahood with this very body and, if so, how it was addressed.

Esoteric Practices and Pure Land Aspirations: Some Unproblematized Combinations

A number of Heian *mikkyō* adepts aspired to birth in the Pure Land, with no apparent sense of incompatibility between the goals of the two doctrinal systems. The very earliest *ōjōden* collection, Yoshishige no Yasutane's *Nihon ōjō gokuraku ki* (Record of those in Japan born in [the Pure Land of] Utmost Bliss, ca. 985), contains several such instances. For example, Zōmyō (843–927), the chief abbot (*zasu*) of Enryakuji, the great Tendai monastery on Mt. Hiei, had been initiated into the threefold rites of Taimitsu practice but also practiced contemplation of Amida; at the end, it is said, he had his disciples chant Amida's name and died facing west.[8] Myōshō, another Hiei monk, "was from the outset drawn to the esoteric teachings" but also died contemplating Amida and chanting the *nenbutsu*.[9] Shinrai, an esoteric adept practicing at Ishiyamadera, had mastered the three secrets. On the day of his death, he initiated his leading disciple into the secret mudrās and mantras of the Diamond Realm (*vajradhātu, kongōkai*) that he had not yet transmitted to him. Then he faced west, contemplating Amida, and passed away.[10] Such examples show that even adepts self-identified with the esoteric teachings sought the Pure Land of Amida as their postmortem goal. While the polemical intentions of the compiler, Yasutane, in representing such eminent monks as Pure Land devotees cannot be ignored, we find similar references in other types of sources as well. For example, we have a notice of resignation from Jōshō (906–983), abbot of the Kongōbuji, the Shingon monastery on Mt. Kōya, and concurrently the chief administrator of Kōfukuji and the Shingon temple Tōji. Jōshō petitioned in 981 to be released from all administrative duties in order to devote his remaining years to practices for achieving birth in Amida's Pure Land.[11] Monks such as Jōshō and those just mentioned from *Nihon ōjō gokuraku ki* were learned clerics and thus surely aware of the differences in orientation between esoteric and Pure Land doctrinal teachings, and yet they are said to have turned their religious aspirations toward Amida's Pure Land as death approached.[12] Such examples suggest that an individual's religious aims and practices were not expected to conform throughout to a single doctrinal system or, perhaps more precisely, that doctrinal systems were more porous and accommodating than contemporary orthodoxy would suggest. Regardless of one's sectarian identity or doctrinal orientation, "aspiring to the Pure Land" was a common vocabulary in which preparation for death was understood.

We also find cases of individuals self-described as Pure Land devotees who incorporated esoteric elements into their customary practices and directed them toward the goal of birth in Amida's realm. Several early instances occur in the short biographical notices contained in the death register (*kakochō*) of the Nijūgo Zanmai-e (Twenty-five Samādhi Society), a fellowship of monks influential in the spread of Pure Land devotion that formed in 986 at the Yokawa precinct of Mt. Hiei for the express purpose of encouraging one another in practices for achieving birth in Amida's Pure Land.[13] These notices show that the society's members freely incorporated a range of practices, including esoteric ones, into their regular disciplines aimed at achieving *ōjō*. For example, the monk Myōfu (d. 1006) practiced both *nenbutsu* and sūtra recitation and at one point conducted a *goma* rite—the offering of oblations in the esoteric ritual fire—for more than a thousand days in order to achieve birth in the Pure Land.[14] Ryōun (d. 1011) regularly practiced an offering rite to the esoteric deity Fudō Myōō (Skt. Acalanātha).[15] Shōnen (a.k.a. Shōkin, d. 1015) for fifteen years chanted the *nenbutsu* ten thousand times at each of the six times of the day (J. *rokuji*) but also twice daily performed the esoteric Amida offering rite (*Amida kuyō hō*); in addition, he recited the *Lotus Sūtra* 4,200 times.[16] Kōshin (d. 1021) repeatedly recited the *Lotus* and *Amida* sūtras, as well as the ten vows of bodhisattva Fugen (Skt. Samantabhadra), Amida's forty-eight vows, and the ten bodhisattva precepts, and also performed the Lotus repentance ritual (J. *Hokke senbō*); in addition, among other practices, he recited numerous esoteric mantras and dhāraṇīs, including the longer and shorter Amida spells, the Wish According (*zuigu*) dhāraṇī, and the Mantra of Light (*kōmyō shingon*), the Superlative Dhāraṇī of the Buddha's Crown (Sonshō Daibutchō; hereafter "Superlative Spell"), the Arorikika mantra, and the mantras of Fudō and Butsugen (Skt. Buddhalocanā).[17]

The *kakochō* entry for Genshin, who was himself active in the group, quotes him as saying with characteristic humility that he lacked the intelligence to study esoteric teachings (J. *shingon*) and preferred to concentrate on the *nenbutsu*, yet he adds that he had regularly recited the spell of the Thousand-Armed Kannon, a dhāraṇī said to confer protection against fifteen types of inauspicious death, and also the Superlative Spell; the biography elsewhere notes that in addition to these two dhāraṇīs, Genshin recited those of Amida, Fudō, and Butsugen, as well as the Mantra of Light.[18] Genshin also refers in his *Ōjō yōshū* to recitation of the Mantra of Light and other dhāraṇis and sūtras of both esoteric and exoteric teachings as supporting practices for achieving birth in Amida's Pure Land.[19]

Another case in point is Genshin's disciple Kakuchō (952/960–1034), also a member of the Nijūgo Zanmai-e, who was celebrated for his esoteric knowledge. According to his *ōjōden* biography, Kakuchō continually practiced the moon-disk contemplation (*gachirinkan* or *gatsurinkan*), an esoteric technique in which one visualizes a Sanskrit A syllable, representing the originally unborn, above a lotus blossom against the background of a white disk, as vehicle for realizing the identity of the practitioner and the cosmic buddha. This account says that Kakuchō died contemplating the Buddha and later appeared in a dream to one of his disciples, announcing that he had been born in the Pure Land.[20] Members of the Nijūgo zanmai-e incorporated esoteric elements not only in their individual practices preparatory for death but also in their funerary rites. The society's regulations specify that at the time of its monthly gathering, after practicing the *nenbutsu* samādhi, members should empower sand by chanting the Mantra of Light and performing the three secrets contemplation. This sand was to be sprinkled over the bodies of any members of the society who had died, to release them from suffering and enable them to be born in the Pure Land.[21]

Similar instances can be found in connection with other monastic settings. Some especially striking examples appear in the *Kōyasan ōjōden*, which contains accounts of the Pure Land aspirants of the Shingon monastery at Mt. Kōya, including both official monks serving in Mt. Kōya's halls and temples and those "*bessho hijiri*" or ascetic holy men practicing in small reclusive communities (*bessho*) that formed on the slopes and valleys of the mountain's sacred precincts.[22] For example, Kyōkai (d. 1093; known also as the "Odawara *hijiri*"), who played an organizing role in the early Kōya *bessho*, is said, as his daily practice, to have cultivated the practices of the two esoteric maṇḍalas, performed the Amida offering rite, practiced the Daibutchō dhāraṇī, and recited the Amida mantra; just before his death, he also copied and consecrated several hundred drawings of Fudō. On his deathbed, he faced west and chanted the *nenbutsu* with his fellow practitioners. Afterward, the monks heard mysterious music receding toward the west, while one dreamt that Kyōkai was ascending on clouds to the Pure Land, escorted by Amida's holy retinue.[23] It will be noted that almost none of the above examples draws a distinction between "exoteric" and "esoteric" practices; all disciplines are equally directed toward birth in the Pure Land.

Hayami Tasuku has argued that whatever the distinctions between Pure Land and esoteric doctrinal teachings, in actual practice, the chanted *nenbutsu* and the mantras and spells of the esoteric repertoire were understood in the same way—as powerful invocations able to effect release from the sufferings of the six paths, to pacify the spirits of the dead, and to bring about birth in a pure land, whether for oneself or for others. That is why, as Hayami demonstrates, both the *nenbutsu* and esoteric mantras were frequently recited in death-related contexts, such as "preemptive funerals" (*gyakushu*)—services for postmortem welfare performed in advance of an individual's death—as well as funerary and memorial rites.[24] It is therefore not surprising that esoteric incantations were also incorporated into practices for the time of death. Since these mantras and dhāraṇīs were considered efficacious in dispelling malign influences or karmic obstructions, one also finds considerable overlap, in the deathbed context, between their contemplative and thaumaturgical functions. To mention a few examples from *ōjōden*: the dowager empress Kanshi (d. 1102) summons monks three days before her death and asks them to recite the name of the bodhisattva Kokūzō (Skt. Ākāśagharbha) and perform the rite of Daiitoku Myōō, an esoteric manifestation of Amida or Monju (Mañjuśrī), to banish hindrances at the time of her death. She herself dies facing west, holding a cord attached to a buddha image.[25] The councilor Ōe no Otomuto (d. 1184) chants the Superlative Spell seven times before he dies.[26]

Other esoteric rituals were also performed at the time of death; the *ajari* (*ācārya*) Yuihan (d. 1095), who at one time served as the chief administrator of Mt. Kōya, has a *goma* rite offering to the esoteric deity Sonshō Butchō performed just before his death to ensure his right mindfulness in his last moments.[27] The monk Shinnō (d. 1096), at the time of his death, has his fellow monks perform the esoteric *rishu zanmai* service, while he himself faces west and chants the *nenbutsu*.[28] *Ōjōden* also offer examples of individuals using esoteric icons as their deathbed *honzon*, or object of worship, in preference to an image of Amida. Enshō (d. 963), the chief abbot of Enryakuji, enshrines at his deathbed images of both Amida and Sonshō Butchō.[29] In the same collection, a woman of the Tomo family, a wife of the governor of Ōmi Province and a devout *nenbutsu* practitioner, has her seat moved on the day of her death before the Womb World (*garbhadhātu*, *taizōkai*) maṇḍala, which presumably served as her deathbed *honzon*.[30] The *ajari* Enkyō (fl. ca. 1076), a monk of Mt. Hiei, enshrines at his bedside a *gachirin*, or "moon disk," on which to focus his final contemplations; an unnamed nun (n.d.) uses a painting of the esoteric *nyoirin* Kannon as her deathbed icon; and the *nyūdō* (lay monk) Myōjaku (d. ca. 1124–1126), a devotee of the bodhisattva Kokūzō and an accomplished esoteric practitioner, hangs near himself at the time of death an inscription of the seed syllable VAṂ, representing Dainichi's wisdom.[31] Other individuals die forming mudrās associated with Dainichi, rather than Amida. Again, in these accounts, no distinction appears to have been made between exoteric or esoteric practices. The individuals depicted simply engage at death in those practices and employ the particular *honzon* of their own preference, and a range of ritual, iconographic, and contemplative elements, including esoteric ones, is unproblematically assimilated to the goal of birth after death in the Pure Land.

All the examples discussed thus far suggest that there were no fixed boundaries between "esoteric adepts" and "Pure Land devotees"; the two categories overlapped to varying degrees and in different ways. There were esoteric practitioners such as Jōshō, who inclined increasingly toward the goal of *ōjō* as they grew older; self-described Pure Land aspirants, like several members of the Nijūgo Zanmai-e, who drew on the perceived power of esoteric ritual to ensure their attainment of *ōjō*; and others, like Kakuchō, who, all along, engaged actively in both modes of thought and practice and sometimes others as well.

Toward an Esoteric Style of Dying

A few *ōjōden* accounts and other hagiographical sources, however, clearly attempt to depict the "ideal death," an incontrovertible proof of *ōjō*, in predominantly or even exclusively esoteric terms. For example, the monk Seien (d. ca. 1074–1077), a native of Izumo who had mastered the rites of the two maṇḍalas, dies sitting erect, forming the mantra of Dainichi and holding a five-pronged *vajra*; there is no mention of him going to a pure land.[32] Such examples occur with somewhat greater frequency in accounts of the practitioners of Mt. Kōya, mentioned above. The monk Shōyo (d. 1167), formerly of Ninnaji but now a resident of Mt. Kōya, announces on the nine hundred ninety-ninth day of a thousand-day Fudō rite that he wishes to complete the entire rite now, because tomorrow he will "be born in the land of Esoteric Splendor." Here, "the land of Esoteric Splendor" (*mitsugon kokudo*), the universal realm of Dainichi's enlightenment, is presented as a postmortem destination.[33] In another example, the monk Nōgan (n.d.) habitually recites both the *nenbutsu* and the esoteric sūtra *Rishukyō*; at death, he faces west and holds the five-colored cords but "with his mind, contemplates the teaching of the three secrets."[34] A particularly intriguing example is the account of the Kōya ascetic Rentai (d. 1098), a *Lotus Sūtra* reciter. One day, someone asks him, "Where have you fixed your aspirations—on [Amida's land of] Utmost Bliss or [Maitreya's Heaven of] Satisfaction?" Rentai responds in part that "the dharma realm is all suchness, so what particular land should I aspire to?" The day after his death, his disciple dreams that the Diamond Realm maṇḍala is unfurled in the sky, and seated in the moon disk of Muryōju Nyorai (Amida) in the space ordinarily occupied by the bodhisattva Saihōin is his master Rentai.[35] This dream is couched, not in the *raigō* imagery typical of most dreams recorded in Heian sources confirming a deceased person's *ōjō*—such as the purple clouds, other-worldly music, and subtle fragrance said to accompany Amida's welcoming descent—but in *mikkyō* iconography. It suggests that the deceased Rentai is indeed in Amida's land—not the remote pure land in the western direction but the "pure land" of the Diamond Realm maṇḍala, in which Amida and his attendants appear as expressions of the cosmic Buddha Dainichi. Without making explicit doctrinal claims, such stories draw on conventions of the Pure Land tradition and rework them in an esoteric mode.

An extremely interesting account, one of many legends concerning the famous poet-monk Saigyō (1118–1190), asserts the existence of a superior, esoteric posture to be observed in dying. Asked about the proper manner in which to die, Saigyō replies, "Those disciples who understand my inner enlightenment (*naishō*) will meet their death facing north. Those who do not know this inner enlightenment will die facing west." Saigyō himself, the narrative goes on to say, dies sitting upright in the posture of meditation, forming the dharma-realm mudrā and facing north. His disciples are distressed and say to one another, "The *hijiri* (holy man) always aspired to [be born in the Pure Land in] the western quarter, but now he is facing north. It must be the work of devils!" And they turn the body so that it is facing west, break the mudrā, and rearrange Saigyō's hands with the palms together in the *gasshō* gesture—the traditional death posture of Pure Land devotees. The narrative dismisses their actions as laughable. While Saigyō was outwardly like a *nenbutsu* practitioner, it explains, inwardly he had mastered the deepest secrets of both Shingon and Tendai *mikkyō* traditions; therefore he faced north and formed the dharma-realm mudrā, a posture that "returns to the source of the three secrets of the dharma realm" and "accords with the quiescent and luminous inner enlightenment that is without periphery or center."[36] This story postulates a distinctly "esoteric" death posture, recognized only by initiates and superior to that of conventional, exoteric deathbed practice.

Esoteric Instructions for Deathbed Practice

The uses of esoteric elements in deathbed practice reviewed thus far are not developed theoretically; practitioners for the most part simply ignored, or at least were not evidently troubled by, doctrinal tensions between notions of birth in a pure land, in which escape from saṃsāra is mediated by death, and the realization of buddhahood with this very body. Even in stories such as those of Seien, Rentai, or Saigyō, where the deathbed practice, posture, or auspicious postmortem signs are clearly cast in an esoteric mode, little theoretical explanation is offered. This does not mean, however, that doctrinal theory was deemed unimportant. For some *mikkyō* scholars, the relationship between *ōjō* and *sokushin jōbutsu* was a problem that required clarifying, and they worked actively to reinterpret Pure Land ideas within an esoteric conceptual framework. Over and against the ethos of "loathing this defiled world and aspiring to the Pure Land," found in *ōjōden* and other Heian Pure Land literature, these Shingon teachers asserted that the Pure Land was inherent in the mind and that "*ōjō*" was not birth after death in a separate realm but the practitioner's union with the Buddha. Of course, they were by no means the first or only Buddhists to put forth non-dual explanations of the Pure Land.[37] The distinctive feature of their arguments lies in their assimilation of Pure Land elements to the esoteric three secrets practices of body, mouth, and mind. Not content merely to work out an esoteric mode of Pure Land thought on a theoretical level, they also produced concrete instructions for deathbed practice that explicitly reflected these esoteric interpretations.

Before turning to examples of these esoteric instructions for deathbed practice, however, let us briefly touch on the Pure Land model they were appropriating. As noted above, deathbed practices aimed at birth in a pure land were first formally introduced to a Japanese readership in Genshin's *Ōjō yōshū*, which outlines *nenbutsu* practice for ordinary times; for special times, such as retreats; and for the moment of death. At the opening of the section on deathbed practice, Genshin cites the passage from the "Chinese tradition" (Ch. *Zhongguo benzhuan*) included in the Vinaya commentary of Daoxuan (596–667) in a section on "Attending to the Sick and Sending off the Dead," discussed by Koichi Shinohara in chapter 3 of this volume.[38] Following the purported conventions of the Jetavana Monastery in India in Śākyamuni Buddha's time, a dying monk is to be removed to a "hall of impermanence" (J. *mujōin*), so that the sight of his familiar surroundings and robe, bowl, and other possessions will not generate thoughts of attachment. There, he should be made to grasp a five-colored pennant fastened to the hand of a buddha image, to help him generate thoughts of following the Buddha to his pure realm.[39] As Shinohara notes, Daoxuan's instructions allow for aspiration to any number of buddha realms, but Genshin frames them in an explicitly Amidist mode. For example, he cites other Chinese predecessors specifically associated with Pure Land practices, such as Shandao (613–681), who recommends that dying persons should be made to face west, visualize the coming of the Buddha Amida to welcome them, and continually recite Amida's name,[40] and also Daochuo (562–645), who stresses the importance of helping the dying to sustain ten reflections on Amida, the minimum contemplation deemed necessary to achieve birth in his Pure Land.[41] Genshin also adds his own recommendations, centering on exhortation to the dying to visualize Amida's physical marks, his radiant, embracing light, and his welcoming descent, together with his holy retinue, to escort the practitioner to the Pure Land. Deathbed practices welding the "Jetavana model" to aspirations for birth in Amida's land are also stipulated in the regulations of the Nijūgo Zanmai-e, whose members were among the first in Japan to conduct such rites in a formalized manner.[42]

Jichihan: Deathbed Contemplation for the Shingon Practitioner

Genshin's instructions for deathbed practice were followed by other works of a similar intent. One of the earliest extant examples, about half a century after *Ōjō yōshū*, is the *Byōchū shugyō ki* (Notes on practice during illness) by the monk Jichihan (a.k.a. Jippan or

Jitsuhan, ca. 1089–1144), known as the founder of the temple Nakanokawa Jōjin'in in Nara and of the Nakanokawa branch of Shingon. Jichihan was versed in Hossō and Shingon teachings and was active in efforts to revive the monastic precepts; at one point, he also studied Tendai doctrine at the Yokawa precinct of Mt. Hiei, where he was exposed to Tendai Pure Land thought.[43] Jichihan was one of the earliest figures to interpret Pure Land ideas from an esoteric standpoint. His *Byōchū shugyō ki*, written during an illness in the winter of 1134, represents the first instructions for deathbed practice to be compiled in Japan in an esoteric mode.[44] In its concluding passage, Jichihan writes:

> [The manner of conducting] a ritual such as this should depend on the individual's inclination. What I have written above is intended solely for myself. Although displaying a holy image and having [the dying person] revere it and hold a colored pennant [affixed to its hand], etc. represent the tradition of the Jetavana Monastery set forth in the Mahāyāna scriptures, these protocols may be adapted according to the occasion and need not necessarily be insisted upon.[45]

This suggests both that the ritual forms of deathbed practice introduced by Genshin were by this time well known in monastic circles and that they were not the first object of Jichihan's concern. What interested him was how the Shingon practitioner should practice at the time of death. While space limitations preclude a detailed review of all the *Byōchū shugyō ki*'s eight articles, let us briefly consider the distinctively esoteric elements in Jichihan's instructions.

One compelling concern of virtually all *rinjū gyōgi* texts is maintaining right mindfulness at the moment of death. As explained in Shinohara's chapter, throughout the Buddhist world, one's thought at the last moment was believed to exert a determinative influence over one's postmortem fate. The *Guanwuliangshou jing*, or *Contemplation Sūtra*, one of the major Pure Land scriptures, says that even evil persons, if able at the time of death to form ten consecutive thoughts of Amida and invoke his name, will thereby eradicate eight billion kalpas of sinful deeds and achieve birth in the Pure Land. However, by the same logic, it was also thought that even a devout practitioner, by a stray deluded thought at the last moment, could in effect negate the merit of a lifetime's practice and plunge into the lower realms. Thus the ability to focus one's mind at this juncture was considered crucial.[46] Jichihan recommends that the Shingon practitioner should always contemplate the deity Fudō Myōō, relying on him to achieve right mindfulness and sustain the aspiration for enlightenment (*bodaishin*) in one's final hours. Fudō is one of the "wisdom king" (*myōō*) deities incorporated into *mikkyō* as a protector. He is often depicted in a fearsome aspect, glaring and tusked, holding a sword to sever delusions and a noose to restrain the passions. "The protection of this wisdom king extends even to realizing the fruit of buddhahood, which is distant," Jichihan writes. "How could he, in his compassionate vow, abandon [practitioners] at the time of death, which is close at hand?"[47] While it is not clear whether or not this was Jichihan's innovation, reliance on Fudō's protection in one's last hours would become a standard feature of virtually all subsequent Shingon deathbed ritual instructions.

Like Genshin's *Ōjō yōshū* and other *rinjū gyōgi* texts, the *Byōchū shugyō ki* recommends that the dying person perform repentance (*sange*) to remove various karmic hindrances that might obstruct one at the time of death. Performing repentance shortly before death seems to have been widespread in Heian Japan, and various methods were used, such as the Lotus repentance rite.[48] Jichihan recommends in particular the efficacy of esoteric spells, such as the Superlative Dhāraṇī of the Buddha's Crown, the Mantra of Light, or the Amida spell. As we have seen, some *ōjōden* accounts mention the recitation of these and other spells as well as the *nenbutsu* at the time of death, both to remove karmic hindrances and to ward off demonic influences; as Hayami has noted, such practices reflect a widespread understanding of the powers of Buddhist incantatory language that did not necessarily differentiate between "Pure Land" and "esoteric" doctrinal categories. Jichihan, however, provides an explicitly esoteric doctrinal explanation: All such recitations are to be performed as part of three secrets practice for uniting the practitioner's body, mouth, and mind with those of the Buddha. One should form the appropriate mudrā with the hands, chant the mantra or dhāraṇī in question with the mouth, and contemplate that mantra with the mind, firmly believing that its essence is the fundamental syllable A, the originally unborn, and that all sins will thereby be eradicated. Or one can simply contemplate the true aspect in accordance with the esoteric teachings, which will lead to the liberating insight that deluded karmic actions, arising through conditions, are without fixed form and thus inseparable from the originally unborn dharma realm.[49]

Jichihan then proceeds to provide an esoteric version of the deathbed contemplation of Amida and his Pure Land set forth by Genshin and his Chinese predecessors. The practitioner must direct his thoughts to Amida, defined here as the "lord of the lotus section," one of the five divisions of the "perfected body" assembly of the Diamond Realm maṇḍala. As for his realm, it is "a land in the western quarter, whose name is Perfect Bliss." It appears here that Jichihan is referring, not to a pure land billions of world-spheres away, but to the lotus section, located west of center in the Diamond Realm maṇḍala, over which Amida presides.[50] Jichihan goes on to describe this land in distinctively esoteric terms; for example, it is composed of the five elements, and its ground, of the seven precious substances. By the empowerment of the syllable HRĪḤ, which is the seed syllable of Amida, the waters, birds, trees, and forests of that land all preach the dharma. Above the Buddha's throne is a moon disk, and upon the moon disk is a lotus; upon the lotus disk is a seed syllable that transforms into the symbolic form (*sanmaya-gyō*) of the object of worship, the Buddha Amida. That Buddha's body is as many *yojana*s in height as six billion *nayuta*s times the number of sands in the Ganges River and possesses eighty-four thousand marks, each with an equal number of excellent qualities, each of which in turn radiates eighty-four thousand rays of light. As Amida's dharma body has four aspects, so does his land. By his supernatural powers, he will appear in differing ways to people of varying capacity, but all these manifestations are in essence equal. In short, the contemplation of Amida recommended here is not meditation on an external savior who will descend and escort the practitioner to his distant pure land but an esoteric visualization sequence in which contemplating, internalizing, and mentally transmuting iconographic imagery serves as the vehicle for realizing one's own identity with the Buddha. Jichihan makes this quite explicit:

> Because there is no discrimination in the single great dharma realm, know clearly that this Buddha is precisely one's own mind. Now, in contemplating the Buddha who is our own mind, know too that his land is also our mind. Truly we will be born into that

> [pure] land that is none other than our mind. The one who contemplates and that which is contemplated, the one who achieves birth and the place where that person is born, are in no way separate from the single great dharma realm.[51]

Continuing his contemplation instructions, Jichihan suggests that the practitioner should visualize the syllable HŪṂ between Amida's brows and envision it transforming into the physical mark of the white curl (Skt. *ūrṇā*; J. *byakugō*), turning to the right, large as five Mt. Sumerus and emitting eighty-four thousand rays of light. Genshin too, in his *Ōjō yōshū*, had emphasized visualization of the radiant light emanating from the white curl between Amida's brows, embracing practitioners and enabling them to eradicate sin, focus their deathbed contemplation, and achieve birth in the Pure Land.[52] Jichihan, however, suggests not only that the white curl should be visualized as a transformation of the letter HŪṂ but also that it is endowed with Amida's four inseparable maṇḍalas: Its pure white color corresponds to the great maṇḍala (*daimandara*); its beneficial manifestations, to the *sanmaya* maṇḍala (*sanmaya mandara*); the insight it produces in becoming a norm of conduct, to the dharma maṇḍala (*hō mandara*); and its light embracing all living beings, to the karma maṇḍala (*katsuma mandara*).[53] In discussing the meaning of the light emanating from this curl and embracing devotees, Jichihan draws on Shandao, who addresses this topic in some detail in his commentary on the *Contemplation Sūtra*;[54] however, as Ōtani Teruo has noted, Jichihan also carefully elides those phrases in Shandao's commentary that suggest a dualistic contrast between a transcendent buddha and the deluded beings who are saved. In short, Jichihan assimilates Shandao's authority as a Pure Land master to an esoteric reading of Pure Land teachings in which the Buddha and the beings are non-dual.[55] Finally, he says, the practitioner should pray to be embraced and brought to awakening by the light emanating from the object of worship (= Amida) that is ultimately identical to one's own mind.

A particular innovation of Jichihan's is his redefinition of the deathbed *nenbutsu* as a form of empowerment through practice of the three secrets (*sanmitsu kaji*), or ritual union with the body, mouth, and mind of an esoteric deity. As Genshin had done for *nenbutsu* practice in his *Ōjō yōshū*, Jichihan similarly defines *sanmitsu* practice for three kinds of occasions, focusing in particular on the basic esoteric practice of A-syllable meditation (*ajikan*). The first letter in the Sanskrit syllabary, A was considered to represent the "originally unborn" (*ādyanutpāda, honpushō*), the true nature of the dharmas.[56] Jichihan's first method, for everyday use, is a traditional three secrets practice in which the practitioner forms the basic mudrā corresponding to the object of worship, recites its basic mantra, and contemplates that mantra as embodying the three inseparable meanings of the syllable A—empty (*kū*), existing (*u*), and originally unborn (*honpushō*)—which constitute the dharma body and are identical to the mind of the practitioner. "Because of inconceivable emptiness, the karmic hindrances one has created are destroyed in accordance with the teaching. Because of inconceivable existence, the Pure Land toward which one aspires is achieved in accordance with one's vows. What is called the 'unborn' is the Middle Way. And because of the Middle Way, there are no fixed aspects of either karmic hindrances or the Pure Land."[57] Jichihan's second kind of *sanmitsu* practice, intended for "when one has extra time, or is physically weak," begins his assimilation of the *nenbutsu* to A-syllable meditation. Here, the practitioner's reverent posture is the paradigmatic "secret of the body"; in this light, all movements of the body are mudrās. Chanting Amida's name is the paradigmatic "secret of the mouth," and on this basis, all words and speech are mantras. The "secret of the mind" is contemplating the meaning of this name, both as a whole phrase (*kugi*) and as three individual syllables (*jigi*). As a whole, it signifies *amṛta* (J. *kanro*), meaning that the Buddha has freed himself from all hindrances, fevers, and poisons, reaching the cool of nirvāṇa, and causes all beings who contemplate his name to become equal to himself. Individually, the three characters in the name "Amida" are equated by Jichihan with three fundamental esoteric meanings of the letter A: *A* indicating the originally unborn, which is the Middle Way; *mi*, the great self that is without self and enjoys perfect freedom; and *da*, moment-to-moment accordance with suchness, which is liberation.[58] Jichihan's third kind of *sanmitsu* practice, to be employed for the moment of death, is a greatly simplified form of what he has already outlined: one should form the mudrā of the object of worship (Amida), chant his name, and single-mindedly take refuge in the myriad virtues of the Middle Way. Here, the elements of visualization and contemplation are vastly simplified, while that of invocation is paramount. Jichihan's synthesis of the *nenbutsu* and the esoteric A-syllable meditation in the context of deathbed practice would be developed by later Shingon figures such as Kakuban and Dōhan and also by teachers of other Buddhist traditions.[59]

Jichihan's Pure Land thought developed over time, and the *Byōchū shugyō ki* may not represent his final word on the subject. Some evidence suggests that, like the esoteric practitioners mentioned above, Jichihan in later life may have framed his postmortem aspirations in terms of birth in Amida's realm.[60] In this writing, however, practice at the time of death is in essence an esoteric three secrets rite for realizing *sokushin jōbutsu* through ritual union with Amida Buddha. Because in this text Jichihan neither explicitly denies exoteric understandings of the Pure Land nor clarifies the relationship between Amida and Dainichi, the cosmic buddha of the Shingon teachings, and because he draws extensively on exoteric sources, such as the works of Shandao and Genshin, some sectarian scholars have been critical of the work as overly indebted to Tendai thought and not sufficiently aligned with Shingon orthodoxy.[61] However, such criticisms overlook how thoroughly the *Byōchū shugyō ki* appropriates Pure Land elements—including Amidist imagery, visualizations, and the deathbed *nenbutsu*—to the non-dual conceptual structure of esoteric three secrets practice.

To a modern sensibility, it might seem counter-intuitive to speak of achieving *sokushin jōbutsu* at the moment of death: What would "realizing buddhahood with this very body" mean if that body was about to perish? We would be wrong, however, to assume that *sokushin jōbutsu* (and its ritual-symbolic apparatus) necessarily implied a purely "this-worldly" orientation. Jichihan's *Byōchū shugyō ki* is not the only text to suggest that this goal might be realized at death, or even after.[62] The distinction drawn by Heian esoteric thinkers such as Jichihan between *sokushin jōbutsu* and *ōjō* was not exclusively or even predominately one of this-worldly versus other-worldly attainments but is more fruitfully understood in other terms. From an esoteric standpoint, the idea of realizing *sokushin jōbutsu* at life's end would of course have been deemed superior to *ōjō*, in that it assimilates the ideal death to the non-dual stance of *mikkyō* doctrine, in contrast to notions of "going" to a separate pure land, which are easily characterized in dualistic terms; moreover, *sokushin jōbutsu* represents full buddhahood, where *ōjō* was understood as merely a stage, although a decisive one, in buddhahood's attainment. But perhaps even more important, *sokushin jō-*

butsu was a state to be achieved *with this body*, the fleshly body born of father and mother, unlike birth in the Pure Land, which is accomplished only in discarding the present body and assuming a more ethereal one. One imagines that for some self-identified esoteric practitioners, positing *sokushin jōbutsu* as a goal to be realized at life's last moment may have represented a reassertion of the embodied, somatic character of esoteric practice and attainment, over and against more "spiritualized" notions of attainment inherent in the idea of *ōjō*.

Kakuban: Deathbed Practice as Ritual Performance

A second important manual of deathbed practice in an esoteric mode is the *Ichigo taiyō himitsu shū* (Collection of secret essentials for a lifetime) by Kakuban (1095–1143), founder of the Daidenbōin lineage of Shingon and systematizer of Kūkai's teachings.[63] He and his followers left Mt. Kōya owing to conflict with the monks of Kongōbuji, the main temple of the mountain, and established themselves at Mt. Negoro; their branch of the tradition would later become known as "new doctrine" (*shingi*) Shingon.[64] Kakuban is arguably the most important Shingon thinker after Kūkai; he is also the key figure in the development of the strand of Shingon thought that later came to be known as *himitsu nenbutsu*, the secret or esoteric *nenbutsu*, which interprets Pure Land elements from a Shingon doctrinal standpoint. His *Ichigo taiyō himitsu shū* in nine articles was clearly inspired by Jichihan's *Byōchū shugyō ki*, which it cites explicitly.[65] This fixes its date of composition in the latter part of Kakuban's life, between 1134, when the *Byōchū shugyō ki* was written, and Kakuban's death in 1143. However, its perspective differs in significant respects from Jichihan's.

The text opens by stressing the critical importance of the last moment, when even evil persons can potentially escape saṃsāra, as well as the efficacy of esoteric ritual and meditative practice in bringing about the mental focus necessary to achieve this:

> Birth in the Pure Land in any of the nine grades depends on right mindfulness at the last moment. Those who seek buddhahood should master this attitude.... By following these protocols for the last moment, even monks and nuns who have violated the precepts are sure to obtain birth in the Pure Land, and lay men and women who have performed evil deeds will also surely be born in [the land

> of] Utmost Bliss. How much more so, in the case of [those monks and nuns] who have wisdom and keep the precepts, or of lay men and women who are virtuous! This is the ultimate point of the mantras and secret contemplations. Believe deeply and do not doubt![66]

Like Jichihan, Kakuban stresses the efficacy of mantras and dhāraṇīs in removing karmic hindrances at the hour of death. He also adopted the idea of deathbed contemplation as a form of three secrets practice, based on either the A-syllable contemplation or the closely related moon-disk contemplation. Kakuban regarded these contemplations as "two but not two," and *ajikan* and *gachirinkan* were often combined in his thought and practice.[67] Here, he says that they enable the practitioner to arouse the *samādhi bodhicitta* (*sanmaji bodaishin*), in which one perfects the three secrets and thus realizes identity with the cosmic buddha.[68] "If [the dying person] forms the mudrā proper to the object of worship and contemplates the Buddha by means of mantra (*shingon nenbutsu*), performing the three secrets without flagging, then that is itself the sign of certain birth in the Pure Land."[69]

Where Jichihan's *Byōchū shugyō ki* is concerned exclusively with the question of how the Shingon practitioner should meditate at the time of death, Kakuban also emphasizes how the Shingon adept should ritually assist others at that juncture. A large portion of his instruction is addressed, not to the dying person, but to the *zenchishiki* (Skt. *kalyāṇamitra*, a "good friend" or Buddhist teacher), here meaning those ritual specialists who attend the dying and assist their practice at the end. In effect, the *Himitsu shū* assimilates deathbed practice to the esoteric rites performed by *mikkyō* adepts on behalf of their aristocratic patrons.

Kakuban repeats the by now familiar conventions of deathbed practice that Genshin had introduced: one should remove the dying person to a separate room or hall, enshrine a buddha image—usually the dying person's personal *honzon*—and burn incense; those who have been drinking alcohol or eating meat or the five pungent roots should be kept away.[70] The dying person is to have secured in advance a promise of assistance from several *zenchishiki*, whose duties and qualifications are clearly specified. The first should "by all means be a person of wisdom, with aspiration for the way." The dying person should imagine this individual as the bodhisattva

Kannon, come to lead him to the Pure Land. This *zenchishiki* should sit close to the dying person, to the west and slightly south, roughly in line with that person's navel. He should keep his eyes fixed on the dying person's face and abide in a spirit of compassionate protectiveness, chanting in harmony with that person. A second *zenchishiki*, someone of long experience and training in practice, should take up his station on the other side of the sick person, near his head—that is, to the east and slightly north—at a distance of about three *shaku*. His task is to recite the mantra of Fudō to ward off demonic attacks or other malign influences that might disturb the dying person's concentration. A third *zenchishiki* should also be positioned to the north, if space permits, or in some other convenient place and strike the gong to set the pace of the chanting. Two more attendants may be on hand to attend to necessities. When the chanting reaches a particular melodic cadence (J. *gassatsu*), all four should join in at the same pitch. "This is the deathbed ceremony for one who seeks the enlightenment of the five kinds of wisdom," Kakuban says. In short, the deathbed scene is to be arranged in a mandalic structure: the four *zenchishiki* assisting the dying person take up their stations around him so that together they reproduce the configuration of the five wisdom buddhas, the dying person occupying the central position of Dainichi.[71]

Kakuban's instructions for practice at the end of life are the first to address explicitly the problem of dying persons who are distracted by pain, mentally confused, or even unconscious and thus unable to form a mindful and liberating "last thought." If the sick person becomes disoriented because of extreme pain, Kakuban says, that person should be made to place the palms together and face the buddha image. It may also happen that although life still remains, the sick person lapses into a state like a feverish sleep and barely breathes. At such a time, the *zenchishiki* are to observe his breathing carefully and match their breathing to his, chanting the *nenbutsu* in unison on the outbreath, for a day, two days, seven days, or as long as necessary until death transpires, never abandoning the dying person even for a moment. "The rite for persons on their deathbed always ends with the outbreath," Kakuban warns. "You should be ready for the last breath and chant the *nenbutsu* in unison." In this way, the dying person can be freed of sins and achieve the Pure Land, because—even when he himself may have ceased to breathe—the attendants chant the *nenbutsu* on his behalf, and Amida's original vow must inevitably respond to the invocation of his name. Moreover, the *zenchishiki* are to visualize their *nenbutsu,* chanted on the outbreath, as the six syllables NA-MO-A-MI-TA-BUḤ in Sanskrit letters, entering the dying person's mouth with the inbreath, transforming into six sun disks, and dispelling with their brilliance the darkness of the obstructions of sins associated with the six sense faculties.[72] This represents Kakuban's esoteric reading of the "meditation on the [setting] sun" (*nissōkan*), the first of sixteen meditations for achieving birth in Amida's Pure Land set forth in the *Contemplation Sūtra*.[73] This synthesis of the *nenbutsu* with esoteric breath meditation and visualization techniques seems to have been Kakuban's innovation.[74] In other writings, Kakuban interprets Amida, conflated with the originally unborn syllable A, as the breath of life itself; with each outbreath, one "returns one's life" (*kimyō,* the translation of "Namu" or Sanskrit "Namo-") to Amida. With this awareness, the act of breathing itself becomes the continuous *nenbutsu*—an idea that would influence subsequent esoteric readings of the *nenbutsu* and also spread beyond Shingon circles.[75]

Kakuban further calls for the *zenchishiki*'s immediate ritual intervention should the death be accompanied by inauspicious signs. Kakuban draws here on a passage from the Chinese esoteric scripture *Shouhu guojiezhu tuoluoni jing* (Sūtra of dhāraṇīs for protecting the nation and the ruler), which enumerates fifteen signs that the dying will fall into the hells (such as crying aloud with grief or choking with tears, urinating or defecating without awareness, refusing to open the eyes, foul breath, or lying face down); eight signs that the dying will fall into the realm of hungry ghosts (such as burning with fever or suffering from hunger or thirst); and five signs presaging a descent into the bestial realm (such as contorting of the hands and feet, foaming at the mouth, or sweating from the entire body).[76] For each of these categories of corporeal signs, Kakuban specifies what sort of ritual counter-action should be performed. For example, having observed any of the signs that the newly deceased person will fall into the hells, the *zenchishiki* should immediately act to rescue that individual by performing the Buddha Eye, Golden Wheel, Shō Kannon or Jizō rituals. Sculpted or painted images should be made of the buddhas or bodhisattas to whom these rites are directed and offerings made to them. Or one may recite the *Rishukyō,* the names of the fifty-three buddhas, or the Jeweled Casket or Superlative Spell, or the Mantra of Light, or perform the Jeweled Pavilion (*hōrō*) rite, or recite the "Bodhisattva Preaching

Verses" chapter of the *Flower Ornament Sūtra*, or the *Lotus Sūtra*, and so forth, as especially efficacious in saving that person from the pains of the hells.[77] Kakuban's instructions thus not only concern the moment of death but also extend into the realm of postmortem rites. With his *Ichigo taiyō himitsu shū*, deathbed practice became no longer a matter merely of the dying individual's contemplation but a ritual service performed by an adept on a patron's behalf. The development of ritual procedures specific to Shingon deathbed rites did not stop with Jichihan and Kakuban but continued throughout the medieval period; eventually, such rites were extended to funeral procedures as well.[78]

A Double Logic

In addition to his ritual innovations, Kakuban also developed the theoretical aspects of deathbed practice from his *mikkyō* perspective, drawing a clear, hierarchical distinction between exoteric and esoteric understandings of the Pure Land. For example, he paraphrases the views of the esoteric master Shanwuwei (Śubhakarasiṃha, 637–735) as follows:

> The exoteric teachings say that [the land of] Utmost Bliss is a buddha land lying tens of billions of [world spheres] away to the west. Its buddha is [A]mida, who has realized the fruit of enlightenment from his practice as the monk Hōzō (Skt. Dharmakāra). But the esoteric teachings say that the pure lands of the ten directions are all the land of a single buddha, and all the tathāgatas are the body of a single buddha.[79]

To which Kakuban adds:

> Apart from this Sahā world, there is no land of Utmost Bliss to contemplate. How could it be separated by tens of billions of other lands? And apart from Dainichi, there is no separate [buddha] Amida. . . . Amida is Dainichi's function as wisdom. Dainichi is Amida's essence as principle. . . . When one contemplates in this way, then, without leaving the Sahā world, one is immediately born in [the pure land of] Utmost Bliss. One's own person enters Amida, and Amida, without transformation, becomes Dainichi. One's own person emerges from Dainichi; this is the subtle contemplation for realizing buddhahood with this very body.[80]

In that it defines Amida as an aspect of the cosmic buddha, Dainichi Nyorai; draws on esoteric sources; and explicitly repudiates the notion of a separate pure land in the west, Kakuban's *Himitsu shū* has often been regarded among Shingon sectarian scholars and others as embodying a more "orthodox" esoteric position than Jichihan's *Byōchū shugyō ki*.[81] Alternatively, Kakuban is said to have effected a true synthesis of *mikkyō* and Pure Land elements, in contrast to Jichihan, whose deathbed ritual has been characterized as "a single-deity rite (*isson hō*) of Amida aiming at *sokushin jōbutsu*" in which "a fusion of the ideas of *ōjō* and *sokushin jōbutsu* is not attempted."[82] Setting aside such hierarchical evaluations of the two works, one does indeed note a difference in perspective between them. Where Jichihan fully assimilates deathbed practice to an esoteric three secrets ritual for realizing one's identity with Amida Buddha, Kakuban maintains that same non-dual perspective but also treats the idea of going to the Pure Land as at least a provisionally real event. Ironically, while Kakuban's *Himitsu shū* has often been deemed more consistent with Shingon orthodoxy than Jichihan's *Byōchū shugyō ki*, it makes a greater accommodation than does Jichihan's deathbed text for notions of the Pure Land as a distinct realm apart from this world.

Kakuban's acknowledgment of two distinct soteriological goals in effect produces a double logic that runs throughout the text. On the one hand, the *Himitsu shū* stresses the inseparability of the Buddha and the Pure Land with the person of the practitioner: by contemplating this non-duality, "without leaving the Sahā world, one is immediately born in [the pure land of] Utmost Bliss." Yet on the other hand, it promises at the very outset a method to escape saṃsāra and achieve "birth in the Pure Land in any of the nine grades," and its ritual instructions to the *zenchishiki* are clearly aimed at negotiating a safe transit for the dying person from this world to a desirable postmortem realm. This oscillation between the two perspectives is also mirrored in the text's claims about what stage practitioners of varying capacities may expect to achieve. For example, in discussing the merits of the A-syllable contemplation, Kakuban writes, "Those of shallow contemplation and limited practice shall, without discarding their present body, achieve the highest grade of superior birth in the Pure Land, while those of deep cultivation and great assiduity shall, without transformation of their present mind, become great radiant Dainichi of [the realm of] Esoteric Splendor"; but he also states, "By relying solely on this contemplation and not cultivating other practices, [even] a negligent person of small capacity can fulfill the great aspiration for birth in the next life in the Pure Land, while an assiduous person of great capacity shall obtain the *siddhi* of realizing buddhahood with this present body."[83] Both passages subsume the goals of birth in the Pure Land and the direct realization of innate buddhahood within the same A-syllable practice, although establishing a clear hierarchy between them. But nonetheless an inconsistency remains: On one hand, to achieve birth in the Pure Land "without discarding their present body" suggests that "birth in the Pure Land" is a level of attainment, albeit an inferior one, to be realized within the limits of this life; on the other, to "fulfill the great aspiration for birth in the next life in the Pure Land" clearly indicates a postmortem goal.

These discrepancies have exercised generations of Shingon exegetes, who, since early modern times, have debated whether Kakuban did in some sense acknowledge birth in a separate pure land as a provisional goal or whether he used this term in an ultimately non-dual sense to denote an achievement inferior to buddhahood but still to be realized with this present body. With minor variations, the present consensus of sectarian scholars assimilates the *Himitsu shū*'s promise of "birth in the next life in the Pure Land" to a non-dual *sokushin jōbutsu* position and seems strongly disinclined to entertain the possibility that Kakuban might have actually been referring to birth after death in a separate realm; *ōjō* is read, for example, as a "skillful means," a concession to the widespread Pure Land beliefs of his day, or is interpreted as "birth" in Dainichi Nyorai's all-pervading "land of esoteric splendor" as an interim stage leading to *sokushin jōbutsu*.[84] The advantage of such readings is that they iron out inconsistencies in the text; indeed, the "reconciliation of contradictions" (*eshaku* or *etsū*) has always been seen as a major task of traditional exegesis. Nonetheless, sectarian orthodoxy represents only one possible approach to the text, and one can also read Kakuban's *Himitsu shū* in a way that not only acknowledges its inconsistencies but also sees them as an interpretive strategy. From this perspective, the *Ichigo taiyō himitsu shū* brings together the two elements—going to the Pure Land (*ōjō*) and realizing buddhahood with this very body (*sokushin jōbutsu*)—not in a way that attempts to reconcile them or subsume one within the other, but in a dynamic tension: on one hand dismantling the very idea of birth in a separate pure land while at the same time prescribing the most efficacious ritual techniques for achieving it. Perhaps because the *Himitsu shū* deals with the specific ritual requirements of the deathbed, in this work, at least, Kakuban's intellectual commitment to non-dual Shingon orthodoxy does not seem to have led him to abandon the notion of death as a potent and possibly dangerous transition to another realm, one whose passage could be negotiated by proper meditative and ritual techniques—especially by the superior meditative and ritual techniques of the esoteric repertoire.[85]

One finds a similar oscillation between the two perspectives in another deathbed ritual text, the *Rinjū yōjin no koto* (Admonitions for the time of death) by the later esoteric figure Dōhan (1178–1252).[86] On the one hand, like Jichihan and Kakuban before him, Dōhan recommends a form of three secrets practice for the practitioner's last hours, centered on the contemplation of some form of non-duality:

> The syllable A as existence arising through conditions corresponds to birth. The syllable A as the emptiness of non-arising corresponds to death. Thus dying in one place and being born in another is nothing other than the letter A.... This is why Vairocana takes this single syllable as his mantra.... Birth and death are nothing other than the transformations of the six elements transmigrating in accordance with conditions. Buried, one becomes dust and is no different from the great earth of the syllable A. Cremated, one becomes smoke and is equal to the wisdom fire of the syllable RA. In contemplating the non-transformation of the six elements, there is no longer arising and perishing, only the naturally inherent four maṇḍalas that are the buddha essence.[87]

Yet at the very same time, Dōhan urges the practitioner, at the hour of death, to offer a vow before an image of Kūkai, the Shingon founder, and implore the aid of his empowerment in reaching the Pure Land of Utmost Bliss.[88] Here too we see a tension, or double logic, in which practice at the last moment is seen both as a ritually controlled transition from the present realm to a pure land *and* in terms of a non-dual metaphysics in which the separate existence of such a pure land must be rejected. The Pure Land conceptual framework that dominated Heian Buddhist approaches to death is thus assimilated to a *mikkyō* orientation on two fronts: deathbed *practice* for achieving birth in the Pure Land becomes esoteric practice, while the Pure Land into which that birth is to be achieved is reconceived in non-dual esoteric terms.[89]

A Minority View

Although their perspectives differed, both Jichihan and Kakuban saw aspiration for the Pure Land—however the "Pure Land" might have been defined—and also deathbed practice as compatible with non-dual esoteric thought. A very different view appears in the *Kakukai Hōkyō hōgo* (Bridge of the Law Kakukai's discourse on the dharma), a short sermon-like tract (*hōgo*) recording the teachings of the Shingon master Nanshō-bō Kakukai (1142–1223).[90] Kakukai served from 1217 to 1220 as the thirty-seventh superintendant of the Kongōbuji on Mt. Kōya. Little is known of him, though he had many gifted disciples, including the above-mentioned Dōhan. This one surviving work of his, the *Hōgo*, rejects both aspiration to specific pure lands and formalized deathbed ritual as fundamentally inconsistent with the insight that the whole universe is Dainichi Nyorai's realm.

Kakukai begins by asserting that "those who truly aspire to unexcelled enlightenment (Skt. bodhi) in accordance with this [Shingon] teaching do not consider in the least where they will be reborn or in what form." This is because, for one awakened to the originally unborn nature of the dharmas, all places are the pure land that is Dainichi's practice hall of Esoteric Splendor (*mitsugon dōjō*). From this perspective, Kakukai argues that the entire notion of fixing one's aspirations on a particular postmortem destination is misguided:

> When we thoroughly contemplate the arising and perishing of the dharmas, in truth we cannot be one-sidedly attached to [Maitreya's] Heaven of Satisfaction, nor to [Amida's land of] Utmost Bliss.... If we simply purify the mind, we shall not feel pain, even if we should assume the forms of such [lowly] creatures as dragons and yakṣas.... Our partiality for the human form and our bias against the strange forms of other creatures is due to our lack of understanding. Regardless of transmigration, we shall suffer no discomfort.[91]

This position leads Kakukai also to reject formalized conventions of deathbed practice designed to control and direct ritually one's passage to the next life, including the attendance in one's last hours of a *zenchishiki*, or religious guide. He continues:

> Nor do I consider what kind of mudrā to make at the moment of death. Depending on my state of mind, I can abide [in right mindfulness] in any of the four postures [walking, standing, sitting, or lying down]. What kind of action is not samādhi? Every thought and every utterance are meditations (*kannen*) and mantras (*shingon*) of attainment (*siddhi, shitsuji*). . . . The practitioner should simply chant the A syllable with each breath and mentally contemplate the true aspect, [that all things] arise in accordance with conditions. The circumstances of our final moments are by no means known to others, and even good friends (*zenchishiki*) will be no help to us. Since one's own and others' thoughts are separate, even if they perform the same contemplation, others' thoughts are likely to differ from one's own. . . . I think it is quite splendid to die as did the likes of [the recluse] Gochi-bō, abiding in a correct state of mind with his final moments unknown to any others.[92]

If we judge solely by this passage, Kakukai does not seem to have regarded death as a unique juncture with its own distinctive dangers and opportunities, requiring mediation by special ritual forms; the simple contemplation of non-duality and interdependent arising is sufficient at the moment of death as it is throughout life. Indeed, from the *Hōgo*'s perspective, to fix one's aspirations for the next life on any specific realm is a form of delusion, betraying one's ignorance that all places and forms are inseparable from Dainichi's practice hall of Esoteric Splendor.

Was the *Hōgo*'s rejection of specific postmortem aspirations and formal deathbed practices made in a particular polemical context? Or was it a statement of Kakukai's abiding personal conviction? Did he in fact act on it in his last moments? Given the lack of reliable biographical information, it is hard to know how to locate this text in the larger framework of his thought.[93] In any event, Kakukai's *Hōgo* is atypical, not in its assertion of an immanent pure land—a common enough doctrinal position—but in its extension of the implications of that position to negate both aspirations for the Pure Land as a postmortem goal and ritualized deathbed practice for achieving it. In this, it is as anomolous as it is logically consistent.

Conclusion

As we have seen above, in Japan's Heian period, esoteric elements were freely and variously incorporated into practices aimed at birth in the Pure Land, usually without theoretical explanation. Many self-defined Pure Land devotees used esoteric contemplations, spells, icons, and so forth in both their deathbed rites and other practices conducted in preparation for the afterlife. And even individuals accomplished in esoteric ritual and meditation frequently framed their postmortem aspirations in terms of birth in Amida's Pure Land. What this suggests is not so much that practice proceeded in disregard of doctrine, as that our own understanding of how doctrine was appropriated may be insufficient. Under the influence of modern sectarian studies, doctrinal systems have come to be defined in rigid, mutually exclusive terms that often belie the permeable, fluid character of denominational categories in the premodern period. Representations of *mikkyō* as "this-worldly" or "world affirming," over and against an "other-worldly" or "world-denying" Pure Land tradition, are especially problematic. Though not highlighted in Kūkai's teachings, the promise of birth in a pure land as a benefit of esoteric practice featured in a number of esoteric sūtras and ritual manuals, and in Japan, as on the Asian continent, *ōjō* represented a generic goal, crossing all boundaries of school and lineage.

A detailed investigation of why the particular soteriological goal of *ōjō* came to predominate—as opposed, say, to direct realization of buddhahood—would require a separate essay. One may imagine that a majority of practitioners saw the ultimate achievement of realizing buddhahood as beyond their capacity. In addition, despite its grounding in sophisticated Mahāyāna non-dual metaphysics, the doctrine of *sokushin jōbutsu* lacks a clear explanation of "what happens" after death and thus, one imagines, might have proved emotionally or even cognitively inadequate in confronting one's own death or the death of close associates. Narratives about going to Amida's Pure Land may in this regard have provided a more attractive basis for conceptualizing postmortem aspirations. Some esoteric practitioners, however, sought to imbue the ideal of a liberative death, dominated at the time by Pure Land thought and imagery, with a distinctively *mikkyō* character; hence the idea of special, esoteric postures to be adopted in death, such as facing north or forming a mudrā associated with Dainichi. And some *mikkyō* scholars addressed on a conceptual level the tensions between the goals of *sokushin jōbutsu* and birth in the Pure Land. Both moves come together in the Shingon instructions for deathbed practice discussed above. Jichihan's *Byōchū shugyō ki* and the *Kakukai Hōkyō hōgo* both resolve the tension between the two soteriological goals in favor of non-dual enlightenment, denying the very idea of "going" to a separate pure land. But they do so in dramatically contrasting ways. In Jichihan's text, while appropriating the chanted *nenbutsu* and other Amidist elements, deathbed practice becomes a meditation ritual for realizing union with the Buddha; any notion of the Pure Land as a separate realm is thoroughly subsumed within what is essentially an empowerment rite for realizing *sokushin jōbutsu*. Kakukai's *Hōgo* adopts the same non-dual perspective but directs it toward a different conclusion altogether, one in which insight into the omnipresence of Dainichi Nyorai's realm must entail a rejection of both aspiration to any specific pure land and any special form of deathbed practice. In marked contrast to both these works, however, Kakuban's *Ichigo taiyō himitsu shū* allows the tension between the two goals to stand, both maintaining a non-dual perspective in which the Buddha does not exist apart from one's own mind and yet also according notions of "going to the Pure Land" at least a provisional validity. This produces a double logic in which non-dual esoteric *doctrine* is used to repudiate the concept of birth in the Pure Land as a separate realm, even as esoteric *practice* is offered as the most efficacious vehicle for achieving it. The result is a dynamic tension in which the two perspectives are asserted concurrently and the opposition between them allowed to stand. While perhaps not as conceptually consistent as either Jichihan's *Byōchū shugyō ki* or Kakukai's *Hōgo*, Kakuban's *Himitsu shū* offers a more complex and, for many, perhaps more emotionally satisfying prospect in which, so to speak, all bases are covered, and the requirements of both goals, direct realization of buddhahood and birth in the Pure Land, can be simultaneously fulfilled.

Notes

Some of the material in this chapter represents a revision of portions of my essay "Death," in *Critical Terms for the Study of Buddhism*, ed. Donald S. Lopez, Jr. (Chicago: University of Chicago Press, 2005), 56–76. I thank the University of Chicago Press for permission to use it here. I would also like to thank Robert Gimello and Ryūichi Abé for their close reading of earlier versions of this chapter and their cogent suggestions for revision.

1. On the construction of *mikkyō* as a category in early Japan, see Ryūichi Abé, *The Weaving of Mantra: Kūkai and the Construction of Esoteric Buddhist Discourse* (New York: Columbia University Press, 1999).

2. See Hisao Inagaki, "Kūkai's 'Principle of Attaining Buddhahood with the Present Body'" (1975), reprinted in *Tantric Buddhism in East Asia*, ed. Richard K. Payne (Somerville, MA: Wisdom Publications, 2006), 99–118. Not all Buddhist teachers identified *sokushin jōbutsu* with the esoteric teachings, however. Kūkai's contemporary, Saichō (766/767–822), founder of the Japanese Tendai school, asserted the same doctrine as a distinguishing feature of the *Lotus Sūtra*. See Paul Groner, "The *Lotus Sutra* and Saichō's Interpretation of the Realization of Buddhahood with This Very Body," in *The Lotus Sutra in Japanese Culture*, ed. George J. Tanabe, Jr. and Willa Jane Tanabe (Honolulu: University of Hawai'i Press, 1989), 53–74.

3. On this point see Motoyama Kōju, "Shingon mikkyō to ōjō shisō," in *Kōgyō Daishi Kakuban kenkyū* (hereafter *KDKK*), ed. Kōgyō Daishi Kenkyū Ronshū Henshū Iinkai (Tokyo: Shunjūsha, 1992), 736–38.

4. Abé Ryūichi, "Mikkyō girei to kenmitsu bukkyō: Myōe-bō Kōben no nyūmetsu girei o megutte," in *Chūsei bukkyō no tenkai to sono kiban*, ed. Imai Masaharu (Tokyo: Daizō Shuppan, 2002), 40–42. As Abé argues, this characterization is linked to a distinction made in Shingon sectarian scholarship between "pure *mikkyō*" (*junmitsu*), based on Kūkai's teaching of *sokushin jōbutsu* and concerned with contemplative practice for realizing the unity of Dainichi Nyorai and the practitioner, and "miscellaneous *mikkyō*" (*zōmitsu*), or rites directed toward other deities for healing, prosperity, or other pragmatic aims—a distinction that also privileges doctrinal writings over ritual manuals. However, recent studies have shown that the hierarchical categories of "pure" and "miscellaneous" *mikkyō* did not appear in Shingon scholarship until the late seventeenth or early eighteenth century and thus reflect notions of *mikkyō* orthodoxy that did not become normative until long after the Heian period. On this issue see Misaki Ryōshū: "'Junmitsu to zōmitsu' ni tsuite," *Indogaku bukkyōgaku kenkyū* (hereafter *IBK*) 15, no. 2 (1967): 535–40, and *Taimitsu no kenkyū* (Tokyo: Sōbunsha, 1988), 146–65, as well as Abé, *The Weaving of Mantra*, 152–54, 178, 271.

5. Several of these scriptures are listed in Izumi Kōyō, "Mikkyō ni

okeru Mida shisō," in *Amida shinkō*, ed. Itō Yuishin (Tokyo: Yūzankaku Shuppan, 1984), 220–24. Izumi categorizes these texts as "miscellaneous *mikkyō*" (*zōmitsu*); again, however, this characterization represents a historically recent notion of Shingon orthodoxy. There is no evidence that Heian practitioners understood rites for achieving birth in the Pure Land to be an adulterated or lesser form of esoteric teaching.

6. *Dale jingang bukong zhenshi sanmeiye jing boru boluomiduo liqushi*, *T* no. 1003, 19:612b–c. On the *Rishukyō*, see note 28 below.

7. *Wuliangshou rulai guanxing gongyang yigui*, *T* no. 930, 19:67c, 69b, and 70b.

8. *Nihon ōjō gokuraku ki* 6, in *Ōjōden, Hokke genki, Zoku Nihon bukkyō shisō* (hereafter *ZNBS*) 1, ed. Inoue Mitsusada and Ōsone Shōsuke, reprint of the 1974 *Nihon shisō taikei* 7 (Tokyo: Iwanami Shoten, 1995), 1:21.

9. *Nihon ōjō gokuraku ki* 19, *ZNBS* 1:30.

10. Ibid., 20, *ZNBS* 1:30.

11. *Shinkō Kōya shunjū hennnen shūroku* 4, ed. Hinonishi Shinjō (Tokyo: Meicho Shuppan, 1982), 56a.

12. For further examples, see Abé, "Mikkyō girei to kenmitsu bukkyō," 39–40.

13. *Ryōgon'in nijūgo zanmai kesshū kakochō* (hereafter *Kakochō*), *Zoku Tendaishū zensho* (hereafter *ZTZ*), *Shiden* 2, ed. Tendai Shūten Hensanjo (Tokyo: Shunjūsha, 1988), 277–91. This record, begun in 1013, records the names of fifty-one monks who belonged to the Nijūgo Zanmai-e. For seventeen of them, a short biography is included, describing their practices during life and at the time of death, as well as their success—or in a few cases, failure—in achieving *ōjō*, such outcomes being communicated in dreams to surviving society members. The purpose of the record may have been to compile just such "proof" that the society's practices did indeed lead to birth in the Pure Land. See Robert F. Rhodes, "Seeking the Pure Land in Heian Japan: The Practices of the Monks of the Nijūgo Zanmai-e," *Eastern Buddhist* n. s. 33, no. 1 (2000): 56–79.

14. *Kakochō*, *ZTZ*, *Shiden* 2:281a.

15. Ibid., 2:282a.

16. Ibid., 2:285a–b. The *Amida kuyō hō* or *Amida hō* was based on the *Wuliangshou yigui* (see note 7) and is said to bring about birth in Amida's Pure Land.

17. *Kakochō*, *ZTZ*, *Shiden* 2:290a. The longer and shorter Amida spells, based on the *Wuliangshou yigui*, are two versions of the Amida dhāraṇī, whose recitation is said to eradicate sins and bring about birth in the Pure Land. The Sonshō Daibutchō or Sonshō Butchō (Skt. *uṣṇīṣavijayā*) dhāraṇī is the dhāraṇī of the Buddha Sonshō Butchō (a.k.a. Butchō Sonshō), a personification of the knot of flesh, one of a buddha's thirty-two superior marks, on the crown of Śākyamuni Buddha's head. Recitation of this

dhāraṇī was said to eradicate sin and prolong life. In translating the name of this dhāraṇī as "Superlative Spell," I follow Paul Copp, "Voice, Dust, Shadow, Stone: Forms of Dhāraṇīs in Medieval China," Ph.D. diss. (Princeton University, 2005), 40–44. The Arorikkia mantra refers to the dhāraṇī of Tara (Skt. Tārā), a manifestation of Kannon. The esoteric deity Butsugen (a.k.a. Butsugen Butsumo)—literally, "Buddha-eye, Buddha-mother"—symbolizes the wisdom of the buddhas.

18. *Kakochō, ZTZ, Shiden* 2:287b, 286b. The fifteen kinds of undesirable death are (1) to die of starvation and poverty; (2) to be put in stocks and tortured to death; (3) to be murdered by someone with a grudge; (4) to die in battle; (5) to be killed by a ferocious animal, such as a wildcat or wolf; (6) to be bitten to death by snakes or scorpions; (7) to be burned to death or to be drowned; (8) to die of poisoning; (9) to die of intestinal worms; (10) to die of madness; (11) to die by falling off trees or cliffs; (12) to die from curses; (13) to die through the acts of evil spirits; (14) to die of evil diseases; and (15) to commit suicide (*Qianshou quianyan dabeixin jing, T* no. 1060, 20:107b; trans. from Robert F. Rhodes, "Pure Land Practitioner or *Lotus* Devotee? On the Earliest Biographies of Genshin," *Japanese Religions* 21, no. 1 (1996): 37n13. See also the biography of Genshin in *Zoku honchō ōjōden* 9, *ZNBS* 1:232–36. On the Mantra of Light, see note 21 below.

19. *Ōjō yōshū, Genshin, Nihon shisō taikei* (hereafter *NST*), 6, ed. Ishida Mizumaro (Tokyo: Iwanami Shoten, 1970), 254.

20. *Zoku honchō ōjōden* 10, *ZNBS* 1:236. Kakuchō is known to have composed a treatise, no longer extant, on the moon-disk contemplation. See entry under "Gatsurinkan" in *Bussho kaisetsu daijiten*, ed. Ono Genmyō (1933–36; rev. ed. Tokyo: Daitō Shuppan, 1964–67), 2:78d.

21. The major textual sources for the Mantra of Light (*kōmyō shingon*) are the esoteric scripture *Bukong juansuo shenbian zhenyan jing* (*T* no. 1092); the ritual manual *Bukong juansuo Piluzhenafo daguanding guangzhenyan* (*T* no. 1002), translated by Amoghavajra; and the ritual manual *Kōmyō shingon giki*, a Japanese apocryphon. Chanting this mantra over sand 108 times and then sprinkling the sand thus empowered over the bodies or graves of the deceased is said to release those dead from the realms of suffering and enable their birth in Amida's Pure Land. On this practice in Heian Japan, see Kushida Ryōkō, *Shingon mikkyō seiritsu katei no kenkyū* (Tokyo: Sankibō Busshorin, 1964), 153–80, and Hayami Tasuku, *Heian kizoku shakai to bukkyō* (Tokyo: Yoshikawa Kōbunkan, 1975), 165–202.

Funerary use of the *kōmyō shingon* is specified in both sets of regulations extant for the Nijūgo Zanmai-e, the 986 *Kishō hachikajō*, attributed to Yoshishige no Yasutane (article 2), and the 988 *Yokawa Shuryōgon'in nijūgo zanmai kishō*, attributed to Genshin (article 4). The critical edition of both texts has been published in Koyama Shōjun, "Tōdaiji Chūshōin shozō

'Yokawa Shuryōgon'in nijūgo zanmai Eshin Yasutane rinjū gyōgi' no saikentō: Sōshobon no goshoku ni yoru mondaiten," *Bukkyōgaku kenkyū* 53 (1997): 56–95 (see 86–87 and 76). On the society's use of the Mantra of Light, see Hayami, *Heian kizoku shakai to bukkyō*, 170–73.

22. On these communities, as well as Pure Land practices on Mt. Kōya more broadly, see Inoue Mitsusada, *Nihon Jōdokyō seiritsushi no kenkyū* (Tokyo: Yamakawa Shuppan, 1956; rev. ed. 1975), 335–82 *passim*; Wada Akio, "Kōyasan ni okeru Kamakura bukkyō," in *Kamakura bukkyō keisei no mondaiten*, ed. Nihon Bukkyō Gakkai (Kyoto: Heirakuji Shoten, 1969), 79–95; and Gorai Shigeru, *Kōya hijiri* (Tokyo: Kadokawa Shoten, 1975).

23. *Kōyasan ōjōden* 1, *ZNBS* 1:696.

24. Hayami, *Heian kizoku shakai to bukkyō*, 183–96.

25. *Shūi ōjōden* II:19, *ZNBS* 1:374.

26. *Zoku honchō ōjōden* 5, *ZNBS* 1:228.

27. *Shūi ōjōden* I:11, *ZNBS* 1:297; cf. *Kōyasan ōjōden* 3, 1:696–97.

28. *Shūi ōjōden* III:13, *ZNBS* 1:369. The *rishu zanmai* service involves chanting of the esoteric scripture *Rishukyō* (Ch. *Liqu jing*), along with other incantations. Reciting the *Rishukyō* was said to remove sins and karmic hindrances and to protect the practitioner from falling into the hells. Several versions of this scripture exist (see *T* nos. 240, 241, 242, 243, 244, as well as fascicle 578 of the 600-fascicle *Dabore jing*, *T* no. 220).

29. *Nihon ōjō gokuraku ki* 16, *ZNBS* 1:27–28.

30. Ibid., 37, *ZNBS* 1:38–39.

31. *Zoku honchō ōjōden* 27, *ZNBS* 1:244–45; *Sange ōjōden* 37, *ZNBS* 1:678; *Kōyasan ōjōden* 7, *ZNBS* 1:698.

32. *Honchō shinshū ōjōden* 6, *ZNBS* 1:684.

33. *Kōyasan ōjōden* 22, *ZNBS* 1:701. The "Land of Esoteric Splendor" (*mitsugon kokudo*, *mitsugonkoku*, *mitsugon jōdo*, etc.) refers to the realm where the body, mouth, and mind of the cosmic Buddha Dainichi are united with the body, mouth, and mind of the esoteric adept through practice of the three secrets. It is mentioned in the *Dasheng miyan jing* (*T* nos. 681 and 682), *Jingangfeng louge yiqie yujia yuqi jing* (*T* no. 867), and *Putixin lun* (*T* no. 1665). The concept of Esoteric Splendor as a pure land undergoes development in the thought of Kakuban, for example, in his *Mitsugon jōdo ryakkan*.

34. *Kōyasan ōjōden* 33, *ZNBS* 1:703. Nōgan's example is significant in light of the adaptations of three secrets contemplation practice to the time of death, discussed below.

35. *Shūi ōjōden* I:17, *ZNBS* 1:305–6; *Kōyasan ōjōden* 4, *ZNBS* 1:697–98. The bodhisattva Saihōin (a.k.a. Kongōin) is one of four bodhisattvas attending Muryōju or Amida as he appears in the perfected body assembly (*jōjinne*), the central assembly of the Diamond Realm maṇḍala. There, Muryō-

ju Nyorai is one of four directional buddhas surrounding Dainichi, each of whom is seated inside a moon disk and attended by four bodhisattvas.

36. *Keiran shūyōshū* 86, *T* no. 2410, 76:781b. The *Kōyasan Daidenbōin hongan reizui narabi ni jike engi*, a biography of the esoteric master Kakuban (1095–1143) said to be have been compiled by one Kakuman of Negoroji in 1292, mentions some disagreement among Kakuban's disciples as to whether he had faced west or north at the time of his death and concludes that he must have faced north (*Kōgyō Daishi denki shiryō zenshū*, 3 vols., ed. Miura Akio [Tokyo: Pitaka, 1977], 1:39). Since both these sources date from around the late Kamakura period (1185–1333), their accounts of the death of Saigyō and Kakuban may represent retrospective claims.

37. For example, the constantly walking samādhi (*jōgyō zanmai*), of one the four samādhis of the Tendai (Ch. Tiantai) school, originally involved the visualization of Amida with the aim of realizing the identity of the practitioner and the Buddha. See Daniel B. Stevenson, "The Four Kinds of Samādhi in Early T'ien-t'ai Buddhism," in *Traditions of Meditation in Chinese Buddhism*, ed. Peter N. Gregory (Honolulu: University of Hawai'i Press, 1986), 45–97 (59–61). (On Mt. Hiei, however, this meditation would be transformed into a rite for eradicating sin and achieving birth in the Pure Land. See Sonoda Kōyū, "Yama no nenbutsu: Sono kigen to seikaku," 1968; reprinted in his *Heian bukkyō no kenkyū* [Kyoto: Hōzōkan, 1981], 163–91, and Paul Groner, *Ryōgen and Mount Hiei: Japanese Tendai in the Tenth Century* [Honolulu: University of Hawai'i Press, 2002], 175–79.) Another example is that strand of medieval Tendai original enlightenment (*hongaku*) literature stressing the non-duality of the Amida and the practitioner and including a number of apocryphal texts on that theme retrospectively attributed to Genshin. See, for example, Hanano Mitsuaki (a.k.a. Hanano Jūdō), "Chūko Tendai bunken to nenbutsu shisō," included in Satō Tetsuei, *Eizan Jōdokyō no kenkyū* (Kyoto: Hyakkaen, 1979), 318–46.

38. The *rinjū gyōgi* section of the *Ōjō yōshū* may be found in *NST* 6:206–17. For a partial translation, see James C. Dobbins, "Genshin's Deathbed Nembutsu Ritual in Pure Land Buddhism," in *Religions of Japan in Practice*, ed. George J. Tanabe, Jr. (Princeton, NJ: Princeton University Press, 1999), 166–75.

39. *Sifenlü shanfan bujue xingshi chao*, *T* no. 1804, 40:144a, cited in *Ōjō yōshū*, *NST* 6:206.

40. *Guannian famen*, *T* no. 1959, 47:24b–c, cited in *Ōjō yōshū*, *NST* 6:207.

41. *Anleji*, *T* 1958, no. 47:11b, cited in *Ōjō yōshū*, *NST* 6:208. The "ten moments of reflection" here refers, on one hand, to the famous eighteenth vow of Amida, which promises birth in his Pure Land to all who aspire to this goal with sincerity and call him to mind "even ten times" (*Wuliangshou*

jing, *T* no. 360, 12:268a). It also refers to the *Contemplation Sūtra*'s claims that even an evil person, if he encounters a good friend (*zenchishiki*) who instructs him at the hour of death so that he is able to sustain ten thoughts of Amida, shall, with each thought, erase the sins of eight billion kalpas and be born in Amida's Pure Land (*Guan wuliangshou jing*, *T* no. 365, 12:346a). Exactly how these "ten thoughts" should be understood was a matter of considerable debate and was embedded in a larger controversy over the respective merits of the contemplative visualization of Amida or the chanting of his name. Genshin took "ten continuous *nenbutsu*" at the time of death to mean reflecting upon Amida, aided by the invocation of his name. While his general approach to Pure Land practice focused upon visualization and contemplation, he also held that under the liminal influence of approaching death, the chanted *nenbutsu* becomes vastly more powerful than it is at ordinary times (*Ōjō yōshū*, *NST* 6:296).

42. These are described in *Kishō hachikajō*, articles 4–6, and *Yokawa Shuryōgon'in nijūgo zanmai kishō*, articles 7–8. See Koyama, "Tōdaiji Chūshōin shozō 'Yokawa Shuryōgon'in nijūgo zanmai Eshin Yasutane rinjū gyōgi' no saikentō," 88–90 and 79–80.

43. On Jichihan, see Satō Tetsuei, "Nakanokawa Jichihan no shōgai to sono Jōdokyō," *Mikkyō bunka*, nos. 71–72 (1965): 21–52, and Marc Bunjisters, "Jichihan and the Restoration and Innovation of Buddhist Practice," *Japanese Journal of Religious Studies* 26, nos. 1–2 (1999): 39–82. I have followed Bunjisters in using the pronunciation "Jichihan."

44. *Byōchū shugyō ki*, *Shingonshū anjin zensho* (hereafter *SAZ*), ed. Hase Hōshū (Kyoto: Rokudaishinbōsha, 1913–14), 2:781–85. I am indebted to James Sanford for introducing me to this text. For discussion, see Ōtani Teruo, "Jichihan *Byōchū shugyō ki* ni tsuite," *Bukkyō bunka kenkyū* 13 (1966): 43–58.

45. *Byōchū shugyō ki*, *SAZ* 2:785.

46. For more on the determinative power of the last thought, see Jacqueline Stone, "By the Power of One's Last Nenbutsu: Deathbed Practices in Early Medieval Japan," in *Approaching the Land of Bliss: Religious Praxis in the Cult of Amitābha*, ed. Richard K. Payne and Kenneth K. Tanaka (Honolulu: University of Hawai'i Press, 2004), 77–119.

47. *Byōchū shugyō ki*, article 3, *SAZ* 2:782.

48. On use of the Lotus repentance rite at the time of death, see Takagi Yutaka, "Ōjōden ni okeru Hokke shinkō," in *Hokke shinkō no shokeitai*, ed. Nomura Yōshō (Kyoto: Heirakuji, 1976), 451–84 (468–77).

49. The notion that "contemplating the true aspect" can dissolve karmic hindrances by awakening insight into their conditioned, nonsubstantial nature is certainly not limited to the esoteric teachings. Cf. the *Guan Puxian Pusa xingfa jing* (Sūtra on the practice of contemplating Bodhisattva Samantabhadra): "The sea of all karmic hindrances/arises from

deluded thought./If you wish to perform repentance,/sit upright and contemplate the true aspect./The myriad sins are like frost and dew,/which the sun of wisdom can dispel" (*T* no. 277, 9:393b). The Tendai school refers to this as "repentance in terms of principle" (J. *risan*) (e.g., *Tiantai sijiaoyi, T* no. 1931, 46:779a).

50. This has been pointed out by Ōtani ("Jichihan *Byōchū shugyō ki* ni tsuite," 50). As Bunjisters notes ("Jichihan and the Restoration," 66), Ōtani's reading stands in diametric contrast to that of other scholars who have taken this statement as indicating that Jichihan was still under the influence of exoteric readings of the Pure Land as a realm far remote from this present world. See, for example, Satō, "Nakanokawa Jichihan no shōgai to sono Jōdokyō," 38, and Kushida Ryōkō, *Kakuban no kenkyū* (Tokyo: Yoshikawa Kōbunkan, 1975), 175–77.

51. *Byōchū shugyō ki,* article 6, *SAZ* 783–84.

52. Contemplation of the white curl is included in the ninth of sixteen visualizations for achieving birth in Amida's land set forth in the *Contemplation Sūtra*. The sūtra speaks of Amida's light emanating from this auspicious mark and embracing all those who think of him; it also suggests the white curl as a point of entry for beginning visualization of Amida's body (*Guan wuliangshou jing, T* 12:343b, c). Genshin assimilates this contemplation to deathbed practice in his seventh and eighth points of encouragement to the dying (*Ōjō yōshū* 2, *NST* 6:212–14).

53. Article 7, *SAZ* 2:784. In the latter Heian period, after Genshin's time, "contemplation of the white curl" (*byakugōkan*) underwent considerable development. Sueki Fumihiko has noted a connection between this reference in Jichihan's *Byōchū shugyō ki* and roughly contemporaneous Japanese Tendai Pure Land works recommending meditation on the white curl between Amida's brows as encompassing various doctrinal categories such as the three bodies or threefold truth (*Kamakura bukkyō keisei ron* [Kyoto: Hōzōkan, 1998], 325–29).

54. *Guan wuliangshou jing shu,* T no. 1753, 37:268a; trans. Julian Pas, *Visions of Sukāvatī: Shan-Tao's Commentary on the Kuan Wu-liang-Shou-Fo Ching* (Albany: State University of New York Press, 1995), 272–73.

55. Ōtani, "Jichihan *Byōchū shugyō ki* ni tsuite," 52–53; see also Bunjisters, "Jichihan and the Restoration," 67–68.

56. For an overview of this practice in Japan and its continental antecedents, see Richard K. Payne, "Ajikan: Ritual and Meditation in the Shingon Tradition," in *Re-Visioning "Kamakura" Buddhism,* ed. Richard K. Payne (Honolulu: University of Hawai'i Press, 1998), 219–48. Payne's observation (221)—that *ajikan* is both meditation *and* ritual—holds true for a number of esoteric rites and practices.

57. *Byōchū shugyō ki,* article 8, *SAZ* 2:784. This interpretative structure is very close to that of the Tendai threefold truth, in which the extremes of

"emptiness" (*kū*) and "conventional existence" (*ke*) are simultaneous affirmed and negated by the Middle (*chū*), and may reflect the influence of Jichihan's Tendai studies.

58. This passage bears some structural similarity to the equation in medieval Tendai thought of the three characters A-mi-da with the threefold truth of emptiness, conventional existence, and the Middle Way. See, for example, Sueki Fumihiko, "Amida santai-setsu o megutte," *Indogaku bukkyōgaku kenkyū* 28, no. 1 (1979): 216–22.

59. Recommendations for simplified forms of deathbed *ajikan*—often simply forming the sound "A" with one's last breath—seem to have been widespread during the latter part of the Kamakura period. See, for example, the references to this practice in *Buppō yume monogatari* by the Shingon master Chidō (latter thirteenth century) (in *Kana hōgo shū, Nihon koten bungaku taikei* [hereafter *NKBT*] 83, ed. Miyasaka Yūshō [Tokyo: Iwanami Shoten, 1964], 222–23, trans. William M. Bodiford, "Chidō's *Dreams of Buddhism*," in Tanabe, ed., *Religions of Japan in Practice*, 242–43; the *Hakuun Oshō yume no ki* of Hakuun Egyō (1223–97), a disciple of the Zen teacher Enni (*Dai Nihon bukkyō zensho* [hereafter *DNBZ*], ed. Suzuki Gakujutsu Zaidan [Tokyo: Suzuki Gakujutsu Zaidan, 1970–73], 48:269b); and the *Kōyōshū*, attributed to Kakuban but almost certainly a later work (*DNBZ* 43:30b–c). Also, Enkyō, abbess of Hokkeji, writing in 1304 about the nuns active in the Kamakura-period revival of her temple, names several women who passed away while contemplating the A syllable (*Hokke metsuzaiji engi, Yamato koji taikan*, ed. Iwanami Kojirō [Tokyo: Iwanami Shoten, 1976–78], 5:142b–143a). I am indebted to Lori Meeks for providing me with this reference. The relevant passage is translated in her "Nuns, Court Ladies, and Female Bodhisattvas: The Women of Japan's Medieval Ritsu-School Nuns' Revival Movement," Ph.D. diss. (Princeton University, 2003), 142–44.

60. When he learned of Jichihan's death, the courtier Fujiwara no Yorinaga (1120–51) noted in his diary that people said the holy man would surely be born in Amida's land, to which he had aspired for many years (*Taiki*, Ten'yō 1 [1144], 9/10, *Zōho shiryō taisei*, ed. Zōho Shiryō Taisei Kankōkai [Kyoto: Rinsen Shobō, 1965], 23:128b). See also Bunjisters, "Jichihan and the Restoration," 75–76.

61. For example, Kushida Ryōkō, *Shingon mikkyō seiritsu katei no kenkyū*, 187–88, and *Kakuban no kenkyū*, 175–77. Outside the realm of sectarian scholarship, a very different view has been voiced by Ryūichi Abé, who sees the *Byōchū shugyō ki* as a "conservative" text, emphasizing Shingon non-dual orthodoxy ("Mikkyō girei to kenmitsu bukkyō," 42).

62. Nichiren, for example, writes that a person of wisdom awakened to the *Lotus Sūtra* who makes offerings before the corpse of a deceased person

enables that individual to achieve buddhahood "in this body" (*Mokue nizō kaigen no koto, Shōwa teihon Nichiren Shōnin ibun*, ed. Risshō Daigaku Nichiren Kyōgaku Kenkyūjo (Minobu-chō, Yamanashi: Minobusan Kuonji, rev. 1988), 1:794. In the early modern period, successful cases of ascetic "self-mummification" were also spoken of as instances of *sokushin jōbutsu*. See Ichirō Hori, "Self-Mummified Buddhas in Japan: An Aspect of the Shugen-dō ('Mountain Asceticism') Sect," *History of Religions* 1, no. 2 (1962): 222–42. When the term first came to be used in this context remains to be determined.

63. The *Ichigo taiyō himitsu shū* is included in *Kōgyō Daishi zenshū* (hereafter *KDZ*), ed. Tomita Kōjun (1935; reprint Tokyo: Hōsenji, 1977), 2:1197–1220, and *Kōgyō Daishi senjutsu shū* (hereafter *KDS*), ed. Miyasaka Yūshō (Tokyo: Sankibō Busshorin, 1977; rev. 1989), 157–76. The *KDZ* version preserves the original *kanbun*; *KDS* has been rendered into Japanese and includes notes.

The *Ichigo taiyō himitsu shū* is virtually identical to the sixth and sole extant fascicle of the *Jūnen Gokuraku iōshū*, compiled by the monk Butsugon (fl. late twelfth century), himself of Kakuban's Denbōin lineage (see Ōya Tokujō, "Butsugon to *Jūnen Gokuraku iōshū*: Fujiwara Kanezane no shinkō ni kansuru gimon," 1924; reprinted in his *Nihon bukkyōshi no kenkyū* [Tokyo: Kokusho Kankōkai, 1927; reprinted 1988], 3:258–76). Entries in the diary of the regent Kujō Kanezane (1149–1207) record that Butsugon showed Kanezane a work in six fascicles called *Jūnen Gokuraku iōshū* and that Butsugon had "compiled it by order of the retired sovereign [Goshirakawa]" (see *Gyokuyō*, Angen 2 [1176], 11/30, and Jishō 1 [1177], 10/2). On this basis, some influential scholars, notably Ishida Mizumaro, have argued that the *Himitsu shū* is not Kakuban's work but Butsugon's (*Jōdokyō no tenkai* [Tokyo: Shunjūsha, 1967], 212–14). Inoue Mitsusada also treats it as Butsugon's work (*Nihon Jōdokyo seiritsushi no kenkyū*, 362–64). However, cogent arguments for Kakuban's authorship had already been advanced by Takase Shōgon, who noted the similarity in content between the *Himitsu shū* and other works of Kakuban related to Pure Land thought, especially the *Gorin kuji myō himitsu shaku* and *Amida hishaku*; he also noted that Goshirakawa had asked Butsugon to "compile" (not "compose") the *Jūnen Gokuraku iōshū*. In all probability, Takase argued, Butsugon had simply included Kakuban's *Himitsu shū* in an anthology and was not himself its author ("Jūnen Gokuraku iōshū kō," *Bukkyōgaku* 1, no. 6 [1924]: 32–48). Kakuban's authorship has also been upheld by Matsuzaki Keisui ("Kōgyō Daishi Kakuban no *Ichigo taiyō himitsu shū* ni tsuite," *IBK* 20, no. 2 [1972]: 251–55); Kushida Ryōkō (*Kakuban no kenkyū* [Tokyo: Yoshikawa Kōbunkan, 1975], 165); Sakagami Masao, "Butsugon-bō Shōshin ni tsuite," *Bukkyō ronsō* 26 (1982): 145–49; and Wada Shūjō, "*Jūnen Gokuraku iōshū* ni tsuite," *IBK* 32, no. 1 (1983): 1–10. Wada gives an especially detailed account of the debate over Kakuban's authorship. I have treated the *Himitsu shū* here as Kakuban's work.

64. On Kakuban, see, for example, Kushida, *Kakuban no kenkyū*, and Matsuzaki Keisui, *Heian mikkyō no kenkyū: Kōgyō Daishi Kakuban o chūshin toshite* (Tokyo: Yoshikawa Kōbunkan, 2002), as well as the essays in *KDKK*. In English, see Ryūichi Abé, "From Kūkai to Kakuban: A Study of Shingon Buddhist Dharma Transmission," Ph.D. diss. (Columbia University, 1991); Hendrik van der Veere, *Kakuban Shōnin: The Life and Works of Kōgyō Daishi* (Tokyo: Nombre, 1998); and, on Kakuban's *nenbutsu* thought in particular, James H. Sanford, "Amida's Secret Life: Kakuban's *Amida hishaku*, in Payne and Tanaka, eds., *Approaching the Land of Bliss*, 120–38.

65. For a detailed comparison of the two texts, see Kushida, *Kakuban no kenkyū*, 159–77.

66. *KDZ* 2:1197; *KDS* 157. The "nine grades" is a reference to nine levels of birth in the Pure Land (*kuhon ōjō*), corresponding to the degree of the practitioner's spiritual cultivation (*Guan wuliangshou jing, T* 12:344c–346a).

67. See Ryūichi Abé, "Bridging Ritual and Text: Kakuban's Writing on Meditative Practice," *KDKK* 1076–1073 (reverse pagination), and van der Veere, *Kakuban Shōnin*, 161–64.

68. Kakuban discusses the two meditations in article 6 of the *Himitsu shū* (*KDZ* 2:1201–13; *KDS* 160–72). Here he follows the *Putixin lun*, which specifies three levels of *bodhicitta*, or aspiration for enlightenment: practice and vows to save living beings (J. *gyōgan bodaishin*); choosing superior teachings over inferior ones (*shōgi bodaishin*); and the *samādhi bodhicitta*, which is equal to the Buddha's own enlightenment (*T* no. 1665, 32:572c–573c).

69. *KDZ* 2:1215; *KDS* 173. Miyasaka notes that the phrase *shingon nenbutsu*—to contemplate the Buddha by means of mantra—has a "secret meaning" (*KDS* 361n60).

70. The removal to a separate hall and the enshrining of the object of worship are discussed in articles 3 and 4 respectively (*KDZ* 2:1199–1200; *KDS* 159). The admonition to bar entry to those who have recently consumed alcohol, meat, or pungent roots (article 8, *KDZ* 2:1215; *KDS* 173) derives from Shandao's *Guannian famen, T* 47:24b–c. Genshin quotes Shandao's admonition in his *Ōjō yōshū* (*NST* 6:207), and it is repeated in the majority of Japanese instructions for deathbed practice.

71. Article 8, *KDZ* 2:1214–16; *KDS* 173. Kakuban draws on the recommendation of Daochuo, also cited in *Ōjō yōshū*, that the practitioner should make a pact in advance with three to five persons of like mind who can assist one another at the time of death (*Anleji, T* 47:11b). The *Himitsu shū* is

ambiguous as to whether the dying person is included among a total of five individuals who have pledged to act together as *zenchishiki* or whether there are to be five *zenchishiki* in addition to the dying person. The above passage specifies tasks for five attendants at the deathbed, but the instruction that "all four should chant together" and the reference to the "five kinds of wisdom" suggest that there are only five persons present *in toto*, including the dying person.

72. Article 8, *KDZ* 2:1216–17; *KDS* 173–74.

73. *Guan wuliangshou jing, T* 12:341c–342a.

74. Kushida, *Kakuban no kenkyū*, 205.

75. See ibid., 201–7, and James H. Sanford, "Breath of Life: The Esoteric Nenbutsu," in *Esoteric Buddhism in Japan* (1994); reprinted in Payne, ed., *Tantric Buddhism in East Asia*, 161–89.

76. *T* no. 997, 19:574a.

77. Article 9, *KDZ* 2:1217–19; *KDS* 174–76.

78. See, for example, Haseo Fumiaki, "Shingonkei rinjū gyōgi ni okeru sōsō to no kanren," *Bukkyō ronsō* 32 (1988): 125–29.

79. Unidentified. This appears to be Kakuban's interpretation, as Shanwuwei, to my knowledge, does not contrast "exoteric" and "esoteric" in this way.

80. Article 7, *KDZ* 2:1214; *KDS* 172.

81. See, for example, Kushida, *Kakuban no kenkyū*, 175–84; Tachibana Nobuo, "*Ichigo taiyō himitsu shū* ni okeru 'rinjū gyōgi' ni tsuite," *IBK* 36, no. 2 (1988): 131; and van der Veere, *Kakuban Shōnin*, 193–95.

82. Motoyama, "Shingon mikkyō to ōjō shisō," 740.

83. Article 6, *KDZ* 2:1211, 1213; *KDS* 169–70, 171.

84. See, for example, Kitao Ryūshin, "Kōgyō Daishi ni okeru ōjō ni tsuite: *Gorin kuji myō himitsu shaku* to *Ichigo taiyō himitsu shū* to no sōi o chūshin toshite," *IBK* 40, no. 2 (1992): 657–60; Tomobechi Seiichi, "Kōgyō Daishi Kakuban no kikonkan (1): Sokushin jōbutsu to jōdo ōjō," *Taishō Daigaku Sōgō Bukkyō Kenkyūjo nenpō* 15 (1993): 47–60; and Matsuzaki Keisui, "Jōbutsu shisō to ōjō shisō," in his *Heian mikkyō no kenkyū*, 599–619. An exception is Motoyama Kōju, who sees the *Himitsu shū* as foregrounding birth after death in a pure land ("Shingon mikkyō to ōjō shisō," 740–41). In regard to this issue, the *Ichigo taiyō himitsu shū* has often been read in conjunction with the *Gorin kuji myō himitsu shaku*, another of Kakuban's later works containing comparable statements relating *ōjō* and *sokushin jōbutsu* to the practitioner's capacity.

85. Kakuban's purely doctrinal writings on Pure Land themes place greater emphasis on the non-dual perspective. See, for example, his *Mitsugon jōdo ryakkan*, trans. in Abé, "From Kūkai to Kakuban," 414–24, or *Amida hishaku*, trans. in Sanford, "Amida's Secret Life," 128–33.

86. *SAZ* 2:792–75. I am indebted to James Sanford for introducing me to this text. For more on Dōhan's esoteric *nenbutsu* thought, see Sanford, "Breath of Life," 175–79.

87. Ibid., 2:793. Dōhan alludes here to A VI RA HŪṂ KHAṂ, the root mantra of Dainichi.

88. Ibid., 2:792.

89. A similar double logic appears in some Tendai texts that simultaneously acknowledge both the immanence of the Pure Land and its existence in the western direction. For example, "Even though one knows Amida Buddha to be one's own mind, one forms a relationship with Amida Buddha of the west and in this way manifests the Amida who is one's own mind. Thus, those who say that one should not contemplate the west because Amida is one's own mind commit a grave error" (*Jigyō nenbutsu mondō, DNBZ* 39:68c).

90. In *Kana hōgo shū, NKBT* 83:55–58; trans. with commentary by Robert E. Morrell in his *Early Kamakura Buddhism: A Minority Report* (Berkeley, CA: Asian Humanities Press, 1987), 89–102.

91. *NKBT* 83:57; trans. from Morrell, *Early Kamakura Buddhism*, 99–100, slightly modified.

92. Ibid.; trans. from Morrell, *Early Kamakura Buddhism*, 100, slightly modified. Gochi-bō Yūgen was a disciple and relative of Kakukai who practiced in reclusion on Mt. Kōya, and, indeed, there is no record of his last moments.

93. Kakukai is said to have died auspiciously, forming a secret mudrā of Dainichi (see entry for "Kakukai" in *Mikkyō jiten*, ed. Mikkyō Jiten Hensankai [Kyoto: Hōzōkan, 1931; rev. 1979], 1:215b). I have not yet been unable to identify the particular biography in which this element occurs.

5

The Deathbed Image of Master Hongyi

Raoul Birnbaum

We begin at the end with a haunting image, very still, a photograph of a Buddhist monk just after death (figure 5.1). He lies on a simple bed, no more than a wooden sleeping platform eased by what looks like a thin, straw-filled mattress. His body lies on its right side, with his right hand cradling his head, just so, his shoes neatly placed together below the bed. A faint smile remains upon his face.

The photo was taken in 1942 in the coastal city of Quanzhou, in China's Fujian Province. It circulated in the Buddhist world and then, in late 1996, resurfaced with a brief commentary in the first issue of *Lao zhaopian* (Old photos), a magazine widely available in large metropolitan bookstores in China. A Chinese poet and literary scholar who bought the magazine in Beijing and happened upon this image sent me a photocopy. The image had an effect on her, and she was not alone in this experience. The response to the deathbed photo was so strong that, remarkably, it was reprinted in *Lao zhaopian*'s second issue with further comments.[1]

Where does the power of this image reside? Since everyone dies and in that sense death is unremarkable, why should this particular photograph catch attention and cause thought and comment? Without knowing whose individual identity is associated with this body, one sees only the composed stillness of the moment.

Viewers in the early 1940s in China lived within a visual culture saturated with images of violent and untimely death resulting from the Japanese invasion and occupation, political assassinations and executions, and civil war and marauding bandits, as well as the sight of famine-defeated peasants collapsed by the roadside. The painter Feng Zikai (1898–1975), ordinarily gentle and even poetic in his work, produced an apt representation from this era, a bitter drawing of the effect of Japanese bombs dropped on the Chinese

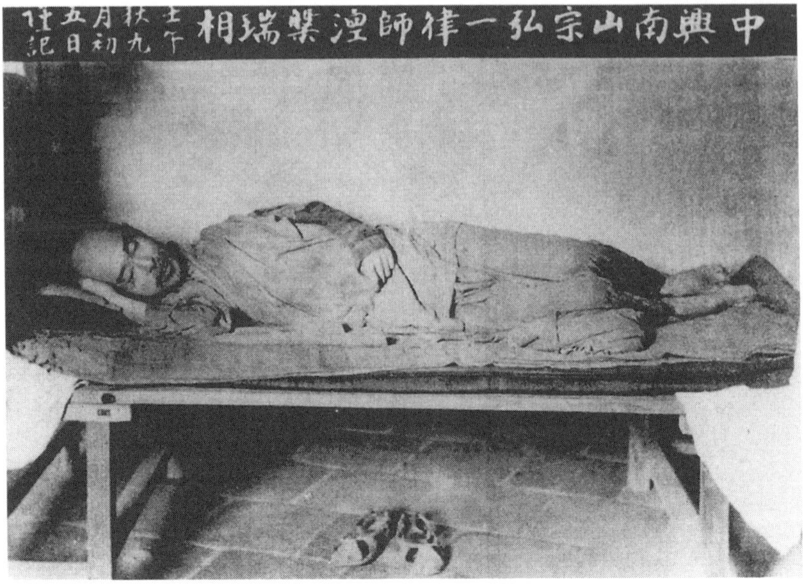

FIGURE 5.1. Master Hongyi on his deathbed, Quanzhou, 14 October 1942.

populace: a child's head blown off his body as his mother tries to carry him to safe shelter. He based it on a news photograph that his university students found amusing, unaccountably so to his way of thinking.[2] In such a difficult time, the deathbed photograph represented an alternative possibility.

Present-day viewers, here in the United States and in urban settings in China, also are accustomed to common grotesqueries in everyday life: the gory results of traffic collisions, suicide/homicide bombings, and wars brought home by television, not to mention the graphic, imagination-filling brutalities of hugely popular cinematic entertainment. And there is the apparatus of violent intervention produced as a matter of course in hospitals and other biomedical settings. How often does one witness a beautiful death?

This photograph does not record the final moments of a "generic monk" whose cremated ashes will be placed in a *putong ta* (common stūpa) and whose name soon will be lost to the winds of time. It is the last photograph of an enigmatic and romantic figure, the renowned Chinese Buddhist master Hongyi (1880–1942). (For an earlier image of the master, see figure 5.2.) Thus it forms part

FIGURE 5.2. Hongyi in 1937.

of his personal history, and it fits into particular contexts that can be explored. In Chinese Buddhist circles, Hongyi has been widely considered one of the most formidable Buddhist practitioners of this past century. He is viewed as a man who embodied Buddhist principles in a profound way in his everyday life. This opens up the realms of meaning that are the principal focus of exploration in this chapter—namely: What is the significance of the photo in thinking about this particular man, and, in a larger sense, what place can it be said to occupy within Chinese Buddhist worlds?

Hongyi was born in 1880 in the northern China city of Tianjin, the son of the youngest of four wives of a prominent salt merchant and banker.[3] Li Shutong (the lay name by which he is best known) grew up accustomed to wealth and privilege, and he was encouraged in his classical studies. His artistic and intellectual talents blossomed early, and by his late teens and twenties he already was well known, with books of poetry and seal-inscriptions published in his twentieth year. Like many ambitious and adventurous young men of his generation, he went to Japan to pursue higher studies. By the time of his return to China in 1910, Li Shutong was thoroughly steeped in what then was understood as "the modern." In his homeland, he was a major force in the transmission of these new views and literary-artistic practices. At age thirty-eight, following a period of internal questioning, discomfort, and even crisis, he became a Buddhist monk, sending a shock wave through the sophisticated world that he left behind.[4]

What did it mean to become a monk? What kind of new engagement, and what kind of disengagement, was expected? In this matter, there is both the invisible and the visible—not only changes in mental stance and habit, but also changes in bodily appearance and deportment. Because the deathbed photograph records the image of a body (this body expressing *something*), let us turn to this visible side of monastic practice.

Some Body Practices

As a privileged young man of a certain time and place, Li Shutong was a well-known habitué of Shanghai's most elegant pleasure-houses. In addition to his early arranged marriage and household in Tianjin, he also married a second wife, a Japanese woman who accompanied him to Shanghai when he returned from studies in Tokyo. In such matters, the general shape of his behavior was not extraordinary for a young man of his background. (After all, his father's household had four wives. There was a forty-eight-year age difference between Shutong's father and mother.)

Interests in the performance of gender resulted in Li Shutong's appearances during his student years in Tokyo as the "leading lady" in such stage dramas (in Chinese translation) as *La dame aux camélias* and *Uncle Tom's Cabin*, apparently to considerable acclaim. Photos record the moment and make clear the ability of the actor to embody a certain vision of femininity, which made possible a convincing portrayal of a female role. These portrayals were of a foreign femininity, the exotic "other" held in fascination and high regard, thus enhancing the dream-like fantasy that his performances embodied.

During his art training in Japan (1905–10), Li Shutong was exposed to Western methods of figure drawing, which require intensive scrutiny of unclothed models in the studio. He was the first to bring these methods to China and was famed for establishing a life-drawing studio for his students at the Zhejiang First Normal College in Hangzhou in 1913. A photograph records this studio, showing the rear view of a male model standing on a platform with students gathered round at work and teacher Li Shutong standing at the back wall.

Later in Hangzhou, Li Shutong complained of *shenjing shuairuo* (nerve weakness or neurasthenia, understood then in particular somatic terms; see below). He sought to cure himself by engaging in body practice and sustained a seventeen-day fasting regime carried out at a monastery at Hupao, a secluded site near Hangzhou's West Lake. According to his own account, it was this experience—a deliberate change in body practices in response to a perceived bodily complaint—that proved pivotal in his turn to Buddhist monastic life.[5]

When Hongyi (formerly Li Shutong) matured as a monk, he turned to the Vinaya, or monastic regulations, as a principal focus of study. Hongyi took seriously the final advice attributed to Śākyamuni Buddha as he prepared for death, when asked how monastic disciples should go on in his absence: "Take the precepts as your master."[6] With this credo in mind, Hongyi made thorough studies of the various systems of Buddhist precepts transmitted to China over many centuries. He sought to identify the most essential aspects and explicate them clearly for monastics and laypersons, so that these precepts could be seen as a viable and coherent set of guidelines for practical use. His studies and lectures on these regulations focused especially on the precepts that guide and restrain bodily activity. In this matter, Hongyi was more than a detached scholar. He was viewed by his peers as an exemplar of these precepts, as a quintessential "monk." He continued to work matters out through his body, as well as through his mind. The change from worldly aesthete to disciplined ascetic was profound. His dedication to self-transformation was severe, even frightening to some in its intensity.

Buddhist practice traditions in China thoroughly engage the body in specific ways. These particular types of engagement are central to the Buddhist monastic enterprise. There is an "ordinary body" created by all monks and nuns, who share certain highly visible characteristics in common. They establish a uniform body surface by regulated garments, scarification through burning on the fore-section of the scalp at the time of full ordination, and twice-monthly head shaving. Thus, an outsider can tell at a glance that this person is a monastic. In addition, many of the basic ways of using the body in daily life are transformed. Gestures, postures, facial expressions; modes of standing, walking, sitting, sleeping, bowing, and prostration: all these are learned and maintained through various disciplinary forces, and many of them are charged with specific meaning that is transmitted through both texts and oral teachings.

The ordinary body not only acts in certain ways, but it is also expected to refrain from certain types of acts. It does not deliberately harm any creature, and it is sustained by a vegetarian diet rather than by taking living creatures as food. It does not drink alcoholic beverages. It does not engage in sexual activity. These at least are basic precepts that all monks and nuns pledge to uphold.

The creation of this ordinary body is basic to the daily practices that are at the core of monastic life. It also is essential to the social maintenance of a Buddhist system within China, for the ordinary body is distinctive in relation to the rest of Chinese society. This ordinary body separates itself from the mainstream of Chinese society, and through the regularity of its features and modes of daily performance, it merges with the order of the Buddhist monastic community.[7]

Against this background of ordinary discipline, to which all monks and nuns are expected to submit, there also are special practices that create extraordinary bodies and mark certain figures with heroic valor in this system: the ascetic bodies of those who hold to the traditional "bitter practices," the singed bodies of those who burn fingers as offerings or mark their arms and torsos with "incense scars" to seal vows, the textualized bodies of those who copy out scriptures using their own blood as ink, the hidden bodies of retreatants, and the highly visible martial bodies of fighting monks.

One expression of Hongyi's commitment and intensity was his custom of going on frequent retreat, from sealed retreats (*biguan*), lasting three to six months, to very quiet periods during the annual summer retreat (*anju*) season. These were periods of especially concentrated internal practice. (Even in times of extensive public activity, when he gave daily lectures, there were periods when he was mainly hidden from view, except for the moment of the lectures.) In such retreats, the body may be made invisible, hidden from the sight of others, but in these circumstances one's mind is especially visible to oneself. This penchant for retreat practices is a sign of a quality of engagement in Buddhist practices that separated Hongyi from dilettantes.

If one truly changes one's body habits, sets down old ways of thinking for an entirely different mental discipline, and does this with firm commitment for twenty-four years, then it is reasonable to expect some sort of result. In Hongyi's Chinese Buddhist world, one expected result, expressed in body and mind, is an excellent death. This particular notion of an excellent death is part of what we can explore here, as prodded by the photo that is at the center of our discussion.

In twentieth-century China (and earlier), outsiders have not necessarily thought of Buddhist monks as men of action, particularly when they are formally dressed in their voluminous, broad-sleeved *haiqing* robes. Indeed, to the eyes of outsiders, those who hold to monastic precepts and practice the ordinary body disciplines may appear "dead," for they have withdrawn from what appear to most as the lively and exuberant pleasures of worldly existence. And those who engage in extraordinary disciplines, such as cultivating the hidden body of retreatants, may seem like the "deader dead." The fact that monks and nuns (especially those on retreat) very commonly live at sites deep in the mountains, where the dead are buried in China, should never be forgotten.

Whether metaphorically dead or alive, all humans eventually will die a physical death, even such complex characters as Hongyi. Let us return to the photograph taken at the end of Hongyi's life.

From this photo, there are a few things that anyone can see. This is a man who died in modest circumstances, resting on an unadorned and scarcely cushioned bed, wearing the plain clothes, perhaps even a bit shabby, of monastic life. For those who know that he was born to wealth and privilege, the lack of material comfort in this photo may seem all the more striking. And further, there is something both peaceful and proper here—there is no disorder apparent, no death struggle. Even his shoes have been carefully set beneath the bed, side by side, just as one is trained to arrange them below the sitting platform in a meditation hall.

One of the aims of Buddhist practice is a calm and conscious death. This kind of death is understood as the result of genuine achievement in one's life, for bodily dignity and control at the moment of death are the natural accomplishments of a person who has attained an unusual degree of interior dignity and mental control. That is one way that this photo can be read.

Deathbed Protocols

Hongyi's Vinaya studies focused most especially on the teachings of the Tang-period master Daoxuan (596–667) and prominent successors in Daoxuan's lineage. (This lineage, the so-called Nanshan Luzong, takes as its basis the regulations transmitted by the Dharmaguptaka lineage of early Indian Buddhism, which Daoxuan had promoted as the standard for monastic conduct.) Hongyi sought to regulate his daily life according to the principles and restraints of this tradition, many key elements of which had by his time been largely abandoned in China, such as the restriction of daily food intake to the hours before noon, a careful following of the rules for summer retreat, twice-monthly group recitation of precepts, and formal confession-repentance. Additionally, Hongyi's methods of daily spiritual cultivation were drawn from the Pure Land tradition. His practice involved mindfulness of Amita Buddha, including chanting practices aimed at achieving this mindfulness, leading to deep levels of samādhi, or profound meditative concentration. From this meditative state, he also performed various acts such as calligraphy, including the copying of scriptures, in order to benefit others. The aims of his Pure Land practices can be seen as twofold, although not separate: to benefit all beings by calling upon the Buddha and various beneficent bodhisattvas and to gain birth in the Buddha's Pure Land.

In the traditions that Hongyi followed, it was understood that birth in the Pure Land (*wangsheng*) could take place on two levels. The capable practitioner with properly focused mind can see the universe as entirely pure. This is a type of "birth in the Pure Land" in this very body. But also, if at the point of death the mind remains unmoved from this state of profound concentration, then it is held that after death, one will be born into Amita Buddha's realm. The moment of death, then, is crucial, but one cannot negotiate that moment properly without thoroughly grounded preparation. Adherence to precepts is essential, since this regulation of body acts creates a basis for stabilizing and purifying the mind, and without a cultivation of secure habits to stabilize and purify the mind, birth in the Pure Land is impossible. If this practice has not yet become a firmly established habit, then in the pain and delirium that often form part of the dying process, it will be difficult to maintain pure and singular focus on mindfulness of the Buddha. Although the Buddha and various bodhisattvas have pledged to assist the dying, if one's mind wavers from concentration on them, then one remains trapped in the Triple World, suffering rebirth again and again.

Hongyi turned to the monk Yinguang (1861–1940) for advice on practice, especially in the early years after he entered the order. They corresponded and on occasion were able to meet. This master, perhaps the preeminent Pure Land teacher of twentieth-century China, had a great influence on Hongyi.[8] Many of Yinguang's teachings were disseminated through the publication of collections of his letters, which most particularly consisted of responses to questions on practice. In addition, he wrote numerous short works, including a manual on deathbed practices published in 1930. As he states in that work's introduction: "Of all the most grievous matters in the world, there is none greater than death. What's more, among all the persons in the world, there isn't a single one who can manage a lucky escape. Therefore, if you want to help yourself and others, then you must plan ahead."[9]

Following Yinguang's lead, Hongyi gave a lecture on deathbed protocols in the twelfth month of the year *renshen* (early 1933) at Xiamen. Quickly revised for publication, it remains among the best known of Hongyi's works intended for wide dissemination. Some specific aspects clearly are intended for laypersons, while the larger principles also apply to monks and nuns. While emphasizing a Pure Land approach, these practices to a certain extent also rest within the Nanshan Lu tradition of Daoxuan, whose teachings on these matters are discussed in some detail in Koichi Shinohara's chapter in this volume. Consistent with his efforts in other areas, Hongyi makes these teachings clear for his generation, producing not an antiquarian approach but a living possibility. Hongyi's text, entitled "Rensheng zhi zuihou" (At the end of life), is divided into seven short sections. Let us turn now to an examination of some of Hongyi's views on how to die an excellent Buddhist death.[10]

The text begins with a brief preface, which gives the text's history and relates how the Vinaya Master Liaoshi, languishing on his sickbed, was inspired upon reading a draft of this text to rise and put all his efforts into religious practice. Then there is a concise formal introduction, in which Hongyi sets the tone for his instructions in a stark and direct manner. He writes:

> An old poem states:
> I see another's death,
> And my heart burns like fire.
> It doesn't burn for that other one:
> I see the wheel turn toward me.
> The last moment at the end of life is a great matter. How could we forget this even for an instant![11]

This approach to death—the sense that it is a presence directly ahead of us that never should be forgotten—is not at all unique to Hongyi; it is basic to a wide range of pan-Asian Buddhist discourse. If we look to present-day Chinese Buddhist visual culture, we can note that death images are found in many monks' rooms to remind them of impermanence, of the urgent need to practice without delay, and of the heedlessness of undue attachment, especially to bodily desires. For example, there may commonly be a black-and-white print of a skeleton, sometimes pasted directly above the doorframe, so that one sees it each time one goes out. One step further, at an Anhui mountain retreat I visited in 1998, a funerary shroud hung right above a monk's bed. This bed in a sense had been transformed into a bier. Memorial photos of deceased teachers and small reliquaries bearing their *sheli* (Skt. *śarīra*, crematory relics) serve many purposes, including the constant reminder of transience. The eminent contemporary Tiantai master Miaojing (1930–2003) trained his students to practice "skeleton meditations," which are Chinese versions of an old Indian Buddhist practice. For a while he had placed a human skeleton at the front of his meditation hall at Fayun Monastery, set there to assist students in their visualization practices. (Now it stands watch in the library. You look up from your book and there it is.) At Baoguo Monastery in Suzhou, where Yinguang carried out a final three-year sealed retreat late in his life, he wrote out with a large brush and deep black ink the character for "death" on a piece of paper, which he then hung on the wall to dominate the room. Yinguang is gone, but the calligraphy remains. Some persons certainly will shudder and see all of this as peculiarly "morbid," but this particular kind of discourse of death, in which death becomes the prodding, ever-present friend who encourages you to practice well, is central to Chinese Buddhist practice traditions.

In "Rensheng zhi zuihou," Hongyi follows his pithy introduction with advice on how to respond to a critical illness. His approach is both explanatory and practical. He speaks to the issue of karma and urges awareness that the pain and suffering of disease arise from karmic obstacles created in past lives, as well as actions of this very life. With a critical illness, the issue is not to recover but to focus the mind entirely on Amita Buddha in preparation for birth in his Pure Land. A panicked state in which one desperately seeks to survive is simply inappropriate. Calm and sustained concentration on the Buddha will enable rapid recovery if that is possible, and if not, it is the method to gain birth in the Pure Land. If the patient is conscious, Hongyi advises that it is useful to speak to that person of all his or her good deeds. In this way the patient is made comfortable and confident and thus can manifest the ability to obtain auspicious rebirth.

We see, then, as is made clear throughout this text, that a person's state of mind through the dying process is the crucial factor—a point also stressed in the chapters by Shinohara and Stone in this volume. The person can be assisted and encouraged but, in the end, must individually, personally manifest this state of mind.

The third section deals with the last period of the dying process, which is a key moment in the practice of seeking birth in the Pure Land. There are three main issues here. First, one should not do anything that causes the dying person to remain attached to this world. All talk of wills and last wishes should have been concluded long ago; now it is too late. Small talk is a distraction. Second, one should help the dying person by chanting Amita Buddha's name (*Namo Omituo fo*) with her or him or by chanting for that person, as he or she can maintain mental concentration on the words even if there no longer is sufficient strength to give voice to recitation. Hongyi gives extensive instruction on which accompanying instruments to use, rhythms, and so forth. (His approach to these matters, and more generally in these deathbed protocols, is more flexible in response to individual needs than that of Yinguang.) A key point here is that before the situation reaches its critical stage, one should ask the dying person precisely what mode of chanting is most comfortable and familiar, so that it will be a support for that person. Here and elsewhere in the text, Hongyi emphasizes the critical importance of preparation, so that there are no distractions when the moment of death arrives.

The third issue in this section is discussion of the body. Hongyi emphatically asserts that one should not touch the dying person's body in any way—whether to change the clothes or to wipe off excrement—without that person's explicit request. Otherwise, the touch will be terribly painful and will distract the person from concentrated recitation.

Hongyi also considers body positions during the dying process. He writes:

> At the time of death, a person may either sit [in meditative posture] or lie down, according to his or her wishes. It is not appropriate to force the person [to take any particular position]. If the dying person feels his or her strength failing, then he or she most certainly can recline on a bed. One should not exert energy to sit or rise in order to make a good appearance. When lying down, the dying person ought to recline on the right side, facing west [toward Amita's Pure Land]. But if there is considerable pain, the person can change position to lie on the back or on the left side, facing east. One should permit the dying person to choose the position naturally, without forcing the issue.[12]

There are social pressures in Chinese Buddhist environments to die sitting in meditative posture. If that is not possible, one should die reclining on one's right side. These are the deaths that, if peacefully achieved, generate respect and elicit favorable comments within the tradition. This kind of death is understood as the result of genuine achievement. The still and composed body reveals at the end of life a settled and collected mind, a visible expression of internal cultivation. Because Hongyi again and again urges that the dying not be forced into any particular position, nor force themselves in order to create an impression, but rather follow what is most natural and comfortable for their particular circumstances, we gain a clear sense that what are described as the basic (and best) postures for dying are in fact not easy to achieve.

The fourth section deals with the time period immediately after death. Here Hongyi returns to the issue of handling the body. At this time in most of China, it was customary to wash the body and to dress the person in good clothes, usually just after death.[13] Hongyi states emphatically that the body should not be handled under any circumstances for at least eight hours after the person has died. He makes clear that the dying process continues for several hours after the last breath. Even though it appears that no consciousness or sensation remains, intense pain is felt when the body is touched during this period. This pain will distract the person, breaking his or her concentration, and thus may well prevent birth into the Pure Land. So after reciting for awhile after the last breath, all persons should leave the room for eight hours and lock the door during this time to prevent anyone from disturbing the body. Only after this time period has concluded may the body be washed and dressed in clean clothes.

Old clothes should be used, and the coffin and tomb should be modest. The person is dead, so there is no benefit gained through grandiose expenditures. If new clothes previously have been set aside for this use, Hongyi recommends that they be given to the poor to gain merit for the deceased.

Section five discusses ceremonies to be carried out in the forty-nine-day period after death and then periodically later on. Given his perception of the deteriorated state of current monastic practice, in which monks often perform such rites as the *fang yankou* in a perfunctory and insincere manner solely as a means of economic support, Hongyi is not keen on such activities. (The *fang yankou,* or "releasing the burning mouths," is a highly theatrical rite to aid hungry ghosts; the merit one gains through sponsoring this performance usually is dedicated to deceased relatives.) Hongyi urges that the most important practice is the simple recitation of the Buddha's name. All persons can do this together with monks and nuns, and thus all will receive some benefit. Merit from all ceremonies should be dedicated to aid all beings, not just to benefit the deceased. This broad and generous view in fact will help the deceased. Again he urges modesty in all activities such as funerary feasts. This preserves the blessings of the deceased.

Section six is very brief. Hongyi encourages people to form associations to assist in recitation at the time of death. He does not give details, but these procedures, such as how to schedule shifts of

FIGURE 5.3. Vinaya master Guanghua at the moment of death, 1996. Superimposed inscription in his calligraphy reads: "Uphold the precepts, be mindful of the Buddha." After *Guanghua lao heshang zhuisi jinian tekan* (Taizhong: Nanlin Chubanshe, 1996), inside front cover.

teams of chanters so that the sound can continue without interruption for several days, are discussed at considerable length in Yinguang's essay. (Figure 5.3 records a contemporary scene of monastic chanting to assist an elderly master as he passes away. This is the moment of death of the esteemed Vinaya teacher and Pure Land practitioner Guanghua [1924–96].)[14]

Hongyi concludes in this way:

> The year is coming to a close. Soon it will be the thirtieth day of the last month, the end of the year. If you have not yet set your finances in good order, then creditors will arrive in a tumult. How can you ward them off? When we approach the end of our life-

> span, it is like the thirtieth day of the last month of a life, the very end of a lifetime. If you have not set your provisions in good order for birth in the Pure Land, then head over heels in flustering chaos you will call out to your father and cry to your mother. And when the bad karma from many past lifetimes appears before you all at once, how can you escape? At the point of death, even though you may rely on others to help you chant and to carry out all matters properly, if you yourself had cultivated [mindfulness] on a daily basis, then you could be in control [of yourself] when you approached the end. Benevolent Ones, I urge you all—you must prepare early. It is much better that way.[15]

Hongyi's essay, originally a lecture, was intended for wide dissemination. It speaks to the needs of laypeople and more ordinary monastic practitioners. When one reads through the collections of "biographies of eminent monks" that have been handed down through the centuries, as well as other tales of monks found in such sources as the mountain monographs of Mt. Wutai and other principal retreat and pilgrimage centers, one finds that descriptions of the deaths of great monks fit within a certain structure. Adherence to this structure constitutes evidence of their greatness. (Of course, many of these texts were originally derived from funerary inscriptions, which dwell upon death with stately cadences.) What we have then is a category of the "special dead."

Generally, monks of this sort are aware of impending death. It does not take them by surprise. Sometimes they foretell the exact day. Aware of the approach of this event, they prepare for it. They may stop eating, and often they stop taking medicine. Some write out a last poem or a bit of calligraphy.[16] Fully prepared, all business complete, they then assume an auspicious posture, either seated in meditative position or reclining on their right side. Body still, mind focused, such clerics may engage in one of their characteristic religious disciplines, such as chanting or meditation, and from that base they then depart in a calm, conscious, and dignified manner. And when their corpse is cremated, relics (*sheli*) are found among the crematory remains: crystalline bits, variously colored, sometimes adhering to bone fragments. In the view of many, this is one of the tests that puts the truth-revealing mirror up to the reputation of an "eminent monk." If no *sheli* are found, perhaps that person's accomplishments were only superficial?

Hongyi's Death

Now let us turn from the generalized and theoretical—how a practitioner ought to die—to the specific: the death of Master Hongyi. Hongyi's health never seemed to be very good. Although records of activities in his younger years and early maturity suggest an energetic person well able to set that energy into motion, photographs make clear that Li Shutong was physically slight, even at his most robust. By his mid-thirties, he was complaining of *shenjing shuairuo*, a label for a constellation of symptoms that includes waves of fatigue and diffused concentration. (*Shenjing shuairuo*, or neurasthenia, was understood at that time simultaneously as a disease of the overworked and overstressed modern "brain worker" and as a way to label a condition traditionally understood as the result of life-force depletion—for example, through excessive sexual activity over the course of one's life.) It was at this point that Li Shutong first experienced Buddhist monastic life, when, as noted above, he retired to a monastery near Hangzhou's West Lake.

This experience set off a chain of internal events, and within two years (by 1918) he had set down his life as an artist, musician, and prominent cultural figure to become a monk. By virtue of his very comfortable family background and upbringing, the exceptional level of his classical and modern education, his cultural prominence, wide network of highly placed friends, and relatively advanced age and experience in the world, Hongyi did not start out the "homeless life" as an ordinary monk. At first, many doors opened to him because he was the former Li Shutong. It would have been possible for him to advance quickly to a comfortable appointment as abbot of one of the great wealthy monasteries of Zhejiang, as was offered to him early in his career. However, he had not become a monk to settle into a life of ease coupled with extensive social obligations. Instead, he embraced a stringent ascetic path that emphasized long hours of religious practice. Unlike most monks of his era, he had no fixed home base but moved from place to place, generally spending at most a few months at each site. As he matured in this monastic life, doors opened not because he was the former Li Shutong but because he was the present Hongyi, well known as a monk of special dedication, equally learned in Buddhist studies and Buddhist practice. His ascetic practices, though, took a further toll on his health.

FIGURE 5.4. Hongyi in 1941.

As photographs record, he seemed to grow more gaunt and frail as the years progressed. When he took ill, he became very ill. By his early fifties he was known as a *lao heshang*, a "venerable reverend," and by his early sixties it appeared that his body had worn out (figure 5.4). A series of grave illnesses, beginning in mid-1932, when he was fifty-two, made clear to him that his years were limited, and already at that relatively young age he began to prepare for his death. In 1932 he wrote to his friend and lay disciple Liu Zhiping with detailed instructions. He asked to be commemorated after his death, not by construction of a stūpa, but by the printing and distribution of two thousand copies of the *Sifenlü biqiujie xiangbiaoji*, his comprehensive diagram-study of the four-part Vinaya that had been explicated by Daoxuan. Hongyi wrote that this was "the most important work composed after I became a monk." Thus, he said, it would be fitting to remember him by it. It is a poignant document—one man's concern for his aftermath, expressed as an attempt to deflect attention from himself to his work.[17]

His lecture "At the End of Life" was given in Xiamen just a few months after this illness. Impermanence had been impressed upon him in a personal way, and his public teachings intensified.

In 1935, while staying at Cao'an, a small temple outside Quanzhou in Pujiang, he once again fell seriously ill. Prepared for the end, he gave these final instructions in writing to the monk Quanguan, his attendant at that time:

> Dying Commands at Cao'an, *yihai* year
>
> Before my death, please assist me from outside the bed curtain by chanting the Buddha's name. There is no need to chant continually. After I die, do not move my body, and keep the door locked for a period of eight hours. After the eight hours have passed, you absolutely must not clean my body nor wash my face. Roll a ruined bed quilt around my body over whatever clothes I happen to be wearing, and then see it off to a mountain hollow behind this building. Let it remain there for a period of three days. If the tigers have eaten it, good. If not, then after the three days, cremate it at that site. (After cremation, then notify others. You absolutely must not notify them earlier.) These matters should be carried out with utmost simplicity before and after my death, and you must rely on these practices [as I have set them forth]. If not, then you are a disobedient disciple.[18]

Hongyi slowly recovered from this illness, however, and returned to a full range of activities for several years. He wrote, gave lectures, and still took time out for strenuous retreats of several months' duration. One can see a significant change at this point in some of his public activities. It was during this recovery that he wrote an autobiographical essay, a brief memoir reflecting back on the circumstances at the time that he became a monk. And it was also at this time that he gave a series of lectures that were very personal in content: his views on the basic principles of calligraphic practices, reflections on his ten years' living in Fujian, etc. These lectures and essay differ from the bulk of his public communications in that here he speaks very deliberately and reflectively from a personal stance, rather than simply presenting expositions of Buddhist principles or explications of scriptures.[19]

In 1937, Hongyi accepted an invitation from the Tiantai master Tanxu (1875–1963) to lecture on the Vinaya at his monastic study center in Qingdao, on the northeast coast. He arrived at the beginning of summer with several disciples to assist him. As Tanxu describes in his memoirs, Hongyi's energy was quite low: he usually lectured for only a half hour or had his disciples lecture on his behalf, following his notes. Even so, by all accounts Hongyi's lectures and personal example had a profound influence on the community. But as winter began to set in, the northern cold became too difficult to bear, and Hongyi returned to the gentler climate of Xiamen, where he continued to write and teach.[20]

Then in 1942, Hongyi grew considerably weaker. Arriving in Quanzhou in early May, he soon moved to a center for the care of elderly monks. A letter composed one month later makes clear that Hongyi was aware that his time soon would come to an end. (In this letter to a lay disciple, Gong Shengxin, Hongyi gives final advice and states that this will be their last communication.)[21] He gave his last public teachings on September 24–25: lectures on the brief, pithy early Mahāyāna scripture *Ba daren jue jing* (Sūtra of the eight realizations of great beings, *T* no. 779) and "Essential Principles of the Pure Land." On October 4, he sought to fulfill requests for calligraphy that had accumulated. He completed a large pillar couplet and then, for students of the Pujiang Middle School, over a hundred sheets (!) of inscriptions.

By October 7 he was fading. That afternoon he wrote some final instructions on the side of a used envelope, entrusting all affairs to his attendant Miaolian and asserting that no one had authority to overrule Miaolian on any decision regarding these matters.[22] The following day at 5:00 p.m., he gave Miaolian specific instructions for how to proceed during the dying process and funerary period. First, his two points regarding the dying process:

1. If I have stopped speaking and breathe in short and rapid breaths, or if my mind has become confused, then you must prepare the necessary materials to assist me in *nian [fo]*, mindfulness [of the Buddha].
2. When it is time to assist me in mindfulness practice, first speak into my ear and let me know, by saying: "I have come to assist you in mindfulness practice." Then proceed to assist me in mindfulness practice. If I am not in the auspicious reclining posture, wait for me to properly assume that posture, and then assist me in mindfulness practice. At the time of assisting me in mindfulness practice, first recite the "Praise-hymn of the Chapter on Puxian's Practices and Vows"—up to the line, "within all the realms of the ten directions." Then chant *"Namo Omituo fo"* ten times (do not strike the wooden fish, chant slowly with a loud voice). Then chant the dedication of merit verse beginning, "I vow to be reborn in the Western Pure Land," up to "... universally benefit all sentient beings." If you see tears in my eyes during this period of chanting scriptures, this is from the feeling of "sorrow [at the suffering of all sentient beings] and joy [at impending birth in the Western Pure Land] intermixed," not from any other reason. Do not misunderstand this.

This was the final body practice of his life, and Hongyi did not assume a random body position for it. The particular manner of lying on one's right side is learned from the very beginning of one's monastic discipline. It is one of the basic elements of the ordinary practices that all monks and nuns are trained to perfect. Many body practices and the mindfulness exercises that accompany them are codified in the *Pini riyong*, or *Vinaya for Daily Use*, a Ming-period text that for several centuries up to the present has been a staple of basic training for novice monks and nuns.[23] In general, Chinese Buddhist monastic training emphasizes that one should maintain alert and concentrated practice whether one is walking, standing, sitting, or reclining. In this text a wide range of specific practices is taught to beginners. These daily practices are maintained by serious practitioners to the end of life. If these practices are fully absorbed, then bodily discipline and mindfulness have become utterly natural.

According to the *Pini riyong qieyao* (the *Pini riyong* with commentary by Jianyue Duti, 1601–79), when one prepares for sleep, one should do the following:

> Prior to sleep, one should clasp one's palms together [in homage], face west and visualize [Amita Buddha], and recite the Buddha's name ten times, a hundred or a thousand times, or ten thousand times. Then one should recite this verse:
>
> At this time of sleep,
> I wish that all living beings
> Will be tranquil and secure in body,
> And undisturbed in mind.
>
> Visualize the character "A" within a disk and recite it twenty-one times in a single breath. Then you should lie down on your right side in the "auspicious sleeping posture." Do not lie facing upwards (on your back), nor on your belly, nor on your left side, nor should you lie undressed to your undergarments or short trousers. Remember to take mindfulness as your fundamental practice.[24]

In his influential training manual, the late-Ming period monk Zhuhong (1535–1615) similarly advised: "When reclining, one should lie on one's right side. This is called 'auspicious reclining.' Do not lie on your back, belly, or left side."[25] It is in this pose of "auspicious reclining" that one falls asleep. One is trained to sleep in a relaxed manner, with knees slightly bent and thus drawn inward. The right hand rests flat on the bed with the palm supporting the head, while the left arm rests along the left side of the body, palm down on the left thigh. Monks and nuns are well aware that this is the position taken by Śākyamuni at the moment of *parinirvāṇa*, for this scene is depicted in paintings or sculptures found in many Buddhist monasteries. These images depict Śākyamuni's body after he has breathed his last. Whatever the auspicious qualities of this position in Indian lore, it is significant that in a Chinese context, one performs this posture repeatedly as part of a process by which one trains one's body to become a buddha-body. And one cultivates this method so that one is prepared to die.

On the subject of posture and the role of assistants in the dying process, it is relevant to consider the example of the death of Yinguang, since he was an eminent monk who had been close to Hongyi. Two years earlier, in 1940, Master Yinguang passed away at Lingyanshan Monastery, the Pure Land center outside of Suzhou where he had presided as spiritual guide in his last years. He died at 5:00 a.m., and by 8:00 that evening, a written record of his death had been prepared. According to this record, when it came time for the eighty-year-old master to die, he rose from his sickbed, washed, and sat upright on a chair. His attendant told him that he was not sitting straight, so he corrected his posture, gave some brief final instructions to the abbot Miaozhen about maintaining Pure Land practice in the monastery, and then chanted the name of the Buddha. With monks chanting around him, he sat for two hours in this way, appearing to enter samādhi, with a smile on his face, and passed away.[26]

In his communication to Miaolian, Hongyi concluded with instructions on how to proceed after his death:

3. Check the window and door, and if they have not yet been closed securely, then close them securely and lock them [after I have died].
4. For the time of encoffining: If the weather is hot, do so after a half-day; if the weather is cool, then you can wait for two or three days. There is no need [for the body] to be dressed in good clothes, just an old pair of short trousers to cover the lower organs. Use a *kan* [a wooden coffin-box used by Buddhist monastics, in which the body is placed in a seated position] of the Yanglao yuan [where Hongyi was then residing], and send it to Chengtian Monastery for cremation.
5. After seven days, seal the door of the *kan* and proceed with the cremation. Divide the bone remains into two portions, one to be placed in the Common Stūpa of Kaiyuan Monastery and one to be placed in the Common Stūpa of Chengtian Monastery. In the period before encoffining, it is not permitted to move the body; let it remain on the bed just as it was. When it has been placed in the *kan*, then it should be moved to Chengtian Monastery. At this time you should take four ordinary small pans, place them under the four legs of the *kan*, and completely fill them with water. This will prevent ants attracted by the odor from climbing up the legs and then losing their lives at the time of the cremation. It is necessary to be very attentive to this. After the

> body has been moved, you should check the water level of the small pans under the *kan* legs on the following days and make sure to keep them full—this is due to concern that the water will dry and the odor will draw ants to climb up into the *kan*.[27]

A couple of points are worth noting here. "Common stūpas" generally are found at large monasteries where there are cremation facilities. The crematory remains of ordinary monks and nuns usually are placed within these architectural structures; eventually, all the ashes and bone fragments become mixed together. A very large monastery may have several *putong ta*. For example, Lingyanshan Monastery outside Suzhou has separate stūpas for the remains of monks, nuns, laymen, and laywomen. The remains of the "special dead," such as those whose bodies are transmuted by fire to produce gem-like relics, often are enshrined in their own individual monuments. (Lingyanshan Monastery has a separate memorial building and walled courtyard dedicated to Yinguang, which houses his remains, with additional stūpas there for several deceased abbots.) Hongyi's request thus modestly asserts that he is not to be placed among the special dead, but the fact that he orders that the remains be divided between two monasteries suggests he certainly recognizes that he will be placed in this category. The equal division of the relics between the two monasteries in Quanzhou, where he had had the most enduring relations, was perhaps not so much a sentimental act as a way to preclude unseemly disputes over ownership.

Hongyi's detailed instructions to protect ants from entering the *kan* might appear oddly emphatic or even unduly scrupulous, but they are entirely consistent with an important area of his teaching. He had strong views about the sanctity of all life, about the need and even duty to cherish all creatures and help them avoid suffering, from the tiniest insects to the largest mammals. His disciple Feng Zikai embarked on a long-term project in collaboration with Hongyi: the preparation of sets of paintings and texts on this theme of "protecting life." Hongyi provided the texts and calligraphy for the first two volumes of this series, with fifty and sixty pairs of text and image respectively; after Hongyi's death, Feng Zikai eventually produced four more volumes in tribute to him.[28]

We return now to our brief chronological account: two days after transmitting these instructions, on October 10, Hongyi asked

Miaolian for writing materials. In a shaky hand, made all the more poignant for his renowned control of the brush, he wrote out four characters: *beixin jiaoji* (sadness and joy intermixed), expressing compassion for the suffering of all beings and the joy of looking toward the Pure Land. These were his last written words. According to Miaolian, the master passed away at 8:00 p.m. on October 13.

Fields of Association

A photograph is both an image and, in many cases, a material artifact, a physical thing. Here I would like to explore two of the many fields of association in which the deathbed image—this thing—may reasonably be placed. First, of course, it is a *portrait*. Second, because it is a postmortem artifact, it finds a natural place among the *remains* of the master.

In its Chinese context, Hongyi's life is remarkable for the depth of documentation available to us, encompassing not only an unusually wide range of written materials, including many handwritten manuscripts, but also numerous photographs. Instead of imagining what Hongyi looked like at various periods in his life or drawing inferences from an artist's sole rendering or a brief written description, one can turn to a substantial body of images for glimpses of a series of captured moments, ranged in an arc across his lifespan.[29] The surviving photos encompass the years of his childhood and youth in Tianjin (the earliest surviving photo was taken in his third year, in 1883), late teenage years and early adulthood in Shanghai, from twenty-five to thirty as a student and actor in Tokyo, to maturity as an art teacher and cultural figure in Hangzhou, through the twenty-four years of his monastic career. We might reasonably think of the deathbed photo as the last in this series.

Hongyi was a man of his time, and he participated in this new cultural practice, one that was entwined with the technology of modernity: his picture was taken often. What is involved in having one's picture taken, what presumptions are made about photographs, and how might that affect views of the deathbed image?

In this period in China and Japan, portrait photography was largely the domain of professionals, who either came to your site to do their work or required that you enter their studio (for the most part, this has been the case until very recent years in China). Thus a certain amount of effort and forethought were required to produce these photos of Hongyi. In order to register a sharp image, the subject was expected to hold still. While the deathbed image was one occasion where this requirement may not have presented a problem, in the other images the subject held still as an act of volition, and so the question is: in what way did he hold still, in what way did he present this stillness to the camera lens? We know that in the years before he became a monk, Hongyi (Li Shutong) liked to perform: he projected a certain image for others to see. He performed on stage in costume, and because he was a schoolteacher, he performed in front of his students on a regular basis to establish his classroom atmosphere. Posed photos require the complicity of the subject, who produces a facial and bodily demeanor to be recorded. Li Shutong was no stranger to this. Later on as a monk, was he still performing when he stood before the camera? Was the last photo a record of the culminating performance of his life?

This image is not the sole after-death photo of this type to circulate from this era. There are not only images of monks, but also, for example, photos of literary-cultural heroes such as Lu Xun (1881–1936).[30] But perhaps none have generated as much interest as Hongyi's deathbed image.

To a certain extent, the world of modernity is a world of "facts," and some of the distinguishing technology of modernity (such as sophisticated optical equipment and other elements of the scientific laboratory) explores and indeed produces this world of facts. Photography records the streaming light of a certain moment, a certain place. One looks at the photographic image and might be assured that it conveys a historical truth—this at least is one of the discourses of modernity.

Photographs, however, can be manipulated beyond the impression that the subject wishes to assert. In Hongyi's day—aside from the interpretive possibilities in the control of a skillful or even a clumsy photographer—this manipulation could be accomplished from two directions: during the printing process in the darkroom and at the site of photography before the shutter was released. For example, one of the most famous and well-circulated historical photos of twentieth-century Chinese Buddhist life depicts the meeting of the two majestic Chan masters of the day. Xuyun and Laiguo stand together, in Shanghai in 1954, in profound stillness and isolation. A less well-known version of the photo, apparently printed from the original negative without alteration, shows them surrounded by additional figures, including Xuyun's attendant Foyuan, with numerous people walking past and behind. It is a boisterous scene, even as the masters are islands of serenity. What facts do we accept here in this record of an event? To move to the deathbed image, which is so striking in what it communicates, we must consider the possibility of manipulation at the scene. Was Master Hongyi's body arranged by his attendant before the photographer did his work, so that it presented the "fact" of a certain type of death?

While the deathbed image, as we have noted, is one of a long series of photos spanning Hongyi's lifetime, it is different from the others in that it is a postmortem artifact. It belongs to the period "after," not "during." It presents a body that is no longer animated, even if it seems to retain traces, a final imprint of that animation.

What other postmortem images were produced? Quite a few, as it turns out. Perhaps the most famous of these images are the one hundred ink drawings of Hongyi made by his disciple Feng Zikai, beginning in 1943, and distributed to friends and disciples of the master.[31] These preserve an artist's memory of the master's essential form, and they continue to be used as authoritative memorial images for acts of ritual remembrance. In addition to paintings and drawings that continue to be produced, there are three-dimensional images—sculptures, some life-size, made of stone, bronze, or resin—that have been established at sites of remembrance of Hongyi. Yet whatever the intended purpose or ultimate function, the difference between record (even if only putative) and interpretation is a profound juncture that separates the postmortem photograph from all other postmortem images.

The deathbed image is an intimate representation of the body after its animating force has departed. It can be thought of as part of the "remains." What became of the body and what relationship did the image have to this corporeal history? Miaolian, entrusted with supervising arrangements in accord with Hongyi's last instructions, later presented a written report, which included the following details.[32] After Hongyi's death, his body remained on the bed for a day. It was placed in a seated position and encoffined on the morning of October 15 and then moved that afternoon to Chengtian Monastery.

If one accepts the veracity of the documented accounts—most especially that Miaolian strictly followed Hongyi's request to ensure that his body was undisturbed until the time to place it in the *kan*—

then it is reasonable to accept that the deathbed photo, which is dated October 14, records precisely that undisturbed scene after the doors were opened. (Several accounts of individuals who gathered at the scene through the night to engage in acts such as burning incense make clear that when the door was opened on the following morning, the master was seen precisely in the auspicious posture recorded in the photo. Indeed, during the night he could be observed in that position through a glass window.)[33]

On October 20 at 7:00 p.m., the assembly at Chengtian Monastery began chanting the *Huayan jing* chapter on "The Practices and Vows of Puxian Bodhisattva," followed by the "Verse in Praise of the Buddha," leading to recitation of Amita Buddha's name—thus taking their cues from the texts Hongyi had recited as he stepped toward death. The cremation began directly at 8:00 p.m. and thus took place seven days after the master's death, to the precise hour.

According to Miaolian's account, the pyre burned for more than two hours, and many observers reported seeing unusual colors and forms in the flames. At midnight, the remaining bone fragments were removed, as well as more than eighteen hundred *sheli* found among the ashes. These were entrusted to Quanzhou's two largest monasteries, Kaiyuan Monastery and Chengtian Monastery.

Sheli (or *shelizi*), as mentioned above, are a particular type of relic found among the crematory remains of the "special dead" in Buddhist China: crystalline bits, variously colored, sometimes adhering to bone fragments. While this is not the place for an extended discussion of relics, some brief explanation is in order. *Sheli* are considered objects of concentrated and mysterious power. As concentrated bodily remains, smelted and refined, their power is related to the dead individual, but also it is separate and independent from that person, as a kind of materialization or concretization of power from another realm. In a sense, they are gifts bestowed by the departed master. *Sheli* ordinarily are enshrined in a special structure, a *sheli ta*, or relic stūpa, which also holds a memory of the master in visible form. While the vast bulk of an individual's *sheli* are set within a single structure (or several structures at places of importance to the deceased), small numbers may be distributed to close disciples. These in turn are ordinarily placed in a small, portable *sheli ta*. (Sometimes monastery treasure rooms will include groups of an individual's *shelizi* displayed in dishes.) In my limited experience viewing such materials, it seems striking that each set of relics appears individualized in its distinctively different visual and affective qualities. The examples of Hongyi's *shelizi* kept by members of his lineage that I have been able to see are small (a bit smaller than a small pea), round, and colored variously deep red or pure white.

Numerous contact relics have also been preserved. These are material objects used by Hongyi—clothes, cloth shoes, his spectacles, a small oil lamp, and so forth. Many such items are preserved at a memorial hall at Quanzhou's Kaiyuan Monastery. Perhaps the photograph lies along the arc of power between these contact relics—rather ordinary objects, made extraordinary by lingering infusion of personal influence—and the crematory *shelizi*. There is somehow a strange syntactical relationship between the deathbed image, which is a visual record of the body at the end, and the smelted, purified remains of that body. But from the point of view of those within the system, there is a kind of magic to the relics, a pure power, that also sets them into their own distinctive category.

A Conclusion

There is far more to say about matters such as Hongyi's last days, about Feng Zikai's memorial portraits and other such posthumous remembrances, but space is limited in this volume. For some attempt at a conclusion, I wish to return to the deathbed photo, which haunts me still. Why does it produce this effect?

Within the discourse of death that is central to Chinese Buddhist practice, every human being who departs becomes an excellent teacher for those who remain. The lesson of impermanence is set forth, again and again, in countless different ways. Beyond this basic teaching, though, in this particular world of understanding, the death of a Buddhist practitioner is viewed as a culminating activity that graphically demonstrates what has been attained.

By all contemporary accounts, Hongyi was an extraordinary monk, and his manner of death fit the pattern for such individuals. But if we remove all the apparatus of "greatness" and simply return to the moment of death, a moment that all humans must face, a moment that most face without much grace or composure, then we can return to the deathbed photograph. And what we can see still etched in a body that no longer breathes is an utterly peaceful moment, absolutely composed. It is ordinary—with no fuss, no bother—in the very deepest sense, and that I believe is why even viewers who know nothing about this person respond to the photo in such an extraordinary way.

Beyond Hongyi's individual accomplishment, the photo is an image that touches on some of the most significant questions in the Chinese Buddhist world. Do the cultivation techniques work? Is the Buddhist path a legitimate response to the modern world? Can modern individuals achieve the goals set forth in ancient texts, or do those texts record a life that now can only be seen as an obscure fantasy or a distant dream? In this context, the photo—itself a product of the modern world—becomes a key element of a discourse that asserts the continued efficacy of these techniques, asserting the powerful value of an alternative approach to the world. Here then is not someone who just says things, however forcefully or beautifully, nor is it one who merely sets out views in writing. Instead, in ways that are intrinsic (and problematic) to this particular medium and its context of reception, the photograph presents a record of experience, a record of something that has been achieved.

Notes

This work is derived from a larger project supported by grants from the National Endowment for the Humanities and the University of California, Santa Cruz. I acknowledge this financial support with gratitude. For comments and materials related to this essay, I most especially thank James A. Benn, Charlotte Furth, Ven. Heng Sure, Yang Lu, Michelle Yeh, and Ven. Yixin.

1. He Yue, "Shengzhe zhi si," *Lao zhaopian* 1 (1996): 30–32; Meng Fanming, "Siwang di yiyi," *Lao zhaopian* 2 (1997): 122–24.

2. For this image, see Xiao Chan, *Feng Zhikai* (Shijiazhuan: Hebei Jiaoyou Chubanshe, 2001), 125. Feng Zhikai has been exceptionally well served by Geremie R. Barmé's recent *An Artistic Exile: A Life of Feng Zikai (1898–1975)* (Berkeley: University of California Press, 2002). For the incident with his students, see 365–66.

3. For some background on Tianjin salt merchants, some of whom were fabulously wealthy, see Kwan Man Bun, *The Salt Merchants of Tianjin* (Honolulu: University of Hawai'i Press, 2001). Popularly known as the "Philanthropist Li" family owing to his father's reputation for good works, Hongyi's family is identified as one of the "Big Eight" extended families that dominated Tianjin economic life in that era (161–62n47).

4. The most important single source for Hongyi's life is Lin Ziqing, *Hongyi dashi xinpu* (Taibei: Dongda, 1993), a revised and considerably expanded edition of his 1944 *Hongyi dashi nianpu*. For extended discussion of this period of Hongyi's life, see Raoul Birnbaum, "Master Hongyi Looks Back: A 'Modern Man' Becomes a Monk in Twentieth-Century China," in *Buddhism in the Modern World: Adaptations of an Ancient Tradition*, ed. Steven Heine and Charles S. Prebish (New York: Oxford University Press, 2003), 75–124.

5. These various matters are discussed at some length in Birnbaum, "Master Hongyi Looks Back."

6. The four-character expression *yijie weishi*, well known to Chinese Buddhists, is a condensation of the leading theme of the *Fo yijiao jing* (*T* no. 389, 12:1110c–1112b, esp. the opening passage at 1110c).

7. In thinking about the construction of this ordinary body and its significance within various social settings, it may be useful to bear in mind Judith Butler's characterization of gender as "the repeated stylization of the body, a set of repeated acts within a highly rigid regulatory frame that congeal over time to produce the appearance of substance, of a natural sort of being." See her *Gender Trouble: Feminism and the Subversion of Identity* (New York: Routledge, 1990), 33. A recent narrative account of life at West Point provides a vivid sense of how, within totalizing circumstances, the body and mind can be transformed over the course of a few short years. Even if the ultimate aims of the military academy's project may differ from Buddhist ideals, the effect is somewhat the same as monastic training, especially when applied to young persons who actively seek a new model for their lives. See David Lipsky, *Absolutely American* (Boston and New York: Houghton Mifflin, 2003).

8. See Hongyi's comments following Yinguang's death, "Lueshu Yinguang dashi zhi shengde," in *Hongyi dashi quanji*, ed. Lin Ziqing (Fuzhou: Fujian Renmin Chubanshe, 1991), 7:380a–381a. (The *Hongyi dashi quanji* is a substantial collection in ten volumes, most set in double registers of small print, of works by Hongyi [vols. 1–8] and documents about him [vol. 10]. Vol. 9 presents a selection of his calligraphy.)

9. Yinguang, "Shu linzhong sanyao," in *Yinguang dashi quanji* (Kuala Lumpur: Malaixiya Jingzong Xuehui, 1999 [reprint of Taibei: Fojiao Shuzhu, 1977]), 5:71. The essay is more commonly known as "Linzhong san dayao." For recent studies on Yinguang, see Shi Jianzheng, *Yinguang dashi di shengping yu sixiang* (Taibei: Fagu Wenhua, 1998), and Chen Jianhuang, *Yuantong zhengdao: Yinguang di jingtu qihua* (Taibei: Dongda, 2002). For an English translation of selected letters, see Thich Tien Tam et al., trans., *Pure-Land Zen, Zen Pure-Land: Letters from Patriarch Yin Kuang* (New York, San Francisco, Niagara Falls, and Toronto: Sutra Translation Committee of the United States and Canada, 1997).

10. For the full text, see *Hongyi dashi jiangyan lu* (reprinted Gaoxiong: Gaoxiong Jingzong Xuehui, 1992), 1–7. This volume collects a number of Hongyi's lectures roughly spanning the mid-1930s to the early 1940s. Quite a few manuscripts of his lectures have now come to light. Based on these materials, we can see that in some cases Hongyi carefully crafted a fully composed lecture, while in others he spoke from an outline, and the published version was based on a disciple's deft recording of the event. The published version of "At The End of Life" is based on a substantially revised transcription; parts of the transcribed manuscript are difficult to read for all the deletions and insertions introduced in Hongyi's distinctive handwriting. Thus this work should be understood as a carefully considered composition, rather than a set of spontaneous comments. For photographic reproduction of the manuscript, see *Wushang qingliang: Hongyi dashi mobao sheli* (Shanghai: Shanghai Renmin Meishu Chubanshe, 2002), 96–99.

11. "Rensheng zhi zuihou," *Hongyi dashi jiangyan lu*, 1.

12. Ibid., 3.

13. See, for example, James L. Watson, "The Structure of Chinese Funerary Rites: Elementary Forms, Ritual Sequence, and the Primacy of Performance," and Susan Naquin, "Funerals in North China: Uniformity and Variation" in *Death Ritual in Late Imperial and Modern China*, ed. James L. Watson and Evelyn S. Rawski (Berkeley: University of California Press, 1988), 12–13 and 39 respectively.

14. For his memorial volume, see *Guanghua lao heshang zhuisi jinian tekan* (Taizhong: Nanlin Chubanshe, 1996).

15. "Rensheng zhi zuihou," *Hongyi dashi jiangyan lu*, 7.

16. For many early examples, see Paul Demiéville, *Poèmes chinois d'avant la mort*, ed. Jean-Pierre Diény (Paris: L'Asiathèque, 1984).

17. Liu Zhiping (1896–1978) had been Li Shutong's music student at Zhejiang First Normal College. For the text of this letter, see *Hongyi dashi quanji* 8:61a. The original is reproduced in color in Li Xianwen, *Hongyi fashi hanmo yinyuan* (Taibei: Xiongshi Tushu Gufen Youxian, 1996), 23. A reproduction of Hongyi's handwritten manuscript of the *Sifenlü biqiujie xiangbiaoji* is found in *Hongyi dashi quanji*, 1:3–193.

18. For this text, see *Hongyi dashi quanji* 8:309a. On exposure of the body as a postmortem practice, see Liu Shufen, "Death and the Degeneration of Life: Exposure of the Corpse in Medieval Chinese Buddhism," *Journal of Chinese Religions* 28 (2000): 1–30. For Quanguan's recollections of this period, see his "Suishi yishi riji," *Hongyi dashi quanji* 10:51b–52b.

19. For example, see "Wo zai Xihu chujia di jingguo" and "Minnan shinian zhi mengying," *Hongyi dashi quanji*, 8:16b–18b and 19a–21b respectively. (The first of these works is translated in full in my "Master Hongyi Looks Back.") See also "Tan xiezi di fangfa" in Li, *Hongyi fashi hanmo yinyuan*, 203–5.

20. Tanxu, *Yingchen huiyi lu* (reprinted Taizhong: Taizhong Lianshe, 2000), 2:203–18; on Hongyi's health, esp. 215. For two additional accounts of this period by monks who participated in the study series, see Huotou Seng, "Hongyi lushi zai Zhanshan," in *Hongyi dashi yonghuai lu*, ed. Xia Mianzun (reprinted Taibei: Longshu Pusa Zengjing Hui, 1991), 56–61, and a 1995 interview with Mengcan, one of Hongyi's attendants during that period, included in Li, *Hongyi fashi hanmo yinyuan*, 86–90.

21. For the letter, see *Hongyi dashi quanji* 8:264a. For a detailed chronology of this year, see *Hongyi dashi xinpu*, 444–62.

22. This document is reproduced in *Wushang qingliang*, 164. The annotations in the upper right corner are Miaolian's record of the date and time that he received these instructions.

23. The *Pini riyong*, credited to the Ming master Xingshi (d. early seventeenth century), is sometimes also known as the *Pini riyong lü*. See *Xu zangjing (*hereafter *XZJ*; reprinted Taibei: Xinwenfeng, 1968–70), 106:105b–128a. The principal commentary ordinarily used is that by Jianyue Duti, the late Ming–early Qing Vinaya master; see *Pini riyong qieyao*, *XZJ* 106:129a–137b. For the source of many of the verses that form the basis of the mindfulness exercises, see chap. 11 of Śikṣānanda's eighty-*juan* translation of the *Huayan jing* (*Avataṃsaka sūtra*), *T* no. 279, 10:69b–72a.

24. *Pini riyong qieyao*, *XZJ* 106:135a.

25. Zhuhong, *Shami luyi yaolue*, in *Lianchi dashi quanji* (Tainan: Heyu Chubanshe, 1999), 2:1947 (retitled photographic reprint of the *Yunqi fahui* [Nanjing: Jinling Kejing Chu, 1898]). In a modern commentary to Zhuhong's work commonly used in the PRC in recent years for training novices prior to full ordination, the Vinaya master Guanghua outlines a method for preparing for sleep and explains that the entire complex is subsumed under the term "auspicious reclining." He explains: "It is called 'auspicious reclining' because it can cause the body to become still, the mind is settled, sleep is not dull, and there are no bad dreams throughout the night." See Guanghua, *Shami luyi yaolue jizhu* (Taizhong: Nanputuo si, 1993), 167.

26. As recorded in the *Yinguang dashi yongsi ji*, in *Yinguang dashi quanji* 5:144–45.

27. These instructions presumably were not written out by Hongyi but were dictated to Miaolian, who carefully gathered together and preserved all materials written by Hongyi in his possession, most especially those from the final days. I have not seen either the original or a photographic reproduction of this document (assuming it is a document). It is quoted in full in Lin Ziqing's 1944 *Hongyi dashi nianpu* and also included in the revised and expanded edition, *Hongyi dashi xinpu*, 460–61.

28. Chap. 6 of Geremie Barmé's *An Artistic Exile* ("Protecting Life and Preserving the Self," 157–90) provides considerable discussion of this project and suggests that Feng Zikai's commitment to it was crucial to his abil-

ity to maintain focus through his difficult last years, when he was subjected to repeated attacks during the Cultural Revolution. For a book-length account of the project, see Chen Xing, *Gongde yuanman:* Husheng huaji *chuangzuo shihua* (Taibei: Yeqiang Chubanshe, 1994). It seems to me that the gentle qualities of Hongyi's death are of a piece with his gentle approach to all creatures. Perhaps it is not so much that the act of creating *Protecting Life* with Feng Zikai had a causative effect on the quality of his death as that the manner of his death was consonant with his manner of life.

29. There are many sources for a wide range of relevant images. Two recent compilations include Chen Xing and Zhao Changqun, *Hongyi dashi yingji* (Ji'nan: Shandong Huabao Chubanshe, 1999), and Jin Mei and Guo Fengqi, *Li Shutong Hongyi dashi yingzhi* (Tianjin: Tianjin Renmin Chubanshe, 2000). For Feng Zikai's account of his preservation of numerous early photos, see "Baiguan Hongyi fashi sheying ji houji," in his *Yuanyuan tang suibi* (reprinted Hangzhou: Zhejiang Wenyi Chubanshe, 2000), 116–20.

30. For Lu Xun's image, see David E. Pollard, *The True Story of Lu Xun* (Hong Kong: Chinese University Press, 2002), xxviii, plate 8. Several extended studies of photographic representations of death have appeared in recent years. For example, see Barbara P. Norfleet, *Looking at Death* (Boston: David R. Godine, 1993), and Jay Ruby, *Secure the Shadow: Death and Photography in America* (Cambridge, MA, and London: MIT Press, 1995). However, these studies focus on the work of European and North American photographers and their social contexts, which may be far distant from Chinese practices, conceptions, and modes of reception during this same time period.

31. These are discussed by Feng Zikai in his memorial essay "Wei qingnian shuo Hongyi fashi," *Hongyi dashi quanji* 10:63c–68a, esp. 64a.

32. Miaolian, "Wanqing laoren shengxi hou zhi zhongzhong," *Hongyi dashi quanji* 10:63a–b.

33. For example, see Ye Qingyan, "Qianjiang yin yue ji," and Huang Fuhai, "Hongyi fashi yu wo," *Hongyi dashi yonghuai lu*, 257 and 269 respectively. In June 2001, together with the monks Yixin (a grandson-disciple in Hongyi's lineage) and Jiexian, I was able to visit the site of Hongyi's passing in Quanzhou. The present residents of this small, deteriorated, single-level building very kindly permitted us full access to their living quarters. Details of the various accounts from 1942 seem entirely reasonable in relation to this physical structure. (The building was scheduled for demolition and perhaps no longer stands today.)

6

Dying Like Milarépa

Death Accounts in a Tibetan Hagiographic Tradition

Kurtis R. Schaeffer

The hagiographic tradition of Milarépa (Mi la ras pa, ca. 1052–1135) reached its height with the redaction of his life story by Tsangnyön Heruka (Gtsang smyon He ru ka, 1452–1507), the "madman of central Tibet." If we may judge from the immense popularity of Tsangnyön's *Life of Milarépa,* this late fifteenth-century religious leader was arguably the most influential hagiographer of the Kagyu (Bka' brgyud) schools of Tibetan Buddhism. In the late fifteenth and sixteenth centuries, Tsangnyön and his disciples actively promoted their school by compiling numerous hagiographies of early Kagyu masters from the eleventh through thirteenth centuries, including Milarépa and his student Réchungpa Dorjé Drakpa (Ras chung pa Rdo rje grags pa, 1085–1161), Lorépa Drakpa Wangchuk (Lo ras pa Grags pa dbang phyug, 1187–1250), and Götsangpa Gönpo Dorjé (Rgod tshang pa Mgon po rdo rje, 1189–1258), as well as their Indian forerunners, Tilopa and Nāropa.

This chapter focuses on death accounts in hagiographies of both Milarépa and Tsangnyön, and in particular on their cremations, marvels accompanying these cremations, and the creation and distribution of their corporeal remains and relics.[1] Tales of the marvelous (*ngo mtshar*) frequently occupy the hagiographer when telling of the deaths of Tibetan holy people, so much so that the funeral proceedings themselves become in great part occasions to engage in creative accounts of apparitions, disembodied sounds, and miraculous events.[2] What were the roles of such relic and miracle accounts in hagiographies of holy men and women in premodern Tibet? In what ways was a Tibetan Buddhist master held to be an active presence in his community even after his passing? What value was placed upon the remains of a deceased yogin, be it a chip of bone, a tiny crystal, a skull, or the skin off his face? If, as a recent scholar of relics and religious life in Carolingian Europe has stated, "relics of saints...had no obvious value apart from a very specific set of shared beliefs,"[3] then hagiographic literature plays a significant role in the structuring of such shared mentalities surrounding relics.

The death accounts of Milarépa and Tsangnyön provide a rich starting point from which to ask these questions, both because they are well-developed hagiographic accounts emphasizing the marvelous deaths of their subjects and because they were popular throughout Tibet in the centuries after their creation, thus allowing us to gain some sense of their influence in later literature. By looking to a single "hagiographic school" or collection of related life stories of Tibetan Buddhist holy men from the fifteenth and sixteenth centuries, I hope to suggest how death and relic accounts may have functioned in the social endeavors of their writers and propagators. It is clear that Tsangnyön drew on a rich tradition of hagiographic materials to create his vision of Milarépa while at the same time adapting and transforming this tradition for a new audience.[4] Yet it is not just the new form of Milarépa's *Life* (as I will generally refer to hagiographic works) itself that makes Tsangnyön's effort so interesting, but the extent to which he self-consciously used the *Life* as a means to expand his network of patrons, disciples, and holy sites. Tibetan hagiographies have as much to say about the contemporary concerns of their authors or compilers as they do about their subjects, who may have lived centuries before their hagiographers. To study the *Life of Milarépa*, composed in the late 1480s by Tsangnyön, is therefore not to study exclusively (or even primarily) the life and times of Milarépa but the life and times of Tsangnyön as well.

It is well known that in creating his *Life of Milarépa*, Tsangnyön Heruka was drawing on a long literary tradition of an already important saint. If we can judge from Gö Lotsawa Zhönu Pel's ('Gos Lo tsā ba Gzhon nu dpal, 1392–1481) late fifteenth-century work, Milarépa's *Life* (in what form, we do not know) was being used at the teaching center of Pakmodru (Phag mo gru) in central Tibet by the mid-twelfth century, only decades after his death.[5] In 1346, almost a century and a half before Tsangnyön's writing, it could be said that Milarépa was the most famous holy man in Tibet.[6] In the mid-fifteenth century, festivals dedicated to Milarépa were being held in Kagyu monasteries such as Taklung (Stag lung), at which the faithful would gather to listen to his songs.[7] As early as the beginning of the fourteenth century, it was rumored that there were 127 different life stories of Milarépa.[8]

Tsangnyön capitalized on this popularity, and it is certainly his promotion of Milarépa as a saint that has earned him renown throughout the Tibetan cultural world—from the southwestern Himalayas to Amdo (A mdo) in the northeast. Using printed texts, paintings, and teachings composed in the style of Milarépa's famous songs, Tsangnyön spent much of his life promoting a cult of devotion to Milarépa. Such missionary work was to have lasting consequences. From the fifteenth to the nineteenth centuries, his telling of Milarépa's tale was carved in new woodblock editions no less that ten times, in southwest Tibet, Bhutan, Dergé (Sde dge), Amdo, Mongolia, Lhasa, and Beijing.[9] Nor was Milarépa's reputation limited to Kagyu circles. He was even considered to be a previous birth of the Gelukpa master Jangya Rölpé Dorjé (Lcang skya Rol pa'i rdo rje, 1717–86), in whose *Life* explicit mention is made of Tsangnyön's efforts at composing and printing the life and songs of Milarépa.[10]

In the largest of three hagiographies dedicated to Tsangnyön,[11] Götsang Répa Natsok Rangdröl (Rgod tshang ras pa Sna tshogs rang grol, sixteenth century) waxes long on the highly realized status of his master, combining classic Mahāyāna descriptions of enlightened beings with an explicit comparison to Milarépa: "With fierce effort that was no different from the Ruler of Yogins, Mila Zhépé Dorjé (Mi la Bzhad pa'i rdo rje) himself, in a single life [Tsangnyön] manifestly achieved the stature of Lord Vajradhara, with the five wisdoms and four enlightened bodies."[12] Götsang Répa even goes so far as to style Tsangnyön as an incarnation of Milarépa.[13] During his relatively short life of fifty-five years, Tsangnyön enjoyed considerable prestige among rulers and wealthy patrons from central Tibet to Kathmandu. He was patronized by the most powerful leader of central Tibet, Rinpungpa Dönyö Dorjé (Rin spungs pa Don yod rdo rje, 1462/63–1512),[14] with whom he even discussed the life story of Milarépa.

If we can judge from Götsang Répa's account, Tsangnyön developed an interest in promoting the tradition of Milarépa early in life. In his early adulthood Tsangnyön traveled to Ngatsa (Rnga rtsa), the birthplace of Milarépa in southern Gungtang (Gung thang). He saw a small red temple and Mila's uncle's house in ruins, and at a renovated temple containing a statue of Milarépa, he met a steward who asked him to compose verses in praise of Milarépa's life. Tsangnyön thus composed an encomium to Milarépa in the form of the twelve acts of the Buddha.[15] In a fascinating passage, Götsang Répa writes of the benefits of Milarépa's life story by attributing the following considerations to Tsangnyön himself:

> There are currently many life stories and song collections of Milarépa. Still, since this extraordinary life story has not been a continuous tradition, it should be clarified and taught for the benefit of my disciples, for teaching its profound and vast dharma and spiritual instructions will surely lead to liberation. They will collect merit. There are kings, ministers, nobles who think that they are great people, and commoners, none of whom have time to practice in accordance with the dharma. Then there are those who do have the time and conceitedly think they are practicing the dharma, but have not taken the spiritual instructions into their experience: They are stirring up bubbles with words. There are those who are so conceited as to think that they are masters who have found the means to achieve the status of a buddha in a single lifetime: In them all virtue will be destroyed.
>
> If this *Life of Milarépa* were to be well known, sense pleasures and things desired in this life would become supports for undertaking ascetic practice, while entertainments in which one wanders would become supports for practicing single-pointedness. [Milarépa's *Life*] would become a perfect example for those who doubt that buddhahood can be attained in a single lifetime, or wonder whether they are meditating at the wrong time. They will have faith in the holy dharma of certain meaning and will be liberated in this life or in the intermediate state. Even those of mediocre capacity can have faith in those who are experienced and provide material support for them. With a pure vow they can go into retreat, gain meditative experience in the next life, and based on that they may gain liberation. Even extremists will give up backward views and develop extraordinary faith, and they will certainly come to the end of saṃsāra. Thus, printing [Milarépa's *Life*] will be of benefit to all beings.[16]

Here Götsang Répa characterizes Tsangnyön as a reformer, using Milarépa's *Life* to counteract hypocrisy and conceit in his day. Milarépa's life story should be engaging for different types of people and should encourage different responses, including everything from patronage to solitary retreat. Block printing is explicitly associated with mass dissemination of hagiographies and thus with the goal of benefiting humanity.

According to Götsang Répa, the *Life of Milarépa* experienced unprecedented popularity due to Tsangnyön's efforts. In the years immediately following the carving of woodblocks of Milarépa's *Life*, prints and paintings were distributed in Mustang, Gungtang, and, thanks to the interest shown by Dönyö Dorjé, in central Tibet. Tsangnyön sent his close disciple Sönam Drüpa (Bsod nams grub pa) on a tour through Ü (Dbus), Tsang (Gtsang), and Tsari (Rtsa ri) with both paintings and block prints "for the benefit of people"—in other words, to missionize on behalf of Tsangnyön.[17] Among the scenes that readers would encounter in this new block print of Milarépa's *Life* or in these new narrative paintings was a fantastic death account, a spectacle the likes of which had not been read (seen, imagined) in previous hagiographies. As Chökyi Wangchuk (Chos kyi dbang phyug, b. 1775), who was well versed in Tsangnyön's work, wrote of Milarépa's death: "The offerings made by the gods and *ḍākinīs* were beyond conception. Where has there been a greater show of magical apparitions than this one in Tibet? Even one just half as good is unknown."[18]

According to most accounts, Milarépa died in the Himalayas just north of the Nepal-Tibet border at the small retreat center of Chuwar (Chu bar/dbar). The death of Milarépa and its aftermath form a substantial portion of Tsangnyön's *Life*. Nearly one-eighth of the *Life* is given over to events *after* Milarépa's death.[19] These events form the third major part of the ninth and last chapter of Tsangnyön's work, dedicated to Milarépa's last acts, the first two being the plot to poison Milarépa by the jealous scholar Geshé Tsukpuwa (Dge bshes Gtsug phud ba) and Milarépa's premonitions of his own death.[20] This chapter also contains sixteen of the work's forty-four or so songs, nine of which occur after Milarépa's death. Furthermore, of these nine songs, all save two deal with issues surrounding Milarépa's relics. Tsangnyön's tale of the post-death events was influential among his circle of disciples. Götsang Répa incorporated it almost verbatim into his lengthy *Life of Réchungpa*, Milarépa's student.[21] By contrast, Réchungpa receives almost no death account in his own *Life*, as if Milarépa's was enough for the both of them.

The Death of Milarépa

Tsangnyön sets the stage for Milarépa's death as two of his disciples ask about the proper way to deal with their master's corpse: "If you must truly depart for the sake of others, how shall we offer worship for your death, worship your corpse, make the figurines, and build a stūpa? Who will guide the order of our tradition? What offering should be made to you on your anniversary?"[22] Milarépa counsels that these external forms of worship are not necessary, for the disciples should focus instead on the internal work of meditation. This marks a pervasive theme in the death and cremation of Milarépa: the conflict between the importance placed upon the physical remains of Milarépa for his disciples and followers and the critique of external crutches for what should ideally be a religious path leading away from saṃsāra, away from desire for worldly goods—relics included. Nevertheless, Milarépa does tell his disciples that even though he may leave no bodily remains, he will bequeath his humble possessions to his closest disciples: Réchungpa should receive his staff and robe, the hat and black aloe staff of Maitripa should go to the "teacher of central Tibet," Gampopa (Sgam po pa), and his wooden bowl, to Zhiwa Ö (Zhi ba 'od). None of these are valuable in any economic sense, states Milarépa, but each will serve as an auspicious connection between himself and his descendants.[23]

As Milarépa's death draws near, marvelous apparitions begin to appear, foreshadowing the spectacle to occur after his death. For each community of disciples, Milarépa manifests a different body so that each may be with him in his last days. On the day of his death, visions appeared all around Chuwar in much the same style as we see in the other Kagyu hagiographies mentioned above, though Tsangnyön creates a scene of minute detail: "The clear sky was filled with a rainbow outline of a Go board, as if one could touch it. And in the center of each square there was a variegated eight-petaled lotus, each with four petals in the cardinal directions. And upon these were three-dimensional maṇḍalas, drawings more amazing and marvelous than any made by expert craftsmen."[24]

No sooner does Milarépa pass away than disputes break out regarding where his body is to be cremated and how his remains (*gdung skal*) are to be distributed. Two rival factions attempt to steal his body, occasioning the first of several appearances by Milarépa from beyond the grave (or rather crematory). In the guise of a divine boy, the master chastises his disciples and patrons for fighting over his corpse (*spur*) and warns that the only way they will receive any remains is through faithful reverence to him.[25] As he disappears once again, he solves the quarrel in a more generous manner by bestowing a second corpse to one of the factions. This corpse is carried to Milarépa's old hermitage of Lapchi (La phyi) and cremated there in just the same manner as the one soon to be cremated at Chuwar. Tsangnyön would thus have the reader imagine the following in stereo, occurring simultaneously in two of the most important sites of Milarépa's activity.

After six days of worshipping the corpse, his disciples are horrified to find that it has begun to disappear. Was it possible that they would be left without any support for their offerings and reverence,[26] without any relics? They thus decide to cremate the corpse before it disappears in order to create the desired relics. They set it upon the funeral pyre, only to find that it will not burn. Why? They had explicitly disobeyed the instructions of their master, who had forbidden them even to touch his body—much less burn it—before his favorite disciple, Réchungpa, arrived. Much as the funeral pyre of the Buddha would not light until Mahākāśyapa could return to pay final homage to his teacher, the funeral of Milarépa could not be completed until Réchungpa was present.

Meanwhile, after learning of his master's passing in a vision, Réchungpa races to Chuwar to pay his last respects, only to be agonizingly barred from viewing Milarépa's corpse by younger disciples who do not recognize him. With a song of lament, Réchungpa beseeches his master to appear one last time. Milarépa returns before the crowd of worshipers a second time to teach them with a song. As he finishes, he fades away once again, and the pyre becomes a divine mansion surrounded by a canopy of light. Flames become goddesses, crackling sparks become celestial music, smoke becomes perfume, and the *ḍākinī*s sing a poetic recapitulation of this imaginative vision as disciples viewing the corpse behold it as various tantric gods—Hevajra, Cakrasaṃvara, Guhyasamāja, and Vajravārāhī.[27]

Now that the pyre is burning, those present wait eagerly for their share of the remains, spending the night by the crematory. When they awake in the morning, however, they find that the *ḍākinī*s have taken all the remains (*gdung*), relics or *ringsel* (*ring bsrel*), and even the cremation ash (*gdung thal*). Outraged, Réchungpa demands that they give Milarépa's human devotees a share of the relics. Their reply is significant: "You great sons have been introduced to the pure mind as the enlightened body of dharma, which is both remains and relics. But if this is not enough, pray to the Master that he may grant you some. Others who did not even see the Master, who was like the sun and moon, as a firefly, will get nothing. This is our share."[28] True yogins, who should be meditating on the empty nature of the mind, the *ḍākinīs* seem to imply, should not really want something as worldly as relics, and the rest of the faithless and quarrelling crowd does not deserve them anyway. Although Réchungpa realizes that the *ḍākinīs* are perfectly right, he beseeches his deceased master for a share of his "remains and *ringsel* relics as supports for faith" (*gdung dang ring bsrel mos pa'i rten*).[29]

Hearing his song, the *ḍākinīs* throw a piece to the crowd, but it transforms into a third post-death manifestation of Milarépa before anyone can touch it. This Milarépa, a miniature seated in a crystal stūpa, is held just out of reach by the *ḍākinīs* as they sing to the crowd, suggesting that the disciples' share of Milarépa's remains (*gdung skal*) is not a piece of his body but their meditative experience and tightly held vows.[30] Milarépa's close disciples are still not convinced of this, however, and Zhiwa Ö begs the *ḍākinīs* to give this crystal stūpa to humanity. Despite these repeated pleas, every trace of Milarépa's corpse is taken away, removed from human hands. All present at the spectacle are heartbroken, not because of the passing of their master, but because they will possess no portion of his corpse for themselves.

Thus, to the great relief of all, in a last-minute reprieve Milarépa returns for a fourth and final time to tell them that he has in fact left something for them. Overjoyed, they search for the "gold" they are sure the Master has left for them under the crematory, only to find a piece of cloth, a knife, a piece of sugar, and a small note. In a final joke from beyond the funeral pyre, Milarépa tells his disciples "to stuff the mouths of those who say Milarépa had any gold with shit!" All reading the note laugh at the master's good humor, despite their state of mourning.

Finally, their departed master proves to be more forgiving than was first apparent, for the cloth when cut with the knife miraculously portions out endless pieces the size of the original, and the sugar grows endlessly as well when divided. These secondary relics of Milarépa are every bit as powerful as the bodily remains of other masters, for through contact with them "the sick and suffering were freed of sickness and suffering, and the deluded and evil-minded became strong in faith, with great wisdom and compassion, and free from bad rebirths."[31] With this final miraculous act of compassion and capitulation, Tsangnyön ends his spectacular account of the death and cremation of Milarépa.

Although this is not the place to undertake a literary history of Milarépa's death account—much less a history of his *Lives* in general—a few examples show that Tsangnyön was engaged in active choices about what scenes to include and what emphasis to place on them. Most important for our purposes, Tsangnyön elaborates Milarépa's death—and the controversy over his relics—beyond what we find in accounts previous to his. Early hagiographies of Milarépa often make no mention of his death, as in the case of Lama Zhang's (Bla ma Zhang, 1123–93) twelfth-century work,[32] or merely make mention of it, as in the *Life* attributed to Gampopa, which states that "as soon as he died he was cremated at both Tisé and Drin."[33] Even more elaborate works such as the *Black Treasury*—a lengthy work comprising elements of what would in Tsangnyön's hands become two separate works, the *Life* and the *Collected Songs* (*Mgur 'bum*) of Milarépa—do not develop the death scene to the extent that Tsangnyön does.[34]

Yet neither is Tsangnyön the only hagiographer to claim that Milarépa's relics were taken away. The ultimate inspiration for this narrative almost certainly comes from death accounts of the Buddha himself. Like the god Sakka in the *Mahāparinibbāna sutta*, the *ḍākinī*s steal Milarépa's relics out of concern that humans will not properly venerate the remains of their master.[35] And in hagiographic compendia of the Kagyu schools, this theme goes back at least several centuries before Tsangnyön's time. In the thirteenth century Gyeltangpa Déchen Dorjé (Rgyal thang pa Bde chen rdo rje) wrote that the *ḍākinī*s took Götsangpa's relics into space, or the greater portion of them at any rate. According to the wishes of Götsangpa himself, several were cast into the Tsangpo River, and the remainder were distributed to disciples, who in turn brought them back to their respective homelands to deliver into the hands of the faithful.[36] The anonymous *Life of Milarépa* included in one of several hagiographic collections of masters in the *Oral Lineage of Cakrasaṃvara* (*Bde mchog snyan brgyud*)—a particular Kagyu tradition of ritual, meditation instruction, and hagiography—also relates that the *ḍākinīs* collect Milarépa's remains and take them "into the sky,"[37] away from human hands, as does Gyeltangpa Déchen Dorjé's account of Milarépa.[38] The theme of disappearing relics was adapted in later tales as well, perhaps drawing on Tsangnyön's *Life*. In Ngawang Namgyel's (Ngag dbang rnam rgyal) 1609 history of Taklung Monastery, Milarépa's remains and relics form into a single mass and disappear,[39] as they do in Chökyi Wangchuk's early nineteenth-century history of Drakar Taso, Milarépa's retreat center in Kyirong.[40]

Not every *Life of Milarépa*, however, ends with the disappearance of his bodily remains. In shorter hagiographies, scenes of Milarépa's death and funeral are entirely absent, as, for example, in Drigung Chöjé Kunga Rinchen's ('Bri gung Chos rje Kun dga' rin chen, 1475–1527) work of 1508,[41] or the collection of Kagyu hagiographies compiled by Möntsépa Kunga Penden (Mon rtse pa Kun dga' dpal ldan, 1408–75).[42] And in stories of Milarépa such as Tséwang Gyel's (Tshe dbang rgyal, fifteenth century) *Religious History of Lhorong* (*Lho rong chos 'byung*, written in 1446), bodily remains are indeed left behind: "Then from the chimney of the crematory a single small piece of the Master came. Lhamen Gyelmo Tséringma (Lha sman rgyal mo Tshe ring ma) took this as an object of devotion for her faith. Half of the ashes were cast into the Tsangpo River, half into the Bongchu River. All the beings who are encountered by the water will be liberated from bad rebirths."[43] Milarépa's humble possessions are also treated as relics in a brief version of his story written some forty years before that of Tsangnyön. Again, Tséwang Gyel offers a variation on a theme:

> From the chimney of the crematory a voice said: "In my storeroom there are many utensils. Dispense of them after I go. Make them great offerings." Master Réchungpa and the other cotton-clad *répa*s went in to his quarters through an open window. Inside there was a single bag, and inside that there was a fire-starting kit, an awl, a small knife, a needle, and three pieces of brown sugar. This was written upon a text: "A beggar leaves a bowl and a walking stick at death. He has abandoned desire for wealth, for karma is collected based upon that. So he has abandoned desire and things." Upon the crematory stones OṂ ĀḤ HŪṂ and the six-syllable mantra appeared where they remain today.[44]

It was left to other redactors of his *Life* to transform these items into self-replicating "contact relics" that feed the hungry, heal the sick, and fulfill the expectations and dreams of Milarépa's disciples through their miraculous power.

The Death of Tsangnyön Heruka

With some sense of Milarépa's death account in several versions, we may now move to the life and death of Tsangnyön himself. Tsangnyön died at Réchung Puk (Ras chung phug), just north of the Yarlung Valley, much closer to the center of the Tibetan cultural world than Milarépa—a fact indicative of the greater role Tsangnyön appears to have played in the politics of central Tibet.[45] The following story of the death, funeral, and relics of Tsangnyön summarizes Götsang Répa's account of his master, the most elaborate account of Tsangnyön's life.[46]

The twenty-eighth day of the fourth month of the water-hare year 1507 finds Tsangnyön quite ill. As death draws near, his disciples and patrons provide him with medicine, and at Tsétang (Rtse thang) his disciples pray to and circumambulate his residence day and night. Someone suggests that they go to Réchung Puk, and at the mere mention of this place Tsangnyön becomes filled with joy: "Now I will go there and the father will die in the son's house," he exclaims, by which I take Götsang Répa to be saying that Tsangnyön as an incarnation of Milarépa would die in the retreat center of his spiritual son, Réchungpa. Sönam Drüpa and fifty disciples travel to Réchung Puk with him. The sun shines upon them as they travel south, and Tsangnyön takes this as an omen that his death will be good. There are marvelous apparitions around Réchung Puk before, during, and after Tsangnyön's death. From the day Tsangnyön arrives in Réchung Puk, the sky remains clear, and in all directions there are rainbows, rain, flowers, and plants. In the midst of this there are mountains of offerings "as in an expertly crafted painting." A five-colored rainbow encircles the sun, from which a blue light streams, pervading all the land. Everyone exclaims that this is Tsangnyön's body dissolving, and they are anxious and unhappy.

On the eleventh day of the fifth month, Tsangnyön tells his close disciple, Sönam Drüpa, that it is finally time for him to die. He urges Sönam Drüpa to take all those disciples who had not been to the holy mountain of Tsari on pilgrimage there. On the thirteenth day of the month, Tsangnyön gives his final teaching to his close disciples. His disciples and patrons feel as if they are actually meeting Milarépa, and they look to the *Life of Milarépa* for strength. On the fifteenth day of the fifth month of the water-hare year 1507, Tsangnyön dies at the age of fifty-five, "like the sun setting on the land of snows."

Three days after Tsangnyön's death, his disciples and others begin to offer prayers "to gather wisdom and merit." After fourteen days, some forty disciples, led by Sönam Drüpa, make fire offerings, while others perform a *gurupūja*, and they offer the corpse to a crematory within a Cakrasaṃvara maṇḍala. The sky is overcast, rain and fierce wind come, and everyone is despondent. When the fire takes to the body, the sky clears, the wind dies down, and flowers fall from the sky like a great snow. Above the corpse, the flames form a rainbow-colored parasol, the shapes of peaceful and wrathful deities, or implements of deities such as turquoise, a *vajra*, a knife, and a staff. Syllables such as HŪṂ! and PHAṬ! resound, beautiful music plays, and a wonderful unknown fragrance "better than either sandalwood or camphor" wafts about.

At these apparitions and sounds, everyone in the region comes to worship in a state of delight. Their rituals in fact have to be truncated because of the large crowds. The circumference of Réchung Puk is surrounded by white light. The sky is filled with non-humans making offerings. People make offerings from their own villages in Yarlung (Yar lung) to the south with butter lamps that can be seen all around the valleys from Réchung Puk. Everyone gathered agrees that there has not been such a wondrous display of marvelous apparitions (*ngo mtshar ba'i ltas*), miraculous acts (*cho 'phrul 'di 'dra'i 'phrin las*), indications of blessing (*byin rlabs kyi rtags mtshan*), or show of faith by the people since the coming of the Zhamarpa (Zhwa dmar pa), the Karmapa, or the great adept Tangtong Gyelpo (Thang stong rgyal po, 1361–1485).

Prayers are made to the crematory for several periods of forty-nine days. At the end of the third period of mourning, the crematory is opened and Tsangnyön's relics distributed. His remaining bones would not be sufficient for the some 2,500 monks and laypeople gathered, so each is given one spoonful of ashes. To some 824 patrons, male and female religious practitioners, and close disciples who had a special connection to him, a piece of cloth, a whole piece of bone, a lock of hair, or many scoops of ash wrapped in paper are given.

The disciples at Réchung Puk then begin distributing relics to people from holy places along the Himalayas in which Tsangnyön was active. Students from Kailash, the Dzong Druk (Rdzong drug), Lapchi, Chuwar, and Tsari and their notable patrons need a share of the relics. Marvelous objects of devotion (*ngo mtshar ba'i rten*) appear: indestructible remains, *ringsel* relics the size of peas in five colors and of various shapes.[47] Ash also appears in the hands of the worthy. Deity-shaped relics as well as "increasing remains" (*'phel gdung*) manifest in the hands of fourteen of Tsangnyön's most important disciples. After these gifts to the faithful are miraculously meted out, festivals are held at both Réchung Puk and the nearby Pakmodru complex. A number of disciples commission a clay statue of Tsangnyön in which his ashes are mixed. Just seeing this statue is said to delight the faithful. Several disciples leave the funeral proceedings and travel south via the Yarlung Valley to the important pilgrimage site of Tsari, where they make further offerings of gold to a certain temple on behalf of Tsangnyön.

Many other marvels are witnessed around Réchung Puk before Tsangnyön's cremation is complete. A dark storm rolls in from the west, but Réchung Puk is protected by a canopy of rainbows shaped like parasols, victory banners, and offerings. All who see this are delighted, and even those who had not met Tsangnyön before become his faithful worshipers. A certain woman who had never seen Tsangnyön beholds him seated on a lion in the middle of a ball of light and dressed as a yogin, just as he had been in life. She instantly develops an unshakeable faith in Tsangnyön, and everyone around Réchung Puk makes prayers to this apparition. On another occasion, a disciple from Kongpo (Kong po) in southeastern Tibet comes to view the remains but in a daze of faith wanders off a cliff. Just as he is about to meet his death, a white light shoots from Tsangnyön's remains and transforms into a piece of wool cloth, while his bones become iron struts to hold the cloth. Everyone looks on as this miraculous emanation catches the faithful Kongpo man, saving his life.

Elsewhere, festivals are held at the holy sites of Milarépa and Tsangnyön dotting the Himalayas. Disciples at Lapchi, Chuwar, Latö Lho (La stod lho), and Latö Jang (La stod byang) hold three-month festivals, and offerings are made in the more distant religious centers of Mt. Kailash and the Dzong Druk. Even the Kathmandu Valley is said to be filled with white light when offerings are made in Tsangnyön's honor at the stūpa of Svayambhū, which he had renovated in 1504. Perhaps most significant, the leader of central Tibet himself, Dönyö Dorjé, travels to Chuwar—the site of Milarépa's death—to pay his respects to Tsangnyön and receive his share of the master's remains.

The months after the funeral also witnessed literary and artistic offerings. Disciples and patrons from Lapchi and Chuwar sponsored statues of Tsangnyön at Chuwar, as well as statues of Vajradhara, Marpa, and Milarépa. The leader of Ngari Dzongkar (Mnga' ris rdzong dkar) commissioned a perfect likeness of the master and installed it at Chuwar. Götsang Répa himself attests to having seen some 340 clay, bronze, copper, and gold statues, as well as paintings. Finally, the patroness Kuntu Zangmo (Kun tu bzang mo)—Tsangnyön's female companion—sponsored the compilation of the master's songs from the notes of disciples, as well as the printing of a life story of Tsangnyön composed by Ngödrub Pelbar (Dngos grub dpal 'bar).[48] The final acts of homage recorded by Götsang Répa are meditation retreats undertaken by Tsangnyön's disciples. If Tsangnyön's body and speech were immortalized through the distribution of relics, the making of statues and paintings, and the writing of his life story, his mind could be properly revered only through strenuous mountain retreats at Kailash, Lapchi, Tsari, and other centers, all undertaken "for the benefit of humanity."

The *Life* of Milarépa after the Death of Tsangnyön Heruka

After hearing these two death accounts, we may stop to consider their interrelations. What, if any, is the relationship between Götsang Répa's account of Tsangnyön and Tsangnyön's account of Milarépa? Clearly Tsangnyön's account of the death of Milarépa had some influence upon the hagiographic literature produced by his students. Götsang Répa was certainly familiar with the death scene in Tsangnyön's *Life of Milarépa*, for as we have seen, he inserted a major portion of it virtually unaltered into his own *Life of Réchungpa*. Yet it does not appear that Götsang Répa explicitly modeled the death account of his own master upon Tsangnyön's famous work. Tsangnyön's account of Milarépa's relics is, at first glance, ambivalent about their value. Ultimately, Tsangnyön would have

Milarépa counsel his disciples, the relic should not be valued, for there should be no need for a physical reminder of Milarépa's inspiring model of solitary contemplation. Yet such solitude in fact relies upon relics, if for no other reason than to provide lay patrons with a concrete incentive to sponsor the more miraculous activities of yogins. The paradox of Milarépa's relic account is that it cautions against overvaluing relics while simultaneously praising their miraculous power and charisma.[49] Milarépa's bodily relics were too valuable for human hands—a claim that makes the relics' possession even more desirable. There is no such ambivalence in the case of Götsang Répa's account of Tsangnyön's relics: as with other Kagyu *Lives*, bodily remains are immensely valuable, and no critique of relics is offered. This is the major difference between Tsangnyön's account of Milarépa's death and those about Tsangnyön himself—Tsangnyön left his body to the faithful, yet Tsangnyön's Milarépa did not.

But are these two approaches really so different? There were, after all, relics associated with Milarépa, and despite the fact that these were "contact relics"—clothing, food, and minor possessions—they are as marvelous (*ngo mtshar ba*) as any *ringsel* relic or bone fragment, with the ability to heal the sick, fulfill the faithful, or release humanity from bad rebirths. By dramatically emphasizing the absence of Milarépa's bodily remains, Tsangnyön in fact endorsed the preeminent importance placed upon relics, a category that could include anything from a lump of sugar to a human skull. Despite the fact that Tsangnyön chose to expand upon the theme of disappearing relics when in all likelihood he knew of alternative accounts, it is likely that his *Life* of the great yogin was a significant element in promoting devotion to Milarépa's relics and that the story of Milarépa's absent but still powerful relics was likewise a significant element in promoting devotion to Tsangnyön himself.

This is not to say that Tsangnyön's literary influence is nowhere felt in Götsang Répa's work. A separate section listing the most important places occurs in the same place as the description of holy places in Tsangnyön's *Life of Milarépa*. Here, important events in Tsangnyön's career are organized and summarized around place, making a ready guide for pilgrims who wish to visit. As was the case with Milarépa, nearly every holy site on the map of Tsangnyön's career lies along the southern border of the Tibetan cultural world. Tsangnyön's "five famous great key places of realization" are Tisé, Lapchi, Tsari, Chuwar, and Swayambhū Stūpa in the Kathmandu Valley.[50] It is not surprising that all of these places are associated with both the marvelous and ascetic activities of Milarépa as well, for locating relics at these places was one way disciples and descendants could maintain the authorizing presence of their master. Götsang Répa provides a clear map of holy sites to which Tsangnyön's remains should be distributed and thus lends continued authority to these sites as places of pilgrimage.

Tsangnyön's *Life of Milarépa* was influential for sixteenth-century relic and miracle accounts in less direct ways, and we can judge Tsangnyön's success from later accounts. By the mid-seventeenth century, for instance, relics attributed to both Tsangnyön and his favorite saint could be found from one end of the Himalayas to the other. One could find loincloths of both Milarépa and Tsangnyön placed side by side with "increasing bone" relics of Śākyamuni Buddha himself in a stūpa in Sikkim and promoted by a Nyingma writer,[51] and statues said to be crafted by Tsangnyön from Milarépa's blood inhabit the pilgrimage sites of Mt. Kailash. The fact that in the most widespread literary account of Milarépa's death the great yogin leaves no relics seems to have had little effect on the presence of Milarépa's bodily relics at pilgrimage sites. Tenzin Chökyi Lodrö (Bstan 'dzin Chos kyi blo gros, 1869–1906) tells us in his 1901 pilgrimage guide to Lapchi that the principal object of devotion at Chuwar was ash from Milarépa's corpse, and at Drin there were also numerous statues of Milarépa made from his ash.[52] In his 1896 guide to pilgrimage sites around Mt. Kailash, the same author relates that in the cave where Milarépa defeated a Bönpo opponent sits a statue of Milarépa crafted by Tsangnyön himself out of Milarépa's blood.[53] Does this mean that Tsangnyön failed in his efforts to convince people that Milarépa left nothing but cotton and sugar? Or perhaps he was successful beyond what he might have imagined at the time of his own death.

To gain some perspective on death and relic accounts among the Kagyupa in the period shortly after Tsangnyön, we may turn to the *Life* of his student, Sönam Lodrö (Bsod nams blo gros, ca. 1460–1541). According to Tsültrim Penden's (Tshul khrims dpal ldan) 1556 *Life of Sönam Lodrö*, he waited on Tsangnyön for more than fifteen years, from around 1490 to Tsangnyön's death in

1507.[54] He was not present at the death of his master Tsangnyön, though he did dream of it one night while in retreat as it was happening. Upon waking, he immediately traveled to Réchung Puk but arrived too late for the ceremonies, much like Réchungpa and Mahākāśyapa before him. Tsültrim Penden tells us that Sönam Lodrö asked passersby to tell him of Tsangnyön's funeral in detail while on the road, suggesting that stories of his death traveled quickly throughout the region.[55]

Tsültrim Penden's account of Sönam Lodrö's own death is substantial, comprising nearly one-tenth of the *Life*. It is well organized and formulaic and contains all the details we have come to expect from such accounts. Tsültrim Penden indulges in certain creative elaborations, particularly when describing the visions (*ltas*) people experienced (*nyams snang*). Some behold Sönam Lodrö seated on a lion and surrounded by *ḍākinīs*, as is Padmasambhava. Some see him seated upon a throne flying from Lapchi to Chuwar, accompanied by women wearing fine silks.[56] Yet the most important aspect of this *Life* for our purposes is not the death account itself but a particular comparison its writer draws: Tsültrim Penden explicitly states that the worship of Sönam Lodrö's corpse by disciples, patrons, and celestial beings is just like the worship of Milarépa.[57] Despite the fact that Sönam Lodrö's corpse produced many relics, despite the fact that the *ḍākinīs* did not take his bodily remains away, his death is likened to that of Milarépa. This key passage strongly suggests that the death account of Milarépa was paradigmatic for the writers of hagiography associated with Tsangnyön's circle in the middle of the sixteenth century, nearly half a century after Tsangnyön's death. If the lack of bodily remains was not appropriated as an explicit theme, the mere comparison with Milarépa's death lent hagiographic accounts of contemporary Kagyupa holy men the authority of the tradition's greatest saint.

Death, cremation, and relic accounts are a principal occasion for what one scholar of early Christianity has termed social formation: the creation of a "complex interplay of many human interests that develop systems of signs and patterns of practice, as well as institutions for their communication, maintenance and reproduction."[58] A central concern of this chapter has been the way in which hagiographic death accounts promote relics. Yet when viewed from the perspective of social formation, relics and hagiographic death accounts promoting relics are really no different from each other. For we must not forget that hagiographies also have physical presence, whether in the form of handwritten manuscripts, block prints, or narrative paintings. All were physical objects with symbolic power, disseminated to inspire and promote "patterns of practice"—ethics, patronage, solitary retreat, pilgrimage—and claim or maintain particular places in Tsangnyön's network of religious institutions. Marvelous visions and accounts of such visions are no different; they too are signs employed by people to support, promote, or even contest practices and institutions. A recent work on relics in Carolingian Europe helps to conceptualize this relationship among relics, marvels, hagiographies, and the development of religious networks by Tsangnyön and his followers: "Miracles . . . advertised the virtues and importance of the saints and thus increased the number of pilgrims to their shrines. More important, saints by their physical presence were a primary means of social integration, identity, protection, and economic support for the communities in which they were found."[59] To this I would add that in the context of the Buddhist cult of the book in Tibet, hagiographies could represent the "physical presence" of the saint.

These possible relationships among relic, text, and saint are suggested in the closing verses of Tsangnyön's *Life of Milarépa*. Just as one should make offerings to the deceased who give rise to such marvels—or, more precisely, to institutions on behalf of the deceased—in the closing verses of the *Life of Milarépa*, Tsangnyön advocates that the faithful should make offerings to the *Life* itself,[60] a *Life* that is also marvelous (*ngo mtshar can*).[61] If a relic is the body of a saint, then *Lives* are the voices of saints, as Tsangnyön so deftly insinuates when he begins his epic tale of Milarépa with the words, "Thus at one time did I hear," the hallmark opening line of Buddhist sūtras.[62] And the powers of the *Life* that Tsangnyön lists in the final verses could well be applied to relics themselves: The words of the *Life* make one's hair horripilate with faith. Seeing the *Life* liberates one from the eight worldly concerns (gain and loss, defamation and eulogy, praise and ridicule, sorrow and joy). Hearing it produces a yielding faith. Remembering it severs attachment and compulsiveness. Touching the *Life* spontaneously fulfills aims for both self and other. Preserving the *Life* fulfills the profound goal of the Kagyu lineage. The *Life* compassionately protects everyone from suffering.[63]

And when one worships the *Life* with offerings and beseeches it to grant blessings, those lying in the sickbed of saṃsāra are healed.[64]

When we view them within this context, we might see the technology of woodblock printing, so prized by Tsangnyön, and the "technology" of relics to be part of the same effort to expand the influence of Tsangnyön's school. Götsang Répa equated block printing with mass dissemination and in turn saw this as an important means to "benefit humanity"—a pleasant Buddhist euphemism for missionizing. For Tsangnyön and his disciples, the new technology of printing was a crucial tool for reaching wider audiences and one that they exploited fully at the beginning of the sixteenth century by carving new editions of numerous hagiographies and religious instructions.[65] The development of printing in fifteenth-century central Tibet requires detailed study to give weight to such a claim. Nevertheless, it is at least clear that Tsangnyön was part of this innovation and that the early prints of his *Life of Milarépa* were among the most important block prints of the late fifteenth century. His is certainly one of the earliest promotions of block printing as a religiously beneficial activity in central Tibetan writings and the most detailed that I have seen. By the time Sönam Lodrö was active in continuing the printing of hagiographic works begun by Tsangnyön, the act of printing was itself an event worthy of the marvelous visions we have come to associate with the accounts of Milarépa's death itself.[66]

The relics, miracle accounts, and block-printed *Life of Milarépa* and *Life of Tsangnyön* likely played a role in central Tibetan politics at the beginning of the sixteenth century as well, though this must be borne out in subsequent studies. Patrick Geary has suggested that in Carolingian Europe, "the relics of . . . sacred persons not only brought hope of cures to the poor and of stability to the great, but because they had a historical past, they could bring political and cultural focus to Carolingian policy."[67] It is equally possible that the Rinpungpa leader, Dönyö Dorjé, sought to utilize relics to aid his attempts at gaining wider control of central and southwestern Tibet. To support Tsangnyön in life was to support an active missionary who, presumably, would promote Dönyö Dorjé's political interests. To promote the memory of Tsangnyön after death by paying homage to his relics was to capitalize on the fame of two transregionally known saints: Milarépa and his hagiographer, the "madman of central Tibet."

Notes

1. Dan Martin: "Crystals and Images from Bodies, Hearts and Tongues from Fire: Points of Relic Controversy from Tibetan History," in *Tibetan Studies: Proceedings of the 5th Seminar of the International Association for Tibetan Studies, Narita 1989*, ed. Ihara Shōren and Yamaguchi Zuihō (Narita: Naritasan Shinshoji, 1992), 1:183–91, and "Pearls from Bones: Relics, Chortens, Tertons and the Signs of Saintly Death in Tibet," *Numen* 44 (1994): 273–324; and Yael Bentor, "Tibetan Relic Classifications," in *Tibetan Studies: Proceedings of the 6th Seminar of the International Association for Tibetan Studies, Fagernes 1992*, ed. Per Kværne (Oslo: Institute for Comparative Research in Human Culture, 1994), 1:16–30, are the most important contributions to the study of Tibetan relics to date.

2. Drawing on Jacques Le Goff (*The Medieval Imagination* [Chicago: University of Chicago Press, 1985], 27–44), I have for the most part used "marvelous" to render the term *ngo mtshar ba*, a Tibetan word that, like "marvelous," often describes apparitions (*ltas*) or other "indescribable" (*brjod par mi lang ba*) or "incomprehensible" (*bsam gyi mi khyab pa*) visual events often present in death accounts. More work should be done on the semantic range of terms such as *ngo mtshar*, *ya mtshan*, *cho 'phrul*, and (to a lesser extent) *rdzu 'phrul*, which appear so frequently in hagiographic literature.

3. Patrick J. Geary, *Living with the Dead in the Middle Ages* (Ithaca, NY: Cornell University Press, 1994), 200.

4. For instance, Gtsang smyon styles Mi la ras pa's final opponent as a Buddhist scholar critical of Mi la ras pa's anti-scholastic ways rather than as the Bon po priest of Rgyal thang pa's thirteenth-century account. See Francis V. Tiso, "The Death of Milarepa: Towards a *Redaktionsgeschichte* of the *Mila rnam thar* Traditions," in *Tibetan Studies: Proceedings of the 7th Seminar of the International Association of Tibetan Studies, Graz 1995*, ed. Helmut Krasser, Michael Torsten Much, Ernst Steinkellner, and Helmut Tauscher (Vienna: Verlag der Österreichischen Akademie der Wissenschaften, 1997), 2:987–95 (994).

5. 'Gos Lo tsā ba Gzhon nu dpal, *Deb ther sngon po* (New Delhi: International Academy of Indian Culture, 1974), 618.3, trans. George Roerich, *The Blue Annals* (Delhi: Motilal Banarsidass, 1976), 707.

6. Tshal pa Kun dga' rdo rje, *Deb ther dmar po rnams kyi dang po hu lan deb ther*, ed. Dung dkar Blo bzang 'phrin las (Beijing: Mi rigs dpe skrun khang, 1993), 79.21.

7. Stag lung Ngag dbang rnam rgyal, *Brgyud pa yid bzhin nor bu'i rtogs pa brjod pa ngo mtshar rgya mtsho* (Lhasa: Bod ljongs dpe yig dpe rnying dpe skrun khang, 1992), 470. Mention of this occurs in the story of the twelfth abbot of Stag lung, Ngag dbang grags pa dpal bzang (1418–96).

8. Karma pa III Rang byung rdo rje, *Rnal 'byor gyi dbang phyug mi la bzhad pa rdo rje'i gsung mgur mdzod nag ma zhes pa karma pa rang byung rdo rjes phyogs gcig tu bkod pa* (Dalhousie: Damchoe Sangpo, 1978), 2:553.6. The attribution of this work to Rang byung rdo rje requires inquiry: the colophon at vol. 2, 553.2–554.1 does not state that the work was composed by Rang byung rdo rje, but rather that it was compiled based upon his work.

9. E. Gene Smith, *Among Tibetan Texts: History and Literature of the Himalayan Plateau* (Boston: Wisdom, 2001), 70–73; Helmut Eimer and Pema Tsering, "Blockprints and Manuscripts of Mi la ras pa's *Mgur 'bum* Accessible to Frank-Richard Hamm," in *Frank-Richard Hamm Memorial Volume*, ed. Helmut Eimer (Bonn: Indica et Tibetica Verlag, 1990), 59–88. Note that Eimer and Tsering's edition "J" of the *Mi la'i mgur 'bum*, a "Xylograph in the British Library, formerly belonging to Heinrich August Jäschke (1817–1883)" (71–72), appears to be a print of the blocks carved by Gtsang smyon's student, Lha btsun pa Rin chen rnam rgyal in the 1550s.

10. Thu'u bkwan Blo bzang chos kyi nyi ma, *Khyab bdag rdo rje sems dpa'i ngo bo dpal ldan bla ma dam pa ye shes bstan pa'i sgron me dpal bzang po'i rnam par thar pa mdo tsam brjod pa dge ldan bstan pa'i mdzes rgyan* (Lanzhou: Kan su'u mi rigs dpe skrun khang, 1989), 43–44. The *Life* of Gtsang smyon is located at 38–45. Blo bzang chos kyi nyi ma used Rgod tshang ras pa's *rnam thar* to write this summary; see Thu'u bkwan Blo bzang chos kyi nyi ma, *Khyab*, 45.9–11; also, for more on this *rnam thar*, see Smith, *Among Tibetan Texts*, chap. 11.

11. Smith, *Among Tibetan Texts*, 60, 285n141.

12. Rgod tshang ras pa Sna tshogs rang grol, *Gtsang smyon he ru ka phyogs thams cad las rnam par rgyal ba'i rnam thar rdo rje theg pa'i gsal byed nyi ma'i snying po*, in *The Life of the Saint of Gtsaṅ* (New Delhi: Sharada Rani, 1969), 8.1.

13. Ibid., 4.5.

14. These dates are taken from Ko shul Grags pa 'byung gnas and Rgyal ba Blo bzang mkhas grub, *Gangs can mkhas grub rim byon ming mdzod* (Lanzhou: Kan su'u mi rigs dpe skrun khang, 1992), 1613–14.

15. Rgod tshang ras pa Sna tshogs rang grol, *Gtsang*, 72.6–73.2. The twelve acts of the Buddha are: (1) descent into the world from Dga' ldan; (2) entry into the womb; (3) birth; (4) miracles; (5) delights with a wife; (6) departure; (7) ascetic practice; (8) going to the heart of enlightenment; (9) becoming a buddha; (10) turning the wheel of dharma; (11) magical apparitions; (12) death. There are variations on this list.

16. Ibid., 137.7–138.7.

17. Ibid., 161.6.

18. Brag dkar rta so Sprul sku Chos kyi dbang phyug, *Grub pa'i gnas chen brag dkar rta so'i gnas dang gdan rab bla ma brgyud pa'i lo rgyus mdo*

tsam brjod pa mos ldan dad pa'i gdung sel drang srong dga' ba'i dal gtam (Nepal-German Manuscript Preservation Project (hereafter NGMPP), no. L940/8), fol. 22a.

19. In Gtsang smyon Heruka, *Rnal 'byor gyi dbang phyug chen po rje btsun mi la ras pa'i rnam thar thar pa dang thams cad mkhen pa'i lam ston* (NGMPP, no. L250/7) (one of at least two Brag dkar rta so block prints), chapter 9 occurs at fols. 83a.6–109a.2. I have used primarily J. W. de Jong, *Mi la ras pa'i rnam thar: Text tibétain de la vie de Milarepa* ('s-Gravenhage: Mouton, 1959), 182–206. For translations, see Lobsang P. Lhalungpa, *The Life of Milarepa* (New York: Arkana, 1979), 173–97; Walter Y. Evans-Wentz, ed., *Tibet's Great Yogī Milarepa* (Oxford: Oxford University Press, 1928), 273–304. For a narrative painting of Mi la ras pa's death, see Toni Schmid, *The Cotton-Clad Mila: The Tibetan Poet-Saint's Life in Pictures* (Stockholm: Statens Etnografiska Museum, 1952), 106–8.

20. Lhalungpa, *The Life of Milarepa*, 155–69 and 169–73.

21. Compare Rgod tshang ras pa Sna tshogs rang grol, *Rje btsun ras chung ba'i rnam thar rnam mkhyen thar lam gsal bar ston pa'i me long ye shes kyi snang ba* (Xining: Mtsho sngon mi rigs dpe skrun khang, 1992), 587–603, with de Jong, *Mi la ras pa'i rnam thar*, 187.12–206. Rgod tshang ras pa composed his work at Ras chung phug (Rgod tshang ras pa, *Rje btsun*, 666).

22. de Jong, *Mi la ras pa'i rnam thar*, 173.29–174.3. See Lhalungpa, *The Life of Milarepa*, 164; Evans-Wentz, *Tibet's Great Yogī Milarepa*, 261.

23. de Jong, *Mi la ras pa'i rnam thar*, 180; Lhalungpa, *The Life of Milarepa*, 170.

24. de Jong, *Mi la ras pa'i rnam thar*, 182–83; Lhalungpa, *The Life of Milarepa*, 173.

25. de Jong, *Mi la ras pa'i rnam thar*, 184; Lhalungpa, *The Life of Milarepa*, 174. This is the ninth song of chapter 9.

26. That is, without any *mchod pa 'bul ba dang gsol ba 'debs pa'i rten*. See de Jong, *Mi la ras pa'i rnam thar*, 184–85.

27. Ibid., 192; Lhalungpa, *The Life of Milarepa*, 183.

28. de Jong, *Mi la ras pa'i rnam thar*, 194; Evans-Wentz, *Tibet's Great Yogī Milarepa*, 289. I take *me khyer* to be correctly translated by Sönam Kazi as firefly. Lhalungpa (*The Life of Milarepa*, 184) leaves this term untranslated.

29. de Jong, *Mi la ras pa'i rnam thar*, 194–95; Lhalungpa, *The Life of Milarepa*, 185.

30. de Jong, *Mi la ras pa'i rnam thar*, 196–98; Lhalungpa, *The Life of Milarepa*, 186–88.

31. de Jong, *Mi la ras pa'i rnam thar*, 205; Lhalungpa, *The Life of Milarepa*, 196.

32. Bla ma Zhang G.yu grag pa Brtson 'grus grags pa (1123–1193),

[Untitled *rnam thar* of Mi la ras pa], in *Writings (Bka' thor bu) of Zaṅ g.yu brag pa Brtson 'grus grags pa* (Tashijong: Sungrab Nyamso Gyunpel Parkhang, 1972), 333.1–352.4 (352.4).

33. Sgam po pa Bsod nams rin chen, *Rje mar pa dang rje btsun mi la'i rnam thar,* in *Selected Writings of Sgam-po-pa Bsod-nams-rin-chen* (Lahul: Topden Tshering, 1974), 18–30 (30). Although recent scholars have attributed this *rnam thar* to Sgam po pa himself, it has no clear statement of authorship in its colophon. I think it is possible that it was in fact written by his biographer, Bsod nams lhun grub (1488–1552), whose work immediately follows the *rnam thar* of Mar pa and Mi la ras pa in all three readily available versions of Sgam po pa's collected works.

34. The death account in the eighteenth and final section of Karma pa Rang byung rdo rje, *Rnal* (2:517–51) bears similarity to that of Gtsang smyon's *Life of Milarepa*. Yet while there are eleven songs in common between the fifteen in the death account of this work and the sixteen in Gtsang smyon's work, it is my impression that Gtsang smyon's rendition is more elaborate in its prose sections. The *Mi la ras pa'i rnam thar* (Newark Museum, Holton Col., acc. no. 36.280), the so-called *Bu chen bcu gnyis Life of Milarepa*, also contains a lengthy death account (fols. 234–43). A critical literary history of these works awaits.

35. Kevin Trainor, *Relics, Ritual, and Representation in Buddhism: Rematerializing the Sri-Lankan Theravāda Tradition* (Cambridge: Cambridge University Press, 1997), 123.

36. Rgyal thang Bde chen rdo rje, *Rje rgod tshang pa'i rnam thar la mgur chen 'gas brgyas pa*, in *Rgyal ba rgod tshang pa mgon po rdo rje'i rnam par thar pa mthong ba don ldan nor bu'i phreng ba* (Xining: Mtsho sngon mi rigs dpe skrun khang, 1993), 305–421 (420.9). See also Sangs rgyas dar po, *Rgyal ba rgod tshang pa mgon po rdo rje'i rnam par thar pa mthong ba don ldan nor bu'i phreng ba* (written in 1540) (Xining: Mtsho sngon mi rigs dpe skrun khang, 1993), 1–304 (290–95).

37. Anonymous, *Rje btsun rin po che mi la ras chen gyi rnam thar,* in *Bde mchog sñan brgyud Biographies: Reproduction of a Collection of Rare Manuscripts from the Stag-sna Monastery in Ladakh* (Darjeeling: Kargyud Sungrab Nyamso Khang, 1983), 133–89 (189).

38. Rgyal thang Bde chen rdo rje, *Rje,* 264, and Tiso, "The Death of Milarepa," 992.

39. Stag lung Ngag dbang rnam rgyal, *Brgyud,* 158.

40. Brag dkar rta so Sprul sku Chos kyi dbang phyug, *Grub,* 22a.

41. 'Bri gung Chos rje Kun dga' rin chen, *Rje btsun mi la ras pa'i rnam thar dngos grub kyi snye ma* (written in 1508), in *Miscellaneous Writings (Bka' 'bum thor bu) of 'Bri-gung Chos-rje Kun-dga'-rin-chen* (Leh: Sonam W. Tashigangpa, 1972), 41–51 (51).

42. Mon rtse pa Kun dga' dpal ldan, *Rje btsun mi la ras pa'i rnam par*

thar pa, in *Dkar brgyud gser 'phreng: A Golden Rosary of Lives of Eminent Gurus* (Leh: Sonam W. Tashigangpa, 1970), 104–65 (164–65).

43. Rta tshag Tshe dbang rgyal, *Dam pa'i chos kyi byung ba'i legs bshad lho rong chos 'byung ngam rta tshag chos 'byung zhes rtsom pa'i yul ming du chags pa'i ngo mtshar zhing bkon pa'i dpe khyad par can* (written in 1447) (Lhasa: Bod ljongs bod yig dpe rnying dpe skrun khang, 1994), 101–2.

44. Ibid., 101. A longer version incorporating these elements appeared at least half a century earlier: Zhwa dmar pa II Mkha' spyod dbang po, *Chos rje dpal ldan mi la ras chen gyi rnam par thar pa byin rlabs kyi sprin phung*, in *The Collected Works of Zwa-dmar II Mkha'-spyod-dbaṅ-po* (Gangtok: Gonpo Tseten, 1978), 1:188–317 (309–16).

45. Ras chung phug was known to 'Jam dbyangs Mkhyen brtse dbang po (1820–1892) as the residence of Gtsang smyon Heruka, whom he considered an incarnation not of Mi la ras pa but of Ras chung pa. See Alfonsa Ferrari, *Mk'yen brtse's Guide to the Holy Places of Central Tibet* (Rome: Istituto Italiano per il Medio ed Estremo Oriente, 1958), 51. In his pilgrimage account of the years 1918–20, Kaḥ thog Si tu Chos kyi rgya mtsho (1880–1924) visited Ras chung phug and reported that the central image of the main temple was a likeness of Gtsang smyon Heruka. See Kaḥ thog Si tu Chos kyi rgya mtsho, *Si tu pa chos kyi rgya mtsho'i gangs ljongs dbus gtsang gnas bskor lam yig nor bu zla shel* (Lhasa: Bod ljongs bod yig dpe rnying dpe skrun khang, 1999), 200–1. Today Ras chung phug is in ruins. During a brief visit there in 1998, I encountered several Kagyu nuns on pilgrimage from Khams who had come there to collect pieces of wood from the temple ruins to bring home as relics.

46. The following is a summary of the last three chapters of Rgod tshang ras pa's *rnam thar* of Gtsang smyon: Rgod tshang ras pa Sna tshogs rang grol, *Gtsang*, 268–82. See Smith, *Among Tibetan Texts*, chap. 5, for an outline of this work.

There are two other hagiographies of Gtsang smyon, which, although they are important in their own right for other reasons, do not add much to our picture of Gtsang smyon's death and its aftermath: Dngos grub dpal 'bar, *Rje btsun gtsang pa he ru ka'i thun mong gi rnam thar yon tan gyi gangs ri la dad pa'i seng ge rnam par rtse ba* (NGMPP, no. L834/2); and Lha btsun pa Rin chen rnam rgyal, *Grub thob gtsang smyon pa'i rnam thar dad pa'i spu slong g.yo ba*, in *Bde mchog mkha' 'gro snyan rgyud (Ras chung snyan rgyud): Two Manuscript Collections of Texts from the yig cha of Gtsang-smyon He-ru-ka* (Leh: Smanrtsis Shesrig Spendzod, 1971), 1–129. Dngos grub dpal 'bar's *Life* was composed and printed shortly after Gtsang smyon's death. While it contains a lengthy account of Gtsang smyon's death (beginning Dngos grub dpal 'bar, *Rje*, fols. 27a.6), Rgod tshang ras pa integrated much of it into his account. Lha btsun Rin chen rnam rgyal's *Life* of Gtsang smyon, printed in 1543, contains only a brief and generic account of the marvelous visions surrounding his death and nothing of his relics. Lha btsun suggests that those wishing to know more about the master's death look at the hagiographies composed by his elder religious brothers (Lha btsun pa Rin chen rnam rgyal, *Grub*, 126.5–27.4).

47. Rgod tshang ras pa quotes a Rnying ma tantra, the *Blazing Remains Tantra, Dpal nam mkha' med pa'i sku gdung 'bar ba chen po'i rgyud*, in *Rnying ma rgyud 'bum* [Mtshams brag ed.] (Thimpu: National Library, 1982), vol. 11 (*da*), fols. 788.2–815.7. See Martin, "Pearls from Bones," 281–82, for an outline of the third chapter of this tantra, which is dedicated to external signs (*phyi rtags*) left by deceased holy people.

48. Yum Kun tu bzang mo is also mentioned at Rgod tshang ras pa Sna tshogs rang grol (*Gtsang*, 281) as one of the participants at the three-month festival at Chu dbar. Compare with the verse from the print colophon of Dngos grub dpal 'bar, *Rje*, fol. 30b.5, in which Kun tu bzang mo's name is integrated.

49. Trainor, *Relics, Ritual, and Representation in Buddhism*, 119–20.

50. Rgod tshang ras pa Sna tshogs rang grol, *Gtsang*, 267.

51. Martin, "Pearls from Bones," 297–98.

52. Elena de Rossi Filibeck, *Two Tibetan Guide Books to Ti se and La phyi* (Bonn: VGH Wissenschafts-verlag, 1988), 133.

53. Toni Huber and Tsepak Rigzin, "A Tibetan Guide for Pilgrimage to Ti-se (Mt. Kailas) and mTsho Ma-pham (Lake Manasarovar)," *Tibet Journal* 20.1 (1995): 10–47 (26). A modern edition of the 1902 block print is now available; see Bstan 'dzin chos kyi blo gros, *Gangs ri chen po ti se dang mtsho chen ma dros pa bcas kyi sngon byung gi lo rgyus mdor bsdus su brjod pa'i rab byed shel dkar me long* (written in 1896), in *Gnas yig phyogs bsgrigs* (Chengdu: Si khron mi rigs dpe skrun khang, 1998), 114–220.

54. Bya bral pa Tshul khrims dpal ldan, *Mkhas grub rdo rje 'chang bsod nams blo gros kyi rnam thar yon tan gyi sbrang rtsi la dad pa'i bung ba rnam par rol pa* (NGMPP, L833/3), fol. 53b.

55. Ibid., fol. 18b.

56. Ibid., fol. 50a.

57. Ibid., fol. 51a.

58. Burton Mack, "Social Formation," in *Guide to the Study of Religion*, ed. Willi Braun and Russell T. McCutcheon (London: Cassell, 2000), 283–96 (283).

59. Geary, *Living with the Dead*, 171.

60. Lhalungpa, *The Life of Milarepa*, 202.

61. de Jong, *Mi la ras pa'i rnam thar*, 22.30.

62. Ibid., 23.1. Lhalungpa, *The Life of Milarepa*, 9, translates this as "The story is heralded by the following preface," thus losing the association Gtsang smyon makes between sūtra and *rnam thar*.

63. de Jong, *Mi la ras pa'i rnam thar*, 209.1–.21; Lhalungpa, *The Life of*

Milarepa, 201–2. Note that my paraphrase differs from Lhalungpa's translation in its treatment of the word *rnam thar*.

64. de Jong, *Mi la ras pa'i rnam thar*, 209.22–10.2. From the fact that de Jong presents this passage as prose without separating each line, it appears that he did not realize that this is a four-line verse with forty-five syllables to the line—an impressive poetic finale!

65. The first printing in central Tibet appears to have been done in 1418–19, less than seventy years before Gtsang smyon printed Mi la ras pa's *Life*. See David P. Jackson, "The Earliest Printings of Tsong-kha-pa's Works: The Old Dga'-ldan Editions," in *Reflections on Tibetan Culture: Essays in Memory of Turrell V. Wylie*, ed. Lawrence Epstein and Richard F. Sherbourne (Lewiston: Edwin Mellen Press, 1990), 107–16 (106 and 114n2). At Dpal 'khor chos sde, the major monastery of Rgyal rtse in Gtsang, a woodblock print of a *dhāraṇī* collection was made during the years 1439–41. See 'Jigs med grags pa, *Rgyal rtse chos rgyal gyi rnam par thar pa dad pa'i lo thog dngos grub kyi char 'bebs* (written in 1479–81) (Lhasa: Bod ljongs mi dmangs dpe skrun khang, 1987), 256–57. Since Gtsang smyon was a student at Dpal 'khor chos sde, it is possible that he was exposed to printing there, though this supposition begs for a history of printing in central Tibet. See also Smith, *Among Tibetan Texts*, 73–79.

66. Bya bral pa Tshul khrims dpal ldan, *Mkhas*, fols. 42b.2–43a.6.

67. Geary, *Living with the Dead*, 191.

7

Fire and the Sword

Some Connections between Self-Immolation and Religious Persecution in the History of Chinese Buddhism

James A. Benn

This chapter addresses a very special form of death—the voluntary termination of life by Chinese Buddhists. Although "martyrdom" is not a category that has much been applied to Buddhist materials, as we reflect on the deaths of certain exemplary individuals in the following pages, it may be useful to keep in mind the possible parallels with types of holy death known in Christianity and Islam. In particular, the concept of martyrdom may help us to understand better how some Chinese Buddhists defined themselves individually and institutionally against a political order that did not always share their interests. According to one standard definition, martyrs are those who "offer their lives voluntarily in solidarity with their group in contrast with another, ideologically contrasting group."[1] The groups considered here are the Chinese imperial state and the monastic community (saṅgha). In the medieval Buddhist world-view, the ideal government was one that supported the dharma. When the state slipped from that ideal function, there was a perceived need to restore the cosmic order, and the actions of self-immolators were incorporated into a larger Buddhist narrative in which rulers and the saṅgha worked together to promote the dharma. We may compare this process with that of the Christian martyrs who "persevered unto death" and died at the hands of an unjust state and whose courage was one granted to them by God.[2] Although martyrdom is not an analytical category that is employed within the Buddhist tradition to define a type or method of death, by using it here, I wish to highlight those political and social aspects of self-immolation that are often obscured by the more passive categories that Buddhist authors employ, such as "relinquishing the body" or "abandoning the self."

Close attention to political, social, and religious contexts in the commemoration of self-immolators shows how their mythic dimension—imitation of certain scriptural ideals of extreme selflessness—intersected with the mundane realities of life and death in imperial China. Buddhist martyrdom was a form of death that disrupted the social order while at the same time reestablishing a cosmic order in which the saṅgha and the state could once again play their correct roles. These intersections and disruptions produced what may be regarded as indigenous Chinese Buddhist myths and indigenous heroes whose importance is crucial to understanding the religious tensions within traditional Chinese society.

To borrow from the genre classification of religious biography developed by scholars of Christianity, in Chinese Buddhist literature the *vita* was always the dominant mode of writing about monks.[3] The *vita* acts as a model of an exemplary life, one that can be admired and imitated by the faithful. The *passio*, or martyrology, on the other hand, provides a dramatic description of trial and death at the hands of secular persecutors. In the historical development of Christian hagiographical literature, the *passio* preceded the *vita*. The existence of a Chinese Buddhist martyrology has so far gone unnoticed, and it was surely never a fully developed genre, but still we may find some traces of a nascent form in the biographies discussed below. It may be that for Buddhists, as for Muslim mystics, martyrology is but part of a larger hagiographical tradition and provides a source of spiritual insight as much as an exemplary form of religious dedication.[4]

Christian martyrs were usually tried and killed by hostile forces. The majority of the monks I shall discuss terminated their lives voluntarily, although at least one was executed. Self-immolation in its strictest sense means "self-sacrifice," derived ultimately from the Latin *molare*, "to make a sacrifice of grain." It does not mean suicide by fire, although the term is now commonly used in that sense.[5] Three Chinese terms in particular are encountered in the sources, and they are used more or less interchangeably: *wangshen*, *yishen*, and *sheshen*. They all mean to relinquish, or to abandon, the body. Here the word *shen* (body) also implies "self," or the person as a whole. Self-immolation may be considered a particular expression of the more generalized Buddhist ideal of detachment from the deluded notion of a self.

Abandoning the body, or letting go of the self, took a variety of forms in Chinese history.[6] For example, *sheshen* can stand for the common Buddhist term *chujia* (to leave the household), which means to become a monk or a nun. The pious Buddhist emperor Liang Wudi (r. 502–49) ransomed himself to the saṅgha on a number of occasions and had to be bought back by his ministers at great expense.[7] This kind of offering of the body is also referred to as *sheshen*. In textual accounts of monks that appeared in collections of hagiographies under the rubric of self-immolation, we find a range of acts such as allowing insects to feed on one's blood, slicing flesh from the body, and burning the fingers or arms. Not all of these necessarily resulted in death. People also terminated their lives by starvation, laceration, drowning, leaping from cliffs or trees, feeding themselves to wild animals, or self-mummification. Burning oneself to death, indicated by terms such as *shaoshen* (burning the body) and *zifen* (self-burning)—and to which I shall refer as "auto-cremation"—was the most common form of terminal self-immolation in Chinese Buddhism.

We shall examine here some cases of self-immolation that appear to be Buddhist responses to persecution, which in China took the form of state-directed attempts to limit the size, and hence the expense, of the saṅgha. In researching a larger project on self-immolation in China, I found about three hundred cases, dating between 398 and 1927; thus, as a proportion of the total number of monks and nuns who lived between these two dates, the six cases I discuss below might seem statistically almost infinitesimal.[8] I would argue that they are nonetheless significant.

In the following six cases, we may detect three basic scenarios. First, in the 570s, monks living under the Northern Zhou regime were forcibly returned to lay life, and those who resisted were hunted down. Biographies of monks living in the Zhongnan mountain range close to the capital show that they responded by placing their faith in the power of sacred text. In one more dramatic case, however, a monk offered the gift of his own body in exchange for a new regime that would again patronize the saṅgha. Second, at the turn of the seventh century, the second emperor of the Sui dynasty announced some reductions in the size of the saṅgha. One monk was so upset by this that he offered his own arm in exchange for the emperor's continued patronage. This scenario appeared again in the 1500s, with a similar outcome. Third, when the city of Luoyang was controlled by an evil tyrant in 618, one devout layman defied him by resigning from office and taking the tonsure. He was executed for his pains. The common thread in all three scenarios is resistance to state persecution or to the loss of state support.

Sacred Biography in Seventh-Century China

In focusing on the problems that the Buddhist monastic community had to face from regimes that were either overtly hostile or less than fervent in their support, let us begin by looking at a few biographies that are contained in the second of the three major medieval collections of monastic biographies, *Xu gaoseng zhuan* (Continued biographies of eminent monks).[9] This work was compiled by the much misunderstood and still insufficiently studied metropolitan monk and prolific author Daoxuan (596–667).[10] This collection contains a significant number of cases of self-immolation in times of religious persecution, and for that reason it is particularly valuable for our purposes here. Like other collections of Chinese monastic biographies, *Xu gaoseng zhuan* is divided into categories of religious specialization. The section on self-immolation is entitled "yishen" and in the form that has come down to us contains twelve main biographies and four supplementary appended biographies. By contemporary standards, Daoxuan emerges as a diligent and very well-informed historian.[11] We know that he went back and corrected and added to earlier drafts of his work when new information on his subjects came to light. But Daoxuan was by no means an impartial recorder of events, and the *Xu gaoseng zhuan* was not compiled in the middle of the seventh century for the benefit of scholars in the early twenty-first. As we shall see, it contained material that was of pressing interest to Daoxuan and his contemporary audience.

There are some textual problems in the *Xu gaoseng zhuan* that concern a number of biographies added after the date of Daoxuan's preface of 645 and some that were added or altered after his death in 667.[12] The section on self-immolation is far from immune from these problems, but for the purposes of this chapter they do not significantly affect the biographies under investigation.[13] Suffice it to say here that Daoxuan's final draft probably contained only ten biographies.

We shall consider five of the biographies in an attempt to delineate some ways in which self-immolation was related to certain religious policies enacted by some rulers in the sixth and early seventh centuries. This will reveal that the biographies in the section on self-immolation, taken as a whole, convey a certain polemical intent on Daoxuan's part. We shall learn that self-immolators did react to religious persecution and that their acts and particularly their deaths may have been understood by Daoxuan and others to have altered the course of history in favor of the Buddhist establishment in China.

Daoxuan was widely traveled and particularly well informed about the religious situation beyond the immediate confines of the capital monasteries. Nevertheless, in the case of the section on self-immolators, there remains a definite geographical bias. Much of his information was drawn from stele inscriptions and eye-witness accounts of monks who lived on Mt. Zhongnan, a mountain range not far from the Tang capital of Chang'an (now the city of Xi'an).[14] Some acts of self-immolation were even investigated by Daoxuan himself on his visits to religious sites there. In time and space, Daoxuan was much closer to the majority of his subjects than any other monastic biographer before or since. The significance of their deaths did not belong to the remote past but was something that Daoxuan and his contemporaries felt acutely. We know that Daoxuan was eager to defend Buddhism against future attacks by the state because he also included a section on "defenders of the dharma" (*hufa*), which had not featured in the earlier *Gaoseng zhuan*.[15]

Northern Zhou Persecution and the Monks of Mt. Zhongnan

The Zhongnan mountain range was an area with which Daoxuan was very familiar, since he resided there on several occasions and finally retired there toward the end of his life.[16] Around 630, Daoxuan withdrew into Mt. Zhongnan in response to the anti-Buddhist policies adopted by the emperor Tang Taizong (r. 626–49).[17] That period in his life, as well as a continued sense of disquiet at the emperor's policies toward Buddhism, may have been on his mind as he was compiling these biographies ten years or so later. Out of a total of ten main biographies of self-immolators in the original text, no fewer than five of them lived and died on Mt.

Zhongnan. As for the *Xu gaoseng zhuan* as a whole, Mt. Zhongnan is mentioned in 55 out of 344 main biographies, about one-sixth of the total.

Let us now examine three of these Mt. Zhongnan biographies: those of Puyuan and his disciples Puji and Puan. In particular, I want to pay attention to the reactions of the two disciples to the persecution of Buddhism by the Zhou emperor Wudi (r. 560–78), which began in 574. This was one of several attacks on the Buddhist community that affected the course of Chinese history, and its impact on the Chinese religious scene was immense.[18] At this time, China had not been unified for hundreds of years, but by the 570s, the Zhou dynasty controlled most of North China. In 574 the Zhou emperor Wudi ordered that all monks and nuns were to return to lay life and that monastic property was to be confiscated and distributed among the Zhou nobility. In 577 this policy was extended across the whole of North China, when the state of Northern Qi fell to the Zhou. One of the effects of this persecution was to drive practitioners from North China, where the Zhou ruled, down to the south, where they met interesting new people and new forms of practice. But what about those who stayed behind? Obviously, they did as any sensible person would: they ran up the nearest mountain and hid. But this was not all that they did, and we may suspect that the inclusion of their biographies was no accident. It seems likely that Daoxuan used the accounts of their deaths to deliver a pointed message about the relationship between the state and Buddhism in his own time, some seventy years later, when China was unified under the Tang dynasty (618–907).

The Zhou Recluse (*Yi*), Śramaṇa Shi Puyuan (fl. ca. 560) of Yongzhou

Let us look first at Puyuan, who is of interest to us here primarily as the master of Puji and Puan.[19] His family background is unknown. Active around central Shaanxi (Northwest China) at the beginning of Wudi's reign, according to his biography, Puyuan was imposing in stature, refined in manner, elegant in his written composition, and well traveled. He concentrated on ascetic practice (Ch. *toutuo*; Skt. *dhūta*)—which in medieval China usually included such austerities as not lying down to sleep, restricting one's diet, and dressing in rags. The biography notes that Puyuan was motivated by compassion and the desire to benefit others. He recited the *Huayan jing* (*Avataṃsaka sūtra*) in a way that his disciples could not recognize until they read the text.[20] He would sit in samādhi (absorption) on his rope bed, and he was so focused on his meditation that he was not aware of the passing of the days. While he occasionally appeared in villages to beg for food, mostly he spent his time practicing meditation in cemeteries (*linmu*).[21] It is worth noting in passing that while cremation-ground contemplations are extolled in Indian Buddhist texts, references to this practice in China are comparatively rare, and it is clear that Puyuan was uncommonly severe in his vocation.

One night Puyuan encountered a powerful and terrifying ghost, which had four eyes and six teeth and body hair that hung straight down.[22] It was holding a twisted club in its hands. Puyuan opened his eyes wide, without any sign of fear, and this caused the ghost to withdraw rapidly. On another occasion, an evil person begged Puyuan for his head. Puyuan was about to chop it off and hand it over, but the other did not dare actually take it and begged for his eyes instead. Puyuan was willing to gouge them out and give them away. Then the person wanted his hand, so Puyuan lashed his wrist to a tree with a rope. He cut off his arm at the elbow and gave it away. He died by the Fan Vale, south of Chang'an. All the villagers lamented at this ascetic act and competed as to who should get his remains, so they divided his body into many pieces and built a stūpa for each of them.[23] The division of the relics recalls what occurred after the Buddha's cremation, as described in John Strong's essay in this volume. However, it must have been a bloodier process, as Puyuan's body had not been reduced to ashes and bones. It has many parallels with the amateur dissections of the bodies of saints in medieval Europe, described so well by Piero Camporesi.[24] The competition to secure fragments of the holy body shows how important these relics were to the medieval Chinese and how taboos on the handling of the corpse could be transcended in the case of these "very special dead."

We cannot really understand Puyuan's death without placing it against the background of stories told about Indian bodhisattva heroes. This extreme form of giving, to anyone who asked, no matter how evil the intention of the asker, was a common theme of the *jātaka* and *avadāna* literature that was popular in North China in the fifth and sixth centuries. The donation of the head or the eyes is often encountered in these stories, and the theme has been explored most productively by Reiko Ohnuma.[25] This particular case seems closest to stories told of two figures, King Śibi and a prince called Candraprabha (Prince Moonlight). Generally speaking, in the Pāli sources, King Sivi (*sic*), who is the Buddha Śākyamuni in a former life, is remembered for giving away his eyes, while in the northern tradition, he is celebrated for giving away all of his flesh. If we look at the story as it appears in a Chinese translation of the *Mahāyāna-sūtrālaṃkāra* of Aśvaghoṣa (*Dasheng zhuangyan lun jing*), we read of a virtuous king known for his generosity.[26] The two gods Śakra and Viśvakarman decide to put his charity to the test. Viśvakarman takes the form of a pigeon, while Śakra becomes a falcon. The pigeon flies away from its pursuer and hides under Śibi's arm. Śibi promises to protect the bird, but the falcon complains that Śibi has stolen his food. Śibi offers the falcon a portion of his own flesh equivalent to the weight of the pigeon, and the falcon agrees to the deal. Śibi places the pigeon on the scale and starts cutting off his own flesh, beginning with his thigh, and adding it to the other side of the balance. But no matter how much flesh he gives, he is unable to match the weight of the pigeon. Śibi ends up giving his entire body. Then the gods reveal their true identity and encourage King Śibi to declare the sincerity of his gift. As a result, Śibi's body is magically restored.

The cycle of stories about Candraprabha is extremely complex, as many different tales concerning offerings of the flesh are associated with this figure.[27] But Puyuan's biography may also recall the story told by Xuanzang (600–64) about the death of the philosopher Nāgārjuna (ca. 150–250), who cut off his head to offer it to a prince who requested it.[28]

This biography represents a reenactment on Chinese soil of stories told about the heroes of Indian Buddhist literature. As such, it displays an imitative quality that is rather unusual in the Chinese sources. Other biographies present forms of self-sacrifice that are usually not so much copies of Indian stories as they are more nuanced reinterpretations of those themes. For example, the evil person or god who demands the head of a bodhisattva is a common character in the *jātaka*s and *avadāna*s but appears very rarely in these biographies. In any case, Puyuan's offering of his own body is not a consequence of religious persecution by the state, but it is important in providing a precedent for his disciples, two of whom did offer to defend the dharma with their own bodies in more perilous times.

The Sui Śramaṇa Shi Puji (d. 581) of Mt. Zhongnan

Puji's biography shows how the power of the ascetic could ward off the depredations of an evil ruler.[29] Puji was from the northern mountains of Yongzhou.[30] When he first became a novice, his master was Puyuan, whom we have just met. He lived alone in the wilds of the forest, unafraid of wild dogs and tigers. He cultivated dhyāna well into his old age but did not eschew scriptural studies, favoring the *Huayan jing* in particular. After the "destruction of the dharma" (i.e., the persecution of Buddhism by Zhou Wudi, which began in 574), he went to live among the peaks of Mt. Zhongnan (referred to here by its alternative name, Mt. Taibai). There he made the following detailed statement:

> He vowed that if the images and teachings [i.e., Buddhism] should flourish, he would relinquish his body in homage (Skt. pūjā). He cultivated the practices of Puxian ("Universally Worthy," the bodhisattva Samantabhadra), so as to be reborn in a most worthy land (*xianshou guo*). At the beginning of the Kaihuang reign period [of Sui Wendi, 581–600], the dharma gate was greatly propagated [i.e., Buddhism was restored], and he considered that his vow had been fulfilled. Then he arranged his own sacrifice. He led a crowd to assemble on the western cliffs of the Tan valley of Mt. Taibai. Loudly pronouncing his great vow, he threw himself off and died. People from afar flocked there, filling the cliffs and valleys. They built a white stūpa for him on a high peak.[31]

Puji's dramatic end offers a rare insight into the way in which the beginning of Sui rule in 581 was probably understood as a momentous and positive event, of truly cosmic dimensions, for monks in the north who had suffered under Zhou Wudi. It seems from his inclusion of Puji's biography that Daoxuan in particular retained some affection for the Sui, despite his subsequent problems, since he owed his own start in religion to Sui patronage.[32] But more than that, the story of Puji suggests that in the minds of Daoxuan and others, Buddhists were able to influence history by bargaining with their own bodies. The phrase "most worthy land" carries within it the sense not only of a pure land established by a buddha, but also, quite literally, "a most worthy state"—i.e., one that propagated Buddhism.[33] Certainly the Sui, at least under the founder Wendi, could be characterized as just such a state.[34] I have found no explicit antecedent in the *avadāna* literature for the life of a bodhisattva being offered in exchange for the restoration of the dharma, and we may see this rather as a particularly Chinese response to persecution. It provides some indication that early Tang Buddhists continued to look with favor on the early years of Sui rule. Might it not also suggest a new and particularly Buddhist way of looking at dynastic legitimation in China—that a dynasty might have to hold, not so much the more traditional mandate of heaven (*tianming*) as a mandate of the Buddha, one that had been obtained less by the founders' own virtues than by the efforts of eminent monks? This would match well with what we know about the patronage of Buddhism by the Sui and Tang royal families.[35]

The Sui Śramaṇa Shi Puan (530–609), Who Was a Recluse to the South of the Capital Suburbs

The biography of another of Puyuan's disciples was probably included here primarily because of that connection and for his miraculous endurance of Wudi's persecution, rather than for any spectacular act of self-immolation.[36] Puan's biography is long and packed with incident, but only a few passages illustrate his body practices. Puan's secular name was Guo, and he was from Jingyang in Jingzhao.[37] He became Puyuan's disciple while still young. Later he is said to have studied under dharma master Ai, most likely Jing'ai (534–75), who in a separate incident sliced up his body and cut out his own heart, leaving behind a long gāthā (verse) composed in his own blood.[38] Although an ascetic by inclination, Puan is said to have completely mastered the *tripiṭaka*, and, like Puyuan's other disciples, he had a particular affection for the *Huayan jing*. He also chanted and practiced dhyāna. Like Puji, he also went into hiding to escape the persecution of Zhou Wudi, and with him sheltered in the Zhongnan mountains dharma master Jingyuan (544–611) and some thirty other renegade monks.[39] The biography describes his attempts to sacrifice himself:

> Also, he cultivated ascetic practices, sacrificing his body for the sake of beings. Sometimes he exposed his body in the grass, donat-

> ing it to mosquitoes and gadflies. Flowing blood covered his body, but he had no fear at all. Sometimes he would lie among discarded corpses, hoping to give himself to wild dogs and tigers. In the hope of giving himself away while still alive, this is what he prayed for as his fundamental intention. Although tigers and wildcats came, they just sniffed at him but would not eat him. He always regretted that his heartfelt vow had not been fulfilled. Alone, he followed the tracks of wild animals, hoping to find one who would eat him.[40]

The donation of the body to insects, which appears at first to be a bizarre invention, is actually based on stories told of King Śibi and others and was to become a common feature in the biographies of later self-immolators.[41] Being eaten by tigers was apparently much harder than it looked in the *jātaka*s, although the implication of the narrative is that by not being eaten, Puan was being saved for an even greater task.[42] Soon, however, failure to be eaten by wild animals was to be the least of his worries, as Puan found himself responsible for the material needs of the monks he was hiding in the forest. Since there was a bounty for the capture of monks at that time, he was taking a considerable risk in showing himself in order to beg for food and clothing on their behalf. He had a couple of narrow escapes, on one occasion being released from custody by Zhou Wudi himself on a technicality.[43] When Jing'ai questioned him about his miraculous good fortune in evading arrest, he attributed it to the power of the *Huayan jing*.[44] Once Buddhism prospered again under the Sui, Puan was free to resume his former solitary and austere way of life, but he continued to be assailed by potential misfortune. These episodes are recounted at length in the biography: there was nearly a nasty accident during the construction of his cliff dwelling; a jealous ascetic attempted to assassinate him; robbers attempted to take his money and, more shockingly, some oil from the pots reserved for the lamps that burned in front of the buddha image. Needless to say, each of these incidents ended happily for Puan, who never failed to attribute the fortunate consequences to the power of his favorite sūtra. He also revived someone from the dead, a feat not commonly attested in biographies of monks.[45]

The last in a series of such tales concerning Puan brings us back to the theme of self-immolation. Troubled by the number of blood sacrifices made at local altars, Puan was in the habit of buying back sacrificial animals so as to save them from slaughter. On one occasion, he attempted to pay the ransom of three pigs. But the villagers wanted the outrageous price of 10,000 pieces of cash for them. Puan could offer only 3,000, and this caused an argument among the crowd. Suddenly a young child, clad in a sheepskin, appeared in order to help Puan to buy back the pigs. When he saw the argument, he asked for some wine. As he danced around drinking, the villagers all lost sight of him, and he mysteriously disappeared. The monk took quick advantage of their confused state:

> Then Puan pulled out a knife. He sliced the flesh of his thigh and said, "Mine and theirs [the pigs'] are both flesh. Pigs eat shit and filth, and you value eating them. Furthermore, if people ate grain, then human flesh would be more valuable." The people of the altar society, having seen and heard this, simultaneously released [the pigs]. The pigs, having attained their escape, circumambulated Puan three times. They snuffled at him with their snouts as if out of love and respect. The result was that within fifty *li* southwest of the suburbs, pigs and chickens had their lineages discontinued [i.e., they were no longer raised domestically].[46]

We can see that this biography makes much of vegetarianism as a mark of conversion to Buddhist faith and a renunciation of the bloody cults of local religion. Here Puan's offering of his own body is responsible for this conversion and the saving of animals' lives. Such was Puan's reputation that in 588, he was invited to the Sui capital, where he served as a mentor to the crown prince.[47] He resided at the Jingfa Monastery, which Princess Zhang (Zhang gongzhu, Sui Wendi's older sister) had founded, although the biography says that he preferred to continue to sleep in the mountains.[48] Given this prestigious connection, it is odd that Daoxuan does not mention this affiliation in the title of the biography. I suspect that he wanted to remind the reader of the fact that Puan was a hero of the Buddhist resistance to the policies of Zhou Wudi, when he was indeed a renegade monk.

On the fifth day of the eleventh month of 609 (Daye 5), Puan died at the Jingfa Monastery, at the age of eighty. A stūpa was raised for his remains on Mt. Zhongnan, by the side of the Zhixiang Monastery. If nothing else, this biography shows that a self-immolator could die of natural causes after a long and eventful life. Why was Puan's biography included here? We must suspect that Daoxuan wanted to make a point about the necessity of state patronage of Buddhism, and he used the Sui as a model example. Puan's heroic reputation and his patronage by the Sui royal family were founded on a combination of resistance to the Zhou persecution and his own willingness to surrender his body to propagate the dharma and protect the saṅgha. His actual death was not required for him to be presented as a model martyr; rather his ascetic practices might be understood as a minor form of martyrdom.

A Martyr for the Saṅgha: The Sui Śramaṇa Shi Dazhi (567–609) of Mt. Lu in Jiujiang

The idea that monks would lay down their lives to protect the saṅgha as a whole against the depredations of the state is nowhere better exemplified than in the biography of Dazhi.[49] The three biographies we have discussed thus far do not focus solely on the monk as martyr; in other words, they remain more *vita* than *passio*. But in Dazhi's biography, we may see how the story of his life and death served as both remembrance and exemplar. In the same way that the Christian *passio* had its roots in the stories (*legenda*) of violent confrontation with secular authority, trial, and death that were read to the faithful on the feast days of martyrs, we shall see how Dazhi's self-immolation was celebrated and remembered by the Buddhist community in the early Tang.[50]

In contrast to most of the self-immolators we have met thus far, Dazhi was a monk of a truly famous lineage, being one of the disciples of the most revered monk of the sixth century, Tiantai Zhiyi (538–597).[51] He came from Shanyin in Kuaiji, and his family name was Gu.[52] The biography contains many references to his physical beauty and elegant speech. When Zhiyi first caught sight of him, he immediately gave him the dharma name Dazhi, which means Great Determination. After his initial training on Mt. Tiantai, Dazhi traveled to Mt. Lu (Lu yue) in 590 and resided at Fengding Monastery.[53] He was a solitary ascetic whose major practices were recitation of the *Lotus Sūtra* and asceticism (Skt. *dhūta*). Like Puan, he tried to offer his body to tigers, but they refused to bite. He established the Jingguan Monastery (*daochang*) south of Ganlu peak on Mt. [Lian]-hua and spent seven years there in uninterrupted meditation. Later, he moved to Fulin Monastery on the same mountain. But in 609, the tranquillity of his life was shattered when Sui Yangdi (r. 604–617) imposed some controls on the numbers of monks, nuns, and monasteries after nearly thirty years of unrestricted growth, first under his father (Sui Wendi, r. 581–604) and then in the earlier years of his own reign.[54] While the official histories make little of Yangdi's measures, there is some evidence from Daoxuan's autobiographical writings of a restriction on monasteries in this period that affected his own training and early career.[55] Dazhi seems to have taken the news rather badly:

> He lamented that the deterioration of the dharma should have reached a point such as this. Then he changed his clothes and inflicted injuries on his body. He wore a mourning cap (Ch. *xiaofu*) on his head and a robe of coarse cloth. In the middle of the Buddha hall, he began to wail mournfully in a loud voice. He continued for three days and three nights without ceasing. When the monks of the monastery came to console him, Dazhi said, "I am lamenting that bad karma should have reached such a state as this! I should exhaust this body of mine in order to glorify the true teaching!"
>
> Accordingly, he went to the Eastern Capital [i.e., Luoyang] and submitted a memorial that said, "My wish is that your majesty might cause the Three Jewels [Buddha, Dharma, Saṅgha] to flourish. In that case, I shall burn one arm on Mt. Song, in order to repay the compassion of the state."[56] The emperor assented to this, and he ordered a great vegetarian feast (*zhai*) to be held, at which the seven assemblies all gathered.[57] Dazhi did not eat for three days. He climbed on top of a large canopied platform (*peng*). He heated a piece of iron until it was red hot and used it to burn his arm, charring it all completely black. He used a knife to cut off the flesh, peeling it off so that the bones were made visible. Then he burned the bones, making them charred black as well. He wrapped them in cloth that was saturated in wax and set fire to them. The light sparkled off the peaks and summits. At that time, a large crowd was watching this performance of austerities. They were all distressed, pierced to the marrow, and felt unsteady on their feet. Yet although he continued to do more burning and branding, neither Dazhi's speech nor his expression changed—he talked and smiled as before. From time to time, he recited verses of the dharma, and sometimes he praised the virtues of the Bud-

> dha. He preached the dharma for the benefit of the crowd, and his speech never faltered. When his arm was completely incinerated, he climbed down from the platform as before. After remaining in dhyāna for seven days, he died in the lotus position. At that time he was forty-three years old.[58]

Dazhi's emotional outburst is in stark contrast to the more stoic attitudes of Puji and Puan, who faced active persecution rather than what appears to have been an expedient measure taken against excessive numbers of ordinations and the consequent weakening of the tax base. He was bold enough to petition Yangdi directly, but the pact made between the emperor and the monk (an arm in exchange for continued patronage) is hard to account for unless we suppose that the biography made a pious fiction out of a public act of defiance. The way in which the biography lingers tenderly over the details of the self-inflicted cutting and burning is unusual in the Chinese context and recalls a similar emphasis on the wounds of the suffering martyr in Christian martyrology.[59] But in Dazhi's case, pain and suffering are explicitly denied—he smiles and preaches the dharma throughout.

At the end of this extremely detailed and slightly gruesome account, Daoxuan appends his own opinions on Dazhi's talent and physical beauty ("his lips looked as if they were painted with cinnabar," for example).[60] After his personal testimonial, we learn that in Daoxuan's own day, Dazhi was still being commemorated at Mt. Lu, nearly forty years after his death:

> He compiled the text of his vow, which was more than seventy pages in length. His purpose was that, through this text, all sentient beings might be his good friends (Skt. *kalyāṇamitra*; Ch. *shanzhishi*). Even those monks who were tough and stubborn and found it hard to uphold [Buddhist practices] with faith, none of them could help shedding tears on reading this votive text. Now, on the peak of Mt. Lu, at the end of every year, the monks who are present in all the monasteries gather together for one night. They read the vow that he left behind, using it to teach both religious and laity. All of them sob with grief.[61]

While one could read this purely in terms of religious practice in memory of a beloved brother, it is certainly tempting to think that the monks were celebrating Dazhi as some kind of martyr. We must suspect that Daoxuan included this contemporary account (clearly drawn from his own knowledge rather than from an epitaph) to make his point clear: the monks remember Dazhi's death, and the Tang state would do well not to forget it either.

Given the amount of personal observation and vividly rendered detail in this biography, we might almost suspect that Daoxuan knew Dazhi personally or at least witnessed his death (he would have been about thirteen at the time of Dazhi's death, and he became a novice at the age of sixteen). But in fact this is unlikely, since there is no record of Daoxuan leaving Chang'an until some years after he was ordained, and Dazhi's death took place near Luoyang. Perhaps Daoxuan knew of this from someone who had witnessed Dazhi's death, or, even more likely, the account as we have it originated as a well-known story, much polished and embellished in the retelling. Like the monks of Mt. Lu, Daoxuan clearly believed that Dazhi's act still carried an important message in his own day. The biography shows us a monk bargaining with his own body for the continuation of the dharma, and this act was being publicly remembered and commemorated in the Tang, when the protection of the saṅgha was still by no means assured. Not only was his personal sacrifice being remembered, but so in a sense was the bargain that had been struck with Sui Yangdi—a bargain that presumably the monks of Mt. Lu and Daoxuan himself wished the Tang rulers would also respect. I believe that Daoxuan's presentation of the biographies of both Puji and Dazhi is no accident; rather they represent almost a kind of moral blackmail—as if saying to the Tang rulers (probably Taizong in particular), "You see what happens when you do not support the saṅgha: eminent monks jump off cliffs or burn off their arms and die."

Dazhi's self-sacrifice apparently continued to resonate with the Buddhist establishment long after the seventh century. We find a strange echo of it in a biography that appears in a much later collection, *Bu xu gaoseng zhuan* (Supplement to continued biographies of eminent monks).[62] The biography of Yonglong (1359–92) in this collection recounts an episode so similar to Dazhi's that it is hard to believe that the text could have been written without knowledge of it.[63] Yonglong was the son of a Mister Shi from Gusu in Jiangsu and was a vegetarian from infancy. He left home at the age of twenty and took the tonsure at Chongfu Monastery on Mt. Yin.[64]

One night, sitting in meditation, he received a visit from the local deity, who told him that the monastery had been founded during the Tianjian era (502–19) of the Liang dynasty but had burned down around thirty years earlier, toward the end of the Yuan (1206–1347). The Buddha had entrusted this god with the defense of the monastery. If Yonglong undertook to have the monastery rebuilt, the deity would protect him. Yonglong took up the challenge and set forth his intentions by writing out both the *Lotus* and the *Huayan jing* in his own blood.[65] As he wrote them, shining *śarīra* (*sheli*, relics) were produced from the brush, and they attracted both reverence and donations from the laity.

As part of the reconstruction of the main hall, boats had to bring timber across the river at Qiantang (in Hangzhou). A typhoon blew them out to sea, much to the alarm of the crew, but Yonglong had faith in the deity's promise, and, sure enough, the wind changed direction and blew the boats back to shore. One of the timber dealers got his fellows to donate a large buddha image in gratitude for this miracle. The reconstruction of the great hall was completed in 1391.

As we can see from these episodes, Yonglong had surely already proved his exemplary dedication to the saṅgha, but his subsequent actions proved yet more heroic and miraculous. The first Ming emperor, Taizu (r. 1368–98), who had himself been a monk before founding the dynasty, attempted to exercise tight control over the size of the saṅgha. In 1373, he ordered that prospective monks and nuns had to take an examination that tested their knowledge of scriptures. In 1391, the Ministry of Rites was ordered to regulate Buddhism and Taoism even more thoroughly, and from then on ordination was to be allowed only once every three years; there was also to be a limit on the number of new monks ordained for each prefecture, department, and district. In order that the saṅgha should not drain away the productive members of society, male ordinands had to be over the age of forty, and females, over fifty. In 1392, as a safeguard against imposture, a monastic register (*sengji ce*) was prepared listing the name, year of ordination, and ordination certificate number of every monk. It is against this background of legislation that the following events occurred.[66]

According to Yonglong's biography, in 1392, there was an imperial ordination for monks, and Yonglong led his disciples to the capital (Nanjing) to be examined on their scriptural knowledge and presented with ordination certificates. More than three thousand novices in total presented themselves for examination, but among them were many who had no knowledge of the scriptures and who wished to obtain ordination certificates by fraud. Taizu was irritated by this deception and dispatched the imperial bodyguard to arrest the novices and conscript them into the army.[67] Yonglong was not unnaturally distressed at this turn of events and submitted a memorial offering to burn his body in order to secure their release.

Taizu, like Sui Yangdi before him, apparently assented to this offer and ordered civil and military officials to escort Yonglong to Yuhua tai.[68] There, Yonglong bowed in the direction of the palace and composed a gāthā:

> As for this thirty-three year old phantom-body,
> the fire of the nature (*xinghuo*) will clearly manifest true reality.
> When the buddhadharma of the great Ming prospers,
> I will pray that the August Lineage (*huangtu*) will last for a
> hundred million years.

In this verse we can see that Yonglong follows a similar logic to that of Puji and Dazhi: the health of the dharma is explicitly linked to that of the state through the offering of the body of the self-immolator. He also took a stick of incense and wrote on it, "The wind and rain will be favorable [for crops]." This he gave to one of the officials and urged him to present it to the emperor, saying that it would be most efficacious if used to pray for rain. Then he burned himself. There was an unusual fragrance, and flocks of cranes soared over the pyre. Many *śarīra* were collected afterwards. The three thousand novices are said to have been pardoned and given ordination certificates as a direct consequence of his autocremation. Sometime later, there was a drought, and Taizu ordered the officials of the Central Buddhist Registry (*senglu si*) to fetch the incense that Yonglong had left behind. The officials prayed for rain for three days and were rewarded with a heavy downfall. Taizu was delighted and told his assembled ministers, "This was truly the rain of Yonglong." He composed a poem, "Luopo seng" (The monk who shed his soul), to commemorate him.[69] Yonglong's disciples took his remains home and interred them beneath a stūpa on Mt. Yin.

This is a very detailed and fascinating account, but so far I have been unable to correlate it with any event known from the official histories. I suspect that something happened in 1392 connected with a protest over state regulated ordination, but I would remain cautious about accepting this version of events uncritically. The biography does show that the ideal of a monk sacrificing himself for the greater community and protests against curtailment of the activities of the saṅgha were still alive and well in the late Ming. It seems that the very special death of the Chinese Buddhist martyr was not something that was unique to the medieval period but could also appear in other times of crisis.

Death at the Hands of a Cruel Tyrant: The Tang Śramaṇa Shi Zhiming (?–619) of the Pseudo-Zheng

The early Tang rulers claimed legitimation in part through their descent from Laozi and so tended to favor Taoism, but they were also shrewd enough to recognize that they could not afford to alienate the Buddhist establishment. Let us now examine how religious persecution and self-immolation were tied into the greater narrative of the founding of the Tang. Although the Tang was officially founded in 618, not everyone in China was keen to accept that fact, and Tang forces were kept busy for another three years in dealing with a number of generals who also fancied ruling the empire after the downfall of the Sui. The Tang was not really secure until it had driven rebel forces out of the city of Luoyang, which it finally did in 621. If we understand the founding of the Tang not as a single act but as something that took some years to secure, then the biography of Zhiming is certainly of some relevance.[70]

I believe that the issue of legitimation is the only way to account satisfactorily for the somewhat unusual status of Zhiming and his biography. The monks we have met thus far left home in their youth, studied under a master, and spent their entire lives cultivating their religious practices. Zhiming was quite a different case. He was a monk only for the very last day of his life, and he seems to have had no formal master but instead was tonsured by his wife. He spent most of his career as a bureaucrat, and he was doubly unfortunate in that he happened to live in the "interesting times" between the end of the Sui and the founding of the Tang and that, in hindsight, he backed the wrong man. His secular name was Zheng Ting, and the biography refers to him by this name throughout, which suggests that his dharma name (Zhiming) may have been given only posthumously.[71] He was from Rongyang and was evidently possessed of some literary talent as a young man.[72] He first entered the service of the Sui dynasty sometime between 586 and 604. Despite his grand sounding title of "commandant of plumed cavalry" (*yujiwei*), this denoted in fact a very junior rank carrying no official responsibilities.[73] Zheng resigned in disgust, made a habit of attending Buddhist lectures, and eventually took up farming in Ningzhou (in present-day Gansu). But in the early years of the Daye reign period (605–17), the vice-director of the Department of State Affairs (*pushe*), Yang Su (d. 606), whom Arthur Wright has so memorably characterized as the "hatchet man" to Sui Wendi and Yangdi, came to Ningzhou on a matter of state and managed to cajole Zheng back into government service.[74] This time he had real responsibility, serving in the office of Sui Yangdi's eldest son, Yuande (Prince Yang Zhao, 579–606).[75] He was promoted to the position of secretary to the heir apparent (*zhongshe ren*), and his office was graded rank five. When Yuande died in 606, Zheng did not serve the prince's successors but wandered around listening to lectures on the Sanlun (three treatise) teachings and the *Lotus Sūtra*.[76]

Unfortunately, some ten or so years later, Zheng made an error of judgment that was to cost him dear. After the death of Sui Yangdi in 617, one of his young sons, Yang Tong (d. 618), the Prince of Yue, was set on the throne as Sui Gongdi by the general Wang Shichong (d. 621). For reasons that are now obscure, Zheng came out of retirement to serve the puppet emperor as censor-in-chief (*yushi dafu*). When Wang Shichong dropped the pretense and declared himself emperor of the Zheng dynasty (618–21), based in Luoyang, Zheng Ting served him in turn, although this may have been under duress.[77] Wang Shichong was the last of the military claimants to the empire to be defeated by the forces of the nascent Tang under Li Yuan (Gaozu, r. 618–26) and his son, Li Shimin (Taizong, r. 626–49), with help from the monks of Shaolin Monastery.[78] Not unnaturally, then, he is portrayed as a cruel and capricious tyrant in Tang sources.[79] The *Xu gaoseng zhuan* biography presents Zheng Ting as an official placed in an intolerable situation:

> Zheng Ting was worn out by this disorder, and he earnestly wished to leave home. He repeatedly requested of the Zheng ruler that he might cultivate the Way for the benefit of the state. But when he

> could not accomplish this intention, he thought only of taking the tonsure and did not worry about the punishment. Therefore, at night he secretly read *vaipulya* (*fangdeng*) sūtras.[80] In the daytime, he continued to discharge his public duties. He did not change his mind even for a moment, so he spent forty days in a complete recitation of the *Lotus Sūtra*. This soothed his heart and made him determined to leave secular life. He also encouraged his wife to take refuge in Buddhism. His words were to the point, so she followed him, and they gave each other the tonsure.
>
> Zheng Ting said to his wife, "My wish has been fulfilled! I will not die and be reborn. I must inform the Zheng ruler. It is not fitting for him to be that way." He put on his dharma robes and picked up his monk's staff (Skt. *kakkhara*). He went to the palace gates and said, "I, Zheng Ting, have just left home! So I have come to pay my respects." Wang Shichong could not overcome his anger, and he ordered him to be executed. When Zheng Ting heard this, he was delighted and said, "Again, my wish has been fulfilled." He smiled imperturbably and joyfully. He walked to the banks of the Luo River. At that time, it was still only daybreak and not yet time for execution. Zheng Ting said [to the executioner?], "If you are my good friend, please deliver me to the other shore as soon as possible. If not, I will soon be released, and thus I will not be able to fulfill my fundamental aspiration." At that time, religious and laity were circumambulating him, and they exhorted him to wait until sunset. But Zheng Ting, with a stern expression and a loud voice, would not agree. So then he was executed. Soon after, there was an imperial order for his release, but this did not save him. [The officials of] the whole court felt regret. This all took place in the early years of the Kaiming reign period of the pseudo-Zheng.[81]

While the two official Tang histories do mention the fact of Wang Shichong's execution of Zheng Ting and Wang Shichong's subsequent regret, they do not recount the circumstances in any detail, and they certainly make no mention of any Buddhist inclinations on Zheng's part.[82] Was Wang Shichong's act particularly anti-Buddhist then? Was Zheng Ting a Buddhist martyr or just another unfortunate victim? There are some indications that Wang Shichong may have severely curtailed Buddhist activities under his regime, but given the biased nature of the sources concerning the founding of the Tang, it is difficult to know how much credence to give this version of events.[83] Indeed, there is also evidence that points in the other direction. One significant fact is that once he occupied the city, Li Shimin returned all monks and nuns in Luoyang to lay life, with the exception of thirty monks and thirty nuns who had shown particular virtue.[84] We may imagine then that by selecting this particular account, Daoxuan was probably trying to show that there was a Buddhist resistance to Wang's regime in Luoyang and that the monks of that city deserved some recognition and protection, rather than further punishment.

If we examine the record of the same event given in that great historical work *Zizhi tongjian* (Comprehensive mirror for the aid of government), we find substantial confirmation for the *Xu gaoseng zhuan* account at the end of the narrative of Li Shimin's campaign against Wang Shichong.[85] This version of events is slightly less laudatory as regards Zheng Ting, since his flattery of Wang Shichong seems a little overblown, even though he was apparently using it as an excuse to escape an intolerable situation. But overall, the compiler, Sima Guang (1019–86), presents Zheng's faith in Buddhism as sincere and his death as heroic and widely admired. His account reads as follows:

> Earlier, Zheng Ting, the censor-in-chief, had grown unhappy with serving Wang Shichong. He often refused to attend state affairs on the pretext of illness. Then he told Wang Shichong, "I, your servant, hear that the Buddha has an indestructible adamantine body. Your majesty is truly like this. I must have many blessings indeed to be reborn during the time of a buddha, and so I wish to resign from office, take the tonsure, and become a śramaṇa and so strive diligently in order to aid your majesty's divine martial ability (*shenwu*)." Shichong said, "Great minister of state, your reputation has long been respected. When you desire to enter the Way, this will come as a great surprise to public opinion. Wait until the battles have ceased, and then you may follow your wish." Zheng Ting made determined requests, but [Wang] would not agree. He went back and told his wife, "I have served in office since I became a man, and in my mind I have aspired to fame and integrity. Due to ill fortune, I have encountered these turbulent times; I have become a refugee here, and I have to stay in this land of danger and death. My intelligence and strength are too weak to protect us.

> People are born, and then they die; what difference is there whether it is sooner or later? If I could follow what I liked, I would have no regrets if I died."
>
> Then he shaved off his hair and put on monk's robes. When Wang Shichong heard of this, he was furious and said, "Is this because you think I am certain to be defeated and you wish to escape by improper means? If I do not execute you, then how can I control the masses?" Accordingly he had Zheng Ting executed in the marketplace. [Beforehand] Zheng Ting laughed and talked unaffectedly, and the onlookers admired his courage.[86]

In contrast with the rather bleak picture presented in this source, according to his *Xu gaoseng zhuan* biography, Zheng Ting had long nurtured the idea of escaping from the horrors of saṃsāra. The biography reproduces a long speech to this effect given in response to a monk who had made a prediction of Zheng's fortune based on his physiognomy at a lecture given by the eminent exegete Jizang (549–623).[87] Since in the biography Zheng speaks of seeing many dead people and since he did live through some remarkably bloody and unsettling times, one can but sympathize with his predicament. The biography, however, seems determined to read his execution as an act of self-immolation:

> Thus when Zheng Ting was on the point of execution he made obeisance to the ten directions and chanted the *Bore* [*jing*] (*Prajñāpāramitā sūtra*). He took up his brush and composed this poem:
>
> Illusory arising returns to illusory destruction.
> But this great illusion does not last beyond the body.
> There is a place where the mind can be pacified,
> One may seek for a "person," but there is no such "person."[88]
>
> After bidding farewell to his friends and acquaintances, he closed his eyes, and in a short while he said, "You may let the blade fall." When they heard his words, they executed him. His expression was mild and pleasant, even more so than usual. His wife became a *bhikṣuṇī* and now resides at Luozhou Monastery.[89]

This is, I believe, the first death verse to be recorded in the context of self-immolation, although there are many more in later accounts, such as the verse that we noted in Yonglong's biography.[90] Like most of the biographies selected by Daoxuan for this section, it is almost impossible to avoid the political implications of this piece. One scarcely has to read between the lines to get the message that only the cruelest of tyrants would refuse to allow a decent man to join the saṅgha. Since Tang Taizong (Li Shimin) had defeated just such a cruel tyrant, he was, in a sense, morally obligated to uphold and patronize his Buddhist allies, rather than punish them for disloyalty. Daoxuan was only too willing to remind Taizong of his obligations, although for obvious reasons he chose an oblique approach rather than direct confrontation. We should also note that Zheng Ting was tried and executed for his decision to become a monk and is thus closest to the type of martyr with which we are familiar from the Christian and Islamic traditions.

Conclusion

The voluntary termination of life in the Chinese Buddhist tradition takes many forms, only some of which I have addressed here. The specific cases I have presented make sense in the contexts in which they occurred. Generally speaking, we can discern the following pattern. At the mundane level, two groups with opposing priorities clashed, and monks offered their bodies and lives in the certain hope and expectation that the dharma would prevail in time. The sacrifices were sometimes conceived of as an exchange of the individual monk's body for the larger body of the saṅgha. On the cosmic level, the deaths of monks were dramatic performances of scriptural models and ideals that were firmly embedded in the literature and praxis of the Mahāyāna. Performance of death meant control over death and a denial of its significance at the individual level by the raising of the performance to the level of the ideal or mythical. For the community left behind by the dead, especially the hagiographer himself, these deaths provided new ideals and new myths, ones that were firmly anchored in historical time and the specific realities of the Chinese Buddhist experience, rather than the sacred time and place of the scriptures.

The particular death rituals and memorial practices described in the biographies were used to construct a strong sense of kinship and identity for the Buddhist community, especially as it emerged from moments of crisis. Indeed, the compilation of biographies itself constitutes a memorial practice that is significant, not just for the individual practitioner and his immediate community, but also for the larger Buddhist establishment and even for potential opponents of Buddhism. The literary representations of the deaths of these monks may have acted to assuage anxieties felt by others about the nature of death itself, but it is equally likely that those representations acted to widen the gulf between exemplary death and ordinary death.

Notes

1. Samuel L. Klausner, "Martyrdom," in *Encyclopedia of Religion*, ed. Mircea Eliade et al. (New York: Macmillan, 1987), 9:230–38.

2. See Peter Brown, *The Cult of the Saints: Its Rise and Function in Latin Christianity* (Chicago: University of Chicago Press, 1981), 68–85.

3. See, for example, Hippolyte Delehaye, *The Legends of the Saints: An Introduction to Hagiography*, trans. V. M. Crawford (Notre Dame, IN: University of Notre Dame Press, 1961), and Thomas J. Heffernan, *Sacred Biography: Saints and Their Biographers in the Middle Ages* (New York: Oxford University Press, 1988).

4. See Carl W. Ernst, "From Hagiography to Martyrology: Conflicting Testimonies to a Sufi Martyr of the Delhi Sultanate," *History of Religions* 24, no. 4 (1985): 308–27.

5. For example, in Sallie King, "They Who Burned Themselves for Peace: Quaker and Buddhist Self-Immolators during the Vietnam War," *Buddhist Christian Studies* 20 (2000): 148n6. King opts to use the term "to refer to religiously motivated self-sacrifice by means of burning oneself to death."

6. The fullest discussion of the variety of meanings of *sheshen* may now be found in Funayama Tōru, "Shashin no shisō: Rikuchō bukkyōshi no ichi danmen," *Tōhō gakuhō* 74 (2002): 358–11 (reverse pagination). I should like to thank Professor Funayama for generously sharing this article with me before it appeared in print. On self-immolation in Chinese Buddhism, see also Jacques Gernet, "Les suicides par le feu chez les bouddhistes chinois de Ve au Xe siècle," *Mélanges publiés par l'Institut des Hautes Études Chinoises* (Paris: Presses Universitaires de France, 1960), 2:527–58; Jan Yün-hua, "Buddhist Self-Immolation in Medieval China," *History of Religions* 4, no. 2 (1965): 243–65; and James A. Benn, "Where Text Meets Flesh: Burning the Body as an 'Apocryphal Practice' in Chinese Buddhism," *History of Religions* 37, no. 4 (1998): 295–322.

7. See Funayama, "Shashin no shisō," 351.

8. For the larger research project, see James A. Benn, *Burning for the Buddha: Self-Immolation in Chinese Buddhism* (Honolulu: University of Hawai'i Press, 2007).

9. The other two collections are *Gaoseng zhuan* (Biographies of eminent monks, compiled by Huijiao, ca. 531) and *Song gaoseng zhuan* (Biographies of eminent monks compiled under the Song, compiled by Zanning, 988; hereafter *SGSZ*). The best introduction to these biographical collections in English is John Kieschnick, *The Eminent Monk: Buddhist Ideals in Medieval Chinese Hagiography* (Honolulu: University of Hawai'i Press, 1997).

10. See Chen Jinhua, "An Alternative View of the Meditation Tradition in China: Meditation in the Life and Works of Daoxuan (596–667)," *T'oung Pao* 88, nos. 4–5 (2002): 332–95. My thanks to Professor Chen for allowing me to see this piece before it appeared in print. In Japanese, see the important series of publications on Daoxuan's life by Fujiyoshi Masumi: "Dōsen no yugyō to nisan no chosaku ni tsuite" 1 and 2, *Sanzō* 189 (1979): 1–8, and 190 (1979): 1–8; "Dōsen no zenhansei," *Chūgokushi to seiyō sekai no tenkai* (Akita: Mishima Shobō, 1991), 73–95; and "Bannen no Dōsen," *Kansai daigaku bungaku ronshū* 41, no. 2 (1991): 29–58. See also Suwa Gijun, *Chūgoku Nanchō bukkyōshi no kenkyū* (Kyoto: Hōzōkan, 1997), 291–300.

11. The early Tang was of course a great period of secular history writing, and Daoxuan's work was in a sense part of the spirit of the age. On official history writing, see Denis Crispin Twitchett, *The Writing of Official History under the T'ang* (Cambridge and New York: Cambridge University Press, 1992). For unofficial histories of earlier dynasties produced in the Sui and early Tang, the tables in Shi Guodeng, *Tang Daoxuan* Xu gaoseng zhuan *pipan sixiang chutan* (Taipei: Dongchu Chubanshe, 1992), 34–36, give some idea of the number of historians working in this period.

12. On this problem, see Ibuki Atsushi, "Zoku kōsōden no zōkō ni kansuru kenkyū," *Tōyō no shisō to shūkyō* 7 (1990): 58–74.

13. See Benn, *Burning for the Buddha*, chap. 2, for a more detailed discussion of the textual history of the section on self-immolation and an account of how later additions have somewhat obscured Daoxuan's original purpose.

14. Daoxuan drew on four types of material for his collection: (1) oral information from travelers and informants; (2) his own personal experiences and investigations; (3) religious and secular historical documents; and (4) funerary inscriptions. These sources are surveyed in Shi Guodeng, *Tang Daoxuan*, 51–91.

15. See the remarks of Shi Guodeng, *Tang Daoxuan*, 149–56.

16. Connections with Mt. Zhongnan are noted throughout the studies of Fujiyoshi Masumi (see note 10 above).

17. Fujiyoshi, "Dōsen no yugyō" 2. On Taizong and Buddhism, see Stanley Weinstein, *Buddhism under the T'ang* (Cambridge and New York:

Cambridge University Press, 1987), 7–11, and Arthur F. Wright, "T'ang T'ai-tsung and Buddhism," in *Perspectives on the T'ang*, ed. Denis Twitchett and Arthur F. Wright (New Haven, CT: Yale University Press, 1973), 239–63. On the relationship of Xuanzang (600–664) with Taizong, see Jan Yün-hua [Ran Yunhua], "Dashi yu Tang Taizong jiqi zhengzhi lixiang tanwei," *Zhonghua fojiao wenhua yanjiu lunji* (Taipei: Dongchu Chubanshe, 1990), 13–41.

18. This purge, its underlying causes, and its immediate and long-term effects have not yet been the focus of a detailed study in any European language. The most comprehensive study in Japanese is Nomura Yōshō, *Shubu hōnan no kenkyū* (Tokyo: Azuma Shuppan, 1968).

19. *Xu gaoseng zhuan* (hereafter *XGSZ*) 27, *T* no. 2060, 50:680b23–c10.

20. It is interesting to note that Mt. Zhongnan was the home of many *Huayan jing* devotees in the sixth and seventh centuries, including Sun Simo (alternative reading Sun Simiao, 581–682), the noted Chinese medical writer whose connections with Buddhism and the *Huayan jing* in particular have been studied by Yoshinobu Sakade, "Sun Simiao et le Bouddhisme," *Kansai Daigaku bungaku ronshū* 42, no. 1 (1992): 81–98. Note also that Sun Simo and Daoxuan were friends. See *SGSZ* 6, *T* 50:790c, and Shi Guodeng, *Tang Daoxuan*, 17–18.

21. Dwelling in cemeteries is listed as one of the thirteen *dhūtagunas*. See, for example, Mochizuki Shinkō, *Bukkyō daijiten*, 10 vols. (rev. ed., Kyoto: Seikai Seiten Kankō Kyōkai, 1954–63), 2335a. On the practice of contemplating corpses in the cremation ground in South Asian Buddhism, see Liz Wilson, *Charming Cadavers: Horrific Figurations of the Feminine in Indian Buddhist Hagiographic Literature* (Chicago: University of Chicago Press, 1996), esp. 41–76.

22. I have been unable to supply this apparition with a name, but see J. J. M. de Groot, *The Religious System of China, Its Ancient Forms, Evolution, History and Present Aspect, Manners, Customs and Social Institutions Connected Therewith* (Leyden: E. J. Brill, 1892–1910), vol. 5, for a good descriptive survey of traditional Chinese demonology.

23. See Kieschnick, *The Eminent Monk*, 46.

24. Piero Camporesi, *The Incorruptible Flesh: Bodily Mutation and Mortification in Religion and Folklore* (Cambridge and New York: Cambridge University Press, 1988), esp. 1–46.

25. See Reiko Ohnuma: "The Gift of the Body and the Gift of the Dharma," *History of Religions* 37, no. 4 (1998): 323–59, and *Head, Eyes, Flesh, and Blood: Giving away the Body in Indian Buddhist Literature* (New York: Columbia University Press, 2006).

26. Fascicle 12, *T* no. 201, 4:321–23, trans. Édouard Huber, *Aśvaghoṣa Sūtrālaṃkāra* (Paris: Ernest Leroux, 1908), 330–41.

27. Hubert Durt unravels some of these in his "Two Interpretations of Human-Flesh Offering: Misdeed or Supreme Sacrifice," *Journal of the Inter-*

national College for Advanced Buddhist Studies (Kokusai Bukkyōgaku Daigakuin Daigaku kenkyū kiyō) 1 (1998): 236–10 (reverse pagination). For sources in Sanskrit and Chinese, see also Étienne Lamotte, *Le Traité de la grande vertu de sagesse de Nāgārjuna (Mahāprajñāpāramitāśāstra)*, 5 vols., Publications de l'institut Orientaliste de Louvain 25–26 (Louvain-La-Neuve: Université de Louvain, Institut Orientaliste, 1944–81), 1:144n3.

28. *Da Tang Xiyou ji* 10, *T* no. 2087, 51:929a–c, and Samuel Beal, *Si-Yu-Ki: Buddhist Records of the Western World* (Delhi: Low Price Publications, 1969 [1884], 212–14. This episode does not appear in earlier Chinese accounts of the life of Nāgārjuna. See Stuart Hawley Young, "The Dragon Tree, the Middle Way, and the Middle Kingdom: Images of the Indian Patriarch Nāgārjuna in Chinese Buddhism" (M.A. thesis, School of Oriental and African Studies, University of London, 2000).

29. *XGSZ* 27, *T* 50:680c11–681a8.

30. Yongzhou occupied the northern part of present-day Shanxi and the greater portion of the northwest of Gansu.

31. *XGSZ* 27, *T* 50:680c16–20.

32. On Daoxuan's early monastic career, see Fujiyoshi, "Dōsen no yugyō" 1.

33. The *Huayan jing* features a bodhisattva by the name Xianshou, and Xianshou is also the name of a chapter in that sūtra. See *Dafangguangfo huayan jing*, *T* no. 278, 9:432c–441b, and *Dafangguangfo huayan jing*, *T* no. 279, 10:72a–80c.

34. On the Sui patronage of Buddhism, see most recently Chen Jinhua, *Monks and Monarchs, Kinship and Kingship: Tanqian in Sui Buddhism and Politics* (Kyoto: Istituto Italiano di Cultura, Scuola di Studi sull'Asia Orientale, 2002). The extensive literature on this topic, nearly all of it in Japanese, is surveyed in Chen's opening pages.

35. On Tang imperial patronage, see Weinstein, *Buddhism under the T'ang*.

36. *XGSZ* 27, *T* no. 50:681a9–682b4 (note variant title in Yuan and Ming editions, *T* 50:678nn13, 14). The title of the biography gives no monastic affiliation, which is very unusual in Daoxuan's collection. Puan's *XGSZ* biography is also reproduced, almost verbatim, in the *Huayan jing zhuanji*, *T* no. 2073, 51:167c–168c.

37. Thirty *li* southeast of present-day Jingyang County in Shanxi.

38. Jing'ai is discussed in Stephen F. Teiser, "'Having Once Died and Returned to Life': Representations of Hell in Medieval China," *Harvard Journal of Asiatic Studies* 48, no. 2 (1988): 437–39, and Jan, "Buddhist Self-Immolation in Medieval China," 252–53.

39. Jingyuan's biography is at *XGSZ* 11, *T* 50:511b–512a.

40. *XGSZ* 27, *T* 50:681a16–21.

41. On this aspect of King Śibi's body practices, see Ohnuma, *Head, Eyes, Flesh, and Blood*, 274–75.

42. The story of Prince Mahāsattva, who offered his body to a hungry tigress, was one of the best-known and most frequently imitated *jātaka*s in China.

43. *XGSZ* 27, *T* 50:681a28–b2.

44. *XGSZ* 27, *T* 50:681b10.

45. *XGSZ* 27, *T* 50.681c7–18.

46. *XGSZ* 27, *T* 50:682a23–27.

47. Presumably Yang Yong, before he was replaced as crown prince by Yang Guang (the future Sui Yangdi, r. 604–18) in 600. See Peter A. Boodberg, "Marginalia to the Histories of the Northern Dynasties," *Harvard Journal of Asiatic Studies* 4, nos. 3–4 (1939): 267.

48. This monastery was located in the Yankang ward in the southeast part of Chang'an. See Victor Cunrui Xiong, *Sui-Tang Chang'an: A Study in the Urban History of Medieval China* (Ann Arbor: Center for Chinese Studies, University of Michigan, 2000), 309.

49. *XGSZ* 27, *T* 50:682b5–c11. Biographies of Dazhi that essentially reproduce the *XGSZ* version are found in *Hongzan fahua zhuan*, *T* no. 2067, 51:25c–26c; *Fahua jing chuanji*, *T* no. 2068, 51:93c–94a (minus Daoxuan's own observations at the end of the *XGSZ* biography); and *Shenseng zhuan*, *T* no. 2064, 50:984a–b (slightly abbreviated). Brief accounts of the Daye purge and Dazhi's reaction to it appear in *Fozu tongji* 39 and 54, *T* no. 2035, 49:362a5–11 and 471a27–29. According to these accounts, Sui Yangdi's edict was not put into effect because of Dazhi's actions. See also *Fozu tongji* 9, *T* 49:198b19–c4, and the brief notice in Leon Hurvitz, *Chih-i (538–597): An Introduction to the Life and Ideas of a Chinese Buddhist Monk*, *Mélanges Chinois et Bouddhiques* 12 (1960–62) (Brussels, 1962), 177.

50. Delehaye: *Legends of the Saints*, 10–12, and *Les origines du culte des martyrs* (New York: AMS Press, 1980), 24–49.

51. On this monk, see Hurvitz, *Chih-i*, and Chen Jinhua, *Making and Remaking History: A Study of Tiantai Sectarian Historiography*, Studia Philologica Buddhica Monograph Series 14 (Tokyo: International Institute for Buddhist Studies, 1999). There is extensive Japanese scholarship on Zhiyi, but note most importantly the work of Satō Tetsuei: *Tendai Daishi no kenkyū* (Kyoto: Hyakkaen, 1961) and *Zoku Tendai Daishi no kenkyū* (Kyoto: Hyakkaen, 1981).

52. Kuaiji was an important center for gentry Buddhism in earlier periods.

53. Mt. Lu, twenty *li* north of present-day Nankang in Jiangxi, had by this time long been an important Buddhist site.

54. On this policy see *Fozu tongji* 9, *T* 49:198b–c, and Daoxuan's *Ji shenzhou sanbao gantong lu* 1, *T* no. 2106, 52:406b21. I have been unable to confirm this action by Yangdi from any official historical source. There is evidence from other sources that Dazhi's protest alone did not persuade Yangdi to reverse this policy. See, for example, the biography of Zhichao

(571–641) at *XGSZ* 20, *T* 50:591c–592c, which seems to indicate that protests over Yangdi's policy continued after Dazhi's death. My thanks to Chen Jinhua for pointing out this information.

55. See Daoxuan's remarks at *Xu zangjing* (hereafter *XZJ*) 62:1024b11–1025a7.

56. Song yue, the Central Marchmount, just south of Luoyang.

57. Vegetarian banquets were, and continue to be, a standard way for laypeople to donate to the saṅgha. The seven assemblies are traditionally given as (1) *bhikṣu* (*biqiu*), fully ordained monks; (2) *bhikṣuṇī* (*biqiuni*), fully ordained nuns; (3) *śikṣamāṇā* (*shichamona*), nuns preparing for full ordination who follow only six of the novice's ten precepts; (4) *śrāmaṇera* (*shami*), male novices; (5) *śrāmaṇerikā* (*shamini*), female novices; (6) *upāsaka* (*youposai*), laymen who take the five precepts; and (7) *upāsikā* (*youpoyi*), laywomen who take the five precepts. The category of *śikṣamāṇā* seems not to have been commonly instituted in Chinese Buddhism and was replaced by other categories, such as *tongxing* (monastic laborer).

58. *XGSZ* 27, *T* 50:682b17–c2.

59. See, for example, the *legenda* of Procopius as discussed by Delehaye, *Legends of the Saints*, 132–34.

60. *XGSZ* 27, *T* 50:682c4.

61. *XGSZ* 27, *T* 50:682c7–11.

62. *XZJ* 134:160b–163a, compiled by Minghe (1588–1641). For a discussion of the title of the collection, see Hasebe Yūkei, *Min Shin bukkyō kyōdanshi kenkyū* (Kyoto: Dōbōsha Shuppan, 1993), 447–48. The self-immolation section of this work is headed *yishen* and contains twelve main biographies, with four appended biographies. Minghe compiled the collection in response to two factors: the inadequacy of the *Da Ming gaoseng zhuan* (Great Ming biographies of eminent monks), which is only eight *juan* in length and has only three categories of religious specialization; and the dominance of hagiographies of Chan masters at the expense of other practitioners.

63. *Bu xu gaoseng zhuan* 19, 161d–162b.

64. Mt. Yin is fifty *li* north of Hang County in Hangzhou.

65. On this practice, see John Kieschnick, "Blood Writing in China," *Journal of the International Association of Buddhist Studies* 23, no. 2 (2000): 177–94.

66. On Ming policy toward Buddhism and especially the regulation of ordination summarized here, see Chün-fang Yü, *The Renewal of Buddhism in China: Chu-Hung and the Late Ming Synthesis* (New York: Columbia University Press, 1981), 155–62, and the scholarship cited therein. For a broader survey of Buddhism under the Ming, see Yü's "Ming Buddhism," in *The Cambridge History of China*, vol. 8: *The Ming Dynasty, 1368–1644*, part 2, ed. Denis Twitchett and Frederick Wade Mote (Cambridge: Cambridge University Press, 1998), 893–952.

67. Something similar happened in 1407. See Yü, *The Renewal of Buddhism*, 158. In 1395, Ming Taizu apparently defrocked all monks who failed a national examination. See *Da Ming huidian*, reprint of 1587 edition (Taipei: Dongnan Shubaoshe, 1963), 104:4a, b.

68. This was just outside the Zhonghua gate of Nanjing. It was so named because of a rain of flowers that fell there in the time of Liang Wudi.

69. I have been unable to verify the existence of this poem from other sources.

70. *XGSZ* 27, *T* 50:682c12–683a24.

71. A somewhat similar case of a biography of a layman in *Xu gaoseng zhuan* is that of Wei Yuansong (fl. ca. 567), who was originally a monk but returned to lay life and turned against his former religion. This case is discussed by Yu Jiaxi, *Yu Jiaxi lunxue zazhu* (1963; Beijing: Zhonghua Shuju, 1977), 238.

72. Rongyang is southeast of present-day Huichang County in Jiangxi. But perhaps Xingyang should be read here rather than Rongyang. The biography says that Zheng was from a powerful and famous clan. The Xingyang Zheng were just such a clan, while we know nothing of any significant Zheng from Rongyang. Because of their similar orthography, the names Rongyang and Xingyang are easily confused, as appears to be the case, for example, at *XGSZ*, *T* 50:625c15 and 644b28.

73. It was the lowest of eight commandant titles conferred on inactive officials (*sanguan*), ranked 9b. The title was established in 586 and discontinued after 604. See Charles O. Hucker, *A Dictionary of Official Titles in Imperial China* (Stanford, CA: Stanford University Press, 1985), 588, and *Lidai zhiguan biao* by Ji Yun (1724–1805), reprinted 2 vols. (Shanghai: Shanghai Guji Chubanshe, 1989), 65/1249a.

74. Yang Su's biography is at *Sui shu* (Book of the Sui, 581–617), 85 *juan*, compiled by Wei Zheng (580–643) et al., in 636 and 656 (Beijing: Zhonghua Suju, 1973), 48/1288–96. See Arthur F. Wright, "The Sui Dynasty (581–617)," in *The Cambridge History of China*, vol. 3: *Sui and T'ang China, 589–906*, part 2, ed. Denis Twitchett (Cambridge: Cambridge University Press, 1976), 69.

75. Yuande's biography is at *Sui shu* 59/1435–37.

76. The Sanlun are three philosophical treatises: the *Madhyamaka-śāstra* (*Zhong lun*), the *Dvādaśanikāya-śāstra* (*Shiermen lun*) by Nāgārjuna, and the *Śata-śāstra* (*Bai lun*) by Nāgārjuna's disciple Āryadeva; all three were translated into Chinese by Kumārajīva (Jiumoluoshi, 344–413 or 350–409). At some time, Zheng also composed a memorial stele for the Sanlun master Bianyi (537–602); see his biography at *XGSZ* 11, *T* 50:510c9–10.

77. On Wang Shichong's short-lived dynasty, see Howard J. Wechsler, "The Founding of the T'ang Dynasty: Kao-Tsu (Reign 618–26)," in Twitchett, ed., *The Cambridge History of China*, vol. 3, 166–67. Hu Sanxing's

(1230–1302) annotation to the *Zizhi tongjian*, compiled by Sima Guang (1019–1086) and others (Beijing: Zhonghua Shuju, 1963), 188/5903–904, says that Zheng Ting had been an official serving Li Mi (582–618), another contender for power at the time, and was captured by Wang Shichong.

78. See Mamoru Tonami, *The Shaolin Monastery Stele on Mount Song*, ed. Antonino Forte, trans. P. A. Herbert, Italian School of East Asian Studies Epigraphical Series (Kyoto: Istituto Italiano di Cultura, Scuola di Studi sull'Asia Orientale, 1990).

79. Li Shimin refers to him as a "murderous bastard" in his instructions to the chief monk of the Shaolin Monastery (Tonami, *The Shaolin Monastery Stele*, 11).

80. *Vaipulya* (extended) in this sense refers to Mahāyāna sūtras.

81. *XGSZ* 27, *T* 50:682c27–683a12.

82. See *Jiu Tang shu* (Old book of the Tang, 618–907), by Liu Xu (887–946), completed in 945 (Beijing: Zhonghua Shuju, 1975), 50/2140, where the case of Zheng Ting is mentioned in a discussion of appropriate punishments conducted in the early years of the reign of Taizong. During the course of this exchange, Taizong remarked that Wang Shichong killed Zheng Ting and only then felt remorse. See also *Xin Tang shu* (New book of the Tang, 618–907), by Ouyang Xiu (1007–1072), Song Qi (998–1061) et al., 1043–60 (Beijing: Zhonghua Shuju, 1974), 46/1409, which says this discussion took place in the fifth year of Taizong's reign, 631. *Zizhi tongjian* 193/6931 says more specifically that the discussion took place in the eighth month of that year but elides Taizong's remarks on Wang Shichong. Wang Shichong's biography in the *Xin Tang shu* also says that he had Zheng Ting executed and later felt remorse (85/2695).

83. See Tonami, *The Shaolin Monastery Stele*, 55 and note 38 in particular, for Li Shimin's distress at the perilous state of Buddhism in Luoyang after his defeat of Wang Shichong.

84. *Zizhi tongjian* 139/5918; also the biography of Huicheng (555–630) at *XGSZ* 24, *T* 50:633c26. Huicheng had been accused of supporting Wang Shichong but was allowed to retain his clerical status.

85. In other words, we have no firm date for this event; we know only that it happened before Wang's defeat.

86. *Zizhi tongjian*, 188/5903–904.

87. *XGSZ* 27, *T* 50:683a14–19. Jizang's biography is at *XGSZ* 11, 513c–515a.

88. Cf. the translation by Paul Demiéville, *Poèmes chinois d'avant la mort*, ed. Jean-Pierre Diény (Paris: L'Asiathèque, 1984), 25.

89. *XGSZ* 27, *T* 50:683a20–24. Presumably she was one of the nuns spared by Li Shimin.

90. On the death verse in general, see Demiéville, *Poèmes chinois d'avant la mort*.

8

Passage to Fudaraku

Suicide and Salvation in Premodern Japanese Buddhism

D. Max Moerman

Religious suicide, as many Buddhists and scholars of Buddhism are quick to point out, is strictly prohibited in the Vinaya. And yet, disciplinary regulations notwithstanding, the hagiographic literature of Buddhist East Asia often reserves the highest praise for those monks, nuns, and laypersons who performed the most extreme acts of self-immolation. Chinese Buddhists were celebrated for throwing themselves out of trees to speed their passage to the Pure Land or for burning themselves alive in emulation of the bodhisattva Medicine King.[1] The earliest Japanese Buddhist sources are similarly full of praise for ascetics who flung themselves off of cliffs, set themselves on fire, or drowned themselves as forms of Buddhist practice.

In Japan, as in China, such practices were informed by the *Lotus Sūtra* and Pure Land cults and followed a model of self-sacrifice that goes back at least as far as the *jātaka* tales. Just as the Buddha in his former lives offered up his body for the hungry tigress and her cubs, so too did Japanese Buddhist ascetics dedicate their bodies as offerings to the Buddha. Moreover, the range of differentiation within the *jātaka* "gift of the body" narratives—perfectly altruistic self-sacrifices, devotional offerings made in ritual contexts, and offerings of the body made in exchange for Buddhist teachings—is found within East Asian hagiography as well.[2] Yet in either cultural context, Buddhist examples of voluntary death are better understood as sacrifices than as suicides.

The subject of this chapter is a particular form of self-immolation performed by Japanese Buddhists from the ninth to the nineteenth centuries: *Fudaraku tokai*, or crossing the sea to Potalaka (J. Fudaraku), the paradise of the bodhisattva Avalokiteśvara (Kannon). Buddhist monks set off from several points along the southern coast of western Japan in small rudderless boats in the hope of reaching Kannon's island paradise, believed to lie across the ocean to the south. The voyagers never returned. According to the accounts of Jesuit missionaries who witnessed the rites in the sixteenth century, the ascetics either dove into the sea with large rocks tied to their bodies and sand and pebbles filling their sleeves or else hastened their journey to paradise by removing wooden plugs from the hulls of their boats once out at sea.[3] Although not a common event, the ritual of *Fudaraku tokai* seems to have been carried out, in much the same manner, for a period of one thousand years. It can therefore hardly be considered an anomaly. In this chapter, I hope to show that *Fudaraku tokai*, as unusual an activity as it may seem, has a meaningful place within the practices, discourses, and representations connected with the Buddhist dead. Furthermore, I hope to suggest that this extreme and perhaps unsettling practice may help us to better understand the central yet ambivalent place of death in the religious landscape of premodern Japan, one in which the dead came to attract rather than to repel the living.

Fire and Water

Accounts of self-immolation are to be found among the earliest Japanese Buddhist literature. One such tale, from the ninth-century *Nihon ryōiki*, a collection of tales illustrating karmic causality, tells of a *Lotus Sūtra* devotee who jumped to his death in the Kumano mountains. When his corpse was eventually discovered, all that was left of the ascetic's body was his tongue, which remained in an otherwise hollow skull and continued to chant the sūtra.[4] A more common method of sacrificial homage to the *Lotus* was the act of self-immolation by fire (*nenshin, shōshin*), modeled after a passage in the sūtra's twenty-third chapter. This chapter, known in Japan as the *Yakuōbon*, describes how, in a previous life, Bodhisattva Medicine King had offered his body as a votive lamp to a buddha of the past who preached the sūtra. The passage describes how the bodhisattva, known in Japanese as Kiken, imbibed and painted his body with fragrant oils, wrapped himself in pure garments, and then set himself on fire. This act is praised as "the prime gift. Among the various gifts, it is the most honorable, the supreme."[5] The Buddha Śākyamuni explains that if one seeking supreme enlightenment "can burn a finger or even a toe as an offering to a Buddha stūpa, he shall exceed one who uses realm or walled city, wife or children, or even all the lands, mountains, forests, rivers, ponds, and sundry precious objects in the whole thousand-million world as offerings."[6] This story from the *Lotus* provided the most common scriptural foundation for East Asian monks and nuns, from medieval to modern times, who lit themselves on fire as Buddhist offerings.

The *Hokke genki*, an eleventh-century collection of miraculous tales related to the *Lotus Sūtra*, contains three examples of this practice. One is that of the tenth-century abbot Jōshō, who, after inadvertently touching a woman, "repented by burning his index finger."[7] Another tells of an unnamed priest of Satsuma Province who, after completing one thousand recitations of the *Lotus*, "looked forward to incinerating himself just as much as the Bodhisattva Kiken."[8] Yet the account that receives the greatest attention is that of Ōshō, "a resident priest of Mount Nachi of Kumano." The *Hokke genki* describes it as "the first example of self-immolation by fire in the country of Japan" and, perhaps because of this inaugural status, provides a highly detailed account:

> Every time he recited the Yakuō chapter of the sutra, Ōshō was so much impressed with the Bodhisattva Kiken's act of self-immolation that he finally wished to burn himself as an offering to the buddhas, just as Bodhisattva Kiken had done. He abstained from cereals, salt, and sweets. In preparation, he purified his interior and exterior self by eating only pine needles and drinking rainwater. Before igniting his funeral pyre, Ōshō donned a new paper robe, held a censer in his hand, sat on the firewood in a posture of meditation facing west, called upon the various buddhas, and vowed, "I offer my body and soul to venerate the *Lotus Sūtra*. My head shall be offered to the buddhas in the upper direction, and my legs to those in the lower direction. My back shall be given to those in the east, and my front to those in the west. My chest shall be received by Great Master Shaka, my right and left sides by Tahō Buddha, and my throat by Amida Buddha. My intestines shall be offered to the five wisdom buddhas, and my other organs to the dwellers of the six worlds." While burning his body, Ōshō made the proper mudrās, and recited the *Lotus Sūtra* with firm faith in the three treasures. Even after his body turned to ashes, his reciting voice did not cease. His burned body did not seem to disperse.

> The smoke did not release an unpleasant odor, but an aromatic fragrance as if the scented jindan wood were burned. A light breeze blew like the sound of delicate music. After the fire was extinguished, the light lingered, illuminating the air in the mountains and valleys. Several hundred unknown and unusual birds gathered and circled about with sounds like the ringing of bells. This was the first example of self-immolation in the country of Japan. All who witnessed it and all who heard of it rejoiced.[9]

Here the sūtra is read and enacted with mimetic precision as a performance text; scripture is taken, quite literally, as script. The literary basis of this act implies a shared readership, both of the sūtra on which it is based and among the future auditors of the tale. For all of the heroism of this sole ascetic, Ōshō was not acting alone. This was a public event. The account begins by identifying Ōshō as "a resident priest of Mount Nachi of Kumano" and concludes by noting that "all who witnessed it and all who heard of it rejoiced." Ōshō had not only fellow priests in residence at Nachi but also a wider audience to witness the act.

The role of spectatorship is not an inconsequential element of such accounts. When Eijo, a monk from Kai Province, incinerated himself at Shuzenji in Izu, "the people from nearby villages saw auspicious purple clouds and said that he had surely been born in the Pure Land."[10] Witnesses do more than contribute to the tale's sense of authenticity. They are willing participants whose presence at the rite carries its own karmic reward. When Kakushin, a resident monk of Rokuharamitsuji, burned his body north of Bodaiji in 995, the retired emperor Kazan and numerous courtiers were there to watch.[11] When, on the very next day, another ascetic incinerated himself at Amidamine, "throngs of people of all status witnessed the spectacle." The *Hyakurenshō* goes on to note that "this was the eleventh such auto-incineration in recent years."[12] Amidamine, located to the east of Kyoto and at whose foot lay the Toribeno cremation grounds, seems to have become a site for such rituals. In the Kōhei era (1058–65), yet another holy man lit himself on fire at the base of this peak, and "men and women high and low gathered to establish a karmic relationship" with the ascetic.[13] And in 1174, when an unnamed holy man burned his body on Mt. Funaoka, another charnel ground outside Kyoto, "People swarmed to see the spectacle and to establish a karmic connection" with the saint.[14]

Another means of self-immolation, one associated more with Pure Land than with *Lotus Sūtra* practices, was that of drowning oneself (*jusui*).[15] It was carried out in lakes and rivers and in particular in the sea at Naniwa beside Tennōji. The western gate of this temple faced the sea and was believed to mark the entrance or the eastern gate of Amida's Pure Land. From this auspicious location, worshipers meditated on the sun setting over the sea as if it were the sun setting in the west of that "other shore" and then sailed out to the open sea to drown themselves. Numerous accounts of this practice are to be found in the *ōjōden* literature, hagiographic collections of those born in the Pure Land.[16] The *Goshūi ōjōden*, for example, tells of a wandering monk determined to drown himself. He sails down the river toward the sea while other monks burn incense, play music, and scatter flowers. When they arrive at the ocean, the monk takes a seat within a bamboo cage, faces west, closes his eyes, and places his hands together in prayer. To the sound of chanting, he is then lowered into the waters.[17]

The *Ippen hijiri-e* offers additional examples of *jusui*, and, as it is a picture scroll (*emakimono*) of alternating panels of text and image, provides some of the few visual representations of the act. The *Hijiri-e* is a hagiography of the priest Ippen (1239–89), founder of the Pure Land order later known as the Jishū, in a twelve-scroll *emakimono* format completed in 1299. The first image of *jusui* appears in the third section of scroll six, often noted for its depiction of Mt. Fuji. Just to the left of the famous peak, however, is another scene depicting a monk from Musashi Province who, having been converted by Ippen's Pure Land teaching, drowns himself in the Fuji River while chanting the *nenbutsu*, the Buddha Amida's name. The other scene is to be found at the end of the tale, in the third section of scroll twelve, which depicts Ippen's death, a scene that follows the standard iconography of pictures of the death of the Buddha (*nehan-e*). The crowds of sorrowful devotees surrounding the teacher are standard elements in such images. What is unusual in the *Hijiri-e* is the depiction of seven of Ippen's followers drowning themselves.[18] The accompanying text describes the scene as "seven people, both members of the Jishū and those with karmic ties (*kechien*), throwing themselves into the sea before them."[19]

As the above examples suggest, the audience itself was very much a part of the performance of self-immolation. It took an active and necessary supporting role. Audience members are as involved as the ascetics themselves and have as much, if not more, at stake in the outcome. The spectator, however, was not driven simply by a voyeuristic urge but by a religious desire to form a karmic connection with the ascetic. Such a bond was of significant religious value. It would allow the positive karma gained by the monk's corporeal offering to be shared by the spectator, as well as allow the spectator's negative karmic burden to be erased, or at least lightened, as it is taken on by the monk's sacrifice.

Fudaraku Tokai in Textual Materials

Fudaraku tokai represents a somewhat different sort of death by water, similar in some respects to those discussed above yet distinctive in many of its detail. This rite occurred most commonly in the waters near the Kumano Nachi shrine, situated on the coast at the southern tip of the Kii Peninsula. Located some hundred miles due south of the capital, Kumano's Nachi shrine was a logical point of embarkation for this final passage. Kumano, as has already been noted, was where *Lotus Sūtra* ascetics first threw themselves from cliffs and lit themselves on fire. Nachi, one of the three Kumano shrines, had since the ninth century been a center of a Kannon cult. Although *Fudaraku tokai* is recorded as having also been performed at other coastal sites in western Japan—such as Muroto and Ashizuri in Shikoku, Izumi near Osaka, and Ariake in Kyūshū—Nachi remained the favored site for those departing for Kannon's paradise. Of the thirty-six instances of *Fudaraku tokai* in which the location is recorded, twenty-four of them took place at Nachi.[20]

References to *Fudaraku tokai* are found in a wide range of textual sources such as chronicles, diaries, prose narratives, and letters. The most comprehensive chronology of the practice, a text known as the *Kumano nendaiki*, lists twenty such journeys from the ninth to the eighteenth centuries.[21] Yet the *Nendaiki* is a rather late compilation, which, as one might expect, provides few details for what it claims as its earliest examples. The description of the earliest *Fudaraku tokai* is a terse entry for the year 868 (Jōgan 10), noting only that on "the third day of the eleventh month, Keiryū Shōnin entered Fudaraku."[22] The *Nendaiki*'s next example, however, offers a little more information and also suggests a wider social context for the rite. The entry for the second month of 919 states that "in the company of thirteen people from Ōshū, Ushin

Shōnin of the Hama no miya Fudarakusanji set off across the sea."[23] It would seem that this Ushin, a resident priest of Fudarakusanji, located on the grounds of the Hama no miya shrine on the beach at Nachi, undertook the passage to Fudaraku alone and that the thirteen people from Ōshū were supporters of the priest (*tokai no ganshu*) who traveled to Nachi to witness the rite.[24]

Although these first references from the *Kumano nendaiki* record the earliest performances of *Fudaraku tokai*, their historicity cannot be independently verified. There are, however, corroborating sources for some of the others from different early medieval sources. Fujiwara no Yorinaga, for example, one of the highest-ranking aristocrats of the mid-twelfth century, has preserved for us one such account. Yorinaga was friendly with a Tendai priest by the name of Kakushū, who had spent one thousand days in ascetic seclusion at the Nachi shrine.[25] Kakushū related the following story to Yorinaga, who included it in his diary entry for the year 1142 (Kōji 1), eighth month, eighteenth day:

> [Kakushū] told me that while he was undergoing seclusion at Nachi, there was a certain lone monk who fervently wished to travel to Mt. Fudaraku in his present body. He carved a statue of the Thousand-Armed Kannon, set it up at the helm of a small boat, and worshipped it for three years. He then prayed that the northern winds not cease for seven days, and, for as many days, the great north winds blew. Rejoicing, the monk boarded his craft and faced south. He did not cease his worship as he traveled far off toward the south. As this was an extraordinary occurrence, the other monks climbed the mountain to watch. This was [an] unfathomable [event]. All said that his vow had been fulfilled.[26]

Kakushū's account is not unlike that of a tale collected in the *Jizō bosatsu reigenki*, tales illustrating the powers of the bodhisattva Jizō (Skt. Kṣitigarbha):

> In the third year of the Chōtaku era (997), Katō Shōnin went to Awa Province and went into seclusion there. After a year or two, he professed a desire to travel to Kannon's paradise of Fudaraku. On the eighteenth day of the eighth month of the third year of the Chōhō era (1001), he boarded an *utsubobune* with his disciple

> Einen and sailed off into the myriad waves. They extinguished the karmic burden of men and women high and low. His remaining disciples expressed their grief at the Cape of Ashizuri, as it is said that this was the site of his departure.[27]

A slightly different version of Katō's story is collected in Kamo no Chōmei's *Hosshinshū* (Tales of religious awakening, 1212–15). It concerns a certain person known as Sanuki no Sanmi, who planned to make a lamp of his body

> but suddenly changed his mind. It might be easy to make a lamp of his body, he thought, but this did not assure birth in the Pure Land. An ordinary person like him might have doubts at the last moment. Yet Mt. Fudaraku was a place in this world where one could go in one's present body, and thus he decided to travel there instead. He went to a place he knew in Tosa Province, acquired a small new boat, and asked a sailor to tell him when a good north wind came. When the wind came, he raised the sail and set off all alone toward the south. Although he had a wife and children, his resolve was so strong it was useless to try and stop him. They could only gaze toward the empty horizon, weeping, in the direction he had gone. All who witnessed the strength of his resolve said that he must have reached his destination. This happened in the era of Ichijōin (986–1011). He was assisted by a disciple and was [later] known as Katō *hijiri*.[28]

Although Katō exhibited some degree of indecision about his means of self-immolation, Chōmei recounts his death with approval. Chōmei's acceptance of this practice, however, was not always unconditional. Another tale from the same volume of the *Hosshinshū* tells of a *hijiri* known as Rengejō, who, like Katō, was similarly "determined to die with single-minded conviction" and so "decided to drown himself in a moment of mental clarity." His priestly attendant tried his utmost to dissuade him, arguing that it was "the kind of thing only a fool does." But, as Rengejō had clearly made up his mind, he "helped with the necessary preparations." Rengejō found a deep spot in the Katsura River, "chanted the *nenbutsu* in a loud voice and sank beneath the waters." A great audience had by then assembled and expressed praise and lamentation. Later, however, Rengejō's attendant was possessed by the spirit of the *hijiri*, who revealed that a lack of mental focus at the last moment had resulted in a rebirth not in paradise, but as a wandering ghost:

> "I had no idea I might change my mind at the last minute, but just as I was about to jump into the water, all of a sudden I was filled with regret. But with so many people looking on, how could I turn back? I looked at you, hoping you could stop me, but you didn't seem to understand and only urged me on. So, terrified that I was about to drown, I had no thought of birth in the Pure Land."[29]

As mentioned in the preceding chapters by Koichi Shinohara and Jacqueline Stone, one's state of mind at the moment of death was thought to be profoundly determinative of one's next life, and thus nothing should be allowed to interfere with one's deathbed concentration on the Pure Land. Chōmei accordingly sees such ascetic histrionics as leading only to perdition. He comments on the tale as follows:

> Because of a desire for reputation, or out of pride or envy, people may foolishly think that they can attain birth in the Pure Land by drowning or by making a lamp of their body. Driven on by such thoughts, they undertake such action. This is the same as the mortification practices of heterodox sects. This is absolute delusion. Self-immolation by fire or by water is extremely painful; it cannot be withstood without the deepest conviction. If there is agony, one cannot maintain a tranquil mind. One cannot maintain correct faith without the assistance of the Buddha. Some people are stupid enough to say things like "I couldn't burn myself alive but drowning is easy." . . . As a *hijiri* once said, "If people think drowning is easy, it's only because they don't know what it's like to die drowning."[30]

The *Heike monogatari* provides what is perhaps the most famous literary version of the rite. The episode entitled "The Drowning of Koremori" (*Koremori no jusui*) recounts how Taira no Koremori, after his clan's final defeat, made a pilgrimage to the Kumano shrines, "garbed as a mountain ascetic," in order to meet his end. At Nachi,

> Koremori boarded a small craft in front of the Hama no Miya shrine and set out into the boundless blue sea. Far in the offing, there was an island. He went to its shore, left the boat, peeled some bark from a large pine tree, and inscribed the words: ..."Middle Captain of the Third Rank Koremori, religious name Jōen, aged twenty-seven, drowns himself offshore from Nachi on the Twenty-Eighth Day of the Third Month in the third year of Juei [1184]." Then he rowed toward the open sea again.... [His priestly attendant] urged the Middle Captain to chant the sacred name. To Koremori it seemed a supremely favorable opportunity for rebirth in the Pure Land. He put away distracting thoughts immediately, intoned Amida's name a hundred times in a loud voice, and entered the sea with "*Namu*!" on his lips.[31]

An even more detailed account is preserved in the *Azuma kagami*, the official chronicle of the Kamakura shogunate. An entry for the year 1233 (Tempuku 1), fifth month, twenty-seventh day, tells of the fate of a warrior named Shimokōbe Rokurō. After embarrassing himself on a hunting expedition with his lord, Minamoto no Yoritomo—he had missed a deer with his arrow—Shimokōbe fled in disgrace. He became a monk, took the religious name Chijōbō, and entered the Kumano mountains, where "he recited the *Lotus Sūtra* day and night." The *Azuma kagami* supplies a number of details missing from the *Kumano nendaiki* accounts. At the time of his passage to Fudaraku, Chijōbō "boarded a small boat and was sealed inside its cabin with wooden planks and nails driven in from the outside, leaving not a crack for light to enter. His provisions consisted of nothing but a thirty-day supply of food and lamp oil."[32]

The most detailed accounts of the rite, however, are to be found in the letters and reports sent by Jesuit missionaries to their superiors in Goa in the second half of the sixteenth century. Although late and by no means unbiased, they provide a surprisingly rich source of information that can help to fill the lacunae left by earlier Japanese accounts. The first such letter to mention the practice of *Fudaraku tokai* was written in 1554 by Pedro de Alcaceva, who had arrived in Japan in August 1552 and spent fourteen months in Bungo and Yamaguchi before returning to Goa, where he wrote the following account.[33] Describing the relationship between acts of self-mortification and fund raising, Alcaceva wrote:

> The most extreme of these ascetic practices by which these demons raise and collect money is to force one of their own to board a boat in which a hole has been drilled and to send it off across the sea. They die somewhere out at sea, but death in this manner is believed to promise salvation. [According to the Japanese,] suicide is a great honor, and their families hold it in great esteem.[34]

Alcaceva concludes by noting that "these matters were described to me by P. Come de Torres." It is thus a second-hand account, but his source, Come de Torres (1510–70), was one of the first missionaries in the country. Torres had sailed to Japan with Francis Xavier in 1549 and worked in Yamaguchi and Bizen.

A letter of 1562 by Caspar Vilela (1525–75), who spent some fifteen years in Japan, is the next to mention the rite and the first to offer a first-hand account. His description is also far more detailed than Alcaceva's:

> After leaving Sakai [in 1561/8,] I have seen the false ways which the Japanese believe will get them to heaven. There was a man with so many troubles in this world that he grew weary of life and, longing for another world of peace and tranquillity, was determined to carry out the practices that would allow him to enter heaven. Just as they believe in a multitude of worlds within this world, the Japanese also believe in a multitude of heavens. Each of these heavens has its own saint, and they believe that this saint will gather up those on earth and return to his heaven. It was said that the heaven to which this man aspired lay beneath the sea and that the saint there is known as Kannon. As preparation for his journey, the man stood at a ritual platform (*pulpito*) for many days without sleeping. He then preached to his followers of the impurities of this world, and those present were encouraged to offer alms. When the final day approached, he preached a sermon to his followers, and then each of them took a drink of *sake*. This act signifies, as it does for us, reciprocal amity. They then all boarded a single empty boat armed with long-handled sickles [*foucegrande*] with which to clear away the vegetation on their passage to heaven. They wore fine clothes newly made, and, in order to quicken the passage to heaven, they were bound to large stones and even stuffed handfuls of stones in the sleeves of their garments. I myself saw seven followers in attendance. My greatest sur-

> prise was that they joyfully boarded the boat and threw themselves into the sea.[35]

The specifics of Vilela's description—the alms, the clothing, the sickle, the stones, and most notably the communal death—are confirmed by an account by Luis Frois (1532–97). Frois, who arrived in Japan in 1563 and remained there until his death thirty-four years later, produced a voluminous corpus of letters, as well as the important *Historio do Japão*. Although Frois' account of the rite comes second hand, he himself witnessed the devotional cult that had developed around these ascetics. In a letter to the mission in Goa dated February 20, 1565, concerning Buddhist funerary practices, Frois provides the following description of *Fudaraku tokai*:

> There is a method of burial alive by which believers hope to attain Amida's [*sic*] glory. While traveling to the capital this year, Luis Dameida and I stopped at a city in Izu Province some forty leagues [22.2 km] from Bungo. We had stayed there previously [in the eleventh or twelfth month of 1564] for six or seven days and had heard that this was a place where they had held the ceremony of offering a living sacrifice to the demons.
>
> Six men and two women wandered through the city prior to their sacrifice, collecting alms for the glory of Amida and then bid their families and friends farewell. Each was dressed in beautiful kimono, and the money they had collected was put in their sleeves. Crowds proceeded with them to the beach, where they boarded a newly built boat. They were then bound by their necks, arms, waist, legs, and feet to large stones and, for a second time, bid farewell to those assembled on the shore. Although the crowd appeared mournful and sobbing, they knew in their hearts that they [the *tokaisha*] were becoming sanctified and wished that they too could be crossing the boundary to beatitude. When they sailed out toward the offing, family and friends followed in a separate boat, and from there wished them a final farewell. When the boat had reached an adequate distance from the shore, they each threw themselves into the deep ocean—or, more accurately, into the depths of hell. Those who came to witness the event then set fire to the boat (figure 8.1).
>
> A small hall was later constructed in their memory. Above the roof of this hall were small poles with narrow strips of paper at-

FIGURE 8.1. Image of *Fudaraku tokai* based on Jesuit accounts. Engraving by John Ogilby from Arnoldus Montanus, *Atlas Japannensis* (London, 1670).

tached. Pillars [stūpas?] with inscriptions were also erected for these famous individuals, and small pine trees were planted in their honor. Many people leave their homes every evening to visit this hall to the eight who martyred themselves for the devil. Those who live in this area come to worship daily at this hall. When Luis Dalmeida and I passed in front of this hall with the young daughter of the family with whom we were staying on the way to her baptism, four or five old women were worshipping there with rosaries in their hands. When they saw that we neither bowed our heads nor offered respects, they laughed at our ignorance and condemned us with stern looks for showing such contempt and disrespect to the martyrs.

Several of those who had thrown themselves into the sea had held long-handled sickles, in order, it was said, to clear away the thick vegetation that obstructed their paths. Those who do not

> throw themselves into the ocean drill a hole in the bottom of the boat and insert a plug that they later remove so that both they and the boat will sink into the sea.[36]

Some of the details of the Jesuit accounts correspond with those found in the Japanese hagiographic literature. For example, the *Goshūi ōjōden* and the *Honchō shinshū ōjōden* both contain the tale of a monk named Gyōhan, who, in the late 1120s, put on purified robes, filled his sleeves with sand, and dove into the ocean in front of Tennōji.[37]

Fudaraku Tokai in Visual Materials

Nachi's position as the primary site of *Fudaraku tokai* in the medieval imagination is represented and reiterated in the *Nachi Pilgrimage Maṇḍala* (figure 8.2). The *Nachi Pilgrimage Maṇḍala* belongs to a genre of religious paintings to which modern scholars refer as *sankei mandara*, or pilgrimage maṇḍalas. Such paintings were produced from the Muromachi (1392–1573) through the Edo (1603–1868) periods to celebrate and advertise the popular pilgrimage sites of the age. At once devotional and promotional in intent, pilgrimage maṇḍalas served as objects of worship for communities of pilgrims far from the sacred sites themselves and as advertisements to encourage travel, veneration, and contributions to these cultic centers. The scene of *Fudaraku tokai* is depicted in all thirty-one extant copies of the *Nachi Pilgrimage Maṇḍala*.[38] This dramatic act of self-immolation, shown with such constancy and adoration in these paintings, was a subject of exposition in the narrative performances of the traveling priests and nuns who circulated the *Nachi Pilgrimage Maṇḍala* and the Kumano cult throughout medieval Japan.

In the *Nachi Pilgrimage Maṇḍala*, the passage to Fudaraku is set, as in our earlier literary accounts, beside Fudarakusanji at the Hama no miya, the subsidiary shrine on the shore of Nachi Bay (figure 8.3). Beneath the shrine's main gate stand three figures wearing red leggings and head coverings (*karasu tokin*, or crow caps), the distinctive garb of Nachi's mountain ascetics. The central figure represents the priest (*tokaisha*) about to embark on his journey to Fudaraku; the two figures on either side are his attendants (*dōgyōsha*). Behind these three stands a group of temple monks, clad in black robes, holding banners and a canopy over the soon-to-be de-

FIGURE 8.2. *Nachi Pilgrimage Maṇḍala* (*Nachi sankei mandara*). Hanging scroll, ink and color on paper. Momoyama period, ca. 1600. 153.5 × 159.4 cm. Courtesy of Kokugakuin University, Tokyo.

parted. To the right are pilgrims and a pilgrimage guide (*sendatsu*), kneeling with their hands pressed together in prayer. Other pilgrims are shown seated apart from this group, wiping tears from their eyes as they look toward the sea at a small sailboat with a red shrine fence (*tamagaki*) and four shrine gates (*torii*) but no person visible on board. The passenger is entombed within its tiny cabin, sealed inside, according to the *Azuma kagami* account, with nails driven in from the outside. Tethered to this vessel are two others, navigated by oarsmen, in which Buddhist monks, shrine priests, and mountain ascetics (*yamabushi*) follow in devotion. They will accompany the priest only to the mouth of Nachi Bay, where, at Kō-

FIGURE 8.3. Detail from *Nachi Pilgrimage Maṇḍala*. Kokugakuin University Collection, Tokyo.

kinshima (Rope-Cutting Island), they will sever their ties and allow the sailboat to drift off to Kannon's southern paradise.

Perhaps the first thing one notices about the scene is its funereal tone. The solemnity of the setting, the audience of priests and mourners, and the boat's ritual appointments all suggest a mortuary rite. The sailboat is laid out like a cremation ground (*hiya*), with the corpse surrounded by a fenced enclosure of forty-nine staves representing the requisite number of days of mourning (*imi*) and the four directional gates (*shimon*) through which the coffin is carried in mortuary rites. The *Shugendō mujō yōshū*, a fifteenth-century Shugendō text of funerary rituals, includes a diagram of the funeral ground nearly identical to the layout of the boat to Fudaraku, with the four gates and forty-nine staves clearly marked (figure 8.4).[39] In some copies of the *Nachi Pilgrimage Maṇḍala*, the four gates are even marked with tablets inscribed with their names: to the east is the *hosshinmon*, the gate of the aspiration of awakening; to the south is the *shūgyomon*, the gate of practice; to the west is the *bodaimon*, the gate of awakening; and to the north is the *nehanmon*, the gate of nirvāṇa. The *Nakasō Fudaraku tokaiki*, a text describing the passage of a certain Kōkai Shōnin, who sailed off from the coast of Hitachi Province in 1531, attempts to clarify the scriptural and ritual connections through numerological association.[40]

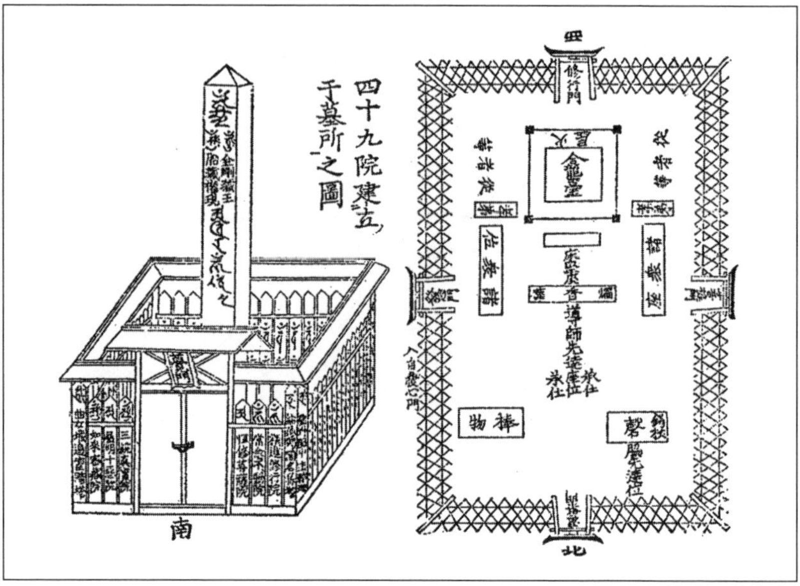

FIGURE 8.4. Diagram of funerary ground from *Shugendō mujō yōshū* identifying the four gates and the forty-nine staves. Reproduced in *Shugendō shōso*, ed. Nihon Daizōkyō Hensankai, 3 vols. (Tokyo: Meicho Shuppan, 1985), 2:342.

> At the center of the boat was a separate room of straw matting. [The surrounding fence] represented the forty-nine days, the thirty-three forms [assumed by Kannon], and the forty-four Sanskrit recitations of the nineteen passages [enumerating Kannon's virtues in the *Lotus Sūtra*]. . . . The four directions were marked by the four gates: the *hosshinmon* to the east; the *shūgyō*[*mon*] to the south; and to the west and east, the *bodaimon* and the *nehanmon*.[41]

These four gates also replicate the four stages of the Buddha's life: Śākyamuni's initial desire for enlightenment, his years of meditation, his awakening, and his *parinirvāṇa*. The pilgrim's itinerary at the Kumano shrines was also, like many other pilgrimage circuits in medieval Japan, marked by a passage through these four gates, offering a topographic correlate to the rite's symbolic structure. Buddhist pilgrimages and Buddhist funerals were thus both mapped by the spatial metaphor of the four gates, and the boat to Fudaraku capitalizes on this double entendre, homologizing the ritualization of enlightenment with the ritualization of death. For this last rite was also, of course, a rite of passage: a journey, to use the Buddhist turn of phrase, from this to the other shore.

The *Nakasō Fudaraku tokaiki* provides Buddhological explanations for the other elements of the boat to Fudaraku as well. The rope is referred to as the "mooring line to be severed," freeing oneself from the world, and the sail is said to have been "inscribed with Sanskrit characters." The mast and rudder are described as being made of the exotic fragrant woods *sendan* and *mukunoki*, which flourish on Kannon's island paradise. However, the most elaborate explications, and those that signal the text's religious affiliations, are reserved for the clothing of the *tokaisha* and his attendants:

> [Kōkai's] robes bore an image of the nine-level Pure Land woven from precious lotus [threads], as large as the [Taima] maṇḍala woven by Chūjōhime, with a host of bodhisattvas on high descending to the living beings below. He was wearing a *kesa* [surplice] of twenty-five *chō*, and, on his head, illuminating all, was a diadem of the twelve radiant buddhas. In the palm of his hands, pressed together [as he chanted the] *nenbutsu* for all living beings, he held the enshrined image of Higoro [Temple]. On his feet, which had walked all over the country, he wore straw sandals with [the markings of] auspicious [dharma] wheels.

In this language of pious exaggeration, the *tokaisha* is clothed, crowned, and shod as if he were a buddha. He wears a pictorial representation of Amida's Pure Land (*hensō-zu*) identical to the Taima maṇḍala woven by the legendary maiden Chūjōhime out of lotus threads provided by Kannon.[42] His *kesa* (Skt. *kasaya*) is gargantuan, the standard *kesa* measuring only seven *chō*. The dharma wheels (*dharmacakra*) on his feet are one of the thirty-two marks of a buddha. With the diadem on his head, the boundaries between priest and buddha begin to dissolve, and while holding the temple's image, he becomes the object of veneration himself.

A more specialized vocabulary of Tendai theory is used for the clothing of monks in the second boat. They are described as wearing such items as "the cloak of the three thousand worlds in a single thought" (*ichinen sanzen*), "the robes of the ten suchnesses within each of the thousand worlds" (*hyakkai sennyo*), "the *kesa* of the integrated identity of the three truths" (*santai sokuze*), and "the sandals of the four meditative practices" (*shishu zanmai*). All of these phrases are drawn from the works of the Tiantai patriarch Zhiyi (538–97). The figures in the third boat, on the other hand, are described as being "in the lineage of En no Ubasoku," the legendary founder of Shugendō. They are thus outfitted in the traditional costume of the *yamabushi* ascetic: "coarse hemp kimono beneath the figured robes with white tassels," worn by "those who have mastered Mt. Ōmine"; "eight-petal straw sandals"; "skull cap of the linked chain of causality"; and they are holding the "conch shell" and "*vajra* staff."

Temple, shrine, and *yamabushi* priests are thus shown joined together in prayer as they see the ascetic off. This is clearly an interdenominational suicide. Such religious pluralism, however, suggests that the pilgrim's goal may have been more than exclusively Buddhist. Fudaraku was not the only paradise at Nachi. The spatialization of death at Kumano was informed by a variety of religious traditions, of which Buddhist cosmologies were an important but far from exclusive element.

Multiple Paradises

In Kumano's religious geography, as in the religious imagination of the early Japanese, the world of the dead had a somewhat unfixed location. One place for this realm, illustrated by both mortuary and literary practice, was in the mountains. The ancient tumuli of the Kofun period, for example, were built on hills or, if on the plains, were themselves constructed as miniature mountains.[43] Even into the Heian period (794–1195), when such burial mounds were no longer erected, imperial mausolea were still referred to as *yama*, or mountains.[44] The less illustrious dead in ancient Japan were similarly relegated to the mountains, to the margins beyond civic boundaries. The Nara legal code stipulated burial in the hills east of the city, and this practice continued after the capital was transferred to Kyoto.[45] The banks of the Kamo and Katsura Rivers were designated as burial grounds, and the charnel fields of Higashiyama and Toribeno at the foot of the capital's eastern mountains marked the limits of this polluted realm.

Japan's earliest literature, the seventh- and eighth-century poetry of the *Man'yōshū*, suggests a similar topography of the other world. The majority of the *banka*, or funeral laments, contained in this collection refer to mountains as the land of the dead, as burial sites, and as the ritual loci and poetic topoi for recalling their spirits. But other poems place this realm in the sky, on islands, across the sea, and even occasionally in an underworld.[46] The location of the other world thus appears less than settled. While the *Man'yōshū* most often identifies mountains as the realm of the dead, as the nexus between the present and future life, and as the site of divine descent and contact, the other world is neither an entirely indigenous nor consistent locale.

The chronicles *Kojiki* (712) and *Nihon shoki* (720) posit the other world with a similar ambiguity. According to these texts, Izanami, the female figure among the two creator deities, was buried atop a mountain in a distant borderland. The *Kojiki* and *Nihon shoki* both render this land of the dead as *yomi no kuni*, or "the land of yellow springs," a Chinese term for the afterworld.[47] Crossing a mountain pass that connects the lands of the living and the dead, the male deity Izanagi sealed his spouse in a dark and cavernous inner chamber that he closed off from the land of the living with a large boulder. But this subterranean land of the dead, resembling a mountain cave or perhaps a stone burial chamber, is not the only image offered by the early chronicles. A different geography of the other world is suggested, in both the *Kojiki* and *Nihon shoki*, by the land called *tokoyo*. At times *tokoyo* shares the qualities of *yomi* as a dark netherworld. But in other instances, it appears as a distant land across the sea, an eternal world of everlasting life. As a realm of the dead located across the sea, *tokoyo* seems to bear an uncanny resemblance to the goal of the *Fudaraku tokai*. In the medieval period, the land across or beneath the sea was often conflated with Buddhist paradises. The submarine palace of the Nāga king, a Buddhist site—which was itself identified with the undersea mansion of the sea god found in native mythologies—was referred to as "the pure land of the dragon palace (*ryūgū jōdo*)."[48] There are also obvious similarities to Mt. Penglai, the mountain isle of immortality in the Daoist tradition. Indeed, in these early sources, *tokoyo* was assimilated to Penglai, known as Hōrai in Japanese. Both the *Kojiki* and *Nihon shoki*, for example, contain the tale of Tajimamori, who is sent by the emperor across the waves to *tokoyo* to retrieve the fruit of immortality. A poem in the *Man'yōshū* recounts a similar story of a fisherman from Urashima who sails off to *tokoyo* only to discover, upon his return, that each year he passed in this land of immortals was equivalent to a century at home. In the *Nihon shoki* version of the Urashima tale, this land of immortality is written with the Chinese characters for Mt. Hōrai, but the interlinear phonetic *kana*, through a literal effort at cultural translation, render this name as *tokoyo*.[49]

What remains significant for our purposes is the degree to which these multiple images of the other world seem to converge at Kumano. According to the *Nihon shoki*, Izanami was "buried at the village of Arima in Kumano, in the province of Kii. In the time of flowers, the local inhabitants venerate the spirit of this goddess by offerings of flowers." Describing rituals for the repose of the dead, the text notes that "they also honor her with banners, drums, flutes, singing, and dancing."[50] Izanami's tomb was identified as the Hana no Iwaya, or flower cavern, near the Kumano Shingū, a cave believed to mark the entrance to the underworld.[51] Izanami's son Susano'o declared his wish to join his mother in a land called *ne no kuni*—literally, the land of the root or origin. According to the *Nihon shoki*, Susano'o, before his final passing, dwelt on Mt. Kumano and from there "eventually entered *ne no kuni*."[52] The death of Sukuna hikona, the helpmate of Susano'o's son Ōkuninushi, is described in a nearly identical manner. The phrasing is the same, but the term for his destination has shifted: *ne no kuni* has become *tokoyo*. Like Susano'o, Sukuna hikona "went to the cape of Kumano and eventually proceeded to *tokoyo*."[53] In a later passage, the *Nihon shoki* associates the ocean off Kumano with the land of *tokoyo*. When Emperor Jinmu encountered stormy seas at Kumano, one of his brothers, Mike Irino no Mikoto, "crossed the waters to *tokoyo*."[54]

Associated as it was with both immortality and death, this land across the sea was marked by a certain understandable ambivalence: it remained an object of both fear and longing. For from this land as well were believed to come deities, mysterious visitors known as *marebito* or deformed and disfigured gods such as Ebisu, who traveled seasonally to Japan's shores, bringing with them blessings and wealth, and returned carrying pollution and disease away from the community.[55] The vessels that ferried these divine figures to and from the land across the sea, replacing defilement with benefit, have much in common with the boats that carried the entombed priests to paradise. Both were known as *utsubobune*—literally, "hollow boats," hermetically sealed vessels, at once empty and full, like the hollow gourds in which Daoist immortals traveled between worlds.[56] In the *Jizō bosatsu reigenki,* it will be recalled, Katō Shōnin sailed off to Fudaraku in an *utsubobune.*

Another example of such ritual expulsion is found in the tale of Awashima *myōjin,* a deity who is sent out to sea in an *utsubobune* by her spouse, the Sumiyoshi *myōjin,* because she suffered from the impurity of vaginal discharge.[57] Her point of departure, the beach at the gate of the Sumiyoshi shrine, was not far from the place where many Pure Land devotees drowned themselves in the sea of Naniwa. The means and the goals of *Fudaraku tokai* were thus profoundly overdetermined. These conflated traditions, of a paradise across the sea to which defilement is expelled and from which blessings rebound, provide a rich subtext for the passage to Fudaraku. They reveal how an ostensibly Buddhist practice may contain latent and multiple meanings.

Scriptural Origins

More canonically Buddhist sources, however, are suggested in the narrative accounts of *Fudaraku tokai.* Yorinaga described the lone monk at Nachi as a devotee of the Thousand-Armed Kannon who hoped to visit Fudaraku in his present life. This pilgrim's desire recalls that of the pilgrim Sudhana, who sailed off to Kannon's paradise in the *Gaṇḍavyūha sūtra,* a topos depicted in the painting, *Manifestation of Kannon at Nachi* (figure 8.5). Yet the cult of Kannon in medieval Japan found its textual basis less in the *Gaṇḍavyūha* than in the *Lotus Sūtra,* the central scripture of Nachi's Tendai Buddhist lineage. The *Azuma kagami,* it will be recalled, noted that Chijōbō "recited the *Lotus* day and night" before his departure. This scriptural source for the rite is often cited in the very scenes of *Fudaraku tokai* depicted in copies of the *Nachi Pilgrimage Maṇḍala.* In many copies of the maṇḍala, the white sail that propels the priest's passage is covered with writing. Kannon's name, for example, is emblazoned on the sail of the boat in the Shōkakuji copy (figure 8.6a). In the maṇḍala belonging to the Kokugakuin Collection, it is Amida rather than Kannon who is singled out for praise (figure 8.6b). Here the sail is inscribed with the characters "*Namu Amida butsu,*" spelling out Koremori's dying words from the *Heike monogatari.*[58] On another copy of the maṇḍala, in the Yoshida Collection, the sail is completely filled with text (figure 8.6c). A total of fifty-one characters in five lines read:

FIGURE 8.5. *Manifestation of Kannon at Nachi*. Hanging scroll, ink and color on silk. Late Kamakura period, fourteenth century. 153.5 × 45.0 cm. Gift and purchase from the Harry G. C. Packard Collection Charitable Trust in Honor of Dr. Shujiro Shimada; Avery Brundage Collection, 1991.56. Asian Art Museum of San Francisco. Used by permission.

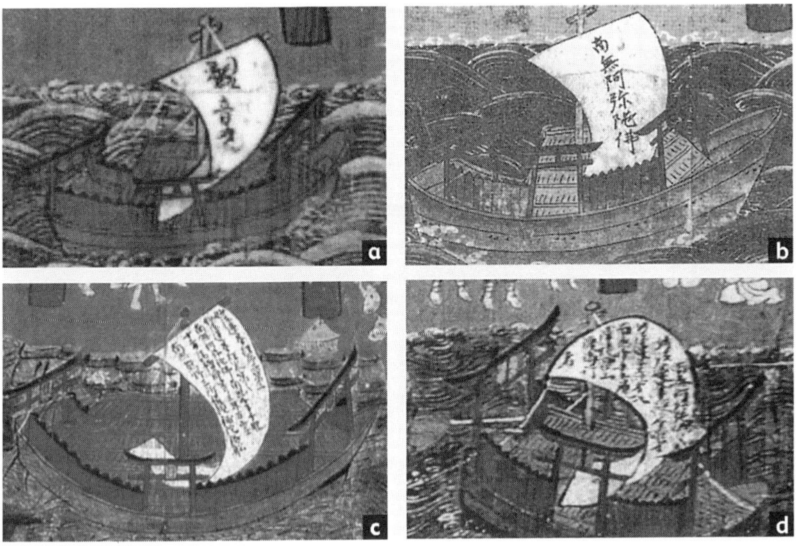

FIGURE 8.6. Details of *Fudaraku bune* sails from *Nachi Pilgrimage Maṇḍala: a*, Shōkakuji Collection, Wakayama; *b*, Kokugakuin Collection, Tokyo; *c*, Yoshida Collection, Okayama; and *d*, Takehisa Collection, Okayama.

Myōhōrengekyō jōbon dai ichi
Myōhōrengekyō kan dai hachi
Namu Amida butsu Namu Senjusengen
Jippō shodanna tō sangai manryō
Namu Kumano sansho gongen Fudaraku bune

First chapter of the *Lotus Sūtra*
Eighth roll of the *Lotus Sūtra*
Hail Amida Buddha, Hail Thousand-Armed Thousand-Eyed [Kannon]
The donors of the ten directions, the myriad spirits of the three worlds
Hail the three Kumano manifestations, the boat to Fudaraku.[59]

A nearly identical inscription is to be found on the *Nachi Pilgrimage Maṇḍala* from the Takehisa Collection (figure 8.6d):

Namu Amida butsu
Myōhōrengekyō jōbon dai ichi

Myōhōrengekyō kan dai hachi
Namu Senju [Kannon]
Fudarakusan tokai gyōja

Hail Amida Buddha
First chapter of the *Lotus Sūtra*
Eighth roll of the *Lotus Sūtra*
Hail Thousand-Armed [Kannon]
The ascetic who crosses the sea to Mount Fudaraku.[60]

The texts on the sails thus name the opening chapter of the *Lotus Sūtra*, the sacred scripture of Nachi ascetics; the eighth roll of the sūtra, which opens with the twenty-fifth chapter devoted to Kannon; Amida, the Buddhist form of the main Kumano deity; and the Thousand-Armed Kannon, the Buddhist form of the Nachi deity, whose paradise represents our pilgrim's goal. In addition, these texts also praise the deities of the three Kumano shrines, the boat itself, and its passenger, who will cross to Fudaraku; and in the reference to "the donors of the ten directions," they announce the recipients of the merit generated by this selfless act. Taken together, the words inscribed on the sails cite, chapter and verse, the scriptural faith of the suicide, the pantheon of the pilgrimage site, the nature and the means of the ascetic's bold endeavor, and, last but certainly not least, the felicitous benefit that it will bring to the larger community.

This last point brings us to a final double meaning still to be considered. The crowds of devotees depicted in the scene and the maṇḍala's larger country-wide audience whom they represent remind us of the public context of the rite. Suicide, as Durkheim argued a century ago, is at once a personal and a profoundly social act. At Nachi, the self-sacrifice of the lone ascetic was supported by a larger institutional order and by an extensive network of provincial patronage. Groups of devotees traveled from across the country—according to the *Kumano nendaiki* reference of 919, from as far as the distant northern province of Ōshū—to sponsor the suicide. Others, according to reports of some Jesuit missionaries, even joined the *tokaisha* in a communal death. As we can see in the maṇḍala, the audience of devoted followers remained more often on "this shore" to witness and receive a share of the merit accrued by the ascetic's self-sacrifice. In giving up his body, the priest assumed and extinguished the karmic burden of his supporters. Donors who formed such a bond received, in the words of one memorial inscription, "peace in this world and reward in the next."[61] Suicide, the most individual of acts, was thus a collective and public event. What the *Lotus Sūtra* called "the prime gift" entailed a ritual and even an economic exchange.

In light of this larger social context, one may wonder to what degree this sacrifice was voluntary and to what degree coerced. That is, are we dealing here with religious suicide or religious homicide? Recalling the local traditions in which a community's pollution was sent off in small boats across the sea, boats that were believed to return bringing blessings and wealth, one might indeed ask whether *Fudaraku tokai* represents a case of ritual scapegoating. A tale from the *Uji shūi monogatari*, a thirteenth-century collection of tales (*setsuwa*), holds out just such a possibility. It tells of "a priest who announced that he was going to drown himself" so as to be reborn in paradise. On the appointed day "the roads were packed with people who came from far and near, and there was a constant stream of carriages back and forth bearing ladies who wished to get a glimpse of the holy man. Even bigger crowds had collected to pay their respects to this holy man who was going to drown himself than there had been in the capital." But as soon as he hit the water, the holy man had a change of heart and madly tried to scramble back to shore. His once worshipful audience was less than pleased with this turn of events and took matters into its own hands, expediting his rebirth by pelting him with stones, "till in the end," the story concludes, "his head was split open."[62]

The passage to Fudaraku, as the dark humor of this tale suggests, was a ritual shot through with ambivalence. It was an act of personal devotion and public spectacle. It involved the priests, the ceremonies, the iconography, and the textual sources of a number of religious traditions. And it belonged to a larger religious culture in which the ritualization of death became, for both participants and observers, a soteriological event.

Notes

Portions of this chapter have appeared in chapter 3 of my book, *Localizing Paradise: Kumano Pilgrimage and the Religious Landscape of Premodern Japan* (Cambridge, MA: Harvard University Asia Center, 2005).

1. For the history of Buddhist self-immolation by fire in China, see Jacques Gernet, "Les suicides par le feu chez les bouddhistes chinois du Ve au Xe siècle," *Mélanges publiés par l'Institut des Hautes Études Chinoises* (Paris: Presses Universitaires de France, 1960), 2:527–58; Jan Yün-hua, "Buddhist Self-Immolation in Medieval China," *History of Religions* 4, no. 2 (1965): 243–68; John Kieschnick, *The Eminent Monk: Buddhist Ideals in Medieval Chinese Hagiography* (Honolulu: University of Hawai'i Press, 1997), 37–50; and James A. Benn, "Where Text Meets Flesh: Burning the Body as an Apocryphal Practice in Chinese Buddhism," *History of Religions* 37, no. 4 (1998): 295–322. See also Benn's chapter in this volume.

2. Reiko Ohnuma: "The Gift of the Body and the Gift of the Dharma," *History of Religions* 37, no. 4 (1998): 323–59, and *Head, Eyes, Flesh, and Blood: Giving away the Body in Indian Buddhist Literature* (New York: Columbia University Press, 2006), 48–50.

3. Mitsuhashi Takeshi, "Iezusukai senkyōshi no mita Fudaraku tokai," in *Kannon shinkō*, ed. Hayami Tasuku (Tokyo: Yuzankaku Shuppan, 1982), 251–81; Nei Kiyoshi, *Fudaraku tokaishi* (Tokyo: Hōzōkan, 2001), 418–36; and Gorai Shigeru, *Nihonjin no shiseikan* (Tokyo: Kadokawa Shoten, 1994), 161.

4. *Nihon ryōiki* III:1, *Shin Nihon koten bungaku taikei* (hereafter *SNKBT*) 30, ed. Izumoji Osamu (Tokyo: Iwanami Shoten, 1996), 129.

5. *Miaofa lianhua jing* 6, *T* no. 262, 9:53b; trans. Leon Hurvitz, *Scripture of the Lotus Blossom of the Fine Dharma* (New York: Columbia University Press, 1976), 295.

6. *T* 9:54a; Hurvitz, *Scripture of the Lotus Blossom of the Fine Dharma*, 298.

7. *Ōjōden, Hokke genki, Nihon shisō taikei* (hereafter *NST*) 7, ed. Inoue Mitsusada and Ōsone Shōsuke (Tokyo: Iwanami Shoten, 1974), 103; trans. Yoshiko Kurata Dykstra, *Miraculous Tales of the Lotus Sutra from Ancient Japan: The Dainihonkoku hokekyōkenki of Priest Chingen* (1983; reprint Honolulu: University of Hawai'i Press, 1987), 66. The misogynistic element of this tale notwithstanding, it should be noted that auto-incinerators were not exclusively male. In 1026, a nun is recorded as having burned herself alive. See *Nihon kiryaku*, Manju 3/5/15, *Shintei zōho kokushi taikei* (hereafter *KT*), ed. Kuroita Katsumi (Tokyo: Yoshikawa Kōbunkan, 1980), 11:265.

8. *NST* 7:72; Dykstra, *Miraculous Tales*, 44.

9. *NST* 7:64–65; Dykstra, *Miraculous Tales*, 38–39, slightly modified. For another example, see *Sange ōjōki* 20, *NST* 7:675.

10. *Sange ōjōki* 23, *NST* 7:676.

11. *Nihon kiryaku*, Chōtoku 1/9/15, *KT* 10:183.

12. *Hyakurenshō*, Chōtoku 1/9/16, *KT* 12:9.

13. *Shūi ōjōden* II:5, *NST* 7:328.

14. *Hyakurenshō*, Shōan 4/7/15, *KT* 12:90.

15. Death by fire and death by water were not necessarily mutually exclusive. One devotee planned to burn his body until a physiognomist informed him that drowning would be more likely in his case. He therefore lit himself on fire on the seashore, but before he was fully consumed by the flames, he threw himself into the ocean to drown (*Honchō shinshū ōjōden* 3, *NST* 7:684).

16. See Sakurai Yoshirō, "Tennōji no umi ni tsuite," in his *Nihon no inja* (Tokyo: Hanawa Shobō, 1986), 79–101.

17. *Goshūi ōjōden* I:4, *NST* 7:645–46.

18. *Ippen Shōnin eden, Nihon emaki taisei* 27, ed. Komatsu Shimegi (Tokyo: Chūō Kōronsha, 1979), 156–57, 333–34.

19. On this scene, see Sunagawa Hiroshi, *Chūsei yugyō hijiri no zusōgaku* (Tokyo: Iwata Shoin, 1999), 77–83.

20. Nei Kiyoshi lists fifty-seven *Fudaraku tokai* from the eighth to the twentieth century. Of these, twenty-five departed from Nachi, six from Ashizuri, five from Muroto, and the balance from unnamed locations (*Fudaraku tokaishi*, 768–69). See also Toyoshima Osamu, *Shi no kuni: Kumano* (Tokyo: Kodansha, 1992), 161.

21. *Kumano nendaiki*, in *Yoshino Kumano shinkō no kenkyū* (*shiryōhen*), ed. Gorai Shigeru (Tokyo: Meicho Shuppan, 1975), 353–408. On the *Kumano nendaiki*, see Yamamoto Nobumi, "*Kumano nendaiki* no seiritsu to shiryō hihan," *Kumano shi* 42 (1996): 153–61.

22. *Kumano nendaiki*, 362.

23. Ibid., 363.

24. The role of such attendants is not always clear and certainly changed over time. Scholars who discuss *Fudaraku tokai* are of differing opinions about whether the attendants, known as *dōgyōsha*, only assisted or actually joined the *tokaisha* on his journey. Jesuit accounts from the late sixteenth century seem to suggest the latter.

25. Kakushū held the ranks of provisional high priest (*gonsōjō*), senior high priest (*daisōjō*), imperial protector (*gojisō*), chief abbot (*chōri*) of Onjōji, and overseer of the Kumano shrines (*Kumano sanzan kengyō*).

26. *Taiki*, in *Shiryō sanshū*, vol. 4, pt. 1 (Tokyo: Zoku Gunsho Ruijū Kanseikai, 1976), 161–62.

27. *Sangoku innen Jizō Bosatsu reigenki* 6.17, *Koten bunko*, vols. 201–8, ed. Yoshida Koichi (Tokyo: Koten Bunko, 1964), 203:172–74.

28. *Hosshinshū* III:5, *Hōjōki, Hosshinshū*, ed. Miki Sumitomo, *Shinchō Nihon koten shūsei* (Tokyo: Shinchōsha, 1975), 137–38.

29. Ibid. III:8, 150.

30. Ibid., 151–52. See also Thomas Blenman Hare, "Reading Kamo no Chōmei, *Harvard Journal of Asiatic Studies* 49, no. 1 (1989): 173–228, esp. 218–20.

31. *Heike Monogatari*, *SNKBT* vols. 44–45, ed. Kajihara Masaaki and

Yamashita Hiroaki (Tokyo: Iwanami Shoten, 1991–93), 45:238–41; trans. Helen Craig McCullough, *The Tale of the Heike* (Stanford, CA: Stanford University Press, 1988), 347–50.

32. *Azuma kagami*, 5 vols., ed. Nagahara Keiji and Kishi Shōzō (Tokyo: Shinjinbutsu Jōraisha, 1977), 4:140–41.

33. Although the letters themselves do not use the term "Fudaraku," the vocabulary was known by the Portuguese in Japan at the time. The Jesuit dictionary *Vocabulario da Lingoa de Iapam com a declaração em Portugues, feito por alguns Padres e Irmaõs da Companhia de Iesu* (Nagasaki 1603) includes entries for "Fudaraku" (*Fudaracu*), "Mt. Fudaraku" (*Fudaracu xen*), "land of Fudaraku" (*Fudaracu xecai*), and "crossing [the sea to] Fudaraku" (*Fudaracu ni wataru*). See *Pari-bon Nippo jisho* (*Vocabulario da Lingoa de Iapam*), ed. Ishizuka Harumichi (Tokyo: Benseisha, 1976), 106.

34. "Carta do Irmão Pedro de Alcaceva, para os irmãos da Companhia de IESV de Portugal, escrita en Goa, no anno de 1554," in *Cartas que os padres e Irmãos da Companhia de Iesu escreverão dos Reynos de Iapão e China aos da messma Companhia da India e Europa, desdo anno de 1549 ate o de 1580*, 2 vols. (Evora, 1598; facsimile edition, Nara: Tenri Central Library, 1992), 1:27. My thanks to Haruko Nawata Ward for her assistance with the Jesuit materials.

35. "Carta do Padre Gaspar Vilela de Iapão, da cida de do Sacáy, pera os padres & irmãos da Companhia de IESV, escrita no Anno de 1562," in *Cartas*, 1:114.

36. "De hũa que o padre Luis Fróes escriveo da cidade do Miáco aos padres & irmãos da Companhia de Iesu, da China, & da India, 20 de Fevereiro de 1565," in *Cartas*, 1:176–77.

37. *Goshūi ōjōden* II:5 and *Honchō shinshū ōjōden* 11, *NST* 7:664, 685.

38. For a list of these collections, see Nei, *Fudaraku tokaishi*, 485.

39. *Shugendō mujō yōshū*, in *Shugendō shōso*, ed. Nihon Daizōkyō Hensankai, 3 vols. (Tokyo: Meicho Shuppan, 1985), 2:342. The diagram is reproduced in Miyake Hitoshi, *Ōmine shugendō no kenkyū* (Tokyo: Kōsei Shuppansha, 1988), 519, and Nei, *Fudaraku tokaishi*, 727. A similar sixteenth-century plan of the cremation ground is reproduced in Anna Seidel, "Dabi," in *Hōbōgirin* (Paris: Adrien Maisonneuve, 1983), 6:583. The use of *torii* in Buddhist funerary rites dates from at least the early fifteenth century. Temporary *torii* made of unhewn hackberry (*enoki*) wood were placed at the four cardinal directions during the funeral of the imperial prince Yoshihito in 1416. See William M. Bodiford, "Zen in the Art of Funerals: Ritual Salvation in Japanese Buddhism," *History of Religions* 32, no. 2 (1992): 153.

40. On this text, see Nei Kiyoshi: "Fudaraku tokaibune no shukyōteki imi," *Indogaku bukkyōgaku kenkyū* 41, no. 1 (1992): 309–12, and "Hitachi

no kuni no Fudaraku tokai," *Sangaku shugen* 13 (1994): 14–32. The manuscript copy in the Ochanomizu University library collection is transcribed and reproduced as an appendix to Nei's *Fudaraku tokaishi*, 756–62.

41. Nei, *Fudaraku tokaishi*, 759.

42. See Elizabeth ten Grotenhuis: *The Revival of the Taima Mandala in Medieval Japan* (New York: Garland, 1985), and "Chūjōhime: The Weaving of Her Legend," in *Flowing Traces: Buddhism in the Literary and Visual Arts of Japan*, ed. James H. Sanford et al. (Princeton, NJ: Princeton University Press, 1992), 180–200.

43. J. Edward Kidder, *Japan before Buddhism* (New York: Praeger, 1966), 146.

44. Ichirō Hori, "Mountains and Their Importance for the Idea of the Other World in Japanese Folk Religion," *History of Religions* 6, no. 1 (1966): 9.

45. Neil McMullin, "On Placating the Gods and Pacifying the Populace: The Case of the Gion Goryō Cult," *History of Religions* 27, no. 3 (1988): 284.

46. Hori, "Mountains and Their Importance," 8. See also Gary L. Ebersole, *Ritual Poetry and the Politics of Death in Early Japan* (Princeton, NJ: Princeton University Press), 81–85.

47. See Donald L. Philippi, trans., *Kojiki* (Tokyo: University of Tokyo Press, 1968), 642.

48. Tanaka Takako, *Gaihō no chūsei* (Tokyo: Sunakoya Shobō, 1993), 129.

49. *Nihon shoki, Nihon koten bungaku taikei* (hereafter *NKBT*), vols. 67–69, ed. Sakamoto Tarō et al. (Tokyo: Iwanami Shoten, 1983), 67:497.

50. *NKBT* 67:91.

51. Toyoshima, *Shi no kuni*, 34–35.

52. *NKBT* 67:129.

53. Ibid.

54. Ibid., 195.

55. See Yoshida Teigo, "The Stranger as God: The Place of the Outsider in Japanese Folk Religion," *Ethnology* 20, no. 2 (1981): 87–99, and Ichirō Hori, "Mysterious Visitors from the Harvest to the New Year," in *Studies in Japanese Folklore*, ed. Richard Dorson (Bloomington: Indiana University Press, 1963): 76–106.

56. See Yanagita Kunio, "Utsubobune no hanashi," in his *Imōto no chikara*, 6th ed. (Tokyo: Sogensha, 1946), 307–42; Cornelius Ouwehand, *Namazu-e and Their Themes* (Leiden: Brill, 1964), 122–23; and Rolf A. Stein, *The World in Miniature: Container Gardens and Dwellings in Far Eastern Religious Thought* (Stanford, CA: Stanford University Press, 1990), 58–77.

57. Tanaka Takako, *Sei naru onna: Saigū, nyoshi, Chūjōhime* (Kyoto: Jinbun Shoin, 1996), 49.

58. Kokugakuin Collection, Tokyo. Reproduced in *Shaji sankei mandara*, ed. Ōsaka Shiritsu Hakubutsukan (Tokyo: Heibonsha, 1987), plate 4.

59. Yoshida Collection, Okuyama. Reproduced in Ōsaka, ed., *Shaji sankei mandara*, plate 7.

60. Takehisa Collection, Okuyama. Reproduced in Ōsaka, ed., *Shaji sankei mandara*, plate 5. The texts from both sails are reproduced in Hagiwara Tatsuo, *Miko to bukkyōshi* (Tokyo: Yoshikawa Kōbunkan, 1983), 74.

61. Gorai Shigeru, "Kumano sanzan no rekishi to shinkō," in his *Yoshino Kumano shinkō no kenkyū* (*shiryōhen*), 165; Toyoshima, *Shi no kuni*, 191.

62. *Uji shūi monogatari*, *Shinpen Nihon koten bungaku zenshū* 50, ed. Kobayashi Yasuharu and Masuko Kazuko (Tokyo: Shogakken, 1996), 352–54; trans. D. E. Mills, *A Collection of Tales from Uji: A Study and Translation of Uji Shūi Monogatari* (Cambridge: Cambridge University Press, 1970), 349–50. This execution may represent something other than disappointment with the monk's performance. On stoning (*tsubute*) as a ritual practice, see Amino Yoshihiko, *Igyō no ōken* (Tokyo: Heibonsha, 1993), 145–96, and H. Byron Earhart, "*Ishikozume*: Ritual Execution in Japanese Religion, Especially in Shugendō," *Numen* 13, no. 2 (1966): 116–27.

9

The Death and Return of Lady Wangzin

Visions of the Afterlife in Tibetan Buddhist Popular Literature

Bryan J. Cuevas

Sometime around the fifteenth century, Tibetans began recounting individual descriptions of the afterlife. The concern in these personal narratives was more about sins and virtues acquired in this life to be tested in the next than it was about the achievement of Buddhist enlightenment, professed in the monastic textbooks as the only true goal of religious endeavor. The central protagonist in this literature is called in Tibetan a *délok* (*'das log*, "passed away and returned"). The *délok* is usually an ordinary person who dies, enters the *bardo* (Tib. *bar do*; Skt. *antarābhava*)—the intermediate state between death and rebirth—tours the netherworld, and returns to report his or her afterlife experiences and to convey messages from the Lord of the Dead about the importance of moral conduct and religious commitment.[1] The biographies of these revenants emphasize the universal Buddhist principles of impermanence and worldly suffering, the fluctuations of karma, and the feasibility of obtaining a favorable rebirth through virtue and merit. As such, these popular narratives are in accord with the basic teachings of Buddhism. But unlike the scholastic and specialized ritual texts, such as those accompanying the celebrated *Tibetan Book of the Dead* (*Bar do thos grol chen mo*), the *délok* stories are aimed almost exclusively at a living non-specialist audience.[2] While parallels can be noted between these popular texts and those of a more technical nature (and indeed the basic concepts in the *délok* narratives are almost always rooted in some aspect of formal doctrine), these personal accounts rarely contain all the particulars described in the theoretical and specialized works. They are, however, rich in detail about everyday anxieties surrounding death and common beliefs about the world beyond. My objective in this chapter is to consider the value of reading the *délok* accounts as social-historical documents that are capable of providing insights into the nature of popular Tibetan perceptions of dying, death, and the hereafter. Though frequently distorting and even contradicting formal Buddhist doctrine, these popular conceptions articulate religious and social values that may have been ultimately more meaningful and compelling to the average Tibetan than those offered in the sophisticated and generally inaccessible literature of the monasteries.

At the level of so-called "lived" tradition, it is clear that religious beliefs are usually only vaguely conceived. Ideas and perceptions are ambiguous and variable, often logically inconsistent with one another, and not always quite what the books say they should be. This results in discrepancies, and very often tensions, between the ideals of the tradition and its practical reality. I will assume here that the learned among Tibetan Buddhist practitioners, regardless of their status as monks or laypeople, would have had more direct access to the formal doctrines of the tradition through written sources and thus were more likely to assimilate many of the details of those formal written doctrines into their own expressions about this world and the world beyond. However, we have to keep in mind that when viewed alongside the religious textbooks, their ideas might still appear to us a bit blurry. Likewise, we must assume that the conceptions of the unlettered Buddhist practitioners, picked up along the way from the teachings of lamas and conversations at home and in village circles, would have been, of course, even less formal but probably still conforming generally to the basic principles and values of the received tradition. Keeping all this in mind, I want to turn now to a category of Tibetan literature that both defines and blurs distinctions between the learned and the unlettered, between formal doctrine and informal understanding, while at the same time revealing in the process something about popular religious ideas, particularly certain common Tibetan Buddhist perceptions of death and the afterlife.

My main source will be a *délok* biography dated to the seventeenth century. The name of our *délok* protagonist is Karma Wangzin (Karma dbang 'dzin), or Lady Wangzin.[3] Karma Wangzin is of special interest not only because she was a female active in a predominantly male religious arena, but also because her case exemplifies quite well the standard form of the *délok* genre in Tibetan literature.

The Délok Narratives: A Synopsis

Most *délok* accounts follow a standard plot, indicating that the written narratives did not change too drastically over time in either form or content.[4] It appears that certain set patterns may have been preserved by continuous literary imitation, and in fact many of the later texts refer explicitly to the influence of earlier *délok* stories.[5] At this point we cannot say which of the earliest texts constitutes the "original" *délok* tale, but it is probably safe to conclude that such a single work may never have existed. These texts represent a conglomerate of traditions that circulated throughout Tibet in both oral and literary form and were worked and reworked over time by the collaborative efforts of multiple parties, including the *délok* themselves; their biographers, editors, scribes, and printers; and other interested groups. For our purposes, one of the most significant aspects of these literary narratives is not so much their universal form but their local texture. Despite a certain generic structure, the biographies provide valuable details about the *délok*'s birthplace, their families, social background, and other information about their local communities. Enough evidence is scattered about in these stories to convince us of the actual existence of the *délok* as historical personalities. All of these, then, can be used effectively as sources for illuminating popular perceptions and attitudes at the local level of Tibetan society, particularly as they pertain to common notions about death and the afterlife, interpretations of the soul, and relations between the living and the dead, as well as certain aspects of the self-consciousness of personality and social identity. I shall begin by introducing some of the standard elements of the basic plot of these Tibetan *délok* biographies.

In most cases the protagonist of the story, who may be a monk or a layperson, male or female, is struck unexpectedly by an illness that leads to a quick death. The individual is not immediately aware that he or she has died and is confused when relatives and friends are seen performing the memorial services or going about their normal business. Confusion turns to anger as the deceased perceives that the group is ignoring his or her attempts to communicate with them. In truth, as we know from the doctrinal literature, the living cannot see or hear the dead. At some point the person comes to realize the facts of his or her predicament and is then transported to the other world, where he or she is guided by a vaguely divine figure, who in some cases is female and in others male. The *délok* visits the regions of hell or the intermediate realm, where he or she is terrified by the tortures of heat and cold, by jagged mountains and dark valleys, and by rivers of blood and fire. In these horrifying places, he or she witnesses the torments inflicted upon the damned by the ferocious attendants of the Lord of the Dead, Shinjé Chökyi Gyelpo (Gshin rje chos kyi rgyal po), the Tibetan form of Yama Dharmarāja. The tortured beings plead desperately with the visiting *délok* to relay messages for their families to perform the necessary rites and prayers so that their sufferings may be quickly alleviated. Sometimes the *délok* witnesses these pitiful beings being delivered by the miraculous chants of a lama or yogi who has traveled there to save them.

Later, the *délok* arrives before the Lord of the Dead himself and sees people being led to judgment, their punishment determined by the nature of their past actions in previous lives. Usually, the *délok* is then joined by two personal advocates, both believed to be born together simultaneously with each individual—a divine spirit (*lhan cig skyes pa'i lha*) holding white pebbles, which represent the *délok*'s virtues, and a demonic spirit (*lhan cig skyes pa'i 'dre*) with black pebbles, which represent accumulated sins. The two spirits are present to help the *délok* argue his or her case before the judge. The Lord of the Dead listens to their case and, after weighing the white and black pebbles on a scale of justice, orders a check of their appeals in the "mirror of karma" (*las kyi me long*), in which is vividly reflected every virtuous and sinful deed. When all is said and done, the Lord of the Dead pronounces judgment and exhorts the *délok* to mend ways and commit to a life of religious service for the welfare of all suffering beings. The journey concludes with the *délok* returning to the living and delivering the messages from the dead for their families and repeating Yama's moral exhortations to pursue a virtuous and devoted life.

Sources and Influences

Broadly speaking, in the context of premodern Tibetan understandings of death and the afterlife, we witness a hybridization of two basic models: one predicated on formal Indo-Buddhist doctrines drawn from both the philosophical and esoteric traditions, with emphasis on correct knowledge and psychophysical control of the dying process, postmortem transition, and rebirth; and a second model founded on widespread Tibetan beliefs and anxieties surrounding the persistence and vulnerability of the soul (*bla*) and the pollution and potential danger of the corpse. Both perspectives share conviction in the possibility of controlling the forces of death and positively affecting the postmortem status of the deceased. Around the late fourteenth and early fifteenth centuries, the hybridization of these two models contributed to the formation in Tibet of a unique liturgical program, the "*bardo* ritual" (*bar do cho ga*).[6] The rituals of this Tibetan Buddhist funeral program, best exemplified in the rites accompanying the specialized texts of the so-called *Tibetan Book of the Dead*, emphasize the purification of sins (*sdig pa*) through ritual actions and prayers that follow the deceased through the frightening *bardo* between lives and into a new existence. A distinctive feature of these *bardo* texts is the portrayal of the journey beyond death.

As noted, narrative descriptions of this postmortem journey can be found in the genre of Tibetan literature about the *délok*, ordinary men and women who have died and returned to life. In general terms, the *délok* narratives relate personal experiences of death and the afterlife. Their accounts reflect the influence of a number of foreign and indigenous traditions. One such tradition is the classical Indian Buddhist doctrine of hell. According to canonical Buddhist cosmology, there are eight types of hell (a model later expanded to sixteen and divided evenly between eight hot and eight cold hells).[7] The primary hells are arranged one on top of the other, and each one has sixteen supplementary places of torment, organized into groups of four around the four cardinal directions.[8] As might be expected, the hells are understood as being like prisons for criminals, where the dead pay for sins committed in former lives. Their suffering, however, is not eternal. Hell in Buddhism is characterized as only one of five or six transient realms of potential rebirth in a continuous cycle of birth and death.

When speaking of hell in Buddhism, we must also draw attention to Yama, the Lord of the Dead, who occupies a central role in Tibetan *délok* depictions of the afterlife, where he appears as Shinjé Chökyi Gyelpo. In India as early as the *Ṛg Veda*, Yama was recognized as the first mortal, the first being to die and travel to the world beyond.[9] In ancient India it was believed that in order to arrive safely in the celestial realm beyond death, the deceased first had to pass Yama's pair of watchdogs, who guarded the entrance to heaven and permitted only a select few to enter.[10] This was the first hint of the judgment seat that Yama would come to occupy in classical Hinduism and later in Tibetan (and Chinese) Buddhism. But even prior to his being identified as the postmortem judge, Yama, the great pioneer of the afterlife, had been transformed into the ruler of the dead. For a variety of reasons, his sovereignty was viewed in economic terms, so this god of death also became the "divine creditor."[11] In that role he and his fearsome entourage (themselves called *yama*s, or *gshin rje* in Tibetan) assumed the authority of registering each individual's death and determining each one's future course. Yama and his retinue had thus become the administrators of death, the underworld magistrates who meted out judiciary verdicts. Yama's image as the supreme judge of the dead appears with great flourish in Chinese accounts of the postmortem bureaucracy,[12] but also frequently in Tibetan ritual and literary traditions having to do specifically with death and the *bardo*, including of course the *délok* narratives.

Among other influences rooted in the classical Buddhist concept of hell, we should note briefly the accounts found in Indian, Chinese, and Tibetan literature of the descent into the netherworld of saintly heroes intent on saving the damned. The tale of the Buddha's disciple Maudgalyāyana might be seen as a prototype of this sort of savior narrative. The story of the hell journey of Maudgalyāyana (Ch. Mulian) to save his suffering mother is widely popular in China, where it forms the framing narrative of the famous "ghost festival."[13] In Tibet, as discussed in Matthew Kapstein's chapter in this volume, we find similar episodes in the popular epic of King Gesar and in the life stories of renowned mystics, such as Guru Chöwang (1212–70).[14] Reports abound in the *délok* texts of beloved lamas harrowing the depths of hell and freeing countless numbers of tormented beings from their shackles.[15] Such dramatic gestures are viewed invariably as testaments to the extraordinary skill and compassion of these accomplished yogis. But although the return-from-death accounts of the *délok* certainly share strong structural parallels with these heroic descent narratives, the *délok* texts themselves must be seen as really quite a different sort of literature. These stories are almost always about ordinary people who just happened to have had an extraordinary otherworldly experience. Their journey is a hapless one and rarely made by choice.[16]

In Tibet, the concept of hell was shaped also by the idea of its being a transitional state of temporary duration for those heavily burdened with karmic sins and defilements. In this regard hell became a way station for the penitent dead and as such could be qualified as a type of "purgatory" in the literal sense of that term, as an interim state in which the sins of the departed are purified. Indeed, the concept of hell is often conflated in popular Tibetan (and Chinese) literature with the Indian Buddhist idea of *antarābhava* (Tib. *bardo*), the transitional period between lives. This conflation of two separate formal concepts, hell and the intermediate state, may be explained in part by the fact that the transitoriness of hell, as seen in light of the traditional Buddhist notion of rebirth, already fulfills a sort of intermediate function. Since hell and the intermediate state are both places where the dead suffer the effects of previous actions while en route to their next place of birth, the two terms essentially came to refer to the same scenario.

This brings us to the second major influence on the *délok* genre—that is, the doctrine of the intermediate state. The earliest Tibetan notion of *bardo* was developed from an Indian Buddhist model expounded in the Abhidharma literature. In that model, following closely the patterns set forth by the Sarvāstivāda school, four stages in the life cycle of a sentient being were acknowledged: birth, the period from birth to the moment of dying, death itself, and the interim (*antarābhava*) between death and rebirth. Over time, interpretations of this fourfold scheme in general and of the interim period in particular were reformulated and embellished in tantric terms, and in Tibet, the intermediate-state doctrine and its attendant rituals became distinctively esoteric.[17]

The history of the concept of the intermediate state is not particularly relevant in the present discussion, but it may be worthwhile to introduce briefly four pertinent characteristics of the intermediate state proper that we encounter in one form or another in the *délok* narratives. First, death is presented as a spatial transition between two states of existence. Second, the duration of this intermediate state is divided into seven short phases, each lasting no more than a week, for a total of up to seven weeks, or forty-nine days. Third, the deceased, the traveler in the intermediate state, is likened to a subtle celestial being called *gandharva* (literally, that which eats odors), because he or she is believed to subsist only on fragrance.[18] Fourth, in the intermediate state, the deceased's senses remain intact, although in subtle forms, and he or she can be seen only by beings of his or her own class.

As for the formal doctrine in the ritual arena, Tibetan funeral rites are timed ideally to coincide with the forty-nine days of postmortem existence. When the complete liturgical program is followed, services are to be performed weekly for the entire seven-week period.[19] The fully developed ritual sequence consists of a variety of offerings, prayers of confession and reconciliation in the purification of sins, and rituals for guiding the deceased through the perilous pathways of the *bardo* and into the next life. The general assumption underlying this series of rituals is that actions performed by the living directly affect the condition of the deceased. The funeral rites are thus designed essentially to provide for the dead a means of expediting safe passage over death's threshold and of ensuring a positive future destiny.

The Tibetan notion of a postmortem intermediate state and of a consciousness that sheds the physical body at death and wanders in search of its next birth was not entirely formulated on Buddhist principles. Indigenous and non-Buddhist concepts also played a significant role in shaping perceptions of death and the afterlife in Tibet. Evidence suggests that throughout Tibet's imperial period (seventh through ninth centuries), the early religion of the court was a highly sophisticated religion of sacred kingship. This ancient royal religion was both a result and reinforcement of ideas about the creative and destructive powers of nature and the constitution and persistence of the soul. In later traditions, this soul is described as a vital physiological and intellectual support principle pervading the entire body and dependent on the respiratory breath (*dbugs*).[20] In life the soul is capable of wandering (*'khyams pa*) away from the body and is particularly vulnerable to being seduced and captured by demons or other evil manifestations.[21] Hence, one of the prime goals of ritual in both ancient and premodern times was to shepherd the soul (*bla 'gugs*), recapture it by means of a ransom (*bla glud*), summon its return (*bla 'bod*), or guarantee its safe passage (*lam bstan*) after death. This rather ancient Tibetan belief in the soul and its vulnerability has survived in the later Tibetan Buddhist ritual traditions, such as the techniques for ransoming the soul (*bla bslu*), calling the life back (*tshe 'gugs*), and guiding (*'dren pa*) the deceased through the *bardo*.[22] Further evidence of the persistence of this indigenous Tibetan notion of the wandering and vulnerable soul lies embedded also in the popular *délok* narratives.

A third major tradition relevant to the *délok* genre that may have inspired some structural aspects of its narrative development in Tibet is the early Indian Buddhist notion of the preta (Pāli, *peta*, frequently translated as "hungry ghost") and the special ritual bond between preta and human being. In the famous anthology of short stories called *Petavatthu* (Stories of the departed), the preta is described as a recently departed tormented being suffering the effects of past actions.[23] To alleviate its pain and to enhance its present circumstances, the preta makes requests to the living that certain virtuous actions be performed for its benefit. Most often these actions include the dedication of merit, almsgiving, and the recitation of Buddhist scripture.[24] This is virtually the same scenario we find in many of the *délok* descriptions of the journey through hell (and occasionally the preta realm), where the traveling *délok* meets and interacts with a host of beings who are suffering there. The damned in these Tibetan accounts request the same sort of pious actions that are recommended in the *Petavatthu* for favorably influencing the effects of karma. Here again we see an underlying principle at work: virtuous actions performed by the living can positively affect the predicament of the deceased.

A fourth tradition influencing the *délok* accounts is the popular cult surrounding the bodhisattva Avalokiteśvara, an omnipresent, omnipotent savior deity beloved throughout Asia.[25] He is believed to possess all virtues and is especially rich in love and compassion. Consequently, he is frequently invoked by devotees to rescue them during times of great crisis, imminent danger, disease, and death. In Tibet early on, as Tibetan historical consciousness was gradually transformed and reconfigured in Buddhist terms, Avalokiteśvara emerged as the country's patron deity linked directly to the role of Tibet's divine kingship.[26] Thus, for example, Emperor Songtsen Gampo (Srong btsan sgam po, ca. 617–649/650), retrospectively identified as Tibet's first Buddhist king, was reconceptualized within this new mythic framework as the compassionate Avalokiteśvara incarnate. The fusion of identities between this Buddhist deity and Tibet's great leaders would persist throughout premodern (and even modern) history, reaching its high point in the person of the Dalai Lama.

From the twelfth century onward, the emerging cult of Avalokiteśvara spread widely among all classes of Tibetan religious practitioners. This popular movement was largely promoted in the public sphere by a disparate group of strolling bards called *maṇi pa*, a name derived from Avalokiteśvara's famous mantra OṂ MAṆI PADME HUṂ.[27] The *maṇi pa* were professional storytellers who wandered around Tibet reciting edifying tales of buddhas and bodhisattvas, the sufferings of sentient beings in the different realms of cyclic existence, the benefits of virtuous action, and the magical effectiveness of the six-syllable *maṇi*-mantra. Their tales were usually intended as a means for soliciting alms. As part of the entertainment value, most *maṇi pa* traveled with colorful props to illustrate their stories, such as scroll paintings (*thang ka*) depicting scenes from the "Wheel of Life" (Skt. *bhavacakra*; Tib. *srid pa'i 'khor lo*).[28] The *maṇi pa* were some of the chief curators and transmitters of the *délok* testimonials, and many of them may have been *délok* themselves.[29]

Lady Wangzin and Popular Perceptions of Death and the Afterlife

In the popular representations of death and the world beyond that we encounter in the *délok* biographies, we see evidence for an extensive variety of common notions, some consistent with formal doctrine and others less so. I want to focus on only a select few—that is, the constellation of beliefs and perceptions clustered around three cardinal events of the *délok*'s experience: dying and departure from the world, the journey beyond death, and return to the body. The narrative examples I want to discuss dramatize these three events and the ideas surrounding them in truly evocative ways, and I hope the examples I have chosen illustrate some of what can be learned from these biographies about popular Tibetan perceptions of death and the afterlife. The selections that follow come from the biography of the *délok* Karma Wangzin.

By way of a brief introduction, Karma Wangzin, a laywoman, was born sometime around the middle of the seventeenth century in the southern Tibetan region of Lhodrak (Lho brag) in a village called Géchu Kunga Ling (Dge bcu Kun dga' gling). Her father was a lama by the name of Tsokyé Dorjé (Tsho skyes rdo rje), and her mother was a chieftain's daughter (*dpon sa*) named Tsering Chözom (Tshe ring chos 'dzom). She may have had more than one sibling, but we know of only a single elder brother—deceased—named Tsangpa Gyentsen (Tshangs pa rgyal mtshan), whom she meets in the *bardo*. When Karma Wangzin was still a young girl, her parents sent her off, against her wishes, to be married to the governor (*sde pa*) of a neighboring district called Okdro ('Og gro). In Okdro, hoping to pursue a religious life, she sought out a number of lamas and yogis and requested religious instruction from them. Among these teachers was a lama by the name of Drupchen Norbu Tashi (Grup chen Nor bu bkra shis). While in retreat at the nearby hermitage of Trapu (Khra/Phra phu), Karma Wangzin had visions of Padmasambhava and Tārā and about a year later developed the illness that led to her *délok* experience. We know very little about her life after she returned from her extraordinary journey.

Here now are passages from Karma Wangzin's narrative, beginning with the account of her departure from the world.

Karma Wangzin's Departure

On the eleventh day of the third month in the dragon year, I was struck with a severe illness. I was repulsed by food, and when I was standing up, I wanted to lie down, and when I was lying down, I wanted to get up. Memories came to mind of my parents, relatives, and close friends. Then on the twelfth day my child servant Sönam Tsering [Bsod nams tshe ring] looked at my face and started crying, "You have shades around your eyes and also your nose is crooked,[30] so would it not be best if I go to your village and ask [your husband] the district governor to come?" I thought to myself, if I can't endure this illness even just a little bit, how will I endure the essential marks of being a religious person, so I wanted to wait until evening before deciding what was appropriate. Then at midafternoon I began shivering, and I was very thirsty. I tried to quench my thirst by drinking water, but it wouldn't go down my throat[31] and spilled out from my nose. The process of the dissolution of the four elements began.

As a sign of flesh and earth dissolving, my body collapsed and I fainted. With the dissolution of blood and water, I became extremely thirsty and my mouth and nose dried up; I no longer had the capacity to drink. With the dissolution of heat and fire, I began shivering and felt cold, even when putting on many clothes. With the dissolution of breath and wind, my breath became raspy, and I couldn't suppress it even when I tried. Because the circle of light around my eyes diminished, I could no longer recognize my friends and companions. Because the sounds in my ears grew faint, I could no longer hear words spoken in my direction. Because the external and internal channels were closed off, I was no longer able to speak. Visions of this life faded as visions arose of my future life; I had reached the borderline [between this life and the next]. Because my awareness was clear,[32] I could remember my close friends and companions and all the joys and goodwill we shared, but now my friends were of no help to me. Now the time had come for me to walk alone. I had no confidence that I was going to the heavens above due to my practice of religion. All the sins I had committed were vividly clear in my mind, and I felt intense remorse. I cried many tears because of this.

At that time there came a very loud roaring and cracking sound. Since the movement of my breath had ceased, I blacked out like a butter lamp smothered with a clay lid.[33] My consciousness [withdrew] into the center of my heart, and I swooned unconsciously without mindfulness. When that happened, I was left in a blank state[34] without cause to fixate on the painful thought of dying, or the joy and sorrow of the thought of not dying, or on any thoughts whatsoever.

Then over yonder came the voice of a woman clear and distinct calling out, "Wangzin! Wangzin! . . . You have crossed over from this world. Do you not know that the impermanence of death has arrived,[35] that you desire and yearn for a body that is illusory? Come rest your mind in the state of reality-itself (Skt. *dharmatā*; Tib. *chos nyid*)!"

Because this voice was so distinct, I regained consciousness. Thinking, "I'm not dead, am I?" I looked around. I saw [above me] only a dusty gray object like an [open] hole in the bottom of a copper cauldron turned face down. Without seeming to move, I [went up through the opening and] arrived suddenly on top of that thing. I didn't know if it was my own head. I became nervous. On top of the object a white light . . . sparkled everywhere like the array of colors on a peacock's feathers, and multicolored rays of light emanated in the ten directions. Upon seeing the light, I became depressed and wept, and the light transformed into nine appearances.

Without the support of a body, my mind stirred about like a feather in the wind. Again I thought about that woman's voice and worried about whether I had died. I searched for my dear friends but couldn't find them. Again, I didn't know if I had died, and I was worried. Because I had been dishonest and slandered the livelihood and reputation [of others], I had not practiced religion. Feeling sad about this, I now wanted to practice, so I thought I needed to return to my village.

I arrived at Okdro and heard loud voices wailing and weeping. [My husband] the district governor and all the men had gone to Trapu and were not there. The women servants were calling out my name, and I thought, "I haven't died. Did the governor scold them?" I grabbed [one of the servants] by the shoulder and lifted her up, but she didn't respond and acted as if she didn't see me. Outside also there were clear and distinct voices wailing. I looked out and heard people saying I had died. Some said I was humble and kind and took care of others. Other people said I was stingy and jealous, and they whispered many secrets about me. My feelings were hurt, and I began to shed tears, even though I tried to hold them back.

Inside some people said, "The mistress has passed away," while others said, "It's a pity the daughter has passed away," and, "It's a pity for the district governor." At that moment [their expressions of sentiment] caused a hail of pus and blood the size of eggs to rain down upon me. I felt suffering in my mind as though my bones had been crushed and my skin had been pierced. Then there came a loud roaring sound. I looked at my body and saw that I was wearing the same clothes as before. As soon as the hail had fallen, I became naked. There came loud cries of unbearable suffering. A disembodied voice said to me, "Go to Trapu!" and suddenly, as soon as the thought of having to go flashed into my mind, I arrived at Trapu.

[My husband] the district governor and his servants had already arrived at Trapu. Vessels of beer had been poured,[36] tea was on the stove, and two monks were laying out scroll paintings and making preparations to set up an altar. There I thought to myself, "Is this a seven-day [funeral] ceremony?" One person after another arrived from the village and went before the governor. All of them offered him beer and expressed their sympathies....

[The district governor] wept many tears and said, "There are books about those in similar circumstances who have returned from death and also many anecdotes about those who were taken and then returned.... [I'm hoping] there's a great chance [my wife] will also return, so it's best to leave her corpse untouched for the duration of the forty-nine day period." There again he wept many tears, and I thought, "I'm not dead, am I?" After the thought of not having died flashed in my mind, I took hold of the governor's hand and exclaimed many times, "I'm not dead. You mustn't suffer!" But [my husband] the district governor and all his servants didn't respond. I thought, "Everyone must be angry with me. . . ."[37]

I thought about the words of [my teacher] Drupchen Norbu Tashi who taught about how this and that vision occurs in the *bardo* at the time of death, and I remembered the way. Thinking, "I seem to have died," I looked at my body to see if it cast a shadow, and it didn't. I stepped back and forth, but there was no sound of footsteps. I thought, "Alas! I've definitely died!" I became depressed, and I stayed for awhile in the human world, which I saw through an opening like a window. I felt a bit thirsty. I had no way to rely on religious practice. Back when I had the free time, I saw no reason to make offerings. Now thinking that the lords of death were coming to seize me, I felt terrible and began crying. I then collapsed.

At that moment a woman appeared dressed in white, her hair tied up in back, holding a rattle-drum (*ḍamaru*). She grabbed me by the shoulders and lifted me up, saying, "O dear, do not suffer! Stand up! When afflictive emotions arise there are no remedies that come, and those who claim to have the religion [to remedy those afflictions] are only speaking lies and harsh words. Birth and death are human merits; they happen over and over again. This death is not your only one. I'll be your companion on this great path we all must travel. Let us go peacefully."[38]

The account of Karma Wangzin's death experience quoted here offers a valuable index of popular Tibetan ideas about what is believed to happen during the dying process and immediately following death. We see in these ideas a familiarity with certain formal doctrines about death and dying that are more fully explicated in the theoretical and specialized literature. We find in Karma Wangzin's case a few imprecise allusions to the formal descriptions of the dissolution of the psychophysical constituents (earth, water, fire, and wind) during the dying process. In the textbooks, that process is said to culminate with the swoon into unconsciousness, followed then by the dawning of the clear light of death, the most fundamental level of reality-itself.[39] Many texts add that this clear light manifests as a panorama of five different rainbow-colored lights, and we also find reference to these five lights in Karma Wangzin's description. Indeed, most of the experiences Karma Wangzin reports here about her own death seem to be inspired by standard textbook descriptions of the psychophysical process of dying and dissolution. Other examples of formal ideas that find expression in Karma Wangzin's account include the notion that the dead are capable of seeing close relatives and friends but are not in turn able to be seen by them and that mourning relatives can cause, through their tears, great pain and suffering for the deceased—in the case of Karma Wangzin, that suffering is externalized and experienced as a painful hail of pus and blood. The notion that the dead keep the same identity and physical appearance that they had while alive and that by a mere thought the dead can travel instantly to any place that comes to mind are also ideas that can be located in the formal canonical literature.

We see, then, that Karma Wangzin's descriptions of her death and departure accord generally with the authorized written sources. But as might be expected, Karma Wangzin's account lacks a degree of formal precision and detail. This is not at all surprising, of course, since we know Karma Wangzin was not a religious scholar or tantric specialist, nor was she a particularly advanced practitioner. What she does say about her experience, however, shows at least some familiarity with the advanced doctrines, though perhaps only informally understood and assimilated as part of her own personalized interpretation of that experience.

We turn now to a few excerpts from Karma Wangzin's description of her journey beyond death to the regions of hell and the *bardo*.

Karma Wangzin's Journey

I covered my forehead with my hands and thought I should go upward, and a forceful wind stood me upright. Powerless, I was raised up into the sky, pulled upward and then thrown down. I had visions of a variety of human-like heads with eyes that looked angry and glaring. Baring fangs, they shook up and down. On their bodies they wore human skins and tiger hides around their waists. They were adorned with bone ornaments and were licking the brains from human skulls that they held in their hands. Some of them were measuring the length of human intestines, some were grasping humans legs, ripping them apart and eating the flesh. Some had a variety of weapons that they raised in the air, shouting "HŪṂ! HŪṂ! PHAṬ! PHAṬ! Strike! Strike! Kill! Kill!" I was caught in the middle of all of them and tossed up and down as if twirled around in a heavy blizzard. At that time I couldn't remember my parents, relatives, or close friends. Instantly, I was led to the edge of a vast plain. When I arrived there, I could feel the wind [like I had before] but could see nothing on the ground. I heard the thunderous roars of "Strike! Strike! Kill! Kill!" and I suffered just a little bit. Memories of my parents, relatives, and close friends came to mind. I cried out the names of my parents and asked, "Where am I going?" There was no advice from their side. My parents didn't tell me where they wanted me to go over here. I said, "I've been sent out alone. How do I cope with this?" and rolled over.

Then that woman from before showed up carrying a rattle-drum. I grabbed onto her clothing and asked her: "Madam, what is the name of this plain? Whose great city is this? What is it called? What is your name? My parents, relatives, and close friends didn't advise me about where they wanted me to go, and I arrived here beyond my control. Now, please accept my jewelry and in exchange give me instructions about how I can get back to my village."

The woman responded: "Because your ignorance is so severe, your own visions rise up as enemies. This plain, as wide open as the sky, is called Desert of Razors. It's also the path that great sinners use to get to the hell realms. That great city over there is called Plain of Vast Expanse. That area is also called Red Element Ridge, or the Great City of the Dead. Do you not recognize me? My secret name is Yeshé Dorjéma [Ye shes rdo rje ma]. Both of us are friends; we're as close as a body and its shadow. You've left behind your own body of flesh and blood, your friends and attendants, food and wealth. You have no control over it. You bear the burden of your sins and defilements coming to fruition, and now you've arrived here in the *bardo* realm. . . ."[40]

I then arrived in the south, and my elder brother, Tsangpa Gyentsen, came out from a small doorway. I was very sad. I held my brother's hand and wept, "Alas! Boy, why have you had to stay here until now? You were born the son of a lama, so you haven't accumulated any sinful karma, have you?"

He responded, "Dear sister, I didn't accumulate the sin of desiring wealth, but since our parents and older brothers viewed me with scorn, I didn't feel encouraged [to pursue] the religious course required of me. Even though I was a lama's son, I had no understanding of religion. I was even forced without cause to tend the cattle herds. Consequently, I had to face verbal abuse and teasing from the wives of the cattle herders. I did become skilled in bleeding cattle. I couldn't recognize [the difference between] virtue and sin. I caught small birds and mice and roasted them alive. As for the ripening of those actions, the area from here to over yonder is called Great Mass of Fire at [the End of the Present] Age. Loud roaring sounds and the voices of people burning in that great fire fill the entire three-thousand-fold universe, and I am very frightened. I was led here beyond my control by Shinjé's attendants. They said to me, "Even though your class and family lineage are good, your behavior has been bad. . . ."[41]

I asked my brother where he was going to go, and he said Chökyi Gyelpo had told him he was going to be reborn at Sengé Dzong [Seng nge rdzong] to the south. I said, "In that case, for your benefit I'll make a community tea offering as well as an offering for the dedication of merit. I'll commission a copy of the *Vajracchedikā* and have it recited. I'll have one hundred thousand *tormas* [*gtor ma*, ritual cake offerings] sent off to the male and female realized yogis and also make prostrations. I'll make sure that you get the fruit of whatever virtues can be achieved through these activities. . . . Now, you're going to Sengé Dzong in accordance with Chökyi Gyelpo's command."

Then with great sadness I held onto my brother's hand and said, "Boy, pull your mind together. Supplicate Dorjé Pakmo [Rdo rje phag mo; Skt. Vajravārāhī], your personal deity, as well as the great Precious One from Orgyen [O rgyan Padmasambhava]. You're a lama's son, but don't slip up!" Just when we started to walk off together, a mountain to our west began to crumble. It was inconceivably frightening. Then a great wind storm rose up and took my brother away beyond his control. I swooned unconsciously, falling into a stupor like heavy darkness, and then my female friend arrived.

"This brother of yours was from a good family, had a clear mind, and wasn't conceited, but since he didn't cultivate the Great Seal [Skt. *mahāmudrā*] meditations, he had to experience for

> awhile the fear and terror of the *bardo*. So there's no need for you to suffer. Stand up!" . . .[42]
>
> [I was led before the Lord of the Dead.] With eyes wide open, Chökyi Gyelpo looked into the mirror of karmic existence and said this to me: "Oh, as to your name there is no error; your name is Trinlé Wangzin ['Phrin las dbang 'dzin]. . . . Now that you've arrived here, should we look closer at your good and evil deeds to tally up your karma? Have you seen the terrors of Shinjé's messengers? Have you understood what virtues should be adopted and what sins should be avoided? Have you understood the messages delivered to you? Do you know that I am Chökyi Gyelpo?"
>
> He continued: "Previously, Lingza Chökyi [Gling bza' chos skyid] returned [from death] because an error had been made in regard to her name and clan. A girl from Dartsendo named Samten [Bsam btan], a Bönpo girl from Kham named Yungdrung Wangmo [G.yung drung dbang mo], and yourself are returning [to the human world], but not because of any error in name or clan. The girl from Dartsendo is returning under the following conditions: I warned her, "If you get distracted by financial profits gained from trading and by worldly activities, then you won't be awakened [to buddhahood]. Don't mix virtue and sin!" With that I sent her back. The Bönpo girl from Kham is returning under these conditions: I told her that the Bön religion doesn't have the fruit of enlightenment, so she should convert to Buddhism. She's returning because it's necessary that she behold the essence of the Great Seal. Now, as for you, encourage the people of Jambuling ['Jam bu gling—i.e., the world] to follow virtue and give them a message about [what happens] in the interim between death and the [next] life. . . . By the power of your previous prayers and the benefits of your virtue, you will return to your body in the human world and work extensively for the welfare of beings."[43]

Here in these excerpts from Karma Wangzin's description of the journey after death, we find several recurring motifs and images: the winds of karma that toss the deceased around uncontrollably; the appearance of Yama's wrathful demons tormenting the dead while shouting, "Strike! Strike! Kill! Kill!"; the tortured screams of the damned; the realm of the dead as a vast landscape filled with extraordinary mountains, valleys, and rivers; the divine guide who leads the deceased along the way; the deceased's meeting with familiar relatives, friends, and local personalities; judgment at the court of the Lord of the Dead; and the mirror of karma that reflects without blemish all the sins and virtues of the dead. Many of these common motifs are clearly borrowed from Buddhist canonical sources, both Indian and Tibetan, while others seem unique to the *délok* genre. Of these, the notions I find most intriguing are the ideas about the geography and spatial organization of the *bardo*, the population of that space, and the externalization and personification of karma.

Throughout Karma Wangzin's journey in the other world, she travels across a vast and varied terrain. In the beginning she is told that she has arrived in the Desert of Razors, the open plain traveled by all sinners on their way to hell. She is then shown a number of impressive landmarks in the Great City of the Dead. From there she travels across an extensive landscape before arriving at the court of Yama, Shinjé Chökyi Gyelpo. The world beyond death depicted in this account is in many respects like the hells described in the classical literature as far back as the *Abhidharmakośa*.[44] Thus, when Karma Wangzin travels through the hells, we expect then that she should see houses of iron and fire, boiling rivers of burning ash, forests of swords, and so forth. What seems exceptional, however, is that her travels through the *bardo* are also described in these same spatial terms. In Karma Wangzin's *délok* account, the *bardo* itself is described as a vast topography with varied boundaries and geographical features, all of which lie at different altitudes that must be either climbed or descended. Such a notion is a far cry from the formal doctrine that narrowly defines the *bardo* as an interim of consciousness, a transitional space of a specific duration between two separate states of conscious existence. We have here a fine example of a popular notion about the afterlife that really only vaguely concurs with ideas explicated in the learned sources.

That the *bardo* is populated by such an enormous number of people and that many of those people are known personally by Karma Wangzin are other concepts that I find provocative in these *délok* accounts. Karma Wangzin, for example, meets a host of folks along the way from her home region. A large proportion of them are nuns, curiously enough, but several are lamas, and others are just simply ordinary people. Many of the souls she meets are tormented by their sins, and a few special visitors are there to help alleviate the suffering. When Karma Wangzin meets her brother,

Tsangpa Gyentsen, he describes the tortures he has to endure for burning animals alive. She promises to dedicate a series of offerings for him so that he might gain some comfort and reprieve from his pain. So one point we can emphasize from of all of this seems to be that in the *bardo*, the dead encounter familiar people in familiar contexts. Karma Wangzin meets local nuns and lamas and various classes of laypeople both from home and from neighboring villages. What we find in these personal details, then, is clear evidence of a move in the *délok* narratives, not only to localize the *bardo* in familiar ways, but also to populate it with hordes of identifiable personalities, a maneuver not characteristically found in the formal literature.

We see this same personalizing move in the descriptions of the trial and judgment before the Lord of the Dead, whereby the sins and virtues of the dead are calculated and weighed and then a verdict delivered. What is most noteworthy about these scenes in Karma Wangzin's account is not so much the trial itself, which can be found portrayed in a variety of Buddhist scholastic sources, but that the nature and quality of the deeds committed are usually described in personal rather than collective terms. The concept of a specific individual's judgment before the Lord of the Dead stands in contrast to other, more conventional depictions of this sort of postmortem scene. Painted images of the "Wheel of Life," for example, tend always to depict the collective judgment of sentient beings as a generic group. The judgment scenes in these paintings are really nothing more than pictorial expressions of the impersonal laws of karmic cause and effect. Because such representations are made to conform to traditional symbols of Buddhist cosmology and are established in accordance with the strict requirements of Tibetan artistic conventions, they are best suited to depict ideal types rather than the personal characteristics of specific relatives and friends, neighbors, and colleagues.

What follows is the individual account of Karma Wangzin's arrival back to the world of the living.

Karma Wangzin's Return

Then I thought to myself, "I will return to my village," and in a flash I arrived in Trapu. There through my doorway I saw the corpse of a dog with a leather shroud covering its eyes[45] and foaming at the mouth. I was frightened and felt sick to my stomach. I ran just a few steps away to the far side [of the room]. After thinking again about it, I felt I could go up to it, and as I became accustomed to the dog's corpse, my mind suddenly entered my body. My recollections were scattered, and I blacked out as though everything had become dark. Then I slightly recovered my presence of mind, but, since my body had no strength, I couldn't move. As my recollections gradually became clearer, I moved just a little bit, and the person keeping watch at my pillow[46] repeated "PHAṬ" three times. When the unforgettable suffering and terror of the hell realms became vividly clear [again in my mind], the palms of my hands shot upward, and the cloth covering my face shifted. The person keeping watch thought, "Is this a zombie animated by a malicious *gyelpo* [*rgyal po*] demon from Okdro?" Removing the veil, he smacked my head many times and then placed his hands on my bosom.[47] I thought about grabbing his hand and telling him I wasn't dead, but because my body had no strength, I wasn't able to grab hold of him, and I couldn't speak. The person keeping watch checked to see if there was any warmth at my heart, and when he noticed a slight bit of warmth he called out to my relatives, "Your daughter has returned. Come here!" My mother came and cried out, "Mother's girl has returned?!," and she untied the stitching of the cloth sack [my body had been bundled in].[48] The old district governor arrived and moved me to another room. I was given a boiled mixture of beer, honey, and brown sugar, but since my tongue and throat had dried out during the seven days that my mind and body were separated, I wasn't able to drink it. As a result, I had to be fed with a spoon a little bit at a time.

The next day I gradually recovered my strength. My family got over [their grief], saying, "Our daughter has returned!," and everyone was overjoyed. They called in two scribes: one of the scribes wrote down and edited my stories about [the dead I had met] from Ü [Dbus], Tsang [Gtsang], and Lhodrak, and the other copied down my series of stories about [the dead I had met] from the Sok region [i.e., Mongolia] and from Mön. I myself planned to travel the country delivering Chökyi Gyelpo's message, but the wife of the high lama spread evil gossip about me, saying, "She's of a very evil class! She left her body in order to steal the breath of people from Ü and Tsang, and now she's returned here!" Listening to this, others also began accusing me, saying, "Yes, she is such a demoness!" They lost faith in me and the evil rumours continued to spread. Then the old district governor... suggested that for the time being I stay quiet and keep my [stories] secret.

Then one day Pönlop Rinpoché [Dpon slob Rin po che] arrived at Tram Khar [Khram khar], and I went there to request religious instruction from him. After about a month of listening to his teachings, I started asking him a number of questions about the direct introduction to [the nature of] mind. I understood the lama's answers, but I told him I found it difficult to generate [experiences] like that. Around that time my servant girl said to the lama, "Certainly, being introduced to [the nature of] mind is easy for her. She's returned from the land of the dead!"

The lama drank from three skull cups filled with beer and, after offering me some, he proclaimed, "First of all, I too have had the experience of traveling to the land of the dead, three times! I traveled there, and this daughter [Karma Wangzin] has traveled there, and both of us have seen a variety of things, so let the daughter tell her story." One by one the lama's students began gathering around me as I related the story [of my journey to the land of the dead]. Pönlop Rinpoché's eyes filled with tears as he listened. For the entire day he postponed his religious classes so that I could finish telling my story about hell and about the messages delivered from the dead.

Afterwards, Pönlop Rinpoché developed great faith in me and said, "Daughter, I'm convinced by what you've told us. I want you to leave here and travel all over the country for the welfare of the people. I'm offering you a riding horse, a pack mule, two servants, and a cook so that you can tell [your story] to the whole world...."

But even though the lama had said this to me, [I recalled] that [back during my journey to the land of the dead] when I arrived before Chökyi Gyelpo, I was frightened by the wrathful gods and goddesses that surrounded him, and in my volatile state [of mind] I prayed for my own liberation. Aside from praying in this way, I wasn't used to praying for the benefit of all beings and so, due to my own self-interest, I was really of no great benefit to people.[49]

It may be stated unequivocally that in premodern Tibetan societies, there was widespread consensus that the world of human beings was overrun by a host of malicious spirits and roaming manifestations of the dead.[50] Consequently, the primary and predominant goal of religious specialists, both lay and monastic, was to remove or contain the aggressive menace of these demonic powers through a variety of exorcism rites and the ritual treatment of corpses. The threat of demonic possession was perceived to be particularly great once the consciousness had left the body. It was feared that evil spirits might enter the corpse and reanimate it, in which case the body might be transformed into a zombie (*ro langs*). To guard against such attacks, the corpse was watched continuously throughout the day and night. Legends of this type of demonic possession can be frequently found in Tibetan oral traditions but less commonly in the literature.[51]

The passages quoted here from Karma Wangzin's biography offer compelling testimony of these sorts of popular ideas about demons and animated corpses that are seldom encountered in the scholastic literature. Two possible insights about death and the *délok* phenomena might be drawn from her descriptions. First, demons and death are intimately linked. There are demons that cause death in humans (these tend to linger near the home) and demons that possess corpses. But apparently there are also certain people who, when possessed by demons, can leave their body temporarily in order to steal the breath away from other living humans.[52] To those left behind, the possessed person appears to have died for a short while, only then to come back to life. This is indeed the type of possessed individual Karma Wangzin had been accused of becoming by a great number of those around her. What then is the difference between this sort of "demoniac" and a *délok*? The religious response should be obvious enough—*délok* are not possessed by demons but have instead undergone an extraordinary journey to the realms beyond death, where they are permitted to communicate with the dead and bring back edifying messages for the living. Society's response, however, seems to have been a bit more ambivalent.

This brings me to the second insight about the *délok* that may be sparked from Karma Wangzin's description of her return to the living. What was the *délok*'s social identity? Relying on the few fragments of information transmitted through the texts, we see that Karma Wangzin was simultaneously feared, vilified, and revered, but in the end she was viewed as a powerful religious personality in her own right, even potentially more influential than the high lama, Pönlop Rinpoché, who had himself traveled to the land of the dead on as many as three separate occasions! But what of her social function? To fully explore that question, we would have to turn to contemporary ethnographic sources. Thus, in concluding, I hope it will suffice to offer here just a few of the observations recorded by the noted Himalayan anthropologist Françoise Pommaret in her pioneering study of the *délok* tradition as "lived" in Bhutan and Nepal.[53] In consideration of the *délok*'s social function, Pommaret distinguishes between features described in the literary sources and those observed in contemporary society. As we have seen in Karma Wangzin's case, the *délok* in the written sources are favorably characterized as messengers of the dead and as preachers of virtuous action and the effects of karma. In lived modern settings, not unlike the women described by John Holt in his chapter in this volume, the *délok* are identified also as "shamans" who undergo the death experience at fixed dates and times, as guides for the dead who save them from evil destinies, and as soothsayers who receive visitors asking for spiritual assistance.[54] The *délok* are also viewed as ritual outcasts who are prohibited from assisting with births and funerals. Presumably, the logic behind such prohibitions stems from the perception of the *délok* as a dangerous and impure liminal being, capable of moving in a world where there are no obstructing borders between the realm of the dead and the realm of the living.

Notes

1. To date less than a handful of critical studies on the *'das log* have appeared in the scholarly literature. The most noteworthy are the studies of Lawrence Epstein, "On the History and Psychology of the 'Das-Log," *Tibet Journal* 7, no. 4 (1982): 20–85, and Françoise Pommaret, *Les revenants de l'au-delà dans le monde tibétain: Sources littéraires et tradition vivante* (Paris: Editions du Centre National de la Recherche Scientifique, 1989); see also Pommaret's summary treatment of the topic in "Returning from Hell," in *Religions of Tibet in Practice*, ed. Donald S. Lopez, Jr. (Princeton, NJ: Princeton University Press, 1997): 499–510. Tulku Thondup provides summary translations of many of the Tibetan *'das log* tales in his *Peaceful Death, Joyful Rebirth: A Tibetan Buddhist Guidebook* (Boston: Shambhala Publications, 2005). For detailed analyses of a similar genre of return-from-death literature in medieval China, see especially Stephen F. Teiser, "'Having Once Died and Returned to Life': Representations of Hell in Medieval China," *Harvard Journal of Asiatic Studies* 48, no. 2 (1988): 433–64;

Robert Ford Campany: "Return-from-Death Narratives in Early Medieval China," *Journal of Chinese Religions* 18 (1990): 91–125, and "To Hell and Back: Death, Near-Death and Other Worldly Journeys in Early Medieval China," in *Death, Ecstasy, and Other Worldly Journeys*, ed. John Collins and Michael Fishbane (Albany: State University of New York Press, 1995), 343–60.

2. See Bryan J. Cuevas, *The Hidden History of the Tibetan Book of the Dead* (New York: Oxford University Press, 2003).

3. Sources for the biography of Karma dbang 'dzin include Khrag 'thung rdo rje, *'Das log karma dbang 'dzin gyi rnam thar* (Delhi: Ngawang Gelek Demo, 1973) (henceforth K1); *'Das log karma dbang 'dzin gyi rnam thar*, in *Two Visionary Accounts of Returns from Death* (Dolanji: Tibetan Bonpo Monastic Center, 1974), fols. 1–303 (henceforth K2); *'Das log karma dbang 'dzin gyi rnam thar*, in *Two 'Das log Manuscripts from the Library of Lhakhang Lama: Rgyal bu Yid 'dzin bzod pa Chos kyi dbang phyug gi rnam thar and a version of Karma dbang 'dzin gyi rnam thar* (Delhi: Don grub rdo rje, 1978), fols. 99–321 (henceforth K3); *'Das log karma dbang 'dzin gyi rnam thar thar pa'i lcags kyu* (Thimphu: Mani Dorji Druk Sherik Parkhang, 1981) (henceforth K4).

4. Although there is literary evidence that attests to the emergence of *'das log* stories in the twelfth century, it seems their development as a distinct literary genre does not get under way until the fifteenth century. See Pommaret, *Les revenants de l'au-delà dans le monde tibétain*, 86. The particular social-historical events of this period that might help to explain this development have yet to be thoroughly examined. The argument of Epstein and Pommaret that the emergence of the *'das log* literature primarily along the southern and eastern border regions was a direct consequence of the rise of Dge lugs pa hegemony in central Tibet is persuasive but requires further investigation. See comments in Epstein, "On the History and Psychology of the 'Das-log," 22–23, and Pommaret, *Les revenants de l'au-delà dans le monde tibétain*, 102.

5. The biography of Karma dbang 'dzin, for example, mentions by name the story of the sixteenth-century *'das log* Gling bza' chos skyid. See K1, 25; K2, 16; K3, 115; K4, 17.

6. See Cuevas, *The Hidden History*, 39–68.

7. The eight hot hells in classical Indian Buddhism are Avīcī (No Respite), Pratāpana (Greater Torment), Tapana (Torment), Mahāraurava (Great Howling), Raurava (Howling), Saṃghāta (Heaping), Kālasūtra (Black-Lines), and Saṃjīva (Reviving). The eight cold hells are Arbuda (Blisters), Nirarbuda (Enlarged Blisters), Aṭaṭa, Hahava, Huhuva, Utpala (Bursting Open), Padma (Lotus), and Mahāpadma (Great Lotus). See *Abhidharmakośabhāṣyam* 3.58–59, translated in Louis de La Vallée Poussin,

Abhidharmakośabhāṣyam, English trans. Leo M. Pruden (Berkeley: Asian Humanities Press, 1988), 457, 459. References henceforth are to Pruden's translation.

8. La Vallée Poussin, *Abhidharmakośabhāṣyam*, 456–58.

9. *Ṛg Veda* 10.14.2, trans. Wendy Doniger O'Flaherty, *The Rig Veda: An Anthology* (London: Penguin, 1981), 43.

10. *Ṛg Veda* 10.14.2. See also Bruce Lincoln, "The Ferryman of the Dead," *Journal of Indo-European Studies* 8, nos. 1–2 (1980): 41–59.

11. See, for example, Charles Malamoud, "La théologie de la dette dans le brāhmanisme," *Puruṣārtha* 4 (1980): 39–62. Accordingly, human beings are born as a debt to Yama, for it is he who has loaned out their bodies; once born, they must begin making payments to him. An individual is released from such debt only by dying. However, to free oneself without having to be destroyed, one must convince Yama to accept a substitute for what is owed him; this one does by ritual sacrifice.

12. See, for example, Laurence G. Thompson, "On the Prehistory of Hell in China," *Journal of Chinese Religions* 17 (1989): 27–41, and Stephen F. Teiser, *The Scripture on the Ten Kings and the Making of Purgatory in Medieval Chinese Buddhism* (Honolulu: University of Hawai'i Press, 1994).

13. See Stephen F. Teiser, *The Ghost Festival in Medieval China* (Princeton, NJ: Princeton University Press, 1988), and Charles Orzech, "Saving the Burning-Mouth Hungry Ghost," in Lopez, ed., *Religions of China in Practice*, ed. Donald S. Lopez (Princeton: Princeton University Press, 1996): 278–83.

14. On Guru Chos dbang, see Guru Bkra shis Ngag dbang blo gros, *Gu bkra'i chos 'byung* (Beijing: Krung go'i bod kyi shes rig dpe skrun khang, 1990), 386–93, and Janet Gyatso, "Guru Chos-dbang's *Gter 'byung chen mo*: An Early Survey of the Treasure Tradition and Its Strategies in Discussing Bon Treasure," in *Tibetan Studies: Proceedings of the 6th Seminar of the International Association of Tibetan Studies, Fagernes 1992*, ed. Per Kværne (Oslo: Institute for Comparative Research in Human Culture, 1994), 275–87. The Tibetan version of the tale of Mulian and its connections to the biography of Guru Chos dbang and the descent into hell of the epic King Gesar are discussed in Matthew Kapstein's chapter in this volume. Versions of the stories of Maudgalyāyana and Guru Chos dbang are included in the Ka shod Mkhar kha blockprint collection of *'das log* stories (collection referred to by Pommaret as "Le *Xylographe Ka shod*"). See *Mnyam med shakya'i rgyal po nyan thos dgra bcom pa mo'u 'gal gyi bus a ma dmyal ba nas bton rab kyi le'u*, text no. 9 (*ta*) in *Xylographe Ka shod*, and *O rgyan gyi rgyal po padma 'byung gnas mchog gi bu chen gter ston gu ru chos dbang kyi yum dmyal khams nas drangs rab kyi rnam thar*, text no. 10 (*tha*) in the same volume. This anthology of blockprints, *Xylographe Ka shod*, dates back to 1948, or possibly but less likely as early as 1888 (the year given as *sa byi*, earth

mouse). The collection was compiled at Bsam gtan chos gling for the aristocratic Ka shod family by one Bya bral Kun dga' rang grol, who also claimed to be a *'das log* himself. The anthology was printed at the Ka shod family estate of Gser lcog in Mkhar kha near Rgyal rtse in southwestern Tibet. Only two copies of this collection exist, preserved on microfilm at the Société Asiatique au Centre d'Études Tibétaines du Collège de France and at the University of Washington.

15. My reference here is to a specific type of advanced tantric practice referred to as "dredging the depths of hell" (*na rag dong sprugs*). See Cuevas, *The Hidden History*, 155–57.

16. As Pommaret's ethnographic research demonstrates, this is not always the case. In the modern Bhutanese context, for example, the *'das log* make the journey regularly by choice. See Pommaret, *Les revenants de l'au-delà dans le monde tibétain*, 125–61.

17. On the concept of the *antarābhava* in India and Tibet, see Bryan J. Cuevas, "Predecessors and Prototypes: Towards a Conceptual History of the Buddhist *Antarābhava*," *Numen* 43, no. 3 (1996): 263–302, and Cuevas, *The Hidden History*, 39–68.

18. La Vallée Poussin, *Abhidharmakośabhāṣyam*, 393.

19. It is not uncommon, however, for the full seven-week sequence to be abbreviated, depending on the wealth of the family.

20. The *bla* is also regarded as one of the three intellectual principles, together with "thought" (*yid*) and "mind" (*sems*). See Samten Karmay, "Soul and the Turquoise: A Ritual for Recalling the *bla*," in his *The Arrow and the Spindle: Studies in History, Myths, Rituals and Beliefs in Tibet* (Kathmandu: Mandala Book Point, 1998), 311.

21. Ibid., 315.

22. On ransom rituals, see Ferdinand D. Lessing, "Calling the Soul: A Lamaist Ritual," *Semitic and Oriental Studies* 11 (1951): 263–84, and Karmay, "Soul and the Turquoise," 310–38. On guidance rituals, see Detlef I. Lauf, *Secret Doctrines of the Tibetan Books of the Dead*, trans. Graham Parkes (Boston: Shambhala, 1977), 127–28; Stan R. Mumford, *Himalayan Dialogue: Tibetan Lamas and Gurung Shamans in Nepal* (Madison: University of Wisconsin Press, 1989), 209–15; and Per Kvaerne, "Cards for the Dead," in Lopez, ed., *Religions of Tibet in Practice*, 494–98.

23. J. Kennedy and H.S. Gehman, "Peta Vatthu: Stories of the Departed," in *The Minor Anthologies of the Pali Canon*, ed. T.W. Rhys Davids (London: H. Milford, 1931), vol. 4; also U Ba Kyaw and Peter Masefield, *Peta-Stories* (London: Pāli Text Society, 1980).

24. On this issue, see John Holt's chapter in this volume and his "Assisting the Dead by Venerating the Living: Merit Transfer in the Early Buddhist Tradition," *Numen* 28, no. 1 (1981): 1–28.

25. In China, Avalokiteśvara became a female deity named Guanyin.

On the history of this gender transformation, see Chün-fang Yü, *Kuan-yin: The Chinese Transformation of Avalokiteśvara* (New York: Columbia University Press, 2001).

26. See discussion in Matthew Kapstein, *Tibetan Assimilation of Buddhism: Conversion, Contestation, and Memory* (New York: Oxford University Press, 2000), 144–55.

27. On the history of this famous mantra, see Alexander Studholme, *The Origins of Oṃ Maṇi Padme Huṃ: A Study of the Kāraṇḍavyūha Sūtra* (Albany: State University of New York Press, 2002); also see Donald S. Lopez, Jr., *Prisoners of Shangri-La: Tibetan Buddhism and the West* (Chicago: University of Chicago Press, 1998), 114–34.

28. Rolf A. Stein, *Tibetan Civilization*, trans. J.E. Stapleton Driver (Stanford, CA: Stanford University Press, 1972), 174, and Pommaret, *Les revenants de l'au-delà dans le monde tibétain*, 20–23. For a history of this image painted on temple walls throughout Asia, see Stephen F. Teiser, *Reinventing the Wheel: Paintings of Rebirth in Medieval Buddhist Temples* (Seattle: University of Washington Press, 2006).

29. See comments in Rolf A. Stein, "Les conteurs au Tibet," *France-Asie* 197 (1969): 143–45.

30. K3, 108.3, has *khyoms*.

31. K3, 108.5, has *gri bar mi 'gro ba sna la lud*. The line in K4, 10.1, *mgrin par mi 'gro bar sna nas lud*, makes better sense.

32. K3, 109.4, *rig pa chu nang las gsal bas a tsa ma*; K4, 10, *rig pa chu nang nya las gsal a tsa ma*.

33. K3, 110.1, has *rdza phug*.

34. K3, 110.1, omits *tho me ba*.

35. K4, 12, *'chi ba mi rtag sleb pa ma shes sam*. K3, 110.4, has *mi rtag sgyu ma zhig pa ma shes sam*.

36. K4, 15, *chang zom la chu blugs*. K3, 113.5, has *chang zom gang sar*.

37. K3, 107.5–116.1; K4, 8–27; cf. also K1, 12–25; K2, 6–18.

38. K3, 123.3–124.5; K4, 25–26; cf. also K1, 38–40; K2, 25–26.

39. These stages are described in some detail in Lati Rinpoche and Jeffrey Hopkins, *Death, Intermediate State and Rebirth* (New York: Snow Lion, 1979), and Geshe Kelsang Gyatso, *Clear Light of Bliss: Mahamudra in Vajrayana Buddhism* (London: Wisdom, 1982).

40. K3, 126.3–129.4; K4, 28–32; cf. also K1, 43–48; K2, 29–32.

41. K3, 167.4–169.1; K4, 73–75; cf. also K1, 109–11; K2, 86–88.

42. K3, 170.4–173.2; K4, 77–79; cf. also K1, 114–18; K2, 90–94.

43. K3, 296.1–299.4; K4, 211–15; cf. also K1, 334–39; K2, 266–71.

44. Again, see *Abhidharmakośabhāṣyam* 3.58–59; La Vallée Poussin, *Abhidharmakośabhāṣyam*, 456–60.

45. According to spelling in K3, 314.4. K4, 231, has *mig ko stong du 'drus pa*.

46. This is a reference to "pillow-guarding" (*sngas srung*), which is the common practice of watching the corpse continuously throughout the day and night to guard against demonic attacks.

47. Literally, "secret or hidden spot." K2, 297.2–3, adds the line, *drod yod med lta ba'i phyir du*, "in order to see whether or not there was heat [in the body]."

48. The bundling of the corpse is a common Tibetan funerary practice. Usually, the spine is broken and the body then wrapped in a crouching position; this is to secure it against demonic possession. See Cuevas, *The Hidden History*, 69–77.

49. K3, 314.3–320.3; K4, 230–36; cf. also K1, 362–71; K2, 296–302.

50. Réne de Nebesky-Wojkowitz, *Oracles and Demons of Tibet* (The Hague: Mouton, 1956).

51. For further details about Tibetan zombies, see Turrell Wylie, "Ro-langs: The Tibetan Zombie," *History of Religions* 4, no. 1 (1964): 69–80; Per-Arne Berglie, "When the Corpses Rise: Some Tibetan Ro langs Stories," *Indological Taurinensia* 10 (1982): 37–44; Michael Walter, "Of Corpses and Gold: Materials for the Study of the Vetāla and the Ro langs," *Tibet Journal* 29, no. 2 (2004): 13–46; and Geoff Childs, *Tibetan Diary: From Birth to Death and Beyond in a Himalayan Valley of Nepal* (Berkeley: University of California Press, 2004), 157–61.

52. These individuals are usually women and are called "living demons" (*gson 'dre*). About these figures, Giuseppe Tucci writes: "There are also human creatures, especially of the feminine sex, who can change themselves into demonic beings. They then become demons in human form and can cause the same misfortune as real demons.... Meeting such women in the evening can trigger off fever and illness. While their body lies lifeless as in sleep their spirit (*bla*) becomes at night a demon (*'dre*) which wanders around restlessly bringing misfortune and lingering illness to those with whom they come into contact. Those who see these demonic women from close up can ascertain their identity." *The Religions of Tibet*, trans. Geoffrey Samuel (Berkeley: University of California Press, 1988), 186–87.

53. Pommaret, *Les revenants de l'au-delà dans le monde tibétain*.

54. On the relationship between *'das log* and shamans, see comments in Tucci, *The Religions of Tibet*, 199.

10

Gone but Not Departed

The Dead among the Living in Contemporary Buddhist Sri Lanka

JOHN CLIFFORD HOLT

HOW THE LIVING regard the significance of death is an issue of such existential import that it might be regarded as an index to the nature of religious meaning per se. How the living regard the dead in Buddhist Sri Lanka is, therefore, an issue of great salience to that religious culture specifically, as well as to the comparative study of Buddhist cultures in general. Wherever Buddhism has wandered and assimilated in the variegated cultures of Asia, it has mixed and mated with a variety of indigenous ideologies and practices. That is, it has transformed and has been transformed in whatever cultures it has taken root. These transformations call into question any view of Buddhist tradition that is based on a reified set of canonical doctrines or practices. This chapter, based upon textual analyses of Theravāda Pāli Buddhist sources and recent fieldwork conducted within rural village settings in the central highlands of Sri Lanka, explores dimensions of religious meaning in relation to the problem of how the dead are often regarded among the living in contemporary settings of Sinhala Buddhist religious culture.

Abstractly, within the philosophical canon of Theravāda Buddhist thought, birth and death are understood as fundamental expressions of the natural ebb and flow of temporal existence: "Whatever is subject to arising is also subject to cessation." Indeed, Buddhagosa's *Visuddhimagga*, a classical exposition that became a normative Theravāda explication of *sīla,* samādhi, and *paññā*, might be read profitably as an extended commentary on the existential significance of time, how birth and death characterize its impermanence, from the momentariness of a single instant to grand cycles constitutive of cosmic aeons. Birth and death, that is, are fundamental facts of temporal samsaric existence.

Within expressive artistic and literary forms of Sinhala culture, the Buddha's enlightenment experience, a mythic and paradigmatic moment central to the formation of Buddhist memory in Sri Lanka, is often understood by bhikkhus and laity alike as a statement of spiritual hope marking nibbāna's ultimate triumph over the forces of death, a final cessation to the *dukkha* intrinsic within the birth/redeath process of saṃsāra. Māra, the Buddha's fearsome nemesis during the three nocturnal watches of his paradigmatic enlightenment experience—who, as his name etymologically signals, is the mythic personification of death—is depicted as a menacing figure whose attacks and defeat are rendered ubiquitously within pictorial registers of temple walls and cave paintings and in various genres of didactic literature portraying this most pivotal of cosmic moments.[1] Here, the Buddha is figured as a culture hero, not only for introducing a moral civilization based on dharma to the island, but also because his insights into the true nature of existence imply the ultimate defeat of death's provenance. So while death may be a fact of samsaric life, its temporary victories are not regarded as final. Those who pass through death's threshold continue on a journey through temporal this-worldly and other-worldly realms until nibbāna brings their karmically fueled peregrinations to an end.

In Sri Lanka, Buddhist teachings about how the living should relate to or care for their dead are as ancient as they are important in contemporary life. According to the Pāli monastic chronicle, the *Mahāvaṃsa*, after Emperor Aśoka's son Mahinda had become an *arahant* (Skt. *arhat*), he magically traveled through the air from Jambudīpa to the Sīlakuta peak of Missaka Mountain (now Mihintale in north-central Sri Lanka).[2] With the help of the local mountain deva, who had assumed the form of a stag to entice the Lankan king, Devānaṃpiya Tissa (who was then on a hunting expedition), Mahinda encountered the king, together with his forty thousand men, and converted all of them to the *sāsana* by preaching the dharma of the *Cūlahatthipadūpama suttanta*. Mahinda then subsequently proceeded miraculously to preach the *Samacitta sutta* in such a sonorous manner that the dharma was heard sweetly resounding throughout the entire island. Hearing the wonderful sounds of truth, all of the island's devas became enraptured and converted to the religion. Soon thereafter, when the women of the royal household heard about the spiritual powers of Mahinda, they requested King Devānaṃpiya Tissa to provide them with a dharma hearing of their own. The king then built a marvelous pavilion within the royal precincts of his capital at Anuradhapura, returned to the Sīlakuta peak of Missaka Mountain "to meet the *thera*s, greeted them reverently, took the almsbowl from the great *thera* Mahinda's hand and led the *thera* into the city, as is the custom in hospitable welcome and homage."[3] After Devānaṃpiya Tissa had provided Mahinda and his accompanying *thera*s with a sumptuous meal, he sent for Queen Anulā, who was also the ranking woman of his court and the chief consort of his younger brother. Anulā appeared with her own five hundred attendants, who bowed down in humility and made bounteous offerings to the saṅgha. In return, Mahinda first preached to this assembly of august women the dharma of the *Petavatthu* and followed this with a preaching of the *Vimānavatthu.* Upon hearing the dharma of the *Petavatthu* and *Vimānavatthu,* Anulā and her followers became the first laywomen (*upāsikā*s) of the dharma and further gained the achievement of becoming "stream enterers," assured therefore of eventually attaining the highest spiritual goal. The *Mahāvaṃsa* concludes the story in this way: "When thus in the isle of Lanka, the peerless *thera,* who is like the Buddha in the protection of Lanka, had preached the true dharma in two places, in the speech of the island, he, the light of the island, thus brought to pass the descent of the true faith."[4]

I have recapitulated this story from the *Mahāvaṃsa* at the outset because it signals a number of motifs connected to the discussion that follows. First, it would seem to indicate the veritable antiquity of the *Petavatthu* and *Vimānavatthu,* texts that were apparently known to the Theravāda Mahāvihāra monk Mahānāma when he redacted the *Mahāvaṃsa* in or about the fifth century CE and chose to give these texts prominence in his account of how the dharma won over the elite rulers of the island. Second, the *Petavatthu* and the *Vimānavatthu,* texts that are fundamentally explications of karma articulated in relation to the fate of departed kin, are understood within this apologetic context to be the most appropriate expression of dharma for the purpose of converting those who are regarded as the prototypical *upāsikā*s (laywomen devotees) of Lanka's Buddhist community. Indeed, unlike much of Pāli literature, women also figure very prominently as protagonists in the stories that comprise the *Petavatthu* and *Vimānavatthu.*[5] Third, this is a myth that purports to recount the first establishment of the dharma in Lanka. There are related myths within the *Mahāvaṃsa* that indicate that Lanka is destined to become the Dhammadīpa, "Island of Dharma," but this story is the first indication in the *Mahāvaṃsa* that reflects something of the dharma's substance. It is significant here because it denotes the fact that among the earliest memories of Theravāda tradition on the island, how the living ought to relate to the dead has been an issue of central importance, especially for the laity. Concern for how the living relate to their familial dead, then, is not just a new dimension of "spirit religion" within a contemporary Buddhism transformed, a popular accretion that is the byproduct of recently wrought social changes in the urban slums of Colombo.[6] Rather, it has been since ancient times, and remains so today, a fundamental focus of lay Buddhist piety in Sinhala culture.

What is, then, this dharma of the *Petavatthu*? It is, on the whole, simply a series of dramatizations in narrative form about the dynamics of karmic retribution: that behavior motivated by malevolent intent in this life will necessarily be played out consequentially in the next. *Peta*s (Skt. preta), specifically, are beings who have lost their humanity, reborn into conditions of other-worldly suffering mirroring the very nature of their malevolent acts in this life. Liars are reborn with putrid mouths, killers are condemned to feed off corpses, thieves and sexual offenders can never satiate their obsessions, etc. But the dharmic lesson is also more than this: in story after story in the *Petavatthu*, the benevolent effects of merit transference are illustrated, showing how selfless acts of giving made on behalf of deceased kin result in the transformation and alleviation of other-worldly suffering and in favorable rebirth. In each of the stories, the same pattern obtains: the dead appear to surviving relations, in dreams in the dead of night or at lonely crossroads at the twilight hour, as grotesquely disfigured and hideous ghosts (usually with long, thin necks and overbearing potbellies) in order to explain the nature and cause of their current suffering. In most, the *peta* makes a plea to a family member to perform a meritorious deed—usually intended for the well-being of the saṅgha on his or her behalf—so that he or she may benefit karmically from the ritual transaction. Thus, what the *Petavatthu* articulates is the bedrock idea behind the practice of ritual merit transference, the legitimating idea behind the elaborate calendar of Sinhala Buddhist ritual almsgivings made to the saṅgha and performed on behalf of the deceased by immediate family members on the seventh day after death, on the third month anniversary, and on the annual anniversary of each year up to ten.

Care and concern for the dead are a centerpiece of lay piety in Sri Lanka, a matter of dharmic duty incumbent upon the living. In many Sinhala homes, it is not rare to display prominently a garlanded photo of one's deceased parents, or even one's deceased brothers and sisters, and to perform acts of remembrance regularly by lighting incense—usually the first ritual act at the beginning of the day. In the same way that the living and the dead seemed to have abided in a reciprocal relationship within the ancient religious culture of Vedic India, so the living and the dead in contemporary Sri Lanka, deemed as destined to continue or to sustain familial relations, are thought to retain a common abiding interest in each other's welfare, so long as peace has been maintained between them. The link between kin, therefore, is not severed finally by death. Moreover, it is also common to find family members claiming that their kinship relations within the family transmigrate through successive rebirths—that is, a family connection persists, though it may not be the same relationship from one lifetime to the next. This is a conception completely congruent with the manner in which relations between the Buddha and his closest followers transmigrate through various rebirths in the *jātaka* stories of his own rebirths. It is also not uncommon for Sinhalas to assert that their individual karmic acts in this present life may also affect the collective rebirth of their family as a whole in the next.[7]

Almsgivings are by far the most common form of familial rites observed in Buddhist Sri Lanka, the occasions par excellence wherein solidarity among family members (dead or alive) is reaffirmed and celebrated. While members of the saṅgha are recipients of almsgivings dedicated to the benefit of the deceased on regularized ritual occasions, monks do little more than make themselves available on these occasions as auspicious fields of merit, worthy objects to receive gifts and thus to enhance the merit that will accrue. But monks do not in any way offer to broker relations between the living and the dead in a priestly guise. Moreover, even *devālaya kapurāla*s (shrine priests) consider themselves mediators only between devotees and deities, so they also will not perform this kind of intermediary service. Instead, the practice of actually facilitating acts of direct mediation or communication between the living and the dead occurs within the more "informal sector" of lay

Buddhist religious culture in Sri Lanka. By "informal sector," I mean those priestly mediators who are not associated with established Buddhist monastic *vihārayas* or with *devālayas* established for the propitiation of the deities, but those priestly practitioners who operate shrines independently, usually within the confines of their own homes or property. While it is impossible to assert with any final degree of certainty, the "informal sector" of religious culture in Sri Lanka seems to be increasingly active and ever more popular in recent decades.

In what follows, I shall provide a brief account of one such "informal sector" priestess I came to know during the course of fieldwork in the upcountry Kandy cultural area in 2000 and 2001. Her work as a medium illustrates the ongoing legacy of relations between the living and dead alluded to in the above discussion of the general trajectory of thought evinced in the *Petavatthu*. It would not be inaccurate to say that this priestess understands herself as a "communications broker" between the living and the dead.

On one of my frequent visits to the Alutnuvara Devālaya (located about five miles southeast of modern Kegalle in the Kandyan culture area of upcountry Sri Lanka) during the spring of 2000, while I was researching the issue of Viṣṇu's legacy within the cult of Däḍimunda Deviyo, I made the acquaintance of a middle-aged woman and her husband who had come to the *devālaya* for the 8:00 p.m. pūjā. She introduced herself to me as "Viṣṇu Kalyāni."[8] During the subsequent pūjā to Däḍimunda Deviyo, Viṣṇu Kalyāni fell into an ecstatic trance during the *kapurāla*'s *yātikāva* (petitionary prayer) as soon as the deity's name was invoked, jerking herself wildly from side to side while simultaneously emitting a series of strident yelps, sounds that were entirely unintelligible but thoroughly emotional in nature. After the pūjā to Däḍimunda, she proceeded in an entranced state to the portico of the abutting Hūniyam *devālaya*, where she began to chant her own *yātikāva* in a frenzied Tamil voice. I spoke with her shortly thereafter.

Her eyes were blurred and bloodshot, her body soaking in sweat, hair completely disheveled and breath panting. She had come to the *devālaya*, she gasped in Sinhala, at "the behest of the god." The god in question was Alutnuvara Deviyo (a.k.a. Däḍimunda, Devatā Baṇḍāra). She and her husband, she continued, were now offering a thanksgiving to Alutnuvara for the new van they had just purchased, and more important, she was also seeking to get her warrant "recharged." I learned that she operated her own *devālaya* about fifteen miles outside of Kandy, and she invited me to come for a visit in the near future. She gave me vague directions and said that I needed only to proceed about ten kilometers down a given road and ask for her whereabouts. People would tell me how to get there, she said.

About a month later, I set out in search of her *devālaya* with one of my research assistants. True enough, we were easily guided to her *devālaya* by helpful villagers. Indeed Viṣṇu Kalyāni was well known in this relatively remote village area, and we had no trouble locating her *devālaya*, despite the fact that it was located about one kilometer off a secondary road on a winding trail that traversed the side of a mountain. In our first meeting, I had learned that she had been considered mad for many years, that she had spent some of those years in forced confinement in mental hospitals, and that she claimed to function as a medium for family members wishing to communicate with departed kin (Sinhala *preta*).

Her *devālaya* was a two-storied, well-constructed building adjacent to her similarly well-constructed house. Actually, her *devālaya* consisted of two *devālaya*s, one on the first floor dedicated to the goddess Pattinī, with a small shrine outside the sanctum for the sorcery-oriented deity Hūniyam. On the top floor, with separate stairs leading up, was another room, containing images of Viṣṇu, flanked on one side by Kataragama Deviyo (a.k.a. Skanda or Murugan) holding a black head in one of his left hands and a fearsome image of Bhadra Kāli on the right. Further to the right was a small effigy of Däḍimunda. She made explicit what the symbolism implied: Viṣṇu was the chief deity who presided over her *devālaya*. Indeed, she said she was simply his "helper," though her power came directly from Däḍimunda.

During the morning of this Saturday *kemmura* day, a milling crowd, which ranged consistently of about seventy people, was in attendance.[9] About fifty of these were middle-aged women. They had generally come from the upcountry region around Kandy, but there were also some people from Colombo, including four businessmen who regaled us with stories about how Viṣṇu Kalyāni had facilitated many contacts with their various departed kin. The morning was taken up with pūjās to the various deities, after which *prasād* was distributed to all. The priestess then engaged in sessions of soothsaying, predicting future events in the lives of her clients.

A prominently displayed sign announced fees of Rs. 105 (then equal to about $1.50) for contact with the departed, but only if the departed had been dead for a minimum of three months or a maximum of ten years. The charge for a generic pūjā, during which vows could be sworn or *sāntiya* (blessing) sought, was Rs. 52.50. The minimum requirement of four separate fruits and a coconut (to be broken on a stone adjacent to the *devālaya*) was also specified. These items could be purchased in a small shop on the first floor of the *devālaya*, along with *tämbili* (King Coconut), tea, Sprite, Fanta, and Coca Cola.

At noon, the nature of activities changed, as did Viṣṇu Kalyāni's function. During the morning, clients had been issued numbers to determine the order of their engagement with the priestess. On this day, the list ran to twenty-four. (I saw that the list of the previous Wednesday *kemmura* was only seven.) The sessions began with the priestess adorning her *halamba* (bangle) and chanting rhythmically for about three minutes before breaking into her familiar yelps. Later, she told us that her yelps indicated when the deceased were either entering her to possess her or when they were exiting from her body. We recorded the first four sessions on tape; here, for reasons of space, I am providing a translation of just the first two. My comments on the significance of these sessions follow after their presentation.[10]

First Session

Dead Father (Viṣṇu Kalyāni): Is it you, son?

Son (Ayurvedic physician): Yes, it's me.

F: Did my daughter come?

S: No, she didn't.

F: And your children?

S: No.

F: Come and sit in front of me. I can't see you properly. Why did you ask me to come?

S: I want to know how you are doing and where you are.

F: I'm in Kataragama now, at Kirivehera. I'm born as a deva now.

S: I'm happy to know that. I know you did a lot of meritorious work while you were alive. We will come to Kataragama very soon.

F: If you come here, give alms to the beggars. You should acquire merits while you are still alive. As the Buddha says, this life and everything else is transient. I had a natural death. My funeral was done properly, and I'm happy for it. I received my seventh-day almsgiving, as well as the third-month and the first-year ones. I came to see my dead body as it was lying in the coffin, and it was in good condition—not deformed. I intend to go to Isipathanaramaya in Dambadīwa. I do not intend to be born again. But I regret that I could not enter the saṅgha. So I do feel like being born again to become a monk. But that will not happen yet. I will remain this way for a kalpa or so. Because if I am born in the human world again, I may get trapped in this hell of violence. Now they kill each other. My times were better, and our generation was a well brought up one. This present generation is corrupted, addicted to alcohol. They reject religion. Thus, the deities are not in favor of them anymore. This period of the human world is in something of a vacuum. I will be born again in this world when there is a good time—that is, when this world is blessed again with a buddha. It will mark the debut of a new era, a new kalpa.

S: I came because my mother and others wanted to know how you are. Did you leave your body and home once you were dead?

F: No. I waited until the funeral and the almsgiving were over. After my death, I did not expect any more merits. I had already acquired enough. While I lived, I had the *varama* of the deity Avushādha (medicine). I cured many people. Who is continuing my profession now?

S: My elder brother.

F: It has been handed down through generations. I feel thirsty often. My armchair that I used to sit in at home is still where it used to be, isn't it?

S: Yes.

F: I have never let my children go astray. I never drank. My children do not, either. I always lived according to the dharma. I do not come to this human world often. But if I see any troubles befalling you, I will see to them and not let any troubles come upon you. I need to go now. It is difficult for me to be seated on the floor like this! [Laughter.] I never used to sit on the floor. You do not need to worry about me. I'm fine. I only want to know if all my children live in peace.

S: Yes, they do. I need to know if we have ever done anything wrong to you. If we have, I hope you will forgive us.

F: No, you have not. You always respected me. I will be leaving this place by *äsala poya* to go to Isipathanaramaya along with Kataragama Deviyo. I think I'll leave now.

Second Session

FATHER (Viṣṇu Kalyāni): *Loku duwa* [elder daughter]?

DAUGHTER: It is me, *podi duwa* [younger daughter].

F: Where is *loku duwa*? Why didn't she come?

D: She is at home.

F: Why did you ask me to come? You are disturbing my sleep!

D: I need to know where you are and how you are.

F: Did you give my first-year almsgiving?

D: Yes, we did.

F: What about the second year?

D: We will give it, too.

F: Did Chuti also come?

D: Who is Chuti?

F: Why, my youngest daughter.

D: No, she couldn't. She had problems.

F: What problems?

D: Her daughter passed away.

F: How? What happened?

D: She met with an accident. She was run down by a train.

F: Who is at home now?

D: Mother and myself.

F: So why did you ask me to come?

D: I want to know if you are short of merits and what we could do for you.

F: I have enough merits. Right now I am born as a *bhūta* [malicious ghost], but soon I will quit this life. I used to come home until you held the third-month almsgiving. After that I stopped coming. Now I stay in Anurādhapura. That is where I get my merits. So, how is your mother? Is she well?

D: No, she is always ill. She has a continuous headache.

F: What about her pains in the joints?

D: Those are okay now.

F: What did the doctors say about her headaches? Didn't they tell you she has a weak vein? That is what she has, so the blood circulation is not proper. See to it. And she thinks too much about things. Tell her not to do so. At this stage, she should relax, do meritorious activities.

D: Do you know that your second son died?

F: No, what happened to him?

D: He died suddenly.

F: Did someone poison him?

D: No, nothing like that. He just died.

F: Did he suffer from any illness?

D: No.

F: Did he drink poison?

D: Of course not.

F: Then how did he die suddenly? I doubt it. Did they conduct a postmortem?

D: No, they didn't.

F: Then just how did he die?

D: I don't know.

F: Then don't tell me about it. This just upsets me a lot now.

D: He died while you were still alive. Nine months before you died. We told you, but you were not conscious of it. You were not aware.

F: No, you never told me about it.

D: No, we did.

F: No, you didn't. No one told me about it until this moment, until I am dead and gone. You shouldn't have told me about this now. I'm very upset. It must have been a previous karma. I still cannot believe he's dead. I'm going to seek his *ātma* [Skt. *ātman*] and go and see him. I was happy that I had a son who was a monk. But now I am upset.

D: We told you all about it, but you were so ill you didn't understand anything going on around you.

F: Yes, I had this terrible wound in my leg. Doctors said that my leg would have to be amputated, but I didn't like it, did I? They said I would have been alive if I allowed them to do so. It was a *hūniyam* done to me. I do not know if they did the same thing to the monk, my son, since he is said to have died without a cause. Shall I leave now? I need to sleep. I cannot properly sleep because I suffer from a terrible headache. I suffered a lot on my deathbed. I hope it will not be the same in the future.

Comments on First and Second Sessions

Viṣṇu Kalyāni is a skilled actress who can change her disposition and presentation almost spontaneously on whatever cue she discerns. Her clients, at least the ones we met, expressed amazement at how she assumed the personalities and knew the details of their dead relations. She claims that Alutnuvara Deviyo has eighteen different *avatāra*s and that these enable her to change herself in eighteen different ways, which correspond to the personalities of the dead.

The substance and pattern of her communications between the living and the dead are rather consistent. It is quite predictable that the basic reason that her clients would seek her out is to inquire into the well-being of their departed kin. She always anticipates this, and she always reciprocates by inquiring into the continued well-being of the family. That is always the structure of the basic exchange. The substantial theme that surfaces throughout these exchanges is the power of karmic retribution, how it determines everyone's well-being now and in future rebirths. The advice that Viṣṇu Kalyāni consistently gives, therefore, is to make merit to assure favorable future circumstances. It is the same advice rendered in the *Petavatthu*: make merit now and transfer it to the departed if they are in need.

But many of the inquiries about the well-being of deceased kin made by family members are not motivated entirely out of pure curiosity or compassion for their dead. In the second exchange noted above, it is clear that the surviving family has experienced some serious tragedies before and after the death of the father. Many of Viṣṇu Kalyāni's clients suffer similarly. They have come to her in order to determine if there is something that has been done specifically in the past that has provoked the anger of their departed kin, suspecting perhaps that it is the anger of the departed that is causing them to experience suffering now. Acts of merit transfer, according to the *Petavatthu*, can assuage the suffering of departed kin. But within this context, it is clear that merit transfer is also a means to placate departed kin who might be wreaking havoc because of their anger or revenge. Even in the relatively smooth exchange of the first session recorded above, the inquiring son wants to know if anyone in his family had done anything wrong to the departed father. Viṣṇu Kalyāni says that departed kin reborn as *bhūta*s or pretas are often responsible for the misfortunes that visit their surviving kin. In these cases, it is necessary to determine the exact or specific grievance that is annoying the departed relation. This is clearly the stated motive in the second example I have provided as well: the deceased's surviving daughter is quick to seek her father's forgiveness if it is needed. Unlike the first case, which could be characterized as amiable, the second interchange between the daughter and father was somewhat sharp and tense. Viṣṇu Kalyāni had assumed a scolding/rebuking stance, and the inquiring daughter was clearly nervous, ill at ease. When the daughter asked if her father was short of merit, this was a way of attempting to determine exactly what could be done to alter the present situation. Viṣṇu Kalyāni's probe about whether the almsgivings had been properly conducted was her own attempt to find a suitable explanation for the family's misfortunes.

While Viṣṇu Kalyāni is able to make a productive living off the belief that pretas and *bhūta*s may inflict harm on the living, it is also true that she believes in the powers of a moral universe. Her advice, more often than not, is for her clients to begin living the moral and therefore meritorious life. After I had spent many hours with her, I began to see the close parallel between the advice she dispenses and the ancient ethic of the *Petavatthu*.

Other motifs that surfaced within the context of the occasions I observed also deserve some comment. The first is that departed kin are almost always understood to be currently dwelling at places deemed sacred to Buddhists in Sri Lanka. In the two instances I have provided above, the departed locate themselves at Kataragama and Anurādhapura, two of the most important sacred places of pilgrimage in Lanka. During the long afternoon of our observances at Viṣṇu Kalyāni's *devālaya*, we noted Kelaniya and Śrī Pāda (Adams' Peak) as other venues that were also frequently mentioned. These are sacred places indicating an auspicious process of favorable progress for the departed in the afterlife. But it also became clear that when the priestess did not mention a sacred venue for the departed, it was an indication that the afterlife condition into which the departed had been reborn was not so favorable at all.

A second motif is that Viṣṇu Kalyāni is a very skilled reader of the clients who present themselves. She seems quite adept at sizing them up before she even begins to respond to them. And she nimbly deflects the course of the exchange if she has turned it in the wrong direction. For instance, in the second session above, it is clear that Viṣṇu Kalyāni was not aware of her client's brother's death. Yet she managed to manipulate the exchange to cover her error. And through observing linguistic conventions, she came to understand that the dead brother was a Buddhist monk. Clients are indubitably more than willing to help her in the process. In these instances, it is clearly a case, as William James once noted in one of his essays, that "faith in the fact helps create the fact."[11]

In addition to observing her work at her *devālaya,* I interviewed Viṣṇu Kalyāni on three other occasions. During one of those visits, her husband showed us her diary. With her permission, I took it and had it translated by one of my assistants.

Just as her work as a medium seems to be dominated by concerns about karma, merit, and rebirth, so it is also the case with her "autobiography." Viṣṇu Kalyāni presents her life as one of great disappointment and suffering, the consequence of bad karma, for which she was responsible in a previous life. She says that it seems as if she was born into this present life to suffer, and the life she has been leading as a priestess is primarily a means of repaying her debts from previous lives. By helping others at her *devālaya,* she is trying to accumulate merit that will pay off her debt in lives to come. Because she has suffered so much in this life, she has tried to commit suicide and also entertains thoughts of becoming a *sīl mäniyō* (robed but lay Buddhist sister) before the end of her present life.

Viṣṇu Kalyāni's visions, like many of those experienced by the protagonists in the stories constitutive of the *Petavatthu,* started with the appearance of a dead relation in her dreams. In her case, it was her grandmother who first appeared, from which time *diṣṭi*s (possessions) became very frequent. In her "autobiography," she says that her powers to practice came about in the following way:

> At this time, Ruk Devi, in the form of a Buddhist monk from Bogahapitiya, gave me the full *varama* [warrant to practice]. Three births ago, Ruk Devi was my father. During the time of Dutugemenu [the second-century BCE Buddhist hero-king], Ruk Devi was also my father and married to my *kiri amma* [literally "milk mother" but referring here to the woman who is now her grandmother]. They were high caste and high officials for the king. At that time, my husband was a servant. One day he abducted me be-

> cause I owed him some pay. Now in this life I am paying off the debt. In fact, all these three past lives I have been with this husband. My work at the *devāle* helps me pay off this debt. Ruk Devi told me about the origins of the village we were living in and helped me to get rid of a yakṣa who was plaguing me due to the *hūniyam* [sorcery] practiced by a neighbor. He dedicated me to Alutnuvara, who was able to command the yakṣa to leave. Alutnuvara can take the form of eighteen *avatāra*s, so he can change me in eighteen different ways that I now have learned to recognize. Ruk Devi stayed here for seven days and told me to go to the local *devāle* each day. After that he told me to go straight to Alutnuvara with seven betel leaves, seven candles, and oil. I got possessed at Alutnuvara and crawled inside the *devāle* on hands and knees, writhing like a serpent. I got the *halamba*. This was on the 27th of August 1988. Only the deity understood my suffering, for which reason I was given the *diṣṭi* [vision].
>
> I was told to build a *devāle* by Ruk Devi. Before this, the *devāle* was inside of our small house for about a year. When I was asked to build the *devāle*, I had no money to do so. The deity sent me to beg to find money for this. I had never known or learned to recite *kāvi* [verses] before, but the deity taught me to sing *virindu*s [a form of song accompanied by the small *rabāna* drum] at little gatherings and on buses. Then he sent me from house to house like a gypsy, singing *virundu*s. In this way, I collected some money that I kept safely. Then I built a small *devāle*.
>
> When I first started predicting, I charged ten rupees. The deity guides me to make correct predictions. I obtained the *varama* first from Alutnuvara Deviyo and then from Kataragama. Then eventually I was given the *varama* by all twelve deities.

It was after a yakṣa was exorcised at Alutnuvara that Viṣṇu Kalyāni began to work successfully as a medium between the living and the dead and also as a soothsayer. She has cultivated a loyal following, despite the fact that her relations with neighboring villagers remain checkered. Like other priestesses I came to know, she has been victimized by *hūniyam* performed by rival practitioners and has continued to have run-ins involving the police.

During one of our interviews, Viṣṇu Kalyāni offered what became a very pertinent way of categorizing the deities of Sri Lanka. At the highest level, Viṣṇu reigns and rules over the planetary movements that can affect our lives. Viṣṇu, however, does not possess human beings. She was insistent on this matter. But below Viṣṇu are what she called the *maheśākhya* deities. These are worldly deities who were originally born as yakṣas but came to worship the Buddha and to learn of his buddhadharma. They have received their *varamas*, or warrants to act in the world, directly from the Buddha. These include Kataragama, Pattinī, Piṭiye, Alutnuvara (Däḍimunda Devatā Baṇḍāra), and Kumara Baṇḍāra. They are the specific deities who have been transformed by the Buddha and his dharma. The deities on the next lower level are those who are in charge of particular areas of the country. They act as they do because they fear the power of the Buddha and thus can be commanded. These include Gāṅga (River) Baṇḍāra, Aiyanar, Kande (Hill) Baṇḍāra, and Gala (Rock) Baṇḍāra.

Viṣṇu Kalyāni's interpretive scheme of the Sinhala pantheon of deities is actually in rough accordance with the hierarchy as it is often portrayed in Kandyan folk literature: an ethical hierarchy stratified on the basis of each deity's perceived proximity to the Buddha, a position derived from the amount of positive karma attributed to each. It is also a scheme that explains the transformation of supernaturals from yakṣa to *devatā* status. It parallels the manner in which pretas can be transformed into *devatās*, and it is the fundamental principle that she imparts in her advice to clients. Note that this principle also shows up in relation to how and where she situates the afterlife residences of the deceased. If the rebirth is favorable, they dwell at a place associated with the power and dharma of the Buddha (e.g., Anurādhapura, Kelaniya, and Śrī Pāda).

Viṣṇu Kalyāni's understanding of the nature of yakṣas also turned out to be surprisingly similar to one developed by a well-known Sri Lankan scholar of Buddhist studies, M. M. J. Marasinghe, who many years ago had been concerned to show how the "popular" meaning of yakṣa had been construed in early Pāli Buddhist literature.[12] Marasinghe noted how the term was defined by Davids and Stede in their *Pāli Text Society Pāli Dictionary*:

> Yakṣa is the name of certain non-human beings, as spirits, ogres, dryads, ghosts, spooks. Their usual epithet and category of being is *anmanussa*, i.e., not a human being (but not a sublime god either); being half deified and of great power as regards influencing people (partly helping, partly hurting).[13]

Marasinghe was specifically interested in the problem that arose when yakṣas were seen in various Pāli *suttas* to be asking metaphysical questions of the Buddha while at the same time they were "not considered capable of any intellectual accomplishments as to understand an exposition of the *Dhamma*, or to ask questions which involve deeper thinking."[14] His answer to this problem was that "yakṣas were not non-human beings, but were those from the yet uncultured tribes, whose presence was a doubtless reality at the time of the Buddha."[15] He says that this explanation renders references in the Vinaya proscribing "sexual intercourse with a female yakṣa [as not being] anything other than a reference possibly to a vagrant tribeswoman."[16] Therefore, in relation to the various exchanges between the Buddha and yakṣas, these figures "would have been at least respectable tribesmen, if not tribal chiefs."[17] He concludes that yakṣas referred to

> in the early Buddhist texts were no more than mere tribesmen, who were of course mythologised at a time much later than that of these *suttas*. The fact that they belonged to tribal societies also goes to explain their "mysterious" character, as has been observed about them in such early texts as the *Ṛg Veda*.[18]

In short, yakṣas were those human beings who had not yet been civilized by either the *brāhmaṇas* or, in this case, the teachings of the Buddha. What brings them into the fold of civilization is an understanding of *brāhmaṇa*, or Buddhist teachings.

This is precisely how Viṣṇu Kalyāni understood the transformation of deities of the second class like Alutnuvara Deviyo, beings who have successfully made the transition from yakṣa to *devatā*. It is also how she explained the manner in which the deceased could be assisted by the living. It is their relation to and understanding of the Buddha and the dharma that transform them. Moreover, what is implied by this principle is that Viṣṇu, by virtue of his position among all of the deities in the pantheon with the possible exception of Nātha, is the deity who is regarded as having the greatest understanding of the Buddha's dharma and the greatest amount of merit.

Viṣṇu Kalyāni understands her own life according to this principle, too. Born to suffer because of her karma, she labors in light of her understanding of the Buddha's teaching to assuage the suffering of others. That much is very clear from the verses of *kāvi* with which she concludes her autobiography:

> I'm born to this world because of karma.
> I've been pushed into this wretched life because of karma.
> Why live without freedom?
> What do I take with me when I die? Only merit and nothing else.
> I do good for people before the deity in my *devāle*.
> I beseech you to help them, to ease their pain and grant them
> their needs.

The world of the "gone but not departed" in Buddhist Sri Lanka pivots on the dynamic power attributed to karma, whether generated by the living before they depart or by the living for those who have departed. Both the living and the dead inhabit a universe that changes (arises and passes qualitatively) according to the principles of a moral economy. Soteriological empowerment is generated, in part, according to moral observance, but power leading to suffering can also be generated by sorcery or by the relative qualitative condition of time itself, measured in terms of proximity to (or distance from) the presence of a buddha and his dharma. But perhaps the most important force characterizing the relation between the living and the dead is the desire on the part of the living to assist the well-being of the dead. Not only may this help to avert misfortune and suffering for both, but it also sustains the bonds of the Sinhala familial pact. Therein lies the link I wish to stress in conclusion: the positive well-being and relative health of the extended family (including relations between the living and the recently dead) are rendered dependent upon realization of the dharma as manifested through karmic actions and their recompense. Morality and merit are the substance of familial religion. Viṣṇu ultimately presides over aspects of this dimension of Sinhala religion as well.

Notes

1. See my *Religious World of Kīrtī Śrī: Buddhism, Art, and Politics in Late Medieval Sri Lanka* (New York: Oxford University Press, 2000), plates 12 and 40, as well as Marie Gatellier, *Peintures murales du Sri Lanka: École*

Kandyan XVII–XIX siècles (Paris: École Française d'Extrême-Orient, 1991), vol. 2, for photos of wall paintings depicting Māra and his hosts. In devotional literature, Māra's defeat is described in the Sinhala *Pūjāvaliya,* trans. H. D. J. Gunawardhana (Colombo: Department of Cultural Affairs, 2000), 29–37, and the Pāli *Anāgatavaṃsa Desanā*, trans. Udaya Meddegama (Delhi: Motilal Banarsidass, 1993), 42.

2. *Mahāvaṃsa*, 13–14.

3. Ibid., 14:51–52.

4. Ibid., 14:65.

5. For a general study of the central dharmic teachings of the *Petavatthu*, especially as these are articulated within the context of female protagonists, see my "Assisting the Dead by Venerating the Living," *Numen* 28, no. 1 (1981): 1–28.

6. See Richard Gombrich and Gananath Obeyesekere, *Buddhism Transformed: Religious Change in Sri Lanka* (Princeton, NJ: Princeton University Press, 1988), 65–200.

7. For a recent discussion of "collective karma," see Jonathan S. Walters in *Constituting Communities: Buddhism and the Religious Cultures of South and Southeast Asia*, ed. John Clifford Holt, Jacob Kinnard, and Jonathan S. Walters (Albany: State University of New York Press, 2003), 9–40.

8. This is an obvious alias. Sinhala parents would most likely never select this kind of name for their child.

9. *Kemmura* days are Wednesdays and Saturdays, days that are generally regarded as inauspicious. As such, these are the days when people will most likely be in need of help. So *devālaya*s are open on these days for people to present their petitions to the gods, since the gods are aware that their assistance may be needed.

10. The Sinhala translations that follow were provided by Vindya Eriyagama, Department of Sociology, University of Peradeniya.

11. William James, "The Will to Believe," in his *Will to Believe and Other Essays in Popular Philosophy* (New York: Dover, 1956 [1897]), 25.

12. M. M. J. Marasinghe, "The 'Yakkhas' in Early Buddhist Literature," *Journal of the Vidyanlankara University of Ceylon* 1 (1972): 103–18.

13. T. W. Rhys Davids and William Stede, *The Pāli Text Society's Pāli-English Dictionary* (London: Routledge and Kegan Paul, 1921), s.v. "yakṣa."

14. Marasinghe, "The 'Yakkhas' in Early Buddhist Literature," 105.

15. Ibid., 108.

16. Ibid., 109.

17. Ibid., 112.

18. Ibid., 116.

11

Mulian in the Land of Snows and King Gesar in Hell

A Chinese Tale of Parental Death in Its Tibetan Transformations

Matthew T. Kapstein

I had never seen anyone use a lanyard.
Or wear one, if that's what you did with them.
But that did not keep me from crossing strand over strand
again and again until I had made a boxy, red and white lanyard
 for my mother.
She gave me life and milk from her breasts,
and I gave her a lanyard.
She nursed me in many a sick room,
lifted teaspoons of medicine to my lips,
set cold facecloths on my forehead
then led me out into the airy light and taught me to walk and
 swim
and I in turn presented her with a lanyard.
"Here are thousands of meals" she said,
"and here is clothing and a good education."
"And here is your lanyard," I replied.
—Billy Collins, "The Lanyard"

They fuck you up, your mum and dad.
They may not mean to, but they do.
They fill you with the faults they had
And add some extra, just for you.
—Philip Larkin, "This Be the Verse"

Pity the parents. In our contemporary cultural imagination, they are inevitably the companions of irredeemable debt, guilt, and error. Though we tend to associate the precise modalities of our anguished relations to our forebears with the historical specificities of our own version of modernity, our poets, in their chants of familial discomfort and pain, have touched a sore nerve that is as close to a cultural universal as ever you'll find. It is in virtue of this ineluctable vein of common experience that the Chinese tales with which I shall be concerned in this chapter struck a chord in Tibet, where they continued to resonate through the generations in Tibetan narrations of the tribulations of parental death. To elucidate this in our present context, I will have to begin with a bit of literary history, but it will be seen that this history is of interest to us precisely for what it discloses of the absolutes of clannish conviction underlying the relative appearances of Buddhist belief.

Mulian in the Land of Snows

It is well known that there was a considerable transmission of Buddhist learning and tradition to Tibet during the period of the old Tibetan empire in the seventh through ninth centuries CE, corresponding to the era of the Tang dynasty in China.[1] But with the exception of the interesting questions surrounding the spread of Chan Buddhism to Tibet, the Chinese contribution to the formation of Tibetan Buddhism has been little studied to date.[2] Rolf A. Stein, to be sure, demonstrated the importance of certain Chinese Buddhist apocryphal scriptures for our understanding of the early development of Tibetan Buddhism and pioneered the investigation of the Dunhuang Tibetan documents in this context.[3] In its text-historical dimension, my concern in this chapter is to extend this line of research, both by bringing to light one group of Chinese popular Buddhist traditions in Tibetan translation that was not considered by Stein and by attempting to trace the legacy of these works in later Tibetan writings.

The elaboration of the legend of the arhat Maudgalyāyana (Ch. Mu[qian]lian) during the course of Buddhism's progression from India through Central Asia to China has long fascinated students of Chinese literature and Buddhism in East Asia. Two of the most famous products of the legend's development are the *Yulanpen jing* (the "Sūtra of the *Yulan* Vessel," *T* no. 685) and the *Damuqianlian mingjian jiumu bianwen*, often referred to in English as the *Transformation Text on Mulian Saving His Mother from Hell* (henceforth the *Transformation Text*).[4] Both of these works derive their inspiration from the ancient but originally quite separate tales of Maudgalyāyana's visionary journeys to the hells and of his ignorance of the realm of his mother's rebirth, and both explore the soteriological crisis that arises when the arhat discovers that contrary to all expectation, she has been born in a miserable state, either as a hungry ghost (in the *Yulanpen jing*) or as a denizen of hell (according to the *Transformation Text*).[5] The Chinese stories of Mulian put into sharp relief the conflict between the properly Buddhist ethic of world renunciation and the claims of family and clan for the filial provision of perpetual material or ritual support.

During the Tang dynasty, when they were at the height of their popularity, these Chinese Buddhist works came to be known in Tibet, where they influenced later Tibetan literary accounts of the life of the Buddha and his disciples and, as I shall argue, Tibetan folklore and literature more broadly. Nevertheless, the Tibetan versions of the Mulian legends have remained obscure. This is due in large part no doubt to the rarity of the texts concerned, though, as will be seen below, there is also evidence that some Tibetan savants did recognize them to be Chinese apocrypha and condemned them as such.

The apparent marginality of the Tibetan Mulian traditions may reflect as well their unimportance for actual religious practice, including in particular rites intended to benefit the deceased. There was never, as far as we know, an institution in Tibet of the "ghost festival" of the fifteenth day of the seventh lunar month, which is promoted in these works as a ritual means for liberating fallen parents and ancestors from evil rebirth. This festival assumed considerable importance in Tang-period China and throughout later Chinese history.[6] The annual Tibetan Yoghurt Festival (*zho ston*), which, like the ghost festival, marks the conclusion of the monks' summer retreat, does seek to appease Māra and his host, for the desequestering of the religious is a time thought to be particularly prone to demonic disturbance.[7] This flows structurally from its being a liminal period characterized by the resumption of interaction between monks and laity after a hiatus of several months, with the attendant moral peril that this entails for weaker or novice monks, as well as for laypersons who may unwittingly or otherwise contribute to the corruption of the clergy. Those familiar with the Chinese ghost festival will perhaps regard this to be a notable point of similarity. Nevertheless, the Tibetan Yoghurt Festival has none of the explicit concern for the salvation of deceased parents and lineal ancestors that is central to its Chinese counterpart.

By contrast, the regular Tibetan Buddhist festival that is most pertinent to the theme of repaying maternal kindness, the Festival of the Descent from the Heavens (*lha babs dus chen*), which falls on the twenty-second of the ninth lunar month, does not revolve around the salvation of parents condemned to infernal abodes but rather commemorates the Buddha's mission to teach his late mother in heaven and his subsequent return to the human world.[8] In the Tibetan ritual cycle, the feeding of hungry ghosts is addressed primarily in the regular—for many devout lay and monastic practitioners, daily—rite of water offering (*chu gtor*) and to varying degrees also in other widely practiced offering rites, such as incense fumigation (*bsang*) and "severance" (*gcod*).[9] Przyluski suggested long ago that the water offering might be related to the Indian ritual background of the Chinese ghost festival, but however that may be, the canonical Indian and later Tibetan rituals of the water offering are not at all related to the tales of Maudgalyāyana that concern us here.[10] The legacy of the Mulian narratives in Tibet has been, as far as I have been able to determine, solely within the sphere of literature and not at all that of religious practice (though, as will be seen below, some types of Tibetan bardic performance may be very distantly related to the Mulian traditions, even if not directly traceable to them). What is certain, nevertheless, is that ritual and practical religious concerns did indeed motivate some of the Tibetan literature with which we shall be concerned, just as they did the earlier Chinese narratives.

The Tibetan version of the *Yulanpen jing* is so far known from just three of the manuscript versions of the Tibetan Buddhist canon, where it is titled "The Sublime Sūtra entitled *Vessel of Complete Protection*" (*'Phags pa yongs su skyobs pa'i snod ces bya ba'i mdo*);[11] it is not found in the printed editions. According to the colophon, it was translated from the Chinese by Gö Chödrup ('Gos Chos grub), the renowned ninth-century translator based in Dunhuang, who is also well known in Chinese as Facheng, a master of both Sanskrit and Chinese Buddhist textual traditions. His extensive corpus of translations and writings includes materials as diverse as a version of the *Avalokiteśvaraguṇa-kāraṇḍavyūha sūtra*, the Korean master Wŏnch'ŭk's great commentary on the *Saṃdhi-*

nirmocana sūtra, and an opuscule explaining the uses of the Sanskrit noun cases.[12]

The translation of the *Yulanpen jing* corresponds closely to the Chinese version of the text as given in the *Taishō shinshū daizōkyō*, though it is clear that (to borrow the catagories employed by Stein) Chödrup chose to translate this sūtra using a Tibetan vocabulary that had been coined to render Indic rather than Chinese Buddhist works.[13] Only a few subtle hints, besides the colophon that plainly states the text to have been translated from the Chinese, suggest that the *Yulanpen jing* in its Tibetan guise is anything but an originally Indian scripture.[14] It is of considerable interest, too, that in the M. A. Stein collection of Tibetan documents from Dunhuang in London, we find a short verse narrative composed by the same Chödrup that is devoted to the story of Maudgalyāyana and that this work is clearly based not on the *Yulanpen jing* but on the *Transformation Text*.[15] Both the Tibetan version of the *Yulanpen jing* and the Dunhuang Tibetan synopsis of the *Transformation Text* are, therefore, attributed to one and the same individual, Gö Chödrup, a.k.a. Facheng. Though many of his translations found their way into the later printed editions of the Tibetan Buddhist canonical collections, other writings and translations by Chödrup were never included therein. The texts considered here are to be found among this latter category.

The origins of the *Yulanpen jing* itself remain mysterious, and it has been proposed that it is a Chinese apocryphon of about the fifth or early sixth century.[16] The mysteries surrounding the sūtra begin with the title, which is based on a term, *yulan* or *yulanpen*, that does not make good sense in Chinese and so has often been interpreted as a foreign—Sanskrit, Pāli, or Iranian—loanword. The Sanskrit *avalambana*, "pendant, hanging down," has been the most frequently suggested source and has been explained in this context as referring to rites for the salvation of souls "hanging downward" in hell. Indeed, it is sometimes assumed that this explanation is so highly plausible, despite the absence of evidence supporting such a use of *avalambana* in known Indic contexts, that writers on East Asian Buddhism have often written of the "Avalambana," using the Sanskrit to the exclusion of the Chinese, as if this were the established, proper name of the ghost festival. The Tibetan translation of the *Yulanpen jing* is of interest to us in the first instance, therefore, because it provides some indication of the manner in which the title was understood by a prominent Tang-period translator who was familiar with contemporary Chinese and Sanskrit Buddhist usage.

Chödrup's rendering of the title in Tibetan is *'Phags pa yongs su skyob pa'i snod ces bya ba'i mdo*, "The Sublime Sūtra entitled *Vessel of Complete Protection*." It is quite clear that the derivation from *avalambana* in the meaning posited for that term does not at all cohere with this interpretation.[17] The Tibetan in this case accords quite well with the overall purport of the sūtra, which teaches that a vase or vessel should be filled with lavish offerings to the saṅgha as a means for assuring the *ritual* redemption of parents who have been *karmically* condemned to an evil rebirth, a key theme throughout the textual corpus that concerns us.[18]

In contrast with Chödrup's synopsis of the *Transformation Text*, which clearly states that the text was composed in connection with the festival of the fifteenth day of the seventh month (see below), there is no similar information accompanying the Tibetan *Yulanpen jing* that would help us to establish the context for its production. We can only imagine that given the considerable popularity that the text and the festival associated with it enjoyed in Tang-period Dunhuang, its translation would have appealed to local Tibetan Buddhists who knew of it through their Chinese correligionists, as well as to Tibetophone Chinese Buddhists, regarding whom something more will be said below. In any event, its occurrence in three widely dispersed manuscript collections stemming from a perhaps fourteenth-century central Tibetan redaction of the Tibetan Buddhist canon demonstrates that its geographical distribution in the Tibetan world was extensive, even if only three examples of the Tibetan *Yulanpen jing* have so far come to light. Though we are therefore certain that this sūtra was sometimes copied, we cannot affirm with similar assurance that the text was ever read. The Chinese Mulian legend in this particular version, though clearly available to Tibetans, remained to all intents and purposes unknown among them.

Transformations of the *Transformation Text*

Given the attention that Sinologists have devoted to the literary genre of transformation texts (*bianwen*), a genre studied largely on the basis of the Chinese Dunhuang documents, it is perhaps surprising that Tibetanists have not yet inquired as to whether or not *bian-*

wen were known in Tibet and, if so, what influence they might have had there.[19] On the surface, at least, it would be surprising if the Tibetans were not familiar with *bianwen*. After all, Dunhuang itself was held by the Tibetan empire for a period of some seven decades or more, and Dunhuang was a center for the production of both Chinese transformation texts and Tibetan translations from Chinese. Moreover, the connection of *bianwen* with oral narration accompanied by paintings of the events described reminds us that such picture tales had a much elaborated tradition in Tibet, a topic to which we shall have occasion to return. Nevertheless, until now, no Tibetan translations have been discovered of Chinese works characteristically identified as *bianwen*. The most that one can say, perhaps, is that there are some early Tibetan writings that, in virtue of their content and form, appear possibly to have have been composed on the model of *bianwen:* the *History of the Cycle of Birth and Death,* studied by Imaeda, might be such an instance.[20] In the case of the *Transformation Text of Mulian Saving His Mother*, however, we are now able to demonstrate Tibetan familiarity with precisely such a work and its contents.[21]

Our earliest example, mentioned above, is the short Dunhuang manuscript in the Stein collection (IOL J Tib. no. 686) written by Gö Chödrup, who provides here a much abbreviated verse summary of the tale of Mulian's rescue of his mother from hell—that is, the story as found in the *Transformation Text*. It is notable that this text, written in the Tibetan language, was composed on behalf of a Chinese devotee, whose name is given as "Hur Sun-cï."[22] As the heading of the manuscript specifies, moreover, the work was commissioned in connection with the ghost festival of the fifteenth day of the seventh month. It therefore contributes to the available evidence concerning the use of Tibetan among Chinese in and around Dunhuang, besides its specifically Tibetological interest.[23] As it provides an essential plot summary of our tale, it may be useful to reproduce it here in full:

The Story Recounted in Brief, Composed on Behalf of Hur Sun-cï for the Full Moon of the First Autumn Month

There was a great land famed as Nyamka (Mnyam dka'),
Whose king was Bimbasāra.
His great minister, the admirable Me'ungelya (Me'u-[d]gal ya),
Dwelt in the town of Shïngtak (Shïng thags).

He had a son called Koleta (Ko le ta).[24]
Once upon a time, when the great Teacher Śākyamuni
Was awakened as Buddha in Rājagṛha,
Sublime Aśvajit, at the Teacher's command,
Converted Me'ungel's son, who became a renunciate monk.
As he practiced with great perseverance,
He put an end to sorrow, attained corruption's cessation.
Among the śrāvakas, he became the most excellent miracle-maker.
Mahā-Maudgalyāyana,
To repay the kindness of his parents,
Well expounded virtue and evil to them both.
Though he preached the doctrine, teaching and making them receptive,
Maudgalyāyana's mother, named Bluish Black Hue,[25]
Was heedless of karma and really devoted to sin.
Desiring others' [possessions], she was stingy and very much envious.
She was dishonest to her son and deceptive.
Without faith in the Three Gems, she blasphemed.
To those who were kind, spiritual friends and preceptors,
She did no honor and turned her mind against them.
Then, when she died and transmigrated,
Driven on by the wind of unvirtuous karma,
She came to experience sorrow in the Avīci domain.
At that time Mahā-Maudgalyāyana
Wondered, "Into which realm of heavenly bliss
Has my mother been born?"
Examining the realms of heavenly bliss in turn
And not finding his mother among them,
He asked the best of men, the Teacher, all about it:
"My mother, her karma exhausted, has transmigrated;
If she is not among the blissful realms of gods and men,
In which destination has she been born?
Omniscient Great Teacher! I pray for your declaration!"
At that, the Teacher, best of men,
Spoke to Mahā-Maudgalyāyana:
"Because your mother practiced unvirtuous deeds,
She has come to experience grief in the Avīci realm.

By my power you must go there
And well assuage your mother's pain!"
Then Maudgalyāyana, by the power of the Teacher,
Miraculously journeyed to the Avīci realm.
At that time mother and son met together,
Embraced one another and wailed.
Maudgalyāyana, seeing his mother's suffering,
Gave varied food and drink to his mother,
But by the power of karma it turned into fire and pus.
Then Maudgalyāyana described his mother's sufferings
To the Teacher in detail.
At that time the Teacher said to Mahā-Maudgalyāyana:
"If you wish to eliminate your mother's pain,
Then, the saṅgha of śrāvakas fully assembled,
At the time of the full moon of the first autumn month,
Worship the Three Gems and make merit!
Thereby, mother's pain will subside,
And she'll be born in the realm of gods and men."
That being so, O you who are intelligent and learned,
Should you wish to abandon the pain of the evil destinies and to
  have bliss,
Then you must very much strive to abandon forever
The ten unvirtuous deeds and the deeds bringing immediate
  retribution,
And to preceptors, teachers and parents
Do appropriate service, honor and respect.
Finis. Composed by the bhikṣu Chödrup.

Chödrup's interpretation of the *Damuqianlian mingjian jiumu bianwen* deserves some attention. Modern commentators have sometimes regarded the *Transformation Text* as emphasizing conceptions of magical saving power, embodied in the quasi-shamanic figure of Mulian, as well as in the rituals of the ghost festival, which are quite contrary to characteristically Buddhist notions of the infallible causal operation of karma.[26] For Chödrup, any such conclusion would have seemed an unacceptable concession to wrong views. In fact, he explicitly warns his readers to avoid any such reading of the story—which is to say that he does clearly see that it *may* be interpreted as affirming the ritual annulment of karma—

and he insists that the tale should be treated above all as an exhortation to adhere to normative Buddhist values. This is quite evident in his closing verses:

> Should you wish to abandon the pain of the evil destinies and to have bliss,
> Then you must very much strive to abandon forever
> The ten unvirtuous deeds and the deeds bringing immediate retribution,
> And to preceptors, teachers and parents
> Do appropriate service, honor, and respect.

We can imagine that Chödrup, as a learned and sophisticated Buddhist monk, was well aware that the ghost festival and the scriptural and literary traditions associated with it did not represent the mainstream of Buddhist scholastic doctrine in all respects. In retelling the story of the *Damuqianlian mingjian jiumu bianwen*, therefore, he attempted to harmonize it with a more orthodox ethical perspective.

Though Chödrup's summary version of the *Transformation Text* had no direct legacy in later Tibetan literature of which we are now aware, it does establish that the *Transformation Text* was known among those literate in Tibetan in Dunhuang. Given that, as we have seen above, the *Yulanpen jing* was also translated into Tibetan there, it seems plausible to hold that later Tibetan knowledge of the Mulian stories was largely derived from ninth-century translations and accounts composed in and around Dunhuang, though we cannot exclude the possibility that some of the materials to which we shall now turn were derived from Chinese works transmitted to Tibet at different times, via different routes.

Unlike the *Yulanpen jing*, the *Transformation Text* was relatively well known in later Tibetan literature, and we can be certain that besides the summary given in the short Dunhuang manuscript considered above, a translation of an extended Chinese version of the tale was produced during the Tang period or soon after and that this work probably still exists. A reference in the writings of the great Sakyapa (Sa skya pa) scholar Pökangpa Rinchen Gyentsen (Spos khang pa Rin chen rgyal mtshan), dated 1427, confirms that there was still knowledge in his day of a scripture entitled *The Sūtra of Maudgalyāyana's Salvation of His Mother from the Hell Realm*

(*Maudgal gyi bus ma dmyal ba nas drangs pa'i mdo*) and that this was regarded as a Chinese apocryphon.[27] It is significant, too, that in the popular life of the Buddha authored by Pökangpa's contemporary Nanam Tsünpa (Sna nam btsun pa, exact dates unknown), the account of the legend of Maudgalyāyana includes the tale of his salvation of his mother and is clearly based upon an elaborate narration of the *Damuqianlian mingjian jiumu bianwen*, though the text is not mentioned there by name. (Nanam Tsünpa's retelling is translated in the appendix below and affords a useful point of comparison with the properly Tibetan stories to be discussed shortly.) The researches of Jampa Samten confirm, moreover, that a version of the *Transformation Text*, entitled *The Sūtra of Maudgalyāyana's Salvation of His Mother from Hell* (*Me'u 'gal gyi bu ma dmyal khams nas drangs pa'i mdo*) and so probably closely similar, if not identical, to the scripture reported in 1427 by Pökangpa, is preserved in the manuscript Kanjur of Orgyen Ling (O rgyan gling) in Tawang.[28] Finally, a detailed verse summary of the story found in the *Transformation Text* is given in an early twentieth-century anthology of *délok* (*'das log*, "return from death," or, as we might now say, "near death") tales preserved in the Bacot collection in Paris.[29] The stories contained in this compilation, like those highlighted by Bryan Cuevas in this volume, concern those who passed into the world of the dead and then were reanimated or else, like Mulian, marvelously were able to voyage among the shades. Significantly, such "returnees from the beyond" typically assume a somewhat shamanic role in Tibetan society, frequently serving as healers and spirit mediums, and thus incarnating some of the very powers attributed to Mulian himself.[30]

When we consider the contents of this anthology of *délok* narratives, it is plausible to suggest that the Mulian *Transformation Text* is in the background of several of these stories. The best example is the tale of Guru Chöwang (Chos dbang), the renowned thirteenth-century "discoverer of spiritual treasure" (*gter ston/bton*), who in general is not considered a *délok* at all but who is included here as the hero of an episode in which he journeys to the hells to rescue his mother.[31] As Guru Chöwang is a figure closely associated with thaumaturgy in the hagiographical literature, it is evident that he is being cast here in some respects as a Tibetan analogue to Maudgalyāyana, the "best in miraculous abilities" among the Buddha's immediate disciples.[32] The probability that the story of Chöwang's salvation of his mother from hell is modeled upon the tale of Mulian indicates that the influence of the *Transformation Text* was wider than the relative rarity of the Tibetan version of that work would itself appear to suggest.[33]

The episode takes for its point of departure, just as does the Chinese *Transformation Text*, the contrast between the hero's virtuous father and sinful mother, who in particular hates all that is connected with charity and religion. Following his father's death and several failed attempts to change his mother's views of religious practice, Chöwang departs to visit Lhasa on a journey of trade and pilgrimage, much as Mulian, in the *Transformation Text*, undertakes a business trip as the story unfolds.[34] In the Tibetan tale, however, his mother's decease occurs before the hero returns home. As will be seen below, this reflects widespread Tibetan anxiety about filial absence on the occasion of parental death, an anxiety that Chöwang expresses in demanding of his boyhood friend Dawö (Zla 'od) whether or not, in his absence, proper funeral rites were held. Dawö assures him that his "mother's bones were not allowed to fall into the mouths of dogs."[35]

Chöwang now takes leave of his friend in order to search for his mother. Entering into a trance, he ascends to heaven, where he meets the god Indra, considered here, in accord with the scheme of the "six sages" (*thub pa drug*) of the Tibetan Nyingmapa (Rnying ma pa) tradition, to be the actual presence of the Buddha among the gods.[36] Responding to Chöwang's search, the god declares that although his mother had put in a brief appearance among the gods, owing to her arrogant hatefulness and greed, she had quickly fallen into the realm of the combatative asuras. Chöwang next encounters his father, who has been graced with a more enduring heavenly station; his father affirms that "when she was in the world, your mother and I were in disaccord in both view and conduct. So now she's gone off to experience the sufferings of the six classes of beings."[37] Here there is an almost verbatim correspondence with the *Transformation Text*.[38]

Realizing that his mother is to be found nowhere but in the hells, Chöwang crosses the Buddhist Styx to meet with Yama himself.[39] The lord of death urges him to give up his quest: "We all enjoy slaughter and butchery! King Chöwang,[40] you'd better be gone from here."[41] But the hero persists and, once more in the manner of Mulian, expresses his determination to take his mother's sufferings upon himself so that she may be released.[42] He is told, however, that in effect the policy of the shop permits neither exchanges nor refunds. The infallible workings of karma are then made clear through a series of judicial proceedings that unfold before his eyes in Yama's court: a virtuous man who had sinned but slightly—with three companions he had once stolen and slaughtered a yak—is mercifully sentenced to a succession of human lives; a young woman who had taken advantage of her husband's trade as a diviner in order to profit from those in distress, particularly in connection with funerals, is condemned to a sealed iron chamber in the nadir of hell; a preacher of Avalokiteśvara leads numbers of female disciples to higher rebirths, while their husbands for the most part descend; and the virtuous wife of a doctor is sentenced to just a week in the poisonous waters of purgatory in order to expiate her husband's crime of imprudently bleeding (in the medical sense) his patients.[43]

After witnessing all this, Chöwang resumes his demand to be reunited with his mother, and after further hesitation on the part of Yama, it is finally revealed to him that she has been consigned to the sealed iron chamber in the very subbasement of hell. The hero manages to penetrate even this dungeon; his appearance there causes the demon-guardians to drop their weapons and faint, but at last he does manage to find his mother among the shades. By reciting Avalokiteśvara's six-syllable mantra, he begins to secure the release of tens of thousands, but his mother proves to be an exceptionally hard case. Coercing her consciousness (*rnam shes bkug*), he elevates her to the realm of the hungry ghosts and from there into the womb of an ass in the possession of a rich Tibetan. Following this, just as in the tale of Mulian, she is condemned to take birth once again, this time as a bitch. In this form, she becomes receptive to her son's teaching of the dharma, and in the end, after returning with him to their ancestral home at Layak in Lhodrak (Lho brag La yag), she gives up her canine form to be reborn in the heavens where her former husband resides.[44]

Throughout most of this, the inspiration of the *Transformation Text* is quite clear. We may ask just what, then, was accomplished by the transposition of the story into a Tibetan setting? Of course, there is much to be said for the merits of retelling a tale in such a way that it seems, for its audience or readership, closer to home than the original; in all cultures, at all times, this has been a hallowed literary device. But it will be noted that in this instance, a Chinese story of Indian inspiration has also been used as a vehicle for addressing some specifically Tibetan concerns. This is clearest in the judgment scene, in which otherwise virtuous Tibetan carnivores are reassured that the butchery of the occasional yak will be treated lightly in Yama's court but that defrauding the public through the divinatory arts is altogether out of bounds.[45] Of particular interest is the treatment of the doctor's wife, who, though herself unimpeachable, must nevertheless suffer a bit on her husband's account. This may only reflect a realistic assessment of the moral complications of marriage, but I think that the apparent exception to the karmic rule in fact speaks to deeper Tibetan concerns. Just what these are will become clearer as we proceed. At this juncture, however, it may be affirmed that the *Transformation Text* in its Tibetan incarnation became naturally assimilated to the genre of *délok* narratives and that, further, it may well have contributed to the very constitution of the genre itself.

King Gesar in Hell

The real impact of the Mulian legend upon Tibetan narratives of parental death and untoward rebirth was, I believe, considerably deeper than even the materials we have examined so far suggest. The proof text for this proposition is none other than the Tibetan national epic, the *Epic of Ling Gesar* (*Gling Ge sar*). I have stated above that there seems to have been no legacy of the Chinese Mulian traditions in Tibetan ritual or performing arts, despite the strong association of the *bianwen* with both of these dimensions of Chinese culture. This seems certainly to be true for the materials we have considered above—in these cases, the evidence we have gathered stems exclusively from the literary tradition. There may, however, have been one significant exception to this representation—that is, one area in which the Mulian tales did enter into Tibetan performance. The hero, however, is no longer named Mulian, or even Maudgalyāyana, but rather Gesar.

The particular type of performance through which the *bianwen* and the Tibetan epic may be related is the picture recitation, in which the bard makes use of a painting depicting scenes from his story in order to guide his audience through the action as it unfolds. The researches of Victor Mair convincingly demonstrate that the

Transformation Text of Mulian was one of the main subjects for such performances in medieval China.[46] Similarly in Tibet, picture recitation became an important vehicle for the diffusion of the Gesar epic, together with *délok* tales and a number of other narrative cycles, all of whose bards, as Stein has shown, have pronounced affinities with the singers of Gesar. In our context, what must be stressed above all is that in these traditions the visionary journey through hell occupies a principal place, whether it be the voyage of the hero or of the bard (and in the lives of the *délok* the two are in fact identical).[47]

The concluding episode of the Gesar epic is called the "Dominion of Hell" (*Dmyal gling*), and in many recensions it is elaborated so as to constitute (as do most of the principal episodes of the epic) an epic tale unto itself. Its enduring popularity may be gauged by its broad geographical distribution no less than by its inclusion in a "young readers" version of the epic recently published in China.[48] Significantly, it is in the "Dominion of Hell" episode of the epic that the resonance of the tale of Mulian for Tibetan mortuary belief and practice is at last fully clarified. Here, Gesar confronts the lord of death himself in order to free his mother—or, according to some accounts, his wife—from the infernal realm into which she has fallen. It is possible to argue, perhaps, that this is simply an instance of a widespread heroic theme in its Tibetan iteration and that it therefore may have no connection with the Chinese story of Mulian. I believe, however, that the similarities between Gesar's and Mulian's interventions in a peculiarly Buddhist hell are far more striking than any resemblance they may both also bear to more generalized narratives of the hero's (or god's) descent into hell.[49] The "Dominion of Hell," too, is known to have been a subject of picture recitation.[50]

The main version of the "Dominion of Hell" to which I refer here was redacted by one Rikdzin Draktsel Dorjé (Rig 'dzin Drag rtsal rdo rje), perhaps during the late eighteenth or early nineteenth century, and seems to have enjoyed an unusually wide circulation.[51] The main narrative elements may have derived from an older tradition, and in his colophon Rikdzin Draktsel Dorjé claims only to have rediscovered an earlier work authored and then concealed by a certain Den Lama Chökyi Wangchuk ('Dan bla ma Chos kyi dbang phyug), who, significantly perhaps in this context, is described as having made use of Chinese paper and ink for his composition.[52]

By both title and content, the work is firmly in line with the great body of far eastern Tibetan recensions of the epic that have been produced during the past few centuries and bear the unmistakable imprint of the "great perfection" (*rdzogs [pa] chen [po]*) teaching of the Tibetan Nyingmapa Buddhist tradition.

According to the tale that we find here, Gesar receives a prophetic injunction from the *ḍākinīs* to travel to India. His mother, Gokza Lhamo/Gokmo ('Gog bza' lha mo/'Gog mo), however, has received prognostications of her impending death and implores her son to stay with her. In connection with the Chinese materials we have surveyed above, it is of some interest that filiality is explicitly invoked here, though in distinctively Tibetan Buddhist terms:

> If my son does not guide me with the *powa* (*'pho ba*) blessing,
> When powerless I struggle in the hells,
> It will be difficult to lead me forward.[53]

Gesar, though much affected by his mother's words, nevertheless receives a renewed prophecy from Ma Drupé Gyelmo (Ma Grub pa'i rgyal mo, "Mother Siddharājñī"), the yoginī particularly associated with the rites of longevity,[54] who declares to him that:

> When it comes time to die,
> A thousand buddhas can't turn things around.
> But if it's untimely death, I can fix it.[55]

Accordingly, Gesar takes his leave and sets off for India. His mother passes away soon after, ironically owing to exhaustion brought on by the numberless prostrations she has performed in the direction of his departure. ("She gave me life and milk from her breasts,/and I gave her a lanyard.") This tragedy—filial absence during the death of a parent—is one that is encountered frequently in Tibetan literature: an excellent example may be found in the splendid autobiography of Shabkar (Zhabs dkar, 1781–1851).[56] Given the relatively large numbers of men who were removed from their parental homes—whether owing to religious vocation, trade, or nomadic movements—this was no doubt a common occurrence, and in suffering the loss of his mother in this way, Gesar exemplifies his role of Tibetan Everyman. In all events, the people of Ling undertake lavish funeral ceremonies on Gesar's mother's behalf, during which the great lamas of Ling seek to secure her rebirth in a pure land. Nevertheless, they are unable to prevent her fall into hell. She is dispatched there, says the text, to offer the means whereby Gesar himself will eventually liberate the infernal realms.[57]

A messenger is sent to Gesar with the news of his mother's passing, including a complete inventory of the rites performed and offerings made as part of her funeral. Thousands of stūpas have been consecrated on her behalf, fresh prayer flags adorn the entire kingdom, and bountiful donations have been distributed among the monks and the entire population, in accord with each one's rank and merit.[58] Of course, by now it should be clear that in accord with the belief system that is in fact represented here, one's rebirth is determined, not as normative Tibetan Buddhist scholastic doctrine would have us imagine, according to the moral weight of one's personal deeds—that is, according to one's own merits—but rather according to the merit that is ritually amassed on one's behalf, particularly by one's descendants. Contemporary Tibetan society offers a clear reflection of the moral universe described in the epic. Thus, in Tibetan families of my acquaintance, parental funerals have always been as enthusiastically documented in photography and video as are weddings, first communions, and bar mitzvahs in American Christian and Jewish culture. The response I have always received on inquiring about this is that "people should know that we have done well by our parents."

His burden thus lightened, Gesar implores his tutelary deities to escort him to the heavens to visit his mother, and he is horrified to learn that she cannot be found in Sukhāvatī or in any other paradise. The search, like Mulian's, takes a descending path through the cosmos, until the hero discovers that his mother has been consigned to the deepest pit in the bottom of hell. Gesar then travels through the infernal regions to confront Yama himself, who proves to be immune to his weapons and threats, for, like Gesar, Yama is an emanation of Mañjuśrī—their meeting is thus a meeting of doubles.[59] Gesar protests that, as his mother was sinless, "If you've sent my mother to hell, it matters not whether there's dharma." Significantly, in this context, he enumerates among his mother's merits the funerary offerings that were made on her behalf.[60] Yama responds that in fact it is not her karma, but instead *his* karma, that counts: his mother is surrounded by all the heroes and warriors Gesar and his armies have slaughtered in battle, and if he wishes to liberate her, he must free them first. Though Gesar may be a buddha, the wars fought by Ling have purposelessly brought death to many, who have fallen into the hells or have continued to wander in the *bardo* between lives. Owing to such conditions, mother Gokmo has also fallen into hell, and the accounting of karma has thus proceeded according to a calculation so fine that one mustard seed may be weighed against a hundred karmic causes and effects.[61] Gesar and Yama continue to spar in a competition of song, only after the conclusion of which does Yama finally teach Gesar a special technique of yoga, a sort of high-powered *powa* in fact, to liberate beings from hells. He assigns one of his assistants, Tiger Head (*stag gi mgo can*), to guide Gesar through the hells. Led on by this strange Virgil, Gesar descends through the cold hells, one by one, and is told of the sins that have led to rebirth in such conditions. Performing the rite Yama has taught him, he liberates the cold hells successively but never finds his mother. The process is repeated through the hot hells, until Gokmo is finally found, like Qingti, Mulian's mother, in Avīci, where she is surrounded by all the enemies her son has slain in battle. It is clear that unlike Qingti, she has fallen into hell owing not to her own sins but rather to those of her son. Gesar performs the rite one last time, liberating both his former enemies and his mother. It is here that the tale of Mulian merges fully with the Tibetan epic—the shamanic journey to the hells to free a fallen parent becomes a martial conquest of the underworld on behalf of all who are imprisoned within it. The narrative thus takes a markedly eschatological turn; the "Dominion of Hell" episode might well have been entitled the *Apocalypse of Gesar*.

Parental Death and the Limits of Renunciation

Though the Chinese ghost festival had no direct legacy, as far as we know, in the ritual life of Tibet, the tales of Mulian that formed a large part of their background nevertheless resonated well with Tibetan anxieties regarding the manner in which the merit and demerit of descendants may affect the status of ancestors—in this moral cosmology, the sins of the children are visited upon the parents. These concerns found their sharpest literary expression, however, not in the borrowed Chinese narratives insofar as these were known in Tibet, but in an indigenous Tibetan literature—and in the epic literature above all—in which earlier Chinese sources of inspiration were assimilated and transformed.

The representations we find here may be thought to doubly contradict Buddhist doctrinal norms; on the one hand, karma is now subordinate to genealogical and ritual orders, while on the other, the continuing role of descendants in maintaining the status of ancestors implies that renunciation can never be perfectly realized. Kinship and the entire nexus of relationships implied by kinship, inclusive of the parental legacy to the progeny and the obligations of successive generations to their forebears—all of this forms a skein from which even the arhat (Maudgalyāyana), even the tantric adept and visionary (Guru Chöwang), even the divinely emanated conqueror of the world (Gesar) can never quite extricate themselves as long as their parents remain bound to the evils of the world. In the system that is implied here, the would-be renunciate has as much chance to be rid of his own shadow as he does of the apparently endless superaddition of debts running up and down the generational chain.

This, however, suggests an alternative way of regarding the matter, one that *prima facie* is more congenial to the views associated normatively with Mahāyāna Buddhism. For it may be held that the impossibility of completely renouncing the world while those to whom one is related remain unfree entails—because in the final analysis all beings have been our mothers at some time or another—an obligation to secure the freedom of all. This, of course, is just what Gesar accomplishes. Read in this manner, the impossibility of perfect renunciation is no longer a source of bondage but rather the very condition enabling universal salvation. What at first seemed a Buddhist concession to naive worldly interests, underwriting the claims of family, honor, and ritual power over and against the billiard ball precision of karmic causation, turns out, on this account, to be an instance of remarkable skill-in-means. And the trick works precisely because the authors of our tales determined to focus our attention upon one familiar but difficult truth: parental death is the oracular mirror in which we presage our own mortality as well.

Appendix: Nanam Tsünpa's Retelling of the *Transformation Text*

When, for the sake of his parents, Maudgalyāyana became an arhat by striving in absorption, he went everywhere [to find their rebirths] and met his father, who had become a Brahma-king. Father and son embraced, and the son asked, "If Father is so happy, wherever can Mother have gone to?"

"I was never without the sūtras in hand and practiced virtue; hence, I was born here. But, because she sinned, she was born in hell."

With that, round midnight, Maudgalyāyana went to the realm of hell for the sake of his mother. On the way, he met up with a rich man named *Zhang Shanhua (Tib. Cang zhan hwa) who had eaten mutton, drunk ale, killed [by hunting] with falcons and dogs, blasphemed the saṅgha, and shouted the command, "Kill!" On the fifteenth of the previous month, he had died, but only after Yama's armies twice attacked. He was surrounded by a thousand *yama*s bearing pitchforks, a rope was tied about his waist, and before him there were five hundred fox-headed [demons] howling. Blood oozed from each one of his pores, and smoke poured out of his mouth. With blood spurting from his nose like an arrow in flight, he cried as he was being led away.

Continuing his descent, [Maudgalyāyana] encountered *yama*s with oxheads and horseheads, but, though he asked them, he could not find his mother. Finally, he met Yamarāja, who sent him to the side of the Lord Who Commands the Five Paths, Wudao Jiangjun (Tib. Mgo de tsang kun).[62] He was wearing golden armor, held a sword, and roared with his eyes bulging. He was terrifying to behold, and surrounded by a company of five hundred, he killed, beat and hacked to pieces beings of human form. Seeing this, [Maudgalyāyana] asked, "Have you seen my mother, Maudgalā?" When [the Commander] passed the inquiry on to his scribe, [the latter responded,] "A certain 'Maudgalā' passed this way three human years ago and is now in Avīci."

Grieving, he proceeded there, but a *rākṣasa* king blocked the way and said, "The Avīci hell is terrifying! Bottom to top, it's made of iron and copper all aflame. Hadn't you better go elsewhere?"

Maudgalyāyana replied, "Who can open its portals?"

He said, "Just three can open it: Yama, Wudao Jiangjun, and the Blessed Lord Śākyamuni!"

Delighted, Maudgalyāyana took up in an instant the Blessed Lord's robes, almsbowl and staff, and before the door of Avīci he thrice shook the rattle of the staff, whereupon the door spontaneously opened. As he shook it again, the watchtower of the iron fortress, together with the key, fell to the ground. From within the door that had spontaneously opened, oxheaded *rākṣasa*s with iron pitchforks came out.

"I have come here to find my mother."

"She's in Avīci," they said.

Then, when he passed through that door, some five hundred *rākṣasa*s refused to let him go on. At this, Maudgalyāyana focused his gaze and while saying, "If I make my home here, what power do you have?" he rattled his staff, whereupon their pikes and pitchforks fell from their hands, and they were unable to stop him. When he arrived before the gate of the iron fortress and again rattled his staff, the sword and spear grove, the mountain of blades, and the needles and thorns on which [the damned] were impaled, continually vomiting flames, disappeared by themselves. But then numberless *rākṣasa*s arrived and there was an exchange of questions and answers as before, after which the *rākṣasa*s led Maudgalā out and brought her beside her son. Her head was the size of a mountain and her throat thin as a thread. She was unable to walk and her body was pierced with 360 nails. When he saw her like this, he spoke choked with tears, "My mother! Formerly you were happy, but now you suffer with blood pouring from the seven orifices. Did you get the things I sent from home?"

His mother replied, "My son! Whatever you send, it's of no use. But if you can, copy the scriptures for my sake. There's no greater benefit than that."

The guards shouted, "Lead her here and put a thousand nails into her body!"

When he heard this, Maudgalyāyana beat himself until blood poured from his mouth and eyes, and he said to the guards, "I will take on my mother's suffering!"

They replied, "How can you change karma?" With that, they led his mother away, and Maudgalyāyana fell to the ground.

The Blessed Lord, who was residing in Sakarjen (Sa dkar can) during the summer retreat and was occupied in taming the evil destinies, knew [what had occurred]. He dispatched Ānanda, who travelled to hell in an instant and raised Maudgalyāyana, who was on the verge of expiring. When [the latter] came before the Blessed Lord, he said, "I pray that you liberate my mother from the sufferings of hell."

The Blessed Lord then projected light into the infernal realms. Indra took hold of a parasol and led the way, while Brahmā followed, holding on to [the Buddha's] golden robes. As soon as they arrived at the gates of hell, the portals all opened by themselves. Iron hammers became jewels, while molten copper cooled, and the denizens of hell took rebirth in the heavens. But despite this, Maudgalā alone was not freed from the sufferings of the evil destinies and instead was reborn as a hungry ghost, pained with great hunger and thirst.

Maudgalyāyana thereupon took his mother to Rājagṛha, where he begged for alms and gave her whatever he received. She greedily stuffed her mouth with food, but it turned into blazing coals, so that she could not eat it. When Maudgalyāyana tried to feed her with a golden spoon, fire poured out of her nose and mouth, and she could not eat. Then, [wandering] in all directions, many tens of thousands of *yojana*s, he led her to a riverbank and bade her drink, while [at the same time] the Blessed Lord projected emanations of some five hundred hungry ghosts, who appeared to be drinking the water of the river. [Seeing them,] Maudgalā ran all about, trying to prevent the hungry ghosts from drinking, owing to which the water, too, turned into blazing coal, so that she could not drink. Her son said, "Mother! Why have you prevented the hungry ghosts from drinking the river water? If, thanks to your desire and greed, you're still unsatisfied, when will you ever be reborn in the higher abodes?"

At this, she became embarrassed before her son. As soon as pangs of regret arose in her mind, she became able to drink the water. She then died right there, on the bank of the river, and took birth in Rājagṛha as an untamable, black, yellow-eyed bitch. Seeing Maudgalyāyana passing by on his alms round, she licked his robes and shed tears. He said to her, "Mother! What's the matter with you that, even though you've become a dog, you can't abandon evil conduct?" And he wept as well.

Maudgalyāyana then went before the Blessed Lord: "As my mother has now become a bitch, what can I do so that she will be free?"

[The Blessed Lord] declared: "If you invite the sublime ones (*ārya*) to recite the scriptures continuously for forty-nine days, she will be liberated."

He did just this, whereupon she transmigrated and was born as a fine young girl in the worldly realm of Light Rays.[63] When the Blessed Lord traveled to Lomajen (Slo ma can), he came to Anavatapta, where Maudgalyāyana saw him and knew that his mother had been tamed by the Blessed Lord. For this reason, he prayed once again and his request was granted:

"By whose miraculous power may I be confident of success?"

"By my miraculous power!"

This said, Mahā-Maudgalyāyana planted a step on the summit of Mt. Meru and, carried by the miraculous power of the Blessed Lord, he travelled on, arriving in Light Rays in a week. When that fine girl saw Maudgalyāyana from a distance, she exclaimed, "I see my son!" The assembled crowd demanded proof, and Maudgalyāyana affirmed that she had been his mother in a former life. After the Blessed Lord, too, had expounded the doctrine, they saw the truth, expressed their acclaim, and offered alms to the Blessed Lord and Maudgalyāyana, which were accepted. Maudgalyāyana then led his mother to the world of Brahmā, where he entrusted her to his father. Afterwards, the Blessed Lord said, "Was Maudgalyāyana confident of success?"[64]

"The Blessed Lord made the journey!"

"By whose miraculous power?"

"By that of the Blessed Lord!"

"Now, think on the Jetavana!"

"Blessed Lord! Shall we go there?"

"Maudgalyāyana himself has already gone; he may be called the 'Miracle Quick Wit.'" So saying, he dwelt in Jetavana.[65]

Notes

For their critical and constructive comments on this chapter, in its various versions presented as talks during the long course of its evolution, beginning in autumn 2000, I extend thanks to Anne-Marie Blondeau, Kuo Liying, Françoise Pommaret, and Geoffrey Samuel. I am grateful to the British Library, London, and to the Société Asiatique, Paris, for making unique documents from their collections available to me in connection with this research. Stephen F. Teiser kindly read the penultimate draft of the essay, providing me with helpful suggestions for its final revision.

1. See my *Tibetan Assimilation of Buddhism: Conversion, Contestation, and Memory* (New York: Oxford University Press, 2000), chaps. 2–5, for general background.

2. Useful orientations to the now extensive literature on the spread of Chan Buddhism to Tibet will be found in Jeffrey L. Broughton, *The Bodhidharma Anthology: The Earliest Records of Zen* (Berkeley: University of California Press, 1999); Paul Demiéville, "L'introduction au Tibet du bouddhisme sinisé d'après les manuscrits de Touen-houang: Analyses de récents travaux japonais," in *Contributions aux études sur Touen-houang*, ed. Michel Soymié (Geneva and Paris: Librairie Droz, 1979), 1–16; Kapstein, *The Tibetan Assimilation of Buddhism*, chap. 5; Lewis Lancaster and Whalen Lai, eds., *Early Ch'an in China and Tibet*, Berkeley Buddhist Studies Series 5 (Berkeley: Asian Humanities Press, 1983); and Guilaine Mala and Kimura Ryūtoku, *Un Traité tibétain de Dhyāna chinois (Chan)*, Bulletin de la Maison Franco-Japonaise, nouvelle série 12/1 (Louvain: Peeters, 1988). Demiéville's *Le concile de Lhasa: Une controverse sur le quiétisme entre bouddhistes de l'Inde et de la Chine au VIIIe siècle de l'ère chrétienne*, Bibliothèque de l'Institut des Hautes Études Chinoises, vol. 7 (Paris: Imprimerie Nationale de France, 1952), and Giuseppe Tucci, *Minor Buddhist Texts*, parts 1 and 2, Serie Orientale Roma 9, (1956 and 1958, reprinted Kyoto: Rinsen Shobō, 1978), remain the fundamental points of departure for the study of Chan in Tibet.

3. Rolf A. Stein, "Tibetica Antiqua I: Les deux vocabulaires des traductions Indo-tibétaine et Sino-tibétaine dans les manuscrits de Touen-houang," *Bulletin de l'École Française d'Extrême-Orient* 72 (1983): 149–236.

4. For background, see Arthur Waley, *Ballads and Stories from Tun-huang* (New York: Allen and Unwin, 1960); Victor Mair: *Tun-huang Popular Narratives* (Cambridge: Cambridge University Press, 1983), and *T'ang Transformation Texts: A Study of the Buddhist Contribution to the Rise of Vernacular Fiction and Drama in China* (Cambridge, MA: Harvard University Press, 1989); and Stephen F. Teiser, *The Ghost Festival in Medieval China* (Princeton, NJ: Princeton University Press, 1988). A discussion of the tale of Mulian in relation to the cult of Kṣitigarbha may be found in Françoise Wang-Toutain, *Le Bodhisattva Kṣitigarbha en Chine du Ve au XIIIe siècle* (Paris: Presses de l'École Française d'Extrême-Orient, 1998), 132–35. It should be noted that the *Yulanpen jing* has often been treated as an authentic Indian work or as one of Central Asian Indo-Iranian Buddhist origin. The canonical Chinese version attributes its translation to the Indian Dharmarakṣa (Ch. Zhu Fahu, 266–317 CE). It seems to me rather more likely, however, that this sūtra is indeed a Chinese apocryphon, though perhaps one that reflects elaborations of the Maudgalyāyana legend that were transmitted via Central Asia. Note that in using the Chinese Mulian to refer on occasion to Tibetan materials concerning Maudgalyāyana in

this chapter, I am taking some liberty (though not *too* much, as Mu[qian]-lian, like Tibetan Mo'u/Me'u dgal gyi bu, is based on the transcription of the Indic). In the present context, this is simply a convenient device to emphasize that the tales here considered are derived from Chinese and not Indian sources.

5. See J.J. Jones, trans., *The Mahāvastu*, vol. 1, Sacred Books of the Buddhists 16 (London: Luzac, 1949), 6–21, for Maudgalyāyana's journeys to the hells, and 22–52, for his peregrinations in other realms. The versions of these episodes known in Tibet, however, were derived from the *Mūlasarvāstivāda vinaya*. On his ignorance of his mother's birth in the divine Marīcilokadhātu, refer to Louis de La Vallée Poussin, *L'Abhidharmakośa de Vasubandhu* (reprint, Brussels: Institut Belge des Hautes Études Chinoises, 1971), 1:2n3; and comments of Yaśomitra on Vasubandhu, *Abhidharmakośam*, ed. Swāmī Dvārikādāsaśāstrī (Varanasi: Bauddha Bharati, 1970–72), 1:7.

6. The ghost festival is studied in detail in Teiser, *The Ghost Festival in Medieval China*.

7. On the *zho ston,* as traditionally conducted, see Thupten Sangay, *Bod kyi dus ston: Festivals of Tibet* [in Tibetan] (Dharamsala: Library of Tibetan Works and Archives, 1974), 50–54, and Hugh E. Richardson, *Ceremonies of the Lhasa Year* (London: Serindia Publications, 1993), 99–107. It is not clear that the festival was originally connected strictly with the close of the summer retreat, and it may have at first just marked the close of the summer herding season, when dairy production is at its peak. In Lhasa at the present time, the authorities of the Tibetan Autonomous Region have made every effort to transform the *zho ston* into a tourist event exemplifying Tibetan folklore. It seems, therefore, that "demonic disturbance" has at last gained the upper hand.

8. Thupten Sangay, *Bod kyi dus ston*, 58; Richardson, *Ceremonies of the Lhasa Year*, 109.

9. Donald S. Lopez, Jr., ed., *Religions of Tibet in Practice* (Princeton, NJ: Princeton University Press, 1997), chap. 15, by Richard Kohn, and chap. 26, by the Nālandā Translation Committee, provide examples of rites of the first two of these categories. On the *gcod,* refer to Giacomella Orofino, *Contributo allo studio dell'insegnamento di Ma gcig lab sgron* (Naples: Istituto Universitario Orientale, 1987), and Jérôme Edou, *Machig Labdrön and the Foundations of Chöd* (Ithaca, NY: Snow Lion, 1996). It is not without interest in this context to note that the Bacot Collection ms. 110, discussed in greater detail below (see note 29), includes a particularly well-known version of the incense fumigation practice, the *Ri bo bsang mchod* of Lha btsun Nam mkha' 'jigs med (1597–1652), as its principal ritual component.

10. Jean Przyluski, "Les rites d'Avalambana," in *Mélanges chinois et*

bouddhiques 1 (1931–32): 221–25. The proposal that the *yulan* ritual might be related to the class of offerings known in Tibetan as *gtor ma* (Skt. *bali*) goes back at least to Ernest J. Eitel, *Handbook of Chinese Buddhism,* 2nd ed. (Hong Kong, 1888; reprint, New Delhi: Cosmo, 1981), 185–86, sub "ullambana."

11. It is no. 266 in vol. 79 of *The Tog Palace Manuscript of the Tibetan Kanjur,* Sherig Dpemzod Series (Leh, Ladakh: C. Namgyal Tarusergar, 1975–80), 109 vols., as catalogued by Tadeusz Skorupski, *A Catalogue of the Stog Palace Kanjur,* Bibliographia Philologica Buddhica, Series Maior 4 (Tokyo: International Institute for Buddhist Studies, 1985), 144. Géza Bethlenfalvy, *A Hand-List of the Ulan Bator Manuscript of the Kanjur Rgyal-rtse Thems Spaṅs-ma* (Budapest: Akadémiai Kiadó, 1982), lists it as Ulan Bator no. 314 and as Tokyo no. 266, following the handlist prepared by Kōjun Saitō. As the *Yulanpen jing* was never included in the printed Tibetan canons, its occurrence in these three manuscripts (though no doubt there are others as well), all ultimately derived from the fourteenth- or fifteenth-century Rgyal rtse *Them spangs ma* manuscript, raises some interesting questions in connection with Tibetan canonical transmission. The text of the Stog Palace Kanjur is, however, the only one that I have actually been able to consult to date, so my remarks are necessarily based on it alone. I have prepared a bilingual Chinese and Tibetan edition of the text, to be published with more detailed philological commentary on a later occasion.

12. On 'Gos Chos grub, or Facheng, see Demiéville, *Le concile*; Shōju Inaba, "On Chos-grub's Tibetan Translation of the *Chien-chen-mi-chung-shu,*" in *Buddhist Thought and Asian Civilization: Essays in Honor of Herbert V. Guenther on His Sixtieth Birthday,* ed. Leslie S. Kawamura and Keith Scott (Emeryville, CA: Dharma Publishing, 1977), 105–13; Daishun Ueyama (with reference to his more detailed work in Japanese) in Lancaster and Lai, eds., *Early Ch'an in China and Tibet*; and Pieter C. Verhagen, "A Ninth-Century Tibetan Summary of the Indo-Tibetan Model of Case-Semantics," in *Tibetan Studies: Proceedings of the 5th Seminar of the International Association for Tibetan Studies, Narita 1989,* ed. Ihara Shōren and Yamaguchi Zuihō (Narita: Naritasan Shinshoji, 1992), 833–44.

13. Refer to note 3 above.

14. Thus, for example, the Chinese *daoyan,* "eye of the path," is literally rendered here in Tibetan as *lam gyi mig.* The sense of the term as it is used in the *Yulanpen jing,* however, seems that of the Sanskrit *divyacakṣuḥ,* the "divine eye," or clairvoyance, translated in standard Tibetan Buddhist terminology as *lha yi mig.* Chos grub, perhaps not entirely sure of the Chinese usage in this case, probably opted to play it safe by calquing the Chinese. Elsewhere we find the Chinese *xiao,* "filial piety," translated as *sri zhu,* a word meaning roughly "courteous behavior, etiquette," without the very precise connotations of the Chinese.

15. IOL J Tib. no. 686, as listed in Louis de La Vallée Poussin, *Catalogue of the Tibetan Manuscripts from Tun-huang in the India Office Library* (Oxford: Oxford University Press, 1962), 221. For a transcription of the text, see my "A Dunhuang Tibetan Summary of the Transformation Text on Mulian Saving His Mother from Hell," in *Dunhuang wenxian lunji*, ed. Hao Chunwen and Zhu Bian (Shenyang: Liaoning Renmin Chubanshe, 2001), 235–47. I should note that because the Tang-period translator Chos grub was well aware that "Mu(qian)lian" was simply a transcription of the Sanskrit "Maudgalyāyana," he used only the Tibetan rendering of the Sanskrit name in his writings—i.e., Mo'u/Me'u dgal gyi bu.

16. Teiser, *The Ghost Festival in Medieval China*, 48.

17. Indeed, the Tibetan version of the sūtra actually begins with an ill-formed "Sanskrit" title: *Ārya-pariśaraṇibhañja*[*sic*!]-*nāma-sūtra*, though the colophon assures us that the text was in fact translated from the Chinese. The pseudo-Sanskrit in this instance is thus best explained as a calque, whether due to Chos grub himself or (as seems far more likely) to some later scribe or editor attempting to supply a Sanskrit equivalent to Chos grub's Tibetan. This in itself, therefore, provides no reliable evidence concerning the interpretation of the meaning of the title in Chinese, for it merely confirms what Chos grub's Tibetan already tells us—namely, that he understood *yulanpen* to mean a "vase of complete protection." Though not at all supporting the derivation of the term from *avalambana*, Chos grub's rendering is nevertheless broadly consistent with another of the proposed Indic etymologies, which holds that the source word might be the Pāli or Buddhist Sanskrit *ullumpana*, "saving, pulling out [of evil circumstances]." It is not clear, however, that Chos grub was himself aware of this explanation. Moreover, for phonological reasons, the transcription of *ullumpana* as *yulanpen* (substituting the short *u* of the second syllable with *a/e*) seems implausible. All in all, it seems more prudent to hold that 'Gos Chos grub understood *yulanpen* as a set expression and translated accordingly.

18. Though I speak of parental death—and indeed the Chinese texts in question do promulgate their rituals for the benefit of one's parents and ancestors "to the seventh generation"—the emphasis is nevertheless clearly on the mother's passing. When both parents are explicitly mentioned, the father is usually depicted as virtuous and therefore reborn in paradise thanks to his own positive karma, without requiring the special ritual intercession needed to save the mother from the fruits of her evil ways. While this gender asymmetry is of considerable interest and merits further reflection, particularly in connection with the image of mother-son relations in the societies with which we are concerned, it is not in itself the main topic of this chapter and so has been left relatively unexplored herein. It is, however, studied with reference to Chinese sources in Alan Cole, *Mothers and Sons*

in Chinese Buddhism (Stanford, CA: Stanford University Press, 1998), where chaps. 5 ("Mothers and Sons in the Ghost Festival") and 8 ("Mu Lian and the Ten Kindnesses of the Mother") are particularly pertinent to our present subject matter.

19. On transformation texts, see especially Mair: *Tun-huang Popular Narratives* and *T'ang Transformation Texts*. Mair's translation of the *Damuqianlian mingjian jiumu bianwen*, given in the former work with copious annotation, has been usefully republished, though without the full apparatus, in Victor Mair, ed., *The Columbia Anthology of Traditional Chinese Literature* (New York: Columbia University Press, 1994), 1093–1127, to which I refer here for reasons of convenience.

20. Yoshiro Imaeda, *Histoire du cycle de la naissance et de la mort* (Geneva and Paris: Librairie Droz, 1981). See, too, the comments on this work in my "Indian Literary Identity in Tibet," in *Literary Cultures in History*, ed. Sheldon Pollock (Berkeley: University of California Press, 2003), 762–67.

21. A fully detailed comparison between the *Transformation Text* and its several available Tibetan retellings must be deferred for another occasion, though a solid beginning, with reference to one of the Tibetan versions, may be found in the contribution of Takasaki Jikidō, cited in note 29 below. This important article is the partial exception to the general Tibetological neglect of *bianwen*. Takasaki, however, considered the *Transformation Text* to be just an extracanonical sūtra (J. *kyō*), without reference to the genre of *bianwen*.

22. Though *hur* has been documented as transcribing *fo*, "buddha," in Old Tibetan documents (refer to my *Tibetan Assimilation of Buddhism*, 200n65), in the present case this is improbable. It could be used to render any one of several characters whose present readings are *fu*, *hu*, etc.

23. Takata Tokio, "Bouddhisme chinois en écriture tibétaine: Le Long Rouleau chinois et la communauté sino-tibétaine de Dunhuang," in *Bouddhisme et cultures locales: Quelques cas de réciproques adaptations*, ed. F. Fukui and G. Fussman (Paris: Presses de l'École Française d'Extrême-Orient, 1994), 137–44.

24. I.e., Kolita, Maudgalyāyana's proper name as given in Buddhist Sanskrit sources. In Chinese, this was usually rendered Luobo, "Turnip," though the basis for this interpretation remains unclear. *Kola-* in Sanskrit refers to the jujube. In any event, it is not without interest that Chos grub chose to use the transcription of the Indic in this context.

25. *Sngo nag mdog* = Ch. Qingti. Because the second syllable of the Chinese makes no sense, Mair speculates that this may be an instance of a meaning + phonetic compound, representing an Indic name that he gives as Nīladhi. It seems to me no less plausible, however, to suppose that the second syllable was added just to give the name an exotic, foreign ring,

much as we find in the plentiful pseudo-Sanskrit expressions with which both Chinese and Tibetan tantric apocrypha are liberally peppered. Note that in contrast with his treatment of the name Turnip, Chos grub has not adopted an Indic usage here.

26. As Teiser, *The Ghost Festival in Medieval China*, 202, puts it, "A strict reading of the doctrine of karma throws into question the efficacy of traditional ancestral offerings." Consider, too, chap. 5, where his theme is "Mu-lien as Shaman," and 203–8, where he takes up the ritual and ascetic power attributed to the monks. Despite the sharp dichotomy between rational and magical sources of agency that seems at play here and that, in my view, must be underscored in analyzing the traditions under discussion, Teiser interprets these and other structural oppositions in terms of what he calls the "'total' socioreligious system" (209), which is held together through interaction, reciprocity, and exchange, whereby, in effect, the hard edge of the law is softened in its applications.

27. Jared Douglas Rhoton, trans., *A Clear Differentiation of the Three Codes* (Albany: State University of New York Press, 2001), 196n103.

28. Jampa Samten, "Notes on the Bka'-'gyur of O-rgyan-gling, the Family Temple of the Sixth Dalai Lama (1683–1706)," in *Tibetan Studies: Proceedings of the 6th Seminar of the International Association of Tibetan Studies, Fagernes 1992*, ed. Per Kværne (Oslo: Institute for Comparative Research in Human Culture, 1994), 393–402; cf. 395–96. I have not, however, been able to verify his identification of this text with the *Rgyal bu kun tu dge zhes bya ba'i mdo* as given in the Stog Kanjur, no. 268.

29. Bacot ms. 110 in the collection of the Société Asiatique, Paris. The tale of Maudgalyāyana is here given as the ninth fascicle (Tibetan marginal siglum *ta*) in eleven folios. As Takasaki Jikidō has shown, this text corresponds very closely to the *Transformation Text* and may in fact be substantially identical to its Tibetan translation: *Indogaku Bukkyōgaku ronshū: Takasaki Jikidō Hakushi kanreki kinen ronshū* (Tokyo: Shunjūsha, 1987), 427–45. I am grateful to Yao Zhihua for having brought this interesting study to my attention. Françoise Pommaret, *Les revenants de l'au-delà dans le monde tibétain: Sources littéraires et tradition vivante* (Paris: Editions du Centre National de la Recherche Scientifique, 1989), 25–29, provides a discussion of Bacot ms. 110 (referred to as "Le *Xylographe Ka shod*") in the context of her investigation of the *'das log* as a living tradition in eastern Bhutan. See, further, chap. 32, the same author's contribution to Lopez, ed., *Religions of Tibet in Practice*, and Bryan Cuevas' chapter in this volume.

30. Pommaret, *Les revenants de l'au-delà dans le monde tibétain*, 123–61, offers a valuable ethnography of a number of such practicing "returnees."

31. Bacot ms. 110, tenth fascicle (Tibetan marginal siglum *tha*) in fourteen folios. Dudjom Rinpoche, Jikdrel Yeshe Dorje, *The Nyingma School of*

Tibetan Buddhism: Its Fundamentals and History, trans. Gyurme Dorje and Matthew Kapstein (London: Wisdom Publications, 1991), 1:760–70, supplies a summary version of Guru Chos dbang's traditional hagiography. The story of his salvation of his mother is not mentioned therein.

32. Reginald A. Ray, *Buddhist Saints in India: A Study in Buddhist Values and Orientations* (New York: Oxford University Press, 1994), surveys many of the pertinent Indian sources.

33. An obvious objection here is that the tale of the hero's descent into hell is a near universal motif of mythology and folklore—consider Dionysius and Orpheus—so that to assume genetic connections among its various instances is therefore questionable. While this is no doubt generally correct, I will be arguing in what follows that there are in fact some very precise indications, above and beyond very general thematic similarities, that demonstrate that the Tibetan story of Guru Chos dbang's rescue of his mother was directly inspired by a version of the *Transformation Text*. If this is right, then it becomes more plausible to consider other Tibetan representatives of the same theme as stemming ultimately from the same source.

34. Mair, *The Columbia Anthology*, 1094.

35. Bacot ms. 110, tenth fascicle, fol. 7a4: *a ma'i rus pa khyi khar ma shor ba*.

36. The "six sages," through whom the Buddha is present in each of the six classes of sentient existence, belong to the Rnying ma pa maṇḍala system of the Peaceful and Wrathful Divinities of the Magical Net (*sgyu 'phrul zhi khro*), which informs, for instance, the *Bar do thos grol*, the so-called *Tibetan Book of the Dead*. The scriptural source from which they are derived is the third chapter of the *Guhyagarbha-tantra (Rgyud gsang ba snying po)*, cited in Dudjom Rinpoche, *The Nyingma School of Tibetan Buddhism*, 1:414. See also 129 of the same work.

37. Bacot ms. 110, tenth fascicle, fol. 8a1.

38. Mair, *The Columbia Anthology*, 1099: "Your mother's activities while she was alive were different from mine. . . . If you search for your mother among the infernal paths of Jambudvīpa, you'll soon find out where she has gone."

39. Unnamed in the Tibetan but clearly the Whathellwedo River of Mair's translation.

40. *Chos dbang rgyal po*. The phrase in fact abbreviates the verse *chos kyi dbang phyug chos kyi rgyal*, from the *Mañjuśrīnāmasaṃgīti*, verse 55, which is always cited in explanation of Chos dbang's name. See Dudjom Rinpoche, *The Nyingma School of Tibetan Buddhism*, 761, and Bacot ms. 110, tenth fascicle, fol. 2b4.

41. Bacot ms. 110, tenth fascicle, fol. 8b5.

42. Ibid., fol. 9a1–2: *bdag gi a ma btang du gsol, a ma'i las ngan bdag gi khur lags so*; cf. Mair, *The Columbia Anthology*, 1116: "My only wish, war-

den, is that you release my mother,/and I myself will bear the endless suffering for her."

43. Bacot ms. 110, tenth fascicle, fol. 9a3–11b6.

44. Ibid., fol. 11b6–13b4; cf. Mair, *The Columbia Anthology*, 1126.

45. It must be stressed that Tibetan moral sensibilities were sorely piqued by animal slaughter. Comments on this, based on ethnographic observation and literary historical study respectively, may be found in Robert B. Ekvall, *Fields on the Hoof: Nexus of Tibetan Nomadic Pastorialism* (New York: Holt, Reinhart and Winston, 1968), 46–51, and my "The Sprul-sku's Miserable Lot: Critical Voices from Eastern Tibet," in *Proceedings of the 9th Seminar of the International Association for Tibetan Studies: Amdo Tibetans in Transition*, ed. Toni Huber (Leiden: Brill, 2002), 99–111. The qualified reassurance offered by our present text, therefore, may be regarded as addressing a real source of anxiety.

46. Refer to the contributions of Mair cited above in note 4. The Indian background of Chinese picture recitation, together with much on its broad distribution, is studied at length in Mair's *Painting and Performance: Chinese Picture Recitation and Its Indian Genesis* (Honolulu: University of Hawai'i Press, 1988). See in particular 116–18 on picture recitation in Tibet.

47. Rolf A. Stein, *Recherches sur l'épopée et le barde au Tibet* (Paris: Presses Universitaires de France, 1959), 322–27.

48. *A stag lha mo*, in the series *Gling Ge sar sgrung gi byis pa'i rtsom rig dpe tshogs* (The children's literary collection of stories of Ling Gesar) (Beijing: Mi rigs dpe skrun khang, 1998).

49. Though it is of course possible that other Tibetan versions of the tale, such as that of Guru Chos dbang, played an intermediate role here.

50. Stein, *Recherches sur l'épopée et le barde*, 324.

51. The text has been published many times in recent years, and the comparison of its several editions remains a desideratum. In the present research I have referred to *Gling rje Ge sar rgyal po'i sgrung dmyal gling rdzogs pa chen po* (Chengdu: Si khron mi rigs dpe skrun khang, 1987) and Rig 'dzin Drag rtsal rdo rje, *Dmyal gling: The Legend of Ge-sar King of Gling's Conquest of Hell* (Thimphu: Damchoe, 1979), referred to respectively as Chengdu and Thimphu in the notes that follow. Other editions include vol. 19 of *The Epic of Gesar: 'Dzam gling Ge sar rgyal po'i rtogs brjod sna tshogs gtam gyi phreng ba*, 31 vols. (Thimphu: Kunsang Tobgyel, 1979–84), with Tibetan introduction by Lopon Pemala and English introduction by R. A. Stein; *Gling rje Ge sar rgyal po'i mdzad sgrungs las Dmyal ba'i le'u: An Episode from the Gesar Epic Cycle Recounting the King of Ling's Conquest of Hell* (New Thobgyal, H. P.: Monastic Centre, 1973); and *'Dzam gling Seng chen Nor bu dgra 'dul gyi rnam thar las Dmyal gling rdzogs pa chen po: The Dmyal Gling Episode of the Gesar Epic Recounting the Conquest of the Realm of the Dwellers of Hell* (Dehra Dun, U.P.: D. G. Khochen Tulku, 1977). Li-

brary of Congress listings for the last two attribute its authorship to 'Dan Bla ma Chos kyi dbang phyug. Stein, *Recherches sur l'épopée et le barde*, 54, shows that the same version of the episode formed part of the Gesar cycle as known at pre-1947 Rwa sgreng, and on p. 66 Stein mentions a Sde dge xylograph of the same. Note, too, that the possible connection of this episode with the tale of Mulian was first proposed, but left undeveloped, by Stein in the same work (45, 323). As his remarks here show, however, he was inclined to see this as an instance of a widespead shamanic motif; cf. note 33 above. Besides the *Dmyal gling rdzogs pa chen po*, other recensions of the episode that have been published in recent years include *Kha-gling and Dmyal-gling: Two Episodes from the Gesar Epic Cycle Recounting the King of Ling's Conquest of the Khache and of Hell* (New Delhi: B. Jamyang Norbu, 1971), and *'Dzam-gling Ge-sar rgyal po'i sgrung: Dmyal gling mun pa rang gsal* (Xining: Mtsho sngon mi rigs dpe skrun khang, 1997).

52. *Dmyal gling* (Chengdu), 351.

53. *Dmyal gling* (Chengdu), 142; *Dmyal gling* (Thimphu), 160–61. On the *'pho ba* rite, used to project the consciousness of the deceased swiftly into a favorable rebirth, see my "A Tibetan Festival of Rebirth Reborn: The 1992 Revival of the Drigung Powa Chenmo," in *Buddhism in Contemporary Tibet: Religious Revival and Cultural Identity*, ed. Melvyn Goldstein and Matthew Kapstein (Berkeley: University of California Press, 1998).

54. She may in fact be the apotheosis of a historical personnage, discussed in Miranda Shaw, *Passionate Enlightenment: Women in Tantric Buddhism* (Princeton, NJ: Princeton University Press, 1994), 117–25.

55. *Dmyal gling* (Chengdu), 144; *Dmyal gling* (Thimphu), 163.

56. Matthieu Ricard et al., trans., *The Life of Shabkar: The Autobiography of a Tibetan Yogin* (Albany: State University of New York Press, 1994), 200–3.

57. *Dmyal gling* (Chengdu), 146; *Dmyal gling* (Thimphu), 166.

58. *Dmyal gling* (Chengdu), 150–54; *Dmyal gling* (Thimphu), 170–77.

59. The phenomenon of the double as it occurs here merits further consideration. On the double as a widespread theme in Indian and Greek mythologies, see Wendy Doniger, *Splitting the Difference: Gender and Myth in Ancient Greece and India* (Chicago: University of Chicago Press, 1999).

60. *Dmyal gling* (Chengdu), 155–56; *Dmyal gling* (Thimphu), 179–80.

61. *Dmyal gling* (Chengdu), 156–57; *Dmyal gling* (Thimphu), 181–82.

62. The Tibetan here pleonastically supplies a Tibetan translation of the title together with the transcription from the Chinese. The representation of Chinese *wu*, "five," as *mgo* is common in Tibetan transcriptions of Middle Chinese and so supports the assumption that the translation of the *Transformation Text*, like the Tibetan *Yulanpen jing* and Chos grub's summary, was a work of the Tang period or very shortly thereafter.

63. This is of course the Marīcilokadhātu mentioned in the Abhi-

dharma (note 5 above). The account we find here thus in effect seeks to reconcile this with the *Transformation Text*.

64. From this point on, the exchange is rather elliptical and its meaning less than perfectly clear.

65. Sna nam btsun pa Skal bzang chos kyi rgya mtsho, *Sangs rgyas bcom ldan 'das kyi rnam par thar pa rmad du byung ba mdzad pa 'khrul pa med par brjod pa bde bar gshegs pa'i spyod pa mchog gi gter* [= *Sangs rgyas mdzad rnam*], Sde dge xylographic edition (Delhi: Tashi Dorje, 1973), fols. 114b–116b (= plates 228–32). A modern typeset edition is given in *Ston pa'i rnam thar chen mo* (Xining: Mtsho sngon mi rigs dpe skrun khang, 1994), 219–23.

12

Chinese Buddhist Death Ritual and the Transformation of Japanese Kinship

HANK GLASSMAN

WHILE THE HISTORY of the transformation of Japanese marriage and kinship practices over the course of the Heian (794–1185) and Kamakura (1185–1333) periods is well known, the role of Buddhist funerary and memorial ritual in the creation of this new model of the family has been largely overlooked. The great changes in burial practices that took place in Japan from the tenth through the fourteenth centuries reveal the sinification of Japanese kinship and gender beliefs.[1] In this article, I examine the role played by Chinese Buddhist notions about the postmortem life of families in fostering the patrilineal model of kinship ubiquitous in late medieval Japan. By looking at the attitudes members of the aristocratic and warrior classes held toward their dead, particularly toward their daughters, sisters, and mothers, we can begin to understand the deep influence that Buddhist rites exerted on the Japanese family.

Women in Japan were not always temporary members of the families of their birth. Once upon a time, women kept their family names after marriage, died as their fathers' daughters, and were buried among patrilineal relatives, their bones revered as ancestral relics by the children and grandchildren of their brothers. As we shall see, however, the period of most intense preoccupation with keeping daughters' bones "in the family" ironically marked the initial entrenchment of agnatic, or patrilineal, principles of descent in Japan. Buddhist funerals and rituals of the ancestral cult, as they were increasingly adopted by the aristocratic and warrior classes, provided a blueprint for this new household, which was built on the foundation of an exclusively male line. Of course, such influence is always a two-way street. As Mark Rowe's chapter in this volume reveals, changing attitudes toward family in contemporary Japan have caused many women to rethink the patterns of burial and memorialization. My argument, however, is that in the case of ancient and medieval Japan, it was Buddhist death ritual that shaped families and not the reverse. Let us begin, then, with a brief survey of the place of the female dead in the Japanese family over time.

A Synoptic History of the Japanese Family

Just one hundred years ago, the practice of posthumous divorce was common in many areas of Japan. This was a custom whereby the corpse of a wife who had committed suicide or who had failed to produce male children was sent back to her natal family.[2] This act signified a severing of ties with the dead woman and put responsibility for her funeral rites, burial, and memorial services back onto the family that had raised her. Barring extreme circumstances such as these, however, the physical and spiritual care required by the dead was, in the case of married women, undertaken by the children of those women and the families of their husbands. Of course, the idea that married women belong with their husbands and sons comes as no surprise. The data on burial and memorial practices gathered by Japanese folklorists early in the twentieth century reveal a great deal of regional variation, but the principle that wives should be buried with their husbands' families is nearly universal.[3]

This simple fact, that under the Japanese kinship system daughters leave their families to live and die among other people, constitutes a kind of common sense for folklorists, anthropologists, and students of gender, as well as for ordinary people in modern Japan. Yet this common sense masks a process of development, of change over time; it forgets older, now lost, ways of living in families. Carrying as it does the implication that things were "always thus," it also closes off avenues to the transformation of the current gender system. A central tenet of feminist history is that examination of the stages in the establishment of patriarchal systems is essential to the effort to dismantle them. What was created over time can also be undone.

My main concern in the following pages is to document the ways in which rituals of kinship—funerals, burials, memorial services, and the creation of genealogies—simultaneously reflect and create social structure. Studies of East Asian funerals and the ancestral cult have tended to view kinship rituals either as indexical to family relationships or, conversely, as a primary driving force behind the transformation of the family.[4] These two perspectives are not mutually contradictory; rather, they reflect the divergent disciplinary concerns of anthropology and social history respectively. While it is my purpose here to argue that death ritual and memorial practices propelled social change, I do not mean to imply that the converse was never the case. Certainly both are true; these ritual forms necessarily function as both cause and effect vis-à-vis kinship structure.

When the history of the Japanese family system is viewed over the *longue dureé*, a general trend from the tenth to the seventeenth century can be observed. Women were early on their fathers' daughters in life and in death, with full property rights and clan membership. Incrementally, they lost their patrimony and came to rely wholly on the families of their husbands. By the Tokugawa period (1603–1868), they were after marriage defined first as brides and later as mothers in the families of their husbands, retaining only a tenuous link to their natal homes. This being said, I rush to note the inadequacy of such a description to capture the great diversity occasioned by class, region, occupation, and other factors. Also, the process of change was not a straight and uninterrupted march to the establishment of the strictly patrilineal model familiar from early modern and modern Japan. Thus, it would be ridiculous to suggest that this process of social change was uncomplicated or that six centuries of history could be encapsulated in a sentence or two. Still, the clear trend toward seeing women as brides who marry out, and thus daughters as only temporary members of their birth families, was one that took shape over these centuries across boundaries of class and region. My aim is to delineate concepts of family membership rather than to make pronouncements on "women's status."[5] With this in mind, I shall provide just a few examples in reverse chronological order that serve to document the shift at various levels of society.

Above I have already mentioned the practice of posthumous divorce during the Tokugawa period. Under normal circumstances, the expectation was that a daughter would leave her family to become a wife and mother in a family with which she would come to be completely identified. At death she would join the family lineage as the consort of the father-cum-ancestor and genetrix of the present link in the patrilineal chain. Katō Mieko has shown that definitions underlying the jural status of women living in the rural villages of Ōmi Province underwent a transformation over the course of the Muromachi period (1392–1573). While in the fourteenth century married women participated in village guilds (*miyaza*) as the daughters of their fathers, by the sixteenth century, the basis of their inclusion was by virtue of their marriage to guild members.[6] Also, Sakada Satoshi has noted that among peasants in Tanba, the fifteenth century saw the end of property separately held by husbands and wives. In the same period, the custom of the wife taking her husband's family name became widespread in the region.[7]

Further back, it is well known that the period from the late Heian through the Kamakura was one of radical change in family structure for the aristocratic and warrior classes. Beginning with the pioneering work of Takamure Itsue, much research has been conducted using the Sino-Japanese (*kanbun*) diaries of male aristocrats, women's prose literature, and the legal documents of the day to trace the history of the Japanese family and the establishment of the *ie*, or patriarchal household system. While until recently the accepted theory was that the *ie* originated in the warrior houses of eastern Japan and spread with their cultural ascendancy, scholars now believe that the transformation began in the imperial house and among the Heian nobility at the close of the tenth century and was only later taken up by provincial warriors.[8] It is here that we can discern the defining role of Buddhist death ritual in this process.

Two central themes of the scholarship on women's history in premodern Japan have been marriage residence and women's control over property. This research reveals a trend away from a traditional system of uxorilocal residence beginning by the close of the Heian period.[9] Uxorilocal marriage, or *tsumadoi-kon*, refers to the arrangement by which married women continued to live with their natal families while their husbands either visited them there or moved in with them and the children. During the Kamakura period, the Japanese family moved away from this system and toward the practice of virilocal residence, in which wives came into their husbands' families as brides. Also, as we have seen, the rights of women to inherit and bestow property were progressively curtailed during the Kamakura period. By the fourteenth century, women were no longer considered permanent members of the house of their birth and so could hold no family property.[10]

Related to the changes occurring in marriage residence and inheritance rules during the late Heian and Kamakura periods, a great transformation was also taking place in the realm of burial practices. It is this subject of graves and the treatment of the dead that we will examine here in an attempt to gain some insight into the meaning of marriage among the aristocracy of the late Heian period. The primary focus of this investigation is the separate burial of husbands and wives of different clan origin. As we shall see, while some have interpreted the inclusion of married daughters in family grave sites as evidence of a lingering matrilineal tendency, others argue that it was this very phenomenon that heralded the birth of the strictly patrilineal and patriarchal *monryū* (house line) system of lineage.

The Separate Burial of Husbands and Wives

There is consensus in the research on the history of burial practices that at least during the eleventh and twelfth centuries, the bodies of married couples of different family origin were sent to separate sites for their final rest. Men and women alike were buried with their fathers' patrilineal family group. There is considerable debate over the significance of this fact, about what went on in earlier periods, and over what kinds of relatives constituted this patrilineal family group. However, the claim, first made by Takamure Itsue, that such couples were not buried together during the late Heian period, is widely accepted.[11] Here I would like to examine several specific cases of this phenomenon of separate burial and offer it as a third indicator, parallel to uxorilocal residence and inheritance by daughters, of women's status during this period as permanent members of their natal families. Indeed, the practice of separate burial is closely linked to these other two features of Heian-period kinship. As we shall see, the development and demise of this custom over a period of two centuries marks the emergence of a new concept of family in Japan, a rethinking of the category of kin. In this new, continental style of imagining the natural family, women became increasingly aligned with their husbands' families and thus came to be ever more narrowly defined as mothers. Motherhood was the mechanism by which they gained membership in these families.

The most famous *shiryō*, or datum, revealing the separate burial of husbands and wives from different clans is the case of Reishi, found in the diary of the courtier Fujiwara no Munetada (1062–

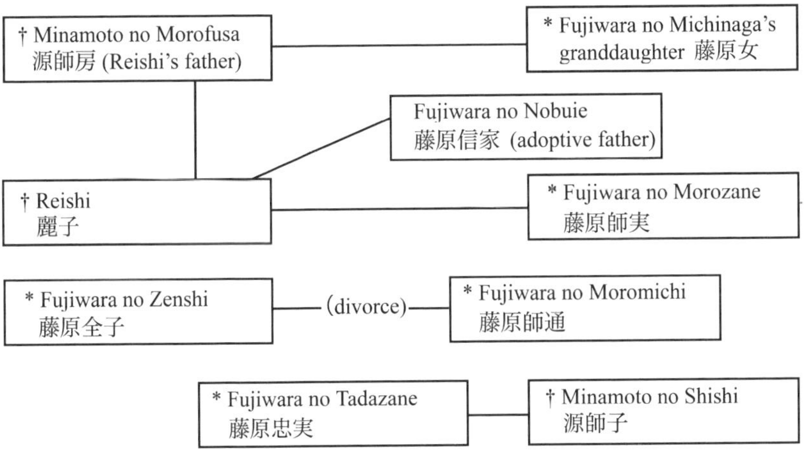

FIGURE 12.1. A chart of marriages among Reishi's close relatives—the separate burial of husbands and wives in unions between Midō line Fujiwara and Murakami Genji (Minamoto) during the eleventh and twelfth centuries. Those marked with an asterisk (*) were buried at Kohota (木幡); those with a dagger (†) were buried at Kita Shirakawa (北白川).

1141), the *Chūyūki* (see figure 12.1).[12] Reishi was the daughter of Minamoto no Morofusa (1008–77) but was adopted at an early age by Fujiwara no Nobuie, was raised at his home, and used the clan name Fujiwara. She came to marry Fujiwara no Morozane, and their son was Moromichi. The entry in the *Chūyūki* concerning Reishi's burial in 1114 states that although she had spent her whole life among Fujiwara clan members and was known as a Fujiwara, her remains were not to be placed at Mt. Kohata in Uji, the ancestral burial ground of the Midō line Fujiwara. Since her father had been of the Murakami Genji, her bones were sent instead to that family's graveyard at Kita Shirakawa. This is a very clear instance of separate burial for a husband and wife of different clan origin. There are numerous examples of this phenomenon throughout the eleventh and twelfth centuries.[13] For the purposes of this illustration, however, let it suffice to note just three more couples from Reishi's immediate family. Each of these cases serves as evidence that during this period, the dead were buried with the members of their fathers' patrilineal family group, regardless of their sex or marital status. Although the examples provided here are described in terms of "couples," polygyny made the actual situation considerably more complex.[14] However, that fact does not affect the meaning of separate burial: women remained members of their fathers' clans after marriage and after death. Whether a woman was a principal wife, a secondary one, or had a more casual tie to a certain man, it did not affect the fact that her bones would in almost every case be placed with those of her father's family.

The grandson of Reishi and Morozane, Fujiwara no Tadazane (1078–1162), married a relative of his mother's, a Murakami Genji, Minamoto no Shishi. These two were buried at Kohata and Kita Shirakawa respectively, as Morozane and Reishi had been. The pattern can also be observed in another case in which the two families are the same but the sexes of the couple are reversed. One of the wives of Reishi's father (Minamoto no Morofusa) was a granddaughter of Fujiwara no Michinaga (966–1027), the most powerful courtier of his day. She was buried at Kohata with her Fujiwara relatives, while Morofusa's bones were sent to Kita Shirakawa. A final example is that of Reishi and Morozane's son, Fujiwara no Moromichi, and his wife, Fujiwara no Zenshi. Moromichi and Zenshi lived with her father, Fujiwara no Toshiie, but they did not get along and were formally divorced shortly after Toshiie's death. After the divorce, Moromichi moved out of Zenshi's home.[15] He later remarried and died in 1099 at the age of thirty-eight. His former wife, Zenshi, died half a century later in 1150 at the age of ninety-one. Her bones were sent to Mt. Kohata in Uji, where Moromichi had been buried. As Kurihara Hiromu points out, within the *ie* system of later periods, it would have been inconceivable that a divorced couple could be buried in the same graveyard.[16] If, for argument's sake, Moromichi had outlived Zenshi and borne her some ill will, he could not have prevented her bones from coming to Kohata, since the propriety of her burial there derived from her relationship to her Fujiwara father, not from her marriage to Moromichi. The determining factor in the place of interment during this period was membership in a patrilineal family group. The dead of either sex were generally buried at the same site as their fathers. Daughters remained members of their natal families after marriage and after death.

Matrilateral Burial: Women as Ancestors

Echoing Takamure's theory that Japan had once been a matrilineal society, Tanaka Hisao has suggested that in earlier periods, until the end of the ninth century, men were customarily buried either matrilocally or uxorilocally.[17] That is, they were buried either with their mothers' families or with the family of one of their wives. This claim is certainly a surprising one in light of the later development of Japanese kinship structure and the fundamental norms of Buddhist/Confucian ancestor worship as it came to be practiced throughout East Asia. According to Tanaka, women were almost invariably buried with their mothers' families. Fukutō Sanae has challenged Tanaka's view and offers many counter-examples. Fukutō's assertion is that there were not, in fact, any strong convictions about burial place vis-à-vis kinship affiliation during this period before the tenth century and that husbands and their main wives were typically buried together at the family graveyard of the first member of the couple to die.[18] Both scholars agree, however, that a great change took place over the course of the tenth century and that there arose a new sensitivity to the relationship between kinship alliances and the burial site. However one interprets the data, the fact remains that until this time, the dead of both sexes were in many instances buried with their in-laws or with their mothers' families, contrary to the practice of later periods. It was at this juncture that Chinese norms regarding kinship began actively to shape Japanese society through Buddhist death ritual. Only during the tenth and eleventh centuries did a system of burial based on patrilineal principles begin to develop. The adoption of Buddhist death ritual by the elites was determinative for the future of Japanese kinship beliefs.

Historians of the family agree that the eleventh and twelfth centuries saw the establishment of a patriarchal family system in Japan.[19] As we shall see below, the practice of establishing temples attached to family graveyards (known as *hakadera* or *bodaisho*) that began in the early eleventh century escalated in the twelfth, with an increasing demarcation of lines of descent within clans. The twelfth and thirteenth centuries saw the proliferation of new "clan temples," or *ujidera*, corresponding to the creation of newly arising branch lineages. This subdivision of clans or "houses" within clans into distinct families (*monryū*, *ichimon*) came to depend in large part upon the dedication of such an institution.[20] As indicated above, it was a practice begun by the aristocrats of the Heian capital and later enthusiastically adopted by the great warrior families.

It was by founding a temple in honor of a parent that a man established his family of descendants—and, by extension, his immediate living family—as a corporate entity distinct from others within the larger clan. Nishiguchi Junko has noted that it was common for men to use the burial and memorialization of their mothers as the occasion for founding an *ujidera* and thus a new lineage.[21] Often the last residence of the mother, used during her retirement as a nun, became the *ujidera* temple building. It is important to note, however, that in the twelfth-century cases that Nishiguchi cites, both mother and son are Fujiwara clan members, and the temples involved are located at Kohata in Uji. This is important because if the mother were not a Fujiwara, she would properly take her final rest with her father's clan, not at the complex of temples and graveyards that by now thrived atop Mt. Kohata. To be of use to a son trying to found a new Fujiwara lineage in this way, a mother would have to be eligible for burial on Mt. Kohata. A particularly instructive case in this regard is that of Fujiwara no Munetada, author of the famous diary *Chūyūki* cited above in the discussion of Fujiwara no Reishi's relatives.[22]

Fujiwara no Munetada was able to coopt the family temple of his mother's Hino line and make it the *ujidera* for a new line, of which he was to become the apical ancestor. This temple was the Kannondō of Hōkaiji on Mt. Kohata, established as the *ujidera* of the Hino line Fujiwara in the 1080s by his maternal grandfather, Sanetsuna. Munetada's mother had died when he was a child; he was lavish in his support of her family temple and commissioned the construction of several buildings to mark the anniversaries of her death. He also had his beloved foster mother buried there, as well as his daughter. After his death, his funeral and memorial services were held there, and it became the temple responsible for the postmortem rites of his descendants.

So, then, during the late Heian period, men and women alike were generally buried with their fathers' kin, regardless of the family origin of their spouse. This was a practice that arose sometime after the beginning of the tenth century, marking a new emphasis on agnatic lines of descent, and by the fourteenth century, women were customarily buried with their husbands' families. The influence of Chinese Buddhist notions concerning the proper disposal and postmortem care of the dead is unmistakable here. It can be discerned in two central aspects of this transformation: (1) a new attitude toward physical remains; and (2) the development of the practice of visiting graves at regular intervals, or *hakamairi*.

The Sacralization of Bones and the Development of Maintained Graves

The new consciousness of lineage and descent that began to manifest itself in Japan from the tenth century can be witnessed in the changing conventions surrounding the burial and memorialization of the dead. As can be observed in the foregoing discussion of burial location, it was only from this time that people began to express strongly held convictions about the location of the burial place. The siting of graves became an explicit statement of family membership and allegiance. Two innovations in mortuary ritual that drove the reformulation and restructuring of the Japanese kinship system first appear in the eleventh and twelfth centuries: the practice of venerating bones and the closely related custom of graveside worship. The introduction of Chinese Buddhist ideas about the postmortem lives of families had ramifications for many generations of men and women to come. An important part of this story is the treatment of the corpse.

Bones, which had formerly been discarded, became the focus of the memorialization of the dead in the late Heian period.[23] The eleventh and the twelfth centuries saw ever-mounting attention to the preservation of bones, their enshrinement (*nōkotsu*), and their veneration (*saishi*). The bones of ancestors became the objects of cult, whereas before then, in the tenth and the early eleventh centuries, the bones of the dead were often pulverized and scattered over the capital's rivers, the Kamo or the Shirakawa, or simply discarded at family graveyards with no monument. Interestingly, the practice called "secondary burial" in the anthropological literature—that is, the collection of bones after they are rid of flesh—was not uncommon. However, whether the bones were taken from the *tamadono*, a structure where the dead were kept temporarily for a period of months or years, or obtained through cremation, they were not preserved.[24] Second burial represented a final disposal of the last remnants of the corpse, not an enshrinement of the bones for purposes of veneration.

The highly endogamous Heian-period aristocracy made no attempt to save the bones after the flesh had rotted away or been burned away by cremation. For them, it was important to dispose of all remains, both flesh and bone. Anthropologists Maurice Bloch and Jonathan Parry have suggested that those who emphasize the distinction between kin and affines are more likely to try to rid the bones of flesh and then make these bones the object of the ancestral cult. In such societies, say Bloch and Parry, "the final triumph over death is also a triumph over the necessity for affines and over the world of sexual reproduction they represent."[25]

In Japan, a new attitude toward bones was inextricably tied to Buddhist notions of kinship and lineage, both real and fictive. We can find the impetus for the initial shift in attitude toward bones in the great attention paid to the proper veneration of the bones of dead masters such as Enchin (814–91) and Ryōgen (912–85).[26] In these cases, the bones are relics, free of any affinal taint. In Japan, before Buddhism, burial had been a family affair. It is essential to note here the ancient taboo, native to Japan, against handling corpses or bones as polluted and polluting substances. People who dressed and buried the corpse would take upon themselves a state of *kegare*, spiritual uncleanness. Thus it was that prior to the tenth century, only family members would be willing to handle a corpse; the dead without immediate family, whatever their station in life, would simply be left where they lay to decompose or become food for dogs and birds. Genshin (942–1017) and the other monks who were members of the famous Nijūgo Zanmai-e, the funeral confraternity based at the Yokawa precinct of the great Tendai monastery on Mt. Hiei, explicitly noted that they were departing from this model by undertaking the burial and memorialization of fellow practitioners not related by blood.[27]

Under the influence first of the *sanmaisō* (funerary priests) of Mt. Hiei and the *Amida hijiri* (wandering Pure Land preachers) of Mt. Kōya and later of Zen and Ritsu priests, the bones of the family dead became the focus of religious practice among the common people in Japan. The Zen and Ritsu sects imported the monastic funerals of Song China and made them available to everyone in Japan as a means of assuring salvation after death and freedom from suffering in the three evil realms of rebirth as animals, hungry ghosts, or hell dwellers.[28] By the late medieval period, deathbed ordination or postmortem ordination had become the norm. In fact, to this day, all the Buddhist dead in Japan are monks and nuns. It is possible to view this change in the treatment of the bones of the dead as a product of their monasticization—that is, as the dead became clergy, their bones became relics.[29] One material outgrowth of the transformation of the status of bones was their permanent enshrinement. Graves, marked by stone monuments such as *sotoba* (*gorintō* or *hōkyōintō*), soon came to be visited and maintained by survivors and descendants.[30]

The custom of regular grave visits did not exist in Japan before the eleventh century. This Buddhist custom, known as *hakamairi* in Japanese, played an important part in redefining the Japanese family. Tanaka Hisao sees the founding of Jōmyōji at Kohata by the Fujiwara clan head Michinaga as the pivotal event in the history of *hakamairi* in Japan. It is here in the early eleventh century that we first see an explicit linking of a Buddhist institution to the care of the graves of a particular family's ancestors. By 1120 we read in the *Chūyūki* of grave attendants called *yamamori*, and in 1167, Taira no Nobunori is given a guided tour of the graves of illustrious dead of the Fujiwara clan at Kohata. He is shown these monuments by a man with the title *hakamori*, "grave keeper."[31]

All this stands in marked contrast to the earlier image of Mt. Kohata seen in a description in the historical tale *Eiga monogatari*. It tells of Fujiwara no Korechika's visit there in 996 to announce his exile before his father Michitaka's grave.[32] Korechika has trouble locating it in the undergrowth, although the moon is shining brightly and the grave is only one year old, so that, as he remarks, "the wood should still look new." The use of wooden grave markers testifies to the fact that the location of the grave was forgotten within one generation, if not sooner. For a grave to be lost among shrubs and weeds after just one year would have been unthinkable in later periods, and a son would know the site well, having visited it on several occasions for graveside ceremonies during that first year of mourning.

Kohata is described as follows in the *ganmon*, or dedicatory text, that Michinaga commissioned for the occasion of the founding of Jōmyōji:

> The old burial mounds are heaped one atop the other in the eerie desolation of the place. One sees no Buddhist ceremonies, only the spring flowers and the autumn moon. One hears no sutras chanted, only the cries of the birds in the valley and the chattering of the monkeys on the peak.[33]

Until the middle of the eleventh century or so, it was only under special circumstances that graves were visited, and the exact place of burial was forgotten after one generation. Michinaga's sentiment embodies the emerging expectation that somehow it should be otherwise. In a similar vein, the *Ōkagami*, another historical narrative, relates the story of Michinaga's boyhood aspiration to build a *sanmaidō*, or mortuary temple, on Mt. Kohata:

> People say Michinaga conceived the plan for the Jōmyōji when he went along on the visit of thanks Kaneie made to Kohata after he became a minister of state. "What a shame that no holy bells ring in a place where so many of our ancestors' bones lie," his Lordship thought, looking about him. "I shall make it my business to erect a Samādhi Hall if I have a successful career."[34]

Graveyards had been deserted and lonely places and were known as such, yet Michinaga feels that there is something inappropriate in this. Here, at the beginning of the eleventh century, we find no evidence of such resident grave tenders as the *yamamori* or the *hakamori* mentioned in twelfth-century sources.

With the calendarization of *hakamairi* in later periods and the development of more permanent stone markers for graves, the site of burial became a site of worship. The place of interment became a place to define the family group and strengthen the bonds of kinship. Both of these phenomena, the preservation of bones and the development of maintained, regularly visited graves, can be viewed as indicators of the sinification of the Japanese kinship practices that took place through the medium of Buddhist death ritual and memorial practice.[35] Chinese ritual encoded a new language of kinship and gender that was to forever change the Japanese family.

The data examined above support Bloch and Parry's hypothesis that the treatment of the corpse can serve as an index to kinship practices.[36] The innovations in mortuary ritual undertaken during the late Heian period—the separate burial of husband and wife, the preservation of bones, and the establishment of a calendar of regular grave visits—were intimately entwined with a newly arising consciousness. In this new way of conceiving of family, agnatic or patrilineal relationships took increasing precedence over affinal ones in defining kin.[37] It was largely over the course of the Kamakura period that women moved from one side of this line of demarcation to the other. Under the influence of Chinese Buddhist death ritual, they had gone from being daughters in their mothers' houses at the beginning of the Heian period to taking their final rest among the dead of their fathers' families at the end of the Heian period. During the Kamakura period, they began to be identified, as wives and mothers, with the family into which they had married rather than the family of their birth. By the end of the Muromachi period, married women lived and died among their husbands' people.[38]

Ancestor worship entered Japan as an imported commodity.[39] It was only with the sinification of the Nara period that names began to be inherited exclusively from the patriline; one finds many instances during this period of men being criticized for "mistakenly" using their mothers' family names. Contrary to the common view—largely the scholarly legacy of Yanagida Kunio—Tanaka Hisao argues that prior to the extensive influence of Buddhism, there was no strong sense of a continuous line of ancestors reaching back to a founding figure. As Tanaka puts it, "Ancestor consciousness in Japan was extremely weak. Only with the importation of the concept of lineage from the Korean peninsula does the history of ancestor worship begin."[40] At first, it was only among the *kikajin*, descendants of Chinese and Korean immigrants, that such a notion existed. Following the example of such clans and under the influence of the Nara-period enthusiasm for things Chinese, awareness of an agnatic line of ancestors developed. This was especially true for members of the highly sinified Fujiwara family.

The Meaning of Separate Burial

The developments of the late Heian period—separate burial for married couples, enshrinement of bones, and *hakamairi*—are inextricably tied to an emerging concept of the family dead as members of an agnatic lineage of ancestors. The context for these social developments was an intensification of lineage consciousness and the consolidation of family groups and subgroups based upon agnatic principles. Peter Nickerson has argued that the institution of uxorilocal residence "crosscut" patrilineal descent during the Heian period to form a fairly stable bilineal system in which competition between agnates was tempered by cooperation with affines.[41] The late Heian period was, however, clearly one of transition for Japanese kinship, and any stability that had existed in the bilineal system was quickly faltering. Nickerson's observations underline the importance of keeping daughters within the patrilineal group at this time of change. The idea that a daughter should stay with her father came to apply to final resting place as it had to marriage residence. The burial of women with their fathers' families does not thus imply a lingering matrilineal tendency but, on the contrary, reveals the victory of agnatic principles over cognatic ones.

Fukutō Sanae has linked the burial of women with their fathers' families and the development of *hakamairi* with the establishment of a patriarchal system in Japan. In this she disagrees with Takamure's suggestion, echoed by Kurihara Hiromu, that the burial of daughters alongside the family dead is evidence of a pre-patriarchal, matrilineal "*uji* system."[42] She argues that by the beginning of the tenth century, the system whereby family was defined primarily by succession from father to son, the *monryū*, was already in place.

Takamure and Kurihara suggest that the burial of women with their fathers is the last vestige of an ancient matrilineal kinship system; in contrast, Fukutō argues that the insistence of fathers and brothers that the bodily remains of daughters and sisters stay with the family represents the triumph of a patrilineal view of family. I would like to suggest that during this transitional phase, it means both. The burial of daughters with their fathers represents the continuing indispensability of women in the avuncular politics of the late Heian period. This political style, still firmly in place during the Kamakura period, in which daughters were through their children the key to family power, does demonstrate a lingering tendency for maternal grandfathers to have great influence over their daughters' children. At the same time, the emphasis on succession from father to son—or, as was often the case, from father to son's son—which gained ascendancy as the basic unit of family in Japan passed from *uji* to *ie* to *ichimon* clearly represents a new enthusiasm for strict patrilineal principles. Fukutō demonstrates that the burial of daughters with their fathers is a product of the *monryū* or *ichimon* model of kinship. It is the tenet of unigeniture embedded in this system that, from this time on, begins to squeeze daughters and non-inheriting sons out of the patrimony.[43] The daughters become the responsibility of their husbands' families, and the sons go on to found new branch lineages. Below, an examination of the relationship between women and property will serve to clarify the former point, that women came to be defined as jural members of their husbands' families. The rise of connubial burial and the proliferation of genealogical charts in the thirteenth and fourteenth centuries serve to illustrate the phenomenon of agnatic splintering.[44]

The process of women's loss of authority in official family matters is dramatically illustrated by the history of women's inheritance patterns in the twelfth and thirteenth centuries. As mentioned at the beginning of this chapter, throughout the Heian period, women had control over their own property, including the freedom to create wills. From the beginning of the Kamakura period, however, women began receiving lifetime use of such holdings, with their heirs stipulated in advance. At the beginning of this period, the majority of women holding such lifetime tenures, or *ichigo*, were widows who had the right to manage their husbands' estates in trust until the succession of a new family head. However, as we have seen, in the later years of the Kamakura period, such measures were taken in bestowing property on daughters, lest they alienate family property to "outsiders."[45] In either case, we can observe an increasing ambivalence over the proper place of women in the kinship system, as well as a deepening dependence of these women upon the benevolence of male relatives, whether agnates or affines.

Not only did Buddhism shape Japanese kinship by dictating new ways of treating the dead, but also new roles were written for surviving family members. As Katsuura Noriko has indicated, during the late Heian period, it became increasingly common for a married woman to become a nun around the time of the forty-ninth-day anniversary of her husband's death. Eventually this became customary. The trend culminated in the fairly rigid medieval image of the widow as a nun who has renounced the world to devote herself to prayers for her late husband's salvation.[46] The widows of the Kamakura period very often became nuns. These *goke-ama*, or widow-nuns, are omnipresent figures in the legal documents of the day, particularly in those cases involving inheritance disputes. Widows were often charged by their children or stepchildren with having altered their husbands' wills or of having taken up a sexual relationship with a man.[47] Taking the tonsure served two purposes (aside from the obvious religious ones) for the widows of the Kamakura period. First of all, it may have helped them avoid a certain degree of scrutiny regarding their sex lives. As the documents show, however, it by no means made them immune to such charges. The act of becoming a nun was in part a symbol that a woman remained bound to her late husband and to the interests of his family. But also—and this is an extremely important point—it marked her status as his primary mourner.

Documents such as wills were not always the sole criteria for determining eligibility for inheritance. The performance of funeral rites and memorial services could be invoked to substantiate or dispute the legitimacy of an inheritance claim.[48] As her husband's principal mourner, a woman strengthened her position vis-à-vis his family property. In her role as mother, she acted as trustee for the inheriting children.[49] As the custodian of her husband's memory and testament, she began to identify herself fully as a member of the family into which she had married, rather than as a member of the family of her birth. This sea change in the family system represents the beginning of the end for women's property rights.

Minegishi Sumio cites a thirteenth-century case in which a man adopted his daughter's son and set him up as his main heir. This case illustrates that although bilineal inheritance was still possible, women were now excluded from the chain of property transmission. Minegishi takes this as evidence that the family system of the warrior class was by this time operating on patriarchal principles of unigeniture with regard to the power of the inheriting son (*chakunan*) to control family property.[50] One aspect of this deepening of the agnatic and patriarchal tendencies that had begun around the tenth century was that a woman eventually became bound to her husband's lineage in life and in death. Of course, this ligature was made firm through the birth of sons.

By the beginning of the thirteenth century, it was not uncommon for wives to be buried alongside their husbands and sons, regardless of their own clan origin.[51] A little more than a hundred years later, it had become the norm. This can be observed in the fourteenth-century diary of Nakahara Moromori; the diary documents the funerals and memorial services performed by Moromori and his brother Moroshige. Here we find that Moromori placed his wife's bones in a grave that already contained his mother's, indicating that these two generations of Nakahara family wives had been buried at a temple belonging to the family of their husbands, a family to which they had contributed sons.[52] While they seem to have been buried with their husbands, the funeral and memorial services for female family members were conducted at a different place than those of the men, foreshadowing the separate funerary temples for men and women known in later periods.[53] This is testimony to the very different positions of men and women in the family, here reflected in the Buddhist cult of ancestors.

During the late Heian period, women's natal relatives performed their funerals, and daughters were buried with their fathers. As long as women continued to hold property and inheritance rights in a system that was becoming increasingly patrilineal, men found it necessary to exert control over the bones of their daughters and their sisters in order to protect agnatic interests. Nishiguchi Junko has suggested that—because during this period the fortunes of families depended in large part upon their daughters' marriage connections and it was women who brought the promise of prosperity to a family—it was natural that families would insist upon keeping the graves of their women close at hand.[54] This is most obviously true in the case of the Fujiwara family. The burial of Fujiwara daughters—daughters who quite often were imperial consorts, mothers, and wet-nurses—at Kohata served to emphasize the connection of these women to their brothers, uncles, and fathers. As we saw above, in his dedication of Jōmyōji, the graveyard temple of Kohata, Michinaga explicitly referred to the fact that the imperial mothers had caused his line to flourish.

The diary *Shōyūki* records an incident of the early eleventh century in which a Minamoto clansman suggests that the bones of Fujiwara no Junshi, a consort of Emperor En'yū (r. 969–84) who had borne no children, might be made into powder and discarded following the recent example of an imperial prince. This Minamoto elder argues that there is really no need to deposit her remains at Kohata. He is rebuffed by the woman's uncle, Fujiwara no Sanesuke, who insists that the prosperity of the Fujiwara still rests upon the imperial mothers and that, for this reason, Junshi must certainly be interred at Kohata.[55] Geomantic beliefs adopted from China held that the proper placement of bones was essential to the prosperity of the family.[56] It is fascinating that the bones of this Fujiwara daughter who bore no children were accorded the geomantic significance of ancestral remains. In China, these beliefs concerned the bones of male ancestors, but in Japan in the tenth and eleventh centuries, women's bones were included. Indeed, the graves of the imperial consorts and imperial mothers at Kohata were more important to family fortunes than were men's graves. Such a perception of the burial place of women's bones was not limited to the Fujiwara family, however. Nakahara Moromoto, in his work *Chūgaisho*, records events of the 1050s, some hundred years earlier, and discusses the burial place of Michinaga's wife Rinshi, a daughter of Minamoto no Masanobu:

> Now that was the site of the funeral of Takatsukasa-den [i.e., Rinshi]. The grave, however, is the place where the bones are kept; it is a place to be deeply revered. Such is not true of the funeral ground. When the bones of the ancestors are placed at their final resting place, they cause future generations of descendants to flourish. Thus the bones of Takatsukasa-den were placed with those of her father Masanobu Daijin for the sake of future prosperity.[57]

During the eleventh and twelfth centuries, the bones of women were seen as the property of the agnatic line of their fathers. It is clear from the two examples above that daughters of the clan were included as ancestors in this lineage. The descendants who are intended to flourish by virtue of Rinshi's interment at the family burial ground at Hōrinji to the north of Ninnaji are not her own children and grandchildren, but rather her nieces and nephews and the sons and daughters of her nephews. Thus, in the late Heian period, daughters were seen as ancestors and regarded as permanent members of their natal families.

Ironically, this appropriation of women's remains by their uncles and fathers and brothers was to be the first step in a process that would eventually make their bodies the property of their husbands' families in life as in death. These bodies that became identified with the husbands' families were by definition maternal bodies. It was the birth of sons that gave a woman a rightful place in the lineage she had provisionally joined at marriage. As we saw at the beginning of this exploration, in later times, the corpse of a woman would be returned to her family only if she were found to be somehow defective. If she were to commit suicide or fail to produce children, for instance, her body would be sent back in a state of disgrace to the family of her birth.

It was only as a wife and mother that a woman could properly find redemption in the Buddhist cult of the ancestors within the family system of the Tokugawa period. Let it be noted that this was not the result of an abrupt imposition of Confucian family ideology by the Shogunate, as some have suggested.[58] While it is true that the Tokugawa government was able to use Buddhist temples to enforce strict adherence to a Chinese model of family, the essential shift in the sex and gender system in Japan took place centuries before, as I have argued above. This change was precipitated by the introduction and adoption of Buddhist death ritual.

The separate burial of husbands and wives in eleventh- and twelfth-century Japan had marked the beginning of a new way of looking at family. A newly emerging lineage consciousness is evident in the developing ideology surrounding burial practice. This agnatic ideology itself came in turn to have a profound effect on the jural status, property rights, and sexual identity of women over the course of the next six centuries. Also, the soteriological status of women shifted with their family membership. A woman's place in the family was now defined as that of outsider, and her blood became dangerous. It could be argued that it was in part the discovery of agnatic kinship reckoning and its logical unfolding through the medieval period that would eventually enable the complete subjugation of women to the families of their husbands during the Tokugawa period. Thus, in a certain sense, women's increasing disempowerment within the family over the course of the medieval period was directly linked to their glorification as mothers. This transformation of the family and of the place of women in the family was sparked by continental ideas of lineage and ancestorhood and supported by the dissemination of Chinese-style Buddhist mortuary ritual throughout the medieval period.

Notes

1. Jane Collier and Sylvia Yanagisako have argued that gender and kinship are mutually constituted fields of inquiry. They are as a single aspect of human experience, inextricably entangled. See Jane Fishburne Collier and Sylvia Junko Yanagisako, "Toward a Unified Analysis of Gender and Kinship," in *Gender and Kinship: Essays Toward a Unified Analysis*, ed. Collier and Yanagisako (Stanford, CA: Stanford University Press, 1987), 14–52.

2. Emori Itsuo, *Kazoku no rekishi minzokugaku: Higashi Ajia to Nihon* (Tokyo: Kōbundō, 1990), 59–65. See also Amano Takeshi, "Shigo no rikon," *Hikaku kazokushi kenkyū*, no. 1 (1986): 100.

3. An exception to this rule is the long-standing practice of adopting a son-in-law as a *muko yōshi*. This was done, and often still is, in families lacking a suitable male heir. However, it should be noted that in the case of son-in-law adoption, a man adopts his wife's family name, and his wife essentially becomes a "bride" in her own home.

4. For the former view, that kinship ritual mirrors social structure, see James Watson, "The Structure of Chinese Funerary Rites," in *Death Ritual in Late Imperial China*, ed. James Watson and Evelyn Rawski (Berkeley: University of California Press, 1988), 3–19. For an example of the latter idea, that kinship ritual can recreate social structure, see Martina Deuchler, *The Confucian Transformation of Korean Society* (Cambridge, MA: Harvard University Press, 1992), 231–81. See also Deuchler's "Neo-Confucianism in Action: Agnation and Ancestor Worship in Early Yi Korea," in *Religion and Ritual in Korean Society*, ed. Laurel Kendall and Griffin Dix (Berkeley: Institute of East Asian Studies, 1987), 26–55, and Mark Peterson, *Korean Adoption and Inheritance: Case Studies in the Creation of a Classic Confucian Society* (Ithaca, NY: East Asia Program, Cornell University, 1996).

5. On the pitfalls of a focus on women's status, see Marilyn Katz, "Ideology and 'the Status of Women' in Ancient Greece," in *Women in Antiquity: New Assessments*, ed. Richard Hawley and Barbara Levick (London and New York: Routledge, 1995), 21–43.

6. Katō Mieko, "Musume no za kara, nyobō no za e," in *Bosei o tou*, ed. Wakita Haruko (Kyoto: Jinbun Shoin, 1985), 204–27.

7. Sakada Satoshi, "Chūsei goki hyakushō no myōji, ie, ie ketsugō," in *Kazoku to josei no rekishi*, ed. Zenkindai Joseishi Kenkyūkai (Sekiguchi Hiroko et al.) (Tokyo: Yoshikawa Kōbundō, 1989), 228–50. On the relationship between the history of women's surnames and female control over family property, see Herbert Plutschow, *Japan's Name Culture* (Folkestone, England: Japan Library, 1995), 181–89.

8. Akashi Kazuki, "Kamakura bushi no ie: Fukei shūdan kara tandokuteki 'ie' e," in *Onna to otoko no jiku: Nihon joseishi saikō*, vol. 2, ed. Kano Nobuko and Itō Seiko (Tokyo: Fujiwara Shoten, 1996), 222–65.

9. On marriage residence in the Heian period, in English, see William McCullough, "Japanese Marriage Institutions in the Heian Period," *Harvard Journal of Asiatic Studies* 27 (1967): 103–67; Peter Nickerson, "The Meaning of Matrilocality: Kinship, Property and Politics in Mid-Heian," *Monumenta Nipponica* 48, no. 4 (Winter 1993): 429–67; and Nishimura Hiroko, "The Family, Communal Ties, and Women in Ancient Times," in *Historical Studies in Japan (VII), 1983–1987*, ed. National Committee of Japanese Historians (Leiden: Brill, 1990), 161–88. On the inheritance rights of women, see Jeffrey Mass, *Lordship and Inheritance in Early Medieval Japan: A Study of the Kamakura Sōryō System* (Stanford, CA: Stanford University Press, 1989); Hitomi Tonomura, "Women and Inheritance in Japan's Early War-

rior Society," *Comparative Studies in Society and History* 32 (1990): 592–623; and Wakita Haruko, "Marriage and Property in Premodern Japan from the Perspective of Women's History," *Journal of Japanese Studies* 10, no. 1 (1994): 73–99.

10. Wakita, "Marriage and Property," 91.

11. Takamure Itsue, "Fūfu no haka," in *Chōseikon no kenkyū* 2, *Takamure Itsue zenshū*, vol. 3 (Tokyo: Rironsha, 1966), 771–76. Takamure's point is developed in detail by Kurihara Hiromu, "Heian chūki no nyūbo kitei to kazoku soshiki," in *Kyoto chiikishi no kenkyū*, ed. Akiyama Kunizō Sensei Tsuitōkai (Tokyo: Kokusho Kankōkai, 1979), 41–66, and further by Fukutō Sanae, "Bochi saishi to josei," in *Shinjin to kuyō*, ed. Ōsumi Kazuo and Nishiguchi Junko (Tokyo: Heibonsha 1989), 81–110.

12. *Chūyūki* (Eikyū 2 [1114], 4/22), in *Shiryō taisei* (Kyoto: Rinsen Shoten, 1965), 12:298. This entry is noted in virtually every secondary source alluding to the practice. This woman's burial place is also mentioned in an entry in the *Heihanki* (Kyūju 2 [1155], 5/10), *Zōho shiryō taisei* 18:315.

13. Kurihara, "Heian chūki no nyūbo kitei to kazoku soshiki," 63–65, appends a chart detailing family and burial place for thirty-nine individuals.

14. See Nishimura Hiroko, *Kodai, chūsei no kazoku to josei* (Tokyo: Yoshikawa Kōbunkan, 2002), 261–66.

15. As noted above, the Heian aristocracy practiced uxorilocal marital residence, and women enjoyed full rights over inheritance, especially over the inheritance of real property in the form of houses. A divorce or the loss of a husband through death or estrangement was not likely to have an adverse effect on a woman's immediate living situation or economic prospects.

16. Kurihara, "Heian chūki no nyūbo kitei to kazoku soshiki," 61.

17. Tanaka Hisao, "Bunken ni arawareta bochi: Heian jidai no Kyōto o chūshin to shite," in *Bochi*, ed. Mori Kōichi (Tokyo: Shakai Shisōsha, 1975), 98. Takamure had also made a similar assertion, stating that prior to the Taika Reform of 645, people were buried with their mother's family ("Fūfu no haka," 771). For an introduction to Takamure's theory of matrilineal descent in ancient Japan and its scholarly reception, see Kurihara Hiromu, *Takamure Itsue no kon'in joseishi-zō no kenkyū* (Tokyo: Takana Shoten, 1994), esp. chap. 4, "*Chōseikon no kenkyū* o chūshin to shita kenkyūshi," 129–68. See also Nickerson, "The Meaning of Matrilocality," 436–44, for an interesting discussion of the possibility of matrilineal descent (as suggested by the inheritance of residences by daughters from their mothers) during the mid-Heian period.

18. Fukutō, "Bochi saishi to josei," 83–88. A tenth-century version of the biography of Prince Shōtoku contained in the *Sanbōe* has Shōtoku remarking lovingly to his consort, a woman of the Kashiwade clan, "When I

die, you and I shall be buried in one grave." See Edward Kamens, *The Three Jewels* (Ann Arbor: Center for Japanese Studies, University of Michigan, 1988), 178. Perhaps the statement is meant to reflect the practice of earlier times, or possibly Shōtoku's reluctance to be separated from his wife even in death was to be understood by a late tenth-century audience as particularly poignant because it was contrary to contemporary custom.

19. For a survey of this consensus, see Nishimura, *Kodai, chūsei no kazoku to josei*, 166–68.

20. Fukutō, "Bochi saishi to josei," 103–6. See also Minegishi Sumio, "Chūsei no ie to saishi," in *Shōja to shisha: Sosen saishi*, ed. Ishikawa Toshio et al. (Tokyo: Sanseido, 1988), 156–59, and Fukutō Sanae, *Ie seiritsu no kenkyū: Sosen saishi, onna, kodomo* (Tokyo: Kōkura Shoin, 1991), 138–48.

21. Nishiguchi Junko, *Onna no chikara: Kodai no josei to bukkyō* (Tokyo: Heibonsha, 1987), 86–88. Mimi Yiengpruksawan has recently published a translation and adaptation of the relevant chapter: Nishiguchi Junko, "Where the Bones Go: Death and Burial of the Heian High Aristocracy," in *Engendering Faith: Women and Buddhism in Premodern Japan*, ed. Barbara Ruch (Ann Arbor: Center for Japanese Studies, University of Michigan, 2002), 417–39.

22. Nishiguchi, *Onna no chikara*, 72–74, 87.

23. Tanaka Hisao, "Heian jidai no kizoku no sōsei: Toku ni jūisseki o chūshi ni," in *Sōsō bosei kenkyū shūsei*, vol. 5, ed. Uwai Hisayoshi (Tokyo: Obunsha, 1979), 183–204.

24. Bernard Faure has pointed out that cremation can be viewed as an accelerated form of secondary burial aimed at securing *śarīra*, the bones or crystalline transformed relics of dead masters. See *The Rhetoric of Immediacy: A Cultural Critique of Chan/Zen Buddhism* (Princeton, NJ: Princeton University Press, 1991), 133–35.

25. Maurice Bloch and Jonathan Parry, eds., *Death and the Regeneration of Life* (Cambridge: Cambridge University Press, 1982), 20–21.

26. See Tanaka: "Heian jidai no kizoku no sōsei," 198–200, and "Bunken ni arawareta bochi," 112–20, for the strong influence of Pure Land Buddhism on Japanese death ritual, beginning in the tenth century and escalating in the eleventh and twelfth.

27. Katsuda Itaru, "Sonraku no bosei to kazoku," in *Kazoku to josei*, ed. Minegishi Sumio (Tokyo: Yoshikawa Kōbunkan, 1992), 202–3. Katsuda also notes the widely held belief that the bones of those born into Amida's Western Paradise were free from any kind of pollution. Nishiguchi Junko cites the eleventh-century *Chūyūki*, in which someone remarks that "white bones"—that is, bones that are more than thirty days old and are no longer linked by any connective tissue—are not a source of pollution (*Onna no chikara*, 93). Both authors also refer to the belief that the bones of women

were no longer female and thus could be interred at places like Mt. Kōya, where the presence of women was forbidden. Women's bones were thus free of the pollution ascribed to women's bodies. This custom represents an interesting twist on the doctrine of *henjō nanshi*, the transformation of the female body to male as a prerequisite to Buddhist salvation (see Katsuda, 206, and Nishiguchi, 79–83). Owing to the practice of *bunkotsu*, or "dividing the bones," it was possible for women to be buried both at such temples and in their ancestral graveyards.

28. On Zen influence on funerals in medieval Japan, see William Bodiford, *Sōtō Zen in Medieval Japan* (Honolulu: University of Hawai'i Press, 1993), 185–210. On the role of Ritsu priests, see Hosokawa Ryōichi, *Chūsei Risshū jiin to minshū* (Tokyo: Yoshikawa Kōbunkan, 1987), and Janet Goodwin, *Alms and Vagabonds* (Honolulu: University of Hawai'i Press, 1994), 120–27. See also Matsuo Kenji, *Kamakura shin bukkyō no tanjō* (Tokyo: Kōdansha, 1995), 103–19, on Zen and Ritsu funerals and the reasons underlying their popularity.

29. Nishiguchi, *Onna no chikara*, 89–97. Nishiguchi points to the influence of the relics cult, which enjoyed great popularity from the end of the tenth century. This begins with the pure remains of the historical Buddha, Śākyamuni, but quickly enough extends to the bones of departed Buddhist masters and from there to those of the "ordinary" dead.

30. For a detailed history of the development of stone grave markers, see Suitō Makoto, *Chūsei no sōsō, bosei: Sekitō o zōryū suru* (Tokyo: Yoshikawa Kōbunkan, 1991), and Janet Goodwin, "Shooing the Dead to Paradise," *Japanese Journal of Religious Studies* 16, no. 1 (1989): 66–67. While Goodwin cites examples of earlier stone monuments, it should be noted that these were probably erected to the memory of apical ancestors or to the dead of the clan in general, rather than for individual family members. Tanaka Hisao distinguishes between the use of stone monuments prior to the Kamakura period and after. Initially, the creation of a *sotoba* was aimed at creating merit for the dead, but the *sotoba* itself was not expected to be maintained and venerated by survivors and future generations. See Tanaka Hisao, "Bukke shakai seiritsu to ujidera, hakadera," in Ishikawa et al., eds., *Shōja to shisha*, 165–67.

31. Tanaka: "Bunken ni arawareta bochi," 81–86, 109–10, and "Heian jidai no kizoku no sōsei," 190. Fukutō points out that during the tenth century, Fujiwara no Tadahira visited his father Mototsune's grave on many occasions; however, these visits were all to announce promotions in rank and did not represent either a calendarization of *hakamairi* or the performance of memorial services at a temple adjacent to the grave site ("Bochi saishi to josei," 95–98). See also Fukutō Sanae, "Heian kizokusō ni okeru hakamairi no seiritsu," in *Haka to kazoku*, ed. Fujii Masao, Yoshie Akio, and Kōmoto Mitsugi (Tokyo: Waseda Daigaku Shuppanbu, 1993), 245–65.

32. Helen McCullough and William McCullough, *A Tale of Flowering Fortunes: Annals of Japanese Aristocratic Life in the Heian Period* (Stanford, CA: Stanford University Press, 1980), 1:187–89.

33. *I Sadaijin kuyō Jōmyōji ganmon*; cited in Tanaka, "Heian jidai no kizoku no sōsei," 187–88. The text, composed by Ōe no Masahira, can be found in the *Honchō monzui*, in *Kokushi taikei* (hereafter *KT*), ed. Kuroita Katsumi (Tokyo: Yoshikawa Kōbunkan, 1929–64), 29:324–26, and *Dainihon shiryō*, ed. Tokyo Daigaku Shiryō Hensanjo (Tokyo: University of Tokyo, 1902–), part 2, 5:511–12. Tanaka quotes the passage as "spring moon, autumn moon," but both texts cited above read as translated here.

34. Helen McCullough, trans., *Ōkagami: The Great Mirror* (Ann Arbor: Center for Japanese Studies, University of Michigan, 1980), 207. See also McCullough and McCullough, *A Tale of Flowering Fortunes*, 2:508–9.

35. On the significance of the development of regular grave visits in Song-period China, see Patricia Ebrey, "The Early Stages in the Development of Group Descent Organization," in *Kinship Organization in Late Imperial China*, ed. Patricia Ebrey and James Watson (Berkeley: University of California Press, 1986), 16–61. Ebrey suggests that Buddhist ideas of lineage deeply influenced Chinese kinship practices. Also, on lineage concerns in early Chan mortuary ritual, see Griffith Foulk and Robert Sharf, "On the Ritual Use of Ch'an Portraiture in Medieval China," *Cahiers d'Extrême Asie* 7 (1993–94): 149–219. For a different view of Song/Yuan China, also see Bettine Birge, *Women, Property, and Confucian Reaction in Sung and Yuan China (960–1368)* (Cambridge and New York: Cambridge University Press, 2002).

36. Maurice Bloch and Jonathan Parry, "Introduction," in Bloch and Parry, eds., *Death and the Regeneration of Life*, 1–44. In the same volume, also see James Watson, "Of Flesh and Bones," 155–86.

37. Of course, there had also been much focus on an ancestral cult within the *uji* system in earlier periods. However, for the *uji*, the only ancestors of importance were the apical or founding ancestor and one's own parents; the emphasis was not on lineage until the end of the Heian period.

38. It is essential to emphasize that this transformation of the family system was process and not event. Some would argue that the process was not complete until the end of the nineteenth century. See, for example, Emori, *Kazoku no rekishi minzokugaku*, 54–55.

39. Tanaka Hisao, "So no imi ni tsuite," in Ishikawa et al., eds., *Shōja to shisha*, 201–56. Tanaka's assertions are evaluated in the same volume by Yoshie Akiko, "Sosen sonchō wa yunyū ni yoru mono ka," 257–62. Both authors agree that during and prior to the Nara period, the character *so*, ancestor, referred equally to men and women. At this time, the character was used in Japan primarily to indicate a person's mother, an observation made early on by Motoori Norinaga (1730–1801). In later periods, the masculine connotations of *so* are unmistakable.

40. Tanaka, "So no imi ni tsuite," 222. See Fukutō, "Bochi saishi to josei," 89, for a late eighth-century document in which three clans descended from a king of Paekche complain of outsiders harvesting lumber on their ancestral lands and neglect of their clan grave sites. They lament, "The place to which the souls of our ancestors have long returned will be lost."

41. Nickerson, "The Meaning of Matrilocality," 452–58. Here I disagree with Nickerson's suggestion that the bilineal system was a stable one and did not mark a transitional phase. However, in support of Nickerson's thesis, see Emori, *Kazoku no rekishi minzokugaku*, 101–5, where he denies that Japanese kinship ever had truly matrilineal tendencies.

42. Fukutō, "Bochi saishi to josei," 105.

43. For an exploration of the meaning of unigeniture in the Kamakura period, see Hayami Akira, "The Myth of Primogeniture and Impartible Inheritance in Japan," *Journal of Family History* 8 (1983): 3–29.

44. The fourteenth century was a time of great proliferation for new houses. Amino Yoshihiko has shown that many families produced genealogies at this time, often with inflated pedigrees. See his *Nihon chūsei shiryōgaku no kadai* (Tokyo: Kōbundō, 1996), 94–95. See also Akashi, "Kamakura bushi no ie," 223.

45. Tonomura, "Women and Inheritance in Japan's Early Warrior Society," 618–20. Note the famous case of Abutsu-ni, who wrote *Izayoi nikki*. She was a poet, the widow of Fujiwara no Tameie, who traveled from Kyoto to Kamakura to argue an inheritance dispute between her son and her stepson. See Helen McCullough, trans., "The Journal of the Sixteenth-Night Moon," in Helen McCullough, *Classical Japanese Prose: An Anthology* (Stanford, CA: Stanford University Press, 1990), 340–76.

46. Katsuura Noriko, "Kikon josei no shukke to kon'in kankei," in Zenkindai Joseishi Kenkyūkai (Sekiguchi Hiroko et al.), eds., *Kazoku to josei no rekishi*, 85. See also Katsuura Noriko, "Josei no hosshin," in Minegishi Sumio, ed., *Kazoku to josei*, 241–71.

47. Tonomura, "Women and Inheritance in Japan's Early Warrior Society," 606–8. See 602 for laws dealing with remarriage and the property rights of widows. For a European parallel, see James A. Brundage, "The Merry Widow's Serious Sister: Remarriage in Classical Canon Law," in *Matrons and Marginal Women in Medieval Society*, ed. Robert R. Edwards and Vickie Ziegler (Woodbridge, England: Boydell Press, 1995), 34–49.

48. See Nishiyaji Harumi, "Chūseiteki tochi shoyū o meguru monjo shugi to hōkanshū," *Nihonshi kenkyū* 320 (1989), esp. 36–40. Nishiyaji demonstrates that counter-claimants in inheritance cases sometimes accused their opponents of failing to inform them of a death or of improperly performing funerals and memorial services when it was not their place to do so. In a modern parallel, Emily Ahern's informants in a village in Taiwan during the early 1970s repeatedly linked the maintenance of ancestral tablets and involvement in the ancestral cult with inheritance rights. Whoever

possessed the tablets could also claim the property. See Emily Martin Ahern, *The Cult of the Dead in a Chinese Village* (Stanford, CA: Stanford University Press, 1973), 139–48.

49. The case of Abutsu-ni is instructive here. She wrote her *Izayoi nikki* to establish her children as the legitimate heirs to her late husband's property, poetry lineage, and ancestral line. Akashi has suggested that the *ie* first grew out of the practice of transmission of lineages in artistic houses. See Akashi, "Kamakura bushi no ie," 225.

50. Minegishi, "Chūsei no ie to saishi," 160–62.

51. Suitō Makoto, "Sengoku jidai no ichi kizoku shisha girei: *Nobutane kyōki* no sōsō, tsuizen no kiji kara," in *Chūsei shakai to funbo*, ed. Ishii Susumu (Tokyo: Meicho Shuppan, 1993), 110.

52. See Itō Yuishin, "*Moromoriki* ni miru chūsei sōsai bukkyō," in Uwai, ed., *Sōsō bosei kenkyūshūsei*, vol. 5, 230. Men continued to hold services on behalf of matrilateral relatives at least into the fourteenth century. See Suitō, "Sengoku jidai no ichi kizoku shisha girei," 164, 167. The point here, however, is that they took responsibility for the funerals and burial of their mothers; it was not left to maternal grandfathers and uncles.

53. Itō, "*Moromoriki* ni miru chūsei sōsai bukkyō," 127–28. Itō notes that apparently the taboo against having more than one set of remains in a single grave was not observed in the case of women (233).

54. Nishiguchi, *Onna no chikara*, 84–85.

55. *Shōyūki*, Kannin 2 (1018), 6/16, *Dainihon kokiroku*, ed. Tokyo Daigaku Shiryō Hensanjo (Tokyo: Iwanami Shoten, 1952), part 5, vol. 10:42, 44.

56. See Watanabe Yoshio, "Haka to kazoku no chirigaku: Fūsuiron no shiten kara," in Fujii, Yoshie, and Kōmoto, eds., *Haka to kazoku*, 81–103. Ōe no Masahira refers specifically to the excellent geomantic properties of Mt. Kohata in his text for the inscription on Jōmyōji's temple bell. See *Seiji yōryaku* (*Nenchūgyōji* 29, twelfth month) in *KT* 29:327, and *Dainihon shiryō*, part 2, vol. 5:514. In Taiwan and Korea, such beliefs continue to be quite important. Families will often move the bones of a family member after a string of bad luck and also credit good fortune to the proper placement of the bones of the ancestors.

57. Quoted in Fukutō, "Bochi saishi to josei," 88. See the *Chūgaishō* in *Zoku gunsho ruijū*, ed. Hanawa Hokinoichi (Tokyo: Keizai Zasshisha, 1879), 11:811a.

58. See, for example, Okano Haruko, "Feminisuto shiten kara no Nihon shūkyō hihan," in *Shūkyō no naka no joseishi*, ed. Okuda Akiko and Okano Haruko (Tokyo: Seikyūsha, 1993), 32–33.

13

Grave Changes

Scattering Ashes in Contemporary Japan

Mark Rowe

The true grave lies in the heart.
—Yasuda Mutsuhiko

In an editorial to the *Asahi* newspaper on September 24, 1990, Yasuda Mutsuhiko, former *Asahi* editor and soon-to-be founder of the Grave-Free Promotion Society, wrote an essay titled "Is Scattering Ashes in the Ocean or in the Mountains Really Illegal? We Are Losing the Freedom of Mortuary Practices, Not Because of Regulations, but Through Preconceptions." Yasuda argued that despite popular belief, the scattering of ashes was in fact not covered under any of the laws then in effect and was therefore not illegal. He then went on to urge people to consider "scattering" as both an environmentally friendly and much more traditional style of burial than the overpriced, family-centered form of ancestral graves that had emerged, along with mandatory temple certification, in the Tokugawa period (1603–1867).

Less than five months later, on February 2, 1991, the first meeting of the Grave-Free Promotion Society (Sōsō no Jiyū o Susumeru Kai; hereafter GFPS or Society) attracted more than three hundred people in Tokyo, and within that same year the Society had conducted its first official scattering ceremony.[1] By its twelfth year, the GFPS had more than eleven thousand members and thirteen branch offices nationwide and, as of December 2002, had conducted 719 "natural funerals" (*shizensō*) for the remains of 1,258 people. While these numbers remain relatively small on a national scale, the group has generated nationwide attention and debate completely out of proportion to its size.[2] Owing in part to its media savvy and timely emergence after the economic bubble of the late 1980s, the Society has had a dramatic impact on public conceptions of mortuary practice. A recent government survey showed that national acceptance of scattering ashes jumped from less than 20 percent in 1990 to almost 75 percent by 1998, with one in eight people saying they would choose a natural funeral for themselves.[3] In 1997, largely in reaction to the Society's success, the Welfare Ministry began investigations into the need for the first change in the grave laws in more than fifty years, and in 1998 the term *shizensō* officially entered the Japanese language with the publishing of the fifth edition of the *Kojien* dictionary.

As one would expect, however, in a country dominated by a patrilineal family grave system, ancestral rites, and Buddhist deathways, support for the GFPS and its objectives has been far from universal. By transgressing the boundaries of graveyards and tradition, natural funerals pose a direct challenge to more than three centuries of Buddhist funerals and memorial rites. Despite Yasuda's claims about historical precedents for scattering in the ancient and medieval periods, the near universal Buddhist mortuary rites and graves for people of all classes—practices dating from the Tokugawa period—are considered by most to constitute proper mortuary tradition in Japan. Further, Yasuda's attempts to connect the Society's version of scattering to wider environmental concerns and issues of personal and religious freedom have provoked opposition from various Buddhist organizations, local civic groups, scholars, and even former GFPS members. The Society's success has also spurred imitation by professional funeral companies, splinter groups, and some Buddhist temples, leading to calls for new regulations for scattering, if not a complete revision of current laws governing burial.

This chapter attempts to place the Society's activities within the wider context of contemporary debate over traditional burial practices and the increasing need for new grave space. With the "graying" of Japanese society, widespread nuclearization of families, an increase in divorce, rising land costs, and growing concern for the environment, Japan is now facing a crisis over insufficient space for the dead. The scattering of remains, new-style "eternal memorial graves" (*eitai kuyō baka*), women's burial associations, high-rise ossuaries, and outer-space burial (*uchūsō*) all speak to changing conceptions of how the dead are to be treated and where they are to be located. Scattering sits at the intersection of legal battles over the ambiguous status of remains, historical debates over what constitutes "traditional" funerary practices, and Buddhist arguments for the necessity of posthumous ordination and memorial rites, as well as social and medical concerns over locating the dead. Despite its limited scale, the GFPS and the debates surrounding it provide valuable insights into changing conceptions of family, religious freedom, self-determination, and the long-standing Buddhist monopoly over death.

The Beginnings of the GFPS

On October 5, 1991, in Sagami Bay near Tokyo, the GFPS quietly held its first official natural funeral. A portion of the cremated remains of a young woman who had killed herself over lost love some thirty years earlier was scattered in the sea, along with flowers, during a short, simple, non-religious ceremony. Present along with Yasuda, the head of the Society, and three other members were former Welfare Ministry official Saitō Nanako, two boat operators, and three private photographers.

Ten days after the ceremony, the Society made an official announcement about the event, and the following day, all the major papers and television networks carried the story. By performing the ceremony before making it public, the Society both avoided a protracted legal battle and revealed its media savvy. Note that there were as many photographers at the ceremony as there were Society members, and having a former Welfare Ministry member present no doubt projected to the public an essential element of credibility if not outright government acceptance. Further, by scattering only a small portion of the remains of a woman who had already been interred for thirty years, the Society eased public concerns over macabre practices. Finally, the love-suicide narrative gave the event a certain romantic appeal.

Yasuda's gamble paid off when the media carried the reaction of the related ministries the day after the Society's announcement. As Yasuda had predicted in his editorial a year earlier, neither the Justice Ministry nor the Welfare Ministry was ready to declare scattering illegal. The Justice Ministry, commenting on Article 190 of the criminal code (*igai ikizai*), which prohibits the discarding of corpses, responded, "Since the aim of this regulation is to protect the religious sentiments of societal customs, as long as this [*shizensō*] is for the purpose of a funeral and takes place with moderation, there is no problem."[4] Further, the ministry conceded that scattering did not constitute the discarding (*iki*) of, and cremation was not equivalent to the destruction (*sonkai*) of, the corpse. Scattering, therefore, did not break any existing laws.[5]

For the Society, the ruling was an "epoch-making" event that was taken as total approbation for the practice of scattering remains. Within the year, it had put out numerous articles and published two books. The first, *You Don't Need a Grave: It's Precisely Because You Love Them That You Should Have a Natural Funeral*—actually published before the first *shizensō*—included a reprint of Yasuda's *Asahi* editorial and reiterated his main arguments on the legality and history of scattering and its relationship to the environment. The most striking aspect of the book is its surreal cover, which shows an old, decrepit, overgrown graveyard with cracked gravestones in complete disarray. The earth hovers in the sky above, forcing the reader to reconsider what planet he or she is actually on. On the back cover, we see only the blue-green earth ordering us to "Bury the dead in the hearts of the living." The second book, *Freedom from "Graves": Natural Funerals That Return Us to the Earth*, was published a mere two weeks after the announcement of the first *shizensō* and offers the first complete manifesto of the GFPS, as well as details on the logistics of scattering and legal advice on all necessary paperwork.

The six-part manifesto of the Society's basic rules includes respect for the wishes of the individual and for religious beliefs, the promise of no discrimination, harmony with nature, and a not-for-profit pledge. Most notable in the list is the following definition of *shizensō*: "The natural funeral, as the final rite for the deceased, returns the remains (ashes) to nature and moreover pays tribute to his or her memory. This is a new creation that takes scattering, a funerary method established in our country since before the Nara period (710–794), and revives it in a form that is appropriate to contemporary custom."[6] We shall return to the question of what exactly constituted pre-Nara scattering below, but it is worth considering here how the Society intended to adapt this putatively honored and ancient tradition to modern sensibilities.

As material objects, human remains require physical treatment and necessitate action. Although it is easy to forget when discussions focus on a "returning to nature" and "funerary freedom," natural funerals involve the basic act of disposing of human remains. In the case of the GFPS, this is most evident in the need to prepare the cremated remains for scattering. Japanese crematoria are designed to burn bodies at a specific temperature that leaves the bones fairly intact. This is to allow the tradition of "picking up the bones" (*kotsuage*) and placing them in a funerary urn for interment.[7] In response to public fears, the GFPS advises that these bones must then be crushed into powder so that there are no pieces larger than five millimeters.[8] The Society offers several methods for crushing the bones, including a wooden stick, a vase, a golf club, or, if available, an electric grinder. One measure of both the success of the Society and the difficulty posed to family members when faced with having to crush the bones of a loved one is indicated by the emergence of funerary companies that, for a nominal fee, will grind the remains.[9]

Once the remains are prepared, they are generally scattered in the mountains or in the sea. In *Freedom from "Graves,"* the reader is given general instructions about choosing the space for scattering, transportation to that spot, the method of scattering, and suitable containers for the ashes. For ocean services, the Society recommends international waters, which begin roughly twenty-two kilometers from land, and for mountain scattering, a remote spot, ideally a place the deceased had visited. In either case, if the ashes are to be placed in any type of container, it must be completely biodegradable. The book also reminds readers that ashes do not settle in any one spot: some are taken by the wind, some are washed away, and some enter the earth. Because the natural funerals advocated by the Society have no fixed religious elements, mourners are told there is no need to have Buddhist rites or Christian hymns.[10]

While the Society was working hard on the promotional front, it also continued to perform funerals. In 1992, it held three more *shizensō*, including the first one on land, and in 1993, there were nine more natural funerals for thirteen people. In spite of these early successes, the legal and social ambiguity of scattering has yet to be clarified. While the Society continues to grow and to arrange natural funerals all over the country, it is still fighting an ongoing battle to gain acceptance for what, despite its claims of tradition, is a revolutionary form of mortuary rites. (Table 13.1 shows the rise in *shizensō* in recent years.)

TABLE 13.1. Natural funerals by year, 1991–2002

Year[a]	Number of *shizensō*	Number of people scattered
1991	1	1
1992	3	5
1993	9	13
1994	16	29
1995	20	40
1996	40	70
1997	72	145
1998	106	187
1999	99	177
2000	128	228
2001	122	196
2002	120	297
Total	736[b]	1,388

[a] Statistical years run from April 1 to March 31.
[b] The chosen locations are as follows: ocean: 552.5; mountain: 162; river: 5; sky: 13.5; private garden: 3. Of these 582.5 were individual services and 153.5 were group services.

From Legality to Regulation

Yasuda made clear in the early days of the Society that he felt the two main hurdles that had to be cleared were (mis)perceptions of the law and of history. Three years before the first *shizensō*, Diet member Ishihara Shintarō focused national attention on the question of the legality of scattering human remains. Asked by his brother, the famous entertainer Ishihara Yūjirō, to scatter his ashes in the ocean, Ishihara consulted various groups and became convinced that scattering was not legal. Ultimately he did not follow his brother's wishes, and the issue of scattering was widely considered to have been settled. It was in reaction to this conclusion that Yasuda wrote his 1990 editorial in the *Asahi*. Yasuda's position, justified by the ministries, was that the grave laws, written in 1948 in response to sanitation concerns in the immediate postwar period, had no provision for the scattering of remains. As for the criminal code prohibition against discarding corpses, Yasuda, employing one of his favorite hyperboles, noted, "If the scattering of ashes in mountains and oceans were covered under this law, then the family that leaves some amount of the remains behind at the crematorium, as well as those workers at the crematorium who dispose of the remains as industrial waste or garbage, are all criminals."[11]

As the Society's success grew and government surveys showed a marked increase in national acceptance of scattering, the debate shifted from arguments over legality to questions of regulation. A spate of articles by Buddhist scholar Fujii Masao and engineer/graveyard specialist Yokota Mutsumi calling for some form of scattering regulation helped bring about a Welfare Ministry roundtable inquiry into contemporary grave practices.[12] Composed of scholars, priests, and professionals, the roundtable, called "An Open Discussion on the Future of Grave Practices," held twelve sessions over fifteen months from February 1997 to June 1998. The committee focused on two concerns: first, the crisis over insufficient grave space and abandoned graves, and second, a clarification of the position of the current grave laws in regard to scattering and a determination on whether some form of regulation were in order. At issue was not only the uncertain status of cremated remains in a country with a 99 percent cremation rate, but also fundamental questions of religious freedom. As the committee report makes clear, the postwar grave laws were intended only to protect public health, and thus to apply a broader interpretation of them in order to regulate what constitutes "acceptable customs" would be highly problematic.

Not surprisingly, when Yasuda and other representatives from the GFPS were invited to speak before the committee, it was on precisely this point that they mounted their defense. Switching tactics from the Society's staple argument that ashes were not covered under the grave law as outlined in Article 4, Yasuda instead focused on Article 1, which, along with the protection of public health and welfare, ensures burial practices that will conform to the "religious sentiments" of the people.[13] As Yasuda put it:

> What exactly is the religious sentiment of the people that is listed in the first article of the grave law? If this is not carefully debated, then this sentiment could be bound up with control by the State. Among all the different religions, is there a single religious sentiment? This is not something that should be regulated by the State, and we would like to discuss this matter carefully. We believe that

> what we are doing in the Society is a manifestation of our religious sentiments.... Natural funerals are a new religious practice and are protected under freedom of expression and belief.... In order to debate problems that would arise if scattering became more common, we must pin down what is meant by religious sentiments. The idea that new practices are strange and therefore must be regulated is a dangerous one.[14]

This bold assertion marked an important shift in the status and policy of the Society. Yasuda's arguments were no longer based on establishing the legality of his fledgling civic group, but rather on fighting for its rights to the same kind of freedom that religious groups are guaranteed under the Constitution. While Yasuda had always argued for freedom of choice, these statements represented a new focus. As we shall see, the claim that scattering represents proper Japanese burial tradition is premised on a vision of family graves as tools of state ideology in the Tokugawa and Meiji (1868–1912) periods. In transposing this argument to the present day and questioning the very essence of religious freedom, Yasuda placed the GFPS in a highly political position vis-à-vis the state by making funerary freedom a battle against state oppression and scattering, the most fundamental of human rights. The potential consequences of these statements regarding freedom of religion and state control are particularly significant in the wake of the Aum affair and subsequent changes in the Religious Corporations Law.[15]

While shying away from strictly defining "religious sentiments," the roundtable committee made clear that it was more concerned with the reactions of the people living in areas where scattering was taking place than with the religious feelings of those doing the scattering. As the committee chairman, Waseda University law professor Urakawa Michitarō, stated, "We are aware of the idea that people 'want daily life and the spirits of the dead to be separate' and that we should consider the religious sentiment of those people who live in areas where ashes are scattered."[16] Along with the need for a clear definition of scattering, some system of authorization, and punishment for breaking the laws, the biggest concern of the committee was with the location of scattering. Specific fears included people shying away from seafood caught in places like Sagami Bay, where scattering often takes place, as well as reports of individuals simply digging holes and dropping in ashes in clear violation of the law. Another potential problem stemmed from the practice of scattering ashes on private land or in gardens and then reselling that property. The grave specialist Yokota, one of the Society's most vocal critics, produced the following imaginary ad to illustrate his opposition: "House for sale: 165 square meters, southeast facing corner lot. Ten years old. Fifteen-minute walk from train station. Human remains included."[17] In the end, the committee recommended to the Welfare Ministry that scattering be regulated at the prefectural level and that there be unified administration of locations, methods of scattering, and records of each case.[18] As of January 2004, there have been no major changes to the grave laws in regard to scattering ashes.

Historical Background

Before we discuss the Society's version of traditional Japanese mortuary history, it is necessary to provide a brief overview of the Japanese grave system and the development of Buddhist funerals. Traditionally, the corpse was seen as something to be feared, as a source of both pollution and possession by malevolent spirits, and it is widely accepted that commoners in rural and urban areas abandoned the dead in mountains, riverbeds, or other noninhabited areas well into the fifteenth century.[19] Early village graveyards were often mere dumping grounds, and in fact scholars have looked at the terms "grave" (*haka*) and "bury" (*hōmuru*) as deriving from terms that meant "throwing away."[20]

According to Hashizume Shinya, most urban residents did not have cemetery plots until the late fifteenth or early sixteenth century. Temple cemeteries developed largely after the Ōnin War (1466–77), as the Buddhist management of the dead became more widespread.[21] While previously commoners would have built communal monuments, from the seventeenth century on, one begins to see commemorative stones dedicated to individuals and couples.[22] With the development of the temple certification system (*terauke seido*) in the seventeenth century, the relationship between temples and commoners was solidified in the so-called parishioner system (*danka seido*), which required all Japanese families to belong to local temples. While this policy was ostensibly implemented to counter the perceived threat of Christianity, it soon transformed Buddhist temples and priests into de facto organs of the state, giving them an inordinate amount of control over the lives of their parishioners, who were beholden to local priests for certifying them as non-Christian.[23] The parishioner also had to visit the temple for death and ancestral rites throughout the year, as well as for the summer *obon* rites to memorialize the dead, the equinoctial weeks, and the death anniversary of the Buddha.[24] According to Andrew Bernstein, "By the end of the warring states period that preceded the Tokugawa, Buddhist death rites had already generated a steady cash flow for temples, but Tokugawa policy created fixed channels for that flow. By registering, processing, and memorializing deaths for captive parishioners, Buddhist temples enjoyed the fruits of total death management, making them both enforcers of social control and enablers of social advancement."[25] The certification system also meant that Buddhist funerals and memorial rites became more or less mandatory.[26] Once one was certified by a specific temple, it was next to impossible to transfer to another temple, and having memorial or death services anywhere else was strictly forbidden.[27]

Temple cemetery plots for urban commoners began appearing in the sixteenth century and became more common after the later implementation of the temple certification system. Tanigawa Akiko, in working on Tokugawa-period grave excavations, has traced a significant mid-eighteenth-century surge in family-centered graves in Edo (modern Tokyo) and surrounding areas.[28] New styles of gravestones in the period "represent the heightening of a family-centered consciousness—a shift in thinking in which the modern extended family (*ie*) became the central unit of society, and for which memorial services for the dead became prevalent."[29] With the family registration law (*koseki*) of 1871, temple certification was officially abolished, but the connection between Japanese families and local temples was now cast in stone. Despite state attempts to promote Shinto funerals and full-body burial as part of the larger, pro-Shinto ideology, the general public was not easily converted. An 1873 proscription of cremation lasted a mere two years.[30]

Until the Meiji period, a wide variety of burial practices existed throughout the country. With the inception of the Meiji Civil Code in 1898, however, a single unified framework of burial and ancestor-based ritual was mandated in order to promote the concept of the extended family and ancestor worship as the cornerstone of the emperor system. "In this way, the incredibly private act of burying the dead and the apparatus of that act, the grave, came under government control and was legalized in the 'right of household succession act' (*katoku sōzoku no tokken*), clause 987 of the Meiji Civil Code."[31]

After World War II, despite the legal dissolution of the *ie* system, many of the premises upon which it was founded still persisted. According to Mori Kenji, the clause concerning inheritance in the current civil code, rewritten after the war, was the result of a compromise between groups that wanted to abolish the household system and those that wanted to preserve it.[32] Clause 897 of the current civil code, which covers the "inheritance of ritual/religious assets" (*saishi zaisan no keishō*), includes a provision stating that "the person who, according to custom, should perform the ancestral rites shall inherit [the grave and Buddhist altar]." As Mori points out, the inclusion of the phrase "according to custom" ensures that the ideals of the household system remain strongly ingrained in the current code.[33] The maintenance of patrilineal descent ideals is plainly evident in the ongoing inability of those without descendants to buy grave space and the difficulty of passing on graves in families without sons. Sociologist and writer Inoue Haruyo argues that the continued influence of the *ie* system also affects the religious choices people are able to make, particularly in the case of a woman who marries and must adopt the religious affiliation of her husband's family in order to be included in the temple grave.

> In this way, "household religion" does not entail, in any true sense, freedom of belief. As for temples, it was not people, but rather graves that were held hostage in order to ensure social stability. Thus, rather than traditional religious activities, it was the household system around which a financial policy based on funerary Buddhism was created. This is why, today, people without descendants encounter discrimination from temples that will not sell them grave space.[34]

When one buys a grave in Japan today, one is actually buying the right to use the land in perpetuity (*eitai shiyōken*). The system is premised on the concept of a continuous, direct descent, localized family that is still implicitly enshrined in civil law. To the present day, the Meiji Civil Code's institutionalization of family graves (*ie no haka*) has defined graves as a central site in family ritual. These graves follow patrilineal lines and are passed through the eldest son, who is expected to maintain upkeep, carry out yearly memorial rites, and visit the grave during the equinoxes and the summer festival of the dead, *obon*, in mid-August. Cremated remains are placed in urns that are interred in the family grave forty-nine days after death, when the traditional Buddhist liminal period ends. The deceased then receive individualized yearly memorial services on the anniversary of death for thirty-three, fifty, or even up to one hundred years, at which point they join the anonymous ranks of ancestors.

Along with complaints against the outmoded grave practices listed above, scholars have also documented a backlash against inflated grave prices and unethical business ties between religious organizations and gravestone producers during the economic bubble of the late 1980s.[35] It was largely in response to these shifting economic and social factors that groups such as the GFPS emerged at the start of the 1990s.

The "Tradition" of Scattering

In addition to legal issues, the second major obstacle that the Society faced was the Japanese attachment to funerary rites and burial practices dating back to the Tokugawa period. It was essential both to show that contemporary practices, viewed as "traditional," were in fact the products of Tokugawa and Meiji government policies, and, at the same time, to establish a link between scattering and the older practice of abandoning corpses. This two-pronged attack of deconstructing family graves and traditionalizing *shizensō*, though overlapping, required different arguments and justifications.

In order to elevate the historical status of scattering, Yasuda provides a variety of precedents, including references to scattering in elegies (*banka*) from the eighth-century poetry anthology *Man'yōshū*; the emperor Junna (786–840), who wrote in his will, "Scatter me in forests and fields and do not build a grave"; and the famous request of Shinran (1173–1262) that his remains be used to feed the fish in the Kamo River.[36] By invoking these well-known markers of "Japaneseness" in almost every Society publication or interview, Yasuda is trying to connect natural funerals to some deeper Japanese essence. There are, however, important distinctions to be made between the abandonment or discarding of complete corpses in mountains owing to fear of death impurity and hiring a boat or helicopter to fly out over the ocean to scatter the carefully prepared, cremated remains of a loved one who has specifically asked for such treatment. Aside from the physical differences between scattering ashes and dumping corpses, these two responses originate in very different motivations. Despite references to romantic tropes uttered by famous historical figures, natural funerals are not a glorious return to a golden mortuary age so much as a modern response to the specific economic, political, and social forces since the early 1990s.

Shima Tōru, a researcher on Japan's Jōmon period (10,000–400 BCE) and former director of the Japanese Buddhist Statuary Society, has written several critiques of the GFPS and of Yasuda's historical claims in particular. Shima summarizes Yasuda's position in five stages:

(1) There was no custom of graves in ancient Japan. From the ancient to the medieval period, commoners would throw away the corpse in mountains, forests, fields, rivers, oceans, or on an island.
(2) From the medieval to the modern period, the corpse changed from an object of aversion that should be discarded to something that was memorialized. During that process, a segment of the ruling class began building graves at temples.
(3) Commoners did not build graves until the institution of the parishioner system of the Tokugawa period. Use of individual and family graves spread among the general populace through public administration via the temples. Temples bound the people to graves and actively promoted funerary rites.
(4) Today's family graves were institutionalized in the Meiji Civil Code of 1898, which set forth graves as the object of family religious services (*ie no saishi*). This transpired against the background of a familial state based on the emperor system (*tennōsei kazoku kokka*) that tried to strengthen the family system through an emphasis on ancestor worship at graves.
(5) The Meiji government forced commoners to memorialize the dead at graves and even dictated funerary styles. Until the Meiji period, regional funerary styles varied widely, but these gradually became homogenized.[37]

Shima proceeds to clarify the Society's statements as indicating that the original funerary method for commoners was simply to throw away the corpse, while the ruling class practiced funerary rituals, maintained graves, and conducted memorial services; the state then mandated these practices as a way to control the masses, with the family grave system becoming merely a tool of state management. The objective of the GFPS thus became achieving freedom from state control through a return to the original practice of discarding the corpse. Shima's response is right to the point: "Why must the making of graves by common people in the medieval period be rejected as a transgression against some original practice?"[38] Certainly the family grave system was tied to state control in the Tokugawa period, but this does not mean that graves were simply imposed from above. Commoners also aspired to the more extravagant rites, graves, distinguished posthumous names, and promises of salvation afforded to the elite classes. As Hashizume Shinya has argued, as temple cemeteries began to spread in urban areas from the sixteenth century, more and more people wanted their tombs as close to the main hall as possible to ensure the "guarantee of continual prayer for their spirits after death."[39]

Possibly the most succinct critique of the Society's readings of history comes from Shingon priest Miyasaka Yūkō, who applies Yasuda's own logic to rice cultivation. "In the Jōmon period, we mainly ate acorns. Therefore, there is no rule that says we must eat rice simply because we are Japanese. Furthermore, acorns don't require the destruction of nature to create cultivated fields, nor is the environment poisoned by pesticides."[40]

Environment

Although Yasuda's historical arguments are premised on a connection between natural funerals and earlier practices of discarding corpses, his defense of the Society hinges on drawing a distinction between simple scattering (*sankotsu*) and the *shizensō* advocated by the GFPS. Integral to this distinction is the Society's environmental platform, which emerged from the idea of a "Forest of Rebirth" (Saisei no Mori). Yasuda initially came up with the idea in response to a debate in 1990 over the destruction of a riverhead in Tamagawa, Yamanashi Prefecture. Locals wanted to build a resort and golf course to revitalize the area, but opposition arose in Tokyo, which was dependent on the river for water. Yasuda later proposed that privately owned groves at the head of rivers be designated Saisei no Mori. Those who wished would pay a basic fee of 100,000 yen (about $800) to have their ashes scattered in the woods.[41] The money collected would be used to protect the woods and revitalize the local area, while at the same time ensuring clean water for major cities. In this way, people from the city would have their ashes "returned" (*kaesu*) to nature, helping to preserve the area and guarantee clean water for future generations. According to Yasuda, the Saisei no Mori was aimed at "having humans and the environment live and be reborn together in the great cycle (*junkan*) of nature."[42]

In 1994, in response to the Society's announcement that it had conducted a *shizensō* for two people in a public grove in Tamagawa earlier that year, the local village applied to ban all future natural funerals. There were three main objections: (1) the land also belonged to the locals; (2) scattering would hurt the image of the area, which was trying to attract tourism; and (3) entering mountains littered with human remains would feel strange.[43] The local protest showed that the Society had to battle not only what it perceived as some mistaken notion of funeral tradition in Japan but also more fundamental taboos and fears of death in general—the same fears that fuel protests against the construction of new funeral parlors, graveyards, and crematoria in local neighborhoods all over the country. One also has to wonder whether Tokyoites would have been happy with a solution that meant their drinking water was being filtered through human remains. The Society now has seven of these forests around the country, but all of them are privately owned, either by the Society itself or by individual members.

A second critique of the Forests of Rebirth comes from the aforementioned Yokota Mutsumi, who questions the entire environmental premise of the GFPS. Yokota is particularly interesting because as a former member of the Society, he has unique insights into its workings. For Yokota, the Society's problems stem from a lack of understanding of the dual position of human remains in Japanese society as an object of both veneration and taboo. He also strongly criticizes the Society's attempts to justify scattering by constantly emphasizing the supposed environmental benefits.[44] As someone who was drawn to the Society because of interest in the problem of insufficient grave space, Yokota felt that the environmental issue was simply "bait" to draw more interest to the cause.

Shima Tōru flatly rejects the notion of the Society as an environmental movement. In the article mentioned above, titled "Some

Doubts about the 'Scattering' Movement: Somewhere between a Community and an Illusory Family," he argues that scattering ashes is a personal choice that should not be tied to larger issues. Shima believes that by equating scattering with environmentalism, the Society is creating a false sense of community centered on environmental issues (rather than treatment of the dead) and projecting a self-righteousness that is ill deserved.[45]

The question then is, what exactly is the concept of nature that the Society is putting forward? One could argue, as critics have, that there is nothing particularly natural about cremating a human body in an oven, crushing the remains into powder with a golf club, and then hiring a motor-driven boat or helicopter to go twenty-two kilometers out to sea to dump the ashes into the ocean. Nor is turning private forests into scattering grounds in order to maintain clean water for cities and income for rural areas particularly "natural." The Society's use of "nature" or "natural" for its rites is, like its use of "tradition," a construct set in opposition to all other forms of mortuary rites. In GFPS rhetoric, returning the ashes to the great blue sea is contrasted with dark, dank, claustrophobic tombs that inevitably fall into ruin.[46] Environmentally beneficial scattering forests are opposed to the growing environmental menace of grave parks, which are devouring the natural countryside much as golf courses did in the 1980s. Nature is something that must be protected and nurtured, as well as something that sets the Society apart from other groups. Indeed, one could argue that the Society's "natural" funerals might more accurately be described as "environmental" funerals (*kankyōsō*).

Buddhist Responses

Soon after the announcement of the first natural funeral, the Buddhist press ran articles headlined, "The Pros and Cons of Scattering Remains: Is the Government's Sanction of Scattering a Threat to Buddhist-Style Graves?";[47] "A Warning Alarm to Japanese Buddhism";[48] and "Arguing for the Centrality of the Spirit of Mourning and Memorial Services... An Object of Veneration Is Essential."[49] Although such concerns are to be expected, given the perceived threat that scattering poses to Buddhist monopoly over mortuary rites and the steady stream of income it generates for temples, Buddhist reactions on the whole have been anything but consistent.

Ranging from damning criticism to approbation, from ambiguity to doctrinal support, the variety of responses says as much about the contentious state of Japanese Buddhist positions on death and burial as it does about the GFPS.

Tendai priest and scholar Katō Eiji, in an article titled "Funerals after Funerary Freedom," agrees that since individual freedom, which includes funerals, is protected under the constitution, people should be allowed to choose their last rites. With this acceptance, however, comes an important caveat: "The funerary process is not limited to the rite alone. There is a 'form' (*kata*) that determines everything from the participants' clothes to words of condolence." Katō argues that rather than "philosophical Buddhism" or Buddhist discourses on the meaning of life, what people really want is the conventional Buddhist funerary form.[50] This form requires Buddhist priests who are able to "take the soul of the deceased (wild spirit, *aramitama*), decisively return it to the other world, destroy its sins, transform it into a buddha (peaceful spirit, *nigimitama*), and perform memorial services."[51] According to Katō, the funerary rite is but one type of cultural "form," which, like an organic entity, does not like sudden changes or discontinuity. By consistently following an unchanging funerary pattern, the form handles the "rupture" of an individual's death and preserves the "continuity" of the social body:

> As long as the communal body continues to exist, it will seek to preserve the continuity of cultural "forms." Today, only Buddhism can provide people with a funeral "form." We really should stop placing so much importance on the debate going on in temples over "funerary freedom" (*sōsō no jiyū*). Isn't it just "freedom *from* funerals" (*sōsō kara no jiyū*) that is being debated?[52]

The continuity that is being protected here is that of Buddhism's monopoly over funerary and memorial rites. The Society is chastised both for its inability to properly pacify and transform the spirits of the dead and for shirking its duties to the departed ancestors. Given the fact that the natural funerals advocated by the GFPS include no Buddhist service, posthumous name, merit transfer (*tsuizen kuyō*), or subsequent memorial rites, it is no surprise that Buddhist critiques of the Society often emphasize the need to make continual offerings on behalf of the dead.

Rinzai Zen priest Ishizaki Yasumune is one of several commentators who place ancestor worship in binary opposition to funerary freedom and then attempt to trace the change from the former to the latter.[53] In a dharma talk on ancestor rites, Ishizaki emphasizes Buddhism's role in explaining causality (*inga*) and the impossibility of an independent condition. This is set up as a counter to what he perceives as the Society's imported Western notions of individuality and self-determination.[54] Ishizaki transposes Buddhism's fundamental tenet of codependent origination onto ancestral rites, arguing that performing memorial rites benefits not only the deceased, but also the descendant, who, through previous generations, is tied to and in some way dependent on, all the life in the universe. For Ishizaki, the Society's abandonment of ancestral rites ignores some fifteen hundred years of Japanese ancestor worship and appears self-centered and selfish. "When you look from the standpoint of this [long history], the trend toward 'funerary freedom' over the last few decades seems like just a flash in the pan."[55]

Shingon priest Komine Michihiko also focuses on what ancestor worship—and, more specifically, Buddhist forms of memorializing the dead—can teach the living. His consideration of natural funerals begins with an extended history of the treatment of human remains in early Mahāyāna Buddhism and then proceeds to the importance of Buddhist stūpas and five-tiered grave markers (*gorintō*). "The meaning of building a five-tiered stone monument above the remains is to pray that the deceased will be embraced by Dainichi Nyorai and become one with his eternal dharma body."[56] According to Komine, the grave, while primarily a site for memorializing the dead, also provides an opportunity for guiding the living toward enlightenment. This is contrasted with scattering, which leaves nothing behind. "Scattering cuts off this important site that leads us to something of value. This is why I have misgivings."[57]

Komine also focuses on the beneficial lessons of causality as part of his critique, though in a different way than Ishizaki. He argues that while both direct cause (*in*), which he interprets as "the power of one's volition," and contributory cause (*en*), "which is the power that surrounds and fosters direct cause," are both essential, it is the latter that is the source of everything we experience. "This reckless scattering, which destroys the opportunity to direct a person's spirit, must be thought of as severing *en*, which for us Buddhists is the most important thing."[58] There is an important conflation here between very different uses of the term *en*. On the one hand, it is a technical Buddhist term that is usually translated as "indirect cause" (or condition/circumstance) and placed in opposition to "direct cause" (*in*) in explaining how phenomena arise in mutual dependence. On the other hand, in common usage, *en* refers to a "relationship" or "bond" and generally takes the form of family (*ketsuen*) or regional (*chien*) ties. We shall return to the question of *en* below, but it is important to recognize here the attempt to connect Buddhist doctrinal concepts and Japanese social forms through the site of the traditional family grave.

Stephen Covell has shown that while it is certainly possible to disregard much of the Buddhist critique of the GFPS as a transparent attempt to protect the economic base of temples, for some Buddhists, such as the Tendai priest quoted below, natural funerals are seen not merely as severing family and social bonds but also as "a threat to the very moral foundations of Japanese culture."[59]

> If we recognize the majesty of human life, it should be clear that the body cannot just be thrown out. Whatever excuse one uses for scattering remains, it comes down to throwing them out. Usually, one visits the grave thinking of the parents. What do people who throw out the remains do? Visit the mountains or forest? . . . The extended family has already collapsed. But I don't think it is all right to destroy parent-child relations as well. Even in a nuclear family, parent-child relations are authoritative. They are tied to good neighborly relations. We should reaffirm the fact that the family line is extended through the grave. . . . The lack of an ethical view is a major problem. Ethical views begin in the family. . . . Set the mind straight, train the body, support your family, govern the country, make all equal under heaven. Are these just too old-fashioned? I think reaffirming the importance of the family and the importance of community relations will shed light on the antisocial nature of scattering remains.[60]

Here again we see the grave as an essential site of family continuity that is now represented as the very basis of morals and ethics, not only for the individual, but also for the entire nation. Scattering remains is no longer simply a reflection of larger social problems but a contributor to the final disintegration of what remains of the traditional family.

While this type of critique of the Society may come as little surprise, Buddhist support for scattering comes from unexpected directions. In an article on the first *shizensō* performed by the Society, the *Bukkyō Times* solicited the opinions of four Buddhist priests and scholars. Despite the "warning bell" headlines noted above, the reactions were not entirely negative, and in fact three of the priests offered at least partial support for the idea of scattering. For Sōtō priest and director of the Buddhist Information Center Suzuki Eijo, scattering has lit a helpful fire of critique that, far from undermining Buddhism, may "provide the key to how individual temples should react to current [funerary] problems."[61] Although he does not specify why, Jōdō Shinshū scholar Ōmura Eishō considers scattering to be both folk religious and an extreme form of secularism. Echoing the criticisms above, he sees natural funerals as "severe individualism" but then admits that as an individual, he too has the desire to have his remains scattered. He then allows, in a surprising but doctrinally consistent statement, that "the leaving behind of bones is of course a type of attachment."[62]

For some priests such as Shinbo Yoshimichi, former head of the Jōdo sect's efforts in Hawaii, scattering is the best way to deal with the increase of individuals who die without descendants to take care of their graves, both in Hawaii and in Japan. Echoing Ōmura Eishō's return to the doctrine of non-attachment, Shinbo argues, "Surely the best method for protecting against the crude handling of ashes is to return them to nature at a suitable time.... Buddhism originally preached emptiness and discarding attachments to all things. Is it not important that we now discard our attachments to bodily remains? If we are going to cling to our bones, then there is no way we should throw away even one fragment of remains after cremation."[63] Shinbo's last statement is of particular interest because it echoes doctrinally the often invoked defense of the legality of scattering made by Society founder Yasuda about the potential criminality of everyone who leaves behind even a small portion of remains at the crematorium.

Another voice that must be included in this debate comes from Buddhists who are also members of the GFPS, such as Shingon Buzan-ha priest Okada Hirotaka. In a special issue of a sectarian research journal, Okada quotes from a 1748 work entitled *A Compilation of Buddhist Rites for Monks and Laity* (*Shinzoku butsuji-hen*), which outlines three ways of dealing with a corpse: earth burial (*dosō*), cremation (*kasō*), and water burial (*suisō*). In a section titled

"The Superior and Inferior Merits of the Three Types of Burial" (*Sansō no kudoku no shōretsu*), the three types of burial are defined in the following way. "Earth burial is an act that disposes of the whole body as it is. Therefore it is a very lonely practice. Cremation involves taking the bones and dividing them among the relatives. This follows the cremation of Śākyamuni. Water burial is a practice that offers the flesh of the body to other living things."[64] These are then ranked so that earth burial is considered a lesser merit (*gebon no kudoku*), cremation is a mid-level merit, while water or forest burial (*rinsō*) offers the highest merit (*jōbon no kudoku*). Though the above classifications are taken directly from the original, Okada then proceeds to equate the sea and forest burials of the text with the natural funerals of the GFPS. "This Buddhist view of placing the body in the water or in a forest as a superior practice comes from a very different historical background from today, but surely we can also value the act of returning powdered cremated remains to mountains and oceans as a 'superior practice.' This is because we can assume that eventually the ashes will become an offering (*fuse*) to living creatures."[65]

Doctrines of emptiness and non-attachment notwithstanding, the Buddhist fascination with bodily remains—seen, for example, in relic cults—appears across a wide variety of cultures and historical periods.[66] In the case of Japanese Buddhism, since the Tokugawa period a devotion to relics has been gradually replaced by a dependence on graves. With the majority of Japanese Buddhist temples' social authority and economic livelihood based on graves and memorial rites, the various sects and individual priests have naturally sought doctrinal justifications for the importance of these traditions. Despite the fact that some Buddhist priests have recognized that the scattering advocated by the GFPS appears to exemplify the ideal of non-attachment, most Buddhist criticisms of *shizensō* can be seen as attempts to maintain a multigenerational attachment to the grave through a focus on continuity, social bonds, and the importance of family. Though such family-oriented arguments may contradict Buddhist doctrine, they are nevertheless a defining characteristic of Japanese Buddhism.

Grave Situations

In order to properly understand the emergence and significance of the Society, its practices, and other similar movements, we must consider the wider context of the current burial situation in Japan. Most professionals, be they religious, funerary, or academic, agree that since roughly around 1990, Japan has been undergoing drastic changes—some say a crisis—in regard to the treatment of the dead. Government and business surveys suggest that a growing number of Japanese have no place to go when they die. In the case of the eight public graveyards serving the Tokyo metropolitan area, the four that are within the city limits (i.e., within the twenty-three Tokyo wards) are no longer accepting applicants, as they are slated to be turned into parks. Despite a leveling off over the last several years of applications to the remaining four graveyards, at about ten thousand per year there are still an average of thirty applications for each grave plot, with this ratio increasing to more than fifty to one for more popular sites.[67]

In addition to exploring the possible regulation of scattering, the Welfare Ministry's 1997 committee on current grave practices also concentrated on the problem of insufficient grave space. According to the committee's report, by 2004, the demand for graves in metropolitan Tokyo would have outstripped supply by 40 percent, potentially resulting in roughly 140,000 corpses going homeless by the end of the following year.[68] A major factor contributing to such a shortage is the large number of "unconnected" or abandoned graves (*muen funbo*). Literally, "graves without ties," this term refers to graves where there are no descendants to take care of them or organize memorial rites. The committee proposed easing requirements for reporting abandoned graves and for subsequent removal of the remains to a communal grave, thus increasing available space.[69] In addition to making it easier to "evict" the dead, the report stressed the need for new graveyard styles, including "spirit parks" (*reien*), communal graves, and "wall style" graves (*kabegata bochi*), which are also referred to as "coin locker graves" because of their physical resemblance to the ubiquitous lockers found at train stations and shopping centers around the country.[70]

The so-called "eternal memorial graves" (*eitai kuyō baka*) have seen a huge boom in the last decade, with several temples throughout the country setting up high-profile "societies" (*kai*) that both fill existing demands for new types of grave space and create new connections between the public and temples.[71] Members of the Society of *En* (En no Kai, founded in 1996) at the Sōtō temple Tōchōji in Tokyo pay 800,000 yen (about $6,400) to have their remains interred and memorialized as individuals for thirty-three years, after which time they are placed in a communal grave treasure tower (*tahōtō*), where they will continue to receive services as ancestors for as long as the temple stands. Members are also given a posthumous name and a grave marker in the form of a twenty-by-ten-centimeter hollow black oblong stone engraved with their actual, as opposed to posthumous, names and placed in small square islands of eighty-one stones in a small pool on the temple grounds.[72] Family members may place memorial items such as reading glasses inside. The ashes and memorial tablet (*ihai*) are placed in the Hall of Arhats (*rakandō*), directly under the main hall. As of July 2002, approximately six years after the En no Kai began, it had roughly 4,850 members, with enough space for up to 7,500. When one realizes that the temple is already considered quite large with its 700 parishioner families, the idea of an additional 7,500 members was staggering at the time, but as of 2006, there were already more than 7,000 members and plans to accept up to 10,000 total. En no Kai also has a quarterly newsletter and offers numerous cultural and educational programs, such as a singing chorus, *zazen* meditation sessions, and lectures on Buddhist culture offered through Tōchōji.

One major impetus for these new styles of graves that do not require descendants to maintain them is a growing number of women who, for various reasons, want the opportunity to own their own graves. The most visible group to call for women's graves, the Society for a Women's Monument (Onna no Hi no Kai), founded in 1979 by Tani Kayoko, was initially formed for women widowed in World War II. The original monument, located at Jōjakkōji, a Nichiren temple in western Kyoto, was engraved with the words, "As long as a single woman lives, we will pray for peace here." According to Tani, the monument expressed the sentiment that "though a women lives alone, once she dies, she wants to rest with her friends."[73] Though the monument was erected in 1979, it was not until ten years later that an ossuary (*nōkotsudō*) was built that could hold the women's remains. The ossuary was named the Shrine of Intentional Bonds (Shienbyō) in order to show that those interred within were joined by bonds (*en*) of purpose, rather than the traditional bonds of family or region. As of early 2000, the Onna no Hi no Kai had more than six hundred members, owing in large part to a noticeable shift in membership that began around 1990, when young single women began joining. Tani sees the change as part of a larger trend toward variety in funerary styles that is allowing not only single and widowed women to make choices, but also married women, who may not wish to spend eternity with their husbands' ancestors. While there are as yet no specific data, it is apparent that there is a growing trend in Japan toward what Inoue Haruyo has termed "posthumous divorce" (*shigo rikon*).[74]

The site that many take as the foundation of Japan's eternal memorial grave boom is Myōkōji, a Nichiren temple in Niigata Prefecture that is the home of the Tranquillity Society (Annon Kai), founded in 1989. Members are interred and prayed for as individuals in a Tranquillity Shrine (Annonbyō), a large octagonal concrete building in the shape of a traditional Buddhist stūpa with a small treasure tower in the center. Demand from across the country for these ossuaries has been so high that as of 2001, the 432 graves in Myōkōji's four Tranquillity Shrines were completely full, and the temple was forced to build an Annon Forest (Mori no Annon) of 240 smaller octagonal graves in 2002. There is also a new Annon Shrine at a Nichiren temple in Kyushu, with plans for another to be built in Kamakura. The success of Annon Kai has come largely from its yearly gathering, the Tranquillity Festival in August, when members take part in memorial services; attend a series of Buddhist memorial rites, cultural performances, lectures, and dharma talks; and dance the "Annon jig," while the head priest, Ogawa, plays the *taiko* drums. Like En no Kai and Onna no Hi no Kai, Annon Kai is successful not simply because of its "open grave" policy but also because of the surrounding network that it offers.

The various burial societies, with their simplified, inexpensive rites; guarantee of postmortem individuality for up to thirty-three years; and memorial rites for "eternity," address new groups of religious consumers that have been emerging since the late 1980s. While the existence of such groups undoubtedly reflects changing conceptions of family and ancestors, it is also worth considering how they are reshaping traditional relationship forms. As noted above, the two most common forms of relationship or bond (*en*) in Japan are those of blood and locale. What is fascinating to note about some of these burial groups is the way they are appropriating the *en* in new ways. The En no Kai offers no modifier for *en* and becomes thus a "Society of Bonds." The use of the term *shienbyō* by the Society for a Women's Monument consciously modifies *en* by adding "will" or "intent," thus allowing its members to form new types of bonds. In both cases, as well as with other burial societies, the traditionally recognized forms of relations are being dramatically expanded, so that friends, acquaintances, and even strangers may now be buried together and memorialize each other. One might then add a third category of relation, "death bonds" (*shien*), to signify this new phenomenon of postmortem social reform.

Building upon the work of Japanese scholars such as Murakami Kōkyō, who has tracked a shift toward the privatization of funerary custom since the 1960s, I have argued elsewhere that we may now speak of the "individualization" of the dead, in which a person's own desires for postmortem treatment take precedence over the wishes of family or the expectations of society.[75] Within this context, the GFPS may be seen as simply another response to widespread uncertainties about what will happen to one's physical remains, but there are essential differences. Despite the new death relationships mentioned above, we must keep in mind that the actions of the various burial societies are still well within the established Buddhist idiom of memorial rites and graves, whereas the GFPS is making a significant break with these practices. Society members may revisit a site, particularly if it is on land, but there are none of the rituals or offerings that accompany traditional yearly grave visits.

Though the Society does not often address itself directly to the question of memorial rites, both Yasuda and individual members are certainly aware of the issue. The Society's quarterly newsletter *Rebirth* (*Saisei*) includes brief letters by members describing natural funerals in which they have taken part and giving their opinions on related issues. A particularly poignant response to the question of memorial rites came from a veteran who wrote of the great number of his fellow navy officers in World War II who had died without funerals in the South Pacific. As if speaking directly to the Buddhist priests, he wrote, "The melody of the endless tide pacifies the departed spirit better than one million sūtra recitations. I hope that I too will be scattered in the azure sea."[76] When I specifically asked Yasuda for his position on ancestor worship, he answered that though he agreed with the concept in general, most people have never even met the generation before that of their grandparents and thus have little connection to ancestors. He also doubted that any ill would come from not continuing to make offerings to the dead, since there was no way a deceased spirit would want to harm his or her own descendants. Despite the apparent logic of this statement, it marks a radical departure from traditional conceptions of the dead. Both the history and physical landscape of Japan are littered with monuments, shrines, and myriad prophylactic rites to ensure the ancestors' continued appeasement.[77]

Locating the Remains

The biggest tradition that scattering overturns is the clear separation between the living and the dead. By slipping through the loophole in current Japanese grave laws, the Society has potentially opened up the entire country to death. With scattering, the boundaries of a graveyard or memorial park are no longer relevant. There is a real fear that somebody's ashes could conceivably be in one's backyard, under a picnic basket, or mixed in with the fish prepared for dinner. The fact that the public at large is reacting so much more strongly to the form and location of scattered remains, rather than to the potential undermining of ancestral rites and family continuity, shows that the location of human remains may be more important than whether or not anyone is memorializing them. Despite finding widespread support for scattering, the Welfare Ministry's 1997 survey also revealed that even among those who accepted scattering, 62 percent felt that fixed rules should be laid down regarding location. More than 80 percent of all surveyed thought that scattering in places such as towns, parks, roads, river heads, and beaches was inappropriate, and 70 percent felt the same way about fishing and farming areas.[78]

Immediately after death, the corpse is in an ambiguous—or, to use van Gennep's term, liminal—state. Neither fully present nor completely gone, the deceased must be ritually removed from both the social and the physical sphere of the living and transferred to that of the dead. What is particularly intriguing about the idea of scattering in public spaces is the way that it may extend the liminal period indefinitely. Although interest in van Gennep's work tends to focus on liminality, we need also to keep in mind the importance of reincorporation.. It is essential that at some point the dead be plainly situated somewhere other than among the living. Note that while for the bereaved family and the GFPS scattering may end the liminal stage, for those who live and work in the area where the remains are scattered, the lack of a clearly defined space for the dead means that they are never *in their place*.

This ambiguity of location that scattering entails carries over into other areas as well. There is the unclear position of scattering in the eyes of the law, neither legal nor illegal, neither prohibited nor fully accepted. The remains are also ambiguous in terms of tradition. Scattered in the ocean or in a forest, they are removed from the cycle of ancestral worship and family obligation—not abandoned (*iki*), but certainly without ties (*muen*). In a sense, scattering solves the problem of *muen*, not simply by reducing the load on overburdened urban graveyards, but rather by providing the deceased with an alternative to the ancestral cycle, that of nature.

Buddhist institutions are also providing alternative cycles and spaces. While maintaining the Buddhist tradition of memorial rites, temples such as Myōkōji, Tōchōji, and Jōjakkōji are creating associations that they argue will transcend the bonds of family and region. Another essential difference between these temples and the GFPS is that the latter ends its relation to the dead as soon as they are "returned" to nature, while the former will continue their interactions for thirty-three years or more. The very impulse toward individual rights and the desire to determine one's fate after death, which the GFPS champions, is leading people to seek alternatives that both let them make choices and keep their individual identities as objects of veneration long after they have died.

Japan is in the midst of a far-reaching transformation vis-à-vis the structure of the family, and this may be nowhere more apparent than in the nation's graves. People who fifteen years ago would have had little choice but to enter a family grave or end up nameless in an ossuary are now in a position to make a wide range of choices about where their remains will end up and how long they will maintain their individuality after death.

What we are witnessing is more than merely a reaction against traditional Buddhist graves and funerals. Though it is tempting to attribute these changes to modernity, this is by no means a simple question of rationalization or secularization. The fact that many people are trying to renegotiate their relationships with temples, whether by joining burial associations or simply by choosing eternal memorial graves that allow them to die Buddhist and as individuals, suggests that the Japanese have not succumbed to a general Weberian disenchantment. At the same time, it is also apparent that Buddhist temples that are entirely dependent on the traditional *danka* system are in serious trouble. Priests whom I have interviewed all speak of the end or at least a fundamental transformation of the parishioner-temple relationship over the next few decades, as the traditional household continues to take new forms. The GFPS, Annon Kai, Onna no Hi no Kai, and others reveal possible directions for the future, not only of burial practices, but also of religious affiliation as a whole. I would posit that the current revolution in Japanese grave and funeral practices does not simply reflect larger societal changes but may provide an essential arena where social norms are first contested.

Notes

I would like to thank Yasuda Mutsuhiko, Ogawa Eiji, Inoue Haruyo, and Soda Yumiko for their help during the researching of this chapter. An earlier version of it appeared in the *Japanese Journal of Religious Studies* 30, nos. 1–2 (2003): 85–118. I would also like to thank the *Journal* for permission to republish it in revised form.

1. The Sōsō no Jiyū o Susumeru Kai officially translates its name into English as the Grave-Free Promotion Society because it feels this best describes its intentions to non-Japanese. A direct translation of the name would be the Society for the Promotion of Funerary Freedom.

2. In 1999 alone, there were almost one million deaths nationwide. *Nihon tōkei nenkan*, ed. Sōmushō Tōkeikyoku Kenkyūjo (Tokyo: Nihon Tōkei Kyōkai, 2003), 33.

3. Mori Kenji, *Haka to sōsō no genzai: Sosen saishi kara sōsō no jiyū e* (Tokyo: Tokyodō Shuppan, 2000), appendix, 1–38.

4. Yasuda Mutsuhiko, "Shizensō no susume," *Bukkyō* 20 (1992): 122–23.

5. Article 190 states the following: "Anyone who damages, discards, or removes the corpse, remains, or hair of the deceased, or an item placed in a coffin, shall be imprisoned for no more than three years." Cited in Inoue Haruyo, *Gendai ohakajijō: Yureru kazoku no naka de* (Nagoya: Osaka: Sōgensha, 1990), 247.

6. Sōsō no Jiyū o Susumeru Kai, ed., *"Haka" kara no jiyū: Chikyū ni kaeru shizensō* (Tokyo: Shakai Hyōronsha, 1991), 176.

7. For details in English on *kotsuage*, see Elizabeth Kenney, "Shinto Mortuary Rites in Contemporary Japan," *Cahiers d'Extrême-Asie* 9 (1996–97): 423; Suzuki Hikaru, *The Price of Death: The Funeral Industry in Contemporary Japan* (Stanford, CA: Stanford University Press, 2000), 117–18; and Mark Rowe, "Stickers for Nails: The Ongoing Transformation of Roles, Rites, and Symbols in Japanese Funerals," *Japanese Journal of Religious Studies* 27, nos. 3–4 (2000): 369.

8. Despite the government's apparent acquiescence on the legality of scattering, there was still much debate in the national press over the actual degree of acceptance given the "within moderation" phrase in the Justice Ministry's opinion. Concerns ranged from the pollution of oceans and mountains to "indiscriminate scattering of remains." Notwithstanding the Society's assurances that human bones are made of calcium phosphate and therefore environmentally beneficial, there remained a fear that someone would now be able to throw away large, recognizable pieces of human bone in public spaces (Yasuda, "Shizensō no susume," 123).

9. For some examples of reactions by Society members when faced with this process, see Yamaori Tetsuo and Yasuda Mutsuhiko, *Sōsō no jiyū to shizensō* (Tokyo: Gaifū, 2000), 96–214.

10. Sōsō no Jiyū o Susumeru Kai, ed., *"Haka" kara no jiyū*, 182.

11. "Haka to sōshiki no jiyū," *Bukkyō* 38 (1997): 116. There are inevitably some remains left over after the process of picking up the bones and placing them in the urn (*shūkotsu* or *kotsuage*). Generally in western Japan, a large percentage of the remains is left over, while in eastern Japan, most of the remains are entombed with only a small amount left behind at the crematorium. However, it is not the case that the remains are simply treated as industrial waste. Some crematoria put the remains in a single memorial grave, and others actually scatter them in the mountains. See Suzuki, *The Price of Death*, 164–67.

12. See Fujii Masao: "Sankotsu to kankyō hogo kisei," *Shūkyō kenkyū* 69 (1995): 211–32, and "Sankotsu no hōkisei o motomeru tame no shogaikoku jirei," *Gekkan jūshoku* 8–9 (1996): 30–52, and Yokota Mutsumi: "Ikotsu wa doko ni demo makeru toshitara dōnaru ka?!" *Gekkan jūshoku*, no. 11 (1996): 56–63, and "Tōtō jitaku no niwa ni ikotsu o makeru jidai ni natta," *Gekkan jūshoku*, no. 2 (1997): 60–63.

13. Article 4 of the laws covering graves and burial states, "Burial or interment of ashes shall not occur in an area outside of a graveyard." Article 1 states, "The intent of this law is to ensure that the management of graveyards, ossuaries, and crematoria, as well as burial and the like, shall, in conformity with the religious sentiments of the people and in accordance with public sanitation and communal welfare, occur without hindrance." Cited in Inoue, *Gendai ohakajijō*, 248–49.

14. http://www1.mhlw.go.jp/shingi/s1023-1.html (accessed January 10, 2003).

15. In March 1995, members of the religious cult Aum Shinrikyō carried out a sarin gas attack on a Tokyo subway, killing twelve people. The government responded in part by revising the Religious Corporations Law in December of the same year, the first amendment to the law in more than forty years. For an excellent analysis of the changes in laws governing religious groups after Aum, see John LoBreglio, "The Revisions to the Religious Corporations Law: An Introduction and Annotated Translation," *Jap-*

anese Religions 22, no. 1 (1997): 38–59. For details on the Aum affair, see Shimazono Susumu, "In the Wake of Aum: The Formation and Transformation of a Universe of Belief," *Japanese Journal of Religious Studies* 22, nos. 3–4 (1995): 381–415, and Ian Reader, *Religious Violence in Contemporary Japan: The Case of Aum Shinrikyō* (Honolulu: University of Hawai'i Press, 2000).

16. *Mainichi shinbun*, August 17, 1998.

17. Yokota Mutsumi, *Ohone no yukue* (Tokyo: Heibonsha, 2000), 113.

18. *Mainichi shinbun*, August 17, 1998.

19. See, for example, Katsuta Itaru, "Samazama na shi," *Nihon tsūshi* 8, *Chūsei* 2, ed. Asao Naohiro (Tokyo: Iwanami Shoten, 1994): 357–73; Hashizume Shinya, "Utopias for the Dead: Cities and the Design of Cemeteries in Japan," *Iichiko International* 8 (1996): 19–39; and Doi Takuji, *Sōsō to haka no minzoku* (Tokyo: Iwata Shoin, 1997), 64–75.

20. Doi Takuji, "Minzoku shiryō ni arawareta bochi," in *Bochi*, ed. Mori Kōichi (Tokyo: Shakaishisōsha, 1975), 125.

21. Hashizume, "Utopias for the Dead," 24–25. For a similar argument, see Tamamuro Taijō, *Sōshiki bukkyō* (Tokyo: Daihōrinkaku, 1964), 211.

22. Andrew Bernstein: "The Modernization of Death" (Ph.D. diss., Columbia University, 1999), 35, and *Modern Passings: Death Rites, Politics, and Social Change in Imperial Japan* (Honolulu: University of Hawai'i Press, 2006), 39.

23. Tamamuro Fumio has done extensive work on the abuses of the temple certification system, including cases of priests who extorted sexual favors from parishioners by threatening not to certify them. See his *Sōshiki to danka* (Tokyo: Yoshikawa Kōbunkan, 1999).

24. Tamamuro Fumio, "Local Society and the Temple-Parishioner Relationship within the Bakufu's Government Structure," *Japanese Journal of Religious Studies* 28, nos. 3–4 (2001): 266.

25. Bernstein, "The Modernization of Death," 37.

26. Buddhist funerals had been spreading among commoners since at least the second half of the fifteenth century, when Sōtō priests, armed with rituals adapted from Song-dynasty monastic funerals, began proselytizing in the countryside. According to William Bodiford, the popularity of these funerals was due largely to the idea of posthumous ordinations that afforded laypeople the rites for a monk and carried a promise of salvation after death that was previously unavailable. See his "Zen and the Art of Funerals: Ritual Salvation in Japanese Buddhism," *History of Religions* 32 (1992): 146–64.

27. Tamamuro, "Local Society and the Temple-Parishioner Relationship," 277.

28. Tanigawa does warn that her findings hold only for the warrior and farmer classes but are not conclusive in regard to the merchant class. See

her "Excavating Edo's Cemeteries: Graves as Indicators of Status and Class," *Japanese Journal of Religious Studies* 19, nos. 2–3 (1992): 293.

29. Ibid., 288–89.

30. Bernstein, "The Modernization of Death," 135–36.

31. Inoue Haruyo and Ogawa Eiji, "Kawaru kazoku to josei to haka" (unpublished survey, 1995), 1. Cited by permission of the authors.

32. Mori Kenji, "Ideorogī toshite no 'sosen saishi' to 'haka,'" in Sōsō no Jiyū o Susumeru Kai, ed., *"Haka" kara no jiyū*, 49–51.

33. The full text of clause 897 reads as follows: "The genealogical records, ritual implements, and the rights to the grave, not bound by previous statutes, shall be inherited by the person who, according to custom, should perform the ancestral rites. However, if the progenitor designates a person to perform rites for the ancestors, then this person shall be the inheritor. In the case where custom is not clear, the family courts will determine the person who shall inherit" (cited in Inoue, *Gendai ohakajijō*, 246).

34. Inoue and Ogawa, "Kawaru kazoku to josei no haka," 1.

35. Mori, *Haka to sōsō*, 5–16. For a general survey of anti-funeral criticism, see Murakami Kōkyō, "Sōgi shikkōsha no hensen to shi no imizuke no henka," in *Sōsai bukkyō: Sono rekishi to gendaiteki kadai*, ed. Itō Yuishin and Fujii Masao (Tokyo: Nonburusha, 1997). For an English translation, see Murakami Kōkyō, "Changes in Japanese Urban Funeral Customs during the Twentieth Century," *Japanese Journal of Religious Studies* 27, nos. 3–4 (2000): 335–52.

36. *Asahi shinbun*, September 24, 1990. Another consistent, though not so ancient, example that the Society uses is that of former U.S. ambassador to Japan Edwin Reischauer, who requested that his ashes be scattered in the Pacific to create a bridge between the two countries.

37. Shima Tōru, "'Sankotsu' undō e no gimon: Kazoku gensō to kyōdōsei no aida," *Seiron* 94, no. 11 (1994): 112–23.

38. Ibid., 115.

39. Hashizume, "Utopias for the Dead," 25.

40. http://www.mikkyo21f.gr.jp/father_shukyo002.html (accessed February 1, 2004).

41. At the time of this writing, exchange rates are calculated at 125 yen to 1 U.S. dollar.

42. Yasuda Mutsuhiko, "Shizensō no Jiyū o Susumeru Kai no ayumi," *Bukkyō* 38 (1997): 114.

43. *Mainichi shinbun*, June 19, 1994.

44. Yokota Mutsumi, "Igi ari! Sōsō no jiyū," *Seiron* 94, no. 2 (1994): 256.

45. Shima, "'Sankotsu' undō e no gimon," 112–13.

46. In Society literature, the verb used to refer to scattering the ashes is almost always "to return" (*kaesu*) rather than "to bury" (*maisō suru*).

47. *Gekkan jūshoku*, no. 12 (1991): 2.
48. *Bukkyō Times*, October 25, 1991, 4.
49. Ibid.
50. Katō Eiji, "Sōsō no jiyū ikō no sōsō," *Gekkan jūshoku*, no. 10 (1993): 61.
51. Ibid.
52. Ibid.; emphasis added.
53. This shift is a central theme in Mori, *Haka to sōsō*.
54. http://www.geocities.co.jp/Bookend-Soseki/5166/senzo.htm (accessed January 10, 2003).
55. Ibid.
56. Komine Michihiko, "Bukkyō wa shizensō o dō kangaeru ka," *Daihōrin* 62 (1995): 119.
57. Ibid.
58. Ibid.
59. Stephen G. Covell, *Japanese Temple Buddhism: Worldliness in a Religion of Renunciation* (Honolulu, University of Hawai'i Press, 2005), 186.
60. *Kōhō Tendai* 10 (1998): 12–13. Quoted in Covell, *Japanese Temple Buddhism*, 186–87.
61. *Bukkyō Times*, October 25, 1991, 4.
62. Ibid.
63. Ibid.
64. Okada Hirotaka, "Ohaka o meguru hōritsu mondai no iroha," Shingon Buzan-ha Kyōka Sentā, *Kyōka Sentā sanka shiryō* 4 (2001): 93.
65. Ibid., 93–94.
66. See, for example, John S. Strong, *Relics of the Buddha* (Princeton, NJ: Princeton University Press, 2004), and David Germano and Kevin Trainor, eds., *Embodying the Dharma: Buddhist Relic Veneration in Asia* (Albany: State University of New York Press, 2004).
67. Sōgi Reien Bunka Kenkyūkai, *Iza to iu toki no sōgi to kuyō jiten* (Tokyo: Nihon Bungeisha, 2000), 272.
68. http://www1.mhlw.go.jp/shingi/s0321–3.html (accessed January 10, 2003).
69. http://www1.mhlw.go.jp/shingi/s9804/s0428–2.html (accessed January 10, 2003).
70. Resembling Western grave parks, *reien* began emerging in the 1930s. They have been referred to as everything from "utopias for the dead" to "subdivisions for the dead." See Bernstein, "The Modernization of Death," 145, and Hashizume, "Utopias for the Dead," 32–34.
71. In 2000, a guidebook to more than 225 eternal memorial graves across the country was published and required a second printing within two months. The third edition, published in 2003, has 328 listings. See Butsuji Gaido Henshūbu, ed., *Eitai kuyō baka no hon* (Tokyo: Rokugatsu Shobō, 2003).

72. Significantly, all of the posthumous names of those who belong to the En no Kai must end in either Shinnyo for women or Shinji for men, both mid-level status titles affixed to the end of posthumous names and traditionally indicating a lay follower. This is in sharp contrast to the common practice of paying large sums for long and prestigious posthumous names seen at other temples and even among the regular *danka* at Tōchōji. One wonders if this was not a conscious decision on the part of the temple to appease the parishioners by inserting a highly visible class break between the two groups.

73. Tani Kayoko, "Onna no Hi no Kai no ayumi kara shien no sōsō o motomete," *Sōgi* 19 (1994): 86.

74. Inoue Haruyo, *Haka o meguru kazokuron* (Tokyo: Heibonsha, 2000), 34.

75. Murakami, "Sōgi shikkosha," and Rowe, "Stickers for Nails."

76. Cited in *Saisei* 41, 19.

77. Examples include Tenmangu shrines, battlefield prayers to pacify the souls of slain enemies, and offerings to wandering spirits, to name but a few.

78. Mori, *Haka to sōsō*, appendix, 28–30.

14

Care for Buddhism

Text, Ceremony, and Religious Emotion in a Monk's Final Journey

Jason A. Carbine

As can be seen in several of the preceding chapters in this volume, Buddhist death practices typically involve one or two very important dynamics, both of which relate to the care that Buddhists show for the dead and living alike.[1] One dynamic occurs largely in the context of funerals for revered exemplars. Buddhist funerals for such exemplars often produce relics that become the focus of continued veneration by the Buddhist community. Indeed, as John Strong has shown, the funeral rites for the Buddha himself were structured around the production of his relics. A second dynamic occurs within the context of virtually any Buddhist death practice, whether it be for ordinary or exemplary dead. When Buddhists perform death practices, they generate merit or positive karmic influence, which can assist particularly but not only the ordinary lay deceased. John Holt has examined this second dynamic as it is borne out in family contexts in Sri Lanka. He highlights the "dynamic power attributed to karma," which can help both the dead and the living avoid suffering.[2]

Clearly, producing relics of revered exemplars and generating family-oriented karma are important aspects of Buddhist care. However, in this chapter I am not primarily interested in relics and karma, at least not in terms of my interpretive focus. Rather, the aspects of Buddhist care addressed here revolve around the very flourishing of Buddhism as such, even in a funerary setting.[3] My objective is to discuss, in the context of Burmese Buddhism, a particular kind of Buddhist communal ethos that harkens back to the days of the Buddha, extends throughout many if not all Buddhist cultures, and takes on the challenge of sustaining words and practices attributed to the Buddha for the present time and for times to come.

My argument has three components. First, akin to Strong's

thesis that producing relics is a governing theme for the Buddha's funeral, I suggest that care for Buddhism is a governing theme for many Buddhist activities, including but hardly limited to funerals—although my focus will be a "cremation volume" or commemorative record of the large-scale funerary events for an exemplary monk. Second, I suggest that the compiling and publishing of such texts and the events they record are meant to be part and parcel of that care; that is, they are meant both to depict and to participate in care for Buddhism. Third, I show how care for Buddhism may involve the active work of different kinds of Buddhist "care groups," ceremonial honors for the exemplary dead, and the nurturing of religious emotion or agitation (Pāli *saṃvega*) among the living. In other words, what I label care for Buddhism can be fruitfully understood as a transgenerational socioreligious project entailing very significant textual, ceremonial, and emotional components.

Buddhist Care in Myanmar/Burma

This chapter discusses Theravāda evidence specifically from the urgent, fraught, and polarized context of contemporary Myanmar/Burma.[4] In a move that is far from unique, Myanmar/Burma's repressive military government has placed itself in line with longstanding Burmese and Buddhist traditions regarding the role of the state as a key protector of the Dispensation (Bur. *Sāsanā*; Pāli *Sāsana*), the corpus of teachings and practices attributed to the Buddha.[5] However, despite military support of Buddhism and despite military attempts to control Buddhist-related activities, the Burmese monastic institution itself remains the largest semiautonomous institution in the country outside military control. This situation, in which there are two dominant spheres of sociopolitical power—one military and one renunciatory—provides a quantity of both fruitful and problematic evidence about how Buddhists have cared, and continue to care, for Buddhism.

On a fruitful side, care for Buddhism thrives in contemporary Myanmar/Burma. Indeed, one can scarcely ignore the extremely large and growing numbers of Buddhist publications in Burmese, Pāli, and other languages; the pagoda renovations; the thriving lay and monastic meditation centers; the expanding monastic communities; the monies funneled into Buddhist education centers; the large-scale, state-backed Buddhist ceremonies; the cultural expressions pertaining to Buddhism, such as "improving," "spreading," and "cleansing" the Dispensation "so that it doesn't vanish," and the like. These and similar activities and expressions current in the country suggest a level of care for Buddhism perhaps unrivaled in the contemporary Southeast and South Asian Theravāda world.

On an especially problematic side, however, when sponsored by the military, the discourses and practices of care for Buddhism are very often forms of propaganda, meant to legitimize military rule in the process of deflecting attention from the military's repressive efforts to maintain power.[6] In an important respect, military-sponsored overtures to care for Buddhism are also in part the product of a culture of paranoia that pervades the military on an internal level. Should the military fail to monitor and/or control Buddhist ceremonies, Buddhist lay organizations, and monastic establishments, it could unwittingly allow them to be used for anti-military activities. In this climate, many monks and novices have been imprisoned, tortured, forced into hard labor, disrobed, or killed by the military. As with lay protests, monastic protests against the military have varied in structure and focus, but some of the most public have involved "overturning the bowl" against the military, a move in which monks and novices refuse to accept alms, one of the cornerstones of traditional Buddhist societies. While many military efforts to care for the manifold "affairs related to the life of the Dispensation" (Bur. *Sāsanā re*") constitute attempts to tap into, foster, and/or rein in the sentiments of the country's predominantly Buddhist populace, it is clear that many people, including monks and novices, continue to resist those attempts.

The contemporary sociopolitical situation in Myanmar/Burma poses several pressing questions for scholars of Buddhist cultures and societies. One such question is this: how can scholars of Buddhism analyze the contemporary Buddhist scene in Myanmar/Burma with reference to the care for Buddhism without overemphasizing the role of the military, even while keeping its activities firmly within the scope of their analyses? Buddhist Studies scholars should, I think, decenter from their analyses both the military and one of the domains of Buddhist thought and practice—meditation—that the military establishment likes most to promote. As important as they are, neither the Burmese "Buddhist" military establishment nor the various traditions of Burmese "Buddhist" meditation exhaust the arena of Burmese Buddhism. Buddhist Studies scholars examining contemporary Myanmar/Burma should not lose sight of either the Burmese military establishment or meditation, but they would do well to go beyond the ways in which both have come to structure much of the recent scholarly inquiry about Buddhism in the country.[7] The topic of care for Buddhism provides one such avenue. Indeed, in the urgent and fraught political circumstances in Myanmar/Burma, it is care for Buddhism that provides a common ground for many people of varied constituencies to articulate their aspirations and concerns, however base or noble those aspirations and concerns may be.

The *Final Journey* and Its Buddhist Care Groups

For illustrative purposes, I focus on a cremation volume or funerary text that offers an excellent source for discussing various aspects of the care for Buddhism in and beyond Myanmar/Burma. The text, *Bhaddanta Indācāra's Final Journey*, commemorates the life and funeral ceremonies for the high-ranking Burmese monk Bhaddanta Indācāra (1897–1993).[8] Indācāra's long and fruitful career included the writing of a number of works dealing with different aspects of Buddhist teaching and practice, tenure as head of a major teaching monastery, and, in 1980, elevation to the position of chairman of a state-backed council responsible for trying to restructure and unify the monastic community.[9]

The *Final Journey* may be described as a local ethnography. While it may lack the critical distance and wide cultural analysis associated with ethnographic work by contemporary scholars, the *Final Journey* provides a number of documentary, biographical, pictorial, and oral materials that bring to life a truly massive series of cultural events honoring a dead monk and the Buddhist tradition he strove to enhance. Indeed, with its array of commemorative sketches, biographical articles, discussions of the life of Buddhism, Pāli poetry and Burmese commentary, four sections of color photographs, and the like, the *Final Journey* provides a literary and visual feast regarding Indācāra and his funeral ceremonies.

In texts like the *Final Journey* and in the activities they record, it is impossible to ignore the presence of the military. For example, members of the military figure prominently in many of the photographs in the volume, especially as a way to showcase themselves as exemplary supporters.[10] However, because of the various kinds of renunciants (monks, novices, and nuns) and laypeople (members of the military, ordinary lay men and women, young and old) depicted in the text, the *Final Journey* does in fact encourage a certain kind of analytical decentering of the military. The text encourages us to set Buddhist discourses and practices of the care for Buddhism within the context of two broad, ideal-typical "care groups," whose interactions stand at the core of the *Final Journey* and thus at the core of the funerary activities it represents: Buddhist renunciants, on the one hand, and laypeople on the other.

In ideal-typical terms, renunciants are understood to be qualitatively different from laypeople. Renunciants have their own systems of discipline, textual study, meditation, ordination, and institutional meetings and gatherings through which they bring themselves together as communities oriented in particular ways around and toward the Buddha's teachings. As Hiroko Kawanami has discussed, the distinction in Myanmar/Burma between nuns and laypeople is more complex and problematic than that between monks and laypeople. For instance, Burmese nuns (Bur. *sīla rhan*, "precept holders") are not recognized as fully ordained nuns (Pāli *bhikkhunī*), largely because lineages of fully ordained nuns are believed to have died out.[11] Nevertheless, like monks, nuns still try to position themselves in relation to the Buddha's teachings in ways that laypeople typically do not. The most obvious markers of a distinctive renunciatory ethos consist of the shaved head and the wearing of the robes, both of which are meant to indicate that one is oriented toward the supramundane (Bur. *lokuttara*) in ways that ordinary laypeople are not. If monks and nuns were once ordinary sons and daughters carrying on family lines, they ideally become religiously and ethically exemplary "sons" and "daughters" of the Buddha when they participate in their monastic communities, which carry on the work of the Buddha and his successors, inasmuch as they care for Buddhism.

The *Final Journey*, like many other Buddhist sources, makes it clear that laypeople are hardly divorced from the patterns of religious practice and social interaction that are involved in the care for Buddhism, and thus also in the formation and activities of particular renunciant communities. Because in any given sociocultural context, laypeople can support only so many renunciants, such renunciants must compete for the continuing, positive attention of laypeople, especially those in positions of sociopolitical power. For their part, laypeople desire to support those renunciants who will provide them with prestige as caregivers for Buddhism. Hence, to encourage additional lay support and to garner mutual prestige, renunciants and their lay supporters often undertake and document large-scale religious ceremonies, such as funerals for exemplars.

Yet in addition to the particular sociopolitical interests that renunciants and laypeople may have in terms of power and prestige—whether individually or collectively or within and across care groups—I suggest that something larger is at work here, on the level of Burmese religious culture. The *Final Journey* and the funeral ceremonies it represents are for the most part the end product of the collective efforts of renunciant and lay care groups as they come together and try to generate continuing support for Buddhism by valorizing those exemplars like Indācāra who are believed to have done great things for the religion. Whatever else it may be—for example, an attempt by the military to enhance its image—the *Final Journey* is an expression of a very powerful and communally widespread ethos among the Burmese, renunciant or lay, exemplary or ordinary: a care for the continuing health and vitality of Buddhism.

An essay by Charles Hallisey offers a useful point of comparison to the perspective on Buddhist care groups offered here.[12] Hallisey approaches issues of care from a different but related angle. To bolster his thesis that preservation constitutes a moral imperative for philosophical study, he highlights a passage attributed to Buddhaghosa, a fifth-century Buddhist philosopher who emphasizes the importance of study "as of a treasurer." Buddhaghosa remarks, "Finally, [there is] the saint, who has acquired a complete knowledge of the aggregates, got rid of the corruptions, developed the Path, penetrated the Fruition of Arahantship . . . [and who] studies merely for the purpose of preserving the tradition, and of guarding the lineage of the doctrine. This is the study as of the treasurer."[13] Hallisey goes on to comment:

> The image of philosophy "as of a treasurer" reminds us that our responsibilities are not only to ourselves, but to past and future generations, and it also reminds us that these responsibilities impress on us certain expectations for how we should approach our expanding intellectual inheritance. . . . We have a responsibility to listen and to "continue the conversation" of tradition, even when

> it leaves us confused and even when we are confident that our reflections have "discovered" conceptual inadequacies within it. . . . [The] incitement to preservation is inherent in the very nature of philosophical understanding, in which ideas and problems received from the past have an autonomous interest beyond what can be explained by reference to their previous historical contexts.[14]

Here, Hallisey emphasizes the significance of a transgenerational philosophical project. As I read him, he suggests that Buddhist (and other) philosophers comprise the groups of scholars who preserve and nurture Buddhist (and other kinds of) doctrine that they inherit as well as pass on to succeeding generations. The type of Burmese material exemplified in the *Final Journey* encourages us to expand on this point by shifting from a religious-philosophical perspective to a religious-social perspective, in which many different kinds of Buddhists (monks, military leaders, and ordinary lay donors) co-participate in the care for Buddhism. While not solely focused on preserving philosophical components in their tradition, many Burmese Buddhists still care for Buddhism in ways similar to people who study as if they were "treasurers." They consider themselves responsible for nurturing (e.g., "improving," "spreading," "cleaning") their religious heritage so that people can continue to access, relate to, and experience Buddhist teaching and practice.

The *Final Journey* and Ceremonial Honor for the Monastic Dead

It is worthwhile to take a closer look at the structure and content of the *Final Journey*. In so doing, we can further comment on how the text relates to the care for Buddhism. The text itself is attractive. A highly stylized green and yellow cover with ornate flourishes on the front and pithy snippets from Indācāra on the back opens up to the monk's radiantly beaming portrait. The portrait is followed by a short introduction, a table of contents, a biographical sketch of Indācāra, a list of his scholastic affiliations, a list of his books, and a list of his ecclesiastical titles and positions, the last of which indicates Indācāra's prominent place among Sudhamma (Good Teaching) monks and among Burmese monks more generally.[15] Immediately following the list of Indācāra's titles and positions, the viewer/reader finds a group of photographs. These photographs provide pictures of Indācāra before his death; his parents; his parents' house; the monastery where he was ordained as a novice and then as a monk; and a trip that he took, in his old age, around the Asian world. These photographs march the viewer/reader toward a lengthy section of articles, attributed to several different people, who praise Indācāra's character and his work on behalf of Buddhism. Titles like "A Hero for the Dispensation" call to mind the death of a great monk whose demise is a considerable loss for Buddhism and for those who knew him.

The articles culminate in a second group of photographs, which catalogue parts of the funerary events for Indācāra. These photographs depict military officials who pay reverence before Indācāra's body; various committees that plan the funeral activities; monks and nuns who come to watch and/or participate in the activities; laypeople who donate money to help defray the cost of the activities; and laypeople who revere Indācāra as he lies in his glass and metal coffin, situated inside the Mahā Pāsāna Cave, where his body was interred for about three weeks before its cremation on May 22, 1993.[16]

After the second section of photographs, the remainder of the *Final Journey* focuses on the three days of official ceremonial activity culminating in the cremation of Indācāra's body at a site near the Mahā Pāsāna Cave. Once his body has been cremated, Indācāra's relics (Pāli *sarīra dhātu*) are deposited in the Yangon River. In recording these events, the compilers of the *Final Journey* included two more sections of photographs; three descriptive articles; several ceremonial verses, addresses, and speeches; excerpts of advice from certain monks, including Indācāra; and the names and functions of the various committees responsible for the proceedings.

Without going into detail about the cremation of Indācāra's body and the post-cremation handling of his relics, I can emphasize that the photographs and text—articles, verses, addresses, speeches, etc.—work together to offer a relatively thorough depiction of the internment of Indācāra's body at the Mahā Pāsāna Cave, the procession of his body to the cremation site, and the cremation proper.

They also vividly depict the fanfare as monks, military leaders, and other lay officials accompany Indācāra's relics out onto the Yangon River.

The *Final Journey* makes it plain, then, that Indācāra's body has been without question cared for.[17] But more than this, the *Final Journey* itself participates in the care for Indācāra's body because it is meant to preserve cultural memories and experiences of the funeral ceremonies. From the text, we see that Indācāra's body was esteemed, valorized, held up amid pomp and circumstance, talked about, visited, venerated, reflected upon, and even, as I will discuss below, lamented over. In brief, for certain periods of time, the *Final Journey* amply demonstrates that his body was placed at the focal point of Buddhist cultic life in order to honor the Buddhist work that he undertook during his life. To push the argument, the *Final Journey* has a pedagogical bent to it. If people want to know what the funeral was like, they can turn to the *Final Journey*. If people want to know how others have cared for the monastic dead, they can turn to the *Final Journey*. If people want to know how they should care for the monastic dead, they can turn to the *Final Journey*. If future military or other lay leaders want to know what role they should play in monastic funerals or see how they might outdo their predecessors in caring for Buddhism by caring for the monastic dead, they can turn to the *Final Journey*.

The *Final Journey* and Religious Emotion

It is crucial to recognize that care for the monastic dead also doubles as care for the living who are left behind. To demonstrate this, I now turn to one of the relationships that the *Final Journey* depicts between the funeral ceremonies for Indācāra, on the one hand, and the experiences of *saṃvega*, religious emotion or agitation, on the other. The *Final Journey* explicitly connects several activities associated with Indācāra's funeral to an increase in *saṃvega-ñāṇ*, which can be translated as "wisdom that comes about in the context and as a result of *saṃvega*." As emphasized by the *Final Journey*, these activities are structured to allow people ample room to express sorrow at the death of their revered teacher (or perhaps any other person), even while pushing them toward states of emotional agitation conducive to religious reflection and advancement. I discuss below a Pāli verse and Burmese commentary that represent this kind of movement. Like other *saṃvega*-oriented moments of Burmese funeral proceedings, the Pāli verse and Burmese commentary help us to understand some of the key religious interactions within Buddhist groups as they care for Buddhism by caring for the living.

According to an article and a photo in the *Final Journey*, both the verse and its commentary were composed by a monk who recited them in front of an audience in the Mahā Pāsāna Cave on the last day of the ceremonies leading up to Indācāra's cremation. By composing and reciting the verse and commentary, the monk is positioned as a primary locus for the Buddhist community's purported experience of *saṃvega*.

Stylistically, the Burmese commentary on the Pāli verse consists of "*nissaya* Burmese," in which Pāli words and phrases are followed immediately by their Burmese translation. In the example explored here, the commentary differs from what can be called the ordinary verbatim *nissaya* type (which contains a minimal number of additions) because it includes a number of embellishments meant to captivate those listening to or reading it.[18] The commentary is meant to captivate its audience in order to agitate listeners or readers, a point emphasized by the fact that the verse itself is labeled "apt to cause emotional agitation" (Pāli *saṃvejaniya*).[19]

Deriving from a verbal root that means to tremble, *saṃvega* applies to those events or places that are likely to induce "some shock [that] inspires an increase in the intensity of religious feelings and intentions."[20] For instance, some Theravādins call the four major places in India associated with the Buddha's life the *saṃvejaniya* places—that is, the places where he was born (Lumbinī), attained enlightenment (Bodhgayā), gave his first sermon (Migadāya), and passed away (Kusinārā).[21]

To better address the salient aspects of the *saṃvejaniya* verse and its commentary, it is helpful to call to mind William Graham's work on the study of orality within the history of religions.[22] Graham advocates moving beyond an oral-written dichotomy by looking at materials that show an interpenetration of oral and written words: "If we postulate a spectrum of religious discourse, with pure oral tradition and the vocal expressions of myth or prayer at one pole, and the written pages of sacred texts at the other, a wide variety of *Mischbildungen*, or intermediate combinations of oral and written word, intervene across the postulated spectrum."[23] While perhaps not a "sacred text" in the sense deployed by Graham, the *Final Journey* exemplifies those kinds of Buddhist materials that offer "intermediate combinations of oral and written word," precisely because the volume includes materials like the *saṃvejaniya* verse and its commentary.

Graham theorizes that the interpenetration of written and spoken words helps to create what he calls the "sensual dimension" of religious experience. This dimension is driven by an intensely personal and emotional engagement of a community with religious texts. Religious texts, he goes on to say, "are not just authoritative documents or sources of doctrinal formulas; they are living words that produce [or are meant to produce] a variety of responses—emotional and physical as well as intellectual and spiritual."[24] Drawing from the *saṃvejaniya* verse and its commentary in the *Final Journey*, we can specify that in the Burmese Buddhist case, such orally directed texts are meant to situate emotions, including sorrow, within specific kinds of Buddhist care for the living.

To fully understand the connection between the verse/commentary, on the one hand, and emotion, on the other, I focus my interpretive efforts on the Burmese commentary itself. The commentary helps us to understand two dynamics involved in the process of Buddhist care for the living as understood within the Burmese context. In one dynamic, people are given the public opportunity to express the sorrow that they may feel when a revered and beloved teacher passes away. Ideally, just as people grieved at the death of the Buddha, so too they grieve at the death of Indācāra; if people did not express such grief, it could possibly mean that they really did not care for Indācāra and/or Buddhism at all. As with the death of the Buddha, a public expression of sorrow becomes a moment that affirms not only the social importance of Buddhism but also the real sense of loss that people may feel at the death of a revered teacher.

In the second dynamic, an intense state of agitation compels people to pursue their religious development, and one way of understanding this process is as follows. The sorrow felt at the loss of a great hero for Buddhism is channeled into a state of emotional agitation. A mind so encompassed by agitation is ripe for religious attainment because the attachments that people have to their life, to the world as they know it, have been exposed in a direct way and are thus more susceptible to being reflected upon and perhaps overcome. The emotional torments that people feel are shown to be an integral part of the problem of being consumed by the fires of saṃsāra, the cycle of rebirth in which people ebb and flow. In effect, the Buddhist community cares for itself in a specifically religious way by offering itself occasions for reflection on cosmological truth. If for nothing else, the *saṃvejaniya* verse offers such an occassion.

With these two dynamics of the Buddhist care for the living in mind, we can explore parts of the Pāli verse and Burmese commentary in detail.[25] The verse and commentary begin by highlighting the arrival of various heavenly beings, led by the King of Gods, Indra. They have reverently come to Indācāra for the purpose of receiving instruction on "the essence of the dhamma," and they invite him back to the heavenly realms while riding on Indra's chariot itself. Present are people identified as "we Burmese people, male and female donors, sunk down in saṃsāra, who cannot uproot our mind and bodies from the river and whirlpool of saṃsāra."[26]

Let us look more closely at part of the verse and commentary. Two lines of the Pāli verse read:

> *āgamitvāna sissānaṃ sametu dukkhavedanaṃ*
> *sokasallena saṃyuttaṃ satiyāva punappunaṃ*

According to the commentary, these Pāli lines carry the following meaning and emphasis:

> Oh Benefactor, Great Noble Lord, please put out the fire called *dukkhavedanā* [sensation of suffering] that torments us. Out of unceasing compassion for your disciples, please put out this fire that violently afflicts us in the basket-husk of our minds and bodies. Please put out this fire that is always paired with the arrow-spike of endless grief, that never stops provoking, grinding and biting intensely in our minds, while our hearts palpitate continuously.

The Pāli lines, then, emphasize the degree to which people may entreat Indācāra to continue to help them overcome the torment they feel because of their existential condition and sense of sorrow. The full word-by-word Burmese commentary on these two lines reads as follows. It begins with an unexpressed subject, *so thero*:

> *so thero*: Our Meritorious Lord who, being tired of the human realm, now enjoys *nat*-hood [here, a *nat* is a kind of heavenly being]

āgamitvāna: having come into this present world as a person

sissānaṃ: of us, the Burmese monastic disciples, etc., who are repeatedly crying, burning with anxiety, stricken with a great deal of inconsolable sorrow, like the cane touched by flame, because our teacher is lost forever, as if each of us were like a fish in too little water, a son without a mother

punappunaṃ: every single moment of the day, over and over again, without missing even 1/60th of an hour, even one minute

satiyāva: just because of our mindfulness, although we miss you a great deal every day

pavakkena [unexpressed adjective of *sokasallena*]: that always exists, because the law is that it will always happen[27]

sokasallena: with the arrow-spike called endless grief that never stops provoking, grinding and biting intensely in our minds, [while] our hearts palpitate continuously

saṃyuttaṃ: that which is always paired side by side with something else, so that no one can separate himself from it

dukkhavedanaṃ: the fire called *dukkhavedanā*, oppressing us to the highest degree, violently burning us, forcefully afflicting us, so that we cannot endure it in the basket-husk of our minds and bodies

sametu: please put it out, P'aya[28]

sametu: please put it out, as you did when you were alive, out of unceasing compassion for your disciples, with the clear white moon of dhamma, so that the stains [of sorrow] stop, [oh] Benefactor, . . . Pegu Myo Ma Sayadaw, Noble Great Lord.[29]

There are at least four interlocking themes in the Burmese commentary that require explanation because each relates to the manner in which the verse is connected to religious emotion/agitation. One theme concerns the human condition. The commentary renders in unambiguous terms a dire picture of the human condition:

a fire of *dukkha*, of suffering, violently burns in the mental and physical husks that people call their minds and bodies. Herein lies the second theme, sorrow, which is an integral part of this fire because existential suffering is itself continually joined with an arrow-spike of endless grief, evident especially when loved ones pass away. In the particular case of the revered monk Indācāra, the sense of loss that people feel upon his death is even compared, in part, to the sense of loss that people feel upon the loss of their own mother. Indeed, Indācāra's disciples are each "like a son without a mother"—a simile that appears to evoke[30] the image of Indācāra as a kind of deceased mother who is no longer immediately available in the human world to continue to care for her son(s).[31]

The third theme is embedded in the first two themes: a subtle but apparent critique of sorrow itself. Sorrow plays a powerful role in preventing people from uprooting their minds and bodies "from the river and whirlpool of saṃsāra." Sorrow reflects attachment, the fuel of rebirth. Thus, the remedy for the existential torment and sorrow—the agitation—that people feel is the "clear white moon of the dhamma," mediated by monks like Indācāra. As the commentary points out, ridden with worry over their condition, people entreat Indācāra, just as when he was "alive as a person," to use the dhamma to quell their *dukkhavedanā*.

The fourth theme relates to the fact that people ask Indācāra to continue his activity in the human world. To understand this theme, we first need to understand what it means for Indācāra to become a heavenly being. In becoming a monastically inclined heavenly being, Indācāra will probably not devote much if any attention to the human world. To emphasize the point, another part of the verse and commentary states that Indācāra "abandons" his followers "without mercy." He leaves them behind without giving them any concern. In effect, he cuts his attachments to them, which is a necessary part of his own journey to enlightenment. He frees himself from the human world so that he can continue his own journey, which now takes him to the heavens. There, he may pursue his Buddhist work by continuing to preach to other beings in the heavens. Indeed, heavenly beings too both want and need to hear the dhamma.

Yet in his heavenly status, Indācāra has become a type of Buddhist saint "who is comparable to the sun," who possesses "all those qualities, with fragrant, nurturing, white, and clean *sīla* [morality] as their base, which spread out beyond the three realms [a reference to various levels of the Buddhist cosmos]."[32] He *does* in fact have the continuing *capacity* to be able to play a role in human and worldly affairs. When people request Indācāra to continue to preach to them as he did when he was "alive as a person," they both acknowledge his persisting capacity to better human life and seem to ask him to pursue his ability. To invoke the title of Holt's chapter in this volume, people believe that Indācāra is dead but not completely departed.

In summary, each of the four themes contributes to the ways in which the Pāli verse and its Burmese commentary relate to the emotional agitation that may prompt people to seek the dhamma. The themes interlock to expose in a graphic way the nature of the human condition, the intensity of human emotion related to the death of a loved one, and the pursuit of dhamma as a soteriological path that can help people sever the bonds imprisoning them in saṃsāra. Ultimately, the themes highlight the role played by emotion or agitation in the turn that people may make both to the dhamma and to those who embody it in this life and the next. For his own part, Indācāra will extend his Buddhist work to places beyond the human realm. Someday, perhaps, he and others like him will return to assist other humans in their time of need as they try to take shelter, as Indācāra himself has done, under "the protective umbrella of the journey to Nirvāṇa."[33]

Depicting and Participating in Care for Buddhism

Like many other Buddhist materials, the *Final Journey* is a textual repository of memories and experiences of care for Buddhism. It is meant to depict and participate in that care by showing, for example, the socioreligious interactions of Buddhist care groups, displaying the ceremonial honors for the exemplary dead, and demonstrating the attempts that people—in this case guided by certain monks—may make to cultivate both emotional agitation and religious insight. Had the Buddha lived, breathed, and died in present-day Myanmar/Burma, we might possibly have seen something like the *Final Journey* produced for him—a *Gautama Buddha's Final Journey*, recording a series of events perhaps far more grand than those held for Indācāra.

Thinking comparatively about the Gautama Buddha's funeral and its commemorative texts (for example, the *Mahāparinibbāna sutta*) from "way back when," on the one hand, and Indācāra's funeral and the *Final Journey* from only a few years "back now," on the other, invites a closing comparison with Strong's thesis that the Buddha's funeral rites are best understood when they are viewed retrospectively from the perspective of the Buddha's relics. They thus have less to do with the treatment of his body and the mourning of his passing than they have with the need to prepare for and preserve those relics. Far from being a postscript, the relics are, in fact, the governing motif that helps determine the whole shape and format of the Buddha's obsequies up to and including his cremation. Drawing on the *Final Journey*, this chapter has argued a complementary thesis that takes the need to prepare for and preserve relics as part of a larger socioreligious agenda. Although the *Final Journey* was produced on the occasion of an eminent monk's death, its governing motif is the living, breathing life of the Buddhist tradition itself. With its depictions of care groups and the various things that they do, the *Final Journey* displays a culture actively participating in care for Buddhism. In the fraught and urgent circumstances of contemporary Myanmar/Burma, Buddhism itself is far from becoming one of the Buddhist dead.

Notes

1. "Death practices" is a category that includes any type of death-related ceremony. "Funerals" are one type of death practice.

2. See John Holt's chapter in this volume.

3. Here, "Buddhism as such" refers to the "thoughts, practices, institutions, and values" that have coalesced around the figure of the Buddha. See Frank E. Reynolds and Charles Hallisey, "Buddhist Religion, Culture, and Civilization," in *Buddhism and Asian History*, ed. Joseph M. Kitagawa and Mark D. Cummings (New York: Macmillan, 1989), 3.

4. Since 1989, the Burmese military, the State Law and Order Restoration Council (SLORC; now called the State Peace and Development Council, or SPDC), has used the name "Myanmar" instead of "Burma" for the country. Many people, especially members of the pro-democracy movement, do not accept this designation. To keep the complexity of the sociopolitical situation to the fore, I have opted to use Myanmar/Burma.

5. For an important discussion, see Juliane Schober, "Buddhist Just Rule and Burmese National Culture: State Patronage of the Chinese Tooth Relic in Myanmar," *History of Religions* 36 (1997): 218–43.

6. In Theravāda societies and especially Myanmar/Burma, care for

Buddhism is almost always a matter of heightened concern when the ruling political order—considered by many Buddhists to be vital in the preservation of Buddhism—is perceived to be in a state of crisis. (Taken in part from F. K. Lehman, private communication.) Studies that have addressed aspects of the history and culture of the political situation in Myanmar/Burma include Donald Eugene Smith, *Religion and Politics in Burma* (Princeton, NJ: Princeton University Press, 1965); E. M. Mendelson, *Sangha and State in Burma: A Study of Monastic Sectarianism and Leadership* (Ithaca, NY: Cornell University Press, 1975); Joseph Silverstein, *Burma: Military Rule and the Politics of Stagnation* (Ithaca, NY: Cornell University Press, 1977); David I. Steinberg, *Burma: A Socialist Nation of Southeast Asia* (Boulder: Westview Press, 1982); Maung Maung Gyi, *Burmese Political Values: The Socio-Political Roots of Authoritarianism* (New York: Praeger, 1983); Gustaaf Houtman, *Mental Culture in Burmese Crisis Politics: Aung San Suu Kyi and the National League for Democracy* (Tokyo: Institute for the Study of Languages and Cultures of Asia and Africa, 1999); Christina Fink, *Living Silence: Burma under Military Rule* (New York: Zed Books, 2001); and Mary Callahan, *Making Enemies: War and State Building in Burma* (Ithaca, NY: Cornell University Press, 2003).

7. The most comprehensive and important account of the politics of meditation in Myanmar/Burma is Houtman's *Mental Culture in Burmese Crisis Politics*. Houtman's book is one of the most important contributions—if not *the* most important—to the field of Burmese Buddhist Studies in recent years.

8. Antima jhāpana kyan" pa re" cī mam khan' khvai mhu ko ma tī, *Bhaddanta Indācāra Antima kha rī"* (Yangon: Antima jhāpana kyan" pa re" cī mam khan' khvai mhu ko ma tī, 1993). A copy of the *Final Journey* is housed in the Library of Congress (LCCN 94917791; BQ964.N52). No publisher or editor(s) is explicitly identified for the volume. A short opening statement regarding the funeral and the publication of the volume is attributed to the planning committee and the information subcommittee. Leading members of these and other committees associated with the funeral are listed on pp. 243–46 of the volume itself. Other commemorative volumes include *Haṃsāvatī charāto bhu rā" krī" e* theruppatti nhaṅ' sā dhu kī ḷa na sa bhaṅ* (Yangon: Icchā sa ya piṭakat puṃ nhip tuik, 1960) and Moṅ phui, *Sai aṅ" gū charāto bhu rā" krī e* antima aggi jhāpana pūjo pvai* (Yangon: Sāsanā re" ū" cī" ṭhāna, 1977).

Apart from the *Final Journey*, materials related to Indācāra's life and death include two works published shortly before his demise, a biography and a collection of his advice/sermons. The biography is Moṅ Cetanā, *Bhaddanta Indācāra theruppatti* (Yangon: Sāsanā re" ū" cī" ṭhāna, 1992); the collection of sermons is Bhaddanta Indācāra, *Sāsanā' sa muiṅ" vaṅ ovāda kathā myā"* (Yangon: Sāsanā re" ū" cī" ṭhāna, 1992). The materials also include a funeral video that closely follows the layout of the photographs contained in the *Final Journey*. As of January 2002, copies of Indācāra's biography and the collection of his advice/sermons were available at what was his home teaching monastery in Pegu. At that time as well, the video of Indācāra's funeral could be purchased in Yangon for much less than a dollar (slightly more than a dollar if the purchaser was a foreigner) at the bookstore near the Mahā Pāsāna Cave (see note 16 below).

9. For a discussion of the 1980 events, see Tin Muang Muang Than, "Sangha Reforms and Renewal of Sasana in Myanmar: Historical Trends and Contemporary Practice," in *Buddhist Trends in Southeast Asia*, ed. Trevor Ling (Singapore: Institute of Southeast Asian Studies, 1993), 6–63.

10. As depicted in the *Final Journey*, members of the military include, for example, Senior General Than Shwe and Lieutenant General Khin Nyunt. In 1992 Than Shwe replaced Saw Maung as SLORC chairman. In August 2003, Khin Nyunt was appointed prime minister; in October 2004, in the midst of a military power struggle, he was replaced as prime minister and put under house arrest. Owing to insurmountable difficulties in identifying the copyright holder(s) and obtaining necessary permissions, I have been unable to include photos from the commemoration volume itself.

11. Hiroko Kawanami, "The Religious Standing of Burmese Buddhist Nuns (*thila-shin*)" *Journal of the International Association for Buddhist Studies* 13 (1990): 17–28.

12. Charles Hallisey, "In Defense of Rather Fragile and Local Achievement: Reflections on the Work of Gurulugomi," in *Religion and Practical Reason*, ed. Frank E. Reynolds and David Tracy (Albany: State University of New York Press, 1994), 121–60.

13. From Buddhaghosa, *The Expositor (Aṭṭhasālinī)*, trans. Maung Tin (London: Pāli Text Society, 1920), 1:29–30, as cited by Hallisey, "Gurulugomi," 149.

14. Hallisey, "Gurulugomi," 150.

15. As evidenced by Indācāra himself, prominent among Burmese renunciants are Sudhamma monks, who comprise the largest, though loosely organized, monastic group in Myanmar/Burma. Sudhamma monks have enjoyed a considerable amount of state backing, at least since the latter part of the eighteenth century, with the rise of the Sudhamma council of monks, which is responsible for the handling of Buddhist monastic law.

16. In northern Yangon stands the Mahā Pāsāna Cave, an artificial construction for the Sixth Buddhist Synod that was held between 1954 and 1956. Just near the cave is the World Peace Pagoda, also built in anticipation of the synod.

17. While funeral participants used ropes to pull Indācāra's sarcophagus to the cremation site, there does not appear to have been a tug-of-war ceremony in the sense explored by Charles F. Keyes in his study of a funeral

for a Thai monk, "Tug-of-War for Merit: Cremation of a Senior Monk," *Journal of the Siam Society* 63 (1975): 44–62.

18. For a study of the ordinary verbatim type of *nissaya* Burmese, see John Okell, "*Nissaya* Burmese: A Case of Systematic Adaptation to a Foreign Grammar and Syntax," *Lingua: International Review of General Linguistics* 15 (1965): 186–227.

19. Antima jhāpana kyan" pa re" cī maṃ khan' khvai mhu ko ma tī, *Bhaddanta Indācāra Antima kha rī"*, 154. The verse and its commentary appear on 164–66.

20. Steven Collins, *Nirvana and Other Buddhist Felicities* (Cambridge: Cambridge University Press, 1998), 593n2.

21. For an example from the contemporary Burmese context, see http://www.myanmar.com/religious/dpps.html (accessed January 22, 2004), which points out that since 1998, the Ministry of Religious Affairs has organized trips to these places.

22. William A. Graham, *Beyond the Written Word: Oral Aspects of Scripture in the History of Religion* (Cambridge: Cambridge University Press, 1987).

23. Ibid., 157.

24. Ibid., 162–63.

25. I would like to express my gratitude to Sayas U Saw Tun and John Okell for their assistance with the translation of the Burmese commentary. Neither is responsible for the interpretations or comments made in this chapter.

26. Antima jhāpana kyan" pa re" cī maṃ khan' khvai mhu ko ma tī, *Bhaddanta Indācāra Antima kha rī"*, 165.

27. "*Pavakkena*" is probably a typographical error for "*pavattena*."

28. P'aya is a term of respect for Indācāra.

29. Antima jhāpana kyan" pa re" cī maṃ khan' khvai mhu ko ma tī, *Bhaddanta Indācāra Antima kha rī"*, 165.

30. I say "appears to evoke" because the passage does not develop the simile in detail. More research remains to be done on this simile, especially given that in Theravāda understanding in Southeast and South Asia, children (especially boys) are said to owe a great debt to their mothers.

31. The portrayal of bereavement here is similar to the image of grieving that occurs when the Buddha passes away. See, for example, the *Mahāparibbāna suttanta*, trans. in T. W. Rhys Davids, *Buddhist Suttas*, Sacred Books of the East Series, vol. 11 (Delhi: Motilal Banarsidass, 1968).

32. Antima jhāpana kyan" pa re" cī maṃ khan' khvai mhu ko ma tī, *Bhaddanta Indācāra Antima kha rī"*, 165.

33. Ibid.

Chinese and Korean Character Glossary

Ai 藹
anju 安居
Ba daren jue jing 八大人覺經
Bai lun 百論
baji raoyi 拔濟饒益
Baoguo Monastery 保國寺
beixin jiaoji 悲欣交集
bianhui 變悔
bianwen 變文
Bianyi 辯義
biguan 閉關
biqiu 比丘
biqiuni 比丘尼
Bore jing 般若經
Bu xu gaoseng zhuan 補續高僧傳
Cao'an 草菴
Chang'an 長安
Chengtian Monastery 承天寺
Chongfu Monastery 崇福寺
chujia 出家
Da Ming gaoseng zhuan 大明高僧傳
Da Ming huidian 大明會典
Damuqianlian mingjian jiumu bianwen 大目乾連冥間救母變文
daochang 道場
Daochuo 道綽
Daoshi 道世
Daoxuan 道宣
Dasheng zhuangyan lun jing 大乘莊嚴論經
Da Tang Xiyou ji 大唐西域記
Daye 大業
Dazhi 大志
Dazhidulun 大智度論
diyiji 第一記
Dunhuang 敦煌
Dunhuang wenxian lunji 敦煌文獻論集
Facheng 法成
Fahua jing chuanji 法華經傳記
Fan 樊
fangdeng 方等
fang yankou 方焰口
fannao 煩惱
Faxian 法顯
Fayun Monastery 法雲寺
Fenbie[da]ye jing 分別「大」業經
Fengding Monastery 峰頂寺
Feng Zikai 豐子愷
Foshuo wuchang jing 佛說無常經
Foyuan 佛源
Fozu tongji 佛祖統紀
Fulin Monastery 福林寺
fuzhu 付囑
Ganlu 甘露
Gaoseng zhuan 高僧傳
gaoyun 告云
Gaozu 高祖
Gongdi 恭帝
Gong Shengxin 龔勝信
Gu 顧
guancha 觀察
Guanghua 廣化
Guanwuliangshou jing 観無量壽經
Guo 郭
Gusu 姑蘇
haiqing 海青
Hongyi 弘一

Hongzan fahua zhuan 弘贊法華傳
huangtu 皇圖
Huayan jing 華嚴經
Huayan jing zhuanji 華嚴經傳記
hufa 護法
Huichang 會昌
Huicheng 慧乘
Huijiao 慧皎
Hupao 虎跑
Hu Sanxing 胡三省
Jiangxi 江西
Jianyue Duti 見月讀體
Jing'ai 靜藹
Jingfa 靜法
Jingguan 靜觀
Jingyang 涇陽
Jingyuan 靜淵
Jingzhao 京兆
Ji shenzhou sanbao gantong lu 集神州三寶感通錄
jishou 稽首
Jiujiang 九江
Jiumoluoshi 鳩摩羅什
Jiu Tang shu 舊唐書
Ji Yun 紀昀
Jizang 吉藏
juan 卷
Kaihuang 開皇
Kaiming 開明
Kaiyuan Monastery 開元寺
kan 龕
Kuaiji 會稽
Laiguo 來果
lao heshang 老和尚
Lao zhaopian 老照片
Laozi 老子
li 里
Liang 梁
Liang Wudi 梁武帝
Liaoshi 了識
Lidai zhiguan biao 歷代職官表
Li Mi 李密
Lingyanshan Monastery 靈嚴山寺
Lingyu 靈裕
linmu 林墓
linzhong 臨終
Linzhong fangjue 臨終方訣
Liqu jing 理趣經
Liqushi 理趣釋
Li Shimin 李世民
Li Shutong 李叔同
Liu Xu 劉昫
Liu Zhiping 劉質平
Li Yuan 李淵
Lu, Mt. 廬岳
"Luopo seng" 落魄僧
Luoyang 洛陽
Luozhou Monastery 洛州寺
Lu Xun 魯迅
Miaojing 妙境
Miaolian 妙蓮
Minghe 明河
Mulian wen jielü zhong wubai jingzhong shi 目連問戒律中五百輕重事
Mu(qian)lian 目(乾)連
Namo Omituo fo 南無阿彌陀佛
Nanjing 南京
Nankang 南康
Nanshan Luzong 南山律宗
nianfo 念佛
Ningzhou 寧州
Ouyang Xiu 歐陽修
peng 棚
pinimu 毗尼母
pini riyong 毘尼日用
Pini riyong qieyao 毘尼日用切要
Puan 普安
Puji 普濟
pushe 僕射
putixin 菩提心
putong ta 普同塔
Puxian 普賢
Puyuan 普圓
qi 期
Qi 齊

Qiantang 錢塘
Qingdao 青島
Qingti 清提
Quanguan 傳貫
Quanzhou 泉州
"Rensheng zhi zuihou" 人生之最後
Rongyang 榮陽
sanguan 散官
Sanlun 三論
sengji ce 僧籍冊
senglu si 僧錄司
Shaanxi 陝西
shami 沙彌
shamini 沙彌尼
Shandao 善導
Shanwuwei 善無畏
Shanyin 山陰
shanzhishi 善知識
Shaolin Monastery 少林寺
shaoshen 燒身
sheli 舍利
sheli ta 舍利塔
shelizi 舍利子
Shengji ji 聖蹟記
shenjing shuairuo 神經衰弱
Shenseng zhuan 神僧傳
shenwu 神武
sheshen 捨身
Shi 施
Shi (monastic surname) 釋
shichamona 式叉摩那
Shiermen lun 十二門論
Shouhu guojiezhu tuoluoni jing 守護國界主陀羅尼經
shuofa liannian 說法斂念
shuofa quanshan 說法勸善
Sifenlü biqiujie xiangbiaoji 四分律比丘戒相表記
Sifenlü shanfa bujue xingshi chao 四分律刪繁補闕行事鈔
Sigao 寺誥
Sima Guang 司馬光
Song gaoseng zhuan 宋高僧傳
Song, Mt. 嵩岳
Song Qi 宋祁
song wangren 送亡人
Sui 隋
Sui shu 隋書
Sui Wendi 隋文帝
Sui Yangdi 隋煬帝
Sun Simo/Simiao 孫思邈
Taibai, Mt. 太白山
Taixu 太虛
Taizong 太宗
Taizu 太祖
Tan 炭
Tang Taizong 唐太宗
Tanxu 倓虛
Tanxuan 曇選
Tianjian 天監
Tianjin 天津
tianming 天命
Tiantai 天台
Tiantai Zhiyi 天台智顗
tongxing 童行
toutuo 頭陀
wangshen 亡身
wangsheng 往生
Wang Shichong 王世充
Wei Yuansong 衛元嵩
Wei Zheng 魏徵
Wŏnch'ŭk 圓測
wuchang qing 無常磬
Wudao Jiangjun 五道將軍
Wuliangshouguo 無量壽國
Wutai, Mt. 五臺山
Xiamen 廈門
Xi'an 西安
xianqian 現見
xianshou guo 賢首國
xiao 孝
xiaofu 孝服
Ximing Monastery 西明寺
xinghuo 性火
Xingyang 滎陽
Xin Tang shu 新唐書

Xuanzang 玄奘
Xu gaoseng zhuan 續高僧傳
Xuyun 虛雲
Yang Guang 楊廣
Yanglao yuan 養老院
Yang Su 楊素
Yang Tong 楊侗
Yang Yong 楊勇
Yang Zhao 楊昭
Yankang 延康
yi 逸
Yijing 義淨
yin 引
Yin, Mt. 尹山
Yinguang 印光
yiqi dayao 一期大要
yiqi yaofa 一期要法
yishen 遺身
Yonglong 永隆
Yongzhou 雍州
youposai 優婆塞
youpoyi 優婆夷
Yuan 元
Yuande 元德
Yue 越
Yuhua tai 雨華臺
yujiwei 羽騎尉
Yulanpen jing 盂蘭盆經
yushi dafu 御史大夫
Za ahan jing 雜阿含經
Zanning 贊寧
zhai 齋
zhanbing songzhong 瞻病送終
zhanbingzhe 瞻病者
Zhang gongzhu 長公主
*Zhang Shanhua 張 ? ?
Zheng 鄭
zhengjian 正見
zhengnian 正念
Zheng Ting 鄭頲
zhengzhi 正智
zhenshiwu 真實物
Zhichao 志超
Zhiman 智滿
Zhiming 智命
Zhixiang Monastery 至相寺
Zhiyi 智顗
Zhongguo benzhuan 中國本傳
Zhonghua 中華
Zhong lun 中論
Zhongnan, Mt. 終南山
zhongshe ren 中舍人
Zhongtianzhu Sheweiguo Qihuansi tujing 中天竺舍衛國祇洹寺圖經
Zhou 周
Zhou Wudi 周武帝
zhuan 傳
Zhu Fahu 竺法護
Zhuhong 袾宏
zifen 自焚
Zizhi tongjian 資治通鑑

Japanese Character Glossary

ajari 阿闍梨
ajikan 阿字観
Amida 阿弥陀
Amida hijiri 阿弥陀聖
Amida hishaku 阿弥陀秘釈
Amida kuyō hō 阿弥陀供養法
Amidamine 阿弥陀峯
Annonbyō 安穏廟
Annon Kai 安穏会
aramitama 荒御魂
Ariake 有明
Arima 有馬
Arorikika 阿嚕力迦
Ashizuri 足摺
Awashima *myōjin* 淡島明神
Azuma kagami 吾妻鏡
banka 挽歌
bessho 別所
bessho hijiri 別所聖
bodaiji 菩提寺
bodaimon 菩提門
bodaishin 菩提心
bodaisho 菩提所
bundan shōji 分段生死
bunkotsu 分骨
Buppō yume monogatari 仏法夢物語
Butsugon 仏厳
byakugō 白毫
byakugōkan 白毫観
Byōchū shugyō ki 病中修行記
chakunan 嫡男
Chidō 知道
chien 地縁
Chijōbō 智定坊
chū 中
Chūgaishō 中外抄
Chūjōhime 中将姫
Chūyūki 中右記
Daidenbōin 大伝法院
Daiitoku Myōō 大威徳明王
daimandara 大曼荼羅
Dainichi 大日
danka seido 檀家制度
dōgyōsha 同行者
Dōhan 道範
dosō 土葬
Ebisu 恵比須
Eiga monogatari 栄華物語
Eijo 永助
Einen 栄念
eitai kuyō baka (or *eitai kuyōbo*) 永代供養墓
eitai shiyōken 永代使用権
emakimono 絵巻物
en 縁
Enchin 円珍
Enkyō (monk of Mt. Hiei) 円慶
Enkyō (abbess of Hokkeji) 円鏡
Enni 円爾
En no Kai 縁の会
En no Ubasoku 役優婆塞
Enryakuji 延暦寺
Enshō 延昌
En'yū 円融
eshaku 会釈
etsū 会通
Fudaraku 補陀落
Fudarakusan tokai gyōja 補陀落山渡海行者

Fudaraku tokai 補陀落渡海
Fudō Myōō 不動明王
Fugen 譜賢
Fujii Masao 藤井正雄
Fujiwara no Junshi 藤原遵子
Fujiwara no Korechika 藤原伊周
Fujiwara no Moromichi 藤原師通
Fujiwara no Morozane 藤原師実
Fujiwara no Munetada 藤原宗忠
Fujiwara no Nobuie 藤原信家
Fujiwara no Reishi 藤原麗子
Fujiwara no Sanesuke 藤原実資
Fujiwara no Tadazane 藤原忠実
Fujiwara no Toshiie 藤原俊家
Fujiwara no Yorinaga 藤原頼長
Fujiwara no Zenshi 藤原全子
Fukutō Sanae 服藤早苗
Funaoka 船岡
fuse 布施
ganmon 願文
gassatsu 合殺
gasshō 合掌
gebon no kudoku 下品の功徳
Genshin 源信
Gochi-bō Yūgen 五智房融源
goke-ama 後家尼
Gokuraku 極楽
Gorin kuji myō himitsu shaku 五輪九字明秘密釈
gorintō 五輪塔
Goshūi ōjōden 後拾遺往生伝
gyakushu 逆修
gyōgan bodaishin 行願菩提心
Gyōhan 行範
Gyokuyō 玉葉
haka 墓
hakadera 墓寺
hakamairi 墓参
hakamori 墓守
Hakuun Egyō 白雲惠暁
Hakuun Oshō yume no ki 白雲和尚夢記（由迷能起）
Hama no miya Fudarakusanji 浜の宮補陀落山寺
Hana no Iwaya 花の窟
Hashizume Shinya 橋爪紳也
Hayami Tasuku 速水侑
Heike monogatari 平家物語
henjō nanshi 変成男子
hennyaku shōji 変易生死
hensō-zu 変相図
Higashiyama 東山
hijiri 聖
himitsu nenbutsu 秘密念仏
hiya 火屋
hōgo 法語
Hōkaiji 法界寺
Hokke genki 法華験記
Hokkeji 法華寺
Hokke metsuzaiji engi 法華滅罪寺縁起
Hokke senbō 法華懺法
hōkyōintō 宝篋印塔
hō mandara 法曼荼羅
hōmuru 葬る
Honchō shinshū ōjōden 本朝新修往生伝
Hōnen 法然
hongaku 本覚
honpushō 本不生
honzon 本尊
Hōrai 蓬莱
hōrō 宝楼
hosshinmon 発心門
Hosshinshū 発心集
Hōzō 宝蔵
hyakkai sennyo 百界千如
Hyakurenshō 百錬抄
ichigo 一期
Ichigō taiyō himitsu shū 一期大要秘密集
ichimon 一門
ichinen sanzen 一念三千
ie 家
ie no haka 家の墓
ie no saishi 家の祭祀
igai ikizai 遺骸遺棄罪
ihai 位牌

iki 遺棄
imi 忌
in (cause) 因
in (*mudrā*) 印
inga 因果
Inoue Haruyo 井上治代
Ippen 一遍
Ippen hijiri-e 一遍聖絵
Ishihara Shintarō 石原慎太郎
Ishihara Yūjirō 石原裕次郎
Ishizaki Yasumune 石崎靖宗
isson hō 一尊法
Izanagi 伊邪那岐
Izanami 伊邪那美
Izumi 和泉
Jichihan (a.k.a. Jitsuhan, Jippan) 実範
jigi 字義
Jinmu 神武
jippō shodanna tō sangai manryō 十方諸檀那等三界万霊
Jishū 時宗
Jizō 地蔵
Jizō bosatsu reigenki 地蔵菩薩霊験記
jōbon no kudoku 上品の功徳
jōgyō zanmai 常行三昧
Jōjakkōji 常寂光寺
jōjinne 成身会
Jōmyōji 浄妙寺
Jōshō 定昭
Jūnen Gokuraku iōshū 十念極楽易往集
junkan 循環
junmitsu 純密
Junna 淳和
jusui 入水
kabegata bochi 壁型墓地
kaesu 還す
kai 会
kakochō 過去帳
Kakuban 覚鑁
Kakuchō 覚超
Kakukai (Nanshō-bō) 覚海（南勝房）
Kakukai Hōkyō hōgo 覚海法橋法語
Kakuman 覚満
Kakushin 覚信
Kakushū 覚宗
kami 神
Kamo no Chōmei 鴨長明
kankyōsō 環境葬
kannen 観念
Kannon 観音
kanro 甘露
Kanshi 歓子
karasu tokin 烏頭巾
kasō 火葬
kata 型
Katō Eiji 加藤栄司
katoku sōzoku no tokken 家督相続の特権
Katō Mieko 加藤美恵子
Katō Shōnin 賀答上人
katsuma mandara 羯磨曼荼羅
Katsuura Noriko 勝浦令子
Kazan 花山
ke 仮
kechien 結縁
kegare 穢
Keiran shūyōshū 渓嵐拾葉集
Keiryū Shōnin 慶竜上人
kengyō 顕教
kesa 袈裟
ketsuen 血縁
kikajin 帰化人
Kiken 喜見
kimyō 帰命
Kita Shirakawa 北白川
Kohata 木幡
Kojiki 古事記
Kōkai Shōnin 高海上人
Kōkinshima 綱切嶋
Kokugakuin 国学院
Kokūzō 虚空蔵
Komine Michihiko 小峰彌彦
kōmyō shingon 光明真言
Kongōbuji 金剛峯寺
Kongōin 金剛因

kongōkai 金剛界
Koremori no jusui 維盛の入水
koseki 戸籍
Kōshin 康審
kotsuage 骨揚げ
Kōya, Mt. 高野山
Kōyasan Daidenbōin hongan reizui narabi ni jike engi 高野山大伝法院本願霊瑞並寺家縁起
Kōyasan ōjōden 高野山往生伝
Kōyōshū 孝養集
kū 空
kugi 句義
kuhon ōjō 九品往生
Kujō Kanezane 九条兼実
Kūkai 空海
Kumano 熊野
Kumano nendaiki 熊野年代記
Kurihara Hiromu 栗原弘
Kyōkai 教懐
maisō suru 埋葬する
Man'yōshū 万葉集
marebito 客人
Mike Irino no Mikoto 三毛入野命
mikkyō 密教
Minamoto no Masanobu 源雅信
Minamoto no Morofusa 源師房
Minamoto no Shishi 源師子
Minamoto no Yoritomo 源頼朝
Minegishi Sumio 峰岸純夫
Miroku 弥勒
mitsugon dōjō 密厳道場
mitsugon jōdo 密厳浄土
Mitsugon jōdo ryakkan 密厳浄土略観
mitsugonkoku 密厳国
mitsugon kokudo 密厳国土
Miyasaka Yūkō 宮坂宥洪
miyaza 宮座
Mokue nizō kaigen no koto 木絵二像開眼之事
Monju 文殊
monryū 門流
Mori Kenji 森謙二
Mori no Annon 杜の安穏
muen 無縁
muen funbo 無縁墳墓
mujōin 無常院
muko yōshi 婿養子
mukunoki 椋の木
Murakami Kōkyō 村上興匡
Muroto 室戸
Muryōju giki 無量寿儀軌
Muryōju Nyorai 無量寿如来
Myōfu 明譜
Myōhōrengekyō jōbon dai ichi 妙法蓮華経序品第一
Myōhōrengekyō kan dai hachi 妙法蓮華経巻第八
Myōjaku 明寂
Myōkōji 妙光寺
myōō 明王
Myōshō 明靖
Nachi 那智
Nachi sankei mandara 那智参詣曼荼羅
naishō 内證
Nakahara Moromori 中原師守
Nakahara Moromoto 中原師元
Nakanokawa Jōjin'in 中川成身院
Nakasō Fudaraku tokaiki 那珂湊補陀落渡海記
Namu Amida butsu 南無阿弥陀仏
Namu Amida butsu Namu Senjusengen 南無阿弥陀仏 南無千手千眼
Namu Kumano sansho gongen Fudarakubune 南無熊野三所権現補陀落船
Namu Senju 南無千手
Naniwa 難波
nehan-e 涅槃絵
nehanmon 涅槃門
nenbutsu 念仏
ne no kuni 根の国
nenshin 燃身
nigimitama 和御魂

Nihon ōjō gokuraku ki 日本往生極楽記
Nihon ryōiki 日本霊異記
Nihon shoki 日本書記
Nijūgo Zanmai-e 二十五三昧会
Nishiguchi Junko 西口順子
nissōkan 日想観
Nōgan 能願
nōkotsu 納骨
nōkotsudō 納骨堂
nyoirin Kannon 如意輪観音
nyūdō 入道
obon お盆
Odawara *hijiri* 小田原聖
Ōe no Otomuto 大江音人
ōjō 往生
ōjōden 往生伝
Ōjō yōshū 往生要集
Okada Hirotaka 岡田弘隆
Ōkagami 大鏡
Ōkuninushi 大国主
Ōmine, Mt. 大峰山
Ōmura Eishō 大村英昭
Onna no Hi no Kai 女の碑の会
onri edo gongu jōdo 厭離穢土欣求浄土
Ōshō 応照
Ōtani Teruo 大谷旭雄
raigō 来迎
rakandō 羅漢堂
reien 霊園
Rengejō 蓮花城
Rentai 蓮待
rinju gyōgi 臨終行儀
Rinjū yōjin no koto 臨終用心事
rinsō 林葬
risan 理懺
Rishukyō 理趣経
Rishushaku 理趣釈
Rokuharamitsuji 六波羅蜜寺
Ryōgen 良源
Ryōun 良運
ryūgū jōdo 竜宮浄土
Saigyō 西行
Saihōin 西方因
Saisei no Mori 再生の森
saishi 祭祀
saishi zaisan no keishō 祭祀財産の継承
Saitō Nanako 斎藤七子
Sakada Satoshi 坂田聡
sange 懺悔
Sange ōjōden 三外往生伝
sankei mandara 参詣曼陀羅
sankotsu 散骨/撒骨
sanmaidō 三昧堂
sanmaisō 三昧僧
sanmaji bodaishin 三摩地菩提心
sanmayagyō 三昧耶形
sanmaya mandara 三昧耶曼荼羅
sanmitsu 三密
sanmitsu kaji 三密加持
sansō no kudoku no shōretsu 三葬の功徳の勝劣
santai sokuze 三諦即是
Sanuki no sanmi 讃岐の三位
Seien 勢縁
sendan 栴檀
sendatsu 先達
setsuwa 説話
shien 死縁
shienbyō 志縁廟
shigo rikon 死後離婚
Shima Tōru 島亨
Shimokōbe Rokurō 下河辺六郎
shimon 四門
Shinbo Yoshimichi 新保義道
shingi Shingon 新義真言
shingon 真言
Shingon Buzan-ha 真言豊山派
Shingū 新宮
shinji 信士
Shinnō 真能
shinnyo 信女
Shinrai 真頼
Shinran 親鸞
Shinzoku butsuji-hen 真俗仏事編
shishu zanmai 四種三昧

shitsuji 悉地
shizensō 自然葬
shōgi bodaishin 勝義菩提心
Shōkakuji 正覚寺
Shō Kannon 正観音
Shōnen (a.k.a. Shōkin) 聖念(聖金)
shōshin 焼身
Shōyo 聖誉
Shōyūki 小右記
Shugendō 修験道
Shugendō mujō yōshū 修験道無常用集
shugyōmon 修行門
shuhō 修法
Shūi ōjōden 拾遺往生伝
shūkotsu 収骨
Shuzenji 修禅寺
so 祖
sokushin jōbutsu 即身成仏
sonkai 損壊
Sonshō Daibutchō 尊勝大仏頂
Sōsō no Jiyū o Susumeru Kai 葬送の自由をすすめる会
sotoba 卒塔婆
suisō 水葬
Sukuna hikona 少彦名
Sumiyoshi *myōjin* 住吉明神
Susano'o 素戔嗚
Suzuki Eijō 鈴木永城
tahōtō 多宝塔
Taiki 台記
Taima maṇḍala 当麻曼荼羅
Taimitsu 台密
Taira no Koremori 平維盛
Taira no Nobunori 平信範
Taishō shinshū daizōkyō 大正新修大藏經
Tajimamori 田道間守
Takamure Itsue 高群逸枝
Takehisa 武久
tamadono 霊殿
tamagaki 玉垣
Tanaka Chigaku 田中智学
Tanaka Hisao 田中久夫
Tani Kayoko 谷嘉代子
Tara 多羅
Tendai 天台
Tennōji 天王寺
tennōsei kazoku kokka 天皇制家族国家
terauke seido 寺請制度
Tōchōji 東長寺
Tōji 東寺
tokai no ganshu 渡海の願主
tokaisha 渡海者
tokoyo 常世
Tōmitsu 東密
Toribeno 鳥辺野/鳥部野
torii 鳥居
Tosotsu 兜率
tsuizen kuyō 追善供養
tsumadoi-kon 妻問い婚
u 有
uchūsō 宇宙葬
uji 氏
ujidera 氏寺
Uji shūi monogatari 宇治拾遺物語
Urakawa Michitarō 浦川道太郎
Urashima 浦嶋
Ushin Shōnin 祐真上人
utsubobune うつぼ舟
Yakuōbon 薬王品
yamabushi 山伏
yamamori 山守
Yanagida Kunio 柳田邦男
Yasuda Mutsuhiko 安田睦彦
Yokota Mutsumi 横田睦
yomi no kuni 黄泉の国
Yoshida 吉田
Yoshishige no Yasutane 慶滋保胤
Yuihan 維範
zasu 座主
zenchishiki 善知識
Zoku honchō ōjōden 続本朝往生伝
zōmitsu 雑密
Zōmyō 増命
zuigu 随求

Contributors

James A. Benn is associate professor in the Religious Studies Department of McMaster University. He studies Buddhism and Taoism in medieval China and is especially interested in the body as a site of religious practice, the cult of relics, interactions between religion and politics, and the religious and cultural aspects of commodities such as tea.

Raoul Birnbaum is professor of Buddhist Studies at the University of California, Santa Cruz, where he also holds the Patricia and Rowland Rebele Chair in History of Art and Visual Culture. His writings consider practices and representations in Buddhist China, from early medieval times to the present day. His work is informed by long-term, continuing field study in Chinese Buddhist communities.

Jason A. Carbine is currently visiting assistant professor at Franklin and Marshall College. His publications include Life of Buddhism (co-edited, University of California Press, 2000), and he is currently working on a book manuscript entitled Negotiating Rupture: Human Labor and the Sasana in a Burmese Buddhist Monastic Tradition.

Bryan J. Cuevas is John F. Priest Professor of Religion at Florida State University. He is the author of *The Hidden History of the Tibetan Book of the Dead* (Oxford University Press, 2003) and co-editor of *Power, Politics, and the Reinvention of Tradition: Tibet in the Seventeenth and Eighteenth Centuries* (Brill, 2006). Currently he is completing a book entitled *Travels in the Netherworld: Buddhist Popular Narratives of Death and the Afterlife in Tibet*. His research interests also include Tibetan history and historiography, monastic politics, and the sociology of ritual.

Hank Glassman is assistant professor of East Asian Studies at Haverford College. He specializes in the religious culture of medieval Japan. His publications include "'Show Me the Place Where My Mother Is!' Chūjōhime, Preaching, and Relics in Late Medieval and Early Modern Japan," in *Approaching the Pure Land: Religious Praxis in the Cult of Amitābha*, ed. Richard K. Payne and Kenneth K. Tanaka (Honolulu: University of Hawai'i Press, 2003), and "The Nude Jizō at Denkōji: Notes on Women's Salvation in Kamakura Buddhism," in *Engendering Faith: Women and Buddhism in Pre-Modern Japan*, ed. Barbara Ruch (Ann Arbor: Center for Japanese Studies, University of Michigan, 2002). Currently he is working on a book about the cult of Jizō.

John Clifford Holt is William R. Kenan, Jr., Professor of the Humanities in Religion and Asian Studies at Bowdoin College. He is the author of *Discipline: The Canonical Buddhism of the Vinayapitaka* (Motilal Banarsidass, 1981); *Buddha in the Crown: Avalokiteśvara in the Buddhist Traditions of Sri Lanka* (Oxford University Press, 1991); *The Religious World of Kīrti Śrī: Buddhism, Art and Politics in Late Medieval Sri Lanka* (Oxford University Press, 1996); and *The Buddhist Visnu: Religious Transformation, Politics, and Culture* (Columbia University Press, 2004). These books have been translated into Sinhala and published in Sri Lanka.

Matthew T. Kapstein is Directeur d'Études at the École Pratique des Hautes Études, Paris, and Numata Professor of Buddhist Studies at the University of Chicago. A specialist of both Indian and Tibetan Buddhism, his recent publications include *The Tibetan Assimilation of Buddhism: Conversion, Contestation, and Memory* (Oxford University Press, 2000); *Reason's Traces: Identity and Interpretation in Indian and Tibetan Buddhist Thought* (Wisdom Publications, 2001); *The Presence of Light: Divine Radiance and Religious Experience* (University of Chicago Press, 2004); and *The Tibetans* (Blackwell, 2006).

D. Max Moerman is assistant professor in the Department of Asian and Middle Eastern Cultures at Barnard College, Columbia University. He is the author of *Localizing Paradise: Kumano Pilgrimage and the Religious Landscape of Premodern Japan* (Harvard University Asia Center, 2005).

Mark Rowe is assistant professor of Japanese religions at McMaster University. His current research focuses on contemporary Japanese Buddhism and changing burial practices. His recent publications include "Where the Action Is: Sites of Contemporary Sōtō Buddhism" (*Japanese Journal of Religious Studies*, 2004) and *Buddhism in Contemporary Japan: Teachings, Doctrines, and Practices* (co-edited, *Japanese Journal of Religious Studies*, special issue, 2004).

Kurtis R. Schaeffer is associate professor in the Department of Religious Studies at the University of Virginia. He is the co-editor of *Power, Politics, and the Reinvention of Tradition: Tibet in the Seventeenth and Eighteenth Centuries* (Brill, 2006) and author of *Himalayan Hermitess: The Life of a Tibetan Buddhist Nun* (Oxford University Press, 2004) and *Dreaming the Great Brahmin: Tibetan Traditions of the Buddhist Poet-Saint Saraha* (Oxford University Press, 2005).

Gregory Schopen is professor of Sanskrit, Tibetan, and Buddhist Studies at the University of California, Los Angeles. His recent publications include *Bones, Stones, and Buddhist Monks: Collected Papers on the Archaeology, Epigraphy, and Texts of Monastic Buddhism in India* (University of Hawai'i Press, 1997); *Buddhist Monks and Business Matters: Still More Papers on Monastic Buddhism in India* (University of Hawai'i Press, 2004); and *Figments and Fragments of Mahāyāna Buddhism in India: More Collected Papers* (Honolulu: University of Hawai'i Press, 2005).

Koichi Shinohara is senior lecturer of Religious Studies at Yale University. His current research centers on the Vinaya commentary and *Further Biographies of Eminent Monks* by the Chinese Buddhist master Daoxuan (596–677). He is also working on sacred places in medieval Chinese Buddhism. His recent publications include "Stories of Miraculous Images and Paying Respect to the Three Jewels: A Discourse on Image Worship in Seventh-Century China," in *Images in Asian Religions: Texts and Contexts*, co-edited with Phyllis Granoff (University of British Columbia Press, 2003); "The Story of the Buddha's Begging Bowl: Imagining a Biography and Sacred Places," in *Pilgrims, Patrons and Place: Localizing Sanctity in Asian Religions*, ed. with Phyllis Granoff (University of British Columbia Press, 2003) and "From Local History to Universal History: The

Construction of the Sung T'ien-t'ai Lineage," in *Buddhism in the Sung,* ed. Peter N. Gregory and Daniel A. Getz, Jr. (University of Hawai'i Press, 1999).

Jacqueline I. Stone is professor of Japanese religions in the Department of Religion at Princeton University. Her primary research field is medieval Japanese Buddhism. She is the author of *Original Enlightenment and the Transformation of Medieval Japanese Buddhism* (University of Hawai'i Press, 1999) and co-editor of *Revisiting Nichiren* (*Japanese Journal of Religious Studies,* special issue, 1999). She is currently writing a study of deathbed practices in premodern Japan and also continuing research on the Nichiren Buddhist tradition.

John S. Strong is the Charles A. Dana Professor of Religion and chair of the Department of Philosophy and Religion at Bates College. He is the author of several books on Buddhism, including *The Legend of King Aśoka* (1983), *The Legend and Cult of Upagupta* (1992), *The Experience of Buddhism* (1994), *The Buddha: A Short Biography* (2001), and *Relics of the Buddha* (2004).

Index

Bold page numbers refer to illustrations.

afterlife: judgment of Yama, 302, 314, 316, 357, 358; location of world of dead, 284–287; popular Tibetan conceptions, 297–298, 300–301, 310–311. See also *bardo*; buddha lands; *délok* tales; hell; rebirth

āgamas, 110–116

Ajātaśatru, King of Magadha, 46, 49, 75

ajikan. *See* A-syllable meditation

Alcaceva, Pedro de, 275–276

Alexander the Great, 33

almsgiving: in Myanmar/Burma, 440; in Sri Lanka, 329–330, 335, 338

Alutnuvara Devālaya, 331, 337, 341, 342

Amida (Amitābha). *See* Pure Land

Ānanda, 42–43, 88–89

anātman. *See* not-self doctrine

anattā. *See* not-self doctrine

ancestor worship, in Japan, 391, 396, 414, 422, 429–430

Annon Kai. *See* Tranquillity Society

antarābhava. See *bardo*

asceticism: Buddhist attitudes, 63; effects on body, 180; extreme practices, 76; of Hongyi, 179; in India, 63; in medieval China, 239; radical, 68. *See also* cemetery-dwelling monks

ash scattering, in Japan: advocates of, 405, 424–425; arguments for, 405, 411–412, 416–419; Buddhist responses, 420–425; debates, 405, 411–413; environmental arguments for, 406, 418–420; GFPS ceremonies, 405, 407, 409; historic roots, 387, 408, 416–418, 424–425; increased popularity, 409; legal issues, 407–408, 410–411, 424, 431; locations, 409, 412–413, 430–431; natural funerals (*shizensō*), 408, 418–419, 420, 429–430; opposition, 406, 412–413, 419–423; preparations, 409; public acceptance, 406, 411; regulation of, 406, 411, 412–413, 430; as religious freedom issue, 406, 411–412. *See also* cremations

Aśoka, King, 35, 61, 327

A-syllable meditation (*ajikan*), 139; in deathbed practice, 146, 149–150, 152, 156–157, 158, 160

"attending to the sick" (*zhanbing*). *See* sick monks, caring for

"Attending to the Sick and Sending off the Dead" (*zhanbing songzhong*). *See* Daoxuan, *Sifenlü shanfan bujue xingshi chao*

Aum Shinrikyō, 412, 433n15

auto-cremations, 35, 236, 267–269. *See also* self-immolation

Avalokiteśvara, 305–306. *See also* Kannon

Avataṃsaka sūtra. See *Huayan jing*

Azuma kagami, 275, 287

Baoguo Monastery, 184
bardo (*antarābhava*): development of doctrine, 303; geography, 315; inhabitants, 315–316, 362; as intermediate state before rebirth, 303–304; Karma Wangzin's journey, 311–316
bardo ritual, 301
Bareau, André, 34, 36, 37–38, 45, 48
bell of impermanence (*wuchang qing*), 121, 122
Bernstein, Andrew, 414
Bhaddā, 39
Bhaddanta Indācāra's Final Journey: care for Buddhism expressed in, 443, 452, 453; depictions of religious emotion, 446–452; as local ethnography, 441; military presence, 441–442, 445; structure and content, 444–446
bianwen. *See* transformation texts
Bka' brgyud schools. *See* Kagyu schools
Bla ma Zhang. *See* Lama Zhang
Bloch, Maurice, 388, 390
Blum, Mark, 9
boats. See *Fudaraku tokai*
bodies: bones, 387, 388–389, 409; bundling, 317, 325n48; division as relics, 240; giving up, 18–20, 235–236, 266; handling dead, 70–71, 187; impermanence, 39; liminal state of corpses, 430; objectification of dead, 96; practices engaging, 179–180, 194–195; as torch, 34, 35, 50. *See also* burials; cremations; death pollution
bones: grinding for scattering, 409; as relics, 388–389; veneration of, 387, 388–389
brahmans, 44, 47, 70–72
'Bri gung Chos rje Kun dga' rin chen. *See* Drigung Chöjé Kunga Rinchen
Brown, Peter, 25, 29n28
Bsod nams blo gros. *See* Sönam Lodrö
Bsod nams grub pa. *See* Sönam Drüpa
Bstan 'dzin Chos kyi blo gros. *See* Tenzin Chökyi Lodrö
Buddha: clothing, 36–37, 63–65, 66–68; marks of Great Man, 42–43; penis, 42–43; preaching to sick monks, 111–116; woman's shroud worn by, 63–65, 67–68, 72
Buddha, death of: death verse on impermanence, 110; as paradigm for Buddhist deaths, 12–15, 17, 23–24, 35, 216; *parinirvāṇa*, 13, 42, 195; reenactment in religious suicide, 18
Buddha, funeral of: cakravartin funerals as model for, 33, 50; commemorative texts, 452–453; cremation, 33, 34–37, 44–45, 50; importance of relic production, 453; iron coffin, 33, 34, 37–41, 50; as paradigm, 23–24; as rite of passage, 32; shrouds wrapped around body, 33–37, 50; site, 52n4; stūpas erected, 33, 48–49, 50; timing of cremation, 38, 41; veneration of body, 41–44, 50; veneration of feet, 43
Buddhaghosa, 2, 34, 45, 50, 326, 443
buddha lands: aspirations for birth in, 134, 144; deathbed practices to achieve birth in, 123–124, 126–127. See also *Fudaraku tokai*; *ōjō*; Pure Land
Buddha relics: collection, 45–46, 50; creation of, 11, 33, 45, 50–51; descriptions, 45; dispute over, 46; division, 40, 46–47; enshrined in stūpas, 48–49, 50; footprints, 44; importance, 453;

power, 13; receptacles, 40–41; separation from ashes, 40; wrapped in cloth, 37. *See also* relics
Buddhism, regional and historical variation, 8–9. *See also* care for Buddhism; Chinese Buddhism; Japanese Buddhism; Tibetan Buddhism
Buddhist modernism, 3–5, 26n6
Bukkyō Times, 424
burials: instructions in *Linzhong fangjue*, 125–126; in mountains, 284–285; secondary, 13, 44–45, 387. *See also* Japanese burial practices
Burma. *See* Myanmar/Burma
Butsugon, *Jūnen Gokuraku iōshū*, 171n63
Bu xu gaoseng zhuan (Supplement to continued biographies of eminent monks; Minghe), 249–252
Bynum, Carolyn Walker, 25
Byōchū shugyō ki (Notes on practice during illness; Jichihan), 144–150, 151, 156, 162

cakravartin kings: funerals, 32, 33, 36, 37, 44, 45, 48, 50; parallel with Buddha, 32, 33, 36, 50, 52n4; veneration of remains, 32–33
Camporesi, Piero, 240
Candraprabha, 241
care for Buddhism: expressed in *Bhaddanta Indācāra's Final Journey*, 443, 452, 453; in funerary rituals, 439; in Myanmar/Burma, 439–440, 442, 443–444, 452, 453; and transgenerational Buddhist community, 443–444
cemeterial cloth, 80–84
cemeteries: family graveyards, Japanese, 385–386, 387, 390, 414; grave attendants, 389, 390; Japanese, 406, 411, 413, 426; meditation in, 240; temple, 413, 414, 418. *See also* burials
cemetery-dwelling (*śmāśānika*) monks: asceticism, 73–74; cannibalism rumors, 78–79, 80, 86, 95; clothing of dead worn by, 74, 76, 85–87, 89–90, 91–92, 93; images among laity, 86; Kālananda story, 87–89, 90–91; Mahākāla story, 76–80, 91; marginalization, 93–94; rules for, 74, 76, 79, 80–84, 87–91, 92–93, 94–96
Chengtian Monastery, 196, 200, 201
China: dynastic legitimation, 243, 252; geomantic beliefs, 395; kinship relations, 385, 387, 397; Tibetan speakers, 350, 351; violence in 1940s, 175–176
Chinese Buddhism: death images, 184–185; funerary rituals, 4; ghost festival, 302, 347–348, 351, 354; influence in Tibet, 346, 347; practices engaging body, 179–180; transformation texts, 350–351. *See also* Daoxuan; Hongyi; self-immolation; Yijing
Chinese Buddhism, relations of saṅgha and state: ideal, 234; in Ming period, 250–252; in Northern Zhou period, 236, 239, 242, 243; persecution, 236, 238, 239, 242, 243; self-immolation as reaction to, 234, 235, 236–238; in Sui period, 236–237, 243, 244, 245, 246, 247, 249; in Tang period, 238, 239, 249, 252, 257
Chökyi Wangchuk (Chos kyi dbang phyug), 212, 217
Chos dbang. *See* Guru Chöwang
Chos kyi dbang phyug. *See* Chökyi Wangchuk
Christianity: dissections of saints' bodies, 240; in Japan, 413–414;

martyrdom, 234, 235, 248, 257; relics, 25, 208–209, 225, 226; religious biographies, 235, 246; similarities to Buddhism, 25
Chūyūki (Fujiwara no Munetada), 382–383, 386, 389
cloth: cemeterial, 80–84, 87–91; discarded, 84–86, 87–89, 91; given to monks, 84
clothing: appropriate to the Bodhisattva, 67; of dead, 70–72, 187, 196; of dead, worn by cemetery-dwelling monks, 74, 76, 85–87, 89–90, 91–92, 93; dressing like the dead, 68; of *Fudaraku tokai* participants, 283–284; monastic robes, 65–66, 68–70; sacred thread (*brahmasūtra*), 72–73; symbolism of changes in Buddha's dress, 64; worn by Buddha, 36–37, 63–65, 66–68
Come de Torres, P., 276
Commentary on the Dīgha Nikāya, 49
contemplation. *See* meditation
Contemplation Sūtra (*Guanwuliangshou jing*), 145, 148, 154
contributory cause (*en*), 422–423
corpses. *See* bodies; cremations
Covell, Stephen, 423
cremations: auto-, 35, 236, 267–269; of Buddha, 33, 34–37, 44–45, 50; of Hindus, 44; of Hongyi, 196–197, 201; in Japan, 409, 411, 416; meaning, 44–45; relics produced in, 11, 189, 197, 201–202; remains left behind, 411, 433n11. *See also* ash scattering
cremation volumes. See *Bhaddanta Indācāra's Final Journey*
crossing the sea to Potalaka. See *Fudaraku tokai*
Cunningham, Alexander, 43–44
Däḍimunda (Devatā Baṇḍāra), 331–332, 341
Dalai Lama, 305
Damuqianlian mingjian jiumu bianwen. See *Transformation Text on Mulian Saving His Mother from Hell*
Daochuo, 128–129, 144
Daoshi, 129–130n6, 133n42
Daoxuan: life, 238, 242, 249; lineage, 182; in Zhongnan mountains, 238; *Zhong tianzhu Sheweiguo Qihuansi tujing*, 129–130n6
Daoxuan, *Sifenlü shanfan bujue xingshi chao*: "Attending to the Sick and Sending off the Dead" (*zhanbing songzhong*), 105, 106–107, 108–110, 116–122, 128; comparison to *Linzhong fangjue*, 122; Hongyi's study of, 192; influence, 105; parts, 106; sources, 106–107, 108, 111, 144
Daoxuan, *Xu gaoseng zhuan* (Continued biographies of eminent monks): accounts of self-immolation, 237–249; Dazhi's biography, 246–249; Puan's biography, 243–246; Puji's biography, 242–243, 249; Puyuan's biography, 239–242; Tanxuan's biography, 128–129; Zheng Ting's biography, 253–255, 256–257; Zhiman's biography, 128–129
Daśaratha, King, 38
Dasheng zhuangyan lun jing (*Mahāyāna-sūtrālaṃkāra*; Aśvaghoṣa), 241
'das log. See *délok*
Davids, T. W. Rhys, 45, 341
Dazhi, 246–249
Dazhidulun (Treatise on perfection of great wisdom), 119, 128
dead, relations with living: actions on behalf of dead, 12, 304,

329–330, 343, 350, 361; communication, 20–22, 330–331; merit transference, 12, 329, 337–338, 361, 362–363; in Sri Lanka, 329–330. *See also* funerary rituals
death: in Buddhism, overviews of, 26n5; Buddhist doctrine concerning, 1; as cross-cultural category in Buddhist Studies, 8–10; good, 115, 181; local variations in beliefs and practices, 9; meditation on, 2, 25–26n3, 125; scholarly discussions of Buddhist doctrines concerning, 24, 31n40; as theme in Buddhist practices, 2; Theravāda understanding, 326; as topic in Buddhist Studies, 3–8
deathbed images: of Lu Xun, 199; of monks, 199. *See also* Hongyi, deathbed image of
deathbed practices: achieving birth in chosen buddha land, 123–124, 126–127; attendants, 121, 152–155, 156, 160, 195–196; chanting, 124, 185–186, 187–188; contradictions with doctrine, 15, 127–129; esoteric, 140–141, 142–143, 144–150, 151–159; at Hall of Impermanence, Jetavana Monastery, 107, 108–110, 113, 119–120, 144; *honzon* (object of worship), 140–141; inauspicious signs, 154; influence of last thoughts on rebirth, 15, 118–119, 121, 122, 127–129, 134–135, 145–146; instructions in *Ōjō yōshū*, 134–135, 144; Kakukai's rejection of formal rituals, 159–161, 162; in *Linzhong fangjue*, 122–125; mindfulness at last moment, 15, 140, 145–146, 151–152, 153–154, 160, 182–183, 185; ordination, 388–389; posture, 142–143, 186, 194, 195–196; Pure Land, 105, 134–135, 142, 143–144, 182–183, 185–186; reflections on impermanence, 110–111, 122, 127–129; repentance performance, 146–147. *See also* moment of death
death pollution: Indian attitudes, 64, 70–72, 96; Japanese attitudes, 388, 413, 419
délok (*'das log*; returnees from death), 297, 319–320
délok tales: audiences, 297; Bacot manuscript, 355–358; Buddhist principles reflected in, 297; descriptions of death and afterlife, 297–298; details about individual *délok*, 299; development of genre, 321n4; of Guru Chöwang, 302, 355–358; influence of *Transformation Text*, 355–356; of lamas, 302; of ordinary people, 302; origins, 299; sources and influences, 300–306; standard plots, 299–300; transmission, 306. *See also* Karma Wangzin
demons: fear of possession by, 319; links to death, 319; Tibetan beliefs, 318–319, 325n52
Devadatta, 75–76
Devatā Baṇḍāra. *See* Däḍimunda
Dharmaguptaka vinaya, 107–108, 110, 111, 120–121
Dharmapāla, Anagārika, 3
Dhūmrasagotra. *See* Droṇa
Diamond Realm maṇḍala, 142, 147
divorce, posthumous, 379, 380, 428
Dmyal gling. *See* "Dominion of Hell"; *Epic of Ling Gesar*
Dngos grub dpal 'bar. *See* Ngödrub Pelbar
Dōhan, 159; *Rinjū yōjin no koto* (Admonitions for the time of death), 158–159

"Dominion of Hell" (*Dmyal gling*), 359–362. See also *Epic of Ling Gesar*
Dpon slob Rin po che. *See* Pönlop Rinpoché
Drigung Chöjé Kunga Rinchen ('Bri gung Chos rje Kun dga' rin chen), 217
Droṇa, 40, 46, 47–48, 50
drowning: self-immolation by, 270, 273–275. See also *Fudaraku tokai*
Dunhuang documents, 349, 350–351, 354
Durkheim, Emile, 290

Edgerton, Franklin, 65
Eiga monogatari, 389
Eijo, 269
eitai kuyō baka. *See* eternal memorial graves
eitai kuyōbo. *See* eternal memorial graves
en. *See* contributory cause
Enchin, 388
Enkyō, 140–141
En no Kai. *See* Society of *En*
Enshō, 140
En'yū, emperor, 395
Epic of Ling Gesar (*Gling Ge sar*), 302, 358–359; "Dominion of Hell," 359–362
esoteric Buddhism (*mikkyō*): deathbed practices, 140–141, 142–143, 144–150, 151–159; doctrines and rituals, 135, 143, 146; double logic of non-duality and Pure Land aspirations, 156–159, 162; funerary rituals, 139, 140; icons, 140–141; ideal deaths, 141–143; Kakukai's rejection of deathbed ritual, 159–161, 162; mantras, 136, 138, 139, 140, 152; *nenbutsu* practice, 140, 148, 151; practices combined with Pure Land aspirations, 136–141, 150, 156, 161–162; Pure Land understanding, 155–158; rituals aimed at birth in Pure Land of Amida, 136; spells, 138, 140, 146; tension between doctrine of realizing buddhahood and aspirations for birth in pure land, 143, 150–151, 156–158, 161; three secrets (*sanmitsu*), 135, 148–150, 152, 158
eternal memorial graves (*eitai kuyō baka*), 426–427
Europe. *See* Christianity
exemplary deaths: as aim, 181–182; esoteric style, 141–143; giving up the body, 18–20; of Hongyi, 202; Hongyi on, 183–184, 185–189; images of, 11, 180; influence of last thoughts on rebirth, 15; Japanese accounts, 135; meaning of death, 10–11. *See also* deathbed practices; *ōjōden*; special dead

Facheng. *See* Gö Chödrup
families. *See* kinship relations; parents
Faxian, 92
Fayun Monastery, 184
Fenbie[da]ye jing (*Karmavibhaṅga sūtra*; Sūtra on the [greater] analysis of deeds), 119
Feng Zikai, 175–176, 197, 200
festival of dead (*obon*), 416
Festival of the Descent from the Heavens (*lha babs dus chen*), 348
Final Journey. See *Bhaddanta Indācāra's Final Journey*
fire: self-immolation by, 35, 267–269, 274. *See also* cremations
Flower Garland Sūtra. See *Huayan jing*
Foshuo wuchang jing. See *Scripture on Impermanence*
Foucher, Alfred, 42

Frois, Luis, 277–279
Fudaraku tokai (crossing the sea to Potalaka): boats, 281–283, 286–287; clothing, 283–284; embarkation sites, 271; fund raising associated with, 275–276; images of, **278**, 279–284, 287–290, **289**; Jesuit accounts, 275–279, 290; mythological sources, 285–287; possible coercion, 291; practice, 266–267; scriptural origins, 287–291; spectators and attendants, 272, 279, 281, 283–284, 290–291; texts on sails, 287–290, **289**; textual accounts, 271–279
Fudō Myōō, 138, 146
Fujii Masao, 411
Fujiwara clan, 386, 389, 391, 395
Fujiwara no Junshi, 395
Fujiwara no Korechika, 389
Fujiwara no Michinaga, 384, 389–390, 395
Fujiwara no Moromichi, 383, 384
Fujiwara no Morozane, 383
Fujiwara no Munetada, *Chūyūki*, 382–383, 386, 389
Fujiwara no Nobuie, 383
Fujiwara no Reishi, 382–383, 384
Fujiwara no Sanesuke, 395
Fujiwara no Tadazane, 384
Fujiwara no Toshiie, 384
Fujiwara no Yorinaga, 272
Fujiwara no Zenshi, 384
Fukutō Sanae, 385, 392
funerary grounds, layouts, 281, **282**
funerary rituals: care for Buddhism in, 439; clerical roles, 2, 3–4; esoteric elements, 139, 140; Hongyi on, 187; Indian, 7, 38, 42; influence on rebirth, 12, 304, 329, 350, 361; instructions in *Linzhong fangjue*, 125–126, 127; merit transference, 12, 329, 337–338, 361, 362–363; as revenue source for temples, 2, 3; as rites of passage, 32; sermons on impermanence, 123; social meaning, 22; in tension with doctrine, 5–7, 8, 28n20; Tibetan, 301, 304, 317, 325n48, 361, 362–363. *See also* Buddha, funeral of; Japanese funerary rituals
funerary texts. See *Bhaddanta Indācāra's Final Journey*

Gampopa, 216
Gaṇḍavyūha sūtra, 287
gandharva, 303–304
Gaozu. *See* Li Yuan
Geary, Patrick, 25, 226
Genshin: burials of Nijūgo Zanmai-e monks, 388; esoteric practices, 138; *Ōjō yōshū* (Collection on the essentials of birth in the Pure Land), 105, 108, 134–135, 138, 144, 148
geomantic beliefs, 395
Gesar, King, epic of, 302, 358–362
GFPS. *See* Grave-Free Promotion Society
ghost festival, Chinese, 302, 347–348, 351, 354
ghosts: hungry, 347, 348, 357; Sri Lankan beliefs, 329. *See also* pretas
Gling Ge sar. See *Epic of Ling Gesar*
Gö Chödrup (Facheng), 348–349, 350, 351
Gö Lotsawa Zhönu Pel ('Gos Lo tsā ba Gzhon nu dpal), 209
Gombrich, Richard, 7
Gongdi, emperor, 253
Gong Shengxin, 193
Goshūi ōjōden, 270, 279
'Gos Lo tsā ba Gzhon nu dpal. *See* Gö Lotsawa Zhönu Pel
Götsangpa Gönpo Dorjé (Rgod tshang pa Mgon po rdo rje), 208, 216

Götsang Répa Natsok Rangdröl (Rgod tshang ras pa Sna tshogs rang grol), 210–212, 218, 221–223, 226
Govinda, Lama Anagarika, 4
Graham, William, 447–448
Granoff, Phyllis, 47
grave attendants (*yamamori*), 389, 390
Grave-Free Promotion Society (GFPS; Sōsō no Jiyū o Susumeru Kai): arguments for scattering ashes, 405, 411–412, 416–419; Buddhist members, 424–425; challenges to tradition, 406, 429–430; critiques of, 417–418; first meeting, 405; Forest of Rebirth proposal, 418–419; publications, 408; rules, 408; scattering ceremonies, 405, 407, 409
graves. *See* burials; cemeteries; eternal memorial graves; Japanese burial practices
graves, visiting (*hakamairi*), 387, 389–390, 416
Group-of-Six monks, 72–73, 81–83, 84, 85–86, 89–90, 91
Gshin rje chos kyi rgyal po. *See* Shinjé Chökyi Gyelpo
Gtsang smyon He ru ka. *See* Tsangnyön Heruka
Guanghua, 188, **188**
Guanwuliangshou jing. See *Contemplation Sūtra*
Guṇaprabha, 71, 91–93, 94
Guru Chöwang (Chos dbang), 302, 355–358
Gyeltangpa Déchen Dorjé (Rgyal thang pa Bde chen rdo rje), 216, 217

hagiographies: Christian, 235; functions, 225; printing technology, 226; promotion of relics, 224–226; self-immolation accounts, 237–238, 266; Tibetan, 208–209, 216–217, 223–226. *See also* Tsangnyön Heruka, *Life of Milarépa*
hakamairi (visiting graves), 387, 389–390, 416
Hallisey, Charles, 443–444
Hall of Impermanence, Jetavana Monastery, 107, 108–110, 113, 119–120, 129–130n6, 144
Hashizume Shinya, 413, 418
Hayami Tasuku, 139–140, 146
Heike monogatari, "The Drowning of Koremori" (*Koremori no jusui*), 274–275
hell: *Epic of Ling Gesar*, 359–362; Indian Buddhist doctrine, 301, 315; Karma Wangzin's journey, 311–316; signs that dying will fall into, 154; Tibetan concept, 303; types, 301, 321n7. See also *délok* tales; Mulian legend
Hertz, Robert, 44–45
Hinduism: cremations, 44; funerary rituals, 8, 47; karmic law, 8; Lord of the Dead, 302
Hokke genki, 268
Honchō shinshū ōjōden, 279
Hongyi: cremation, 196–197, 201; death, 198, 200, 202; family, 177, 178, 190, 203n3; final instructions, 192, 194, 196–197; health, 179, 190–193; ink drawings of, 200; lectures, 180, 183, 192, 193, 205n10; personal history, 176–179; photographs of, **177**, **191**, 192, 198–199; practices, 180–181, 182, 190; preparations for death, 192, 193–194, 196–198; relics, 201–202; "Rensheng zhi zuihou" (At the end of life), 183–184, 185–189; retreats, 180–181; on sanctity of life, 197; sculptures of, 200; *Sifenlü biqiujie xiang-*

biaoji, 192; study of Vinaya, 179–180, 182, 192, 193; turn to monasticism, 178, 179, 190
Hongyi, deathbed image of, **176**; exemplary death shown, 181; as part of remains, 198, 200–201, 202; peacefulness, 181, 202–203; as portrait, 198–199; power of, 175; publication in *Lao zhaopian*, 175; relationship to relics, 202; time when photographed, 200–201
honzon (object of worship), 140–141
Horner, I. B., 61–62, 63
Hosshinshū (Tales of religious awakening; Kamo no Chōmei), 273–274
Huayan jing (*Avataṃsaka sūtra*; *Flower Garland Sūtra*), 121, 240, 243
hungry ghosts, Chinese understandings of, 347, 348, 357. *See also* pretas
Hyakurenshō, 269

Ichigo taiyō himitsu shū (Collection of secret essentials for a lifetime; Kakuban), 151–158, 162, 171n63
ie. *See* patriarchal household system
illness. *See* sick monks, caring for
Imaeda, Yoshiro, 351
images. *See* deathbed images
impermanence: bell of, 121, 122; of body, 39; reflections on, 110–111, 122; reminders of, 110, 112–113, 121, 127–128, 184, 202; sermons on, 123. *See also* Hall of Impermanence; not-self doctrine
Indācāra, Bhaddanta: career, 441; cremation, 445–446; funerary rituals, 445–447, 453; grieving for, 448, 451; as heavenly being, 451–452; portrait, 444; relics, 445–446. See also *Bhaddanta Indācāra's Final Journey*
India: attitudes toward death, 64, 70–72, 96; funerary customs, 7, 38, 42. *See also* Hinduism
Indian monasticism: development, 60–61, 93–94; relations with laity, 61–62, 70, 73, 86, 93–94. *See also* cemetery-dwelling monks
Inoue Haruyo, 415, 428
Ippen, 270
Ippen hijiri-e, 270
Ishihara Shintarō, 410
Ishihara Yūjirō, 410
Ishizaki Yasumune, 422
Islamic martyrdom, 234, 257
Izanagi, 285
Izanami, 285, 286

James, William, 339
Jampa Samten, 355
Japan: ancestor worship, 391, 396, 414, 422, 429–430; Aum affair, 412; clans and lineages, 385–386, 391–392, 397; history of kinship relations, 379–382, 391–392; Justice Ministry, 407–408; matrilineal kinship system, 392; Meiji Civil Code, 414–415, 417; patriarchal household system (*ie*), 381, 384, 385–386, 392, 394, 415–416; patrilineal descent, 378, 415–416; uxorilocal marriage, 381, 382; virilocal residence, 381; Welfare Ministry, 406, 407, 411–413, 426, 430
Japanese Buddhism: clan temples, 385–386, 397; fluidity of doctrinal categories, 137, 161; modern criticism of clerical focus on funerals, 3–4; monastic funerals, 388;

monopoly over mortuary rites, 420, 421, 431–432; parishioner system, 413–414, 432; relationship with state, 413–414; responses to ash scattering practices, 420–425; Ritsu sect, 388; self-immolation, 266, 267–271; temple certification system, 413–414; Zen sect, 388. *See also* esoteric Buddhism; *Fudaraku tokai*

Japanese burial practices: abandoned grave problem, 426; care of graves, 389; contemporary changes, 406–407, 424, 426–429, 431–432; eternal memorial graves (*eitai kuyō bakao* or *eitai kuyōbo*), 426–427; family graves, 415–416, 417, 418; family graveyards, 385–386, 387, 390, 414; grave attendants, 389, 390; grave laws, 406, 410–412, 414–415, 417, 433n13; grave monuments, 389, 414, 422; history, 413–415, 424–425; individual choices, 429, 431; influence on kinship relations, 378, 385, 389–391, 397, 423, 428–429; law prohibiting discarding corpses, 407–408; locations, 395–396; matrilateral, 384–385; in mountains, 284–285; separate burial of husbands and wives, 382–384; shortages of grave space, 406, 411, 426; spirit parks, 426, 436n70; temple cemeteries, 413, 414, 418; Tranquillity Shrines, 428. *See also* Japanese women

Japanese funerary rituals: abandonment of corpses, 416–418; benefits for family members, 422; Buddhist monopoly, 420, 421, 431–432; changes in treatment of bodies, 387–389, 390–391; Chinese influences, 385, 386–387, 390, 397; cremations, 409, 411, 416; deathbed or postmortem ordination, 388–389, 434n26; festival of dead (*obon*), 416; modern criticism of clerical focus on, 3–4; of monks, 388; posthumous names, 427, 437n72; Shinto, 414; social function, 421; veneration of bones, 387, 388–389; visiting graves, 387, 389–390, 416; of women, 394–395. *See also* ash scattering

Japanese women: burials with father's family, 378, 382–384, 386, 391, 392, 395; burials with husband's family, 379, 386–387, 394, 415; burials with mother's family, 385, 391; contemporary burial practices, 427–428; funerary rituals, 394–395; graves owned by, 427–428; imperial consorts, 395–396; leaving father's family at marriage, 379, 380–382, 391, 392, 394, 397; maternal role, 396–397; membership of father's families, 378, 380, 381, 382; posthumous divorce, 379, 380, 428; property and inheritance rights, 380, 382, 393–394, 395; treatment of bodies after death, 395–396; widows as nuns, 393–394

Jesuits, accounts of *Fudaraku tokai*, 275–279, 290

Jetavana Monastery, Hall of Impermanence, 107, 108–110, 113, 119–120, 144

Jianyue Duti, 195

Jichihan, *Byōchū shugyō ki* (Notes on practice during illness), 144–150, 151, 156, 162

Jizang, 256

Jizō bosatsu reigenki, 272–273, 287

Jōjakkōji, 427, 431
Jōmyōji, 389–390, 395
Jōshō, 137, 141, 268
Jūnen Gokuraku iōshū (Butsugon), 171n63
Junna, emperor, 416
Justice Ministry, Japan, 407–408

Kagyu (Bka' brgyud) schools: hagiographies, 208–209. *See also* Milarépa
Kaiyuan Monastery, 196, 201, 202
Kakuban, *Ichigo taiyō himitsu shū* (Collection of secret essentials for a lifetime), 151–158, 162, 171n63
Kakuchō, 138–139
Kakukai: death, 174n93; disciples, 159; *Kakukai Hōkyō hōgo* (Bridge of the Law Kakukai's discourse on the dharma), 159–161, 162
Kakushin, 269
Kakushū, 272, 293n25
Kālananda, 87–89, 90–91
Kamo no Chōmei, *Hosshinshū* (Tales of religious awakening), 273–274
Kannon (Avalokiteśvara): cult of, 287; at Nachi, 287, **288**, 289, 290. See also *Fudaraku tokai*; Thousand-Armed Kannon
Kanshi, dowager empress, 140
Karma dbang 'dzin. *See* Karma Wangzin
Karmavibhaṅga sūtra (*Fenbie[da]ye jing*; Sūtra on the [greater] analysis of deeds), 119
Karma Wangzin (Karma dbang 'dzin): death experience, 307–311; *délok* tale, 298, 307–320; family, 306–307; journey to hell and *bardo*, 311–316; life of, 306–307; return to world of living, 316–320
karmic relationships, 269–270
karmic retribution, 8, 185; kinship relations and, 361–362, 363; overcoming, 126, 140, 146, 152, 271, 350; tales illustrating, 267, 329; Viṣṇu Kalyāni's understanding of, 337, 342–343. *See also* hell; rebirth
Kāśyapa, 117. *See also* Mahākāśyapa
Katō Eiji, 421
Katō Mieko, 380–381
Katō Shōnin, 272–273, 287
Katsuura Noriko, 393
Kawanami, Hiroko, 442
Kieschnick, John, 35
Kiken, 267–268. *See also* Sarvasattvapriyadarśana
kings. *See* cakravartin kings
kinship relations: Chinese norms, 385, 387, 397; history in Japan, 379–382, 391–392; influence of Japanese burial practices, 378, 385, 389–391, 397, 423, 428–429; Japanese clans and lineages, 385–386, 391–392, 397; karmic retribution and, 361–362, 363; matrilineal, 392; patrilineal descent, 378, 415–416; persistence through successive rebirths, 330; Tibetan views, 360, 363; uxorilocal marriage, 381, 382; virilocal residence, 381. *See also* Japanese women; parents
Kohata, Mt., 386, 389–390, 395
Kojiki, 285
Kōkai Shōnin, 281–282
Komine Michihiko, 422–423
Kōshin, 138
Kōya, Mt., 139, 141
Kōyasan ōjōden, 139
Kūkai, 135, 158, 161
Kumano, 286, 290. *See also* Nachi shrine
Kumano nendaiki, 271–272, 290
Kun tu bzang mo. *See* Kuntu Zangmo

Kuntu Zangmo (Kun tu bzang mo), 221
Kurihara Hiromu, 384, 392
Kyōkai, 139

Laiguo, 199–200
Lalitavistara, 63–65, 66–68, 70, 72
Lama Zhang (Bla ma Zhang), 216
land of Esoteric Splendor (*mitsugon kokudo*), 141–142, 166n33. *See also* practice hall of Esoteric Splendor (*mitsugon dōjō*)
Lao zhaopian (Old photos), 175. *See also* Hongyi, deathbed image of
Le Goff, Jacques, 25
Lévi, Sylvain, 75
lha babs dus chen. *See* Festival of the Descent from the Heavens
Liaoshi, 183–184
Life of Milarépa. *See* Tsangnyön Heruka, *Life of Milarépa*
Lingyanshan Monastery, 197
Linzhong fangjue (Instruction for the moment of death; Yijing), 122–127
Liqu jing. See *Rishukyō*
Liqushi. See *Rishushaku*
Li Shimin. *See* Taizong
Li Shutong, 177–179. *See also* Hongyi
Liu Zhiping, 192
Li Yuan (Gaozu), 253
loin-cloth, of Buddha, 63–65
Lo ras pa Grags pa dbang phyug. *See* Lorépa Drakpa Wangchuk
Lord of the Dead. *See* Yama Dharmarāja
Lorépa Drakpa Wangchuk (Lo ras pa Grags pa dbang phyug), 208
Lotus Sūtra: and ascetic practitioners, 267, 287, 290; Sarvasattvapriyadarśana (Kiken) story, 35; *Yakuōbon* (Medicine King chapter), 267–268
Lu Xun, 199
Mahākāla, 76–80, 91
Mahākāśyapa, 38, 42–44, 48, 69–70. *See also* Kāśyapa
Mahānāma, 328
Mahāparinibbāna sutta, 216, 452–453. See also *Mahāparinirvāṇa sūtra*
Mahāparinirvāṇa sūtra: account of Buddha's funeral, 32, 34, 37, 40, 41, 48, 51–52n2; cakravartin funerals, 33; death of Buddha, 110; final stanza, 50–51; readings, 49; themes, 39
Mahāvaṃsa, 327–329
Mahāyāna-sūtrālaṃkāra (*Dasheng zhuangyan lun jing*; Aśvaghoṣa), 241
Mahinda, 327–328
Mair, Victor, 358–359
Mallas of Kuśinagarī, 41–43, 44, 45–46, 48, 50
Mānavadharma-śāstra, 71
maṇḍalas: Diamond Realm, 142, 147; *Nachi Pilgrimage Maṇḍala*, 279–281, **280**, **281**, 287–290, **289**; pilgrimage, 279
Manifestation of Kannon at Nachi, 287, **288**
maṇi pa (storytellers), 306
mantras, 136, 138, 139, 140, 152
Man'yōshū, 284–286, 416
Māra, 327, 347
Marasinghe, M. M. J., 341–342
marriage. *See* Japanese women; kinship relations
martyrdom: Christian, 234, 235, 248, 257; Islamic, 234, 257. *See also* self-immolation
material possessions: attachment to, 119–121; contact relics of Hongyi, 202; contact relics of Milarépa, 213, 217–218. *See also* clothing
Maudgal gyi bus ma dmyal ba nas drangs pa'i mdo (*Sūtra of Maudgalyāyana's Salvation of His Mother from the Hell Realm*), 354–355

Maudgalyāyana. *See* Mulian
meditation: A-syllable, 139, 146, 149–150, 152, 156–157, 158, 160; in cemeteries, 240; on death, 2, 25–26n3, 125; esoteric practices, 154; in Myanmar/Burma, 439, 440–441; on non-duality, 158, 160; right (*zhengnian*), 112; skeleton, 184
mediums, 20. *See also* Viṣṇu Kalyāni
Meiji Civil Code, 414–415, 417
memorial rituals. *See* funerary rituals
Menander, King, 33
merit transference, 12, 329, 337–338, 361, 362–363
Miaojing, 184
Miaolian, 193–194, 196–198, 200–201
mikkyō. *See* esoteric Buddhism
Mi la ras pa. *See* Milarépa
Milarépa (Mi la ras pa): birthplace, 210–211; cremation, 213–214; cult of, 210–212; death, 212–218; fame, 209–210; festivals dedicated to, 209; life stories, 209–210, 211, 216–218; possessions, 213; post-death appearances, 213–214, 215; relics, 212, 214–218, 221–222, 223; statues of, 223; students, 212; Tsangnyön compared to, 210. *See also* Tsangnyön Heruka, *Life of Milarépa*
Minamoto no Masanobu, 396
Minamoto no Morofusa, 383, 384
Minamoto no Shishi, 384
mindfulness, at last moment, 15, 140, 145–146, 151–152, 153–154, 160, 182–183, 185
Minegishi Sumio, 394
Ming dynasty, relations of saṅgha and state, 250–252
Miyasaka Yūkō, 418
Mogharāja, 121
moment of death: mindfulness, 15, 140, 145–146, 151–152, 153–154, 160, 182–183, 185; power of mental state, 119; in self-immolation, 274. *See also* deathbed practices
monasticism: practices engaging body, 179–180, 194–195. *See also* Indian monasticism; ordination; Vinaya
monastic robes, 65–66, 68–70
monks: death images, 184–185; Group-of-Six, 72–73, 81–83, 84, 85–86, 89–90, 91; Japanese funerary rituals, 388; leaving household, 236; position for sleep, 194–195; roles in funerary rituals, 2, 3–4. *See also* cemetery-dwelling monks; sick monks, caring for
Mon rtse pa Kun dga' dpal ldan. *See* Möntsépa Kunga Penden
Möntsépa Kunga Penden (Mon rtse pa Kun dga' dpal ldan), 217
Mori Kenji, 415
mortuary sites. *See* cremations
mothers: roles in Japan, 396–397. *See also* Mulian legend; parents
mountains: burials in Japanese, 284–285; scattering ashes in, 409. *See also* Zhongnan mountains
Mūlasarvāstivāda vinaya: Buddha on monk's clothing, 66, 69; concern with public image of monks, 93–94; Devadatta stories, 75–76; discouragement of cemetery-dwelling, 74; influence, 94; instructions for handling dead bodies, 70–71; literary qualities, 75; Mahākāla story, 76–80; practices adjusted to lay values, 62; rule on wearing sacred thread, 72–73; rules for cemetery-dwelling monks, 80–84, 85–91; stories of monks' clothing, 68–70

Mulian (Maudgalyāyana) legend: Chinese versions, 346–347; influence on *délok* tales, 355–358; influence on *Epic of Ling Gesar*, 358–359, 362; influence on Tibetan mortuary practice, 359, 362–363; journey to hell to save mother, 302, 351–353; Tibetan versions, 347, 348, 354–355. See also *Transformation Text on Mulian Saving His Mother from Hell*

Mulian wen jielü zhong wubai jingzhong shi (Mulian's five hundred questions on precepts), 119–120

Muṇḍa, King, 39

Murakami Kōkyō, 429

Muryōju giki (*Wuliangshou yigui*), 136

Mu'u 'gal gyi bu ma dmyal khams nas drangs pa'i mdo (*Sūtra of Maudgalyāyana's Salvation of His Mother from Hell*), 355

Myanmar/Burma: Buddhist communal ethos, 438; care for Buddhism, 439–440, 442, 443–444, 452, 453; military government, 439, 440–442, 445; persecution of Buddhists, 440; relations of saṅgha and state, 439, 440–442. See also *Bhaddanta Indācāra's Final Journey*

Myōfu, 138

Myōjaku, 141

Myōkōji, 428, 431

Myōshō, 137

Nachi Pilgrimage Maṇḍala, 279–281, **280**, **281**, 287–290, **289**

Nachi shrine, 271, 272, 274–275, 287, 290

Nāgārjuna, 241

Nakahara Moromori, 394, 396

Nakasō Fudaraku tokaiki, 281–282, 283–284

Nanam Tsünpa (Sna nam btsun pa), 355, 364–367

Nanshō-bō Kakukai. *See* Kakukai

natural funerals (*shizensō*): ceremonies, 405, 407, 409; definition, 408; distinction from simple ash scattering, 418–419; use of term, 420. *See also* ash scattering

navaśrāddha rites, 47. See also *piṇḍa*s; *sapiṇḍīkaraṇa* ceremony

nenbutsu practice: combined with esoteric practices, 138, 139–140, 142, 143, 149–150, 154; on deathbed, 137, 139, 140, 144, 146, 148, 153–154; esoteric, 151, 152; in funerary rituals, 140; Pure Land, 134–135

nenshin. *See* self-immolation

Ngag dbang rnam rgyal. *See* Ngawang Namgyel

Ngawang Namgyel (Ngag dbang rnam rgyal), 217

Ngödrub Pelbar (Dngos grub dpal 'bar), 221

Nickerson, Peter, 391, 392

Nihon ōjō gokuraku ki (Record of those in Japan born in [the Pure Land of] Utmost Bliss; Yoshishige no Yasutane), 136–137

Nihon ryōiki, 267

Nihon shoki, 285, 286

Nijūgo Zanmai-e (Twenty-five Samādhi Society), 137–139, 141, 144, 388

Nishiguchi Junko, 386, 395

Nōgan, 142

non-duality: contemplation of, 158, 160; Pure Land aspirations and, 156–159, 162

Northern Zhou dynasty, 236, 239, 242, 243

not-self doctrine (Skt. *anātman*; Pāli *anattā*), 5–7, 8, 27n15, 28n20

nuns: Burmese, 442; Japanese widows as, 393–394
Nyanatiloka, 5

obon. *See* festival of dead
Ōe no Otomuto, 140
Ohnuma, Reiko, 18, 241
ōjō (achieving birth in a pure land): aspirations, 134, 161; distinction from *sokushin jōbutsu*, 150–151; meaning in esoteric Buddhism, 143, 157; proof of, 141–143. *See also* buddha lands; Pure Land
ōjōden (accounts of those born in the Pure Land), 135, 136–137, 139, 141, 270, 279
Ōjō yōshū (Collection on the essentials of birth in the Pure Land; Genshin), 105, 108, 134–135, 138, 144, 148
Okada Hirotaka, 424–425
Ōkagami, 390
Ōmura Eishō, 424
Onna no Hi no Kai. *See* Society for a Women's Monument
orality, in religions, 447–448
ordinary dead, distinction from "special dead," 10, 11–12
ordination: deathbed or post-mortem, 388–389, 434n26; regulation of, 250–252
Ōshō, 268–269
Ōtani Teruo, 148

parents: presence at death of, 356, 360; relations with, 345–346; and renunciate ideal, 22, 31n39, 362–363. *See also* kinship relations; mothers
Parry, Jonathan, 388, 390
passio, 235, 246
patriarchal household system (*ie*), 381, 384, 385–386, 392, 394, 415–416
Paxton, Frederick, 25
peta. *See* pretas
Petavatthu (Stories of the Departed), 305, 328, 329, 337, 338, 339
'Phags pa yongs su skyobs pa'i snod ces bya ba'i mdo. See *Yulanpen jing*
photography: manipulation of, 199–200; portrait, 198–199. *See also* Hongyi, deathbed image of
picture recitation, 358–359
pilgrimage maṇḍalas, 279. See also *Nachi Pilgrimage Maṇḍala*
*piṇḍa*s, 47, 77, 78, 79. See also *navaśrāddha* rites; *sapiṇḍīkaraṇa* ceremony
Pini riyong (*Vinaya for Daily Use*), 194–195
Pini riyong qieyao (*Pini riyong* with commentary by Jianyue Duti), 195
Plutarch, 33
Pökangpa Rinchen Gyentsen (Spos khang pa Rin chen rgyal mtshan), 354–355
Pommaret, Françoise, 320
Pönlop Rinpoché (Dpon slob Rin po che), 318, 319
popular religion, 7, 28n21
Potalaka. See *Fudaraku tokai*
practice hall of Esoteric Splendor (*mitsugon dōjō*), 159. *See also* land of Esoteric Splendor (*mitsugon kokudo*)
precepts. *See* ordination; Vinaya
pretas (*peta*; hungry ghosts), 305, 329, 332–339, 341
printing, woodblock, 210, 226
"Protestant Buddhism," 26n6
"Protestant presupposition," 5, 27n13
Przyluski, Jean, 32–33, 34, 36, 38–39, 41, 48, 348
Puan, 239, 243–246
Puji, 239, 242–243, 249
Pure Land, esoteric and exoteric understandings, 155–158

Pure Land aspirations: biographies of monks achieving birth in, 128–129; combined with esoteric practices, 136–141, 156, 161–162; deathbed contemplations, 147–148; deathbed practices related to, 125, 134–135, 182–183, 185–186; in Heian Japan, 134–135; non-duality and, 156–159, 162; preparations, 182–183. See also *ōjō*
Pure Land Buddhism: combined with esoteric practices, 150; deathbed practices, 105, 134–135, 142, 143–144, 182–183, 185–186; esoteric elements in practices, 137–141; Hongyi's practices, 182, 183; *nenbutsu* practice, 134–135, 270; Nijūgo Zanmai-e, 137–139, 141, 144, 388; self-immolation, 270
Puyuan, 239–242, 243

Quanguang, 192

Rahula, Walpola, 6
Ras chung pa Rdo rje grags pa. *See* Réchungpa Dorjé Drakpa
Ratnamegha sūtra, 94–96
realizing buddhahood with this very body (*sokushin jōbutsu*), 135, 143, 150–151, 156–158, 161, 162
rebirth: of bodhisattvas, 11; in chosen buddha land, 123–124, 126–127; influence of deathbed actions, 8; influence of funerary rituals performed by others, 12, 304, 329, 361; influence of last thoughts, 15, 118–119, 121, 122, 127–129, 134–135, 145–146; ordinary, 11–12; samsaric cycle, 1, 11–12, 105, 123, 134, 326. *See also* karmic retribution; *ōjō*; Pure Land aspirations
Réchungpa Dorjé Drakpa (Ras chung pa Rdo rje grags pa), 208, 212, 213, 214–215
reien. *See* spirit parks
Reischauer, Edwin, 435n36
relics: bones as, 388–389; Christian, 25, 208–209, 225, 226; cults, 425; disappearances, 214–215, 216–217, 222, 223; distribution, 201–202; enshrining as secondary burial, 13; of Hongyi, 196–197, 202; in medieval China, 240; of Milarépa, 212, 214–218, 221–222, 223; political role, 226; power, 201; produced in cremations, 11, 189, 197, 201–202; promoted by hagiographic death accounts, 224–226; as reminders of impermanence, 184; of Tsangnyön, 219–220, 222, 223, 226. *See also* Buddha relics
religious emotion or agitation (*saṃvega*), 446–452
Rengejō, 273–274
"Rensheng zhi zuihou" (At the end of life; Hongyi), 183–184, 185–189
Rentai, 142
renunciants, in Myanmar/Burma: care groups, 442–444; differences from laypeople, 442; relations with laypeople, 442–443. *See also* monks; nuns
Reynolds, Frank E., 1
Rgod tshang pa Mgon po rdo rje. *See* Götsangpa Gönpo Dorjé
Rgod tshang ras pa Sna tshogs rang grol. *See* Götsang Répa Natsok Rangdröl
Rgyal thang pa Bde chen rdo rje. *See* Gyeltangpa Déchen Dorjé
Rig 'dzin Drag rtsal rdo rje. *See* Rikdzin Draktsel Dorjé
Rikdzin Draktsel Dorjé (Rig 'dzin Drag rtsal rdo rje), 359

Rinjū yōjin no koto (Admonitions for the time of death; Dōhan), 158–159
Rinpungpa Dönyö Dorjé (Rin spungs pa Don yod rdo rje), 210, 212, 221, 226
Rin spungs pa Don yod rdo rje. *See* Rinpungpa Dönyö Dorjé
Rishukyō (*Liqu jing*, Sūtra of the guiding principle), 136
Rishushaku (*Liqushi*), 136
Ritsu sect, 388
royalty. *See* cakravartin kings
Ruk Devi, 339–340
Ryōgen, 388
Ryōun, 138

Saigyō, 142–143
saints. *See* special dead
Saitō Nanako, 407
Sakada Satoshi, 381
saṃvega. *See* religious emotion or agitation
saṃvejaniya verse, 447–452
samsaric cycle, 1, 11–12, 105, 123, 134, 326
sanmitsu (three secrets), 135, 148–150, 152, 158
Sanuki no Sanmi, 273
sapiṇḍīkaraṇa ceremony, 28n24, 47. See also *navaśrāddha* rites; *piṇḍa*s
Sarvasattvapriyadarśana, 35. *See also* Kiken
Sarvāstivāda vinaya, 116–118
scattering of ashes. *See* ash scattering
Schmitt, Jean-Claude, 25
Schopen, Gregory, 50
Scripture on Impermanence (*Foshuo wuchang jing*), 122, 123, 125–126, 127
sea: scattering ashes in, 407, 409. See also *Fudaraku tokai*
secondary burial, 13, 44–45, 387
Seien, 141
self-immolation: auto-cremations, 35, 236, 267–269; commemorations, 235, 248–249, 257–258; Daoxuan's accounts, 237–249; of Dazhi, 246–249; death verses, 256–257; by drowning, 270, 273–275; eaten by tigers, 244, 246; by fire, 35, 267–269, 274; images of, 270; in Japan, 266, 267–271; literary accounts, 268–269; *Lotus Sūtra* story, 35; meaning, 235–236; means, 236; patterns, 257; performances of death, 257; political aspects, 234–235, 242–243; as response to state persecution, 234, 236–238; spectators or attendants, 269, 270–271, 273–274; state of mind at moment of death, 274; of Yonglong, 249–252; of Zhiming, 252–257. See also *Fudaraku tokai*
Shabkar (Zhabs dkar), 360
shamans: *délok* as, 320; Mulian as, 353; in Tibet, 355
Shandao, 144, 148
Shanwuwei (Śubhakarasiṃha), 155
Sharf, Robert, 23–24
sheli. *See* relics
Shima Tōru, 417–418, 419–420
Shimokōbe Rokurō, 275
Shinbo Yoshimichi, 424
Shingon school. *See* esoteric Buddhism
Shinjé Chökyi Gyelpo (Gshin rje chos kyi rgyal po), 300, 301, 313, 314, 315, 316. *See also* Yama Dharmarāja
Shinnō, 140
Shinrai, 137
Shinran, 416
Shinto funerals, 414
shizensō. *See* natural funerals
Shōnen (Shōkin), 138
shōshin. *See* self-immolation

Shouhu guojiezhu tuoluoni jing (Sūtra of dhāraṇīs for protecting the nation and the ruler), 154
Shōyo, 141–142
Shōyūki, 395
shrouds: Buddha on, 89–90; defects, 89, 91; woman's worn by Buddha, 63–65, 67–68, 72; worn by living, 72, 89–90, 91–92; wrapped around Buddha's body, 33–37, 50
Shugendō mujō yōshū, 281
Śibi, King, 241, 244
sick monks, caring for: Daoxuan on, 106–107; instructions in *Linzhong fangjue*, 123; origin of practice, 107–108; reminders of impermanence, 110, 112–113, 121, 127–128; sermons to, 113, 116–117, 120, 121–122; sūtras on, 110–116; treatment of bodily impurity, 109–110
sickness scriptures, 111–116
Siddhārtha, Prince, reaction to sight of corpse, 2. *See also* Buddha
Sifenlü biqiujie xiangbiaoji (Hongyi), 192
Sifenlü shanfa bujue xingshi chao. *See* Daoxuan
Sima Guang, *Zizhi tongjian* (Comprehensive mirror for the aid of the government), 255–256
skeleton meditations, 184
śmāśānika monks. *See* cemetery-dwelling monks
Sna nam btsun pa. *See* Nanam Tsünpa
Society for a Women's Monument (Onna no Hi no Kai), 427–429
Society of *En* (En no Kai), 426–427, 428, 437n72
sokushin jōbutsu. *See* realizing buddhahood with this very body
Sönam Drüpa (Bsod nams grub pa), 212, 218–219
Sönam Lodrö (Bsod nams blo gros), 223–224, 226
Songtsen Gampo (Srong btsan sgam po), Emperor, 305
Sōsō no Jiyū o Susumeru Kai. *See* Grave-Free Promotion Society
soul, Tibetan concept, 301, 304–305
special dead: category inspired by Peter Brown, 29n28; contact with, 20–22; meaning of death for, 10–11; patterns of great monks' deaths, 189; relationships with living, 12, 20–22. *See also* exemplary deaths; Hongyi; Indācāra, Bhaddanta; Milarépa; relics; Tsangnyön Heruka
spells, esoteric, 138, 140, 146
spirit parks (*reien*), 426, 436n70
Spiro, Melford, 6–7
Spos khang pa Rin chen rgyal mtshan. *See* Pökangpa Rinchen Gyentsen
Śramaṇa Shi Dazhi. *See* Dazhi
Śramaṇa Shi Puan. *See* Puan
Śramaṇa Shi Puji. *See* Puji
Śramaṇa Shi Puyuan. *See* Puyuan
Sri Lanka: almsgiving, 329–330, 335, 338; Alutnuvara Devālaya, 331, 337, 341, 342; hierarchy of deities, 340–341; informal religious sector, 330–331; introduction of Buddhism, 327–329; relations between living and dead, 329–330, 343; sacred places, 338; understanding of Buddha's enlightenment, 327. *See also* Viṣṇu Kalyāni
Srong btsan sgam po. *See* Songtsen Gampo
state, relations with saṅgha: in Japan, 413–414; in Myanmar/Burma, 439, 440–442; persecution of Buddhism in

China, 234, 236–238, 239, 242, 243; persecution of Buddhism in Myanmar/Burma, 440. *See also* Chinese Buddhism, relations of saṅgha and state
Stede, William, 341
Stein, Rolf A., 346, 359
storytellers (*maṇi pa*), 306
stūpas: Buddha relics enshrined in, 33, 48–49, 50; common, 196, 197; meanings, 422
Sublime Sūtra entitled *Vessel of Complete Protection* (*'Phags pa yongs su skyobs pa'i snod ces bya ba'i mdo*). See *Yulanpen jing*
Sudhana, 287
suicide, as social act, 290
suicides, religious: by fire, 35, 236, 267–269; giving up the body, 18–20, 235–236, 266. See also *Fudaraku tokai*; self-immolation
Sui dynasty: beginning, 242; downfall, 252; relations of saṅgha and state, 236–237, 243, 244, 245, 246, 247, 249; Zheng Ting's service, 253–255
Sūtra of Maudgalyāyana's Salvation of His Mother from Hell (*Mu'u 'gal gyi bu ma dmyal khams nas drangs pa'i mdo*), 355
Sūtra of Maudgalyāyana's Salvation of His Mother from the Hell Realm (*Maudgal gyi bus ma dmyal ba nas drangs pa'i mdo*), 354–355
Sūtra of the *Yulan* Vessel. See *Transformation Text on Mulian Saving His Mother from Hell*; *Yulanpen jing*
sūtras: Chinese *āgamas*, 110–116; sickness scriptures, 111–116
Suzuki Eijō, 424

Taira no Koremori, 274–275
Taira no Nobunori, 389
Taixu, 4
Taizong, emperor (Li Shimin), 238, 253, 255, 257
Taizu, emperor, 250, 251
Takamure Itsue, 381, 382, 392
Tanaka Chigaku, 3–4
Tanaka Hisao, 384–385, 389, 391
Tang dynasty: defeat of Wang Shichong, 253; founding, 252; persecution of Buddhism, 238; relations of saṅgha and state, 238, 239, 249, 252, 257
Tanigawa Akiko, 414
Tani Kayoko, 427–428
Tanxu, 193
Tanxuan, 128–129
temple cemeteries, 413, 414, 418
temple certification system, 413–414
temples: clan, 385–386, 397; revenue from funerary rituals, 2, 3
Tenzin Chökyi Lodrö (Bstan 'dzin Chos kyi blo gros), 223
Thailand, funerary rituals, 84
Thousand-Armed Kannon, 138, 272, 287, 290. *See also* Avalokiteśvara; Kannon
three secrets (*sanmitsu*), 135, 148–150, 152, 158
Tiantai Zhiyi, 246
Tibet: demons, 318–319, 325n52; imperial period, 304, 351; picture recitation, 359; popular conception of afterlife, 297–298, 300–301, 310–311; soul concept, 301, 304–305
Tibetan Book of the Dead, 4, 26–27n10, 301
Tibetan Buddhism: Avalokiteśvara cult, 305–306; *bardo* doctrine, 303–304, 311–316, 362; Chinese influences, 346, 347; Festival of the Descent from the Heavens, 348; funerary rituals, 301, 304, 317, 325n48, 359, 361, 362–363; hagiog-

raphies, 208–209, 216–217, 223–226; hell concept, 303; importance of presence at parental death, 356, 360; introduction of Buddhism to Tibet, 346; marvels accompanying funerals of holy people, 208, 213, 219, 220; perspective on death, 4; Yoghurt Festival, 347–348. See also *délok* tales; Milarépa
Tibetan politics, 218, 226
tigers, 244, 246
Tōchōji, 426, 431
torch, body as, 34, 35, 50. *See also* cremations; self-immolation
Tranquillity Society (Annon Kai), 428
Transformation Text on Mulian Saving His Mother from Hell (*Damuqianlian mingjian jiumu bianwen*), 346–347; Dunhuang Tibetan synopsis (Gö Chödrup), 349, 350, 351–354; influence on *délok* tales, 355–356; Nanam Tsünpa's retelling, 355, 364–367; performances of, 358–359; Tibetan versions, 354–355
transformation texts (*bianwen*), 350–351, 358–359
Tsangnyön Heruka (Gtsang smyon He ru ka): accounts of life, 210–212, 218, 221–223; cremation, 219; death, 218–221; disciples, 212, 218–219, 220, 221, 223–224; patrons, 210, 221; post-death appearances, 220; promotion of Milarépa cult, 210–212; relics, 219–220, 222, 223, 226; statues, 220, 221
Tsangnyön Heruka, *Life of Milarépa*: death account, 212–216; influence, 211–212, 221–222, 223, 224; popularity, 208, 212; woodblock editions, 210; worship of, 225–226
Tséwang Gyel (Tshe dbang rgyal), *Religious History of Lhorong*, 217
Tshe dbang rgyal. *See* Tséwang Gyel
Tshul khrims dpal ldan. *See* Tsültrim Penden
Tsültrim Penden (Tshul khrims dpal ldan), *Life of Sönam Lodrö*, 223–224
Twenty-five Samādhi Society. *See* Nijūgo Zanmai-e

Uji shūi monogatari, 291
Urakawa Michitarō, 412
Uttarasena, King of Udyāna, 47

van Gennep, Arnold, 32, 430
Vaudeville, Charlotte, 34, 36
vegetarianism, 180, 245
Vilela, Caspar, 276–277
Vimalakīrti-nirdeśa sūtra, 118
Vimānavatthu, 328
Vinaya: composition, 62; *Dharmaguptaka vinaya*, 107–108, 110, 111, 120–121; Hongyi's study of, 179–180, 182, 192, 193; importance of lay values, 61–63; *Pini riyong* (*Vinaya for Daily Use*), 194–195; *Sarvāstivāda vinaya*, 116–118. See also *Mūlasarvāstivāda vinaya*
Vinaya-kārikā (Viśākhadeva), 94
Vinaya-saṃgraha (Viśeṣamitra), 94
Vinaya-sūtra, 71, 73, 91–93
Viśākhadeva, *Vinaya-kārikā*, 94
Viśeṣamitra, *Vinaya-saṃgraha*, 94
Viṣṇu, 332, 340–341, 342, 343
Viṣṇu Kalyāni: autobiography, 339–340, 343; *devālaya*, 332, 340; life, 342–343; as medium, 332–339, 340; meeting with, 331–332; sessions as medium, 333–336, 337–338
vita, 235

Waldschmidt, Ernst, 34, 38, 39, 43
Walshe, Maurice, 45

Wang Shichong, 253–256
Wangzin, Karma. *See* Karma Wangzin
Welch, Holmes, 4
Welfare Ministry, of Japan, 406, 407, 411–413, 426, 430
Wendi, emperor, 245, 247, 253
Wilson, Liz, 18–20
women. *See* Japanese women; Karma Wangzin; mothers; Viṣṇu Kalyāni
woodblock printing, 210, 226
Wright, Arthur, 253
Wudi, emperor, 239, 242, 243, 244
Wuliangshou yigui. See *Muryōju giki*

Xuanzang, 38, 47, 241
Xu gaoseng zhuan. *See* Daoxuan, *Xu gaoseng zhuan*
Xuyun, 199–200

yakṣas, 341–342
Yama Dharmarāja (Lord of the Dead), 300, 301 302, 315, 316, 356, 357, 358, 361–362. *See also* Shinjé Chökyi Gyelpo
yamamori. *See* grave attendants
Yanagida Kunio, 391
Yangdi, emperor, 247, 248, 249, 253, 262–263n54
Yang Su, 253
Yasuda Mutsuhiko, 405, 406, 407, 408, 410–412, 416, 418, 429–430
Yijing, *Linzhong fangjue* (Instruction for the moment of death), 122–127
Yinguang, 183, 184, 195–196, 197
Yoghurt Festival (*zho ston*), 347–348
Yokota Mutsumi, 411, 413, 419
Yonglong, 249–252
Yoshishige no Yasutane, *Nihon ōjō gokuraku ki* (Record of those in Japan born in [the Pure Land of] Utmost Bliss), 136–137
Yuihan, 140
Yulanpen jing (Sūtra of the *Yulan* Vessel), 346–347, 348–350, 354; Tibetan version, 348. See also *Transformation Text on Mulian Saving His Mother from Hell*

Za ahan jing (Saṃyuktāgama), 110–111; entry 1025, 113–116, 122, 128; entry 1028, 111–113
zenchishiki (attendants of dying), 152–155, 156, 160
Zen sect, 388
Zhabs dkar. *See* Shabkar
Zheng dynasty, 253–256
Zheng Ting (Zhiming), 252–257
Zhiman, 128–129
Zhiming (Zheng Ting), 252–257
Zhongnan mountains, monks in, 237–246, 260n20
zho ston. *See* Yoghurt Festival
Zhou dynasty. *See* Northern Zhou dynasty
Zhuhong, 195
Zizhi tongjian (Comprehensive mirror for the aid of the government; Sima Guang), 255–256
Zōmyō, 136–137

Kuroda Institute
Studies in East Asian Buddhism

Studies in Ch'an and Hua-yen
Robert M. Gimello and Peter N. Gregory, editors

Dōgen Studies
William R. LaFleur, editor

The Northern School and the Formation of Early Ch'an Buddhism
John R. McRae

Traditions of Meditation in Chinese Buddhism
Peter N. Gregory, editor

Sudden and Gradual: Approaches to Enlightenment in Chinese Thought
Peter N. Gregory, editor

Buddhist Hermeneutics
Donald S. Lopez, Jr., editor

Paths to Liberation: The Margā and Its Transformations in Buddhist Thought
Robert E. Buswell, Jr., and Robert M. Gimello, editors

Sōtō Zen in Medieval Japan
William M. Bodiford

The Scripture on the Ten Kings *and the Making of Purgatory in Medieval Chinese Buddhism*
Stephen F. Teiser

The Eminent Monk: Buddhist Ideals in Medieval Chinese Hagiography
John Kieschnick

Re-Visioning "Kamakura" Buddhism
Richard K. Payne, editor

Original Enlightenment and the Transformation of Medieval Japanese Buddhism
Jacqueline I. Stone

Buddhism in the Sung
Peter N. Gregory and Daniel A. Getz, Jr., editors

Coming to Terms with Chinese Buddhism: A Reading of The Treasure Store Treatise
Robert H. Sharf

Ryōgen and Mount Hiei: Japanese Tendai in the Tenth Century
Paul Groner

Tsung-mi and the Sinificataion of Buddhism
Peter N. Gregory

Approaching the Land of Bliss: Religious Praxis in the Cult of Amitābha
Richard K. Payne and Kenneth K. Tanaka, editors

Going Forth: Visions of Buddhist Vinaya
William M. Bodiford, editor

Burning for the Buddha: Self-Immolation in Chinese Buddhism
James A. Benn

Production Notes for Cuevas and Stone / The Buddhist Dead

Cover and interior design by
University of Hawai'i production staff

Composition by Asco Typesetters

Printing and binding by The Maple-Vail Book Manufacturing Group

Printed on 60# Glat. Offset B18, 420 ppi